Hilkhot Mo'adim

Understanding the Laws of the Festivals

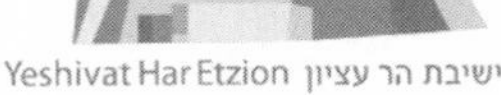

David Brofsky

HILKHOT MO'ADIM

UNDERSTANDING THE LAWS OF THE FESTIVALS

Maggid Books

Hilkhot Mo'adim
Understanding the Laws of the Festivals

First Edition, 2013

Maggid Books
An imprint of Koren Publishers Jerusalem Ltd.

POB 8531, New Milford, CT 06776-8531, USA
& POB 4044, Jerusalem 91040, Israel
www.korenpub.com

The publication of this book was made possible
through the generous support of *Torah Education in Israel.*

ISBN 978 159 264 352 3, *hardcover*

A CIP catalogue record for this title is
available from the British Library

Printed and bound in the United States

Dedicated in loving memory of

Richard J. Silvera, z"l

by his children
Hillel, Albert, and Michelle

בס"ד

02-9933644 :משרד
052-5456060 :נייד
rimonim613@gmail.com

יוסף צבי רימון
רבה של אלון-שבות דרום
ור"מ בישיבת הר-עציון

רחוב: קבוצת אברהם 10
אלון שבות, מיקוד: 90433

TRANSLATION: LETTER BY RABBI YOSEF ZVI RIMON

2 Tammuz, 5773

Rav David Brofsky *shlit"a,* a member of our community here in Alon Shevut, has been blessed with unique aptitude in the study of Torah, and exceptional skill in writing and in teaching. He is a *Talmid Ḥakham* and *yireh shamayim,* who learns and teaches Torah with deep-seated halakhic commitment, accompanied by perceptive awareness of modern-day realities.

In his book, *Hilkhot Mo'adim,* Rav Brofsky succeeds in presenting, clearly and lucidly, the underlying principles of the *halakhot* from the sources, starting with the Gemara and *Rishonim,* and continuing on to modern-day *posekim.* He integrates all of this together with *torani,* yeshiva-style analysis and insights, adeptly illuminating his ideas through philosophical principles. Rav Brofsky's book overflows with sources and penetrating insights, presented in a lucid and enlightening fashion, and serves as an excellent means of preparing for the *ḥagim.* May Hashem bless the author so that he may continue learning, teaching, and publishing additional works, so that Am Yisrael may continue to benefit from his profound and beautiful Torah.

Yosef Zvi Rimon

Rav, Alon Shevut South
Rosh Merkaz HaHalacha VeHaHora'a
Ram, Yeshivat Har Etzion

בס"ד

LETTER BY RABBI MICHAEL ROSENSWEIG

5 Tammuz, 5773

I am pleased for the opportunity to congratulate Rabbi David Brofsky, a cherished and talented *talmid,* on an impressive achievement, the completion of his *sefer* on *Hilkhot Mo'adim.* Typically, halakhic works are divided into two distinct genres. Some studies focus on the details of halakhic observance, while others examine the principles and underlying themes of a particular subject. The capacity to integrate conceptual analysis and practical implementation in a mutually illuminating manner reflects impressive halakhic scholarship and significant halakhic ambition. The introduction of Rabbi Brofsky's *sefer,* which highlights the dual *kiyum* of studying *hilkhot mo'adim* – both before and on the *regel* – and which situates his work within the broader context of different contemporary and classical genres, embodies and establishes the tone of this important multiple agenda. In keeping with this program, the book effectively melds broad motifs with specific details. The fact that the rigorous analysis of the topics is also highly accessible is particularly noteworthy. May the author continue to make important contributions to both Torah learning and halakhic observance both by his teaching and his writing.

Bevirkat HaTorah,

Michael Rosensweig

Rosh Yeshiva and Rosh Kollel
Yeshivat R. Yizhak Elhanan, Yeshiva University

CONTENTS

YOM KIPPUR

SUKKOT

ḤANUKKA

PURIM

PESAḤ

SEFIRAT HAOMER — SHAVUOT

FAST DAYS

INTRODUCTION

THE TALMUD CITES two passages that emphasize the importance of studying the laws of the festivals. The first instructs us to "inquire about and investigate (*sho'alin vedoreshin*) the laws of Pesaḥ [beginning] *thirty days prior* to Pesaḥ" (Pesaḥim 6a–b). This source clearly emphasizes the value of studying the numerous halakhot of each festival before the festival. The second source relates that "Moshe instituted for Israel that they study the laws of Pesaḥ on Pesaḥ, those of *Atzeret* [Shavuot] on *Atzeret*, and those of *Ḥag* [Sukkot] on *Ḥag*" (Megilla 32a). This passage seems to emphasize the value of studying the laws of each festival on the festival itself. The *Rishonim*, as we shall see,[1] note the apparent disagreement between these two sources, and discuss the relationship between these two passages.

The simple resolution of this contradiction reveals a very obvious yet important message. There are multiple reasons for learning about the festivals. Through learning the laws *before* the festival, one prepares to fulfill its numerous halakhot; through learning the halakhot *on* the festival, one understands and internalizes its spiritual messages.

Indeed, an in-depth study of halakha prepares one for the proper fulfillment of a mitzva, and potentially adds greater depth and meaning to its performance. Halakhic literature, over the past millennium, has oscillated between halakhic codes that present the halakhic rulings, and works that offer the breadth and depth of the halakha. In recent years, books on halakha, both Hebrew and English, have reflected the former, as treatises that focus upon all areas of Jewish law, including the laws of Shabbat, Yom Tov, *kashrut*, family purity, *berakhot, ribbit,* and even *shiluaḥ haken* fill the shelves of local Jewish book stores. Two styles dominate these code-like books. Some list halakha after halakha, often containing almost encyclopedic footnotes. Others explain and organize the halakhot, usually presenting one practical approach, while relegating background information and dissenting opinions to footnotes or endnotes.

These books provide a great service to the observant community, in that they make the details of halakha accessible to all. One who wishes to observe the laws of Shabbat or *kashrut*, for example, can simply purchase a halakhic guide book, and study. However, these books often do not present the origins or development of a specific practice. They do not provide the reader with an opportunity to learn a topic in depth. When disagreement arises, the author chooses which position to present as authoritative, and dissenting opinions, even those which are practiced by some, are often not even mentioned.

This volume, which focuses upon the laws of *mo'adim,*[2] begins each topic with its primary sources, be it a talmudic passage, a comment of the *Geonim*, or a practice instituted by the *Rishonim* or *Aḥaronim*. Each section traces the halakha through the *Rishonim* and *Aḥaronim*, including relevant debates among the *posekim* regarding contemporary applications. At times, historical and philosophical sources, as well as traditional "*lomdut,*" are woven into each chapter. This book, however, is still committed to presenting the "bottom line" practical halakha. Although at times the simplicity of direct instruction is sacrificed, a deeper, richer, and more accurate understanding is gained. This is the method I use to teach my students; it is a method I believe in strongly.

The Jewish calendar, both in its form and content, can be described in one word: dynamic. Each month, at the sight of the new moon, the Jewish people, as represented by the Sanhedrin, sanctify time and establish the beginning of each month. The calendar is marked by festivals, holidays, and days of mourning. Adherence to the ever-changing lunar cycle, as opposed to the static solar cycle, sets a model for our lives as individuals and as a nation. God is at times distant, just as the moon at times cannot be seen. However, just as the moon will always "return" at the start of each month, and increase in size and illumination, so too God's presence will wane, and then return to our lives as individuals and as a nation.

This dynamic Jewish calendar provides constant religious challenges and spiritual opportunities. It allows us to focus on the birth of our nation, our travels in the desert, our relationship to God, and the giving of the Torah. We mourn the tragedies of the past, and pray for a better future. We coronate God as the King of the world, and dedicate a day to introspection and repentance. And all of these are achieved through the performance of mitzvot, as is written in the *Sefer HaḤinukh* (published anonymously in thirteenth-century Spain), *aḥarei hamaasim nimshakhim halevavot* – "our hearts are influenced by our actions."[3]

Unfortunately, many do not internalize the spiritual messages offered through halakhic observance. I believe that through the in-depth study of Torah, and in our case, more specifically of the halakhot of the *mo'adim,* one can and should enrich one's personal, religious, and spiritual experience. That is the primary purpose of this book.

I embarked upon this project almost five years ago, when I began writing *shiurim* on the festivals for Yeshivat Har Etzion's Israel Koschitzky Virtual Beit Midrash (VBM). I would like to thank R. Reuven Ziegler, and the staff of the VBM, for enabling me to write, and disseminate, classes on *kashrut,* prayer, the holidays, and blessings through this medium. I also appreciate their cooperation and support in the publication of this volume.

I have been blessed with the opportunity to have studied in Yeshiva University, and to have learned from Rav Michael Rosensweig. In addition, I spent close to eight years studying, and later, teaching in Yeshivat Har Etzion. Yeshivat Har Etzion remains my spiritual home, and its guiding lights are Rav Aharon Lichtenstein, under whom I studied during those years, and Rav Yehuda Amital z"l. I feel forever indebted to the Yeshiva for its contribution to my growth. The Jewish people have benefited from the many graduates of the Yeshiva, and Judaism is a richer religion due to its teachings.

Throughout my research I consulted with the many modern halakhic compendiums and treatises written on the festivals, as well as numerous articles published in halakhic journals or available on the Internet. I sincerely hope that I dutifully cited all those who provided sources, ideas, or references, in fulfillment of the words of our sages, "Whoever says a thing in the name of he who [originally] said it brings redemption to the world."[4] If I unintentionally omitted an author, a journal, or a *sefer*, I express my sincere apologies.

I would like to thank my friends and colleagues, R. Yitzi Blau, R. Zvi Hirschfield, Mrs. Sally Mayer, Dr. Ethan Rotenberg, and R. David Silverberg, who reviewed sections of this book. In addition, I appreciate the diligent work of Mrs. Meira Mintz, who edited the first few drafts of this book.

I would like to acknowledge and thank Mr. Matthew Miller, Publisher at Koren Publishers, Ms. Gila Fine, Editor in Chief of Maggid Books, and R. Reuven Ziegler, Chairman of the Koren Editorial Board, for their efforts in printing this volume. I would also like to thank Ms. Tomi Mager, Ms. Sara Rosenbaum, Mrs. Nechama Unterman, Ms. Leah Khukhashvili and Mr. Robert Cook for their work editing and proofreading this book.

I would also like to thank my parents, Jarrett and Arlene Brofsky, who have always supported my desire to learn, and my in-laws, Dr. Mark and Leah Adler, who have been a constant source of encouragement.

Finally, I am indebted to my wife, Mali, who not only encouraged me in this, and other endeavors, but is also a constant source of personal and spiritual support and inspiration. I pray for many more years of partnership and companionship, and that our children, Yehuda, Shira, Yonatan, and Hadar, will grow up to learn, fulfill, and live the words of the Torah.

David Brofsky
Fall 5773/2013
Alon Shevut

Yom Tov

CHAPTER 1

Prohibited Labors on Yom Tov and *Okhel Nefesh*

ALTHOUGH EACH FESTIVAL has its own individual identity and halakhic obligations – such as eating *matza* on Pesaḥ, and sitting in a *sukka* and taking the *arbaat haminim* on Sukkot – we are also commanded to relate to each festival as a "Yom Tov," during which one may not violate any of the forbidden labors (*melakhot*). In that sense, Yom Tov seems quite similar to Shabbat.

Shabbat and Yom Tov, however, differ in at least three significant ways. Firstly, one who intentionally performs any of the thirty-nine *melakhot* on Shabbat violates both a positive (Ex. 23:12) and negative (20:10) commandment, and, under certain conditions, incurs capital punishment (35:2). If these conditions are not met, one incurs the punishment of *karet* (31:14). Furthermore, one who unintentionally violates the Shabbat must bring a *korban ḥatat*.[1] However, one who intentionally performs a prohibited *melakha* on Yom Tov violates a negative commandment (12:16) and possibly a positive commandment,[2] but only incurs *malkot* (lashes).

Second, the Gemara teaches that on Shabbat, there is "*ḥiluk melakhot*" – that is, if one were to unintentionally violate numerous *melakhot* on Shabbat during one period of unawareness ("*he'elem eḥad*"), he must bring a **separate** *korban ḥatat* for each *melakha* (Makkot 21b). On Yom Tov, however, there is no "*ḥiluk melakhot*"; one who violates numerous *melakhot* on Yom Tov *behe'elem eḥad* incurs only one punishment.

Third, one may perform *melakhot* for the sake of *okhel nefesh* on Yom Tov. The Torah states: "No work is to be done on those days, except to prepare food for everyone to eat – that is all you may do" (Ex. 12:16). We learn from this verse that one may perform *melakhot* necessary for the preparation of food on Yom Tov. Furthermore, the Mishna teaches: "The only difference between Shabbat and Yom Tov is *okhel nefesh*" (Megilla 7b), implying that the central difference between Shabbat and Yom Tov lies in the permissibility to cook on Yom Tov.

To what can we attribute these differences between Shabbat and Yom Tov? Seemingly, the *issur melakha* accomplishes two goals. By refraining from *melakha,* one remembers the creation of the world, when God ceased "working" on the seventh day (Gen. 2:1–3). This is particularly true on Shabbat, whose primary theme is the commemoration of creation. Because one who violates the Shabbat denies God's role in the creation of the world, he is "cut off" (*karet*) from this world, and each and every labor performed is significant.

Furthermore, abstaining from *melakha* contributes to an atmosphere of "*mikra'ei kodesh*" (Lev. 23:1–2). The *Sefer HaḤinukh* explains:

> The purpose of this mitzva [is to ensure] that the Jewish people will remember the great miracles that God wrought for them and their forefathers, and so that they should discuss them and inform their children and grandchildren. Through refraining from worldly matters, they will be free to engage in this. If one could work on the festival, even light labors, each person would focus on his business, and the respect for the festival would be forgotten by the adults and their offspring. There are other benefits from refraining from labor as well – the entire nation gathers in their houses of worship and houses of study to hear words of wisdom, and the communal leaders can guide and teach them.[3]

On Yom Tov, the prohibition to work plays a secondary role; it provides the proper atmosphere for one to celebrate the particular festival. For that reason, *melakha* on Yom Tov is prohibited by an ordinary negative commandment, and it is not accompanied by capital punishment or *karet*. In addition, as we shall see, Yom Tov is observed not only by fulfilling the mitzvot specific to each festival, but also through eating, drinking, and rejoicing physically and spiritually. The halakha therefore places less emphasis on each individual *melakha* (*ein ḥiluk melakhot*), and even permits those *melakhot* that may enhance the atmosphere of the day (*okhel nefesh*).[4]

In the following chapters, we will discuss the laws of Yom Tov related to *okhel nefesh*, the *melakhot* permitted in order to prepare food for the festival, as well as the other laws of Yom Tov, including the proper celebration of Yom Tov, *Eiruv Tavshilin*, and Yom Tov Sheni (for one who resides outside of Israel, as well as for a visitor there).

WHICH *MELAKHOT* ARE PERMITTED ON YOM TOV?

According to the mishna cited above, *okhel nefesh*, the permissibility of cooking on Yom Tov, encapsulates the difference between Yom Tov and Shabbat. Indeed, this difference is stressed by the Torah, as we noted above: "No work is to be done on those days, except to prepare food for everyone to eat – that is all you may do" (Ex. 12:6).

Which *melakhot* may one perform in order to prepare food? Although one might intuitively suggest that all *melakhot* necessary for the preparation of food are permitted, the Gemara rules that not all *melakhot* are permitted for *okhel nefesh* purposes.[5] What, then, are the criteria in determining the scope of the *heter okhel nefesh*?

Some *Rishonim* explain that only *melakhot* that *must* be performed on Yom Tov are permitted, because if those *melakhot* were to be done before Yom Tov, one would not achieve the same result. Rambam, for example, explains:

> Whenever it is possible to perform a labor on the day prior to the holiday without causing any loss or inadequacy, our sages forbade performing such a labor on the holiday itself, even if it is performed for the sake of [the preparation of] food.
>
> Why was this forbidden? This was a decree [instituted], lest a person leave for the holiday all the labors that he could have performed before the holiday, and thus spend the entire holiday performing those labors. Thus, he will be prevented from rejoicing on the holidays and will not have the opportunity to [take pleasure in] eating and drinking.
>
> For this very reason, [our sages] did not forbid transferring articles on a holiday, although the transfer of all [articles] is a task that could be performed

> before the holiday. Why was this not forbidden? To increase our festive joy, so that a person can send and bring anything he desires, and thus fulfill his wants, and not feel like someone whose hands are tied. With regard to other labors that are possible to be performed on the day before the holiday, since they involve [prolonged] activity, they should not be performed on a holiday.
>
> What is implied? On a holiday, we do not harvest, thresh, winnow, separate, or grind grain, nor do we sift [flour]. For all these and any similar activities can be performed on the day prior to the holiday without causing any loss or inadequacy.
>
> We may, however, knead, bake, slaughter, and cook on a holiday, since if these activities had been performed on the previous day, the taste would be adversely affected. For warm bread or food that is cooked today does not [taste] the same as bread or food that was cooked the day before. Similarly, meat that is slaughtered today does not [taste] the same as meat slaughtered on the previous day. The same rules apply in all analogous situations.
>
> Similarly, when it would be detrimental for subsidiary activities [involved in the preparation] of food to be performed on the day [before the holiday] – such as grinding spices and the like – they may be performed on the holiday.[6]

Rambam also writes:

> We may not make cheese on a holiday, for cheese will not lose its flavor if it is prepared on the day before the holiday. In contrast, one may crush spices in the ordinary manner [on a holiday], for if they were crushed before the holiday, they would lose flavor.[7]

According to Rambam, although *mideoraita* all *melakhot* necessary for the preparation of food are permitted on Yom Tov, the sages only permitted those *melakhot* that cannot be done as effectively before Yom Tov, lest one be "prevented from rejoicing on the holidays and will not have the opportunity to [take pleasure in] eating and drinking." Rashi implies that these *melakhot* are biblically prohibited.[8]

Other *Rishonim*, however, explain that *melakhot* that are usually performed on a large scale, in order to prepare food for a longer period of time, are prohibited. Rosh, for example, explains:

> Since one is accustomed to cut [the grapes of one's] vineyard and to cut [the wheat of one's] field together, and to grind a lot [of wheat] and to crush

> domain to another] and *hav'ara* [the kindling of a fire]. Since it is permitted to transfer articles for the sake of [the preparation of] food [on Yom Tov], [this activity] was permitted even when it is not necessary for [the preparation of] food. Therefore, it is permitted to transfer an infant, a Torah scroll, a key, or the like from one domain to another. Similarly, it is permitted to kindle a fire, even though it is not for the purpose of [the preparation of] food.
>
> With regard to the other forbidden labors, [the following principles apply:] Whenever the activity is necessary for [the preparation of] food – e.g., slaughter, baking, kneading, or the like – it is permitted. If it is not necessary for [the preparation of] food – e.g., writing, weaving, building, and the like – it is forbidden.[25]

Rambam explicitly applies the principle of *mitokh* to *hotzaa* and *hav'ara,* but not to the other *melakhot* necessary for the preparation for food. What is the difference between these two labors and the other *melakhot okhel nefesh*?

Maggid Mishneh explains that according to Rambam, there are three categories of *melakhot. Melakhot* inherently connected to the preparation of food, such as *bishul* (cooking) and *sheḥita* (slaughtering), were not prohibited at all on Yom Tov. *Hotzaa* and *hav'ara,* which are not inherently related to food preparation, but are, at times, certainly necessary for *okhel nefesh,* are also permitted even for non-food preparation due to the principle of *mitokh. Melakhot* which are not related to food preparation at all, such as *kotev* (writing) and *kosher* (tying a knot), are never permitted on Yom Tov. Therefore, according to *Maggid Mishneh,* Rambam adopts both of the conceptual positions that we have outlined.[26]

The *Shulḥan Arukh* rules that one may carry a child, lulav, *sefer Torah,* and utensils, "since it was permitted for [food-related] purposes, it was also permitted for non-[food-related] purposes."[27] The *Mishna Berura* applies this principle to *hav'ara, sheḥita, afiya,* and *bishul* as well.[28]

DEFINING "*LETZOREKH KETZAT*": CARRYING ON YOM TOV

We learned above that according to *Beit Hillel,* one may carry a lulav, a *sefer Torah,* and even a child in a *reshut harabbim* (public area), even though they are not needed for "*okhel nefesh*." Although Rashi permits carrying for no specific need or purpose, other *Rishonim* insist that the *mitokh* principle only permits one to carry for some, even slight, need. What is considered to be a legitimate need?

Rabbeinu Ḥananel (990–1053) implies that one may only do these *melakhot* for the sake of a mitzva: One may carry a lulav or *sefer Torah* for their respective mitzvot, and a child in order to perform a *Brit Mila*.[29] Tosafot reject this narrow definition of "*tzorekh*," and maintain that one may even carry a child in a public area on Yom Tov for a "*tiyul*."[30] Rosh cites Rabbeinu Tam (1100–1171), who explains that one who wishes to walk to the *Beit Knesset*, or even for a "*tiyul besimḥat Yom Tov*," and cannot leave his child at home, may carry a child through a public area on Yom Tov.[31] Indeed, Tosafot even record that people play ball in a public area, as this is also considered to be a "*tiyul*," which is permitted.[32]

Rosh also permits carrying *Maḥzorim* and Siddurim home from the synagogue, as "*hitiru sofan mishum teḥilatan*" – they permitted certain actions lest one otherwise not be able to perform the mitzva at all.[33] Maharshal objects to this leniency unless one truly fears that they may be stolen if left in the synagogue.[34]

Finally, Rosh cites the *Geonim*, who prohibit carrying keys that do not open boxes for food or jewelry. He bases this position upon passages from the Yerushalmi and Tosefta.[35] Maharshal argues that based upon these sources, one should not carry keys to one's chests or rooms because one fears that his property may be stolen. Rather, he argues, one should preferably remain at home and not violate the Torah prohibition of carrying for no purpose on Yom Tov (Beitza 1:18). *Beit Yosef*,[36] however, cites *Hagahot Rabbeinu Peretz*,[37] who permits carrying keys to chests containing money, since avoiding anxiety may also be considered to be a "*tzorekh hayom*" (a legitimate need).

Rema cites the position of Tosafot, that one may play ball in a public area on Yom Tov. He also cites Rabbeinu Peretz, and rules that one may carry on Yom Tov, "when there is [even] a small need, or he fears that they may be stolen, or another loss."[38] He concludes that one who lives in an area surrounded by an *eiruv* may carry anything that is considered functional (that is, any item that is not considered to be *muktze*).

BATHING ON YOM TOV

The Gemara (Ketubot 7a) further limits that application of *mitokh*:

> Are you then of the opinion that it is permitted to burn spices [on Yom Tov], because burning is permitted in a case of need and should therefore be permitted even if there is no need? R. Papa responded: Regarding this, the verse states: "For what is *ye'aḥel lekhol nefesh* [literally: edible by all people], that alone may be done for you" – only something which is of benefit to all (*shaveh lekhol nefesh*) may be done.

The Gemara concludes that the principle of *mitokh*, which permits labors generally done for food purposes (*hotzaa, hav'ara, sheḥita, bishul,* and *afiya*), only applies when the *melakha* is *shaveh lekhol nefesh* – burning spices was not viewed as a universally enjoyed activity. The majority of *Rishonim* rule in accordance with this passage.

The *Rishonim* discuss the principle of "*davar hashaveh lekhol nefesh*" regarding the permissibility of heating up water for bathing purposes on Yom Tov. Before we address bathing on Yom Tov, we must first discuss whether one may bathe on Shabbat.

Bathing on Shabbat poses a number of problems. First, heating up water on Shabbat is clearly prohibited, as it violates the *melakha* of *bishul*. The use of hot water in most homes is thus prohibited, as one would most likely directly turn on a heating element, thereby violating the *melakha* of *hav'ara,* and/or heat up cold water (either directly or when it enters the boiler to replace the hot water taken from the tap), violating the *melakha* of *bishul*. But may one bathe in hot water that was heated up before Shabbat? The Gemara relates:

> At first, people used to wash in pit water heated on the eve of Shabbat; then, bath attendants began to heat the water on Shabbat, maintaining that it was done on the eve of Shabbat. So [the use of] hot water was forbidden. (Shabbat 39b–40a)

Thus, although one may wash his face, hands, and feet in water that was heated before Shabbat, one may not wash his entire body. This *gezeira* is known as the *gezeirat merḥatzaot* or the *gezeirat balaniyot*.

Regarding bathing in cold water on Shabbat, R. Yaakov b. Moshe Moelin (1360–1427), known as Maharil, records that it is customary not to bathe in rivers on Shabbat.[39] He attributes this custom to the fear that one may squeeze water from his hair, carry, or swim. Many *Aḥaronim* cite this practice.[40] Some *Aḥaronim* assume that it is customary to refrain from showering in cold water as well.[41] R. Moshe Feinstein (1895–1986), however, argues that the custom not to bathe in rivers does not apply to showers. He acknowledges that most people do not shower even in cold water on Shabbat, but questions whether that is simply because they are not used to showering in cold water or because they are under the mistaken impression that there is an actual custom not to shower on Shabbat.[42] The *Aḥaronim* agree that one who is experiencing great discomfort may certainly bathe in cold water on Shabbat, as long as he is careful not to violate other Shabbat prohibitions (*seḥita, memare'aḥ*, etc.).[43]

Regarding Yom Tov, the Mishna[44] records that *Beit Hillel* permits heating water on Yom Tov in order to wash one's face, hands, and feet.[45] Why does the Mishna imply that one may not heat water in order to bathe one's entire body on Yom Tov? Why doesn't the principle of *mitokh* permit bathing in warm water? We will present two approaches. First, Tosafot explain that one may not heat water in order to wash one's entire body for the following reason:

> We [only permit heating water for] a *davar hashaveh lekhol nefesh*, and this [heating water in order to bathe one's entire body] is only for a finicky individual, while [washing] one's hands and feet is considered to be *shaveh lekhol nefesh*.

In other words, the principle of *davar hashaveh lekhol nefesh* limits our ability to apply *mitokh* to heating water. Therefore. one may only heat water for the purpose of washing one's limbs.

According to this logic, Tosafot would seemingly permit bathing in water that was heated before Yom Tov. Rosh, however, rules that one may not even bathe in water heated up before Yom Tov.[46] Ran explains that just as the *gezeirat merḥatzaot* extends the biblical prohibition of heating water on Shabbat in order to bathe one's entire body to water heated up before Shabbat, the *gezeirat merḥatzaot* applies to water heated up before Yom Tov as well, as it is not considered *shaveh lekhol nefesh* to bathe in hot water on Yom Tov and thus fundamentally prohibited.[47]

Rif[48] and Rambam[49] disagree. They explain that heating water on Yom Tov for bathing is permitted, due to the principle of *okhel nefesh*. Nevertheless, the *gezeirat merḥatzaot* of Shabbat was extended to Yom Tov, prohibiting using water that was heated on Yom Tov for full-body bathing. One may, however, bathe in water that was heated up before Yom Tov. Since there is no biblical prohibition of heating water on Yom Tov, the *gezeirat merḥatzaot* was only applied to Yom Tov itself.[50]

The *Shulḥan Arukh* rules in accordance with Rif and Rambam, and permits washing one's entire body with water heated before Yom Tov.[51] Rema implies that he adopts the position of Tosafot, prohibiting heating water on Yom Tov because bathing is not considered *shaveh lekhol nefesh*, as well as that of Rosh, prohibiting using water heated before Yom Tov.[52]

Nowadays, when we are accustomed to bathing with greater frequency, may we be more lenient regarding bathing on Yom Tov? Perhaps bathing in warm water is now considered *shaveh lekhol nefesh*, and thus permissible on Yom Tov according to Tosafot and Rosh? According to the *Shulḥan Arukh*, it seems that the prohibition of bathing in hot water on Yom Tov is related to the *gezeirat merḥatzaot*, and not to the principle of *shaveh lekhol nefesh*. There would thus be no compelling reason to be lenient, despite the change in common practice. According to this opinion, however, one only may bathe in water that was heated before Yom Tov. Some view water heated in a "*dud shemesh*" (using solar panels, a common means of heating water in Israel) as water heated before Yom Tov, since it is not directly heated on Yom Tov in a prohibited fashion.[53] According to Rema, however, who prohibits bathing in hot water on Yom Tov because full-body bathing in hot water was not considered to be *shaveh lekhol nefesh*, might we permit such bathing nowadays, when it is standard for people to bathe daily in hot water?

This may depend upon a broader question regarding the application of *shaveh lekhol nefesh*: is the definition of *shaveh lekhol nefesh* subjective? Some *Aḥaronim* certainly imply that *shaveh lekhol nefesh* is not an objective, unchanging standard, but rather may be subject to time and place. For example, the *Biur Halakha* questions whether one may heat water to wash one's feet nowadays, as washing one's feet daily is no longer a common practice.[54] Similarly, Rema[55] and *Magen Avraham*[56] debate whether bathing a child is considered *shaveh lekhol nefesh*, which would allow one to heat water in order to wash a child. It would seem that the very fact that there is a debate highlights that *shaveh lekhol nefesh* must be subjective.

R. Shlomo Zalman Auerbach questions if one would be permitted to heat water in order to bathe in a case in which one is sufficiently filthy that everyone would bathe in hot water.[57] R. Yehoshua Neuwirth, author of *Shemirat Shabbat KeHilkhata*, suggests that nowadays, warm showers may be considered a *davar hashaveh lekhol nefesh*.[58] Furthermore, R. Neuwirth mentions that nowadays, when one turns on the hot water for a shower, he often does not heat the water to be used for the shower, but rather uses water that was already heated. Cold water then enters the boiler and may be heated, and this water may be used for another permitted purpose, such as washing one's limbs or washing the dishes. (Some heating systems, however, heat the water immediately, and this rationale would not apply.[59]) In the text of his *Shemirat Shabbat KeHilkhata*, however, R. Neuwirth does not accept these leniencies.[60]

Some *Aḥaronim* imply that one may bathe in *mayim poshrim*, lukewarm water, on Shabbat and Yom Tov,[61] but others disagree or limit this leniency to the specific situation of *mikveh* immersion. *Shaar HaTziyun* cites *Beit Meir*, who considers heating water "*lehafig tzinatan*" (in order to remove the chill) as certainly *shaveh lekhol nefesh*.[62]

One who follows Rema may certainly bathe on Yom Tov when experiencing discomfort. Furthermore, one who wishes to bathe in warm water on a two- or three-day Yom Tov has upon whom to rely, and may certainly bathe in water heated slightly in order to remove the chill. One who bathes on Yom Tov must avoid other Yom Tov prohibitions, such as wringing out one's hair and using bar soap.[63]

Needless to say, this discussion applies to a situation in which the method of heating up water does not entail the violation of other prohibitions, such as a boiler filled with hot water. It may be prohibited to use some hot water systems of Yom Tov due to the prohibition of *hav'ara.*

SMOKING ON YOM TOV

Before we begin our discussion of smoking on Yom Tov, it is important to note that as time passes and the dangers of smoking become increasingly clear, it seems quite difficult to justify smoking at all. The recent consensus of *posekim* seems to prohibit smoking completely.[64] That being said, we will still dedicate the next few paragraphs to discussing the permissibility of smoking on Yom Tov, as it was discussed by numerous Torah sages over the past four hundred years, as it relates to our discussion of *shaveh lekhol nefesh.*

One of the earliest authorities to address smoking on Yom Tov was R. Chaim Benveniste (1603–1673) in his *Knesset Gedola,* who prohibits smoking due to the *melakha* of *mekhabeh* (extinguishing).[65] R. Avraham Gombiner (1633–1683), in his *Magen Avraham,*[66] adds that smoking should be similar to burning spices (*mugmar*), which was prohibited because it was not *shaveh lekhol nefesh.*

This discussion continued into the next century. R. Yaakov Yehoshua Falk (1680–1756), in his commentary to the Talmud, the *Penei Yehoshua,* argues further that smoking is healthy and good for the digestion (!), and therefore *shaveh lekhol nefesh.*[67] R. Netanel Weil (1687–1769), however, in his commentary to Rosh, the *Korban Netanel,* insists that smoking is not *shaveh lekhol nefesh* and harshly criticized those who smoke on Yom Tov.[68]

This debate continued further. R. Avraham Danzig (1748–1820) prohibits smoking on Yom Tov in his *Ḥayei Adam,*[69] while R. Chaim Mordechai Margulies (1780–1820), in his *Shaarei Teshuva,* cites others who rule leniently.[70] Interestingly, he records that *Ḥakham Tzvi,* R. Tzvi Hirsch Ashkenazi (1656–1718), smoked on Yom Tov in his youth, but refrained in his older years. Due to the great discomfort he experienced from not smoking, he was counseled to resume smoking, as not smoking detracted from his *simḥat Yom Tov*.

This debate reflects the dynamic definition of *davar hashaveh lekhol nefesh*. Those who smoke on Yom Tov nowadays assume that smoking is considered to be an activity categorized as *shaveh lekhol nefesh*. However, as more and more countries legislate against smoking in airplanes and other public places, it becomes increasingly difficult to consider smoking a universally enjoyed activity. In a posthumously published responsum, R. Moshe Feinstein grapples with this question, and concludes:

> Since there are many who do not smoke, as they assume it to be dangerous … therefore smoking cigarettes today is certainly not *shaveh lekhol nefesh*, although it is difficult to rule against the practice of the world …. Therefore, although a *baal nefesh* should certainly be stringent, it is difficult, halakhically, to prohibit it.[71]

Others, such as R. Shlomo Zalman Auerbach, R. Yosef Shalom Elyashiv, and R. Moshe Sternbach,[72] prohibit smoking on Yom Tov, as it is not considered to be a *davar hashaveh lekhol nefesh*. This was apparently the view of *Ḥazon Ish* as well.[73]

CHAPTER 2

Cooking on Yom Tov for the Next Day: *Marbeh BeShiurim* and *Eiruv Tavshilin*

COOKING ON YOM TOV FOR A WEEKDAY

The Torah permits cooking and other *melakhot* on Yom Tov for the sake of food preparation. There are, however, certain limitations upon the allowance of *okhel nefesh*.[1] The Gemara discusses whether one may cook on Yom Tov for the following weekday.

> It was stated: [With regard to] one who bakes [food] on a festival for [consumption on] a weekday, R. Ḥisda said: He receives lashes; Rabba said: He does not receive lashes. R. Ḥisda said: He receives lashes [because] we do not say that since (*ho'il*) if guests visited him, it would be fit for him [to eat on the festival itself]. Rabba said: He does not receive lashes, [because] we say that since [if guests visited him, he could serve them this food]. (Pesaḥim 46b)[2]

Rabba maintains that we may view one who cooks on Yom Tov for a weekday as if he in some respect is cooking for Yom Tov itself due to the principle of "*ho'il*" – "since (*ho'il*) if guests visited him, it would be fit for him." In other words, since guests may visit this person after he has cooked on Yom Tov, and he would then serve the food that he originally cooked for the following day to these guests, we view one who cooks on Yom Tov for a weekday as one who cooks for Yom Tov itself. R. Ḥisda, however, rejects this principle, stating that cooking on Yom Tov for the next day is prohibited *mideoraita*.

The *Rishonim* debate whether the halakha is in accordance with Rabba[3] or R. Ḥisda.[4] Practically, however, both opinions agree that one may not cook on Yom Tov for the next day; the question is whether the prohibition is *mideoraita* (R. Ḥisda) or *miderabbanan* (Rabba).

COOKING ON YOM TOV FOR SHABBAT

Although the Talmud clearly prohibits cooking on Yom Tov for the next day, the Gemara permits, under certain circumstances, cooking on Yom Tov for Shabbat. The Mishna describes how one who prepares an "*Eiruv Tavshilin*" before Yom Tov may cook on Yom Tov for Shabbat (Beitza 15b). The gemara cited above continues:

> Said Rabba to R. Ḥisda: According to you, who maintain that we do not say "*ho'il*," how may we bake on a festival for the Sabbath? On account of *Eiruv Tavshilin*, [R. Ḥisda] answered him. [Rabba questioned:] And on account of an *Eiruv Tavshilin* we permit a biblical prohibition?! [R. Ḥisda] responded:

> By biblical law, the Shabbat needs may be prepared on a festival, and it was only the Rabbis who forbade it, lest it be said that you may bake on a festival even for weekdays; but since the Rabbis necessitated an *Eiruv Tavshilin* for it, he has a distinguishing feature.

The Gemara assumes that the permissibility of cooking on Yom Tov for Shabbat is understandable according to Rabba, who maintains that *mideoraita*, one may cook on Yom Tov for the next day. The Gemara questions, however, how this would be permissible according to R. Ḥisda, who maintains that cooking on Yom Tov for the next day is biblically prohibited. How could the rabbinically instituted *Eiruv Tavshilin* permit a biblically prohibited activity? The Gemara explains that R. Ḥisda maintains that "*tzorkhei Shabbat naasin beYom Tov*" – *mideoraita*, Shabbat needs may be prepared on a festival. Since it was the Rabbis who forbade this practice, they were able to permit it through the execution of an *Eiruv Tavshilin*.

What is the basis for R. Ḥisda's assertion that one may cook on Yom Tov for Shabbat? Rashi explains that an adjoining Yom Tov and Shabbat are considered to be "*kedusha aḥat*" – one long day. Therefore, he writes, just as one may cook for Yom Tov on Yom Tov, one may cook for Shabbat as well.[5] Ri, however, cited by Tosafot, offers a different approach.[6] He explains that since one is commanded to prepare for Shabbat,[7] and this mitzva may only be fulfilled on Yom Tov in this situation, preparing for Shabbat is actually considered to be a Yom Tov need, and is therefore permitted on Yom Tov.

Both Rabba and R. Ḥisda maintain that *mideoraita*, one may cook on Yom Tov for Shabbat, but the Rabbis prohibited preparing on Yom Tov for Shabbat. Since the need to prepare for Shabbat on Yom Tov is considered to be a *she'at hadeḥak* (extenuating circumstances), the Rabbis permitted preparing on Yom Tov for Shabbat, provided one first performs an *Eiruv Tavshilin*.

Tosafot raise a practical difference between the opinions of Rabba – who maintains that cooking on Yom Tov for Shabbat is biblically permitted due to the principle of *ho'il* – and R. Ḥisda – who maintains that it is biblically permitted due to the principle of *tzorkhei Shabbat naasin beYom Tov*: According to Rabba, if one prepares the food too late in the day for it to be eaten by guests, the reasoning of *ho'il* would not apply, and thus, such cooking would be prohibited even *mideoraita*.[8]

Indeed, R. Avraham Gombiner rules in his *Magen Avraham* that if, like Rabba, we accept the reasoning of *ho'il* and reject that of *tzorkhei Shabbat naasin beYom Tov*, it is prohibited to cook on late Friday afternoon of Yom Tov for Shabbat. Furthermore, he explains that it is customary to begin Shabbat early when Yom Tov falls on Friday in order to ensure that people do not cook too close to dark.[9] Although many *Aḥaronim*, including the *Mishna Berura*, cite this stringency, the *Mishna Berura* writes that in extenuating circumstances, one may rely upon those who rule in accordance with R. Ḥisda[10] and prepare food for Shabbat even close to the evening.[11] The *Arukh HaShulḥan* (527:3) reports that the custom is not to be concerned with this stringency.

PERMISSIBLE METHODS OF COOKING ON YOM TOV FOR THE NEXT DAY: *MARBEH BESHIURIM*

Although one may not cook on one day of Yom Tov for the second day, even for Shabbat, the Gemara suggests two methods through which one may cook on Yom Tov for another day – "*marbeh beshiurim*" and "*Eiruv Tavshilin*":

> Our Rabbis taught: One may not bake on the first day of a festival for the second. In truth they said: A woman may fill the whole pot with meat, although she only needs one portion, and a baker may fill a barrel with water, although he only needs one handful, but as for baking he may bake only what he needs. R. Shimon b. Elazar says: A housewife may fill the entire oven with loaves, because bread is baked better in a full oven. Said Rabba: The halakha is as R. Shimon b. Elazar. (Beitza 17a)

R. Shimon b. Elazar permits one to cook larger quantities than one actually needs on Yom Tov in order to prepare for the following day. As long as one cooks or bakes a larger quantity in the same pot or oven, this is not considered to be cooking for the next day and is permitted.

The *Rishonim* grapple with a number of fundamental and practical questions. First, why is it permitted to cook additional food on Yom Tov for the next day, while this is forbidden on Shabbat? Regarding Shabbat, the Gemara prohibits cutting a stem with more figs than one needs to aid a sick person (Menaḥot 64a). In both cases, one is performing a permissible act (cooking on Yom Tov or performing a *melakha* for a sick person), but doing more than absolutely necessary. Rashba explains that *mideoraita, marbeh beshiurim* is permitted both on Shabbat and on Yom Tov. The Rabbis, however, prohibited *marbeh beshiurim* on Shabbat, when the prohibition of *melakha* is more severe, and did not prohibit *marbeh beshiurim* on Yom Tov.[12]

Ran, however, distinguishes between cooking on Yom Tov and performing a *melakha* for a sick person on Shabbat. He explains that there is an essential difference between the nature of *pikuaḥ nefesh,* the permission to violate a prohibition in order to save a life, and the permission to cook on Yom Tov.[13] He offers two explanations. In his first answer, Ran explains that on Shabbat, the prohibition of *melakha* is "*deḥuya*" – suspended or set aside – in order to save a life. Therefore, one may only do that which is absolutely necessary in order to save the life. On Yom Tov, however, certain *melakhot* that pertain to *okhel nefesh* are "*hutra*" – completely permitted – and it is therefore permissible to add on to the *melakha*. In his second answer, Ran explains that since the Torah permitted certain actions for the sake of *okhel nefesh,* one is not required to "weigh and measure in order that one does not cook more than one needs."

The *Aḥaronim* discuss a possible difference between these two reasons. If one carries an item on Yom Tov for a permissible reason, may he carry other items that are not needed as well? For example, may one carry a key chain on Yom Tov that contains keys needed on Yom Tov along with others that are not? Seemingly, according to Ran's first explanation, which maintains that *melakhot okhel nefesh* are "*hutra*," as long as one carries for the sake of *okhel nefesh,* the action is completely permitted; it should not matter what or how much one carries. According to the second reason, however, the halakha of *marbeh beshiurim* does not indicate that certain *melakhot* are absolutely permitted on Yom Tov, but rather that one need not account for every quantity that one carries for Yom Tov. Therefore, although one may carry more food than necessary, one may not carry items that have no use on Yom Tov.

R. Moshe Feinstein writes that one may carry a full pack of cigarettes on Yom Tov, even though one may not intend to smoke all of them.[14] Based on this responsum, the *Shemirat Shabbat KeHilkhata* assumes that R. Feinstein would permit carrying keys that are not needed on Yom Tov as well.[15] In a later responsum, however, R. Feinstein rules that one may not carry a key chain with extra keys.[16] Others do permit one to carry a key chain with "additional" keys on Yom Tov.[17]

The *Aḥaronim* also disagree as to when the Gemara's case of adding more food to a pot is permitted. R. Yaakov b. Asher (1270–1340), *Tur*, cites a debate regarding whether one may add additional food even if one explicitly states that his intention is to cook for the next day.[18] *Beit Yosef* explains that the answer depends on the reason that *marbeh beshiurim* is permissible.[19] According to some opinions, such as *Maggid Mishneh*,[20] one may be *marbeh beshiurim* and add more meat even after the food has been placed on the fire because the additional food enhances the taste of the entire dish. *Beit Yosef* notes that *Tur* concludes in accordance with this explanation.[21] Thus, one may add food even after explicitly stating his intention to prepare food for the next day, since the extra food enhances the entire dish regardless of his intention. Rashi, however, maintains that *marbeh beshiurim* is permitted because it is performed in one "exertion" ("*keḥad tirḥa sagi*").[22] Accordingly, the extra meat could only be added at the same time as the food needed for Yom Tov is placed in the pot. Furthermore, Rashi might maintain that if one explicitly declares his intentions of cooking the food for the following day, the act would be prohibited even though it is performed in one action. *Tur* concludes by citing Baal HaIttur, who prohibits increasing the quantity of food after one has already eaten, as that certainly constitutes an act of cooking for the next day.

The *Shulḥan Arukh* rules that one should only add food before the morning meal. After the meal, the food is clearly added for the next day, and to add more food is thus strictly forbidden. After the fact (*bediavad*), however, the food would still be permitted.[23] The *Mishna Berura* rules that the food must be cooked at one time and not added later.[24] Furthermore, he adds that one should not increase his efforts in order to prepare for the next day. Therefore, for example, one should not prepare and fry extra chicken cutlets, as this requires extra effort and they are cooked separately.[25]

Finally, the *Aḥaronim* question whether the entire scenario described by the Gemara refers to one who intends to eat some of the food on Yom Tov or to merely taste the food in order to be able to add additional food to be eaten the next day. The *Mishna Berura* records that it is it customary to be lenient, although one who is strict regarding this matter "should be blessed."[26]

EIRUV TAVSHILIN

The Mishna teaches that "[If] a festival fell on the eve of Shabbat… he may prepare a dish on the eve of the festival and rely upon it [to prepare food] for the Shabbat" (Beitza 15b). One who prepares and designates a dish before Shabbat may then continue to prepare for Shabbat on the festival. This method is called "*Eiruv Tavshilin*." The Gemara records a dispute regarding the reason for this enactment:

> Whence do we know this? Shmuel said: Because Scripture says, "Remember the Sabbath day to keep it holy" – remember it in view of another festival that comes to make it forgotten. What is the reason [for the institution of the *eiruv*]? Said Rava: In order that he may choose a fine portion for the Shabbat and a fine portion for the festival. R. Ashi said: So that people might say: You may not bake on a festival for the Shabbat – how much the more [is it forbidden] on a festival for a weekday!

Rava and R. Ashi disagree as to whether the *Eiruv Tavshilin*, which permits the rabbinically prohibited cooking on Yom Tov for Shabbat, protects the honor of the festival by reminding a person that he may not cook on Yom Tov for the next day (R. Ashi), or the honor of Shabbat by ensuring that a person adequately prepares for Shabbat (Rava).

R. Zeraḥia HaLevi (1125–1186), Baal HaMaor, suggests that this debate may be related to the previously mentioned dispute regarding the permissibility of cooking on Yom Tov for the following day. Rava (though Baal HaMaor insists that this is, in fact, Rabba) accepts the principle of *ho'il*; therefore, *mideoraita*, one may cook on Yom Tov for the following day. The Rabbis, however, prohibited cooking on Yom Tov for the next day, but they feared that one may thus not properly prepare for Shabbat. They therefore permitted cooking for Shabbat through the mechanism of *Eiruv Tavshilin*. R. Ḥisda, on the other hand, who ruled that cooking on Yom Tov for the following weekday is forbidden *mideoraita*, maintained that the Rabbis feared that one who cooks for Shabbat, as "the Shabbat needs may be prepared on a festival," may mistakenly believe that one may also cook for a weekday. They therefore required an *Eiruv Tavshilin* to correct this false impression.[27]

R. Betzalel Zolti (1920–1982), former Chief R. of Jerusalem, suggests that this discussion relates to another debate regarding the origin of the term "*Eiruv Tavshilin*."[28] The *Rishonim* offer different interpretations of the phrase. Rambam, for example, writes:

> Why is this called an *eiruv*? [Because it creates a distinction.] The *eiruv* that is established in courtyards and lanes on the day before Shabbat is intended to create a distinction, so that people will not think that it is permitted to transfer articles from one domain to another on Shabbat. Similarly, this portion of food creates a distinction and a reminder, so that people do not think that it is permitted to bake food on a holiday that will not be eaten on that day. Therefore, the portion of food is referred to as an *Eiruv Tavshilin*.[29]

Rambam maintains that the term "*eiruv*" is borrowed from the halakha of *Eiruv Ḥatzeirot*. Just as an *Eiruv Ḥatzeirot* creates a distinction that reminds people that they may not carry from one domain to another on Shabbat, the *Eiruv Tavshilin* is also a distinction or reminder. Raavad disagrees, insisting that the term "*eiruv*" is not borrowed, but rather describes how one "mixes (*eiruv*) the needs of Shabbat with the needs of Yom Tov together."[30] Or as Ritva explains, "They called it an '*eiruv*' because it is as if he combines Yom Tov and Shabbat, combining them and making them into one sanctity, as if when he prepares for Shabbat it is as if he prepares for Yom Tov."[31]

R. Zolti explains that Rambam follows the opinion of R. Ḥisda, who maintains that although one may cook *mideoraita* on Yom Tov for Shabbat, one may not cook for a weekday. The *Eiruv Tavshilin* therefore serves as a "reminder" that one may generally not cook on Yom Tov for the next day. Raavad, however, follows the reasoning of Rabba, who views one who cooks on Yom Tov for the next day as actually cooking for the purposes of Yom Tov due to the principle of *ho'il*. By beginning one's preparations for Shabbat early by preparing an *Eiruv Tavshilin*, one "mixes" or "combines" Yom Tov and Shabbat preparations. One who cooks for Shabbat is therefore viewed as if he is cooking for Yom Tov.

The *Rishonim* suggest practical differences between the two reasons for an *Eiruv Tavshilin*. Rosh, for example, writes that according to Rava, who believes that the *Eiruv Tavshilin* is intended to ensure that one properly prepares for Shabbat, the *eiruv* must be prepared immediately before the festival that precedes Shabbat. According to R. Ashi, however, who maintains that the *eiruv* protects the integrity of Yom Tov, one may prepare the *Eiruv Tavshilin* even long before Yom Tov. In fact, he writes that one may make an *Eiruv Tavshilin* on the Wednesday before the first Yom Tov of Sukkot, which will suffice for the second Yom Tov (Shemini Atzeret)/Shabbat as well, as long as he says so explicitly.[32] R. Meir b. R. Yekutiel HaKohen of Rothenburg (1260–1298), author of the *Hagahot Maimoniyot*[33] cites Raavya, who apparently agrees with Rosh's explication of R. Ashi, but adds that one may not make one *Eiruv Tavshilin* for the entire year. *Beit Yosef*,[34] however, insists that Rosh, as well as *Tur*,[35] would maintain that as long as the *eiruv* still exists, one may rely upon it for the entire year! *Kol Bo*[36] cites Rabbeinu Netanel, who disagrees and maintains that one may only prepare the *Eiruv Tavshilin* on Erev Yom Tov, as implied by the Mishna and Gemara. The *Shulḥan Arukh* rules that one should preferably not rely upon Rosh, but should rather prepare a new *eiruv* for each Yom Tov that precedes Shabbat.[37]

R. Mordekhai b. Hillel HaKohen, the *Mordekhai* (1240–1298), raises another possible difference between the opinions of Rava and R. Ashi. He relates that R. Shmuel of Bunberg once ruled that one who forgot to prepare the *Eiruv Tavshilin* before Yom Tov may make an *eiruv* on Friday, Yom Tov Sheni, before Shabbat. He reasons that one may rely upon Rava, the more lenient opinion, who maintained that the *eiruv* ensures that one properly prepares for Shabbat. This would not be permitted according to R. Ashi, who holds that the purpose of the *eiruv* is to preserve Yom Tov.[38] R. Yosef Karo rejects this possibility in his *Beit Yosef* and does not cite it in the *Shulḥan Arukh*.[39]

WHAT IS THE *EIRUV TAVSHILIN*?

The Mishna cites a dispute between *Beit Shammai* and *Beit Hillel* regarding whether the *Eiruv Tavshilin* must consist of one or two food dishes:

> [If] a festival fell on the eve of Shabbat, one may not at the outset cook on the festival for Shabbat, but he may cook for the festival, and if any is left over it remains for Shabbat; and he may prepare a dish on the eve of the festival and rely upon it [to prepare food] for Shabbat. *Beit Shammai* says: two dishes [are required for this purpose], while *Beit Hillel* says: one dish. (Beitza 15b)

This Mishna clearly implies that according to *Beit Hillel*, one must only prepare one dish for the *eiruv*. However, the Gemara elaborates:

> Now a *Tanna* deduces it from the following: "Bake that which you will bake, and cook that which you will cook" [Ex. 16:23] – from this, R. Eliezer concluded [that] you may bake only [in dependence] upon what is [already] baked and you may cook only [in dependence] upon what is [already] cooked.

This passage implies that one who wishes to cook and bake must prepare two dishes, one cooked and one baked.

The *Rishonim* differ as to how to interpret this gemara. Rabbeinu Tam rules that one who wishes to bake must also prepare a baked item for the *eiruv*.[40] Most *Rishonim*, however, disagree and rule that the *eiruv* consists of one cooked food alone.[41] Tosafot cite Ri, Rabbeinu Tam's nephew, who remarked that "I cannot bring myself to violate the words of my uncle; rather, one should prepare two dishes, one cooked and one baked, and the halakha is in accordance with him."[42]

Here, too, R. Zolti suggests that this debate may relate to a more fundamental debate. If the *Eiruv Tavshilin* merely comes to serve as a reminder, then one dish would certainly suffice. However, if the *eiruv* constitutes the beginning of one's preparations for Shabbat, then assuming that cooking and baking are viewed as separate forms of preparation, we might suggest that one must begin each form of preparation before Yom Tov in order to continue those activities on Yom Tov. The *Shulḥan Arukh* rules that one should preferably prepare both a cooked and baked food, although if one only prepared a cooked food, that is sufficient.[43]

The Gemara also relates to the size of the *Eiruv Tavshilin*:

> R. Abba said: An *Eiruv Tavshilin* must be the size of a *kezayit* (olive}. They asked: [Does that mean] one *kezayit* for all [the participants together], or a *kezayit* for each one separately? Come and hear: For R. Abba said in the name of Rav: An *Eiruv Tavshilin* must be the size of a *kezayit,* whether for one or for one hundred. (Beitza 16b)

Although the *Shulḥan Arukh* cites this passage,[44] Rema relates that some, based upon the Talmud Yerushalmi, require that one prepare a *kebeitza* of bread. He records that this is the custom.[45]

Finally, the *eiruv* must remain intact in order for it to enable one to cook or bake for Shabbat. The Mishna teaches that, "[If] he ate it or it was lost, he may not rely upon it, but if he left over any [small] portion of it, he may rely on it [to cook] for the Sabbath" (Beitza 15b).

It is customary to prepare a *ḥalla* and a cooked dish as one's *Eiruv Tavshilin.* The *Arukh HaShulḥan* notes that when Yom Tov falls on Thursday and Friday and the *Eiruv Tavshilin* must be prepared on Wednesday, the cooked dish may spoil before Shabbat, thereby disqualifying the *Eiruv Tavshilin.* Therefore, he writes, one should use a hardboiled egg, which will not spoil before Shabbat.[46] Although nowadays food can be stored in a refrigerator, many are still accustomed to set aside a cooked egg as one's *Eiruv Tavshilin.*

One should not eat the *Eiruv Tavshilin* until all of the preparations for Shabbat have been completed, preferably, as we shall see, including the *hadlakat neirot*. Therefore, one should not eat the *eiruv* until Friday night. R. Shlomo Luria (1510–1573), known as Maharshal, relates that the Maharam of Rothenberg would eat the *Eiruv Tavshilin* at the third meal of Shabbat.[47]

WHAT DOES AN *EIRUV TAVSHILIN* PERMIT?

Which ordinarily prohibited preparations does the *Eiruv Tavshilin* permit? Tosafot write that when one recites the *Eiruv Tavshilin* formula ("with this *eiruv*, let it be permitted for us to bake, cook"), one must add "*ule'adlukei*" ("and to light candles"). In addition, they explain that one who does not prepare an *Eiruv Tavshilin* may not light more than one candle.[48] Rosh[49] and Ran[50] concur. The *Mordekhai*, however, seems to disagree, as he notes that the Yerushalmi only requires one to mention baking and cooking, implying that one may light without an *Eiruv Tavshilin*.[51] Similarly, neither Rif[52] nor Rambam[53] mention lighting in their texts of *Eiruv Tavshilin*. The *Shulḥan Arukh* cites two opinions regarding whether one who did not prepare an *eiruv* may light a candle for Shabbat.[54] It is customary to mention lighting in the formula of the *Eiruv Tavshilin*.

The authorities debate whether an *Eiruv Tavshilin* permits *melakhot* performed for Shabbat needs unrelated to food. For example, may one carry a *Maḥzor* to synagogue on Friday that one intends to use on Shabbat? Furthermore, may one engage in preparations for Shabbat that do not involve a *melakha*? For example, may one wash dishes on Friday to be used on Shabbat? May one roll the *sefer Torah* to the proper place for the Shabbat reading? May one make beds and set the table for Shabbat? It is customary to permit these preparations for Shabbat.[55] The *Shulḥan Arukh* rules that the *Eiruv Tavshilin* only permits one to prepare for Shabbat on Friday, but not on Thursday, of Yom Tov.[56]

ONE WHO FORGETS TO PREPARE AN *EIRUV TAVSHILIN*

The Talmud rules regarding one who did not prepare an *Eiruv Tavshilin*:

> He who has not set an *Eiruv Tavshilin* may neither bake nor cook … neither for himself nor for others; nor may others bake or cook for him. (Beitza 17a)

The Gemara offers, however, a number of suggestions for one who forgot to make an *Eiruv Tavshilin*.

One Who Remembers Before Sunset

One who forgot to prepare an *Eiruv Tavshilin* and has already left for synagogue should preferably return home to make the *eiruv*. If this is impossible, one may call home and ask someone at home to make the *eiruv*. If this too is impossible, R. Yisrael Lipschitz (1782–1860) writes in his commentary to the Mishna, *Tiferet Yisrael*:

> In my humble opinion, if he has bread and a cooked item in his home he may, in the *beit midrash*, say, "The bread and the cooked food that I will take when I return home should from this moment be designated as an *Eiruv Tavshilin*." And although this person has many loaves of bread and many cooked dishes in his house, regarding laws of rabbinic origin we apply the principle of "*bereira*" – and when he returns home, he will separate a loaf of bread and a cooked item and set them aside for Shabbat.[57]

Although some *Aḥaronim* disagree,[58] others rule that in extenuating circumstances, one may rely upon *Tiferet Yisrael*, but one should not recite the blessing in this case.[59]

Tenai (Condition)

The Gemara discusses the possibility of establishing an *Eiruv Tavshilin* on the first day of Yom Tov that falls on Thursday, instead of the day before. (This, of course, is only relevant outside of Israel.)

> Rava said: A man may prepare an *Eiruv Tavshilin* on the first day of a festival for the second and stipulate. (Beitza 17a)

Rashi explains that one would say: "If today is a weekday and tomorrow is the festival, then my *eiruv* should be an *eiruv*. If, however, the opposite is true, then I do not need an *eiruv* at all."[60]

The *Rishonim* discuss when and how this condition may be made. For example, Ran[61] cites Rabbeinu Efraim, who insists that one may make a condition only if there is food prepared from the day before. *Tur*[62] and *Baḥ*[63] disagree. Furthermore, R. Yitzchak b. Abba Mari of Marseilles, France (author of the *Sefer HaIttur*), notes that this condition would certainly not apply to Rosh HaShana,[64] which the Gemara describes as "one long day" (Beitza 6b).

Rambam raises an interesting point, ruling that nowadays, when we do not really observe the second day of Yom Tov out of doubt but rather because of the established custom, one may not make this condition on the first day of Yom Tov.[65] Raavad disagrees.

The *Shulḥan Arukh* rules that one who forgot to make an *Eiruv Tavshilin* may prepare one on the first day of Yom Tov and recite the standard text of the *eiruv,* adding the condition mentioned above.[66] The *Mishna Berura,* however, cites a debate among the *Aḥaronim* regarding whether one should recite the blessing over this *eiruv*.[67] The *Shulḥan Arukh* also cites the dispute regarding whether one must have food prepared from the previous day. The *Mishna Berura* rules in accordance with *Tur* – even one who did not begin cooking the day before may prepare this *eiruv*.[68] One may not make an *Eiruv Tavshilin* in this fashion on Rosh HaShana, as we view the two days of Rosh HaShana as "one long day."

Relying on the Rabbi's *Eiruv*

The Talmud also discusses the possibility of relying upon someone else's *eiruv*. The Gemara states that the rabbinic authority of the city should prepare an *Eiruv Tavshilin* for the inhabitants of the city who do not prepare their own.

> Come and hear: For the father of Shmuel used to set the *eiruv* for the whole of Nehardea; R. Ammi and R. Assi used to set the *eiruv* for the whole of Tiberias. R. Yaakov b. Idi proclaimed: He who has not set an *Eiruv Tavshilin,* let him come and rely upon mine. (Beitza 16b)

The Gemara implies, however, that not everyone may rely upon this *eiruv*:

> There was a certain blind man who used to recite *baraitot* in the presence of Mar Shmuel. When he noticed that he was gloomy, he asked him: Why are you gloomy? He replied: Because I have not set an *Eiruv Tavshilin*. Then rely upon mine, he rejoined. The following year, he [again] noticed that he was gloomy. He said to him: Why are you gloomy? He answered him: Because I have not set an *Eiruv Tavshilin*. [Then] said he to him: You are a transgressor – to everyone else it is permitted, but to you it is forbidden.

This passage implies that one who is a "transgressor" (*poshe'a*) – in this context, one who forgot to prepare an *Eiruv Tavshilin* twice – may not rely upon the *Eiruv Tavshilin* prepared by the head of the city.

Some *Rishonim* do not cite this passage, and apparently maintain that one may always rely upon another person's *eiruv* prepared on his behalf.[69] Other *Rishonim* disagree, but differ as to how to understand this passage. Rosh, for example, explains that each person should prepare his own *Eiruv Tavshilin,* and one may not intentionally rely upon the *eiruv* prepared by the local rabbi. One, however, who intentionally neglects to prepare his own *eiruv,* intending to rely upon the rabbi's *eiruv,* is considered to be a transgressor, and he may not rely upon the *eiruv*.[70]

Beit Yosef writes that according to Rashi's explanation of the Gemara,[71] the *eiruv* does not work in such a case because the one who prepares the *eiruv* for the inhabitants of the city does not have transgressors in mind. If, however, he were to have in mind those who intentionally do not prepare an *eiruv,* the *eiruv* would, indeed, work for them.[72] The *Arukh HaShulḥan* maintains that even Rosh would agree with this conclusion.[73] The *Shulḥan Arukh* rules:

> It is incumbent upon every individual to prepare an *eiruv*. It is also incumbent upon the prominent figure in the city to prepare [the *eiruv*] for all the inhabitants of his city, in order [to help] one who forgot, or was unable [to prepare an *eiruv*], or one who prepared an *eiruv* but it was lost [and also for the ignorant who do not know that they must make an *eiruv*]. However, one who is able to prepare an *eiruv* and does not, but rather wished to rely upon the *eiruv* of the prominent figure in the city, is considered to be a transgressor and may not rely upon it.[74]

The *Aḥaronim* disagree regarding who is considered a "transgressor" and may therefore not rely upon someone else's *Eiruv Tavshilin*. The *Kaf HaḤayim* writes that only one who forgets to prepare an *Eiruv Tavshilin* for two consecutive festivals is considered to be a "transgressor,"[75] but *Ḥayei Adam* writes that one who forgets to prepare an *Eiruv Tavshilin* twice, even for nonconsecutive festivals, may not rely upon the rabbi's *Eiruv Tavshilin*.[76] The *Arukh HaShulḥan* argues that nowadays, the rabbis have in mind even one who consistently forgets to prepare an *Eiruv*

Tavshilin. He suggests that Mar Shmuel only referred to the specific person in the anecdote cited in the Gemara, who should have known better and whose forgetting surely expressed negligence.[77] The *Mishna Berura* suggests that *bediavad*, in order to ensure *simḥat Yom Tov*, one may rely upon those opinions that permit one to rely upon the rabbi's *eiruv*.[78]

One who prepares an *eiruv* for others must have them in mind when making the *eiruv*. In addition, when preparing an *eiruv* for others, someone must "acquire" the *eiruv* on their behalf. This person lifts the *eiruv* at least a *tefaḥ* above the ground, and the person making the *eiruv* takes it from him and recites the blessing "*al mitzvat eiruv*," followed by the formula recited over the *Eiruv Tavshilin*, adding "for us and for all of the inhabitants of this city." Preferably, the rabbi's wife or other family member should not be the one to acquire this *eiruv* on behalf of the community, as discussed elsewhere by the *Shulḥan Arukh*.[79]

As we have seen previously, in the absence of an *Eiruv Tavshilin*, one who must prepare food on Yom Tov for Shabbat may do so by cooking a larger amount than one needs for the Friday Yom Tov meal (in one pot). If this option proves unsatisfactory, the *Aḥaronim* discuss whether it is preferable to rely on the rabbi's *eiruv* or to prepare an *eiruv* conditionally (on the first day of Yom Tov outside of Israel).[80]

EIRUV TAVSHILIN FOR GUESTS

Must one's children or guests prepare a separate *Eiruv Tavshilin*? R. Avraham David Wahrman of Buczacz (1770–1840) writes that although one may not rely upon another's *Eiruv Tavshilin*, the head of the household prepares the *Eiruv Tavshilin* for all those who are eating his food. Therefore, one's children and guests need not prepare an *Eiruv Tavshilin*.[81]

If a family eats all of their Yom Tov meals at another person's house but sleeps in their own home, or if they stay at a hotel for Yom Tov, must they prepare their own *Eiruv Tavshilin*? In his commentary to the *Shulḥan Arukh*, *Maamar Mordekhai*, R. Mordechai Karmi (1749–1825) discusses whether one who has no intention to personally cook or bake for Shabbat must make an *Eiruv Tavshilin*. He claims that this question depends upon whether one may light candles for Shabbat without preparing an *eiruv*, as we discussed above. As this is subject to debate, he concludes that one in this situation should prepare the *eiruv* and recite the formula, but should not recite the blessing due to the principle of *safek berakhot lehakel* (when in doubt whether to recite a blessing, one should refrain from doing so).[82]

R. Menashe Klein, in his Responsa *Mishneh Halakhot*, discusses whether a married couple who eat all of the Shabbat meals at their parents' home should prepare an *eiruv*. He concludes that if they sleep at their parents' home, it is customary to rely upon their parents' *eiruv*, but if they sleep in their own home, they should prepare an *eiruv* without reciting the blessing. He bases this conclusion in part upon the *Maamar Mordekhai* cited above.[83] Similarly, R. Ovadia Yosef[84] and R. Bentzion Abba Shaul[85] (1924–1998) conclude that one should preferably prepare an *eiruv* without a blessing in order to permit lighting candles for Shabbat.[86]

MAKING THE *EIRUV TAVSHILIN*

One who makes an *Eiruv Tavshilin* holds both a baked and cooked food prepared before Yom Tov and recites the blessing of "*al mitzvat eiruv*." He then recites the formula, "With this *eiruv*, let it be permitted for us to bake, cook, insulate, light candles, make preparations, and do all of our needs on Yom Tov for Shabbat." Although the text is traditionally recited in Aramaic, one who does not understand the text should say it in a language he understands.[87]

CHAPTER 3

The Celebration of Yom Tov

SIMḤAT YOM TOV

The Torah commands in three places that one should "rejoice" on Yom Tov. Regarding Shavuot, the Torah says:

> And you shall rejoice before the Lord your God, you, and your son, and your daughter, and your man-servant, and your maid-servant, and the Levite that is within your gates, and the stranger, and the fatherless, and the widow who are in your midst, in the place which the Lord your God shall choose to cause His name to dwell there. (Deut. 16:11)

The Torah mentions the obligation to rejoice twice in the context of Sukkot:

> And you should rejoice in your festival, you, and your son, and your daughter, and your man-servant, and your maid-servant, and the Levite, and the stranger, and the fatherless, and the widow who are within your gates. Seven days you should keep a feast unto the Lord your God in the place which the Lord shall choose; because the Lord your God shall bless you in all your increase, and in all the work of your hands, and you shall be altogether joyful. (Deut. 16:14–15)

The *Rishonim* offer different suggestions for the source of the obligation of *simḥa* on Pesaḥ.[1]

The Gemara describes how in the days of the *Beit HaMikdash*, the mitzva of *simḥat Yom Tov* was fulfilled through eating the meat of the various *korbanot* offered on the festival:

> Our Rabbis taught: [It is written,] "And you shall rejoice in your feast." This includes all kinds of rejoicings as [festival] rejoicing. Hence the sages said: Israelites may fulfill their obligation with *nedarim*, *nedavot*, and *maaser*

> *behema*; and the Kohanim [fulfill their obligation with] the *ḥatat* and *asham*, the *bekhor*, and the breast and the shoulder [given to the Kohanim]. One might [think] also with bird-offerings and meal-offerings; [therefore,] Scripture teaches: "And you shall rejoice in your feast" – only with those [offerings] from which the *ḥagiga* can be brought. These [bird- and meal-offerings], then, are excluded since the *ḥagiga* cannot be brought from them. R. Ashi said: It is to be deduced from [the expression]: "And you shall rejoice"; these, then, are excluded because there is no [festive] joy in them. (Mo'ed Katan 14b)

Does the mitzva of *simḥat Yom Tov* apply nowadays, after the destruction of the *Beit HaMikdash*, and if so, in what way? The Gemara teaches:

> We learned in a *baraita*: R. Yehuda b. Beteira said: When the *Beit HaMikdash* is standing, *simḥa* is only with meat, as the verse says, "And you shall slaughter peace offerings and eat them there and be joyous before the Lord your God," and when the *Beit HaMikdash* is not standing, *simḥa* is only with wine, as the verse says, "And wine shall gladden the hearts of man." (Pesaḥim 109a)

This passage implies that although we can no longer fulfill the mitzva of *simḥa* through eating the meat of the *korbanot*, one may still fulfill the mitzva of *simḥa* in a different manner. Furthermore, the Gemara says:

> The Rabbis taught: A person is obligated to make his children and the members of his household happy on Yom Tov, as the verse says, "And you shall be joyous in your holiday." And how does he make them happy? With wine. R. Yehuda said: Men with what is appropriate for them and women with what is appropriate for them. Men with what is appropriate for them – with wine. And women with what? R. Yosef taught: In Bavel, with colored clothing and in Eretz Yisrael, with pressed flax clothing. (Pesaḥim 109a)

This passage similarly describes how one may fulfill the mitzva of *simḥa* through drinking wine and buying gifts for one's spouse. Does the *simḥa* achieved through drinking wine, and buying gifts for one's family, fulfill the biblical obligation of rejoicing on the festival? Tosafot maintain that these passages refer to a rabbinic obligation; nowadays, when the festival sacrifices (*shalmei simḥa*) are no longer offered, the mitzva of *simḥa* on Yom Tov is only *miderabbanan*.[2]

Rambam disagrees, however, ruling that the biblical mitzva of *simḥat Yom Tov* is in force even today:

> Even though the *simḥa* mentioned here refers to the *korban shelamim,* as we explain in *Hilkhot Ḥagiga,* included in this *simḥa* is to make one's children and members of his household joyous, each one according to his means. How? For children, one gives roasted kernels and walnuts and candies. For women, one buys clothing and pleasant jewelry based on what one can afford. And men eat meat and drink wine, for *simḥa* is only with meat and wine.[3]

R. Chaim Soloveitchik explains that according to Rambam, there are actually two types of *simḥa* – objective and subjective joy. One fulfills the objective mitzva of *simḥa* through eating the *korbanot.* However, the subjective form of *simḥa,* which applied during the time of the *Beit HaMikdash,* as it does nowadays as well, is fulfilled in the manner described by Rambam.[4] Similarly, R. Aryeh Leib Gunzberg explains in his *Shaagat Aryeh*:

> It seems to me that since the mitzva of *simḥa* that we were commanded to fulfill on the festival is not a specific mitzva, but rather a general mitzva that one is obligated to be happy on Yom Tov in all ways that he is able to rejoice, it is not similar to other mitzvot, regarding which all people are equal – the rich person should not increase and the poor person should not reduce. For this *simḥa,* each and every person is obligated to rejoice according to his means.[5]

Furthermore, he notes that according to many *Rishonim,* the permissibility of cooking on Yom Tov and the extension of this permissibility to other activities through the concept of *mitokh* results from the mitzva of *simḥat Yom Tov.*[6]

Since one may fulfill the mitzva of *simḥat Yom Tov* nowadays through various other means, must one eat meat or drink wine on the festivals? The Gemara states that "when the *Beit HaMikdash* is not standing, *simḥa* is only with wine, as the verse says, 'And wine shall gladden the hearts of man'" (Pesaḥim 109a). Some question whether one who achieves *simḥa* through other means must still drink wine,[7] but other sources indicate that one should preferably drink wine on Yom Tov regardless.[8] Some Torah scholars were accustomed to drink wine even on Ḥol HaMo'ed!

Interestingly, Rambam writes that one should "eat meat and drink wine," as "*simḥa* is only with meat and wine."[9] This ruling is somewhat puzzling, as the gemara cited above refers only to wine. Maharshal defends this position. He explains that certainly, "*ein simḥa ela bevasar*" – the primary fulfillment of *simḥat Yom Tov* is through eating meat at the Yom Tov meals. During the days of the *Beit HaMikdash,* consuming the meat of the *shelamim* was sufficient. Nowadays, however, when one cannot visit the *Beit HaMikdash* and partake of the meat of the *korbanot,* one should supplement his Yom Tov meal, during which one eats meat, with wine as well.[10] R. Yoel Sirkis (1561–1640), in his commentary to *Tur,* the *Bayit Ḥadash,*[11] as well as R. Barukh HaLevi Epstein (1860–1941) in his *Torah Temima,*[12] concur.

In *Beit Yosef,* R. Yosef Karo disagrees with this position,[13] and in his *Shulḥan Arukh,* he does not mention an obligation to eat meat on Yom Tov.[14] Many *Aḥaronim* write, however, that one should preferably eat meat on Yom Tov,[15] and some discuss whether one may fulfill this mitzva with fowl.[16] This question arises in particular in the context of the custom of eating dairy foods on Shavuot, as we shall discuss.[17]

In addition to the mitzva of *simḥa,* the mitzvot of *kavod* and *oneg* apply to Yom Tov as well.[18] As a result, Rambam implies that one must eat three meals on Yom Tov, just as one eats three meals on Shabbat.[19] *Tur* disagrees,[20] and the *Shulḥan Arukh* writes that it is not customary to eat three meals on Yom Tov.[21] One should, however, recite the blessing of *hamotzi* on two loaves, fulfilling the mitzva of *leḥem mishneh* at each meal. The *Shulḥan Arukh* adds that one's clothing for Yom Tov should be even nicer than one's clothing on Shabbat.[22]

In analyzing the nature of *simḥat Yom Tov,* R. Soloveitchik adds two additional points.[23] First, he explains that in Rambam's view, the mitzva of *simḥa* is fundamentally an internal experience. One cannot observe *aveilut* (mourning) during a festival, because the internal happiness of *simḥat Yom Tov* contradicts the internal anguish that a mourner feels.

Second, R. Soloveitchik explains that the joy of Yom Tov emerges from "standing before God," as the Torah describes:

> And you shall take you on the first day the fruit of goodly trees, branches of palm-trees, and boughs of thick trees, and willows of the brook, and you shall rejoice before the Lord your God seven days. (Lev. 24:40)

While *simḥa* has an external expression, fulfilled through eating, drinking, and merriment, the source of this joy emerges from one's closeness to God. Similarly, R. Aryeh Pomeronchik explains that while wine and meat may arouse joy, the real *simḥa* of Yom Tov is rejoicing with God. He insists that those who rejoice with the Torah on Simḥat Torah but do not rejoice in the festival itself may not fulfill the mitzva of *simḥat Yom Tov* at all![24]

ḤETZYO LAKHEM

In addition to the joy derived from dining on meat and wine and participating in festive Yom Tov meals, the Talmud discusses another element of *simḥat Yom Tov* – joy that comes from focusing on spiritual matters:

> For it was taught: R. Eliezer says: On a festival, a man should either eat and drink or sit and learn. R. Yehoshua says: Divide it – half of it for the Lord [and] half of it for yourselves. R. Yoḥanan said: Both drew their inference from the same scriptural verse[s]. One verse states: "A solemn assembly to the Lord your God" [Deut. 16:8] and another verse reads: "You shall have a solemn assembly" [Num. 29:35]. How is this [to be reconciled]? R. Eliezer is of the opinion: Either the whole of it is for the Lord or the whole of it is for yourselves; while R. Yehoshua is of the opinion: Divide it – half of it is for the Lord and half of it is for yourselves. (Beitza 15b)

According to R. Eliezer, one may choose how to spend his time, but R. Yehoshua argues that one must divide his time between personal and spiritual enjoyment (*ḥetzyo LaShem veḥetzyo lakhem*). The halakha follows R. Yehoshua's opinion.

Interestingly, the Gemara insists that all agree that on Shavuot, the day upon which we celebrate the giving of the Torah, one must dedicate at least part of the day to physical enjoyment (*lakhem*) (Pesaḥim 68b).

Rambam describes how one should divide his time evenly between these activities:

> Although eating and drinking on the holidays are included in the positive commandment [to rejoice], one should not devote the entire day to food and drink. The following is the desired practice:
>
> In the morning, the entire people should get up and attend the synagogues and the houses of study, where they pray and read a portion of the Torah pertaining to the holiday. Afterward, they should return home and eat. Then they should go to the house of study, where they read [from the Written Law] and review [the Oral Law] until noon. After noon, they should recite the afternoon service and return home to eat and drink for the remainder of the day until nightfall.[25]

Although Rambam implies that "*ḥetzyo LaShem veḥetzyo lakhem*" applies to Ḥol HaMo'ed as well,[26] *Tur* limits this principle to Yom Tov itself and he writes simply that one should divide his time between his personal (*lakhem*) and spiritual (*LaShem*) activities. He implies that one must simply spend a significant or meaningful portion of the day on each type of activity.[27]

The *Shulḥan Arukh* cites *Tur* and omits the Yom Tov program described by Rambam.[28] Some *Aḥaronim*[29] cite Maharshal (Ḥullin 1:50), who criticizes *ḥazanim* who unnecessarily lengthen the service since their singing is not to be considered a fulfillment of "*lakhem*"!

Rambam discusses two additional aspects of *simḥat Yom Tov*. First, he notes that rejoicing on Yom Tov does not mean that one should lapse into frivolity:

> When a person eats, drinks, and celebrates on a festival, he should not let himself become overly drawn to drinking wine, mirth, and levity, saying: Whoever indulges in these activities more is increasing [his observance of] the mitzva of rejoicing. For drunkenness, profuse mirth, and levity are not rejoicing; they are frivolity and foolishness.
>
> And we were not commanded to indulge in frivolity or foolishness, but rather in rejoicing that involves the service of the Creator of all existence. Thus, the verse states, "Because you did not serve God, Your Lord, with happiness and a glad heart with an abundance of prosperity" [Deut. 28:47]. This

> teaches us that service [of God] involves joy. And it is impossible to serve God while in the midst of levity, frivolity, or drunkenness.[30]

Second, Rambam reminds us that one's celebration must not only include his family, but must also include those who are in need of support on Yom Tov:

> When a person eats and drinks [in celebration of a holiday], he is obligated to feed converts, orphans, widows, and others who are destitute and poor. In contrast, a person who locks the gates of his courtyard and eats and drinks with his children and his wife, without feeding the poor and the embittered, is [not indulging in] rejoicing associated with a mitzva, but rather the rejoicing of his gut. And with regard to such a person [the verse] is applied: "Their sacrifices will be like the bread of mourners, all that partake thereof shall become impure, for they [kept] their bread for themselves alone" [Hos. 9:4]. This happiness is a disgrace for them, as [implied by the verse (Mal. 2:3)]: "I will spread dung on your faces, the dung of your festival celebrations."[31]

These beautiful passages place the obligation of rejoicing into its proper context and perspective.

GREETING ONE'S TEACHER ON THE FESTIVAL

In addition to rejoicing on the festival, the Talmud teaches that one should pay his respects to his teacher on each festival:

> R. Yitzḥak further said: It is incumbent on a man to go to pay his respects to his teacher on festivals, as it says, "Why do you go to him today? It is neither Rosh Ḥodesh nor Shabbat" [II Kings 4:23], from which we infer that on Rosh Ḥodesh and Shabbat one ought to go. (Rosh HaShana 16b)

The prophet relates how the husband of the *Isha Shunamit* asked his wife, who intended to visit the prophet Elisha with her dead son, why she was going to the prophet, as "it is neither Rosh Ḥodesh nor Shabbat" – implying that on those days, she would visit the prophet.

The commentators ask a number of questions about this proof. First, how does the Gemara derive that one must visit one's teacher on Yom Tov from a verse that speaks of Rosh Ḥodesh and Shabbat?

Second, what is the reason behind, and the nature of, this halakha? Rabbeinu Ḥananel implies that he had a different text of the Gemara, as he writes:

> And we ask, "Didn't we speak of a festival?" And we answered, "If his teacher lives nearby, then he is obligated to visit him each Rosh Ḥodesh and Shabbat, and if he lives far away, one must visit him only on the festival."[32]

According to this text, the Gemara asked our question, concluding that one's proximity to his teacher should determine the frequency of his visits. Ritva agrees that one should visit his teacher each Rosh Ḥodesh or each Shabbat, if possible; he even suggests that, if possible, one should visit his teacher every day![33]

According to this interpretation of the Gemara, there is no inherent connection between the obligation to visit one's teacher and the festival itself. Rather, the principle of *kevod rabbo* (respecting one's teacher) entails that one should visit his Rav as often as possible, and Shabbat, Rosh Ḥodesh, and Yom Tov are simply convenient times, depending on one's proximity.

This understanding emerges from the language of Rambam as well. In the context of discussing the laws of honoring one's teacher, Rambam writes:

> A person is obligated to stand before his teacher from the time he sees him – as far away as he can see – until [he passes beyond his field of vision] and is hidden, his figure no longer visible. Then, [the student] may sit. A person is obligated to visit his teacher during the festivals.[34]

Rambam clearly views the obligation to visit one's teacher on the festival as an expression of *kevod rabbo*, respecting one's teacher. Similarly, Rashi explains that "one is obligated to show respect to one's teacher by visiting him."[35]

R. Yechezkel Landau (1713–1793), offers a different explanation in his work of responsa, the *Noda BiYehuda*. He claims that ideally, one should visit his teacher on Rosh Ḥodesh and Shabbat due to the additional sanctity of those days, upon which the *korban musaf* is offered. On those days, the teacher's potential to influence his student is also increased. It is impractical to mandate that one visit one's teacher each Shabbat and Rosh Ḥodesh, however. Moreover, such a demand would also imply that one's respect for his teacher is greater than his regard for God, whom one visits only three times a year in the *Beit HaMikdash*.[36]

According to this interpretation, nowadays, when one is not able to "visit" the *Shekhina* at all, one is not obligated to fulfill this mitzva and to visit one's teacher each festival. Indeed, as the *Noda BiYehuda* notes, *Tur* and the *Shulḥan Arukh* omit this halakha entirely![37]

Interestingly, R. Yehonatan Eybeschutz (1690–1764) offers a completely opposite approach. In his homiletic work, *Sefer Ye'arot Devash*, he explains that greeting one's teacher is akin to greeting the *Shekhina* (Y. Sanhedrin 11:4). During the times of the *Beit HaMikdash*, one would visit the "home" of the *Shekhina* each Yom Tov, so there was no need to visit one's teacher as well. The obligation to visit one's teacher is actually meant to replace *aliya leregel*, and is therefore *only* applicable nowadays![38]

Thus, we may understand the obligation to visit one's teacher on the festival as an expression of *kevod rabbo* (respect for one's teacher), an outgrowth of the mitzva of *talmud Torah*, or as a replacement for *aliya leregel* and visiting the *Shekhina*, which is central to the Yom Tov experience. Aside from the distinctions mentioned above, one might also question whether this mitzva applies to one's "*rav muvhak*" (his main teacher), any teacher, or to any inspiring religious figure, as we shall see regarding the hasidic practice of visiting the "rebbe" on the festival.

As mentioned above, *Tur* and the *Shulḥan Arukh* omit this halakha entirely, generating much discussion among the *Aḥaronim*. Interestingly, the *Shulḥan Arukh* does mention the mitzva of visiting one's teacher in the context of Shabbat.[39] The *Magen Avraham* insists that although one is obligated to visit one's teacher on the festival, it is still considered a "mitzva" on Shabbat. Furthermore, the *Magen Avraham* writes that women are also obligated in the mitzva; the example brought by the Gemara was, after all, a woman – the *Isha Shunamit*.[40]

Must one visit his teacher on the festival if this would entail leaving behind his wife and family? The Gemara relates:

> Our Rabbis have taught: It once happened that R. Ilai went to pay his respects to R. Eliezer his master in Lydda on a festival. He said to him: Ilai, you are not of those that rest on the festival, for R. Eliezer used to say: I praise the indolent who do not emerge from their houses on the festival, since it is written, "And you should rejoice, you and your household."
>
> But it is not so? For did not R. Yitzḥak say: From where do we know that a man is obliged to pay his respects to his teacher on the festival? From Scripture, which said, "Why do you go to him today? It is neither Rosh Ḥodesh nor Shabbat," from which we infer that on Rosh Ḥodesh and Shabbat one ought to go.
>
> There is no difficulty. The latter refers to when he can go and return [to his house] on the one day, the former to when he cannot go and return on the same day. (Sukka 27b)

This passage clearly implies that one may only visit his teacher on the festival if he returns the same day. Furthermore, we might infer that even if a woman permits her husband to travel, he may still be exempt from doing so, as R. Eliezer did not even inquire as to whether R. Ilai had received his wife's permission to come!

In his mention of the mitzva to visit one's teacher on the festival, Rambam does not distinguish between one who can return home on the same day and one who cannot. *Kesef Mishneh* explains that Rambam maintained that R. Yitzḥak disagreed with R. Eliezer, maintaining that one may fulfill this mitzva even if he cannot return home the same day.[41] R. Simḥa Bunim Sofer (1842–1907), the grandson of R. Moshe Sofer (known as Ḥatam Sofer), raises this point in his discussion of the custom of Hasidim to leave their families in order to visit their "rebbe" on the festival.[42] This would impact upon the propriety of the modern phenomenon of husbands traveling to Uman, the city of R. Naḥman of Breslav's grave, for Rosh HaShana.

PURIFYING ONESELF BEFORE THE FESTIVAL

The Gemara cited above continues to quote R. Yitzḥak, who maintains that one must purify himself in a *mikveh* for the festival.

> R. Yitzḥak further said: A man should purify himself for the festival, as it says, "And their carcasses you shall not touch" [Lev. 11:8]. It has been taught to the same effect: "And their carcasses you shall not touch" – I might think that [ordinary] Israelites are cautioned not to touch carcasses. Therefore it says, "Say unto the Priests the sons of Aaron" [21:1] [which shows that] the sons of Aaron are cautioned not to defile themselves, but ordinary Israelites are not cautioned. May we not then argue a fortiori (*kal vaḥomer*): seeing that in the case of a serious uncleanness, while the Priests are cautioned Israelites are not cautioned, how much less [are they likely to be cautioned] in the case of a light uncleanness! What then am I to make of the words, "And their carcasses you shall not touch"? On the festival. (Rosh HaShana 16b)

What is the reason for this obligation, and does it apply nowadays? On the one hand, Rambam implies that R. Yitzḥak refers only to the time of the *Beit HaMikdash*:

> All of Israel are enjoined to be pure on each festival, because they must be prepared to enter the *Mikdash* and to eat sacrifices, and this is what the Torah means, "And their carcasses you shall not touch" – only on the festival, but during the rest of the year, one is not [commanded to be pure].[43]

Seemingly, according to Rambam, this obligation would not apply nowadays. Similarly, R. Abraham b. Isaac of Narbonne (1085–1158), in his *Sefer HaEshkol*,[44] cites R. Hai Gaon (939–1038), who rules that one must only be concerned with being "*tahor*" (ritually pure) during the time of the *Beit HaMikdash*, when one intends to enter the *Mikdash*. Other *Geonim* and *Rishonim* concur.[45]

On the other hand, perhaps purification is desirable even after the destruction of the Temple as a sort of "*zekher laMikdash*." We might even suggest that R. Yitzḥak demands that one elevate himself both spiritually and physically for the festival, and that this obligation may have existed during the time of the *Mikdash* even for those who did not ascend to Yerushalayim. Indeed, *Tur*, citing Raavya's interpretation of a Yerushalmi, implies that one must certainly purify oneself for Rosh HaShana, upon which one was not obligated to visit the *Beit HaMikdash*.[46] Elsewhere, however, *Tur* cites his father, Rosh, as requiring that one immerse before Yom Kippur.[47]

The *Shulḥan Arukh* omits this halakha, and it is not the normative practice to immerse in a *mikveh* before festivals. However, R. Yoel Sirkis explains that although one who immerses before Yom Tov does not recite the *berakha*, since it is not possible to completely purify oneself from *tumat met* (impurity from contact with a dead body), R. Yitzḥak teaches that one should still do "all that is possible" in order to purify oneself, even before Rosh HaShana.[48] Similarly, R. Shmuel Feivish (1640–1698), in his *Beit Shmuel* commentary to the *Even HaEzer* section of the *Shulḥan Arukh*, also implies that one should immerse before Yom Tov, even nowadays.[49]

CHAPTER 4

Yom Tov Sheni

INTRODUCTION

The first commandment given to the Jewish people was the mitzva of the sanctification of the new moon – "This month will be for you the first of the months" (Ex. 2:2) – the prerequisite for establishing the Jewish lunar calendar. Each month, the moon completes a cycle around the earth. At the beginning of each month, the moon is only slightly visible due to its position; it grows larger and larger until the middle of the month, at which time the entire moon may be seen (a "full moon"), and then it gradually decreases in size throughout the rest of the month. At the end of each month, the moon completely "disappears" from our vision.

A lunar month is between twenty-nine and thirty days long. Rosh Ḥodesh, the first day of the next month, upon which the *musaf* sacrifice is offered (and the Musaf prayer is recited in our day), falls on either the thirtieth or thirty-first day. Each month, witnesses who saw the appearance of the new moon (the "*molad*") would travel to the *beit din* in Jerusalem and testify that they had seen it. Based upon their testimony, the *beit din* would declare that the new moon had been sighted, and proclaim it the first day of that month, Rosh Ḥodesh (Rosh HaShana 21b–25b). By sanctifying the new month, the *beit din* also indirectly determined the proper day of the festivals, such as Sukkot and Pesaḥ, which fall on the fifteenth day of their respective months.

The Mishna relates that after declaring the new month, the *beit din* would light torches on the tops of the mountains, thereby conveying the message that Rosh Ḥodesh had been declared from mountaintop to mountaintop all the way from the Land of Israel eastward, toward Babylonia. Most communities were thus informed which day was declared Rosh Ḥodesh, and they were therefore able to determine the proper days upon which to celebrate the festivals. Apparently, those communities that did not learn when the new month was declared observed two days of Yom Tov out of doubt (Rosh HaShana 22b).

The Mishna relates that a group of antagonistic residents of the Land of Israel known as the *Kutim* (Samaritans) purposely disrupted the system of lighting fires by lighting fires on the wrong days. The Yerushalmi relates that as a result of this sabotage, R. Yehuda HaNasi discontinued the practice of using fires to announce the declaration of Rosh Ḥodesh (Rosh HaShana 2:1). The Rabbis therefore had no choice but to send out messengers to inform the communities regarding the exact day of Rosh Ḥodesh. These messengers did not reach the communities in the Diaspora, and these areas would therefore observe two days of Yom Tov, as they did not know the proper day of the festivals.

YOM TOV SHENI NOWADAYS

Sometime during the later amoraic period, Jewish communities began to observe Rosh Ḥodesh and the festivals based upon a fixed calendar. (The establishment of this calendar and its halakhic basis are the subject of great debate, both rabbinic and academic, and lie far beyond the scope of this chapter.[1]) Even after the establishment of the calendar, it was customary for communities outside of Israel to observe two days of Yom Tov, while those in Israel only observed one. The Gemara records that some questioned this practice:

> Now that the calendar is fixed, what is the reason for which we observe two days of Yom Tov? They send from there [from the Land of Israel to Babylonia]: Be careful in maintaining the custom of your forefathers, lest a foreign government issue a decree [thereby preventing knowledge of the Jewish calendar] and it will cause confusion [in ritual]. (Beitza 4b)

The Gemara mentions two reasons for this practice: *minhag avot*, maintaining the custom of one's forefathers, and *kilkul*, the fear that a government might issue a decree that would lead the community to forget the calendar and become confused regarding ritual. The *Rishonim* differ as to which is the primary reason to observe Yom Tov Sheni. Interestingly, the Yerushalmi only mentions that it is a *minhag*, and not the fear of a government issuing a decree (Y. Eiruvin 3:9).

In addition, the *Rishonim* question whether to view the observance of Yom Tov Sheni as a *minhag*, an ancient custom,[2] or a formal rabbinic enactment, a *takana*.[3] Some confusion surrounds the position of Rambam.[4] This question is not merely academic; it may be relevant to the discussion regarding the proper practice of a resident of the Diaspora who travels to Israel for Yom Tov.

One might suggest that even in the Diaspora, one should only observe one day of Shavuot; as after all, the day of Shavuot is set by counting fifty days from the second day of Pesaḥ, and one surely would have known the proper day of Pesaḥ weeks after Rosh Ḥodesh Nissan. Some explain, however, that the Rabbis did not wish to distinguish between the festivals.[5] Ritva adds that we do not observe two days of Yom Kippur, especially after the establishment of the fixed calendar, as this would constitute an enactment that the majority of the community could not fulfill.[6]

Before the establishment of the set calendar, Rosh HaShana was observed for two days even in the Land of Israel. Even if the *beit din* declared the thirtieth day of Elul to be Rosh Ḥodesh/Rosh HaShana, the messengers were unable to inform anyone outside of the *beit din*. Everyone else therefore had to assume the Rosh HaShana might not actually be until the next day; it was thus necessary to observe two days.

There is a disagreement, however, as to whether the communities in Israel should continue to observe two days after the establishment of the calendar.

R. Hai Gaon, responding to an inquiry from R. Nissim, acknowledges that the contemporary custom (eleventh century) of many in the Land of Israel was to observe one day of Rosh HaShana, but he argues that they should return to the original custom of their forefathers and observe two days.[7] Similarly, Rabbeinu Ḥananel implies that the residents of the Land of Israel should keep two days of Rosh HaShana.[8] Rif[9] and Rambam[10] concur.

Rosh cites Rif's student, Rabbeinu Efraim, who disagreed, ruling that only one day of Rosh HaShana should be observed in the Land of Israel.[11] Baal HaMaor agrees, and insists that the custom in Israel had always been to keep one day of Rosh HaShana, as the above-cited responsum from R. Hai Gaon implies, although the influence of Provençal scholars had brought about a change in that practice.[12] Ramban, however, defends the position of Rif, insisting that although the custom in Israel was, indeed, to keep one day of Rosh HaShana, this was a mistaken custom brought about by the long exile of the Jewish people.[13] The current practice is in accordance with Rif, and even in Israel, all observe two days of Rosh HaShana.[14]

Although the obligation to observe Yom Tov Sheni is of rabbinic origin, or possibly even a custom, the Rabbis did not distinguish between the halakhot of the first and second day of Yom Tov in order to prevent people from not properly observing, or possibly demeaning, Yom Tov Sheni. Therefore, on Yom Tov Sheni, one recites the *berakhot* of Yom Tov, including Kiddush, the lighting of the candles, and the Yom Tov prayers, despite the prohibition of reciting a blessing in vain (Shabbat 23a). Furthermore, one does not lay *tefillin* on Yom Tov Sheni, thus forgoing the fulfillment of a biblical commandment in order to protect the integrity of the day. Finally, one who violates Yom Tov Sheni is punished, and even excommunicated, by the *beit din*.[15]

Nevertheless, there are some differences between Yom Tov Rishon and Yom Tov Sheni. For example, on Yom Tov Sheni, one may violate a rabbinic prohibition for the sake of a *ḥoleh she'ein bo sakkana,* a sick person facing no mortal danger (Beitza 22a). (This leniency does not apply to the second day of Rosh HaShana.) Similarly, if a person died on Yom Tov Sheni, one may prepare him for burial, and even actually bury him (6a). Finally, if a relative is buried on Ḥol HaMo'ed, the last day of the festival, Yom Tov Sheni is considered the first day of the seven days of mourning, due to its lower status.[16]

WHERE IS YOM TOV SHENI OBSERVED?

As described above, Yom Tov Sheni is observed outside of Israel, where the messengers sent by the *bet din* did not reach. The Gemara, however, does not clearly explicate how to determine which communities observe one day and which communities observe two. Which borders of Israel are relevant for a discussion of Yom Tov Sheni?
Rambam writes:

> When the Sanhedrin functioned and the calendar was established based on the sighting [of the moon], the inhabitants of the Land of Israel, and [similarly, the inhabitants of] all the places where the messengers of Tishrei would arrive, would celebrate the holidays for one day only. The inhabitants of the distant places that were not reached by the messengers of Tishrei would celebrate two days because of the doubt involved. For they did not know the day that the inhabitants of the Land of Israel established as [the beginning of] the new month.
>
> Thus, the principles governing this matter can be summarized as follows: Whenever the distance between Jerusalem and a particular place exceeds a ten-day journey, the inhabitants should observe [the holidays] for two days, as was their previous custom, for the messengers sent out for Tishrei [cannot be guaranteed] to reach places other than those within a ten-day journey from Jerusalem.
>
> [The following rules apply for] places that are a ten-day journey or less from Jerusalem, to which it is possible that the messengers could have reached: We see whether that place is [located in the portions of] the Land

> of Israel that were inhabited by Jews during the time the calendar was established on the basis of the sighting [of the moon] during the second conquest [of the land] – for example, Usha, Shefaram, Luz, Yavneh, Nov, Tiberias, and the like. [The inhabitants of these places] should celebrate only one day. If the place is part of Syria – for example, Tyre, Damascus, Ashkelon, and the like – they should follow the custom of their ancestors. If [the custom was to celebrate] one day, [they should celebrate] one day. [If the custom was] two days, [they should celebrate] two days.
>
> When a place is located within a journey of ten days or less from Jerusalem, and it is part of Syria or the Diaspora, and [its inhabitants] have no [established] custom conveyed [from previous generations], they should celebrate two days, as is customary in the world at large. [The same rules apply to] a city that was created in the desert Land of Israel, or a city first populated by Jews in the present era.[17]

Rambam clearly maintains that only places within a ten-day journey of Jerusalem, which could have been reached by the messengers and which were actually inhabited during that time, may observe one day of Yom Tov. Communities farther than a ten-day journey from Jerusalem, or new communities that did not exist in the time of the Talmud, must observe two days. Based on this opinion, some suggest that even places within the Land of Israel that were not inhabited during the time of the Talmud should observe two days of Yom Tov according to Rambam.[18]

Ritva disagrees and explains that when the Rabbis established the obligation to observe Yom Tov Sheni, they decided that since most of the communities in the Disapora observed two days, all communities outside of Israel should observe two days. Similarly, since most communities within the Land of Israel observed one day, all communities within Israel should observe one day.[19]

Some question whether communities in the Southern Negev, including Eilat, should observe two days of Yom Tov. After all, Eilat is farther than a ten-day journey from Jerusalem, and messengers were most likely not sent to Eilat, even according to Ritva. Furthermore, it is questionable whether Eilat was conquered during the initial conquest of the Land of Israel and whether it should be viewed as part of "Israel" for this matter.

R. Yechiel Michel Tukachinsky (1874–1955), Rosh Yeshiva of Yeshivat Etz Chayim in Jerusalem and author of many books relating to halakhic observance in the Land and State of Israel, addressed this issue. He describes how he sent this question to eighteen prominent rabbis in Israel; the majority responded that in Eilat, one may observe one day (the others didn't even respond). He cites the former Chief Rabbis of Israel, R. Yitzchak Herzog (1888–1959) and R. Bentzion Uziel, as well as the *Ḥazon Ish,* as ruling leniently.[20] R. Eliezer Waldenberg (1916–2006) also deals extensively with this issue, ruling that one may observe only one day of Yom Tov in Eilat.[21] Others, however, maintain that there is a true doubt regarding whether one may observe one day of Yom Tov in Eilat, and therefore one should be stringent on the second day and refrain from *melakhot.*[22] The custom is in accordance with the lenient position.

VISITORS TO ISRAEL FOR YOM TOV

Due to increased travel between Israel and the Diaspora, the question of Yom Tov Sheni for the traveler has received much attention in recent years. How many days must one observe if he is visiting Israel during Yom Tov and intends to return thereafter to his home in the Diaspora? Conversely, how many days must an Israeli observe if he visits a Diaspora community for Yom Tov and intends to return to his home in Israel? We will begin by discussing a resident of the Diaspora, a *ben Ḥutz LaAretz,* who visits Israel.

A Visitor to Israel: Two Days

The *Rishonim* and *Aḥaronim* differ regarding a *ben Ḥutz LaAretz* who visits Israel for the festivals. His status will determine not only whether or not he may perform *melakha* on the second day of Yom Tov, but how he prays, whether or not he lays *tefillin,* when he recites Havdala, and sometimes whether or not he must prepare an *Eiruv Tavshilin.*

As we mentioned above, some view the practice of Diaspora communities observing two days of Yom Tov as fundamentally a custom. If so, we might compare this case to one in which a person who observes one custom visits a place where they observe a different custom. The

Mishna discusses a case in which a person travels from one place to another:

> One who goes from a place where they work to a place where they do not work, or from a place where they do not work to a place where they do work – we lay upon him the restrictions of the place from which he departed and the restrictions of the place to which he has gone. A man must not act differently [from local custom] on account of the quarrels [which would ensue]. (Pesaḥim 50a)

The Mishna teaches that one who travels from one place to another should retain the customs of his place of origin, but not violate the customs of his destination, in order not to cause "*maḥloket*." R. Ashi explains that this refers only to one who intends to return to his place of origin; one who does not intend to return to his place of origin should accept the customs of his new home, even in private (Pesaḥim 51a). Rosh adds that one may accept upon himself the customs of his new place regardless of whether they are more lenient or more stringent than his original customs.[23]

Applying this principle in the context of Yom Tov Sheni, R. Yosef Karo concludes in his Responsa:

> One who leaves Eretz Yisrael to go to *Ḥutz LaAretz* and has intention to return, it is as if he were still in Eretz Yisrael; similarly, one who comes from *Ḥutz LaAretz* to Eretz Yisrael with the intention to return is in the category of one who lives in the Diaspora.[24]

The question posed to R. Karo assumed that one who visits Eretz Yisrael should observe two days, as R. Karo notes is customary, and asks regarding the appropriateness of holding public Yom Tov prayers, since the population does not observe Yom Tov Sheni. R. Karo rules that a visitor to Israel should observe a full two days of Yom Tov and sanctions holding public Yom Tov Sheni prayers. The Rabbis were concerned that deviating from the *minhag hamakom* may lead one to violate a prohibition, such as a prohibited *melakha*, but that is not a fear in this case.

Interestingly, R. Yosef Karo omits this ruling in his *Shulḥan Arukh*, discussing only one who travels from Eretz Yisrael to *Ḥutz LaAretz*.[25]

Most contemporary *posekim* accept this view,[26] ruling that one who visits Eretz Yisrael should observe two days of Yom Tov. However, these authorities must grapple with a host of questions.

First, these authorities must determine who is considered in the category of "*ein daato laḥzor*," one whose intention is not to return to his place of origin. Often, one's intention is not clear, even to the person himself. In addition, other factors may be considered in determining whether one's relocation, or intent to return, is taken seriously. For example, the *posekim* discuss the case of one who leaves Eretz Yisrael with his family in order to work, but intends to return to Israel. The *Magen Avraham* cites Radbaz, R. David b. Solomon ibn Avi Zimra (1479–1573), who maintains that one who relocates with his wife and children cannot be considered to have in mind to return to his place of origin.[27] R. Moshe Feinstein, however, insists that nowadays, when traveling from one place to another is much simpler, whether we consider one to have relocated depends on his intentions, and not on the mere fact that he moved with his wife and children.[28] We must determine whether one who relocates for an extended period of time for business purposes or studies is nevertheless considered to be a resident of his place of origin.

The *posekim* also discuss whether students who come to study in Israel must observe Yom Tov Sheni. Although students have traveled to Eretz Yisrael for centuries in order to learn Torah, this phenomenon has increased dramatically over the past forty years. R. Chayim Yosef David Azulai (1724–1806), known as Ḥida, discusses this question in his responsa, *Ḥayim Shaal*.[29] He cites a well-known debate among his predecessors regarding whether students who come to study in Israel with the intention of returning to *Ḥutz LaAretz* should observe one or two days. He notes that although a number of prominent rabbis from Tzefat ruled that these students should observe two days, many great rabbis of Jerusalem, including R. Yaakov Ḥagiz (1620–1674),[30] rule that an unmarried man should observe one day, as he may eventually find a spouse and stay in Israel. R. Ovadia Yosef rules accordingly.[31] *Magen Avraham*, however, writes that a student who comes to Eretz Yisrael to study for two to three years must still observe two days of Yom Tov.[32]

In other words, when a visitor reaches a town, which the *Mishna Berura* defines as a town with Jewish population,[57] he must refrain from doing *melakha*. However, if he is not in a populated area or an area not populated by Jews, he may perform *melakha*.

As we discussed above, one must determine how to establish his status as a resident of Eretz Yisrael and how to assess whether he truly intends to return to Eretz Yisrael. The *posekim* discuss whether Israeli families who travel to *Ḥutz LaAretz* for business or as emissaries for the government or a Jewish agency and intend to return to Israel after their allotted time abroad should be considered *benei Ḥutz LaAretz* or *benei Eretz Yisrael*.[58]

According to this ruling, one who visits *Ḥutz LaAretz* should refrain from doing *melakha* on Yom Tov Sheni in order to avoid deviating from the local norm. He should therefore also dress in Yom Tov clothing.[59] However, he should pray the weekday prayers silently and lay *tefillin* in private. The *Rishonim* disagree regarding whether he must observe these stringencies in private as well. Rashi implies that work is only prohibited in public, where others can see him,[60] but Tosafot rule that work is prohibited in private as well.[61] *Taz* rules in accordance with Rashi,[62] but *Magen Avraham*[63] and *Mishna Berura*[64] accept the position of Tosafot.

Even those who are stringent permit one to perform *melakhot* that the observer would assume are permitted. For example, when Yom Tov falls on Thursday, a visitor may cook on Friday without having made an *Eiruv Tavshilin*, as the observer will assume that he prepared an *Eiruv Tavshilin*. Similarly, one may move a *keli shemelakhto le'issur*, as the observer may assume that he is moving the *muktze* object for a permitted purpose. R. Moshe Feinstein suggests that one may even turn on a light privately, as many set their lights on a Shabbat clock.[65] One may shower on Yom Tov Sheni even in a manner prohibited on Yom Tov, as the observer will assume that he showered in a permissible manner. Unfortunately, many Israelis who visit *Ḥutz LaAretz* for Yom Tov are not careful regarding this matter. Even those who permit performing *melakhot* in private do not permit driving or other public violations of Yom Tov Sheni.

May an Israeli fly from Israel after Yom Tov ends there and arrive in *Ḥutz LaAretz* on Yom Tov Sheni? Some *posekim* prohibit taking such a flight, as landing in an airport would be a violation of the local custom in *Ḥutz LaAretz*. Others view an airport, even within the vicinity of a city with a Jewish population, as "extra-territorial," and therefore one would be permitted to land and stay in the airport. However, one would certainly not be permitted to drive to a town with Jewish residents, as that certainly deviates from the public observance of Yom Tov.[66]

Ḥol HaMo'ed

CHAPTER 5

Issur Melakha on Ḥol HaMo'ed

ISSUR MELAKHA ON ḤOL HAMO'ED

The Talmud dedicates an entire tractate to the laws of Ḥol HaMo'ed, the intermediate days between the first and last days of Yom Tov. The Gemara teaches that one must refrain from performing *melakhot,* actions normally forbidden on Shabbat and Yom Tov, unless a specific, legitimate need arises. In addition, the Rabbis prohibited other actions, such as those that involve great effort, as well as laundering and haircuts, in order to protect the integrity of the festival. According to *Tur,* one is permitted to perform *melakhot* on Ḥol HaMo'ed for one of five reasons:

(1) If one will incur a financial loss by refraining from doing so (*davar haaved*).

(2) For the sake of *okhel nefesh.*

(3) For an individual need related to the festival (*tzorekh hamo'ed*), as long as the *melakha* is not a *maase uman* (a *melakha* ordinarily performed by a professional).

(4) For the sake of public need (*tzorkhei rabbim*).

(5) One may hire a worker who has nothing to eat in order to support him.[1]

At times, one must also take into account the degree of skill and effort necessary to perform the *melakha,* as well as whether the *melakha* was deliberately scheduled to be performed on the festival.

The Talmud suggests numerous sources for the prohibition of *melakha* on Ḥol HaMo'ed. The final *baraita* brought by the Gemara states:

> Another [*baraita*] taught: "Six days you shall eat unleavened bread; and on the seventh day shall be restraint [of work] unto to the Lord" [Deut. 16:8]. Just as the seventh day is under restraint [in respect of work], so the six days are under restraint [in respect of work]. If [you should think that] just as the seventh day is under restraint in respect of all manner of work, so the six days are under restraint in respect of all manner of work, therefore Scripture teaches: "And on the seventh day shall be restraint [of work]" – only the seventh day is under restraint in respect of all manner of work, but the six days are not under restraint in respect of all manner of work. Thus, Scripture left it to the sages to tell you on which day [work] is forbidden and on which day it is permitted, which manner of work is forbidden and which is permitted. (Ḥagiga 18a)

The search for a biblical source for the *issur melakha* on Ḥol HaMo'ed strongly implies that his prohibition is *mideoraita*. Indeed, the Gemara elsewhere explicitly describes the prohibition of *melakha* on Ḥol HaMo'ed as such (Mo'ed Katan 11b).

The *Rishonim*, however, note difficulties in maintaining that *melakha* is biblically prohibited on Ḥol HaMo'ed. First, a number of passages imply that the *issur melakha* is only *miderabbanan*. For example, the Gemara implies that the sages prohibited *melakha* on Ḥol HaMo'ed because it entails strenuous activity (*tirḥa*) (Mo'ed Katan 13a). Similarly, the Yerushalmi cites R. Abba b. Mamel, who said:

> If my colleagues would join me, I would permit *melakha* on Ḥol HaMo'ed. The only reason it is prohibited is in order that people rejoice in the festival and spend their time immersed in learning Torah. Nowadays, though, people eat and drink excessively and act frivolously during the festival. (Y. Mo'ed Katan 2:3)

This passage clearly implies that *melakha* was forbidden by the Rabbis, and therefore R. Abba b. Mamel relates that with the proper support, he would permit *melakha* on Ḥol HaMo'ed.

Second, the laws of Ḥol HaMo'ed are not consistent with other biblical laws. For example, Rabbeinu Tam notes that the Rabbis permitted certain *melakhot* on Ḥol HaMo'ed if refraining from them may lead to financial loss, known as a "*davar haaved*." He asks, "Where do we find a biblical prohibition which is at times prohibited and at times permitted?"[2] Similarly, the *Mordekhai* asks how the Rabbis would be so lenient in establishing which *melakhot* to prohibit and which to permit if the prohibition is *mideoraita*.[3]

These questions and others led many *Rishonim* to conclude that the verses cited in the passage above should be understood to be "*asmakhtot*," attempts to match a rabbinic prohibition to a biblical verse; the prohibition of *melakha* on Ḥol HaMo'ed is in fact only *miderabbanan*.[4]

Some *Rishonim* provide the reason for this prohibition and explain the Rabbis' dispensations accordingly. For example, Ritva explains:

> The reason for the prohibition of *melakha* on Ḥol HaMo'ed is because of strenuous activities (*tirḥa*) and in order to ensure that one does not minimize the rejoicing of the festival (*simḥat haregel*). Therefore, the Rabbis permitted that which is for the sake of the festival or that which may lead to financial loss, so that a person should not be concerned with his loss and limit his enjoyment of the festival. For that reason, they permitted paying a worker who does not have enough to eat.[5]

Furthermore, the Yerushalmi cited above implies that the Rabbis prohibited *melakha* on Ḥol HaMo'ed so that one may spend one's time "immersed in Torah."

Other *Rishonim* imply that the *issur melakha* of Ḥol HaMo'ed is *mideoraita*.[6] They would apparently agree, however, that the Torah entrusted the sages to determine "which manner of work is forbidden, and which is permitted." Some *Rishonim* maintain that some *melakhot* are biblically prohibited, while others are rabbinically prohibited. *Nimukei Yosef*, for example, records:

> [Ramban] struck a compromise and said that all *melakha* which is not necessary for the festival and does not entail financial loss is prohibited *mideoraita*... and the Rabbis prohibited some of these *melakhot*, as has been explained.[7]

Rashba[8] and Ritva[9] concur.

Rambam's' position has received much attention. He writes:

> Although Ḥol HaMo'ed is not referred to as a Sabbath, since it is referred to as "*mikra kodesh*" (a holy convocation) and it was a time when the *ḥagiga* sacrifices were brought in the Temple, it is forbidden to perform *melakha* during this period, so that these days will not be regarded as ordinary weekdays that are not endowed with holiness at all. A person who performs forbidden labor on these days is given lashes for rebelliousness (*makkot mardut*), for the prohibition is rabbinic in origin (*midivrei soferim*). Not all the types of "servile labor" forbidden on a holiday are forbidden on it, for the intent of the prohibition is that the day not be regarded as an ordinary weekday with regard to all matters. Therefore, some labors are permitted on it and some are forbidden.[10]

Many commentators conclude that Rambam believes that the prohibition of *melakha* on Ḥol HaMo'ed is of rabbinic origin, "so that these days will not be regarded as ordinary weekdays." Some, however, challenge this interpretation. R. Yitzchak of Karlin (1784–1852), *Keren Ora*, notes that Rambam, in his commentary to the Mishna, refers to the prohibition of *melakha* on Ḥol HaMo'ed as coming from "tradition" (*bekabbala*), a term often used to describe commandments "received" at Sinai and passed down generation after generation. In fact, the term "*midivrei soferim*," which he used in the *Mishneh Torah* also may be used to describe biblical commandments derived through rabbinic exegesis.[11] *Keren Ora* concludes that Rambam maintains that *melakha* on Ḥol HaMo'ed is fundamentally biblically prohibited so that one can devote his energies to fulfilling the mitzvot of the festival. The specific prohibitions, however, were defined by the Rabbis, as implied by the Talmud (Ḥagiga 18a).[12]

TEFILLIN ON ḤOL HAMO'ED

Interestingly, the question of whether *melakha* is biblically or rabbinically prohibited on Ḥol HaMo'ed relates to a broader question regarding the nature of these days. Put simply, to what extent are these days fundamentally "*ḥol*" (weekdays) with certain aspects of *mo'ed* (such as *simḥa* and Musaf), or, are they days of *mo'ed* that resemble weekdays in some respects? The *Rishonim* relate to this issue explicitly in their discussion regarding wearing *tefillin* on Ḥol HaMo'ed. The Talmud records a debate regarding whether one must put on *tefillin* on Shabbat and Yom Tov (Eiruvin 96a). The Gemara cites a disagreement regarding the reason for those who rule that one should not wear *tefillin* on those days:

> It was taught: It is written, "And you shall observe this ordinance in its season from day to day" [Ex. 13:10]. "Day," but not night; "from day," but not all days; hence the Sabbaths and the festivals are excluded. This is the view of R. Yose HaGlili. R. Akiva says: This ordinance refers only to the Passover offering! He derives it from the text from which R. Akiva derives it. For it was taught: One might have thought that a man should put on the *tefillin* on Sabbaths and on festivals. Scripture therefore says, "And it shall be for a sign upon your hand, and for frontlets between your eyes" – that is, [only on those days] which stand in need of a sign [are *tefillin* to be worn], but Sabbaths and festivals are excluded, since they themselves are a sign. (Menaḥot 36a)

R. Yose HaGlili explains that the verse implies that there are days on which one wears *tefillin* and others on which one does not. R. Akiva suggests a more fundamental approach: Man needs a constant "sign" (*ot*) reflecting the relationship between him and God. During the week, *tefillin* play this role. On the Shabbat and festivals, however, one need not wear *tefillin*, as these days themselves are a "sign" of the relationship between man and God.

Must one wear *tefillin* on Ḥol HaMo'ed? Some *Rishonim* derive from a passage in the Talmud, which teaches that one may write *tefillin* on Ḥol HaMo'ed "for oneself" (Mo'ed Katan 19a)[13] that one must wear *tefillin* on Ḥol HaMo'ed just as one wears *tefillin* on a weekday.[14] They explain that the *issur melakha* on Ḥol HaMo'ed, the prohibition of eating *ḥametz*, and the obligation to sit in the *sukka* do not constitute an "*ot*" that would obviate the need for *tefillin*. Many *Rishonim*, however, explain that one need not wear *tefillin* on Ḥol HaMo'ed, as Ḥol HaMo'ed also constitutes an "*ot*."[15] They disagree, however, as to whether it is the prohibition of *melakha* on Ḥol HaMo'ed that serves as the "*ot*" or the mitzvot of *sukka* and *matza*, which apply during Ḥol HaMo'ed as well. Some *Rishonim*, uncertain about whether or not one should wear *tefillin* on Ḥol HaMo'ed, argue that one should wear *tefillin* without a blessing.[16]

R. Yosef Karo records that Sephardic Jews originally wore *tefillin* on Ḥol HaMo'ed, until they discovered a kabbalistic passage, the *Midrash Ne'elam*, which prohibits wearing *tefillin* on Ḥol HaMo'ed.[17] He rules accordingly in the *Shulḥan Arukh*.[18] Rema, however, rules in accordance with *Tur*'s father (Rosh) that one must wear *tefillin* on Ḥol HaMo'ed and quietly recite the blessing.[19] *Taz* recommends wearing *tefillin* without a blessing on Ḥol HaMo'ed.[20]

In practice, Sephardic Jews do not wear *tefillin* on Ḥol HaMo'ed, in accordance with the *Shulḥan Arukh*. Many Ashkenazim do wear *tefillin* on Ḥol HaMo'ed, following the position of Rema, although they do not generally recite the *berakhot*, as cited above. Interestingly, the Vilna Gaon (R. Eliyahu b. Shlomo Zalman, 1720–1797) ruled that one should not wear *tefillin* on Ḥol HaMo'ed,[21] and this position became increasingly popular in Lithuania, as recorded by the *Arukh HaShulḥan*.[22] R. Soloveitchik records that his father and grandfather, R. Chaim Soloveitchik, following the custom of the Vilna Gaon and of the Volozhin Yeshiva, rejected the long-standing Ashkenazic practice and did not wear *tefillin* on Ḥol HaMo'ed. He explains that it is not the *issur melakha* that precludes *tefillin* on Ḥol HaMo'ed, but rather its *kedushat hayom* (sanctity). Therefore, just as one does not put on *tefillin* on Shabbat and Yom Tov, one does not put on *tefillin* on Ḥol HaMo'ed.[23] Interestingly, this is also the practice of many Hasidim, based upon the ruling of R. Yitzchak Luria (Arizal, 1534–1572).[24] This also became the standard practice of all Jews in Eretz Yisrael.

While there are clearly many variables in determining whether or not to wear *tefillin* on Ḥol HaMo'ed, as we have demonstrated, the status, nature, and source of the *issur melakha* on Ḥol HaMo'ed may certainly play a role in this question.

CHAPTER 6

Haircuts and Laundry on Ḥol HaMo'ed

INTRODUCTION

Ḥol HaMo'ed is a festive time, or, as Rambam describes it, a "mikra kodesh."[1] Some Rishonim note that the mitzva of simḥat Yom Tov applies on Ḥol HaMo'ed as well. For example, Rambam writes:

> It is forbidden to fast or recite eulogies on the seven days of Pesaḥ, the eight days of Sukkot, and the other holidays. On these days, a person is obligated to be happy and in good spirits; he, his children, his wife, the members of his household, and all those who depend on him, as [Deut. 16:14] states: "And you shall rejoice in your festivals." The "rejoicing" mentioned in the verse refers to sacrificing peace offerings, as will be explained in Hilkhot Ḥagiga. Nevertheless, included in [this charge to] rejoice is that he, his children, and the members of his household should rejoice, each one in a manner appropriate for him.[2]

In fact, *posekim* discuss whether one must eat a meal with bread on each day of Ḥol HaMo'ed[3] or whether a meal of fruit suffices.[4] They also discuss whether one must drink wine and eat meat each day of the festival.[5] Some even teach that one should wear nice clothing on Ḥol HaMo'ed.[6] The *Mishna Berura* concludes that although one need not eat a meal of bread, nor must one wear Shabbat clothing, one should treat the days of Ḥol HaMo'ed with greater respect than one treats a weekday.[7]

The Rabbis were concerned with treating Ḥol HaMo'ed with the proper respect and honor, and they feared that one might engage in unnecessary labors on these days. In this context, one can understand why they prohibited taking a haircut and laundering on Ḥol HaMo'ed, due to these concerns.

HAIRCUTS AND SHAVING ON ḤOL HAMO'ED

The Mishna lists those people who may take a haircut during Ḥol HaMo'ed:

> And these [people may] take haircuts during Ḥol HaMo'ed: One arriving [home] from abroad, or from a place of captivity or one coming out of prison, or one under a ban to whom the sages have [just] granted absolution. And likewise, one who applied to a sage and was absolved [by him], and a Nazirite or a leper on emerging from his [state of ritual] impurity to [begin] his purification. (Mo'ed Katan 13b)

These people were either physically or legally unable to cut their hair before the festival and are therefore permitted to take a haircut during Ḥol HaMo'ed.

The Gemara explains that the sages forbade taking a haircut during the festival "so that they do not enter upon the festival in a state of untidiness." In other words, this enactment ensures that people take haircuts before the festival, in honor of the festival. The Gemara then questions the extent of inability to cut one's hair before the festival that would justify taking a haircut during Ḥol HaMo'ed:

> R. Zeira inquired: Suppose one had lost something on the day before the festival? [Do we say,] since he was prevented [from attending to himself before], he may [take a haircut], or perhaps, as the reason is not obvious, he may not? (Mo'ed Katan 14a)

Although the Gemara leaves this question unanswered, *Tur* and *Beit Yosef* rule stringently.[8] Accordingly, only in one of the cases enumerated by that mishna may one take a haircut during Ḥol HaMo'ed. Ritva explains that the Gemara assumes that although "*giluaḥ*" is technically a *melakha*, since one takes a haircut for the sake of one's appearance, it is considered to be a form of *okhel nefesh*. Therefore, had the Rabbis not forbidden taking a haircut, it would have been permitted.[9]

The *posekim* discuss the scope of this prohibition. For example, one may certainly wash and comb one's hair, even though this will certainly entail pulling out some hairs.[10] Furthermore, one may cut hair for medical reasons, such as hair around a wound.[11] A man may trim his moustache,[12] and woman may remove body hair that she normally removes.[13]

In recent years, shaving has become a societal norm in many places, and it is certainly common for observant men to shave daily in a permissible manner. Does the prohibition of taking a haircut during Ḥol HaMo'ed apply equally to shaving? Seemingly, the *gezeira* described above, which prohibited taking a haircut during Ḥol HaMo'ed in order to ensure that one properly prepare for the festival, should not apply to shaving, as even one who shaves before the festival will need to shave again a day or two later! Furthermore, one might even suggest that not shaving causes the ordinarily clean-shaven man discomfort, and may even be seen as a lack of respect for the festive days of Ḥol HaMo'ed.

Initially, we might base a lenient position upon an opinion cited and rejected by numerous medieval German *Rishonim*,[14] which claims that one who took a haircut before Yom Tov may certainly have his hair cut during Ḥol HaMo'ed, as he demonstrated proper respect for the festival. *Tur*[15] and later authorities attribute this position to Rabbeinu Tam. *Tur* rejects this opinion, arguing that it is not publicly known that one took a haircut before Yom Tov. Furthermore, he wonders why such a leniency, if applicable, did not appear in the Mishna. The *Shulḥan Arukh* does not mention this position.

Although the *posekim* do not accept the position attributed to Rabbeinu Tam, R. Yechezkel Landau rules that one who shaved before the festival may hire an "*ani she'ein lo ma yokhal*," an impoverished barber, to shave him during Ḥol HaMo'ed. He argues that those who reject Rabbeinu Tam's rationale maintain that one who shaved before Yom Tov, and thus afforded Yom Tov its due respect, is still prohibited to shave because shaving is a prohibited labor on Ḥol HaMo'ed. However, one may hire an impoverished worker to perform a labor on Ḥol HaMo'ed, and therefore, in this case, such behavior should be permitted.[16] R. Moshe Sofer, known as Ḥatam Sofer,[17] and most other *Aḥaronim*, reject this leniency.

Most authorities prohibit shaving during Ḥol HaMo'ed unless one risks facing financial loss.[18] Two of the last century's Torah giants, however, permitted shaving during Ḥol HaMo'ed.

R. Moshe Feinstein argues forcefully that in a society in which it is customary for a man to shave daily, there is simply no prohibition to shave during Ḥol HaMo'ed. He insists that the Mishna's prohibition does not apply to one who clearly shaves every day, and insists that even those who reject the position attributed to Rabbeinu Tam would agree to this logic. He concludes, however, as follows:

> Therefore, it is clear, in my humble opinion, that in our times, and in our country, in which people who ordinarily shave do so every day… that there is no prohibition at all…. In any case, I do not generally permit [one to shave] unless one has a great need or one suffers great discomfort. [However,] if one wishes to rely upon this even for his appearance, he should not be criticized, as according to the letter of the law, it is permitted, in my humble opinion.[19]

R. Yosef Dov Soloveitchik also permitted shaving on Ḥol HaMo'ed. R. Hershel Schachter summarizes R. Soloveitchik's position:

> Regarding those who shave every day, it is obvious that they may shave on Ḥol HaMo'ed as well, since it is clear from the explanation of the Mishna given in Mo'ed Katan 14a that every case where it is obvious to all that a person is under duress, and thus cannot shave, that a person may shave on Ḥol HaMo'ed. All know that a clean-shaven person cannot, on the eve of a holiday, shave those hairs that have not yet appeared.[20]

Not only is shaving *permitted* on Ḥol HaMo'ed, R. Soloveitchik argues, but "one who is permitted to shave on Ḥol HaMo'ed *must* shave, so as not to be appear unkempt on Ḥol HaMo'ed and so as to avoid entering the last days of the festival looking repugnant." This is the practice and ruling of many of R. Soloveitchik's students.

LAUNDRY ON ḤOL HAMO'ED

Just as the Rabbis prohibited taking a haircut during the festival in order to ensure that one cut one's hair before Yom Tov, the Mishna similarly teaches that one may not launder during Ḥol HaMo'ed (Mo'ed Katan 13b).

In addition to the cases listed above regarding haircuts, the Mishna enumerates other situations in which one may launder during Ḥol HaMo'ed.

> Hand towels, barbers' towels, and bath towels [may be washed]. *Zavim* and *zavot*, as well as menstruate women or women after childbirth and all those emerging from [a state of ritual] impurity to [begin] their purification, are allowed [to wash their garments]; but all other men are forbidden.

The Gemara explains that even one who has more than one of these garments may wash them if they are soiled, as they become dirty quickly (Mo'ed Katan 18a). Furthermore, the Gemara cites R. Yoḥanan, who said that "one who has only one garment is allowed to wash it during the festival." Similarly, some *Rishonim*[21] cite the Yerushalmi (Y. Mo'ed Katan 3:2), which permits washing children's clothing, as this case "is akin to one who has only one garment."

The *Shulḥan Arukh* rules that one may wash all of these garments on Ḥol HaMo'ed. However, one should only wash according to one's need, and therefore one who is not accustomed to change his sheets or towels every day should not wash them during Ḥol HaMo'ed.[22] However, handkerchiefs,[23] as well as other items that are changed daily, such as pantyhose and stockings, may be laundered according to one's needs. When washing in a washing machine, some *Aḥaronim* permit adding other clothes which one needs for the festival.[24]

In our day, people change their undergarments daily, especially in hot weather. Therefore, some write that just as the Mishna permits washing hand towels, which become dirty each day, one may wash underwear in a case of need during Ḥol HaMo'ed.[25] Some permit washing all clothing which one is accustomed to change every day.[26] A hotel may wash sheets and towels on Ḥol HaMo'ed, as guests are not expected to use dirty towels and linens. Similarly, a hospital may wash sheets, towels, and linens, as aside from the consideration raised above, not doing so may pose a health risk. One may remove stains on Ḥol HaMo'ed, as this is not considered to be a form of laundering.[27] Furthermore, if a garment becomes stained and cannot be cleaned unless it is washed immediately, it may be washed, as the situation entails financial loss.[28] If one's Yom Tov or Shabbat shirt has been stained, one may wash one's shirt for Yom Tov.[29] One may iron one's clothing on Ḥol HaMo'ed. Similarly, one may shine one's shoes on Ḥol HaMo'ed.[30] One who leaves his home for the entire festival is not required to take enough clothing to last the entire festival. Rather, he should take with him a normal amount, and if he or his family runs out, he may launder in accordance with the rulings stating above.[31]

Rosh HaShana

CHAPTER 7

Elul in Prayer and Custom

ELUL: THE NAME SAYS IT ALL

R. Shlomo Ganzfried (Hungary, 1804–1886) records numerous explanations for the name of the sixth month of the Hebrew calendar, Elul.[1] First, he cites R. Yitzchak Luria (Arizal), who explains that the four letters of the word "Elul" (*aleph-lamed-vav-lamed*) correspond to the initial letters of the words "*inna leyado, vesamti lekha*." This is a part of a verse that refers to one who kills another person unintentionally and must seek shelter in one of the cities of refuge (*arei miklat*): "And if a man does not lie in wait, but God *causes it to come to hand; then I will appoint you* a place where he may flee" (Ex. 21:13). Arizal explains that Elul is a propitious month to repent for sins committed throughout the year, adding that the *remez* (allusion) from the verse indicates that one should especially repent for unintentional sins.

R. Ganzfried also cites the *dorshei reshumot*,[2] those who interpret the law symbolically for the sake of edification and instruction, as asserting that the letters of "Elul" correspond to the initial letters of "*et levavekha ve'et levav*," from the verse, "And God will circumcise *your heart and the heart* of your seed" (Deut. 30:6). He adds that the letters of "Elul" also match the initial letters of the phrase "*Ani ledodi, vedodi li*" – "I am my beloved's, and my beloved is mine" (Song. 6:3). Finally, he suggests that the initial letters of the phrase "*ish lere'ehu umatanot la'evyonim*" – "each to his fellow and gifts to the poor" (Est. 9:22) – also allude to Elul.

R. Ganzfried notes that these last three interpretations highlight the three central themes of the High Holy Days, "repentance, prayer, and charity" (Y. Taanit 2:1). These three activities should be assiduously practiced during the month of Elul. He apparently views the month of Elul as a period of preparation for the repentance of Rosh HaShana and Yom Kippur. We must begin the arduous process of repentance a full month before the High Holy Days.

While this is certainly true, one might suggest a more precise description of the spiritual experience of Elul. As we mentioned above, Arizal draws a connection between the unintentional killer, who must flee to a city of refuge, and the month of Elul. What is the experience of such a person, and how does it relate to Elul?

While the month of Elul certainly prepares us for the holidays of Tishrei, during which repentance and absolution are major, and perhaps primary, themes, the essence of Elul is "spiritual crisis," as reflected by the prayers and the shofar. One who flees from his victim's relatives, fearing retribution, and runs to the exile of a city of refuge, seeks protection, shelter, and safety because of his transgression. Similarly, one who sins seeks refuge with God, hoping and praying that his remorse and repentance will be accepted. Thus, while the last three verses allude to one's behavior during Elul, Arizal captures the true experience of Elul: fleeing one's sins in fear and desperation, in search of divine protection.

THE BLOWING OF THE SHOFAR DURING ELUL

One of the most well-known customs of the month of Elul is the blowing of the shofar. From the first day of Elul until the day before Rosh HaShana, congregations customarily blow the shofar, sounding the straight *tekia*, broken *shevarim*, and staccato *terua* upon concluding the morning prayers. What is the origin and meaning of this custom?

Pirkei deRabbi Eliezer, a post-talmudic aggadic collection, connects this practice to the giving of the second set of tablets (*luḥot*). After shattering the first set of tablets in response to the sin of the Golden Calf and praying on behalf of the people, Moshe was summoned to ascend Mount Sinai, again, on Rosh Ḥodesh Elul, to receive the second set of *luḥot* (Deut. 10:1). He returned to the people forty days later, on Yom Kippur.

> On Rosh Ḥodesh [Elul], the Holy One, Blessed be He, said to Moshe: "Ascend the mount to Me." And they sounded the shofar in all the camp [to notify the people] that Moshe had ascended the mount, so that they should not stray again after idols. And the Holy One, Blessed be He, ascended in that shofar, as it is written, "God ascends in a *terua*" [Ps. 47:6]. Thus, the sages established that the shofar should be sounded every Rosh Ḥodesh [Elul].[3]

Interestingly, the Midrash does not explain how the shofar prevents the nation from returning to their idolatrous ways, nor does it fully explain why the sages enacted that the shofar should be blown each Rosh Ḥodesh Elul. Does the shofar merely "remind" us of Moshe's actions? As we shall demonstrate in the next chapter, blowing the shofar signals crisis and engenders fear, as the prophet Amos describes, "Shall a shofar be blown in the city, and the people not tremble?" (Amos 3:6). The prophet Zephaniah further connects the blowing of the shofar with crisis and distress:

> That day is a day of wrath, a day of trouble and distress, a day of waste and desolation, a day of darkness and gloominess, a day of clouds and thick darkness, a day of shofar and *terua*. (Zeph. 1:15–16)

Moshe Rabbeinu apparently hoped that this sense of alarm and impending disaster would prevent the people from returning to idolatry, and in future situations it would lead the nation (Num. 10:9) and individuals[4] to repent. This is the overwhelming feeling of the month of Elul, and it is similarly expressed through the shofar blasts.

Based upon the Midrash, R. Avraham b. Natan HaYarḥi (Provence, twelfth to thirteenth century) records in his *Sefer HaManhig* that while the original enactment entailed blowing the shofar yearly on Rosh Ḥodesh Elul, in France, the shofar was blown throughout the entire month.[5] R. Yaakov b. Asher cites the passage from *Pirkei DeRabbi Eliezer* in *Tur,* explaining that we sound the shofar in order to urge the Jewish people to repent and to "confuse the Adversary." He records that Ashkenazic communities blow the shofar each morning and evening after their prayers.[6] Rema cites the practice of blowing the shofar each morning during Elul,[7] and the *Aḥaronim* record different customs regarding whether one should begin from the first day of Rosh Ḥodesh Elul (the thirtieth of Av) or the second day (the first of Elul). It is customary to blow the shofar each morning of Elul, beginning on the second day of Rosh Ḥodesh.[8]

SELIḤOT

Tur cites three customs regarding *Seliḥot,* the penitential prayers recited before Yom Kippur.[9] R. Amram Gaon endorses the custom of the great Babylonian yeshivas to recite *Seliḥot* between Rosh HaShana and Yom Kippur. R. Hai Gaon records a custom to recite *Seliḥot* during the entire month of Elul. Finally, *Tur* notes the Ashkenazic custom of reciting *Seliḥot* beginning on the Saturday night before Rosh HaShana.

Today, Sephardic Jews recite *Seliḥot* each morning of the entire month of Elul, continuing until Yom Kippur.[10] Ashkenazic Jews begin reciting *Seliḥot* on the Saturday night before Rosh HaShana, unless Rosh HaShana falls on a Monday or Tuesday, in which case they begin the previous Saturday night in order to recite *Seliḥot* for at least four days before Rosh HaShana.[11]

What is the nature of this unique prayer, and why is it befitting for the month of Elul? This question may relate to a broader understanding of the nature of prayer. Seemingly, one can identify two fundamentally unique types of prayer: the daily prayer and the prayer recited in times of need. Regarding the first type, the *Rishonim* question the origin of the daily obligation of prayer. Rambam rules that there is a biblical obligation to pray each and every day;[12] Ramban[13] and Rashi[14] disagree. Ramban notes, however, that while daily prayer is of rabbinic origin, another type of prayer is biblically mandated:

> [This derivation] may be…instructing us that included in the service [of God] is that we must…pray to Him in times of crisis. Our eyes and hearts should turn toward Him alone, like the eyes of slaves to their masters. This

> is similar to what the Torah states, "And when you go to war in your land against the adversary that oppresses you, then you shall sound a *terua* with the trumpets; and you shall be remembered before the Lord your God, and you shall be saved from your enemies" [Numbers 10:9]. It is a mitzva to respond to every crisis which the community faces by crying out to Him in prayer.

According to Ramban, there is a biblical obligation to respond to crisis with prayer. Rambam seems to concur, as he writes:

> There is a positive commandment to cry and call out with the trumpets upon every crisis which confronts the community.... This is the way of repentance, that during a crisis they should cry and call out; they should know that their condition is a function of their bad behavior.... This is what will allow them to avert the crisis. This is the way of repentance, that when a crisis comes, [the nation] should cry and call out, and all should realize that because of their deeds, their situation has worsened.[15]

What type of prayer is the *Seliḥot* service? On the one hand, it begins with the recitation of *Ashrei* and concludes with *Taḥanun*, giving the appearance of a standard service. However, R. Soloveitchik notes that the content of *Seliḥot* differs from our regular prayers. He contrasts *tefilla* (prayer) with *tze'aka* (crying out):

> In halakhic liturgy, prayer at the stage of "*tze'aka*" is called "*Seliḥot*." There are four distinctive characteristics of "*Seliḥot*:" (1) Recital of the Thirteen Attributes of Mercy; (2) Confession; (3) Repetition of short sentences, distinguished by simplicity of form; (4) Reading of prophetic verses of petition or praise.[16]

The main distinction between "*tefilla*" (represented by the *Shemoneh Esreh*) and "*tze'aka*" (as represented by *Seliḥot*) lies in the absence of strict formulation in the case of the latter. While "*tefilla*" is a meditative-reflective act, "*tze'aka*" is immediate and compulsive. The content of *Seliḥot* can be summed up by one of the concluding supplications: "*Aneinu, Hashem, aneinu*!" – "Answer us, God, answer us!" R. Soloveitchik points to the lack of order or articulation in the *Seliḥot*. *Seliḥot*, he explains, are frantic prayers of crisis said in response to the spiritual uncertainty and fear brought about by the approaching High Holy Days. Thus, *Seliḥot* capture and characterize the essence of the month of Elul. How fortunate are the Sephardic Jews who recite *Seliḥot* each morning of the month!

THE THIRTEEN ATTRIBUTES OF MERCY

The Thirteen Attributes of Mercy, as R. Soloveitchik notes, are both central to and define the *Seliḥot* service. The Torah refers to God's attributes of mercy, which are employed as supplications to assuage God's anger, in two contexts. After the sin of the Golden Calf, God reveals these attributes as He forges a "new" covenant with the Jewish people:

> Then God passed by in front of him and proclaimed, "**Lord, Lord, God, compassionate and gracious, slow to anger, and abounding in lovingkindness and truth; who keeps lovingkindness for thousands, who forgives iniquity, transgression, and sin; yet He will by no means leave the guilty unpunished, visiting the iniquity of fathers on the children and on the grandchildren to the third and fourth generations.**" Moshe made haste to bow low toward the earth and prostrate. He said, "If now I have found favor in Your sight, God, I pray, let God go along in our midst, even though the people are so obstinate, and pardon our iniquity and our sin, and take us as Your own possession." Then God said, "Behold, I am making a covenant. Before all your people I will perform miracles which have not been produced in all the earth, nor among any of the nations; and all the people among whom you live will see the working of God, for it is an awesome thing that I am going to perform with you." (Ex. 34:6–10)

In addition, after God threatens to destroy the Jewish people in the wake of the sin of the spies, Moshe pleads with God, concluding:

> But now, I pray, let God's power be great, just as You have declared, "**Lord is slow to anger and abundant in lovingkindness, forgiving iniquity and transgression; but He will by no means clear the guilty, visiting the iniquity of the fathers on the children to the third and the fourth generations.**" Pardon, I pray, the iniquity of this people according to the greatness of Your lovingkindness, just as You have forgiven this people from Egypt even until now. (Num. 14:17–19)

The Talmud elaborates upon these events:

> "Then God passed by in front of him and proclaimed" – R. Yoḥanan said: Were it not written in the text, it would be impossible for us to say such a thing! This verse teaches us that God wrapped Himself like the prayer-leader and showed Moshe the order of prayer. He said to him: Whenever Israel sin, let them perform this service before Me, and I will forgive them.... R. Yehuda said: There is a covenant made concerning the Thirteen Attributes, that they never return empty-handed, as it is written, "Behold, I am making a covenant." (Rosh HaShana 17a)

This passage implies that whenever the Jewish people sin – or, according to other sources, whenever the Jewish people are in crisis[17] – they are instructed to recite the Thirteen Attributes of Mercy, and they will be redeemed.

Ein Yosef (Rosh HaShana 17a) cites R. Moshe Alshikh (Tzefat, 1508–1593), who questions the Talmud's statement. Many people have recited the Thirteen Attributes of Mercy, he observed, without witnessing results! He explains in the name of the author of *Livnat HaSappir*:

> For this very reason, it does not say "*recite* this service," but rather, "*perform* this service" – implying that [forgiveness] is not dependent upon speech alone, but rather upon performance.... If you emulate these attributes, they will not return empty-handed.

Indeed, R. Moshe Cordovero (Tzefat, sixteenth century) bases his entire *Tomer Devora*, a book of ethical teaching, on how to emulate the Thirteen Attributes. The Thirteen Attributes of Mercy are not a magical formula for attaining forgiveness, but rather a spiritual and ethical program that should make a person worthy of forgiveness.

SELIḤOT WITHOUT A *MINYAN*

R. Amram Gaon[18] cites R. Natan, who records that it is customary for an individual praying without a *minyan* to omit the Thirteen Attributes of Mercy. R. Shlomo ibn Aderet, Rashba, concurs, explaining that the Thirteen Attributes are considered a *davar shebikedusha,* a "matter of holiness" similar to Kaddish and *Kedusha*. Such prayers are only recited with a *minyan*.[19] *Tur*, however, questions why reciting the Thirteen Attributes should be any different from ordinary study of Torah, as the prayer is based upon an excerpt from the Torah. One should thus be permitted to recite the Attributes even when praying alone.[20]

In his *Beit Yosef* commentary on *Tur*, R. Yosef Karo cites Rabbeinu Yona, who similarly disagrees with Rashba's opinion. In the *Shulḥan Arukh*, however, R. Karo rules that one praying alone should *not* recite the Thirteen Attributes. He stipulates that one may recite them "as if he were merely reading" ("*derekh keria be'alma*").[21] R. Moshe Feinstein explains that one praying alone should recite the entire verse (until "*ve'al ribbe'im*") and should avoid chanting the verse to the tune of supplicatory prayers, using instead a tune ordinarily used for learning.[22] Some cite Arizal's opinion that one should completely omit the passage of the Thirteen Attributes when praying alone.[23]

Rema adds that "an individual should not recite *Seliḥot* or '*VaYaavor*' [the verse preceding the Thirteen Attributes]."[24] *Taz* questions why reciting *Seliḥot* should be prohibited: "Is it prohibited for an individual to say the supplications he wishes?" He concludes that although an individual should refrain from reciting prayers that even mention the Thirteen Attributes, prayers that do not mention the Attributes may be said privately.[25] *Baḥ* and the *Mishna Berura*[26] disagree with Rema, insisting that all of the supplications may be recited by an individual. However, one should omit the Thirteen Attributes themselves, beginning from "*VaYaavor*," as mentioned above. The *Mishna Berura* writes that one should also refrain from reciting the Aramaic supplications that appear toward the end of the *Seliḥot* service, such as "*Maḥei UMassei*" and "*Maran DeVishmayya*," without a *minyan*.[27]

MAKHNISEI RAḤAMIM

One passage in *Seliḥot* has caused great controversy over the centuries. R. Yehuda b. Betzalel Loew (Prague, 1525–1609), Maharal, writes that one should not recite the passage "*Makhnisei Raḥamim*," in which we beseech the angels to carry our prayers to God.[28] Maharal insists that one must not employ intermediaries when praying to God, and that this prayer is therefore inappropriate.

Ḥatam Sofer writes that according to Maharal, one should refrain from reciting the liturgical poems "*Malakhei Raḥamim*" and "*Shelosh Esreh Middot*" as well, as they also address the angels. He concludes that while his congregation includes these prayers, he personally recites a lengthy *Taḥanun* in order to avoid reciting "*Makhnisei Raḥamim*."[29] Interestingly, R. Tzedkia b. Avraham HaRofeh (Italy, thirteenth century), the author of the *Shibbolei HaLeket*, raised this question centuries before Maharal did. He cites R. Avigdor Kohen-Tzedek, who brings talmudic passages to support his assertion that one may directly address angels and request that they pray or argue on one's behalf.[30]

THE PROPER TIME FOR *SELIḤOT*

Another question that raises great controversy is the proper time for the recitation of *Seliḥot*. The *Shulḥan Arukh* writes[31] that "it is customary to rise early in the last three hours of the night[32] to recite *Seliḥot*." Ashkenazic Jews, who begin reciting *Seliḥot* the week of Rosh HaShana, usually recite the first *Seliḥot* on Saturday night after midnight. This custom appears in *Leket Yosher*, a fifteenth-century work authored by R. Yosef b. Moshe, a student of R. Yisrael b. Petaḥya Isserlein (1390–1460), *Terumat HaDeshen*. The *Aḥaronim* have offered different explanations for this practice.

In recent generations, it has become popular to recite *Seliḥot* nightly, before midnight. The *Shaarei Teshuva*,[33] citing the *Birkei Yosef*, writes that if one finds himself in a congregation that recites *Seliḥot* before midnight, he should "not recite the Thirteen Attributes... [but rather] sit silently or say Psalms; but one may recite *Viduy*." Similarly, *Magen Avraham* cites Arizal, who strongly censures those who recite *Seliḥot* before midnight.[34] R. Ovadia Yosef also strongly criticizes the practice of reciting *Seliḥot* before midnight based upon kabbalistic sources.[35] These sources seem to view reciting the Thirteen Attributes before midnight as a particularly negative, if not damaging, act.

R. Moshe Feinstein notes that the primary objection raised by the *posekim* is kabbalistic, not halakhic. He suggests that while the recitation of the Thirteen Attributes may be "less effective" before midnight, it certainly should not be worse than any other prayer. R. Feinstein concludes that a congregation that might not otherwise recite *Seliḥot* or participate in activities aimed at inspiring repentance may, as a *horaat shaa* (temporary measure), recite *Seliḥot* before midnight. He adds that it may be preferable to recite *Seliḥot* between the second and third evening watch, which he calculates to be around 10:15–10:20 PM in New York.[36] R. Ovadia Yosef disagrees with this conclusion, suggesting that it might even be preferable to recite *Seliḥot* before Minḥa the next day!

It is noteworthy that members of various hasidic sects, such as the Gerrer and Talner Hasidim, recite *Seliḥot* after Maariv, well before midnight.[37] Similarly, R. Soloveitchik reportedly regularly participated in the early *Seliḥot minyan* of his son-in-law (Rabbi Dr. Yitzchak Twersky, the Talner Rebbe) in Boston, as well as the early *Seliḥot minyan* at Yeshiva University.[38]

LEDAVID HASHEM ORI

The *Kitzur Shulḥan Arukh* records:

> It is also customary in these lands to recite each morning and evening, from the second day of Rosh Ḥodesh Elul until Shemini Atzeret, the Psalm [27] "*LeDavid, Hashem ori veyish'i,*" in accordance with the Midrash, which derives, "'God is my light (*Hashem ori*)' – on Rosh HaShana; 'And my salvation (*veyish'i*)' – on Yom Kippur"; "and He hides me in His shelter (*besukko*)" [v. 5] – which is a hint to Sukkot.[39]

Incidentally, the original midrash does not include the reference to Sukkot.[40] While the Midrash clearly finds reference to the High Holy Days in this psalm, is that allusion merely incidental? We may suggest a deeper interpretation of the Midrash and of the custom to recite "*LeDavid*" during Elul.

The first verse, which is expounded upon by the Midrash, is followed by this passage (vv. 2–4):

> When evil-doers came upon me to eat up my flesh, my adversaries and my foes, they stumbled and fell. Though a host may encamp against me, my heart shall not fear; though war may rise up against me, even then will I be confident. One thing have I asked of God, this will I seek: that I may dwell in the house of God all the days of my life, to behold the graciousness of God, and to come early to His Temple.

The entire psalm describes King David's response to crisis and his attempt to deepen his connection with God and seek His shelter and protection. Therefore, the recitation of this psalm is consistent with the theme of Elul, which, as demonstrated above, is reflected by its name, the blowing of the shofar, and the *Seliḥot.*

While we have focused upon the sense of crisis and despair, there is another aspect of Elul that deserves mention. R. Shneur Zalman of Liadi (known also as the "Alter Rebbe" and the "Baal HaTanya"), the founder and first rebbe of the Chabad branch of Hasidim, discusses the uniqueness of the month of Elul in his *Likkutei Torah.*[41] He explains that unlike Shabbat and the festivals, Elul is a month when "*haMelekh basadeh*" – "the King is in the field." Even the simplest person, in the simplest clothing, can approach and become close to the King. Despite, or parallel to, our spiritual fears and anxieties, the days of Elul, similar to the days between Rosh HaShana and Yom Kippur, are days of divine immanence and proximity. It behooves us to take advantage of this opportunity.

CHAPTER 8

The Experience of Rosh HaShana

ROSH HASHANA IN TANAKH

Rosh HaShana, as it appears in Scripture, is somewhat mysterious. The Torah commands:

> And in the seventh month, on the first day of the month, it shall be a holy convocation (*mikra kodesh*) for you; you shall do no servile work; it shall be a day of *terua* for you. (Num. 29:1)

While the celebration of Rosh HaShana does not entail the pilgrimage component of the other festivals, it shares an *issur melakha*, the prohibition of labor, as well as the title of "*mikra kodesh*." The uniqueness of Rosh HaShana seems to lie in its being a "*yom terua*," a "day of *terua*," the ululating sound that is variously described in Scripture as emanating from the shofar, trumpets, or human throats. Similarly, the Torah teaches elsewhere:

> And God spoke to Moshe, saying: "Speak to the Israelites, saying: In the seventh month, on the first day of the month, it shall be a solemn rest for you, a *terua* memorial (*zikhron terua*), a holy convocation. You shall do no servile work, and you shall bring a fire-offering to God." (Lev. 23:23–25)

Here, too, Rosh HaShana is described by the term "*terua*." While our sages understand this to refer to the mitzva of shofar, the Torah uses the term to describe the day itself. In what way does "*terua*" characterize the day? What does blowing a shofar or trumpet symbolize?

Throughout Tanakh, we can identify two distinct, yet apparently contradictory, descriptions of these sounds, and thus, of Rosh HaShana itself. On the one hand, the prophet Zephaniah describes the horrors that will befall the Jewish people as follows:

> Hark ... the great day of God is near; it is near and hastens greatly, the sound of the day of God, wherein the mighty man cries bitterly. That day is a day of wrath, a day of trouble and distress, a day of waste and desolation, a day of darkness and gloominess, a day of clouds and thick darkness, **a day of shofar and *terua*,** against the fortified cities, and against the high towers. (Zeph. 1:10, 14–16)

The terms "shofar" and "*terua*" are clearly employed here to depict alarm and distress. Similarly, Amos describes the blowing of the shofar and the people's response: "Shall a shofar be blown in the city, and the people not tremble? Shall evil befall a city, and God has not done it?" (Amos 3:6). Indeed, when the Jewish people go out to war, they are commanded to make this sound:

> And when you go to war in your land against the adversary that oppresses you, then you shall sound a *terua* with the trumpets; and you shall be remembered before Lord your God, and you shall be saved from your enemies. (Num. 10:9)

These verses strongly imply that "a day of *terua*" is a day of alarm, crisis, and distress.

On the other hand, the trumpets are also sounded on festive days, as the very next verse in Numbers notes:

> And on the day of your joy, and on your appointed seasons, and on your new moons, you shall blow the trumpets over your burnt-offerings and over the sacrifices of your peace-offerings; and they shall be for you as a memorial before your God: I am Lord your God. (Num. 10:10)

Similarly, we find the following description of Ezra's joyous reading of the Torah on Rosh HaShana:

> And Ezra the Priest brought the Torah before the congregation, both men and women, and all that could listen with understanding, on the first day of the seventh month.... And Nehemiah, who was the governor, and Ezra the Priest, the Scribe, and the Levites who taught the people said to all the people, "*This day is holy to the Lord your God; neither mourn nor weep!*" For all the people were weeping, as they heard the words of the Torah. Then he said to them, "Go on your way. Eat the fat, and drink the sweet, and send portions to

> him for whom nothing is prepared; *for this day is holy to our God; do not be sad, for God's gladness is your strength.*" So the Levites stilled all the people, saying, "Hold your peace, for the day is holy; do not be sad." And all the people went their way to eat, to drink, to send portions, and to make great joy; because they had understood the words that were said to them. (Neh. 8:2, 9–12)

Nehemiah commands the people to overcome their grief over their failure to keep the Torah. Instead, it is time to celebrate, because "this day," Rosh HaShana, "is holy to our God."

In summary, Tanakh portrays Rosh HaShana as both "a day of *terua*" – of fear and apprehension – and a day of great joy.

HALLEL AND *SIMḤAT YOM TOV* ON ROSH HASHANA

The uncertainty regarding whether Rosh HaShana is a day of alarm and distress or one of happiness and joy continues in the halakhic literature. The Gemara instructs us to recite Hallel on the festivals and the eight days of Ḥanukka. The Gemara then questions why Hallel is not mandated on other special days, such as Rosh Ḥodesh, Ḥol HaMo'ed Pesaḥ, and Purim. Rosh HaShana and Yom Kippur seem to meet the requirements for Hallel; they are "appointed seasons" with a prohibition of labor. Why are they excluded?

> R. Abbahu said: Is it seemly for the King to be sitting on His Throne of Judgment, with the Books of Life and Death open before Him, while the people sing joyful praises to Him? (Arakhin 10b)

From the fact that the Gemara asks why Hallel is not recited on Rosh HaShana, it seems to assume that it would certainly be appropriate, if not obligatory, to recite the joyous prayer of Hallel on Rosh HaShana. The Gemara's answer, however, is somewhat unclear. Does the Gemara intend to deny Rosh HaShana any aspect of joy or happiness, or merely to temper it by omitting Hallel? Interestingly, Rambam writes:

> However, we do not recite Hallel on Rosh HaShana and Yom HaKippurim, as they are days of repentance (*teshuva*), fear (*yira*), and dread, *not days of excessive joy* (*simḥa yeteira*).[1]

Rambam describes Rosh HaShana as a day of repentance, characterized by "fear and dread," yet he still implies that there is some mitzva to rejoice.

Indeed, the *Rishonim* disagree as to whether the mitzva of *simḥat Yom Tov*, the command to rejoice on the festivals, applies to Rosh HaShana. The Torah instructs, "*Vesamaḥta beḥagekha*" – "And you shall rejoice on your holiday" (Deut. 16:14). Is this mitzva limited to the consumption of the *shalmei simḥa*, the joyous peace-offerings brought on the *Shalosh Regalim* (the Three Pilgrimage Festivals) for the purpose of rejoicing, in which case it would not apply to Rosh HaShana, or does it extend to other expressions of happiness as well?

Tosafot assume that the obligation of *simḥat Yom Tov* may only be fulfilled through the consumption of *shalmei simḥa*. The obligation ro rejoice on the festivals nowadays, in the absence of the Temple, must be rabbinic in nature.[2] On the other hand, Rambam writes:

> A person is obligated to rejoice on these days – he, his children, his wife, his grandchildren, and all those who have joined his family – as the Torah states, "And you shall rejoice on your holiday." Even though the Torah is referring to the obligation to offer and consume peace-offerings (the *shalmei simḥa*), *included in this obligation to rejoice is for a person and his entire family to rejoice in the manner that is appropriate for him.* How is this practiced? One distributes parched grain, nuts, and delicacies to the children. One purchases, depending on what he can afford, clothes and beautiful jewelry for the women in the family. The men eat meat and drink wine, as there is no rejoicing without meat and wine.[3]

Rambam expands the parameters of the mitzva of *simḥat Yom Tov* to include other expressions of joy as well. Clearly, Tosafot cannot maintain that the obligation to rejoice on festivals applies to Rosh HaShana, when there is no obligation to offer *shalmei simḥa*. Rambam, however, who expands the definition of *simḥat Yom Tov*, might apply this mitzva to Rosh HaShana. Indeed, as we saw above, he describes Rosh HaShana as a day without *excessive* happiness, but with happiness, nonetheless. Furthermore, he implies elsewhere[4] that the mitzva applies to festivals other than Pesaḥ and Sukkot, seemingly referring to Shavuot, Rosh HaShana, and Yom Kippur.

R. Aryeh Leib b. Asher Gunzberg discusses this issue in his *Shaagat Aryeh*,[5] concluding that there must be a mitzva of *simḥat Yom Tov* on Rosh HaShana since one is allowed to perform certain types of labor necessary for producing food ("*okhel nefesh*") on Rosh HaShana. If not for the commandment to rejoice, he assumes, it would be prohibited to cook on Rosh HaShana.

MOURNING ON ROSH HASHANA

The Mishna discusses which holidays pre-empt the first seven (*shiva*) and first thirty days (*sheloshim*) of mourning observed after the burial of a close relative (Mo'ed Katan 19a). The *ḥakhamim* and Rabban Gamliel dispute whether only the *Shalosh Regalim* cancel *shiva*, or if Rosh HaShana and Yom Kippur do so as well.

R. Aḥai Gaon (eighth century) explains that Rabban Gamliel, who rules that "Rosh HaShana and Yom Kippur are akin to the festivals," maintains that the commandment of *simḥat Yom Tov* also applies on these days. R. Aḥai Gaon clearly assumes that it is the mitzva to rejoice that cancels *shiva*.[6]

Ramban derives from the verse in Nehemiah cited above that there is "*simḥa* and a prohibition to be sad" on Rosh HaShana, and the observances of *shiva* and *sheloshim* are thus put to an end by Rosh HaShana.[7] The *Shulḥan Arukh* rules in accordance with Rabban Gamliel; Rosh HaShana and Yom Kippur cancel *shiva* and *sheloshim*.[8]

FASTING ON ROSH HASHANA

The halakhic ambivalence toward the nature of Rosh HaShana is found once again regarding one's demeanor while eating on the holiday. The *Shulḥan Arukh* writes:

> They eat, drink, and rejoice, and they do not fast on Rosh HaShana and Shabbat Shuva. However, they should not eat to satiety, in order that they not become lightheaded – "that the fear of God should be upon their faces" [cf. Ex. 20:16].[9]

The *Mishna Berura* explains that although Rosh HaShana is a "day of judgment," the commandment of *simḥa* obligates one to eat and drink, as stated in Nehemiah.[10]

Rema,[11] however, cites the *Terumat HaDeshen,*[12] who asserts that some consider it "a mitzva to fast on Rosh HaShana." *Magen Avraham,* in his introductory comments to this chapter, cites *Baḥ,* who relates that Maharshal would not eat fish on Rosh HaShana, as he especially enjoyed this dish and he wished to restrict himself in some way. *Magen Avraham* also cites a discussion regarding the propriety of eating meat and wearing festive clothing on Rosh HaShana.

In opposition to this opinion, the *Mordekhai*[13] cites R. Naḥshon Gaon, who prohibits fasting on Rosh HaShana due to its inherent *simḥa,* and *Taz*[14] and *Mishna Berura*[15] concur.

TEFILLA ON ROSH HASHANA

The question of the nature and experience of Rosh HaShana may also impact upon the text and recitation of the day's prayers. Rosh[16] and his son, the Baal HaTur,[17] record different customs regarding the text of the *Shemoneh Esreh* and Kiddush of Rosh HaShana. They cite R. Sar-Shalom, R. Paltoi Gaon, and R. Shmuel b. Ḥofni, who report that in the two major Babylonian yeshivas, the standard *Shalosh Regalim* formula was recited on Rosh HaShana, thanking God for giving us "***mo'adim lesimḥa,*** *ḥagim uzemanim lesason*" – "appointed seasons for rejoicing, holidays and times for jubilation." *Tur* concludes, however, that the custom is in accordance with R. Hai Gaon, who omits the references to *simḥa.* Clearly, these scholars are debating the very nature of Rosh HaShana.

Interestingly, the *posekim* also discuss the manner in which one should pray on Rosh HaShana. The *Kitzur Shulḥan Arukh,* for example, records that some are accustomed to praying the silent prayers of Rosh HaShana and Yom Kippur while bowed, with their heads lowered. He personally recommends praying upright, with a "bent heart and with tears."[18]

R. Ovadia Yosef also discusses this issue: should one pray with happiness and elation, or out of "fear of judgment," while crying?[19]

He cites R. Ḥayim Vital, who testifies that Arizal would cry during his Rosh HaShana and Yom Kippur prayers. Alternatively, he notes that the Vilna Gaon maintains that one should not cry during the prayers on Rosh HaShana and that the cantor should lead the prayers with a traditional festival melody.[20] R. Yosef concludes that one who is naturally overcome by tears may cry, but one should not bring himself to weep; rather, one should pray with happiness and great focus.

CONCLUSION

Rosh HaShana surely emerges as a confusing holiday. From the sages to the later *Aḥaronim*, our greatest minds have grappled with its nature and experience. It would seem that this confusion is no accident. In fact, all service of God, as King David relates, reflects this dialectic. In his Tehillim, we find both, "Serve God with joy; come before His presence with singing" (Ps. 100:2) and "Serve God with fear, and rejoice with trembling" (2:11). *Midrash Tehillim* asks:

> "Serve God with joy" – another verse says, "Serve God with fear." If [one serves] with joy, how is it with fear? And if [one serves] with fear, how is it with joy?[21]

The Midrash records different resolutions to this quandary. R. Aḥa suggests that one should serve God in this world with fear in order to reach the next world with happiness. Similarly, R. Aivu distinguishes between *tefilla*, during which joy is the primary feeling, and other activities, during which fear dominates. The Midrash suggests another type of solution as well: "'With joy' – is it possible without fear as well? The verse therefore teaches, 'with fear.'" In other words, joy and fear do not necessarily contradict each other; rather, they are crucial and complementary components of our service of God.

When we discuss the different reasons for the mitzva of shofar, we will note that Rosh HaShana is "*yom harat olam*," "the day of the world's creation," during which we coronate God as King over humanity. Standing before God and accepting upon ourselves His service inspires not only feelings of fear and trepidation, but feelings of joy and happiness as well. These seemingly contradictory feelings are natural for one who truly experiences and internalizes Rosh HaShana, setting the proper tone for the entire year, during which our service of God vacillates between *simḥa* and *yira*, and at times is even made up of of both.[22]

CHAPTER 9

The Reason for and Nature of *Mitzvat Tekiat Shofar*

REASONS FOR THE MITZVA OF SHOFAR

The fourteenth-century Spanish scholar R. David b. Yosef Abudraham records that R. Saadia Gaon (tenth century) enumerates ten reasons for the blowing of the shofar on Rosh HaShana. Many *Maḥzorim* (High Holy Day prayer books) include these reasons before the blowing of the shofar. We will focus on three of them.

Coronation

According to R. Saadia Gaon, one function of blowing the shofar, as it appears in the Bible, is to praise God and to crown Him as our King. When a king is crowned at the beginning of his rule, trumpets and horns are blown to announce his coronation. Similarly, we coronate God through the blowing of the shofar on Rosh HaShana. Indeed, the Book of Psalms states, "With trumpets and the sound of the shofar, shout before the King, God" (Ps. 98:6) and, "Praise Him with the blowing of the shofar; praise Him with the psaltery and harp" (150:3). Furthermore, Bileam tells Balak, "Nor has He seen perverseness in Israel; God, his God, is with him, and the king's shout (*teruat melekh*)" is in him" (Num. 23:21).

The Gemara, discussing the three central blessings of the Musaf prayer, also implies that this is a function of the shofar blowing:

> And you should recite before Me *Malkhuyot, Zikhronot,* and *Shofarot. Malkhuyot,* in order that you should coronate Me for you; *Zikhronot,* in order that your remembrance should rise to Me with favor. And how? Through the shofar. (Rosh HaShana 16a)

Elsewhere, the Gemara relates a debate between R. Eliezer and R. Yehoshua regarding whether the world was created in Tishrei or Nissan (Rosh HaShana 10b). The Gemara records that our prayers follow the opinion of R. Eliezer, as we say in the Musaf prayer, "This is the day, the beginning of Your work, a remembrance for the first day" (27a).

This reason for blowing the shofar on Rosh HaShana may be indicated by a comparison to another command to blow the shofar. Interestingly, the Torah never states explicitly that we blow the shofar on Rosh HaShana; rather, it simply describes the day with the term "*terua*" (Lev. 23:23–25; Num. 29:1). The Torah only explicitly commands us to blow a shofar on Yom Kippur of the *Yovel* (Jubilee) year:

> And you shall number seven sabbaths of years for you, seven times seven years; and there shall be for you the days of seven sabbaths of years – forty-nine years. Then shall you make proclamation with the **shofar of *terua*** on the tenth day of the **seventh month**; on the Day of Atonement shall you make proclamation with the shofar throughout all your land. (Lev. 25:8–9)

The Gemara derives that all of the laws of the shofar in "the seventh month" (i.e., those written regarding Yom Kippur of a *Yovel* year) apply equally to Rosh HaShana (Rosh HaShana 33b).

Is the relationship between *Yovel* and Rosh HaShana merely coincidental, or do they share a common theme? Rambam writes:

> And it is known that this blowing on the *Yovel* is to publicize the freedom [of the slaves]... as it says, "And you shall proclaim liberty" [Lev. 25:10] – and it is not similar to the sounding of the shofar on Rosh HaShana, which is a remembrance before God; whereas this [*Yovel*] is to release the slaves, as we have explained.[1]

According to Rambam, we should not search for the meaning of the shofar in the laws of the *Yovel.*

The *Sefer HaḤinukh,* however, a work that systematically discusses the laws, and some reasons for, the 613 mitzvot, offers a different perspective. The *Ḥinukh* offers the following reason for blowing the shofar on the *Yovel*:

> The reason for this mitzva, according to the simplest understanding, is that God wishes to declare to His nation that everything is His, and that everything which He wishes to bestow will ultimately be returned, because the land is His.... The message of *Yovel* is similar to that which earthly kingdoms practice, that the lord of the land periodically takes control of the fortified cities he has given to his vassals, in order to instill in them fear of their lord.[2]

The *Ḥinukh* does not believe that this is the reason for the shofar on Rosh HaShana, but based upon this reason, we might suggest that just as the shofar on *Yovel* is meant to declare the kingship of God, the shofar of Rosh HaShana similarly crowns Him.

Repentance

R. Saadia Gaon offers a second reason for the shofar:

> The second reason is that the day of Rosh HaShana is the first day of the *Aseret Yemei Teshuva* (the Ten Days of Repentance), and we blow the shofar... as if to warn: Whoever wishes to repent should do so; and if not, he will suffer the consequences.

The prophet Amos's description of the blowing of the shofar, "Shall a shofar be blown in the city, and the people not tremble?" (Amos 3:6), illustrates the potential impact of the shofar upon those who hear it. Similarly, Rambam writes:

> Even though the blowing of the shofar on Rosh HaShana is a decree of the Torah, there is a hint in it, as if to say: Awake, sleepers, from your sleep, and slumberers from your slumber! Search your actions and repent, and remember your Creator!... Because of this, the entire house of Israel maintains the custom of increasing their charity, good deeds, and involvement in mitzvot from Rosh HaShana until Yom Kippur, above the level of the rest of the year.[3]

The *Ḥinukh* elaborates on this, describing the impact of the shofar sound:

> Because a physical being will only awaken to certain things upon being called…on Rosh HaShana, which is a day designated from antiquity for judging all creatures…the sound of the shofar wakes the heart of all who hear it, **and certainly the sound of the *terua*, that is, the broken sound**. And not only should a person be aroused, a person should remember to break his evil inclination to desire the pleasures of the world and to sin **when he hears the broken sounds**.[4]

Prayer

Shofar blowing fulfills a third function: its serves as a vessel or instrument of prayer. The Torah relates the numerous functions of the trumpets in the desert (Num. 10:1–10). For example, they were sounded in order to signal the camps to move, or even merely to assemble the people. It is in this context that we first encounter the scriptural term "to blow" – "litko'a" – from which the talmudic word for a straight note, *tekia*, is derived. It appears only as a verb in Tanakh; in fact, the Torah even uses the verb form of *tekia* to command us to blow a *terua*!

When the Torah describes the preparations before going out to war, it relates that the trumpets are also blown:

> And when you go to war in your land against the adversary that oppresses you, then **you shall sound a *terua*** with the trumpets; and **you shall be remembered** before the Lord your God, and you shall be saved from your enemies.

Apparently, the sounding of the trumpets in this context is meant either to arouse the nation to repent or possibly to serve as the vehicle of prayer itself. In fact, as we have previously noted, Ramban derives from this verse that prayer in times of crisis is a biblical obligation.[5] Rambam similarly writes:

> There is a positive commandment to cry and call out with the trumpets upon every crisis which confronts the community.… This is the way of

> repentance, that during a crisis they should cry and call out; they should know that their condition is a function of their bad behavior.... This is what will allow them to avert the crisis. This is the way of repentance, that when a crisis comes, [the nation] should cry and call out, and all should realize that because of their deeds, their situation has worsened.[6]

As we saw above, this may be the intention of the Gemara that describes the shofar as the tool for bringing our remembrance before God (Rosh HaShana 16a).

THE NATURE OF THE MITZVA OF *TEKIAT SHOFAR*

Understanding the halakhic nature of the blowing of the shofar may shed light on the reason for the mitzva. There are actually two components of the mitzva of shofar: *tekia* and *shemia*, blowing and hearing the shofar. The *posekim* have struggled for generations to understand the relationship between these two elements, attempting to determine whether the *tekia* or the *shemia* defines the mitzva. To do this, we must examine cases in which either the blowing or hearing is problematic.

On the one hand, the Mishna teaches that one who blows a shofar into a hole or pit has only fulfilled his obligation if he heard the sound of the shofar itself, not its echo (Rosh HaShana 3:7). This mishna seems to strongly indicate that even if one properly blows the shofar, one must still *hear* its pure sound. On the other hand, other sources indicate that this may not be so simple. For example, another mishna teaches:

> A deaf person, a mental incompetent, and a minor cannot fulfill the public's obligation. This is the rule: [only] one who is obligated in a matter can fulfill the public's obligation. (Rosh HaShana 3:8)[7]

Who is the deaf person (*ḥeresh*) mentioned in the mishna who cannot blow the shofar for another? Is he a deaf-mute, who is generally exempt from all mitzvot, or even a deaf person who can speak, who may be obligated in mitzvot that are not affected by his condition?

Me'iri cites two divergent opinions regarding this question,[8] which may be dependent upon our discussion. R. Yonatan of Lunel rules that the mishna is speaking of a deaf-mute; a deaf person, however, who can speak *may* fulfill another's obligation.[9] This implies that the main point of the mitzva is blowing, not hearing, the blasts. The *Shulḥan Arukh,* however, strongly implies that a deaf person may *not* exempt others,[10] implying that *shemia* is the crucial aspect of the mitzva. The latter position is faced with a perplexing difficulty: if *shemia* is the focal point of the mitzva, why does it matter if the person blowing the shofar is technically obligated or not? As long as one hears the shofar blasts, he should fulfill the mitzva. The dispute among the *Rishonim* regarding this issue extends to other aspects of *tekiat shofar* as well.

BIRKAT HASHOFAR

Rambam rules that the listener should recite the blessing "*lishmo'a kol shofar,*" "to hear the sound of the shofar."[11] This alone may not irrefutably indicate how Rambam understands the mitzva of shofar, but a number of other sources do. For example, Rambam introduces *Hilkhot Shofar* by noting the mitzva "to *hear* the sound of the shofar on the first of Tishrei." In a responsum, he states this explicitly:

> The mitzva that is commanded is not the *tekia*, but rather hearing the *tekia*.... If the mitzva would have been the *tekia* [alone], each and every male would be obligated to sound [the shofar], just as each and every male is obligated in the mitzvot of *sukka* and lulav; and one who listens but does not blow would not have fulfilled his obligation... Similarly, one who blows but does not hear – for example, one who covers his ears – would fulfill his obligation!... [Rather,] we only blow in order to hear... and therefore we recite the blessing "to hear the sound of the shofar," and not, "on the blowing of the shofar."[12]

Rambam clearly maintains that the mitzva is to *hear* the shofar, not to blow the shofar. He also raises another fascinating point: since the mitzva is to hear, the congregation does not fulfill their obligation through the principle of *shome'a keoneh,* which equates listening to a sound with actually producing it, as the Gemara implies (Rosh HaShana 27b), but rather by simply hearing the sound of the shofar.

Seemingly, the principle of *shome'a keoneh* cannot apply to the mitzva of shofar, as it is performed with one's body, and not one's speech.

The *Shulḥan Arukh* rules in accordance with Rambam (as well as *Behag*, Raavya, and Rosh); one should recite the blessings of "*lishmo'a kol shofar*" and "*Sheheḥeyanu*," the blessing over new or seasonal experiences, before blowing the shofar.[13]

Rabbeinu Tam[14] disagrees. He maintains that one should recite the blessing "*al tekiat shofar*" – "on the blowing of the shofar" – because "*asiyata hi gemar mitzvata*" – "its performance is the conclusion of the mitzva." R. Aḥai Gaon[15] and *Semag*[16] also rule that one should recite "*al tekiat shofar*" before blowing the shofar. It seems at first glance that Rabbeinu Tam believes that the *tekia* is the primary component of the mitzva. This understanding is questionable, however, given his explanation that "*asiyata hi gemar mitzvata*." We might suggest that Rabbeinu Tam maintains that one recites blessings over the performance of a mitzva's act (*maase*), rather than over the fulfillment of its aim (*kiyum*). Thus, even though the goal of the mitzva is hearing the blasts, the blessing is recited over the act of blowing them.[17]

THE STOLEN SHOFAR

The Yerushalmi questions why one may not fulfill his obligation with a stolen lulav, but one may do so with a stolen shofar:

> R. Yosa said: Regarding a lulav, it says, "And you shall take for yourself" [Lev. 23:40] – that which belongs to you, and not that from which it is prohibited to derive benefit. But here [regarding shofar, it says,] "It shall be a day of *terua* for you" [Num. 29:1] – in any way.
>
> R. Lazar said: There, he fulfills the mitzva with [the object] itself; here, he fulfills the mitzva with its sound, and no prohibition exists to benefit from a sound. (Y. Sukka 3:1)

Rambam rules in accordance with R. Lazar: "There is a positive commandment *to hear* the sound of the shofar of Rosh HaShana ... one who blows a stolen shofar has fulfilled his obligation, as the mitzva is fulfilled through the sound ... and the sound cannot be stolen"[18] Once again, it is clear that Rambam maintains that *shemia* is the dominant component of the mitzva. Raavad, commenting on Rambam,[19] adopts R. Yosa's opinion: "Even if a sound could be stolen, the verse says, 'It shall be a day of *terua* for you' – in any way." Raavad may be alluding to a fundamentally different approach to the entire mitzva of shofar, as we shall see shortly. *Hagahot Asheri*[20] cites the *Or Zarua*, who rules that a stolen shofar may *not* be used for the mitzva. Seemingly, he believes that the mitzva of shofar is no different than the mitzva of lulav; both mitzvot are fulfilled through an action performed with the object – in the case of the shofar, the *tekia*.

Each approach, in truth, seems to fall short. Rambam, for example, does not explain why one must hear the sound of the shofar from a person who is obligated in the mitzva, the problem we noted above (Rosh HaShana 29a). Furthermore, the Gemara quotes R. Zeira as telling his friend, "Have in mind; sound the shofar for me" (28b). Some maintain that this gemara must be understood according to those who maintain that commandments must be fulfilled with intent (*mitzvot tzerikhot kavana*); thus, the blower must also have intent to fulfill his obligation.[21] Others maintain, however, that the gemara implies that one needs intent in order to fulfill another person's obligation of shofar.[22] In fact, Rambam rules[23] that both the person blowing the shofar and the person listening must have in mind to fulfill the mitzva, and the one blowing must have in mind to fulfill the obligation of the listener.

Why is this necessary if the mitzva is fulfilled merely by listening? Some suggest that R. Zeira merely reminded his friend to blow the shofar for the public properly, not merely "to play around." He is not referring specifically to the intention to fulfill his own or another's obligation. Some interpret Rambam's statements in this manner. In any case, Rambam's position remains difficult.

Still, those who focus upon the *tekia*, such as R. Aḥai, *Semag*, and Rabbeinu Tam, must explain why a deaf person (who is not also mute) is unable to fulfill the mitzva; after all, he is capable of blowing the shofar, even if he cannot hear it. Furthermore, they must also explain the Mishna's assertion that one who blows the shofar into a pit and hears the echo has not fulfilled his obligation. If the mitzva is fulfilled through the *tekia* alone, then one should fulfill his obligation in that case as well. Finally, those who maintain this approach assume that the listeners fulfill their obligation through the principle of *shome'a keoneh*. They must thus confront Rambam's question: How can the principle of *shome'a keoneh* apply to a mitzva performed with one's body?

The *Aḥaronim* grapple with these questions and offer numerous solutions. Some attempt to adhere to the extreme positions, suggesting, for example, that although the mitzva may be the ***shemia***, the hearing of the shofar, one must still hear a halakhically recognized *kol shofar*, which can only be produced by a person obligated in the mitzva of blowing a kosher shofar. The *shemia* is only valid if the blasts were blown properly. Alternatively, some suggest that although the mitzva is fulfilled through the ***tekia***, the blowing of the shofar, one must still produce a sound that may be heard. The *tekia* is only valid if the blasts were heard properly. Maharam Alashkar (1466–1542), for example, explains that:

> For those who state that there is a mitzva to blow… nevertheless, one must blow in a way that the sound reaches his ears, as we find by the recitation of the *Shema* and similar mitzvot, that although the mitzva is reading, it must be a reading that is audible.[24]

Others suggest a more moderate approach, explaining that all must agree that *both* the *tekia* and *shemia* are integral components of the mitzva of shofar. R. Yosef b. Moshe Babad (1801–1874), author of the *Minḥat Ḥinukh*, writes:

> See what the later commentators have written regarding this mitzva, that both the hearing and the blowing are part of the mitzva, and one without the other is insufficient. For one who hears from someone who is not obligated, e.g., from women and the like, does not fulfill his obligation. Thus, the mitzva is not only hearing; one must also blow, and thus he can fulfill his obligation only via someone who is obligated. Similarly, blowing without hearing is not sufficient, as is explicit in Tractate Rosh HaShana: "One who blows into a pit…"[25]

Accordingly, the *Rishonim* cited above disagree as to the *primary* aspect of the mitzva, not as to which is the *only* component of the mitzva.

One of the most intriguing and innovative suggestions is offered by R. Yonatan of Lunel:

> It does not say, "And you shall blow the shofar," as it says regarding lulav, "And you shall take..." [Lev. 23:40]; rather, [it says] "*zikhron terua*" [ibid., v. 24] and "*yom terua*" [Num. 29:1]. Therefore, if one hears the sound from his friend, it is a "*yom terua*" and it is a "*zikhron terua*."[26]

Apparently, R. Yonatan of Lunel believes that the mitzva is neither to blow nor to hear the shofar. Rather, the mitzva is to create "**a day of *terua*,**" which is accomplished by a person obligated in the mitzva blowing a kosher shofar. This may also be the view of Raavad, cited above, who disqualifies a stolen shofar due to the verse, "It shall be a day of *terua* for you" (Num. 29:1).

CONCLUSION

Perhaps we can correlate the reasons offered for the mitzva of shofar with the differing perspectives regarding the nature of the mitzva. Those who maintain that the primary reason for the mitzva is the shofar's role in the coronation of God or as an instrument of prayer may be inclined to focus more upon the blowing of the shofar and less upon hearing the shofar. It is the act of blowing that accomplishes the coronation or the prayer. Alternatively, those who view the sounding of the shofar as a call to repent may be more inclined to focus upon the "hearing" of the shofar. Rambam, for example, who explains that the shofar is a "wake-up call" to repent,[27] also strongly asserts that the mitzva lies in the *shemia*, not the *tekia*.[28]

CHAPTER 10

The Laws of the Shofar and Its Sounds

PHYSICAL CHARACTERISTICS OF THE SHOFAR

Horns and Antlers

As we have previously noted, the Torah does not explicitly state that one must blow a shofar on Rosh HaShana. Rather, the Torah states that the day should be a "*zikhron terua*" (Lev. 23:24) or "*yom terua*" (Num. 29:1), a "remembrance" or "day" of *terua*. The Gemara derives the obligation to blow a shofar, as well as the types and number of sounds required, from the shofar blown on Yom Kippur of the *Yovel* year (Rosh HaShana 33). Regarding Rosh HaShana, the Torah instructs, "And in the **seventh month**, on the first day of the month… it shall be a day of *terua* for you" (Num. 29:1). The Gemara derives that the term "*terua*" refers to a sound produced by a shofar, as it says regarding *Yovel*, "Then shall you make proclamation with the **shofar of *terua*** on the tenth day of the **seventh month**" (Lev. 25:9). Just as the ***terua* of the seventh month** of the *Yovel* year is produced by a shofar, so too, the *terua* of the **seventh month** of every year, on Rosh HaShana, is generated by a shofar.

What is a shofar, and from which animals may it be taken? It is crucial for our purposes to understand the difference between a "horn" and an "antler." A "horn" is a hollow sheath, made of keratin and other proteins, which covers a small core of living bone. Horns are generally found on animals from the Bovidae family, which includes cattle, sheep, goats, and antelopes. Horns begin to grow soon after birth, and they continue to grow throughout the animal's lifetime. An "antler" is a bony, solid outgrowth of the head, found only in males, which is shed each year after the mating season. They are large and complex, and they are commonly found on deer.[1]

Theoretically, antlers can be hollowed out and used as an instrument, but they are disqualified nonetheless for use as a shofar. Ramban (Rosh HaShana 26a) explains that the word "shofar" refers to a hollow horn, not a bone. An antler is therefore inherently disqualified. Ramban also notes that while an antler is disqualified, as it is simply not a horn, there are other horns that the Gemara disqualifies for other reasons, as we shall see.

Which Horns are Valid?

The Mishna teaches:

> All shofarot are kosher, except for the shofar of a cow, because it is a *keren* (horn). R. Yose said: All shofarot are called *keren*. (Rosh HaShana 3:2)

This Mishna seems to present two opinions. R. Yose apparently sanctions the use of *all* shofarot, while the *Rabbanan* (the first opinion) disqualify the shofar of a cow.

The Gemara offers a few interpretations of the *Rabbanan*'s position. First, the Gemara suggests that while R. Yose makes a valid point, the shofar of a cow is unique, and therefore disqualified; unlike other species, whose horns are called both *keren* and shofar, the horn of a cow is referred to *only* as a *keren*, and not as a shofar. Ula then suggests that aside from the linguistic reason, the horn of a cow should not be used because it recalls the sin of the Golden Calf. Similarly, a *Kohen Gadol* (High Priest) may not enter the Holy of Holies on Yom Kippur to plead the case of the Jewish people while wearing garments of gold, as "*ein kategor naase sanegor*" – "a prosecutor cannot serve as a defender" – and the gold adornments "remind" God of the sin of the Golden Calf. Thus, a shofar, which also symbolically pleads our case before the Heavenly Court, should not be made from a cow's horn for the same reason.[2] Abaye explains that there is a physical disqualification of the cow's horn; it grows in a manner that makes it appear like multiple shofarot. In any case, both opinions presented in the Mishna seem to agree that almost all shofarot are valid, and they disagree *only* regarding the horn of a cow.

However, the next mishna, which discusses the various horns used on Rosh HaShana in the Temple, fast days, and the Yom Kippur of *Yovel*, teaches:

> The shofar on Rosh HaShana is that of a *ya'el* (ibex), straight and with a mouthpiece covered in gold.... R. Yehuda says: The shofar of Rosh HaShana is that of a male [ram]. (Rosh HaShana 3:3)

The Gemara adds that R. Levi agrees with R. Yehuda – "the mitzva of Rosh HaShana...is to blow a bent [shofar]," explaining further:

> In what do they argue? R. Yehuda maintains that on Rosh HaShana, the more one bends himself, the better...while the Tanna Kamma (the first opinion) maintains that on Rosh HaShana, the more one is outstretched, the better. (Rosh HaShana 26b)[3]

Many *Rishonim* question the relationship between the first mishna, which sanctions the use of all horns with the possible exception of that of a cow, and the second mishna, which mentions only the straight horn (of an ibex) or a bent one (of a ram). Furthermore, another passage teaches:

> R. Abbahu asked: Why do we only blow on the shofar of a ram? The Holy One, Blessed be He, says, "Blow for Me a ram's shofar, and on account of it I will remember the binding of Yitzḥak [and the ram that was sacrificed in his place]. I furthermore will consider it as if you bound yourselves up before me like Yitzḥak." (Rosh HaShana 16a)

What does this passage teach us about the permissibility of using horns from animals other than a ram? Rambam rules that *only* the shofar of a ram may be used on Rosh HaShana.[4] The commentaries on Rambam and other *Rishonim* question this position, especially since the Gemara never even implies that there is a debate regarding this issue.

Most *Rishonim* disagree with Rambam's opinion, maintaining that all horns (except the horn of a cow, according to the Tanna Kamma) are acceptable.[5] They explain that the second mishna discusses which horn should *preferably* be used. They rule in accordance with R. Yehuda, especially in light of R. Abbahu's comments, preferring the use of a ram's horn. According to these *Rishonim*, there are three categories of bony cranial protrusions: those which are disqualified, either inherently (antlers) or by species (cow horns, according to the Tanna Kamma); other horns, which may be used when necessary; and the ram's horn, which is preferable.

Some *Rishonim* question whether it is preferable to use the horn of a ram, in accordance with R. Abbahu, or any bent horn, as R. Yehuda implies. Ran, for example, explains that R. Yehuda and the Tanna Kamma do not refer exclusively to an ibex or a ram, but rather to any horns that are "straight" or "bent."[6] The *Mordekhai* also suggests that while one should preferably use the horn of a ram, *bediavad* (if there is no alternative), one may even use the horn of an ibex or goat, *as long as it is bent.*[7] In other words, despite that fact that the Gemara describes the horn of an ibex as *pashut* (straight), if it is somewhat curved, it may be used, when necessary.

In order to saw off and prepare the end of the shofar as a mouthpiece, modern shofarot are heated and then straightened somewhat. They are therefore not as "curved" as described by the Mishna, and their shape has been altered. R. Yosef Kapaḥ (1917–2000), a great Torah scholar and Yemenite halakhic authority, challenges the status of these shofarot.[8] Some of his Yemenite followers use a ram's horn with a full curvature, in accordance with his opinion. Common custom, however, is to allow the use of the semi-straightened shofarot.

The *Shulḥan Arukh* concludes:

> The mitzva of the Rosh HaShana shofar should be fulfilled with [the horn] of a ram, which is bent. In extenuating circumstances, all shofarot are acceptable, straight or bent, although there is a greater mitzva to use a bent shofar. The shofar of a cow is not acceptable in any case, nor are the antlers of most undomesticated animals, as they are made of bone and are not hollow.[9]

Aside from those Yemenites who follow R. Kapaḥ and use a fully curved ram's horn, most Yemenite communities use the horn of a greater kudu, native to eastern and southern Africa. This custom is especially surprising due to the Yemenite community's general strict adherence to Rambam's halakhic rulings. As we have seen, while most *Rishonim* tolerate, *bediavad,* the use of other bent shofarot, Rambam seems to disqualify them under any circumstances! This widespread Yemenite practice has generated much halakhic discussion.[10] R. Natan Slifkin, author of many essays and books on zoology and Judaism, discusses the use of horns originating from exotic animals.[11]

THE SHOFAR BLASTS

How Many Notes Must One Blow?

Not only does the Torah not state clearly that the *terua* must come from a shofar, it also does not explicitly teach which and how many notes must be blown! The Gemara teaches that each *terua,* which we have established must be blown with a shofar, must be preceded and followed by a *tekia* (Rosh HaShana 33b). A *terua,* the Gemara assumes, is a broken sound, while the *tekia* is a smooth, level sound. The Gemara offers a few attempts to derive this practice. One source is Leviticus 25:9, in which the term "*haavara*" is found both preceding and following the word "*terua.*" *Haavara* implies a flat, simple sound, described by the sages as a "*peshuta.*" This series – *peshuta-terua-peshuta,* or *tekia-terua-tekia* – is known as a "*tarat*" (or "*karak,*" as it appears in some *Rishonim*).

How many times must one sound a *tarat* series on Rosh HaShana? The Gemara derives that since the term *terua* appears three times in the context of Rosh HaShana and *Yovel,* and each one must be preceded and followed by a *tekia,* one must blow three sets of *tarat,* or nine sounds. The *Amora'im* debate whether *mideoraita* (biblically) one must blow two sets or three, which would determine whether all nine sounds are of biblical or rabbinic origin. Rambam,[12] *Tur,*[13] and *Shulḥan Arukh*[14] rule that one must hear all nine sounds *mideoraita.*

While the sound of the *tekia* is relatively self-evident – smooth and flat – the broken sound of the *terua* is somewhat unclear. Does it refer to medium, tremolo blasts, what we refer to nowadays as "*shevarim*" (breaks)? Or does it refer to very short, staccato blasts, what we call a *terua*? Or does it refer to a combination of the two? The Gemara records that R. Abbahu confronted this question and enacted in Caesarea (c. 300 C.E.) that one should blow all different possible variations (Rosh HaShana 34a). Since a biblical *terua* reflects human weeping, which can be tremolo groaning, staccato wailing, or the former leading to the latter (but not the reverse), we must sound all three variations. Rif therefore summarizes:

> Thus, it is now the case that we blow *tekia-shevarim-terua-tekia* three times, and we blow *tekia-shevarim-tekia* three times, and we blow *tekia-terua-tekia* three times.[15]

These thirty sounds make up the basic obligation of shofar blowing. We will relate to the thirty sounds blown before Musaf, as well as the sounds blown during and after Musaf, which total the customary one hundred sounds. However, first we must discuss the nature of R. Abbahu's enactment and the definition of the sounds themselves.

R. Abbahu's Enactment: Thirty Sounds

The *Rishonim* question the necessity of R. Abbahu's enactment requiring one to blow thirty sounds. R. Hai Gaon,[16] for example, asks the following powerful question: "Before R. Abbahu came, had the Jewish people not fulfilled their obligation of *tekiat shofar*?" He answers:

> There is no doubt that the law was clear to them, as it is not possible that regarding a mitzva [such as shofar], which is performed each year, they would not know the truth, and they would not have observed each other, and it would not have been properly transmitted since Moshe Rabbeinu.... Rather, the biblical *terua* may be fulfilled in any of these ways... as the Torah's intention of *terua* is to create sounds and broken tones, and originally, some would blow tremolo and some staccato... as they saw fit, and they would all fulfill their obligation as such.... And then the masses began to believe *mistakenly* that there is a difference between the sounds, and that some could not fulfill the obligation of others.... Therefore, in order to remove doubt from the simple people and to establish a uniform practice, R. Abbahu established that each group should blow like the other groups as well.... Because it seemed to the simple people to be a debate, the Talmud presents it as if there were a doubt.

This fascinating position of R. Hai Gaon implies that no matter which *terua* one blows, one has fulfilled his obligation. This explains the medieval custom of not sounding each variation during Musaf, which we will soon discuss.

Rambam disagrees with R. Hai Gaon and explains,

> Due to the great passage of time and the extended exile, we are no longer sure as to the nature of the *terua* mentioned in the Torah. We do not know whether it is similar to the wailing of weeping women; or the slow, deep sobbing of someone heavily burdened; or whether it is like a sobbing which naturally turns into a wailing. Therefore, we perform all three variations.[17]

According to Rambam, R. Abbahu responded to a bona fide biblical doubt (*safek deoraita*); he therefore enacted to blow thirty sounds to ensure that everyone fulfills his biblical obligation.

Interestingly, the Gemara explains that simply blowing three sets of *tashrat* would not suffice, as the "wrong" *terua* would constitute an interruption (*hefsek*) between the first *tekia,* the proper biblical *terua,* and the final *tekia.* This makes sense according to the opinion of R. Yehuda, who rules that one must hear the nine blast of the shofar without interruption (Sukka 53b–54a). However, the Gemara rules in accordance with the *Rabbanan,* that "one who hears nine blasts in a period of nine hours" has fulfilled his obligation, implying that he has performed the mitzva even if he does not hear the nine blasts uninterrupted! According to that opinion, why must we be concerned about a *hefsek*?

Rabbeinu Tam[18] suggests that R. Abbahu's fear of *hefsek,* which led him to insist that one blow thirty blasts as opposed to twelve (three sets of *tashrat*), was out of concern for R. Yehuda's position. He notes that according to R. Hai Gaon, the point of the edict was to bring about unity among the various customs; therefore, R. Abbahu showed concern for the rejected opinion of R. Yehuda as well. Practically speaking, however, the halakha is in accordance with the *Rabbanan,* and one would even fulfill the obligation through three sets of *tashrat.*

Ramban, and subsequently many of the Sephardic authorities, disagree with Rabbeinu Tam. They insist that R. Abbahu's enactment must certainly be according to the position of the *Rabbanan*. They explain, therefore, that when the *Rabbanan* posit that "one who hears nine blasts over a period of nine hours" has fulfilled his obligation, they mean that *time* does not constitute an interruption. However, another blast of the shofar between the opening and closing *tekiot* of each set would constitute a *hefsek*. The *Shulḥan Arukh* mentions both views,[19] but, as we will see, he clearly endorses the stringent one.[20]

Definition of *Shevarim* and *Terua*

The *Rishonim*, based upon the Gemara (Rosh HaShana 33b), discuss and debate the precise definition of and relationship between the *shevarim* and the *terua*. Most *Rishonim* understand that the minimum length of *tekia* equals the minimum length of the sounds contained within (i.e., the *terua*). They disagree, however, as to how long they must last. Rashi, for example, claims that the *terua* consists of three short blasts; therefore, the *tekia* must equal the length of those three sounds.[21] This interpretation leads Riva and Rivam to warn that according to this view, one should not blow a *shever* the length of three short blasts, as then it would equal the *tekia* which surrounds a *terua*.[22] Therefore, a *shever*, according to this opinion, should not exceed two beats. Alternatively, Riva and Rivam agree that the length of the *tekia* should equal the length of the sound contained within; however, they maintain that a *terua* should consist of nine short blasts, equaling the length of three *shevarim* and one *tekia*. In fact, some *Rishonim* add that the quantity of sounds is less important than the length, and one may even blow four or five *shevarim*, as long as the *tekia* is as long. Rambam has a completely different reading of the gemara, and he concludes that a *terua* is twice as long as a *tekia*.[23]

In order to illustrate the differences, let us demonstrate how each would blow a *tashrat*:

Rashi's *tashrat* would be:

"---------" "-- -- --" "- - -" "---------"

Tosafot's *tashrat* (that of Riva and Rivam) would be:

“ ------------------ ” “ --- --- --- --------- ” “ ------------------ ”

Rambam's *tashrat* would be:

“ --------- ” “ --- --- --- --------- ” “ --------- ”

While Rashi, Riva and Rivam, and Rambam disagree regarding the length of the *shevarim*, they agree that the *tekia* is measured somehow relative to the inner blasts.

Raavad disagrees,[24] maintaining that one *always* blows a *tekia* for nine *terumitin* (beats), regardless of the length of the *terua*. The *Arukh HaShulḥan* concludes that one should always blow a *tekia* for a minimum of nine *terumitin* in order to fulfill all of the opinions.[25] The *Shulḥan Arukh* cites the first two opinions.[26] It is customary to follow the second opinion, that of Riva and Rivam.[27]

Definition of *Shevarim-Terua:* One Breath or Two?

Ran writes that one should blow all the beats of the *shevarim* or *terua* in one breath.[28] He cites a debate regarding the *shevarim-terua*, which combines both possibilities of a biblical *terua*. Rabbeinu Tam asserts that they need *not* be blown in one breath, as “people certainly do not moan and then wail in one breath.”[29] Ramban[30] disagrees, explaining that the *shevarim-terua* combination is “one *terua*,” and should therefore be blown in one breath.

The *Shulḥan Arukh* cites both opinions and then writes that one who is “God-fearing” should attempt to fulfill both opinions; he should blow the *shevarim-terua* in one breath during the *tekiot before* Musaf, and in two breaths *during* Musaf.[31] Rema records that the common custom is to blow the *shevarim-terua* in two breaths and that one should not diverge from this custom.[32]

The *Aḥaronim* differ as to which custom people should follow. The *Mishna Berura* notes that *Ḥayei Adam* omits Rema's ruling; indeed, it may be preferable to follow the *Shulḥan Arukh*'s ruling, as it covers all of the opinions.[33] The *Arukh HaShulḥan* testifies that this is the custom of many communities.[34] R. Soloveitchik, as recorded by R. Hershel Schachter, argues that the *shevarim-terua* should be blown in one breath, as it constitutes one sound.[35] He therefore instructed the *toke'a* (the one sounding the shofar) to blow them in one breath throughout the entire *tefilla*. During the *tekiot after* the repetition of Musaf, the *toke'a* would blow three *tashrat* sets with two breaths, totaling 102 sounds.

Regarding the *tarat* (*tekia-terua-tekia*), the Yerushalmi rules that if one blows the entire set of *tarat* "*binfiḥa aḥat*," in one breath, one has fulfilled his obligation (Y. Rosh HaShana 4:10). The Tosefta differs, stating that one has not fulfilled his obligation in such a case (Tosefta 2:12), and Rosh rules accordingly.[36] The *Shulḥan Arukh* cites both opinions.[37]

The Sound of the *Tekia, Shevarim,* and *Terua*

The *Shulḥan Arukh* rules: "If the sound is particularly thick or thin, it is still acceptable, as *all sounds are acceptable for the shofar.*"[38] The *Aḥaronim* differ regarding the status of the blasts if the sound changes in the middle of a specific *tekia, shevarim,* or *terua*. R. Yehoshua Yehuda Leib (Maharil) Diskin (1818–1898), a leader of the Old Yishuv community in the late-nineteenth century, was extremely stringent regarding this question. He stressed that the *Shulḥan Arukh* refers to *different* sounds and blasts, but he would not rule leniently if one would alter the sound within one specific *terua* or *tekia*. Common practice is in accordance with the *Ḥazon Ish* and others, who are not concerned with this change of tone, but many scrupulous individuals are strict regarding this issue.[39]

There are different customs concerning the sound of the *shevarim*. Some communities blow smooth/flat sounds. Others break each *shever* in the middle, creating a "*tu-a-tu*" or "*a-tu*" sound, often described as *oleh veyored*, "ascending and descending." Because there are so many variations and opinions regarding the length and sound of the blasts and the number of breaths, some, especially in yeshivas, are accustomed to blow extra sounds after Musaf in order to fulfill many, if not all, of the opinions.

Interruptions (*Hefsek*) Between the Sounds

We noted above that the *Rishonim* differ as to whether or not one must hear the shofar blasts uninterrupted. While the *Shulḥan Arukh* cites both opinions,[40] elsewhere, the *Shulḥan Arukh* assumes that one may *not* interrupt between the sounds with invalid notes.[41] Assuming that one may not interrupt in this manner, what constitutes an invalid note? And if one must "return," to where should one do so?

The *Shulḥan Arukh* rules that if one inadvertently inserts the wrong sound, such as a *terua* instead of a *shevarim*, he must return to the opening *tekia*. The same would apply even if one repeats the same sound, such as an extra *shevarim* (after taking a breath) after the required *shevarim*.[42] However, if, for example, one successfully blows two sets of *tashrat* and errs during the third, one need not repeat all three sets, but rather only the final set.[43]

What if one began to blow a *terua* or *shevarim* but cannot produce the proper sound? The *Arukh HaShulḥan*[44] and the *Mishna Berura*[45] rule that this does *not* constitute an interruption and one need only return to the beginning of that specific sound. Knowledge of these laws is crucial for the *toke'a*, as well as for the *makri*, the one who announces and approves each sound.

CHAPTER 11

The Timing of the Shofar Sounds and the Relationship Between *Tekiat Shofar* and Musaf

WHEN DO WE BLOW THE SHOFAR?

"Confusing Satan"

We saw previously that due to a doubt regarding the precise sound of the shofar blast called "*terua*," R. Abbahu enacted that one should blow thirty sounds: three sets of *tashrat* (*tekia, shevarim, terua, tekia*), three sets of *tashat* (*tekia, shevarim, tekia*), and three sets of *tarat* (*tekia, terua, tekia*). We also discussed the debate over whether R. Abbahu's enactment responded to a true *safek deoraita,* a doubt regarding a law of biblical origin, for which the law always dictates stringency (Rambam), or not (R. Hai Gaon).

However, as we know, we blow many more than thirty blasts! What is the source of our practice? The Gemara (Rosh HaShana 16b) asks why we blow the shofar while "we are sitting," that is, before beginning the Musaf prayer, and then again "while standing," during Musaf itself. The Gemara concludes, "in order to confuse Satan (the accuser)."

This passage raises a number of questions. First, what does the Gemara mean by its conclusion, "to confuse Satan"? Second, which sounds actually fulfill our obligation of shofar and which are considered to be the "extra" sounds? Tosafot[1] cite the *Arukh,* who cites the Talmud Yerushalmi, which explains that when Satan, the accuser who petitions against us before the Heavenly Court, hears the persistence of the shofar when it is blown twice, he will be startled, as he will think that he hears the shofar of the final redemption.

Other *Rishonim* offer less esoteric explanations. Rashi and Rabbeinu Ḥananel explain (Rosh HaShana 16b) that when the Jewish people demonstrate their love for the commandments by blowing the shofar more than necessary, Satan is unable to petition against us. Alternatively, Ran explains that Satan refers to each and every individual's *yetzer hara,* the evil inclination; by repeatedly blowing the shofar, we battle our *yetzer hara* and remind ourselves to repent.[2] This explanation is particularly befitting of Rambam's understanding of the shofar blasts as a call to awaken ourselves spiritually.

In any case, the Gemara clearly requires us to blow additional sounds. The first set, blown before Musaf, are known as the *tekiot demeyushav,* the *tekiot* sounded while sitting; the sounds blown during Musaf are known as the *tekiot deme'umad,* the *tekiot* sounded while standing. As we shall see, the *Rishonim* differ as to how many sounds should be blown.

Which *Tekiot* are Primary?

It would seem that the fact that the *tekiot demeyushav* are blown first and the blessing is recited upon them implies that they are the primary fulfillment of the mitzva. Indeed, Rif[3] and Rambam[4] record that during Musaf, we blow only one set of sounds for each blessing. Rif explains that although one could not fulfill his obligation with so few sounds, the number of blasts of the *tekiot deme'umad* is limited because the members of the congregation have already fulfilled their obligation of blowing the shofar with the *tekiot demeyushav*. We therefore refrain from blowing so large a number of blasts a second time so as "not to inconvenience the congregation." Similarly, Rashba[5] and Ritva[6] explain that one fulfills the mitzva of *tekiat shofar* through the *tekiot demeyushav*.

However, Ran[7] and the *Tur*[8] write that the first *tekiot* are intended to "confuse Satan"; one actually fulfills the mitzva through the second blowing. This, of course, raises a question regarding the placement of the blessing on the mitzva of blowing the shofar (*birkat hashofar*). Why do we make the *berakha* before the *tekiot demeyushav* and not during Musaf, prior to the more important *tekiot deme'umad*? Indeed, if the *tekiot deme'umad* are the actual fulfillment of the mitzva, one would need to avoid interrupting between the *birkat hashofar* and the final *tekiot* of Musaf. Tosafot write explicitly that

> The same *birkat hashofar* that one recites upon the *tekiot demeyushav* works for the *tekiot deme'umad*, which are the essential ones, and which are performed while reciting the order of the *berakhot* [*Malkhuyot, Zikhronot*, and *Shofarot*].[9]

Interestingly, the Baal HaMaor, troubled by this question, writes:

> It appears to me that our custom of blowing *tekiot demeyushav* and reciting on them the blessing of *tekia* is not in accordance with the custom of the talmudic sages. It is rather a custom introduced by later generations so that people who leave prayer prior to Musaf can still fulfill the mitzva of shofar. To this end, the earlier *tekiot* [*demeyushav*] were introduced, as well as a condensed version of the blessing of *tekia*. In fact, however, the primary blessings are those of Musaf: *Malkhuyot, Zikhronot*, and *Shofarot*.[10]

In this shocking passage, Baal HaMaor suggests that there was originally no *birkat hamitzva* for the shofar, nor were there any *tekiot demeyushav*. These blasts were introduced later for the benefit of those who could only stay for the *tekiot demeyushav*. Baal HaMaor clearly reveals a belief that the primary *tekiot* are the sounds blown during Musaf.

As we shall see, this debate over which *tekiot* fulfill the primary obligation of shofar blowing may impact upon other halakhot relating to the shofar blasts, such as whether one may talk between the first thirty blasts and those blasts blown during Musaf. Furthermore, we might also suggest that this debate depends upon our understanding of the exact halakhic relationship between the Musaf prayer and the accompanying *tekiot*.

THE SOURCE OF *MALKHUYOT, ZIKHRONOT*, AND *SHOFAROT*

Rosh HaShana boasts a unique Musaf prayer. While the usual Shabbat and Yom Tov *tefillot* consist of the three opening and three closing blessings of the *Shemoneh Esreh*, with an additional middle *berakha* devoted to the sanctity of the day (*kedushat hayom*), during the Musaf of Rosh HaShana, we insert three *berakhot* in between the opening and closing blessings. In addition, we blow the shofar during the recitation of these *berakhot*.

What is the source for the obligation to recite these three middle blessings? How are we to understand their structure and composition? And finally, which *tekiot* are blown during Musaf and why? The Gemara, at first glance, seems to send a somewhat mixed message regarding the source of *Malkhuyot, Zikhronot*, and *Shofarot* (henceforth, MZ"V). On the one hand, one passage states simply that "God said that we should recite them" (Rosh HaShana 32a). Along these lines, the Gemara records this:

> The Holy One, Blessed be He, said…"Recite before Me on Rosh HaShana *Malkhuyot, Zikhronot*, and *Shofarot*. *Malkhuyot* in order that you will coronate Me as your [King]; *Zikhronot* in order that your remembrances should come before Me with favor. And how? Through the shofar." (Rosh HaShana 16b)

On the other hand, the Gemara elsewhere teaches thus:

> The mitzva of blowing is greater than reciting the blessings [of MZ"V]. How so? If there are two cities, and in one of them they blow the shofar and in the other they recite the blessings, one should go to the place where they blow [the shofar].
>
> That is obvious?! One [obligation] is of biblical origin [the shofar] and the other of rabbinic origin [the *berakhot* of MZ"V]?! It is necessary [to teach us this law for a situation in which] one place is certain and the other is a doubt [even in the case of doubt, one should go to the city where he may be able to hear the shofar]. (Rosh HaShana 34b)

This source clearly asserts that the *berakhot* of MZ"V are *miderabbanan.*

Indeed, most *Rishonim* assume that the *berakhot* are of rabbinic origin. Rashi[11] implies that the biblical verse "*zikhron terua*" refers to the blessings of MZ"V, but Ramban, based upon the final passage we cited from the Gemara, rejects Rashi's implication, suggesting that even Rashi must accept that the interpretation is no more than an *asmakhta,* a biblical "hint."[12]

R. Soloveitchik suggests that even if recitation of the *berakhot* of MZ"V does not constitute an independent biblical mitzva, it may nevertheless have import for biblical law in the role of enhancing the fulfillment of the biblical mitzva of shofar.[13] We will discuss the significance of this opinion shortly.

THE *TEKIOT DEME'UMAD*

The *Rishonim* record numerous customs regarding which and how many blasts are blown during Musaf. Many *Rishonim*[14] record that the early custom, apparently from geonic times, was to blow one set of *tashrat* for *Malkhuyot,* one set of *tashat* for *Zikhronot,* and one set of *tarat* for *Shofarot,* equaling altogether an additional ten blasts. Some question the correctness of this practice, as according to R. Abbahu, who enacted that one should blow thirty sounds (three sets of *tashrat,* three sets of *tashat,* and three sets of *tarat*), proper blasts should be sounded during each of the Musaf *berakhot.* This question is easily resolved according to Rif, who writes, as we mentioned above, that while in theory we might have required thirty blasts for each blessing, since the congregation fulfilled their requirement before Musaf, only one set is blown after each *berakha* of Musaf so as not to burden the congregation. Furthermore, R. Hai Gaon, as we also discussed above, believed that fundamentally all of the types of *terua* are correct and that R. Abbahu's concern was with communal unity and not with halakhic doubts. Accordingly, a halakhically correct set was blown for each blessing. However, according to Rambam, who views R. Abbahu's doubt as a true *safek deoraita,* the question remains. Ramban[15] offers yet another explanation:

> The truth is that halakhically, one has already fulfilled the obligation of *tekiat shofar* with the *tekiot demeyushav* [before Musaf], and the *tekiot* blown with the order of the *berakhot* do not come to fulfill the commandment of shofar, but rather [to fulfill] the mitzva of communal prayer – to raise prayer with the blast [of the shofar], as is done on communal fast days.

Here Ramban claims that the *tekiot* blown during Musaf are not meant to fulfill the mitzva of shofar, but rather to enhance the *tefilla.*

The *Shulḥan Arukh* accepts this position and adds that it is customary to blow each set three times, for a total of thirty extra sounds.[16] Elsewhere, he records the Sephardic custom to blow a final blast – a "*terua gedola*" – after Musaf, for a total of sixty-one blasts.[17]

Rabbeinu Tam disagrees with these *Rishonim,*[18] as he is troubled by the question we raised above, that according to R. Abbahu, one must blow proper blasts by each *berakha.* He therefore established that we should blow a *tashrat* for each *berakha,* for a total of forty-two additional sounds.[19] Rema records that this is the custom for Ashkenazic Jewry.

R. Yeshayahu HaLevi Horowitz (1565–1630), known as *Shela HaKadosh* ("the Holy *Shela*") after his work *Shenei Luḥot HaBerit,* insists that the proper practice is to blow a *tashrat, tashat,* and *tarat* after each *berakha,* totaling an additional thirty blasts.[20] Most congregations seem to follow the position of the *Shela,* blowing three sets for each *berakha.*

ONE HUNDRED BLASTS

As we have seen, according to the original geonic custom, the *tekiot deme'umad* consisted of only ten sounds; according to Rabbeinu Tam's practice, they consisted of twelve sounds; and according to the *Shulḥan Arukh*'s practice, as well as that of the *Shela*, they consisted of thirty. Together with the thirty *tekiot demeyushav* blown before Musaf, a total of forty, forty-two, or sixty blasts were blown, respectively.

However, the prominent custom of most communities nowadays is to blow one hundred blasts. What is the origin of this practice? Tosafot[21] cite the *Arukh*, who cites what is an apparently non-extant midrash that records a practice to blow one hundred sounds to parallel the hundred wailings of the mother of Sisera, the Canaanite general defeated and killed by Barak and Devorah. The Book of Judges describes Sisera's mother waiting in anticipation of her son's return: "Through the window she looked forth, and cried, the mother of Sisera, through the lattice: 'Why is his chariot so long in coming? Why tarry the wheels of his chariots?'" (Judges 5:28). Indeed, elsewhere (Rosh HaShana 33b), the Gemara derives from this verse that the word "*terua*" refers to the short, throbbing cries:

> The Torah states: "It shall be a day of *terua* for you." The Targum translates the phrase as "*yom yevava*," a day of sobbing, based on the verse: "At the window Sisera's mother looked out and cried" [Judges 5:28].

The commentaries attempt to understand this halakhic derivation. Some seek to understand how this verse can serve as a source for the requirement to sound one hundred wailings, suggesting, for example, that the *gematria* (numerical value) of the word "*haḥalon*" (the window), which is exactly 99, implies that had Sisera's mother wailed just once more, for a total of one hundred times, her son might have been saved. Others try to understand the relationship between Sisera's mother's whimpers and our sounding of the shofar. One might suggest that just as Sisera's mother, standing by the window, cried out of an intense feeling of uncertainty regarding what would become of her son; when the books of life and death are open and our future is at stake, we similarly cry by means of the shofar, expressing our fears and uncertainties to God and praying for a positive judgment. While this practice apparently did not become customary during the Middle Ages, the *Shela* endorsed it, testifying that it was the practice in Jerusalem, and the *Mishna Berura*[22] and *Arukh HaShulḥan*[23] confirm its acceptance.

Interestingly, R. Binyamin Shlomo Hamburger, in his *Shorshei Minhag Ashkenaz,* after summarizing the different positions from a historical and geographical perspective, defends the long-standing German tradition of adhering to the geonic position and blowing only ten blasts during the Musaf repetition.

According to our custom of blowing one hundred blasts, how are these blasts distributed throughout the *tefilla*? There are different customs regarding this question. Some communities, generally of non-hasidic, Ashkenazic origin, do not blow at all during the silent *Shemoneh Esreh,* and therefore blow thirty blasts during the repetition. The final forty blasts are blown after Musaf (thirty) and after the final *Kaddish Titkabel* (ten).[24] Other communities, generally those of Sephardic and hasidic origin, blow during both the silent *Shemoneh Esreh* (thirty) and the repetition (thirty), and the final ten blasts are blown either after the final Kaddish or before the stanza of "*titkabel,*" in which we petition God to accept our prayers.

INTERRUPTING BETWEEN *BIRKAT HASHOFAR* AND THE FINAL SHOFAR BLASTS

Our discussion above may impact upon a very practical question regarding the *tekiot* of Musaf. May one speak during the Musaf prayer, or is there a problem of interrupting between the *birkat hashofar* and the later *tekiot*? Indeed, it is customary to refrain from speaking between the *birkat hashofar* and the *tekiot* after the final Kaddish. But why?

R. Saadia Gaon writes that "the one who blows the shofar is not permitted to speak until the conclusion of the entire service."[25] Similarly, in another fascinating geonic responsum, the congregation is warned against talking until the conclusion of the service, as the blessing recited over the shofar is "*lishmo'a,*" to hear, and not "*litko'a,*" to blow. Rosh cites this position as well.[26]

Rif is the primary source for this stringency. At the end of his commentary to Rosh HaShana,[27] he cites a Reish Metivta who criticizes those who speak "before one blows with the recitation of the *berakhot* [MZ"V]." He equates this to the case of one who speaks between putting on the *tefillin shel yad* and the *tefillin shel rosh*; in that case, the Gemara rules (Menaḥot 36a) that although one has sinned, he does not need to repeat the blessing. Rosh[28] and Rambam[29] cite this ruling. Rabbeinu Simcha[30] rules that one who speaks before the conclusion of the *berakhot* (MZ"V) should, in fact, repeat the *birkat hashofar*!

The anonymous Reish Metivta cited by Rif makes two assumptions. First, he assumes that one may not speak after reciting a *birkat hamitzva* until the *conclusion* of the mitzva. Second, he assumes that the *birkat hamitzva* of shofar covers the *tekiot* blown during Musaf.

Ran, citing Baal HaMaor, rejects the first assumption.[31] He claims that one sins when one interrupts between putting on the *tefillin shel yad* and the *tefillin shel rosh* because in that case, he must recite an additional *berakha*, "*al mitzvat tefillin.*" He maintains, however, that once one generally begins the performance of a mitzva, there is no prohibition of talking until its completion. In fact, he forcefully asserts that one who begins searching for *ḥametz* after reciting the blessing upon *bedikat ḥametz* is certainly not prohibited from speaking until its completion. He concludes, however, that, out of deference to the Reish Metivta who uttered the ruling, one should still refrain from speaking. The second assumption of the stringent opinion is that the *tekiot* blown with the *berakhot* of MZ"V are covered by the *birkat hashofar*. As we have seen, some opinions maintain that the mitzva is already fulfilled through the *tekiot demeyushav*, while the *tekiot deme'umad* are "extra." In that case, interruption between the *berakha* and the *tekiot deme'umad* would not be problematic.

Despite the apparent absence of any talmudic source for the stringent position, the *Shulḥan Arukh* rules that

> One should not speak, not the person blowing the shofar, nor the congregation, between the *tekiot demeyushav* and the *tekiot deme'umad*.[32]

Taz defends this position against that of Ran, maintaining that the primary fulfillment of the mitzva of shofar occurs during Musaf and that one must not interrupt until the conclusion of the entire mitzva.[33]

While a full discussion of "interruptions" (*hefsek*) throughout halakha is beyond the scope of this chapter, we will briefly discuss some other considerations related to this question.

The *Aḥaronim* debate whether the congregation is obligated to hear the blessings of MZ"V in their entirety in order to fulfill the obligation of the *tekiot deme'umad* (R. Chaim Soloveitchik), or whether merely hearing the *tekiot* blown during the *berakhot*, even without hearing the repetition of the *berakhot* themselves, is sufficient (*Ḥazon Ish*[34]). Seemingly, according to R. Chaim, one must not interrupt during the *berakhot* in order to fulfill the mitzva of the *berakhot* as well! One may question, based on R. Chaim's approach, whether one should hurry his silent prayer in order to hear the entire repetition and whether the first three *berakhot* of Musaf are also included in this mitzva. Furthermore, according to those who blow the shofar during the silent *Shemoneh Esreh*, one might question whether one must conclude the *berakha* before hearing the *tekiot* or may simply pause to listen.

It is further noteworthy that *Kol Bo*, a medieval work on Jewish ritual and traditions, explains that one should not talk between the *tekiot* before Musaf and those blown during Musaf, "in order that [people] should focus their hearts on the *tekiot*."[35]

Finally, we noted previously that due to the many opinions regarding the proper manner of blowing the shofar, some are accustomed to blowing differently each time in order to accommodate a variety of opinions. For example, some blow a "*shevarim-terua*" in one breath for some of the blasts, while they blow it in two breaths for others; some blow a straight "*shevarim*" for some blasts and an "*oleh veyored*" (*tu-a-tu*) for others. In such a case, one might not be allowed to interrupt unnecessarily until after all of the *tekiot*, even those blown after Musaf, are blown. Until that point, one is still in doubt as to whether he has fulfilled his obligation, as he has not yet blown all of the possible combinations of sounds.

What constitutes a *hefsek* (a halakhically offending interruption) regarding this question? Clearly, one may recite Musaf and its *Kedusha*. Furthermore, it is customary to recite various "*piyutim*" during the repetition. Rema implies that one should not speak "*devarim betelim*," idle chatter. The *posekim* discuss whether one who uses the bathroom during Musaf may recite the blessing *Asher Yatzar*. *Penei Yehoshua*[36] seems to equate this with the law during Hallel and Megilla reading, during which one may not recite *Asher Yatzar*, and during which one may interrupt only out of "fear or respect" for another. Others rule leniently,[37] equating this issue to interrupting during *Pesukei DeZimra*, during which we permit one to say *Asher Yatzar*.[38]

THE RELATIONSHIP BETWEEN THE SHOFAR AND MUSAF

Why do we integrate the shofar blasts into the blessings of Musaf at all? Why did the sages insist that both mitzvot be performed together, and what role does each component play in this combination? We may propose two possible understandings. Perhaps the shofar blasts are employed to enhance our prayers. Indeed, we have already seen that a major aspect of the mitzva of shofar is prayer. For example, as the verse describes, trumpets are used during wartime:

> And when you go to war in your land against the adversary that oppresses you, then you shall sound an alarm with the trumpets; and you shall be remembered before the Lord your God, and you shall be saved from your enemies. (Num. 10:9)

We have suggested that the origin of the shofar, as well as its shape, may be so crucial for the very reason that we are utilizing the shofar as an instrument of prayer. Finally, as we saw above, Ramban explains explicitly that although we may not fulfill our mitzva of shofar during the Musaf blasts, they "[fulfill] the mitzva of communal prayer, to raise prayer with the blast [of the shofar], as is done on communal fast days."[39] If the shofar is an instrument of prayer, it makes sense to incorporate the blowing of the shofar into the Musaf. Apparently, the wordless shofar blasts contribute something that the three lengthy, articulate blessings do not. What the shofar adds may be the sense of emergency that is expressed by the sounding of an alarm. Alternatively, it may be that after verbal prayer expresses all that it has in its power to express, the shofar articulates those prayers and hopes that transcend words.

A second approach to explaining why we incorporate blowing shofar into Musaf suggests that although mitzvot are generally fulfilled even if lacking an awareness of the reason behind the mitzva,[40] nevertheless, some mitzvot may be elevated or enhanced when fulfilled within a certain understanding and context. For example, *Baḥ* insists that mitzvot for which the Torah explicitly mentions a reason should preferably be fulfilled while aware of that reason.[41] Therefore, he rules that one should think about the redemption from Egypt while fulfilling the mitzva of *sukka* on the first night of Sukkot, as it says in the verse, "in order that your generations may know that I made the children of Israel to dwell in booths, when I brought them out of the land of Egypt" (Lev. 23:43).

Along similar lines, Ramban[42] explains R. Gamliel's famous statement about the first night of Pesaḥ – "Whoever did not say these three things on Pesaḥ has not fulfilled his obligation. And these are they: Pesaḥ, *matza,* and *marror*" (Pesaḥim 116a) – in an innovative way. While we generally assume that R. Gamliel refers to three essential components of the mitzva of *sippur yetziat Mitzrayim,* the mitzva to relate the story of the exodus from Egypt, Ramban suggests that without fully comprehending these components, one's fulfillment of the mitzvot of *eating* the Pesaḥ, *matza,* and *marror* are lacking!

Similarly, perhaps the mitzva of shofar should ideally be performed while reciting the *berakhot* of MZ"V, as the *berakhot* provide the proper mindset for the performance of the mitzva. In fact, as noted above, R. Soloveitchik suggests that this may be Rashi's intention in interpreting "*zikhron terua*" as referring to MZ"V – MZ"V may be *mideoraita* when integrated unto the mitzva of blowing the shofar.

How do the *berakhot* of *Malkhuyot, Zikhronot,* and *Shofarot* enhance the mitzva of shofar? The themes of these *berakhot* – the coronation of God (*Malkhuyot*), reward and punishment (*Zikhronot*), and divine revelation (*Shofarot*) – are central themes of the mitzva of shofar. Thus, reciting these *berakhot* together with the shofar blasts may heighten one's performance of the mitzva of shofar.

Interestingly, the fifteenth-century Spanish philosopher, R. Yosef Albo, in his *Sefer HaIkkarim*,[43] claims that the *berakhot* of Musaf on Rosh HaShana correspond to three basic principles of faith: The existence of God, the divine origin of the Torah, and reward and punishment. *Malkhuyot* affirms the existence of God, *Zikhronot* relates to *sekhar veonesh* (reward and punishment), and *Shofarot* recalls the divine revelation. In our Musaf of Rosh HaShana, in the opening prayer of the New Year, we affirm our belief in these three fundamental principles. What emerges from our discussion is an understanding of a truly unique ritual – the Musaf blessings of *Malkhuyot, Zikhronot,* and *Shofarot* accompanied by the blowing of the shofar.

Yom Kippur

CHAPTER 12

The Laws and Practices of Erev Yom Kippur

INTRODUCTION

Many customs and laws occupy us on the day preceding Yom Kippur. Some have the custom of visiting cemeteries before Yom Kippur,[1] others participate in *kapparot,* swinging a live chicken or a small sack of money above their heads,[2] and some even have the custom of receiving *malkot* (lashes).[3] In this chapter, we will focus on a number of central laws and customs observed on Erev Yom Kippur: asking for forgiveness, immersion in a *mikveh, Viduy* (confession), and eating.

ASKING FOR FORGIVENESS BEFORE YOM KIPPUR

It is customary to ask for forgiveness from one's fellow man before Yom Kippur. The Gemara relates that for thirteen years, Rav visited R. Ḥanina on the day before Yom Kippur to beg his forgiveness (Yoma 87b). This practice is based upon the following mishna:

> For sins between man and God, Yom Kippur atones, but for sins between man and his fellow, Yom Kippur does not atone until he appeases his fellow. R. Elazar b. Azaria derived [this from the verse]: "From all your sins before God you shall be cleansed" [Lev. 16:30] – for sins between man and God, Yom Kippur atones, but for sins between man and his fellow, Yom Kippur does not atone until he appeases his fellow.

The Gemara continues:

> R. Yitzḥak said: Whoever aggravates his fellow even through words is required to placate him.... R. Yose b. Ḥanina said: Whoever beseeches forgiveness from his friend should not beseech him more than three times. And if he died, [the offender] brings ten people and must stand them by his grave and he says, "I have sinned against the Lord, the God of Israel, and so-and-so whom I wounded." (Yoma 87b)

Furthermore, the Talmud teaches that one should be quick to forgive:

> From where can we learn that should the injured person not forgive him, he would be [stigmatized as] cruel? From the words, "So Avraham prayed unto God and God healed Avimelekh" [Gen. 20:17]. (Bava Kama 92a)

In fact, the Gemara relates that "When R. Zeira would have grounds [for a grievance] against someone, he would pass in front [of the offender], thereby making himself available to him so that he would come and appease him" (Yoma 87a). Similarly, Rambam writes, "This is the way of the Israelite people and their principled heart."[4] Indeed, Rava asserts, "Anyone who passes over his measures [i.e., relinquishes his rights and does not judge those who have wronged him], they [God] pass over all of his sins" (Rosh HaShana 17a). Only under certain circumstances, such as for the benefit of the offender (Yoma 87b) or if one was publicly maligned, is the victim not obligated to forgive,[5] although it is certainly proper to do so.[6]

Some *Aḥaronim* question whether one who knows that he has been forgiven must still ask for forgiveness. Are we concerned merely with the victim forgiving the offender or with the offender actually asking for forgiveness as part of the process of repentance? If the offender must ask for forgiveness as part of his process of repentance, then he must seemingly beg forgiveness even if he knows that he has been forgiven. However, if we are simply concerned that one person forgives the other, then asking for forgiveness in this case would be superfluous.

This question relates as well to a most uncomfortable situation: What if a person does not know that he has been offended, and by asking for forgiveness, the offender may actually cause him distress?

R. Yisrael Meir Kagan (Lithuania, 1838–1933) writes this in his *Sefer Ḥafetz Ḥayim*:

> One who sinned against his friend without his knowledge but did not cause him any embarrassment or distress or damage, as those who heard rejected his words, does not have to ask for forgiveness from his friend. This is considered a sin between man and God, and he should express remorse, and accept upon himself not to speak *lashon hara* in the future. However, if he spoke ill of someone without his friend knowing and he was embarrassed by this . . . even if his friend doesn't know this, he must still reveal to him what he has done and ask forgiveness from him.[7]

Ḥafetz Ḥayim rules that if the person experienced some loss, or even distress, as a result of one's words, one must ask for forgiveness, even if his friend did not know that he spoke ill of him.[8]

R. Yisrael Salanter reportedly disagreed with this last point, and even confronted Ḥafetz Ḥayim regarding this stringency.[9] R. Salanter argues that one should thoroughly consider one's actions, as at times merely asking someone for forgiveness may constitute a sin of causing someone distress. R. Binyamin Zilber[10] and others[11] rule in accordance with R. Yisrael Salanter.

R. Avraham Danzig, author of *Ḥayei Adam*, formulated and popularized the famous opening supplication of Yom Kippur, *Tefilla Zakka*.[12] This moving prayer, recited by individuals before *Kol Nidrei*, bemoans how man has misused his God-given abilities; instead of using them for the service of God, he has used them for sin. The climax of this prayer, which even those who do not have sufficient time to recite the entire *Tefilla Zakka* should recite, reads:

> I know that there is no one so righteous that they have not wronged another, financially or physically, through deed or speech. This pains my heart within me, because wrongs between humans and their fellow are not atoned by Yom Kippur until the wronged one is appeased. Because of this, my heart breaks within me, and my bones tremble; for even the day of death does not atone for such sins. Therefore, I prostrate and beg before You to have mercy on me and grant me grace, compassion, and mercy in Your eyes and in the eyes of all people. For behold, I forgive with a final and resolved forgiveness

> anyone who has wronged me, whether in person or property, even if they slandered me or spread falsehoods against me. So I release anyone who has injured me either in person or in property, or has committed any manner of sin that one may commit against another, except for legally enforceable business obligations, and except for someone who has deliberately harmed me with the thought, "I can harm him because he will forgive me." Except for these two, I fully and finally forgive everyone; may no one be punished because of me. And just as I forgive everyone, so may You grant me grace in the eyes of others, that they, too, forgive me absolutely.

The reader forgives anyone who has wronged him in the hope of both enabling others to be forgiven and to receive divine grace himself.

Why is it customary to appease one's fellow man specifically on the eve of Yom Kippur? The simple explanation is that while one should always appease someone who has been wronged,[13] there is certain urgency before Yom Kippur. *Tur,*[14] however, cites *Pirkei DeRabbi Eliezer,*[15] which explains differently:

> Samael [the accusing angel of God] sees that there is no sin in them on Yom Kippur. He says to God: Master of the worlds, you have one people on earth who are like the ministering angels in Heaven. Just as the ministering angels are barefoot, so Israel is barefoot on Yom Kippur; just as the ministering angels neither eat nor drink, so Israel does not eat or drink on Yom Kippur; just as the ministering angels cannot bend, so Israel stands all Yom Kippur; just as with the ministering angels, peace serves as an intermediary between them, so with Israel, peace serves as an intermediary between them on Yom Kippur; just as the ministering angels are free of all sin, so Israel is free of all sin on Yom Kippur. God hears the testimony of Israel from their accuser and He atones for the altar and for the Temple and for the Priests and for the entire congregation.

Tur explains that on Yom Kippur, there is a special motivation to bring peace among the Jewish people – so that God will reject the arguments of the accuser.

IMMERSION (*TEVILA*)

The *Rishonim* cite an ancient custom to immerse in the *mikveh* on Erev Yom Kippur.[16] Some *Rishonim* rule that one should even recite a *birkat hamitzva* (blessing over a commandment) before immersing![17] The *Arukh HaShulḥan* suggests[18] that these *Rishonim* may understand the command of "You shall be clean before the Lord" (Lev. 16:30) literally. Most *Rishonim* reject this opinion, however, and rule that immersion is performed without a blessing.[19]

Rosh explains, based upon the *Pirkei DeRabbi Eliezer* cited above, that on Yom Kippur we attempt to emulate the angels; just as they are pure, we similarly become pure. The precise reason for this immersion, however, remains unclear. While Rema writes that one immerses to remove the impurity of "*keri*" (seminal emission),[20] *Magen Avraham* cites those who view this immersion as an act of *teshuva*, repentance.[21] Indeed, R. Akiva draws a comparison between *teshuva* and the *mikveh*:

> R. Akiva said: Fortunate are you, Israel! Before whom do you cleanse yourself? And who cleanses you? Your Father in Heaven! And it also says, "The *mikveh* of Israel is God." Just as a *mikveh* cleanses the contaminated, so does the Holy One, Blessed be He, cleanse Israel. (Yoma 85b)

The question of whether the goal of this *tevila* is *tahara* (purification) or *teshuva* leads to a number of practical ramifications. While Rema writes that one should immerse himself only once, the *Mishna Berura* writes that since one immerses for the purpose of *teshuva*, one should dunk three times.[22] Some are even accustomed to immerse thirty-nine times![23] Furthermore, while Rema writes that one immerses without saying *Viduy* (confession), some are accustomed to recite the *Viduy* while in the *mikveh*.

VIDUY AND OTHER PRAYERS

The Talmud teaches that one should recite the *Viduy* before the meal on Erev Yom Kippur:

> The Rabbis taught: The obligation of confession takes effect on the eve of Yom Kippur with the approach of dark. But the sages said: One should confess before he eats and drinks, lest he lose his mind at the meal. And although he confessed before he ate and drank, he should confess again after he eats and drinks, lest something unseemly happens at the meal. (Yoma 87b)

Rashi explains that the sages were concerned lest one become intoxicated during the meal,[24] while Rambam writes that they were concerned lest he choke and die before repenting.[25]

The *Rishonim* debate whether the second confession is to be recited after the meal, before the onset of Yom Kippur, or on Yom Kippur evening. Ran[26] cites Ramban, who explains that the mitzva is to confess on Erev Yom Kippur before dark. The sages were concerned lest one become intoxicated at the meal and therefore instituted a *Viduy* before the meal, but they did not replace the confession meant to be recited before nightfall. Most *Rishonim* disagree, however, and the halakha is in accordance with their view. A second *Viduy* is not recited before dark.[27] Some suggest reciting another *Viduy*, and explain that the recitation of *Tefilla Zakka* fulfills Ran's opinion.[28] R. Soloveitchik relates that in Khaslavitch, where he grew up, it was customary to recite the *Viduy* before saying the *Tefilla Zakka*. The Rav maintained this custom in Boston as well.[29]

The *Geonim* discuss whether the *Viduy* recited at Minḥa before Yom Kippur should also be recited by the *sheliaḥ tzibbur* in his repetition.[30] Raavya, R. Eliezer b. Yoel HaLevi (d. 1225), suggests that the *sheliaḥ tzibbur* does not repeat the *Viduy*, as there is nowhere to insert the *Viduy* in the weekday *Shemoneh Esreh*. He also suggests that since the *Viduy* is only recited at Minḥa lest one become intoxicated or choke at the *seuda mafseket*, the final meal before Yom Kippur, it was not incorporated into the *ḥazan*'s repetition. Apparently, on Yom Kippur itself, the *Viduy* is an integral part of the day's prayers, and is therefore included in the repetition, while on Erev Yom Kippur, the *Viduy*'s relationship with Minḥa is coincidental, and is therefore not incorporated into the repetition. R. Amram Gaon, however, insisted that that the *Viduy* be repeated in order to fulfill that obligation of those who are unable to pray on their own.

THE MITZVA TO EAT

The Talmud teaches:

> R. Ḥiyya b. R. Difti taught: It says, "And you shall afflict yourselves on the ninth" [Lev. 23:32]. Now on the ninth do we fast? Do we not fast on the

> tenth? Rather, this is to tell you that anyone who eats and drinks on the ninth, the Scripture considers it as if he fasted on the ninth and the tenth.[31]

Indeed, the Gemara records that "Mar the son of Ravina would sit at all times in fast except for the days of Shavuot, Purim, and Erev Yom Kippur" (Pesaḥim 68b).

The Gemara teaches that there is a mitzva to eat on the day before Yom Kippur and that eating on Erev Yom Kippur and then fasting on Yom Kippur is somehow tantamount to fasting for two days. What function does this mitzva fill? How are we to understand the Talmud's equation between eating on the ninth of Tishrei and fasting on Yom Kippur? And does this mitzva somehow reflect the true nature of Yom Kippur? The *Rishonim* differ as to how to understand this mitzva. Some view the obligation as a form of preparation for the fast. Rashi, for example, explains:

> And the verse says, "And you shall afflict yourself on the ninth," implying [that you should] prepare yourself on the ninth in order to be able to fast on the tenth. And since the Torah employed the language of "affliction," it teaches that it is as if one fasted on the ninth.[32]

Rashi understands that one eats on the ninth of Tishrei in order to prepare for Yom Kippur. For this extra preparation, one receives "credit" as if one fasted on both days.[33] Rosh concurs, explaining:

> In other words, "prepare yourselves on the ninth, rejuvenate and strengthen yourselves through eating and drinking, in order that you will be able to fast tomorrow." This is in order to demonstrate God's affection for Israel, similar to a person who has a beloved child who must fast for a day; he will give him food and drink the day before the fast in order that he will tolerate [the fast]. Similarly, God does not normally command the Jewish people to fast, except for one day, for their own good, to atone for their sins.[34]

Rosh understands the mitzva, like Rashi, as a preparation for the fast, but he adds that it demonstrates God's affection for the Jewish people and His desire that they should not suffer.

Conversely, *Shibbolei HaLeket* suggests that one who eats "well" on the day before Yom Kippur will experience more discomfort on Yom

Kippur itself.[35] Similarly, R. Barukh HaLevi Epstein explains in his *Torah Temima*:

> Based upon what appears in Taanit 27b, that the *anshei mishmar* [the Kohanim on duty] in the Temple would not fast on Sunday... and according to one [reason] in order that they should not go from rest and enjoyment [on Shabbat] to discomfort and fasting. And the commentators explain that a fast which comes after a day of excessive eating and drinking is more difficult and therefore they would not fast then. Similarly, it is now understood that one who eats and drinks on the ninth, it is as if he fasted for the ninth and the tenth, because the fast on the tenth is harder for him ... and therefore the fast on the tenth counts for him for two fasts.[36]

While this opinion fits in nicely with the words of the Gemara, it is predicated upon the assumption that "*inui*" refers literally to physical affliction and that one should maximize one's personal affliction on Yom Kippur. We will examine this assumption when we discuss the afflictions of Yom Kippur. Interestingly, *Torah Temima*'s father, R. Yechiel Michel Epstein (1829–1908), cites both reasons in his *Arukh HaShulḥan,* insisting that while the fast may be difficult due to excessive eating the day before, one's ability to fast successfully will still be enhanced by eating on Erev Yom Kippur.

Given this discussion, we might question the permissibility of ingesting pills before a fast that are purported to relieve the discomfort of the fast. Indeed, R. Chaim Chizkiyah Medini, (1833–1904), in his *Sedei Ḥemed,* cites a scholar who discouraged engaging in *segulot* (spiritual remedies) intended to ease the fast.[37] Most *posekim,* however, insist that there is no reason to be stringent, especially since according to Rashi, the entire intention of this mitzva is to ease the fast the next day.[38]

After citing the views of Rashi and the Rosh, Rabbeinu Yona (Spain, 1180–1263) presents an alternate perspective of this mitzva. He writes:

> If a person transgressed a negative commandment and repented, he should be concerned with his sin and long and wait for the arrival of Yom Kippur in order that God will be appeased.... And this is what they meant [Rosh HaShana 9a] [when they said that if] one who eats a special meal on the eve

> of Yom Kippur it is as if he was commanded to fast on the ninth and tenth and did so, as he demonstrated his joy that the time for atonement has come, and this will be a testimony for his concern for his guilt and his anguish for his sins.... Second, on other festive days, we eat a meal for the joy of the mitzva... and since the fast is on Yom Kippur, we were commanded to designate a meal for the joy of the mitzva on the day before Yom Kippur.[39]

Ritva paraphrases Rabbeinu Yona, explaining that the mitzva to eat on Erev Yom Kippur is meant "to demonstrate that this day is holy to our Lord, and it is appropriate to eat sweet foods, like on Rosh HaShana, but the Torah commands us to abstain on this day from physical pleasures in order that we should be like angels, as the Midrash says."[40] Rabbeinu Yona clearly believes that we are not to view the mitzva to eat on Erev Yom Kippur as a preparation for the fast, but rather as an independent commemoration or celebration of Yom Kippur that was "pushed up" to the day before.

The *Aḥaronim* discuss these two approaches – whether the mitzva is intended as a preparation for the fast of Yom Kippur or as a separate commandment – at great length. They raise a number of potential differences between these approaches. R. Akiva Eiger (1761–1837), for example, questions whether women are obligated in this mitzva. He was asked to rule regarding an ailing woman who was warned by her doctors not to eat, lest her condition deteriorate. He writes:

> God forbid, she should not eat. And since you say that she is learned, and fears the word of God and will hardly listen to you, my advice is to take a servant or two to tell her that a letter arrived from me prohibiting her from eating anything more than she is accustomed to each day.

He concludes with the following thought:

> While this ruling must not be delayed, I am somewhat curious regarding healthy women [as well], whether they are obligated to eat on Erev Yom Kippur, as possibly they may be exempt, as they are exempt from all time-bound commandments.... Or possibly, since the verse employs the phrase "the ninth of the month," implying that it is as if one fasted on the ninth and the tenth, therefore all who must fast on the tenth, to fulfill "and you shall

> afflict yourselves," must fast on the ninth.... This question requires further thought for a less busy time.[41]

Other *Aḥaronim* discuss this question as well.[42] In his commentary on R. Aḥai Gaon's *She'iltot,* R. Naftali Tzvi Yehuda Berlin (1816–1893), Netziv, supports the understanding that one eats on the ninth in order to prepare for the fast on the tenth.[43] Indeed, the text of the *She'iltot* reads, "One who eats and drinks on the ninth and fasts on the tenth, the Scripture considers it as if he fasted on the ninth and the tenth," implying that one eats on the ninth in order to successfully fast on the tenth. If so, Netziv questions whether one who is confident in his ability to fast must still eat and drink on the ninth. Conversely, must one who is unable to fast on Yom Kippur eat on the ninth?

R. Avraham Shmuel Binyamin Sofer (1815–1871), *Ketav Sofer,* also asks whether one who is unable to fast on Yom Kippur must still fulfill this mitzva on Erev Yom Kippur.[44] He concludes that an ailing woman who cannot fast on Yom Kippur would certainly not be obligated to eat. He argues that if the obligation relates to the fast, then she should be exempt, as she will not fast the next day, and if this halakha constitutes and independent obligation, she should be exempt because it is a time-bound commandment.

Finally, should one strive to eat a meal with bread on Erev Yom Kippur? It would seem that those who view this mitzva as a preparation for the fast would see no reason to prefer one manner of eating over another. However, those who view this mitzva as a "*seudat mitzva*" or even a "*seudat Yom Tov*," might be inclined to prefer a more festive meal made over bread. Similarly, *Minḥat Ḥinukh* questions whether there is a minimum amount that one must eat. He concludes, creatively, that since the halakha defines "*inui*" on Yom Kippur as abstaining from food the size of a date (*kakotevet*), one should similarly eat a minimum of a "date" on Erev Yom Kippur, when one's eating also fulfills the commandment of "*inui*."[45]

Traditionally, one partakes of a large festive meal, known as the *seuda mafseket,* after reciting Minḥa and the *Viduy,* and before the onset of the fast. R. Avraham Yitzchak HaKohen Kook analyzes this mitzva in his *Ein Aya*, a commentary on the aggadic sections of the Talmud.[46] He begins by asserting that there are two dimensions of *teshuva* that are alluded to in verses from the Torah:

> And it shall come to pass when all these things come upon you, the blessing and the curse that I have set before you, and you will take it to your heart among all the nations where the Lord your God has driven you. And you will return unto the Lord your God and hearken to His voice, according to all that I command you this day, you and your children, with all your heart and with all your soul.... And the Lord your God will circumcise your heart and the heart of your children to love the Lord your God with all your heart and with all your soul, so that you may live. (Deut. 30:1–2, 6)

If one "returns" to God, then why must God "circumcise his heart" in order to bring about "the love of the Lord your God"? R. Kook explains that sin impacts upon a person in two ways. First, the person has violated the will of God. Second, the person has distanced himself from God, decreasing the love and fear of God in his heart. The process of repentance, therefore, must both correct the sin as well as restore the love and fear of God to one's heart. These two goals of *teshuva* are accomplished in different ways.

The *teshuva* of restoring one's personal relationship with God can best be achieved without the distractions of the physical world. However, fixing what one has wronged cannot be fully accomplished while detached from the world; rather, he must be immersed in this world. The Rabbis teach:

> What is the definition of a *baal teshuva* (a person who has repented)? R. Yehuda said: One who has the opportunity to do the same sin [implying that circumstances are such that his desire to do the sin is the same] and this time does not do it! He is a *baal teshuva*! (Yoma 86b)

If so, R. Kook claims, "One must be involved in business dealings and in his day-to-day dealings and [still] act according to God's Torah and its commandments" in order to perform *teshuva* properly. One might therefore claim that the abstinence of Yom Kippur, through which one restores his personal relationship with God, does not actually achieve full and complete *teshuva*. We thus eat and drink on the day before Yom Kippur, "and are careful in the service of God, placing the fear of God upon us so that we do not stumble with regard to any prohibition, even through eating and drinking, and we therefore engage in active repentance, and only afterward can we increase our repentance with added sanctity."[47] This beautiful idea explains why the Talmud equates the ninth and tenth days, as together they compose the complete experience of Yom Kippur.

CHAPTER 13

Kol Nidrei and Teshuva

INTRODUCTION

The Torah explicitly mentions the theme of atonement in the context of Yom Kippur: "For on this day shall atonement be made for you, to cleanse you; from all your sins shall you be clean before the Lord" (Lev. 16:30). Furthermore, the *avodat Yom HaKippurim*, the sacrificial service performed in the *Beit HaMikdash*, clearly entails confession and atonement, as the Torah states:

> And Aaron shall lay both his hands upon the head of the live goat and confess over him all the iniquities of the children of Israel and all their transgressions, even all their sins; and he shall put them upon the head of the goat and shall send him away by the hand of an appointed man into the wilderness. (Lev. 16:31)

What is the nature of this repentance and atonement, and does it differ at all from the general commandment of *teshuva*? The *Rishonim* grapple with the fundamental question of whether the Torah can demand that one repent for his sins. They also discuss technical questions relating to the source and means of repentance. Rambam, who devotes an entire section to the laws of *teshuva*, writes:

> If a person transgresses any of the mitzvot of the Torah, whether a positive command or a negative command, whether willingly or inadvertently, when he repents and returns from his sin, he must confess before God, blessed be He, as it states, "If a man or a woman commit any of the sins of man…they must confess the sin that they committed" [Num. 5:6–7]. This refers to a verbal confession. This confession is a positive commandment.[1]

Rambam's emphasis upon the *Viduy* (confession) generated much discussion among the commentators. Some insist that Rambam does not say that one is obligated to repent; he rather holds that the Torah provides the proper means for one who wishes to return in the form of *Viduy*.[2] Others explain that while the *Viduy* is the "means" to repentance (the *maase*), the fulfillment (the *kiyum*) is achieved through honest and soulful penitence.[3] Rambam himself explains: "There is one positive commandment: that the sinner should repent from his sin before God, and confess."[4]

Yom Kippur, as along with the days preceding it, is an auspicious time for repentance, as Rambam writes:

> Even though repentance and calling out are desirable at all times, during the ten days between Rosh HaShana and Yom Kippur, they are even more desirable and will be accepted immediately, as it states, "Seek God when He is to be found" [Hos. 55:6].[5]

Furthermore, Rambam records a unique obligation to repent on Yom Kippur:

> Yom Kippur is the time for repentance for every individual and for the many [the nation], and it marks the final pardon and forgiveness for Israel. Therefore, all are obligated to perform repentance and confess on Yom Kippur. The mitzva of the Yom Kippur confession begins on the eve of the day, before one eats.[6]

It is noteworthy that Rambam cites this obligation in his general treatment of *teshuva*, *Hilkhot Teshuva*, and not in the more specific laws of Yom Kippur. Apparently, the obligation on Yom Kippur is more urgent, but it is not necessarily qualitatively different than the general requirement.

Incidentally, Ramban insists that the mitzva of *teshuva* should be derived from a different source:

> For you shall obey the Lord your God to observe His commandments and statutes that are written in this book of the Torah, for you shall return to the Lord your God with all your heart and with all your soul. For this mitzva which I am commanding you today – it is not removed from you, nor is it distant. It is not in heaven, [for you] to say, "Who will ascend for us to heaven, and take it for us that we will hear it and fulfill it?" It is not across the sea, [for you] to say, "Who will cross for us to the other side of the sea, and take it for us that we will hear it and fulfill it?" For the matter is very close to you, in your mouth and in your heart to fulfill it. (Deut. 30:10–14)

Ramban explains that "this mitzva" refers to the mitzva of *teshuva*.[7] Rabbeinu Yona disagrees in his famous work on *teshuva*, *Shaarei Teshuva*. He writes:

> There is a positive biblical commandment for a person to arouse his spirit to repent on Yom Kippur, as it says, "You shall be purified from all your sins before the Lord" [Lev. 16:30].[8]

Apparently, R. Yona believes that on Yom Kippur, not only is there a unique imperative to repent, but its character differs from the general year-long commandment of *teshuva*. On Yom Kippur, we not only "return"; we are "purified."

In the context of a broader discussion in which he distinguishes between *kappara* (acquittal) and *tahara* (purification), R. Soloveitchik explains:

> Indeed, true *teshuva* not only achieves *kappara* (acquittal and erasure of penalty); it should also bring about *tahara* (purification) from *tuma* (spiritual pollution), liberating man from his hard-hearted ignorance and insensitivity.

> Such *teshuva* restores man's spiritual viability and rehabilitates him to his original state.[9]

THE *TESHUVA* OF YOM KIPPUR

The difference between the *teshuva* of Yom Kippur and that of the rest of the year may be illustrated by two disagreements regarding *Viduy* that are noted by the Talmud. First, the Rabbis debate whether one should include sins from previous years in the current year's *Viduy*.

> It was taught: Sins which a person confessed [i.e., recited *Viduy* about] on this Yom Kippur, one should not include in his *Viduy* on another Yom Kippur. If one repeated [the sins], then one must confess it again on another Yom Kippur. If he did not repeat them, and still confessed them, the verse says regarding this person, "As a dog that returns to his vomit, so is a fool that repeats his folly" [Prov. 26:11].
>
> R. Eliezer b. Yaakov says: How much more so is he worthy of praise [if he repeats the *Viduy* the next year], as it says, "For I know my transgressions; and my sin is ever before me" [Ps. 51:5]. (Yoma 88b)

Ostensibly, the first opinion, which states that one should not confess prior sins on Yom Kippur, makes perfect sense. Indeed, it would seem that to confess again might even be misinterpreted as a lack of faith in the power of repentance on the part of the sinner! Why should one repent for prior sins, which already have been forgiven? The Talmud cites another debate regarding the extent to which one must specify each sin when reciting the *Viduy*.

> And one must specify each sin, as it says, "And Moshe returned unto the Lord, and said: 'Oh, this people have sinned a great sin, and have made them a god of gold'" [Ex. 32:31]; these are the words of R. Yehuda b. Baba.
>
> R. Akiva said: "Happy is he whose transgression is forgiven [literally, "covered"], whose sin is pardoned" [Ps. 32:1]. (Yoma 88b)

While R. Yehuda b. Baba says that one must specify each sin in his confession, R. Akiva states that a general confession is sufficient.[10] Here, too, one may wonder why one should *not* confess all of one's sins!

R. Menaḥem Me'iri (1249–1310) sheds light on this debate in his *Ḥibbur HaTeshuva*. After discussing the various opinions regarding the final halakha, he concludes:

> Some of the *Geonim* rule that if one wishes to repent for a specific sin and his *teshuva* relates at that moment to that specific transgression, then he should specify the sin. However, one who intends to repent in a more general manner and to confess all of his sins does not need to specify each transgression. Rather, they should be before him, inscribed in his heart, and he should have in mind to include them in the general statement "*ḥatati*" (I have sinned). That was the intention of the *Viduy* from the geonic era, which was made up of of four words: "We have sinned, become guilty, caused perversion, caused wickedness."[11]

Me'iri distinguishes between a general overhaul of one's spiritual fabric, for which one should confess in a more general sense, and a more specific repentance, for which one should specify the sin.

Interestingly, Rambam writes regarding *teshuva* in general:

> If one transgressed any commandment of the Torah, whether a positive or a negative one, whether deliberately or accidentally, then when one repents, one must confess verbally to God.... This means verbal confession, which is a positive commandment, and is performed by saying, "O Lord, I have sinned, transgressed, and rebelled before You, and have done such-and-such, and I am ashamed by my actions and will never do it again." This is the main part of verbal confession, and expanding on it is praiseworthy.[12]

Rambam rules that one should specify the sin. However, regarding Yom Kippur, he writes:

> The Day of Atonement is a time of repentance for all, whether individually or with the community, and completes the pardoning and forgiving of Israel. Therefore, one is obligated to confess and repent on the Day of Atonement.... The confession which all Jews recite starts, "For we have sinned," etc. This is the core of confession. Any sins which one confessed on the Day of Atonement, one confesses on the following Day of Atonement, even though he has maintained his repentance, for it is written, "For I acknowledge my transgressions, and my sin is ever before me."[13]

Here, Rambam cites the more general *Viduy*, which does not specify each and every individual sin. Furthermore, he also rules that one should repeat mention of prior sins in each year's *Viduy*. Why? Rambam may believe that the *teshuva* of Yom Kippur differs from the regular, day-to-day *teshuva*. During the course of the year, our *teshuva* focuses upon specific transgressions. On Yom Kippur, however, we direct our *teshuva* toward our entire personality. On Yom Kippur, our performance of *teshuva* is not meant only to acquit or remove the need for punishment. Rather, we search for the cause of our sins. Yom Kippur offers a full spiritual "tune-up." For that purpose, one must recount all of one's sins, even past ones, in order to understand what led and continues to lead one to sin.

This distinction between repentance and purification, between the *teshuva* of the entire year and the *teshuva* of Yom Kippur, may help explain the enigmatic prayer of *Kol Nidrei*, the first prayer of Yom Kippur.

KOL NIDREI

Each year, we begin Yom Kippur with the somewhat mysterious prayer of *Kol Nidrei*. Its haunting tune is accompanied by a rush of emotions and feelings, as it ushers in the Day of Atonement. *Kol Nidrei* is no more than an annulment of past vows and a declaration that future vows should be null and void. It is, in fact, somewhat curious that this legal procedure should open the holiest day of the year!

The Torah emphasizes the obligation to keep one's word. For example, we learn:

> If a man vows a vow to the Lord or swears an oath to impose an obligation on himself, he shall not break his word; according to all that comes out of his mouth, he shall do. (Num. 30:3)

Similarly, the Torah says elsewhere:

> When you make a vow to the Lord your God, do not delay fulfilling it, for the Lord your God will require it of you and [if you don't fulfill it] you will have

> incurred a sin. But if you refrain from vowing, you will not have incurred a sin. That which has come from your lips you shall observe and do, what you have voluntarily vowed to the Lord your God which you spoke with your mouth. (Deut. 23: 22–24)

Indeed, the Talmud censures those who do not keep their word in business dealing.

> They [the sages] said: He who punished the generation of the flood and the generation of the dispersion will take vengeance on one who does not stand by his word. (Bava Metzia 47b)

Since vows are taken so seriously, how is it possible for us to publicly and ceremoniously annul our vows? Furthermore, the notion that Jews may not only annul their past vows but may also stipulate that future vows should not be binding was a source of great antagonism between Jews and non-Jews throughout the ages. Jewish apostates and enemies of the Jews have used *Kol Nidrei* to cast suspicion upon the honesty and trustworthiness of Jews and their oaths for hundreds of years.

In the famous Disputation of Paris in 1240, held at the court of Louis IX, for example, R. Yeḥiel of Paris debated the convert Nicholas Donin, and he was forced to counter this claim. He responded:

> We only annul the unintentional vows, in order that a person should not transgress with his vows or oaths…and only those [vows] which relate exclusively to himself, and not to others. However, vows which involve other people may not be annulled.[14]

In 1875, the Russian Czar issued a special *ukase*, a proclamation that recognized the rabbinic interpretation of the prayer. The rabbis, responding to the government, wrote:

> In the name of God, and according to the Torah, we annul vows and oaths in which a person prohibits upon himself.… However, God forbid that anyone should think that we annul vows and oaths which we swear to the government and in courts, or vows and oaths which we take between other parties.[15]

These rabbinic responses highlight the dilemma that *Kol Nidrei* raised.

Indeed, the criticism of *Kol Nidrei* was so great that not only did the Reform movement unanimously decide to abolish *Kol Nidrei* at the rabbinical conference held at Brunswick in 1844, but even R. Samson Raphael Hirsch, the leader of the neo-Orthodox community in Germany, omitted the recitation of *Kol Nidrei* in Oldenburg in 1839 (although he later retracted). The claim that *Kol Nidrei* demonstrates the way Jews relate to their commitments was repeated as recently as 1964.[16] Our task in this chapter, however, is not to trace the historical development of this prayer, but rather to present its halakhic significance and attempt to explain its centrality in the traditional Yom Kippur liturgy.

Source and Reasons

The earliest references to *Kol Nidrei* appear in the geonic literature. R. Natronai Gaon, who served as the head of the Sura academy in the middle of the ninth century, records that while he had heard that some were accustomed to recite *Kol Nidrei* on Yom Kippur, this was not practiced in the "two academies" in Babylonia, and he had never seen such a practice.[17] His student and successor, R. Amram Gaon, records the *Kol Nidrei* in his Siddur, but comments, "But the holy academy sent word that this is a foolish custom and it is forbidden to practice it."

Apparently, *Kol Nidrei* became a widely accepted part of the Yom Kippur liturgy toward the turn of the millennium (although it goes unmentioned by Rambam), despite constantly attracting all sorts of criticism.

The *Geonim*, as well as many *Rishonim*, expressed great difficulty with this custom. General unease about vows, uncertainty regarding the right to annul them, and a general fear of both the internal educational message and external perception of such an apparent loophole led many to oppose its recitation. In addition, many raised halakhic objections. *Hatarat nedarim* (nullification of vows) requires a *beit din* of three judges (in the absence of an outstanding individual scholar), as well as regret and specification of the vows or oaths being nullified. If so, our question grows even stronger: How and why do we recite *Kol Nidrei* on the eve of Yom Kippur?

Some *Rishonim* defend the traditional understanding of *Kol Nidrei* – that the congregation annuls their vows before the onset of Yom Kippur. This is supported by the language of *Kol Nidrei,* which is phrased in the past tense. Raavya, for example, insists that *Kol Nidrei* does actually annul one's past vows. The entire congregation

> Aligns their intentions with that of the *sheliaḥ tzibbur,* as if they said explicitly "and we regret the vows we have made, and we request annulment," and he releases them with the consent of the community, as an individual cannot absolve vows unless he is an expert (*mumḥe*).[18]

In other words, with the consent of the community, the *ḥazan* serves as an individual judge, empowered to annul vows and oaths.

Rabbeinu Tam, however, disagrees and raises many objections to the traditional understanding of *Kol Nidrei.*[19] He insists that *Kol Nidrei* does not affect the past by annulling previous vows, but rather stipulates that any vow that one will take in the future should not be binding. Indeed, the Talmud teaches:

> And he who desires that none of his vows made during the year shall be valid, let him stand at the beginning of the year and declare, "Every vow which I may make in the future shall be null." [His vows are then invalid,] provided that he remembers this at the time of the vow. But if he remembers, has he not canceled the declaration and confirmed the vow? ... Rava said ... Here the circumstances are, for example, that one stipulated at the beginning of the year, but does not know in reference to what. Now he vows. Hence, if he remembers [the stipulation] and he declares, "I vow in accordance with my original intention," his vow has no reality. But if he does not declare thus, he has canceled his stipulation and confirmed his vow. (Nedarim 23b)

According to this Gemara, one may declare each year that all vows that one makes during the year should not take effect. Those vows will then be invalid as long as one remembers this stipulation at the time of the vow. Other *Rishonim* still questioned the validity of *Kol Nidrei.* Some even write that one who relies upon *Kol Nidrei* and then violates his vows transgresses the biblical prohibition of violating one's word (*bal yaḥel*).

Rabbeinu Tam explains that *Kol Nidrei* fulfills this talmudic recommendation. In fact, Rabbeinu Tam altered the text of *Kol Nidrei*. While the original text read, "All personal vows we are likely to make, all personal oaths and pledges we took from the last Day of Atonement until this one, we publicly renounce," Rabbeinu Tam amended the text to read, "All personal vows we are likely to make, all personal oaths and pledges we are likely to take between this Yom Kippur and the next Yom Kippur, we publicly renounce."

R. Tzedkia b. R. Avraham HaRofeh, the author of the *Shibbolei HaLeket*, suggests that *Kol Nidrei* may simply serve as a reminder to keep all of one's commitments before the Festival of Sukkot, during which time one traditionally fulfills one's vows.[20] He suggests that since "*avon nedarim*," the sin of not discharging one's vows, is so great, we petition God in *Kol Nidrei* for forgiveness, both for those vows which went unfulfilled and for those which were kept. In other words, *Kol Nidrei* does not annul vows at all, but rather begs God's forgiveness for not keeping them.

Kol Nidrei and the *Teshuva* of Yom Kippur

As noted above, the Rabbis express great ambivalence, and often unease, regarding vows in general. For example, the Talmud cites the following debate regarding *nedarim*.

> For it was taught: "Better it is that you should not vow, than that you should vow and not pay" [Eccl. 5:4]. Better than both [vowing and paying] is not to vow at all; thus said R. Meir. R. Yehuda said: Better than both is to vow and repay. (Nedarim 9a)

Elsewhere, taking vows is equated with building illegal altars:

> For it was taught: R. Natan said: Whosoever makes a vow is as though he had built an unlawful altar (*bama*), and who fulfills it, is as though he burned incense thereon. (Nedarim 60b)

Furthermore, one who vows is considered by some to be a sinner.

> Rava said to R. Naḥman: Behold, Master, a scholar came from the west [the Land of Israel] and related that the Rabbis gave a hearing to the son of

> R. Huna b. Avin and absolved him of his vow, and then said to him, "Go, and pray for mercy, for you have sinned." For R. Dimi, the brother of R. Safra, learned: He who vows, even though he fulfills it, is designated a sinner. R. Zeved said: What verse [teaches this]? "But if you shall forbear to vow, it shall be no sin in you" [Deut. 23:23]; hence, if you have not forborne, there is sin. (Nedarim 77b)

Vows were generally taken to forbid a person from doing something that was ordinarily permitted. This practice was also criticized:

> Shmuel said: Whoever fasts is termed a sinner. He is of the same opinion as the following *Tanna*. For it has been taught: Eleazar HaKappar b. Rebbi says: What is Scripture referring to when it says [of the Nazirite], "And make atonement for him, for he sinned by reason of the soul?" [Num. 6]. Against which soul did he sin? [It must refer to the fact that] he denied himself wine. We can now make this inference from minor to major: If this man [Nazirite] who denied himself wine alone is termed a sinner, how much more so he who denies himself the enjoyment of ever so many things. (Taanit 11a)

What do the Rabbis find so problematic with taking vows? Rambam explains:

> Whoever makes vows in order to discipline his moral disposition and to improve his conduct displays commendable zeal and is worthy of praise.... All such vows are ways of serving God, and of them and their like, the sages have said, "Vows are a fence around self-restraint."
>
> Yet in spite of the fact that vows are ways of serving God, one should not multiply prohibitory vows nor employ them regularly.... Indeed, the sages have said, "Whosoever makes a vow is as though he had built an unlawful altar."[21]

Vows and oaths are a means of dealing with one's moral and spiritual weaknesses. While at times they may be necessary, and even praiseworthy, they do not solve the problem. Ideally, one should change his behavior through thorough examination and introspection, leading to sincere repentance, and not through the artificial means of a vow.

On Yom Kippur, we cast aside our vows and oaths and state before God: We are willing to purify ourselves and to get to the bottom of our moral and spiritual failings, once and for all. We no longer need vows and oaths to keep us from sinning. We will plumb the depths of our personalities, searching for that which motivates us to sin. The *teshuva* process that begins on Yom Kippur evening with *Kol Nidrei* aims to rehabilitate our weak personalities, rendering the need for vows null and void. Only this type of repentance leads to purification, as the Torah teaches, "For on this day shall atonement be made for you, to cleanse you; from all your sins shall you be cleansed before the Lord" (Lev. 16:30).

CHAPTER 14

"You Shall Afflict Your Souls"

THE TORAH REFERS to appropriate behavior on Yom Kippur in three places:

> And it shall be a statute forever unto you: In the seventh month, on the tenth day of the month, you shall afflict your souls, and shall do no manner of work, the home-born or the stranger that sojourns among you. For on this day shall atonement be made for you, to cleanse you; from all your sins shall you be clean before God. It is a Sabbath of solemn rest (*Shabbat Shabbaton*) for you, and you shall afflict your souls; it is a statute forever. (Lev. 16:29–31)
>
> On the tenth day of this seventh month is the Day of Atonement; there shall be a holy convocation for you, and you shall afflict your souls; and you shall bring an offering made by fire unto the Lord. And you shall do no manner of work in that same day; for it is a day of atonement, to make atonement for you before the Lord your God. For whatever soul that shall not be afflicted on that same day shall be cut off from his people. And whatever soul that does any manner of work on that same day, that soul will I destroy from among his people. You shall do no manner of work; it is a statute forever throughout your generations in all your dwellings. It shall be unto you a Sabbath of solemn rest (*Shabbat Shabbaton*), and you shall afflict your souls; in

> the ninth day of the month in the evening, from evening unto evening shall you keep your Sabbath. (Lev. 23:27–32)
>
> And on the tenth day of this seventh month, you shall have a holy convocation and you shall afflict your souls; you shall do no manner of work. (Num. 29:7)

In these verses, the Torah does not specifically prohibit eating, drinking, or other pleasures, but rather commands that one should "afflict" (*ve'initem*) oneself on Yom Kippur. What is the definition and nature of this "affliction" and what is its purpose? In addition, the Torah describes Yom Kippur as a "*Shabbat*," and even more puzzling, the Torah juxtaposes the phrase "*Shabbat Shabbaton*" with the command of "*ve'initem*." What, if any, is the relationship between "*ve'initem*" and "*Shabbat Shabbaton*"?

THE FIVE AFFLICTIONS

The Mishna teaches:

> On Yom Kippur it is prohibited to engage in eating and drinking, in washing oneself, in anointing [one's body with oil], in wearing shoes, and in marital relations. The king and a bride may wash their faces, and a new mother may wear shoes. These are the words of R. Eliezer. But the sages prohibit this. (Yoma 73b)

The Gemara proves that the phrase "*inui*," as used in the Torah, refers to depriving oneself of eating and drinking (Yoma 74b). Thus, all agree that these two prohibitions are biblically prohibited; only they incur the punishment of *karet* if violated.

Regarding the other four prohibitions, the Talmud asks:

> To what do these five afflictions correspond? R. Ḥisda said: They correspond to the five [times] afflictions are stated in the Torah.... These are only five, yet we learned in the Mishna there are six [afflictions]? Drinking is included in "eating." (Yoma 76a)

The *Rishonim* debate whether the other four prohibitions are prohibited *mideoraita* (biblically) or *miderabbanan* (rabbinically). Most *Rishonim* argue that these prohibitions are *miderabbanan.*[1] These *Rishonim* bring numerous proofs to support their claim. First, the language of the gemara above, which asks, "To what do these five afflictions correspond?" and not "What is the source for these afflictions?" implies that the Gemara viewed these prohibitions as rabbinic in origin. Second, the *Rishonim* point to the halakhic differences between the prohibitions of eating and drinking and the other afflictions. Only eating and drinking on Yom Kippur incur the punishment of *karet*. Furthermore, in the Mishna, R. Eliezer permits a king and a bride to wash their faces and a new mother to wear leather shoes. Had the prohibition of washing been *mideoraita,* we would not expect to find such exceptions. Similarly, the Gemara teaches that if one was soiled with mud or excrement, one may wash himself, and one who has scabs on his head may anoint himself as he usually does (Yoma 77b). Again, had the prohibition been of biblical origin, we would not expect to find these exceptions. *Tosafot Yeshanim* suggests that this discussion may actually be the basis for the debate between R. Eliezer and the sages, although he rejects this possibility.

Due to the problems raised above, it would seem quite difficult to maintain that the other *inuyim* are prohibited *mideoraita,* unless we were to either redefine what exactly is prohibited *mideoraita* or reevaluate our assumption that a biblical law cannot tolerate exceptions. R. Eliezer of Metz, author of the *Sefer Yerei'im,* argues that *mideoraita,* only bathing most of one's body for pleasure is prohibited. *Miderabbanan,* however, one may not bathe even a small part of one's body for pleasure. A king and a bride who wash only part of their body (the face) were excluded from this prohibition, as was one who washes part of his body that has become soiled.[2] Similarly, *Tosafot Yeshanim* suggests (and rejects) the possibility that the Torah only prohibited wearing a "*minal,*" shoes that cover the entire foot, while a "*sandal,*" which only partially covers the foot, is prohibited only *miderabbanan,* but permitted for a new mother.[3]

R. Naftali Tzvi Yehuda Berlin (Netziv), in his commentary to *She'iltot,* defends R. Aḥai Gaon, who rules that all five afflictions are *mideoraita.*[4] He explains that while eating and drinking entail "*aveidat nefesh*" – life depends on them – the other four afflictions generally entail refraining from enjoyment. Washing, anointing, or wearing leather shoes in situations that do not involve "pleasure" were not prohibited by the Torah, but rather *miderabbanan*. Therefore, R. Eliezer permitted a king and bride to wash their faces and a new mother to wear shoes, as they do not do so for enjoyment. Similarly, the *She'iltot* explains that one may wear leather shoes in order to walk in an area with scorpions, as in that case, the shoes are not worn for enjoyment, but rather for protection. This theory enables Netziv to explain the halakhic discrepancies between eating and drinking and the other *inuyim*.

While these opinions attempt to resolve the apparent difficulties in asserting that the other *inuyim* are biblically prohibited and to explain the halakhic discrepancies between eating and drinking and the other afflictions, Ran offers a unique approach, redefining how we understand the notion of a "biblical prohibition":

> Therefore, it seems to me that all of the afflictions are *mideoraita* ... and the Scriptures gave over the authority to the sages and they were lenient, as they saw fit, and permitted that which wasn't done for pleasure.[5]

In other words, while the core prohibition of "and you shall afflict" is *mideoraita*, its specific details were determined by the sages. The sages, therefore, determined that a king and a bride, as well as one who wishes only to remove dirt, may wash.[6]

The *Aḥaronim* discuss the position of Rambam at length, debating whether he agrees with those who view the other prohibitions as being of biblical or rabbinic origin. Rambam writes:

> It is a positive commandment to refrain from all work on the tenth [day] of the seventh month, as it states, "It shall be a Sabbath of Sabbaths for you" [Lev. 16:31].
>
> There is another positive commandment on Yom Kippur to refrain from eating and drinking, as it states, "You shall afflict your souls" [Lev. 16:29]. According to the Oral Tradition, it has been taught: What is meant by afflicting one's soul? Fasting.
>
> Whoever fasts on this day fulfills a positive commandment. Whoever eats or drinks on this day negates the observance of [this] positive commandment and violates a negative commandment, as it states, "Any soul that

> does not afflict itself will be cut off" [Lev. 23:29]. Since the Torah punishes a person who does not fast with *karet*, we can derive from this that we are forbidden to eat and drink on this day.
>
> Similarly, according to the Oral Tradition, it has been taught that it is forbidden to wash, anoint oneself, wear shoes, or engage in sexual relations on this day. It is a mitzva to refrain from these activities in the same way one refrains from eating and drinking. This is derived from [the exegesis of the expression] "a Sabbath of Sabbaths." "A Sabbath" implies refraining from eating [according to another version, "with regards to work"]; "of Sabbaths" implies refraining from these activities. One does not incur *karet* or become obligated to bring a sacrifice except [for violating] eating and drinking. However, if one washes or anoints or wears leather shoes or engages in marital relations, one receives rabbinical lashes (*makat mardut*).[7]

On the one hand, Rambam writes that one who violates one of the four afflictions receives "*makat mardut*," implying that the other *inuyim* are only *miderabbanan*. On the other hand, Rambam writes, "It is a mitzva to refrain from these activities in the same way one refrains from eating and drinking" – seemingly equating the prohibitions of eating and drinking and the other afflictions. Ran insists that Rambam prohibits the other afflictions *mideoraita*.[8] *Maggid Mishneh* disagrees,[9] explaining that Rambam distinguishes between eating and drinking, which are prohibited *mideoraita*, and the other *inuyim*, which are prohibited *miderabbanan*. Interestingly, Rambam, both in his *Sefer HaMitzvot*[10] and in his *Perush HaMishna*,[11] writes that the five afflictions are known "through tradition" (*min hakabbala*), implying that they are *mideoraita*.

R. Moshe Soloveitchik, as cited by his son R. Yosef Dov Soloveitchik, notes an intriguing point in this Rambam. Rambam implies that the phrase "Shabbat" applies equally to refraining from labor and refraining from eating, drinking, and the other *inuyim*. In other words, the prohibition against "*melakha*" and the requirement to fast emerge from essentially the same halakhic origin. R. Soloveitchik raises numerous ramifications and expressions of this principle. For our purposes, we will note that according to Rambam, the Torah does not prohibit eating, drinking, or other pleasures, but rather demands that we "rest," or abstain from these activities, just as we refrain from prohibited labor. Indeed, as we mentioned above, the Torah repeatedly mentions the commandment regarding the afflictions along with the theme of *Shabbaton*.

If so, then how are we to understand the "afflictions" of Yom Kippur? What role do they play, and why are they referred to as "*Shabbaton*"?

THE NATURE OF THE *INUYIM*

Ostensibly, "*ve'initem et nafshoteikhem*" (Lev. 16:31, 23:27, 23:32; Num. 29:7) should be translated literally: "And you shall afflict your souls." The apparent purpose of the *inuyim* is to afflict, to cause discomfort, in order to motivate the person to repent. Indeed, this assumption seems to guide the Gemara, at least initially, in the following discussion:

> The Rabbis taught: "You should afflict yourselves" [Lev. 16:29]. It might be thought that this means that one should sit in the [hot] sun or in the cold in order to suffer. To advise otherwise, the Torah then states, "And you shall not do any work" [ibid.]. [The linking of the two verses teaches:] Just as [the injunction against] work is a command to sit and not do, so too, the commandment of afflicting oneself is a command to sit and not do. But say in a case where one sits in the sun and becomes hot, we would not say to him, "Get up and sit in the shade." Or where one sits in the shade and becomes cold, we should not say to him, "Get up and sit in the sun!" [The Gemara answers: The mitzva of afflicting oneself is] similar to [refraining from] work: Just as you do not differentiate concerning work, so too, you do not differentiate regarding affliction. (Yoma 74b)

At first, the Gemara clearly understands the obligation of "you shall afflict yourselves" as an imperative to cause oneself discomfort. Afterward, the Gemara suggests that while one need not actively cause discomfort, one should certainly not improve one's state of comfort. Finally, the Gemara concludes that just as "work" refers to specific labors that are always prohibited, "affliction" refers to specific forms of *inui*, or abstentions, which apply in all situations.

The Gemara does not indicate, however, the extent to which it clings to its initial assumption. In other words, does the Gemara still understand the primary goal of *inui* as causing discomfort? We have previously discussed the mitzva to eat on the eve of Yom Kippur. We noted that the *Shibbolei HaLeket* and the *Torah Temima* suggest that the Torah wants one to eat excessively the day before a fast in order that he will suffer even more on the day of the fast itself. Clearly, *Shibbolei HaLeket* and *Torah Temima* understand "*ve'initem*" literally – one should ideally suffer great discomfort on Yom Kippur.

Most *Rishonim* (Rashi, Rosh), however, explain that the Torah commands the Jewish people to eat on Erev Yom Kippur so that they should experience *less* discomfort during the fast, or to express one's joy upon the opportunity to receive absolution (Rabbeinu Yona, Ritva). These *Rishonim* seem to disagree with the first opinion; they do not view experiencing discomfort as the goal of the day.

Furthermore, according to Rambam, as we explained above, *inuyim* are a fulfillment of "Shabbaton," similar to refraining from doing *melakha*. Apparently, the *inuyim* would be better described as abstentions from the physical world – a withdrawal from day-to-day activities – than an attempt to cause discomfort. Indeed, *Pirkei DeRabbi Eliezer*, which compares the Jewish people to the ministering angels who are completely removed from physicality and devoted to fulfilling God's commandments, more accurately portrays the function of the *inuyim*.[12] In order to repent fully and achieve complete forgiveness, the Torah commands us to withdraw from the physical world and to focus upon the world of spirit, if only for a day. Afflicting oneself literally is not the intention of the Torah.

CHAPTER 15

The Afflictions of Yom Kippur: Practical Applications

EATING AND DRINKING ON YOM KIPPUR

The Mishna discusses the amount that one must eat or drink in order to be culpable on Yom Kippur.

> One who eats the equivalent of a large date (*kakotevet hagasa*), i.e., the equivalent of it and its pit, or drinks a quantity of liquid equal to the fill of his cheeks (*melo lugmav*) is liable. All foods combine for the [volume] equivalent of a large date, and all beverages combine for the [volume] equivalent of the fill of his cheeks. But eating and drinking do not combine. (Yoma 73b)

The measurements (*shiurim*) for Yom Kippur differ from those generally used in other contexts – we usually define eating by the volume of an olive (*kezayit*) and drinking by a *revi'it* of liquid. Regarding Yom Kippur, the Gemara explains:

> R. Zevid said: The "*kakotevet*" (a large date) whereof they spoke is smaller in size than an egg, for we learned ... the quantity of an egg will satisfy one, the size of a big date will still one's hunger. (Yoma 76b)

A *kakotevet*, an ordinary date, is slightly smaller than the volume of an egg. Modern authorities estimate the volumetric measurement of a *kotevet gasa* to be about 1.5 fl. oz. [44 ml].[1] Similarly, regarding drinking, the Gemara explains:

> R. Yehuda said in the name of Shmuel: The Mishna does not mean the actual fill of his cheeks, but rather any amount that were he to remove it to one side [of his mouth], it would appear as if his cheeks were full.

The Gemara is aware of the subjective nature of this measurement, and concludes:

> What is the difference between eating, [in the context of which] the measure for everyone is a *kakotevet* (the volume of a date), and for drinking everyone [measures according to] his own [cheek-full]? Abaye said: It has been accepted by the Rabbis that with such [a volume of food], one's mind is put at ease, and with less than that one's mind is not put at ease. But with regards to drinking, with one's own cheek-full his mind is put at ease, but with the cheek-full of his friend, his mind is not put at ease.

Finally, the Gemara concludes that just as regarding prohibited foods one must consume a *kezayit* (an olive's volume) within the amount of time it takes to eat half of a loaf of bread (*bikhedei akhilat peras*), one must similarly eat the date's volume of food in this time span in order to incur *karet* on Yom Kippur, as "it has been accepted by the Rabbis that when a date's volume is eaten in such a time span, one's mind is put at ease" (Yoma 80b). The *Rishonim* debate whether this refers to the time it takes to eat the volume of three eggs (Rambam) or four (Rashi).

The *Aḥaronim* further attempt to define this time span. Ḥatam Sofer, for example, rules that "*kedei akhilat peras*" is the equivalent of nine minutes,[2] and the *Mishna Berura* cites this ruling.[3] R. Shneur Zalman of Liadi, author of the *Shulḥan Arukh HaRav*, reportedly estimated this time at eight minutes, while the *Arukh HaShulḥan* suggests that this period may be between six and seven minutes.[4] Others accept even shorter periods, from four,[5] three,[6] or even two minutes.[7]

The *Shulḥan Arukh* cites two opinions regarding drinking. While some say that the time frame for drinking is identical to that of eating, that is, *kedei akhilat peras*, others say that it is much shorter – *kedei shetiyat revi'it*, the amount of time it takes to drink a *revi'it* (roughly four ounces) of liquid.[8]

While the details of the size of the forbidden *shiur* and the time span in which it must be eaten are relevant to determining if one is deserving of divine punishment, one may not eat even a smaller amount of food or the *shiur* over a longer time span. Indeed, the Talmud cites a debate regarding whether "*ḥatzi shiur*," that is, eating less than the proscribed amount, is prohibited *mideoraita* or *miderabbanan*.

> Regarding "*ḥatzi shiur*" – R. Yoḥanan said that it is biblically prohibited. Reish Lakish said that it is rabbinically permitted. R. Yoḥanan said that it is biblically prohibited, for since the half measure is fit to combine with more of the same forbidden food, he is considered to have eaten prohibited food. Reish Lakish said it is rabbinically permitted, as the Torah referred to "eating," and there is no eating. (Yoma 73b–74a)

The Gemara concludes, however, that even Reish Lakish agrees that there is a rabbinic prohibition against eating a *ḥatzi shiur*. Interestingly, the Yerushalmi suggests that Reish Lakish, who generally rejects the concept of *ḥatzi shiur*, would concede that it is forbidden on Yom Kippur (Y. Terumot 6:1). Apparently, the Yerushalmi believes that on Yom Kippur, any experience which prevents *inui* is forbidden, even if performed with less than a *shiur*. This discussion may be significant for one who must eat on Yom Kippur due to illness.

THE SICK, INFIRM, OR PREGNANT ON YOM KIPPUR

The Tosefta teaches, "Nothing stands in the way of saving one's life (*pikuaḥ nefesh*)" (Tosefta, Shabbat 9:22). While the Talmud does discuss limitations to this principle, as a general rule, *pikuaḥ nefesh* takes precedence over other mitzvot and prohibitions. The Gemara searches for a source for this principle:

> It once happened that R. Yishmael, R. Akiva, and R. Elazar b. Azaria were traveling on the road with Levi the organizer and R. Yishmael, the son of R. Elazar b. Azaria, following behind them, when the following question was asked before them: From where do we know that saving a life overrides the law of Shabbat?

After citing numerous possibilities, the Gemara cites a final opinion:

> R. Yehuda said in the name of Shmuel: Had I been there, I would have said that mine [source] is better than theirs. [It is written,] "[You shall guard My

> decrees and My laws that man shall carry out] and he shall live by them" [Lev. 18:5] – but he should not die on their account. (Yoma 85a)

The Talmud explicitly permits one who is dangerously ill to eat and drink on Yom Kippur (Yoma 82a). Just as one violates the Sabbath or any other commandment in order to preserve one's life (except for the three cardinal sins of murder, illicit sexual relations, and idolatry), one may, and is even required to, eat or drink on Yom Kippur in order to preserve one's life. Indeed, Ran writes:

> A sick person who has been instructed by experts to violate the Shabbat – it is not an act of piety to refrain, but rather this person sheds blood. The Talmud Yerushalmi says, "[When it comes to life-saving,] the hasty is praiseworthy, the one who is asked a question [about life-saving] is a disgrace, and the one who asks a question is a murderer."[9]

How much may one eat and drink on Yom Kippur in order to preserve one's health? The Gemara states, "The Rabbis permitted a pregnant woman to eat less than a *shiur* due to the danger" (Keritot 13a). In other words, she may consume less than the volume of a date (*kakotevet*) in the time it takes to consume half of a loaf of bread.

Many *Rishonim* apply the principle stated in this gemara to all sick individuals.[10] They rule that a sick person should preferably try to limit his eating, when possible, to less than a *kotevet gasa bikhedei akhilat peras*, or less than a *melo lugmav* in that period (or, according to some, in less than *bikhedei shetiyat revi'it*). Rosh stipulates that if a doctor insists that the *ḥoleh* must eat more than that amount, he should eat normally.

The *Shulḥan Arukh*[11] rules in accordance with Ran,[12] who writes that when one feeds a sick person on Yom Kippur, one should give him approximately two thirds of the size of an egg, slightly less than the volume of *kakotevet*. Based on this, one who is ill and must eat on Yom Kippur should eat approximately 1 fl. oz. (30 ml) – approximately the size of a small box of matches – of food every nine minutes.[13] R. Moshe Feinstein recommends waiting four and a half minutes between each portion when necessary.[14] One who must drink on Yom Kippur should drink less than a cheek-full of liquid every nine minutes.[15] If necessary, one may drink every six minutes[16] or every four or two minutes (see above).

Interestingly, Netziv insists that Rif and Rambam do not accept the ruling of the *Rishonim* who extended the Gemara about pregnant women to *ḥolim* as well.[17] Netziv argues that the Gemara only instructed a pregnant woman to eat small amounts, as the concern is to reduce her hunger cravings and ensure the safety of her fetus. The Gemara never meant to limit the eating of a dangerously ill person. Such *ḥolim* may eat normally on Yom Kippur.

R. Chaim Soloveitchik also rules leniently.[18] He explains that one who must eat in order to avoid becoming seriously ill should eat in small amounts. However, one who is already dangerously ill should eat normally. He bases this ruling upon *Maggid Mishneh*'s comments on Rambam's statement that one may violate the Sabbath even in order to care for the non-critical needs of a person who is dangerously ill (*ḥoleh sheyesh bo sakana*).[19] Indeed, R. Chaim ruled accordingly when he served as the rabbi in Brisk. When challenged, he would often respond, "I am not ruling leniently regarding Yom Kippur, but rather strictly regarding *pikuaḥ nefesh* (saving one's life)."[20] R. Yosef Dov Soloveitchik[21] and R. Yechezkel Abramsky[22] rule like R. Chaim Soloveitchik,[23] but the *Arukh HaShulḥan*,[24] *Shemirat Shabbat KeHilkhata*,[25] and R. Ovadia Yosef[26] do not. One should consult with his doctor and a halakhic authority, when possible, before eating or drinking on Yom Kippur to avoid being unnecessarily lenient or stringent.

A "*ḥoleh she'ein bo sakana*" – a sick person whose life is not in danger but who must continue to take medications, such as antibiotics, or one who suffers from a chronic condition but is not presently sick and therefore must fast – should try to swallow his medicines without water. Some suggest that one who is unable to swallow medicines without water should mix a bit of water with a bitter substance and take the medicine with that water.[27] Swallowing a pill with a bit of mouthwash should also suffice. Some suggest wrapping pills, especially pleasant-tasting pills, in thin paper and then swallowing them.[28] R. Moshe Feinstein permits one who must take medicine in order to prevent the development of a serious medical condition, and certainly one who suffers from a potentially life-threatening situation, to swallow his pills with a bit of water.[29]

Rema writes that one who is sick may shower normally on Yom Kippur.[30]

ANOINTING ON YOM KIPPUR

As mentioned previously, the Torah never explicitly specifies the afflictions of Yom Kippur. In fact, the *Rishonim* debate whether the other four afflictions that appear in the Mishna (Yoma 73b) – abstention from washing, anointing, wearing leather shoes, and engaging in marital relations – are of biblical or rabbinic origin.

The Gemara offers two sources for the prohibition of anointing. In Yoma, the Gemara asks:

> From where do we know that [abstaining from] washing and anointing are considered acts of affliction? For it is written, "I ate no desirable bread, and meat and wine did not enter my mouth, and I did not anoint myself with an anointing" [Daniel 10:3]. And from where do we know that this is considered an affliction? For it is written, "And he said to me, 'Do not fear, Daniel, for from the first day that you set your heart to understand and to afflict yourselves before God, your words have been heard; and I have come because of your words'" [v. 12]. (Yoma 76b)

The Mishna in Shabbat provides another source prohibiting anointing on Yom Kippur, comparing it to drinking.

> How do we know that anointing is the same as drinking on the Day of Atonement? Although there is no proof of this, yet there is a "*remez*" (suggestion) thereof, for it is said, "And it came into his inward parts like water, and like oil into his bones" [Ps. 109:18]. (Shabbat 86a)

Tosafot question the necessity for two sources prohibiting anointing on Yom Kippur, especially since the Gemara admits that one of them is not more than a "*remez*."[31] Gra suggests that the Mishna in Shabbat comes to prevent a mistaken conclusion that anointing is literally akin to drinking; anointing is similar, but not identical, and therefore, on Yom Kippur, one who anoints does not incur "*karet*."[32]

R. Soloveitchik offers a different approach.[33] He suggests that there may be two types of "anointing" prohibited on Yom Kippur – anointing that is akin to drinking (*sikha kashtiya*) and anointing done for pleasure (*sikha shel taanug*). Thus, it would seem that even *sikha* done not for the purpose of pleasure should be prohibited on Yom Kippur! Indeed, Rambam rules:

> One may not anoint even part of one's body on Yom Kippur, regardless of whether the anointing is done for pleasure or not, although one who is sick, even though he is not in danger, or a person with scabs on his head, may anoint normally.[34]

Rambam delineates three types of anointing: anointing for pleasure, anointing not for pleasure, and anointing for a sick person. He prohibits the first two types and permits the third. Tosafot disagree, prohibiting only anointing for pleasure.[35] This distinction may yield a practical ramification. The *Shulḥan Arukh* writes:

> It is prohibited to anoint even part of one's body, even if he only intends to remove filth. However, one who is sick, even if he doesn't face any danger, or one who has scabs on his head, may [anoint].[36]

The *Biur Halakha* notes that while on Tisha B'Av, the *Shulḥan Arukh* only prohibits anointing for the purpose of pleasure, on Yom Kippur all anointing is prohibited.[37] Some *Aḥaronim* thus deduce that one may apply deodorant, whose purpose is to "remove filth," on Tisha B'Av, but not on Yom Kippur.

WASHING ON YOM KIPPUR

The Gemara continues to search for a source to prohibit washing on Yom Kippur:

> We have found anointing; from where do we know washing?... R. Ashi said: Washing is derived from the verse itself, as it says, "And I did not anoint myself with anointing." (Yoma 76b)

This passage, as well as the Gemara elsewhere (Mo'ed Katan 15a), views washing as a form of anointing. However, unlike anointing, the Gemara seems to only prohibit washing for the purpose of pleasure.

> The Rabbis taught: It is forbidden to wash part of one's body just as it is forbidden to wash all of one's body. But if he was soiled with mud or excrement, he need not be concerned.[38]

The *Rishonim* debate the extent of this prohibition and the definition of "washing for the purpose of pleasure." As we saw regarding anointing, there may be three types of washing: washing for pleasure, not for pleasure, and to remove dirt or for medicinal purposes. May one wash not for the purpose of pleasure, but not necessarily to remove dirt?

The *Rishonim*, for example, discuss whether one may wash one's hands in the morning upon rising, as one does every morning. Rambam rules that since washing is prohibited on Yom Kippur, one does not recite the blessing of "*al netilat yadayim*" in the morning.[39] Ran disagrees,[40] ruling that for the sake of a mitzva,[41] such as washing one's hands upon rising, one may wash and recite the *berakha*. Rabbeinu Tam and others concur.[42] The *Shulḥan Arukh* rules that one should wash his hands in the morning up to the knuckles and recite the blessing.[43] Similarly, the *Shulḥan Arukh* rules than an "*istinis*," one who is extra sensitive, may wash his face.[44] Rema records that it is customary to be stringent.[45]

Finally, Rema writes that it is customary not to rinse one's mouth on Yom Kippur.[46] Some *Aḥaronim*[47] express concern that one might accidentally swallow some of the water. This might lead us to the conclusion that a liquid that is not fit for consumption may be used for rinsing one's mouth on Yom Kippur. R. Moshe Feinstein suggests that washing out one's mouth on Tisha B'Av may be prohibited because of "*reḥitza*" (bathing).[48] The *Minḥat Yitzḥak* prohibits rinsing one's mouth out on Tisha B'Av, but permits brushing one's teeth with "powder" in order to reduce discomfort.[49] What about rinsing one's mouth with a liquid unfit for consumption, like vinegar, or even mouthwash, on Yom Kippur? R. Efraim Zalman Margolis (1762–1828), in his *Mateh*

Efraim, a *sefer* devoted to the ritual laws to be observed from the beginning of the month of Elul until after Sukkot, writes that one should not even rinse his mouth with a liquid unfit for consumption on Yom Kippur. Brushing one's teeth with a dry toothbrush, however, is certainly permitted.

WEARING SHOES ON YOM KIPPUR

The Mishna lists "*ne'ilat hasandal*," wearing shoes, as one of the five *inuyim* of Yom Kippur (Yoma 73b). What type of shoes does the Mishna prohibit? Does the Mishna prohibit shoes of certain materials specifically or of a certain level of comfort? The Talmud reports that many *Amora'im* would wear non-leather footwear on Yom Kippur.

> And they inquired further: What is the law regarding going out with a sandal made of cork on Yom Kippur? R. Yitzḥak b. Naḥmani rose to his feet and said: I once observed R. Yehoshua b. Levi going out with a sandal made of cork on Yom Kippur.... R. Yehuda went out with [sandals made from] *hitni*. Abaye went out with [sandals made from] palm leaves. Rava went out with [sandals made from] grass. Rabba b. R. Huna would wrap a kerchief around his foot and go out.

The Gemara then questions:

> Rami b. Ḥama retorted: An amputee may go out [on Shabbat] with his wooden foot; these are the words of R. Meir. R. Yose prohibited. And a *baraita* taught in reference to this: But they both agree that it is forbidden to go out [with a wooden foot] on Yom Kippur! (Yoma 78b)

In other words, the Mishna prohibits an amputee to wear his wooden prosthetic on Yom Kippur, despite the fact that it is not made from leather. The Gemara cites Rava, who refutes an answer offered by Abaye and concludes, "In truth, all agree that a [wooden foot] is considered a 'shoe.'"

The *Rishonim* debate how to understand Rava's conclusion. Baal HaMaor explains that all footwear that provides protection, including that worn by the *Amora'im* mentioned above, is prohibited, except for the kerchief worn around one's foot.[50] Rashi disagrees, explaining that the Gemara prohibits shoes made from leather and wood, similar to the amputee's prosthetic, but permits footwear fashioned from other materials, in accordance with the *Amora'im* noted above.

Rif[51] and Rosh[52] rule that only wearing leather shoes constitutes "*ne'ilat hasandal*." Therefore, one may wear all other types of footwear, even shoes made from other comfortable materials. Interestingly, Rambam writes:

> It is permitted to wear on Yom Kippur shoes made from cork or from rubber, and a person may even wrap a cloth around his feet and go out to a public area, as *the firmness of the ground reaches his feet and he feels as if he is barefooted*.[53]

Rambam seems to permit shoes made from other materials only if one can still feel the hardness of the ground.

The *Shulḥan Arukh* rules in accordance with Rif and Rosh, permitting all shoes that are not made of leather.[54] R. Moshe Sternbach suggests a distinction between leather and other materials. He argues that in the olden days, when people walked on dirt and not asphalt, it was customary to wear leather shoes all year round. Therefore, he argues, leather shoes represent the standard shoes that people wear outside. Nowadays, many wear comfortable sneakers, and one should therefore refrain from wearing these shoes on Yom Kippur, even if they are not made of leather.[55]

Similarly, some *Aḥaronim* discourage wearing comfortable shoes through which one cannot feel the ground. R. Meir Eisenstadt (1670–1744), for example, writes in his *Panim Me'irot* that a God-fearing person should not wear non-leather shoes that are both protective and comfortable.[56] Ḥatam Sofer concurs.[57] *Baḥ* writes that one should even refrain, when possible, from wearing a cloth around one's feet, and he reports that his teachers were accustomed to walk barefoot on Yom Kippur. The *Mishna Berura* cites the *Aḥaronim*, such as the *Eliya Rabba*, who rule stringently, concluding that it is proper for one to be stringent and to wear a soft cloth slipper, as opposed to a comfortable shoe.[58]

R. Ovadia Yosef[59] and R. Shlomo Zalman Auerbach,[60] however, permit wearing all shoes not made of leather, in accordance with the popular custom. Similarly, R. Shimon Gruenfeld (1860–1930), known as Maharshag, writes:

> In my opinion, it seems that even from the strictest point of view, there is no reason to be stringent.... There is no great level of piety and one who is stringent in order that it should be more of an "affliction" and so that he should suffer more is a "foolish pious man," and he has no capability of understanding the depth of our holy Torah.... It is clear to me that one who walks on Yom Kippur while suffering due to not wearing shoes, [such as one] who walks in a cold area in order to suffer more through walking barefoot, does not receive additional rewards and is only considered a fool and simpleminded.... In addition, it seems to me that one who does an action in order to suffer on Yom Kippur, even involving one of the five afflictions, in a way that the Torah would permit, and he would to be more stringent in order to increase his discomfort, will be punished because for denigrating the festival.[61]

This position stands in sharp contrast to that of the *Mishna Berura* cited above.

Some *Aḥaronim* point out that many shoes are made of many materials; even if leather is used only for the soles or for other parts of the shoe, they are still prohibited.[62] *Kaf HaḤayim*, however, permits wearing shoes which are merely laced with leather shoe laces.[63]

At times, one is permitted to wear leather shoes. For example, the Gemara (Yoma 78b), explaining the Mishna (Yoma 73b), teaches that "a new mother may wear shoes because of the cold." Similarly, the Gemara continues, "Shmuel said: Because of the danger of a scorpion, it is permitted [to wear leather shoes]." R. Yehuda Aryeh Leib Alter (1847–1905), author of the *Sefat Emet*, points out that Shmuel's leniency does not refer to a life-threatening situation, in which case this would certainly be permitted. Rather, Shmuel allows one to walk in an area where there may potentially be scorpions and wear leather shoes; he does not require one to remain at home to avoid having to wear shoes.[64]

Rema writes that if it is raining and one wishes to walk to synagogue or to return home, and he is an "*istinis*" (an extremely sensitive person), he may wear shoes until he reaches his destination.[65] The *Mishna Berura* writes that one who knows that his feet will become soiled may walk out in shoes, but he should remove them immediately upon arriving at his destination.[66]

MARITAL RELATIONS ON YOM KIPPUR

The Mishna prohibits engaging in marital relations on Yom Kippur (Yoma 74b). Some *Rishonim* write that one should observe the precautionary prohibitions of the laws of *nidda* (*harkhakot*) as well. For example, *Beit Yosef*[67] cites the *Mordekhai*,[68] who writes that on Tisha B'Av and Yom Kippur it is prohibited to sleep in the same bed as one's wife. Similarly, the *Sefer Agudda* writes that one should avoid all physical contact with one's wife on the night of Yom Kippur.

The *Shulḥan Arukh* writes that one should refrain from physical contact with one's wife and not sleep in the same bed.[69] *Taz* rules that the *harkhakot* generally observed during the period of "*nidut*," aside from sleeping in the same bed, apply only at night, and not during the day.[70] The *Mishna Berura*,[71] however, citing Maharil, writes that one should observe all of the *harkhakot* of the laws of *nidda*[72] for the duration of Yom Kippur.

CHAPTER 16

The Conclusion of Yom Kippur

THE *TEKIAT SHOFAR* OF YOM KIPPUR

For many, the concluding moments of Yom Kippur are the most powerful part of the day's prayers – the congregation declares "*Shema Yisrael*" and "*Hashem Hu HaElokim*" in unison, the *ḥazan* concludes *Ne'ila* with the festive Kaddish, the shofar is sounded, and all join in singing "*Leshana habaa biYerushalayim*." The blowing of the shofar stands out

– why is the shofar, generally associated with Rosh HaShana, sounded on Yom Kippur? Furthermore, shouldn't it be prohibited to sound the shofar on Yom Kippur, just as it is prohibited when Rosh HaShana falls on Shabbat? (Rosh HaShana 29b).

We find numerous suggestions regarding the reason for this practice. Tosafot[1] record that contemporary *Maḥzorim* (prayer books) related this practice to the blowing of the shofar on Yom Kippur of the *Yovel* year.[2] They reject this suggestion – if the shofar blowing is really related to the *Yovel* year, then it should not be blown every year![3] *Hagahot Maimoniyot* adds that according to this reason, one should blow the shofar on Yom Kippur itself, and not at its conclusion. Alternatively, he suggests that the custom to blow shofar is based upon the midrash that teaches that at the conclusion of Yom Kippur, a heavenly voice (*bat kol*) proclaims, "Go and eat your food in happiness" (Eccl. 9:7). Similarly, Tosafot explain that the shofar is blown to declare that the fast has concluded, and therefore children may be fed and the festive meal to be eaten after the fast should be prepared.[4]

Others offer different interpretations. R. Elazar of Worms writes in his Roke'aḥ that the blowing of the shofar symbolizes our victory over the "Satan."[5] R. Aharon b. Yaakov of Lunel explains in his *Kol Bo* that the shofar is intended to "confuse Satan," who regains "control" after Yom Kippur.[6] Finally, *Semag*[7] writes that the blowing of the shofar corresponds to the *Shekhina*'s ascent through the seven heavens, parallel to each "*Hashem Hu HaElokim*" that we declare, as the verse says, "And God ascends with the *terua*" (Ps. 47:6).

There are two customs cited by the *Rishonim*[8] regarding this shofar blowing – blowing one long sound, or blowing a set of *tekia-shevarim-terua-tekia* (*tashrat*). The *Shulḥan Arukh* rules that one should blow a *tashrat* upon concluding *Ne'ila*, while Rema records that it is customary to sound one long blast.[9] These customs appear to correspond to the reasons we have suggested. If the sounding of the shofar corresponds to the ascent of the Divine Presence or serves as a proclamation regarding eating or preparing food, then one long sound should suffice. However, if the blowing of the shofar parallels the blowing of the shofar on Yom Kippur of the *Yovel* year, then a proper set of *tashrat* should be blown.

As for the permissibility of blowing the shofar, the *Rishonim* explain that blowing the shofar is a "*ḥokhma*" (a skill) and not a *melakha* (labor), and it is therefore permitted during twilight (*bein hashemashot*) of Yom Kippur.[10] While some question this practice, as generally this leniency only applies before Shabbat begins, during *bein hashemashot*, and not as Shabbat ends, it is customary to blow the shofar before the fast is completely over. Some explain that one may certainly blow the shofar twenty minutes after *shekia*, the time established by the *Geonim* as *tzeit hakokhavim* (the halakhic end of the day).

KIDDUSH LEVANA

Birkat HaLevana, known as "*Kiddush Levana*," may be recited within the first sixteen days after the appearance of the new moon (the *molad*). While the *Shulḥan Arukh* writes that one should not recite the blessing until at least seven days have passed since the *molad*,[11] the *Aḥaronim* rule that one may recite this blessing as early as three full days (i.e., seventy-two hours) after the appearance of the *molad*.[12]

The *posekim* cite different opinions regarding whether *Kiddush Levana* should be recited before or after Yom Kippur. Rema records that one should not recite *Kiddush Levana* until after Yom Kippur.[13] Some explain that one who fears the upcoming judgment cannot recite the *Birkat HaLevana* with the appropriate joy and happiness. After Yom Kippur, however, when one's sins have been absolved, one should recite the *Kiddush Levana*.

Many *Aḥaronim* disagree. R. Mordekhai Yoffe (1530–1612) explains in his *Levush Malkhut*:

> The custom is to not to sanctify the new moon until after Yom Kippur because we are suspended in judgment and sanctifying requires happiness. I heard from one sage that on the contrary, it is preferable to sanctify the moon during this time so as to add this mitzva to one's merits and perhaps tip the scales in favor of one's merits.[14]

In other words, *Levush* argues that one should preferably perform the mitzva during the *Aseret Yemei Teshuva* in order to "tip the scales" in his favor. Similarly, R. Eliyahu b. R. Binyamin Wolf Shapiro (1660–1712), author of the *Eliya Rabba* (an important commentary on the *Shulḥan Arukh*), wrote in his commentary on *Levush,* known as the *Eliyahu Zuta*:

> There is a story of a person who encountered an idolater at night, and the idolater wished to kill him. The Jew requested from his captor that he be allowed to perform one mitzva before his death, whereupon he sanctified the new moon; while jumping up and down, as is customary, a miracle occurred and the wind picked him up and took him away to safety. I also heard that one who recites the sanctification of the moon is guaranteed to survive the month. I cited this to support *Levush*'s argument that it is better to sanctify the moon before Yom Kippur so as to ensure that a decree of death will not be issued against you for the coming year.[15]

In *Eliya Rabba,* he similarly rules that one should preferably recite *Kiddush Levana* before Yom Kippur.[16] Gra concurs.[17]

Nevertheless, common practice seems to be to recite *Kiddush Levana* after Yom Kippur. The *Mateh Efraim* suggests eating a bit before reciting *Kiddush Levana,* although he acknowledges that one should not separate from the community if they recite the blessing immediately after the fast.[18]

HAVDALA ON MOTZA'EI YOM KIPPUR

On Motza'ei Yom Kippur, like after Shabbat and Yom Tov, one must recite Havdala both in one's *Shemoneh Esreh* and over wine (or grape juice). The *Rishonim* discuss the differences between the Havdala recited after Yom Kippur and the Havdala recited after Shabbat. On Motza'ei Shabbat, we recited a blessing over a fire and over *besamim* (spices) in addition to the Havdala blessing recited over a cup of wine (Berakhot 51b). Although the *Mordekhai* implies that one should recite the blessing over *besamim* on Motza'ei Yom Kippur as well, in accordance with the custom of Rabbeinu Gershom,[19] most *Rishonim* disagree. It is therefore customary *not* to recite the blessing over *besamim* after Yom Kippur.

The Gemara explains the reason for the blessing recited over fire on Motza'ei Shabbat – God intended to give man fire on the sixth day, but He waited until after the first Sabbath instead:

> R. Yose said: ... The Holy One, Blessed be He, bestowed understanding upon Adam HaRishon ... and he took two stones, rubbed them one upon the other, and fire emerged. (Pesaḥim 54a)

Each and every Motza'ei Shabbat, we acknowledge God as the one who endowed us with the ability to create and use fire by reciting the blessing "*borei meorei ha'esh*" (Blessed be He ... who created the lights of the fire)." Since the fire used for Havdala on Motza'ei Shabbat commemorates both the phenomenon of fire and its creation by Adam HaRishon after the first Sabbath, one may use a pre-existing flame that remained lit for the duration of Shabbat – known as a "*ner sheshavat*" – or a newly lit flame – known as an "*esh hayotzei min ha'etzim umin haavanim*" – for the Havdala flame.[20]

The Gemara explains that after Yom Kippur, however, one must use a *ner sheshavat* (Pesaḥim 54a). The flame used after Yom Kippur comes to contrast *kodesh leḥol* – on Yom Kippur, lighting this fire was prohibited; it is now permitted. What is considered a "*ner sheshavat*"? It would seem that a *ner sheshavat* refers to a fire that remained lit for the entire duration of Yom Kippur. Rashi, however, explains that "[even] if it was lit in a permissible manner [on Yom Kippur], such as for a new mother or a sick person ... one may recite the blessing upon it after Yom Kippur."[21]

The *Rishonim* write that one may also recite the blessing over a fire that was lit from a pre-existing flame. Nevertheless, the *Maggid Mishneh*[22] cites Ramban, who writes that although on Motza'ei Shabbat one may recite the blessing of *borei meorei ha'esh* over a fire lit from a flame which was lit on Shabbat by a non-Jew, on Motza'ei Yom Kippur, one may not. The *Shulḥan Arukh* concurs.[23] R. Avraham b. Natan HaYarḥi, in his *Sefer HaManhig,* records a custom to light extra-long candles before Yom Kippur in order to recite the Havdala blessing upon them after the fast.[24]

Some *Rishonim* record that it was customary to recite the blessing over the candles in the synagogue, which remained lit for the entire Yom

Kippur. Rema cites two opinions regarding whether one may recite the blessing over these candles, as they were lit for "*kavod*," and not in order to provide light. He concludes that one should preferably light another candle from that fire, and then combine them and recite the blessing over both flames, in which case one's blessing includes both the original *ner sheshavat* as well as a flame lit exclusively for light.[25] The *Arukh HaShulḥan*, however, records that it was customary to recite the blessing over the candles of the *beit knesset*, as they are also generally lit in order to provide light.[26]

May one, *bediavad*, recite the blessing on a flame that was lit after Yom Kippur, which did not "rest" for the duration of Yom Kippur? Some *Rishonim*[27] cite a view that permits one to recite the blessing over a flame that was lit from a fire lit after Yom Kippur. The *Shibbolei HaLeket* cites a similar view in the name of R. Yehudai Gaon.[28] The *Shulḥan Arukh* cites this view,[29] although he seems to reject this opinion further on.[30] Some *Aḥaronim* rule that in extenuating circumstances, one may rely upon the opinion cited and recite the blessing of "*borei meorei ha'esh*" on a flame lit from a new fire.[31] The *Mishna Berura*,[32] R. Ovadia Yosef,[33] and R. Moshe Feinstein[34] write that one should not rely upon this minority opinion, but rather one should simply recite Havdala over the wine, and recite the blessing of "*borei meorei ha'esh*" if and when a *ner sheshavat* becomes available.

HAVDALA ON MOTZA'EI YOM KIPPUR ON MOTZA'EI SHABBAT

How should one perform Havdala when Yom Kippur falls on Shabbat? The *Kol Bo* rules that one does not recite the blessing over the *besamim* on Motza'ei Yom Kippur, even if Yom Kippur falls on Shabbat.[35] He explains that one ordinarily smells *besamim* on Motza'ei Shabbat in order to comfort oneself upon the loss of the "*neshama yeteira*," the "extra soul" that each Jew possesses on Shabbat.[36] One does not experience this "*neshama yeteira*" on Yom Kippur due to the fast, so no blessing should be recited on *besamim* at Havdala. Others, however, rule that one should say the blessing over *besamim* when Yom Kippur falls on Shabbat.[37]

The *Shulḥan Arukh* rules that one should not recite the blessing over the *besamim* when Yom Kippur falls on Shabbat.[38] The *Aḥaronim,* however, disagree, and rule that one should say the blessing over the *besamim.*[39] Although the *Mishna Berura* writes that one should not instruct the community to say this *berakha,*[40] the *Arukh HaShulḥan* records that it is customary to say the blessing.[41] Sephardim do not recite this blessing.

Raavya writes that one does not need a *ner sheshavat* for Havdala of Yom Kippur that falls on Shabbat, as on an ordinary Motza'ei Shabbat one may recite Havdala upon a new fire.[42] The *Mishna Berura* writes that while one may certainly use a newly lit fire for Havdala after a Yom Kippur which fell on Shabbat, it is customary to use a *ner sheshavat.*[43]

The *Aḥaronim* discuss whether one may recite the *birkat haner* of Havdala over an electric light. The blessing certainly cannot be recited over a fluorescent light, which contains no actual "fire." The glowing filament inside an incandescent light bulb, however, may possibly be considered to be "*esh*."[44] Some nevertheless prohibit using a light bulb for Havdala,[45] while others permit it.[46] R. Moshe Sternbach rules that according to those who permit using electric lights for Havdala in general, one may also use an electric light on Motza'ei Yom Kippur as a *ner sheshavat* when necessary.[47] Interestingly, R. Eliezer Waldenberg disagrees, arguing that a filament "fueled" by the constant flow of electricity does not constitute a *ner sheshavat.*[48]

While one should generally not eat or drink before Havdala, one who is thirsty or weak may drink water after the conclusion of the fast even before hearing Havdala. This is especially pertinent to women whose husbands may be delayed at the synagogue. Furthermore, they may also make their own Havdala and then eat or drink regularly.

Rema writes that one should eat and drink on Motza'ei Yom Kippur, as it is a "minor Yom Tov."[49] *Beit Yosef* attributes this to the midrash cited above, which describes the heavenly voice that declares upon completion of the fast: "Go your way, eat your bread with joy, and drink your wine with a merry heart; for God has already accepted your works" (Eccl. 9:7).

The *Geonim*,[50] as well as the *Rishonim*,[51] record that it is customary not to recite *Viduy* or *Taḥanun* during the months of Nissan and Tishrei (after Yom Kippur). Rema writes that *Taḥanun* is not recited until Sukkot,[52] although it is customary to omit *Taḥanun* until after Rosh Ḥodesh Ḥeshvan.

Finally, Rema records that "the meticulous should begin building the *sukka* immediately after Yom Kippur, in order to go from mitzva to mitzva."[53] We will discuss the mitzva of building the *sukka* and why the meticulous begin to buld their *sukkot* immediately after Yom Kippur in the next chapter.

Sukkot

Chapter 17

The Mitzva of Building a *Sukka*

INTRODUCTION: THE REASONS FOR THE MITZVA OF *SUKKA*

The Torah teaches in two places that one must "dwell" in a *sukka* for seven days:

> You shall dwell in booths seven days; all that are native in Israel shall dwell in booths; that your generations may know that I made the children of Israel to dwell in booths, when I brought them out of the land of Egypt – I am the Lord your God. (Lev. 23:42–43)
>
> You shall keep the feast of Sukkot seven days, after you have gathered in from your threshing-floor and from your winepress. And you shall rejoice in your feast, you, and your son, and your daughter, and your man-servant, and your maid-servant, and the Levite, and the stranger, and the fatherless, and the widow, that are within your gates. Seven days shall you keep a feast unto the Lord your God in the place which the Lord shall choose; because the Lord your God shall bless you in all your increase, and in all the work of your hands, and you shall be altogether joyful. (Deut. 16:13–15)

The Torah explains the reason for the commandment to dwell in *sukkot*: "That your generations may know that I made the children of Israel to dwell in booths, when I brought them out of the land of Egypt."

The Talmud records a debate about what exactly we are enjoined to remember:

> For it has been taught: "I made the children of Israel to dwell in booths." These were clouds of glory, so said R. Eliezer. R. Akiva says: They made for themselves real booths. (Sukka 11b)

R. Eliezer and R. Akiva disagree regarding whether this verse refers to the *ananei hakavod,* the "clouds of glory" that guided and protected the Jewish people during their forty years of wandering in the desert,[1] or to the booths that the Jews made for themselves during their travels. According to R. Eliezer's explanation, we commemorate the divine protection of the Jewish people during their wandering in the desert. Apparently, *mitzvat sukka* is intended to arouse the memory of the Exodus from Egypt in general, and more specifically, God's supernatural protection of the Jewish people throughout their travels in the desert. However, according to R. Akiva, why is it worth commemorating the booths that the Jewish people made for themselves?

Ramban explains that through remembering the *sukkot* that the Jewish people made for themselves in the desert, we remember that God provided for all of the needs of the Jewish people in the desert.[2] According to this explanation, R. Eliezer and R. Akiva agree that *mitzvat sukka* commemorates the divine protection that the Jewish people merited in the desert. If so, what is the difference between their opinions? Ostensibly, while R. Eliezer focuses upon the miraculous and supernatural protection of the Jewish people in the desert, symbolized by the *ananei hakavod,* R. Akiva focuses upon the day-to-day shelter that God provided through the natural order. This protection, although not supernatural, was no less extraordinary.

Alternatively, we can explain that while R. Eliezer focuses upon the divine protection afforded to the Jewish people, R. Akiva notes the Jewish people's active involvement in furthering the redemption – they made booths for themselves. As the prophet Jeremiah described, "Go, and cry in the ears of Jerusalem, saying: Thus says the Lord: I remember for you the affection of your youth, the love of your espousals; how you followed after Me in the wilderness, in a land that was not sown" (Jer. 2:2). The mitzva of *sukka* highlights the Jewish people's dedication and loyalty to God throughout their travels (with, admittedly, a few exceptions), and their response to the divine gesture of *yetziat Mitzrayim.* As we read in *Megillat Eikha,* "Turn us unto You, O Lord, and we shall turn [toward You]" (Lam. 5:21).

Finally, we might also suggest that the Torah focuses upon the "booths they made for themselves" because the purpose of the mitzva of *sukka* is to recall and to relive the experience of the Jewish people in the desert. Indeed, Rashbam writes:

> "That your generations may know" – Its plain meaning is like those who say in Tractate Sukka: an actual *sukka*. And this is what it means: You shall make for yourself a Festival of Booths when you gather from your threshing floor and your wine-press, when you gather the corn of the field and your houses are filled with every good, grain, wine, and oil, that you shall remember that I made the Children of Israel dwell in booths in the wilderness for forty years without settlement and without inheritance. And from this you will offer thanksgiving to Him, who gave you an inheritance and your houses filled with every good, and you will not say in your hearts, "My power and the might of my hand have gotten me this wealth"... And therefore we go out of our houses that are filled with every good at the time of the [harvest] gathering and we dwell in *sukkot* as a reminder that they did not have an inheritance in the wilderness, nor houses to dwell in. And for this reason, God established the Festival of Sukkot at the time of gathering from the threshing floor and the wine-press, so that their hearts not swell on account of their houses that are filled with every good, lest they say, "Our hands have gotten us this wealth."[3]

Rashbam explains that we celebrate Sukkot during the "gathering" season in order to impress upon the Jewish farmer the goodness which God has bestowed upon him, in contrast to the bare existence of the Jewish people as they left Egypt.

In other words, we are commanded to experience the sense of transience, the exposure to the elements, and the uncertainty of nomadic life in the desert. R. Akiva challenges us to realize the truth of our existence – even our permanent homes are really "*dirot arai*" (temporary dwellings), and that which appears secure and permanent is actually vulnerable and ephemeral. Only God's providence secured the Jewish people's personal and national existence in the desert, and this is true in our day as well. While Rashi, Ramban, and Onkelos,[4] and subsequently *Tur* and *Shulḥan Arukh*,[5] accept R. Eliezer's opinion, Rashbam argues for R. Akiva's understanding.[6] Although seemingly there should be no practical difference between these two views, some *Aḥaronim* point to a possible halakhic ramification, discussed below.

INTENTION FOR THE MITZVA OF *SUKKA*

Tur observes that the Torah links the mitzva of *sukka* to *yetziat Mitzrayim*, the Exodus from Egypt, an event which undoubtedly demonstrates God's existence and involvement in this world. R. Yoel Sirkis notes that it is uncharacteristic of *Tur* to discuss the reason for a mitzva, and he suggests a reason for *Tur*'s interest in the reason behind the mitzva of *sukka* specifically:

> It seems to me that he must believe that since the verse says, "that your generations may know," one has not fulfilled the mitzva in its entirety (*ketikuna*) if he does not know the intention of the mitzva of *sukka* according to its simple understanding (*kefi peshata*). Therefore, [*Tur*] explained, according to the *peshat*, that the primary intention that one should keep in mind while fulfilling the mitzva of *sukka* is to remember the Exodus from Egypt.[7]

R. Sirkis understands that whenever the Torah links a mitzva's performance with its intention – *lemaan yedu* (in order that you shall know) – the Torah wishes to teach that the awareness of the mitzva's reason is an integral part of its performance. (He further explains that *Tur* seems to require one to have the proper intention when fulfilling the mitzvot of *tzitzit*[8] and *tefillin*,[9] as the Torah also links the performance of these mitzvot with their reasons [Num. 15:40; Ex. 13:9].)

The *Mishna Berura* writes that one should preferably keep in mind the Exodus from Egypt and the *ananei hakavod* during the performance of the mitzva of *sukka*.[10] Based upon the debate cited above, one should preferably keep both understandings of the mitzva of *sukka* in mind while performing the mitzva.

Seemingly, lack of this awareness should not prevent the fulfillment of the mitzva; rather, performing these mitzvot with their proper intention constitutes a "*mitzva ketikuna*" – a mitzva fulfilled in its entirety. R. Yaakov Ettlinger (1798–1871), in his treatise on the laws of *sukka*, rules that if one did not keep these reasons in mind while eating in the *sukka* on the first night of Sukkot, he should preferably eat another *kezayit* of bread in the *sukka* with the proper intention.[11] The *Mishna Berura*, however, rejects this conclusion.[12]

IS THERE A MITZVA TO BUILD A *SUKKA*?

While there clearly is a mitzva to sit in the *sukka*, as the verse teaches, "You shall dwell in booths seven days," is there a mitzva to build a *sukka* as well? The Torah does command, "You shall keep the Feast of Sukkot seven days, after you have gathered in from your threshing floor and from your wine-press," but "you shall keep" (literally, "you shall make") apparently refers to keeping the festival, and not building the *sukka*, per se. Indeed, Ḥatam Sofer explains that there is no mitzva to build a *sukka*.[13] There are numerous indications, however, that point to a mitzva of some sort to build a *sukka*. R. Aḥai Gaon writes this in his collection of homilies on Jewish law and ethics, the *She'iltot*:

> The Jewish people are obligated to construct a *sukka* and to dwell in it for seven days, as it says, "You shall keep the Feast of Sukkot seven days" – and it [also] says, "You shall dwell in booths seven days."[14]

R. Naftali Zvi Yehuda Berlin explains in his commentary to the *She'iltot*, *Haamek She'ala*:

> It seems that we can derive from his language that even though the primary mitzva is to sit [in the *sukka*], and the construction [of the *sukka*] is only preparatory, still there is a mitzva [in the building], as this preparation is written in the Torah and is more important than other preparations for mitzvot that are not mentioned in the Torah, and the building of a *sukka* and the writing of a *sefer Torah* and mezuzot, regarding which it says "and you shall write."[15]

Based upon this, many are accustomed to participate in the building of their own *sukka*,[16] in fulfillment of the talmudic dictum, "*mitzva bo yoter mibisheluḥo*," which teaches that one who is obligated to fulfill a mitzva should preferably fulfill the mitzva himself, and not through an agent (Kiddushin 41a).

It would seem that if we view the building of the *sukka*, and not only dwelling in it, as a mitzva, then it should certainly be worthy of a *berakha*. Indeed, the Yerushalmi teaches that one who builds a *sukka* for himself (*le'atzmo*) should recite a *birkat hamitzva* of "*laasot hasukka*" (to make a *sukka*) (Y. Sukka 1:2; Berakhot 9:3). The Talmud Bavli does not record this opinion, however. The *Or Zarua* explains that according to the Yerushalmi, one recites a blessing upon making an article that is to be used for a mitzva if the process of making that item must be done "*lishma*," with special intention.[17] The Talmud Bavli rejects this assumption, and even questions whether the construction of the *sukka* must be *lishma* (*Beit Hillel* rules leniently) (Sukka 9a). Alternatively, the Yerushalmi may simply maintain that the building of one's own *sukka* constitutes a mitzva of some sort, and this mitzva warrants a blessing.

While the Talmud Bavli does not instruct one to recite a *birkat hamitzva* upon building a *sukka*, the Gemara does imply that the blessing of *Sheheḥeyanu* should be said upon building a *sukka*:

> Our Rabbis taught: One who makes a *sukka* for his own use shall recite the benediction, "Blessed are You who has kept us in life, etc." [*Sheheḥeyanu*]. When he enters to take up his abode in it, he says, "Blessed are You who has sanctified us," etc. If it was already erected, he may recite the benediction if he can make some renovation in it; and if not, he recites two benedictions [i.e., the *birkat hamitzva* and *Sheheḥeyanu*] when he enters to take up his abode in it. R. Ashi stated: I observed that R. Kahana recited all of them over the cup of Kiddush. (Sukka 46a)

The Gemara first cites a Tosefta that teaches that one who builds his own *sukka* should recite *Sheheḥeyanu* (Tosefta, Berakhot 6:14), and then relates that R. Kahana would recite both the blessing of "*leishev basukka*" and "*Sheheḥeyanu*" upon reciting the Kiddush on the first night of Sukkot.

How should we understand the position of the Tosefta that one should recite *Sheheḥeyanu* upon building the *sukka*? On the one hand, we might assert that the actual building of one's own *sukka* warrants the blessing of *Sheheḥeyanu*. Of course, then we must explain why we recite *Sheheḥeyanu* and not a *birkat hamitzva*! On the other hand, we might suggest that the *birkat Sheheḥeyanu* is actually recited upon the Festival of Sukkot when encountering it in a meaningful way for the first time. Indeed, Tosafot rule that one who recited *Sheheḥeyanu* upon building one's *sukka* should not repeat *Sheheḥeyanu* during Kiddush on Yom Tov![18]

How are we to understand the position of R. Kahana, who recited the *birkat Sheheḥeyanu* over Kiddush and not when building his *sukka*? Some insist that one should certainly recite the *Sheheḥeyanu* upon building one's *sukka* and once again on Yom Tov. R. Kahana never intended to rule that one should not recite *Sheheḥeyanu* upon building his *sukka*, but rather to teach that one can recite the blessing on Yom Tov over both the building and the sanctity of the day.[19] Others explain that R. Kahana maintains that one should not recite *Sheheḥeyanu* upon building a *sukka* at all.[20] Rosh writes that since erecting a *sukka* is a preparation for the festival, we delay reciting the *Sheheḥeyanu* until the festival itself.[21] Finally, the *Mordekhai* suggests that since so few people actually build their own *sukkot*, it is customary for everyone to simply recite *Sheheḥeyanu* during Kiddush.[22]

The *Shulḥan Arukh* rules that although theoretically one should recite *Sheheḥeyanu* upon building one's *sukka*, it is customary to recite the *Sheheḥeyanu* during Kiddush on the first night.[23] This entire discussion implies that many *Rishonim* understand that, at least theoretically, the building of one's *sukka* warrants the blessing of *Sheheḥeyanu*, and therefore should be viewed as a mitzva on some level.

THE PROPER TIME TO BUILD THE *SUKKA*

Rema writes in the concluding laws of Yom Kippur: "The meticulous should begin building the *sukka* immediately after Yom Kippur, in order to go from mitzva to mitzva."[24] In the next chapter, Rema begins the laws of *sukka* by teaching that "it is a mitzva to fix (*letakein*) the *sukka* immediately after Yom Kippur: *mitzva habaa leyadkha al taḥmitzena* – when a mitzva comes your way, do not allow it to ferment. In other words, one should build the *sukka* immediately after Yom Kippur because when the opportunity to do a mitzva arises, one should do it quickly. Incidentally, *Shaarei Teshuva* cites those who recommend building, or at least starting to build, one's *sukka* before Yom Kippur in order to accumulate more mitzvot before the Day of Judgment.[25]

Why does Rema mention twice that one should build the *sukka* immediately after Yom Kippur, one chapter after another? *Magen Avraham,* most likely responding to this question, explains that the second passage refers to *completing* the *sukka.*[26]

Alternatively, we might suggest that the first passage, taught in the context of Yom Kippur, teaches that after Yom Kippur, one should go "from mitzva to mitzva" – a message appropriate for the conclusion of Yom Kippur. The second passage, however, refers to the laws of Sukkot: Since building a *sukka* constitutes a mitzva of sorts, one should perform it without delay.

CHAPTER 18

The Dimensions of the *Sukka*

THE LAWS REGARDING the *sukka* itself, which can be found in the first two chapters of Tractate Sukka, concern the walls, dimensions, and structure of the *sukka,* the *sekhakh,* the sanctity of the *sukka* and its decorations, and the time and order of the construction of the *sukka.* These laws are numerous and complex. In this chapter, we will attempt to summarize the central and relevant halakhot of *sukka* construction.

THE DIMENSIONS OF THE *SUKKA*

Ḥayei Adam writes that it is a *mitzva min hamuvḥar,* halakhically preferable, to construct a *sukka* of four complete walls.[1] The Talmud, however, records that a *halakha leMoshe miSinai* teaches that when constructed properly, two walls and an additional piece may suffice. In this chapter, we will first discuss the general principles relating to the dimensions of a standard *sukka* of three or four complete walls. We will then discuss how to construct a *sukka* consisting of fewer than three complete walls.

In order to understand the detailed laws regarding the dimensions of the *sukka,* we must first establish the equivalent contemporary measurements of the Talmud's typical measurements – the *tefaḥ* and *ama.* The *Aḥaronim* disagree as to whether a *tefaḥ* (handbreadth) is approximately 8 cm (R. Chaim Na'eh) or approximately 10 cm (*Ḥazon Ish*). As a result, three *tefaḥim,* the measurement of "*lavud,*" ranges between 24 and 30 cm; seven *tefaḥim,* the minimum length of the *sukka*'s walls, ranges between 56 and 70 cm; and ten *tefaḥim,* the minimum height of the *sukka*'s walls, is between 80 and 100 cm. We will also encounter the measurement of four *amot* (190 cm–232 cm), ten *amot* (470 cm–590 cm), and twenty *amot* (940 cm–1200 cm). While some claim that one should preferably adopt the larger measurement of *Ḥazon Ish* for matters of biblical origin, others insist that the halakha is in accordance with R. Chaim Na'eh.

Understanding of some talmudic concepts is also essential before we explore the laws of the *sukka.* The Gemara records that a *halakha leMoshe miSinai* teaches that two components separated by a gap of less than three *tefaḥim* are considered to be "*lavud,*" connected (Shabbat 97a; Sukka 6b). Thus, if a wall is separated from the ground, another wall, or the *sekhakh* by less than three *tefaḥim,* we overlook the gap and consider the wall to be connected to the other *sukka* component. Another concept that may or may not be relevant to the laws of *sukka,* as we shall see below, is "*gud asik meḥitzta.*" If a wall constitutes a valid *meḥitza* (partition), we consider it as if it extends both upward and downward.

Minimum Height

The Talmud teaches that the walls of the *sukka* must be at least ten *tefaḥim* high.[2] Based on the concept of *lavud,* the Gemara also teaches that the walls may be suspended within three *tefaḥim* of the ground (Sukka 16b). Thus, one may theoretically use walls slightly more than seven *tefaḥim* high and suspend them slightly less than three *tefaḥim* from the ground in order to achieve the necessary height of ten *tefaḥim.*

Furthermore, the Gemara relates that even a wall of slightly more than four *tefaḥim* may be used by relying on *lavud*:

> R. Ḥisda stated in the name of Abimi: "A mat slightly more than four *tefaḥim* [wide] is permitted as a *sukka* wall." How does one place it? One suspends it in the middle, less than three [*tefaḥim*] from the ground and less than three from the top [where the *sekhakh* is], and whatever [space] is less than three *tefaḥim* is treated as *lavud*. But is this not obvious? One might have said that we apply the law of *lavud* once, but we do not apply *lavud* twice [to the same wall]; therefore, he informed us of this. It was objected: A mat slightly more than seven [*tefaḥim*] is permitted as a *sukka* wall! With reference to what was this taught? With reference to a large *sukka*.

In other words, when constructing a tall *sukka*, one may use a wall of slightly more than seven *tefaḥim* suspended within three *tefaḥim* from the ground. When building a short *sukka* of only ten *tefaḥim* high, one can even use a wall of slightly more than four *tefaḥim*, suspended within three *tefaḥim* of both the ground and the *sekhakh*, using the principle of *lavud* twice.[3]

The Talmud further teaches that the walls of the *sukka* do not have to reach the *sekhakh* as long as they line up with the *sekhakh* (Sukka 16a). Many people rely on this leniency when building *sukkot* using pre-existing walls (such as on a balcony). What is this leniency based upon? Ritva suggests that this leniency relies on the halakhic principle of *gud asik meḥitzta*. If a *sukka* wall is at least ten *tefaḥim* tall, and thus a valid *meḥitza*, we consider it as if it projects upward or downward, and therefore as though it actually reaches the *sekhakh*.[4]

Interestingly, however, the Gemara cites a dispute regarding whether and to what extent this principle can be applied to the laws of *sukka*. For example, R. Yaakov maintains that one can place *sekhakh* on four poles positioned on the top of a building; the four walls of the building, projecting upward, will serve as the walls of the *sukka* based on the principle of *gud asik meḥitzta*. The sages, however, disagree and maintain that such a *sukka* is invalid. Furthermore, the Gemara questions whether, according to R. Yaakov's position, one must align the poles and the *sekhakh* with the outer walls of the building or whether the poles and *sekhakh* may even be positioned in the middle of the roof. The latter suggestion clearly calls into question that the principle of *gud asik meḥitzta* is the source for the leniency (Sukka 4b).

Rambam rules in accordance with R. Yaakov; one may employ the principle of *gud asik meḥitzta,* but only at the edge of the roof.[5] Rosh, however, rules that such a *sukka* is invalid regardless of whether the poles are on the edge of the house or the center.[6] Ran explains that if we reject R. Yaakov's position completely, then there is no application of *gud asik meḥitzta* in the context of the laws of *sukka.*[7] The *Shulkhan Arukh* cites both opinions,[8] and the *Mishna Berura* rules stringently.[9]

The *Aḥaronim* note that according to Ran, who seems to completely reject the application of *gud asik meḥitzta* to the laws of *sukka,* we must find an alternate basis for allowing walls of ten *tefaḥim* that do not reach the *sekhakh.*[10] We might suggest that the four walls of the *sukka* do not, even theoretically, need to reach the *sekhakh*; the Gemara never intended that the four walls would fully enclose the *sukka,* but merely that they demarcate the area of the *sukka.* As long one uses halakhically valid *meḥitzot* of ten *tefaḥim,* the *sukka* is valid.

The question of why we permit ten-*tefaḥ*-high walls that do not reach the *sekhakh* may have a practical ramification. The Mishna teaches that if the walls of the *sukka* do extend to the height of the *sekhakh,* the *sukka* is valid even if the walls do not actually touch the *sekhakh,* as long as the *sekhakh* begins within three *tefaḥim* of the walls (Sukka 17a). *Tur*[11] and *Shulḥan Arukh*[12] extend this ruling even to walls that are ten *tefaḥim* high and are not directly under the *sekhakh.* Since ten-*tefaḥ* walls are valid even if they do not reach the height of the *sekhakh* and *lavud* "connects" them to the *sekhakh,* the *sukka* is valid as long as the walls are within three *tefaḥim* inward or outward of the *sekhakh.*

R. Akiva Eiger challenges this ruling, questioning whether one may rely upon the leniencies of both *lavud* and *gud asik meḥitzta* simultaneously.[13] Ran, for example, suggests that one may not rely upon both *lavud* and another leniency when validating a *sukka.*[14] R. Eiger and other *Aḥaronim* attempt to resolve this apparent contradiction, but this question only applies if we assume that ten-*tefaḥ* walls that do not reach the *sekhakh* are valid due to *gud asik meḥitzta.* If we allow such walls simply because that is the base requirement of the walls of the *sukka* and not because we view them as projecting upward, the *sukka* described by the *Shulḥan Arukh* does not rely on two leniencies.

Maximum Height

The Mishna records the following debate:

> A *sukka* that is more than twenty cubits high is not valid. R. Yehuda, however, declares it valid. (Sukka 2a)

The Gemara offers three explanations of the first view:

> Whence do we know this? Rabba answered: Scripture says: "That your generations may know that I made the Children of Israel to dwell in *sukkot*." [With a *sukka*] up to twenty *amot* [high], a man knows that he is dwelling in a *sukka*, but with one higher than twenty *amot*, he does not know that he is dwelling in a *sukka*, since his eye does not see it. R. Zeira replied: From the following verse: "And there shall be a booth for a shadow in the daytime from the heat." [With a *sukka*] up to twenty *amot* [high], a man sits in the shade of the *sukka*; but with one higher than twenty *amot*, he sits not in the shade of the *sukka*, but in the shade of its walls.... Rava replied: [It is derived] from the following verse: "You shall dwell in booths seven days." The Torah declared: "For the whole seven days, leave your permanent abode and dwell in a temporary abode." [With a *sukka*] up to twenty *amot* [high], a man makes his abode a temporary one; [in one] higher than twenty *amot*, a man does not make his abode temporary, but permanent.

The Gemara explains that there are numerous halakhic differences between these views. For example, what if the *sukka* is more than twenty *amot* high but the walls reach the *sekhakh*? According to Rabba, one may still be conscious of the *sekhakh* in this case, but according the R. Zeira and Rava, the *sukka* is still invalid. Alternatively, what if the *sukka* is higher than twenty *amot*, but the *sukka* is also wider than four *amot*? According to R. Zeira, the *sukka* may be valid, as one sits in the shade of the *sekhakh*, but according to Rabba and Rava, the *sukka* would still be invalid.

Assuming that the halakha is in accordance with the view in the Mishna and a *sukka* taller than twenty *amot* is invalid, which reason offered by the *Amora'im* is accepted? While some accept the view of Rabba,[15] Rif and Rambam rule in accordance with Rava: the *sukka* must be a temporary abode, and a *sukka* taller than twenty *amot* is therefore invalid, regardless of whether the walls reach the *sekhakh* or the width of the *sukka* exceeds four *amot*.[16] The Gemara discusses numerous ways of validating a *sukka* whose walls are over twenty *amot* high (Sukka 4a).

Minimum Area

The Gemara records three opinions regarding the minimum area of a *sukka* (Sukka 3a). Rebbi holds that the minimum area of a *sukka* is four *amot* by four *amot*; *Beit Hillel* maintains that a *sukka* into which one can fit one's head and most of one's body (about six *tefaḥim* by six *tefaḥim*) suffices; and *Beit Shammai* rules that the *sukka* must also be able to hold a small table (at least seven *tefaḥim* by seven *tefaḥim*). The Gemara rules in accordance with *Beit Shammai*. One may construct a *sukka* of other shapes, such as a circle, as long as a *sukka* of seven *tefaḥim* by seven *tefaḥim* can fit inside of it.[17] The *Aḥaronim* discuss whether a *sukka* that is longer than seven *tefaḥim* but narrower than seven *tefaḥim* is valid. The *Mishna Berura* writes that most *Aḥaronim* agree that this *sukka* is invalid.[18]

CONSTRUCTING A *SUKKA* FROM TWO WALLS

The Tosefta (in Sukka 1:6), cited in the Gemara, brings a debate regarding the minimum amount of walls halakhically required for a *sukka*:

> Our Rabbis taught: Two [walls] must be of the prescribed dimensions (*shenayim kehilkhatan*), and the third [may be] even one *tefaḥ*. R. Shimon says: Three walls must be of the prescribed dimensions, and the fourth [may be] even one *tefaḥ*. (Sukka 6b)

The Gemara suggests different reasons for this debate and rules in accordance with the first view, which requires a minimum of two full walls and another partial wall.

Based upon what we learned above, a *sukka* consisting of three walls, each at least seven *tefaḥim* long, is valid. According to the Gemara, if one has only two full-length walls, one may still construct a valid *sukka* using a partial wall. How and where must one construct the third partial wall? The Gemara discusses two scenarios of "*shenayim kehilkhatan.*" In the first scenario, two walls are placed at a right angle to each other:

> Where is this *tefaḥ* [of a wall] placed? Rav said: It is placed at a right angle to one of the projecting [walls].... It was also stated: Shmuel said in the name of Levi: It is placed at right angles to one of the projecting [walls], and so it is ruled in the *Beit HaMidrash* that it is placed at a right angle to one of the projecting [walls]. R. Shimon, or some say R. Yehoshua b. Levi, ruled: One makes [the additional wall of the width of] a "loose *tefaḥ*" [i.e., slightly more than a *tefaḥ*] and places it within three *tefaḥim* of the wall, since whatever is less than three *tefaḥim* from the wall is regarded as joined to the wall. (Sukka 6b–7a)

According to this Gemara, the third wall may consist of a piece of material slightly larger than a *tefaḥ* placed at a right angle to one of the walls. Placed slightly less than three *tefaḥim* from the wall, the *lavud* gap and the piece of wall together constitute a majority of a valid *meḥitza* (four out of seven *tefaḥim*).

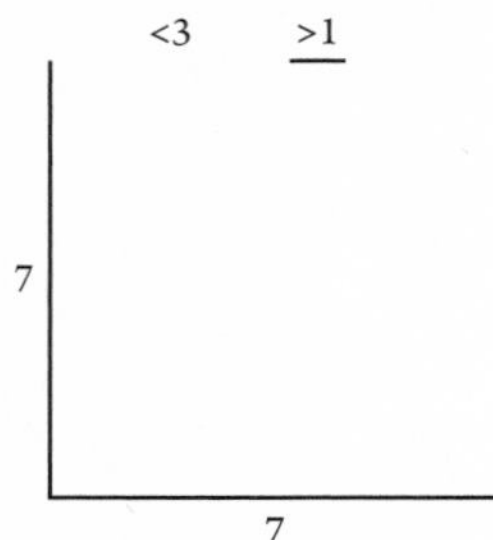

The gemara that follows brings three opinions regarding whether one must add a "*tzurat hapetaḥ*" to the third wall, and the *Rishonim* discuss this matter in great depth. The *Shulḥan Arukh* concludes:

> Regarding the walls of a *sukka*: If there are two [walls] at a perpendicular angle, one should take another wall, slightly wider than a *tefaḥ*, and place it within three *tefaḥim* of one of the walls. Then one places a vertical beam opposite that *tefaḥ* and makes a doorway and places a cross beam above it and above the *tefaḥ* [of wall], and [the *sukka*] is valid.[19]

According to the *Shulḥan Arukh*, in addition to the piece of wall slightly more than a *tefaḥ* long and ten *tefaḥim* high placed within three *tefaḥim* of the wall, one must add a doorway, a *tzurat hapetaḥ*, composed of a vertical beam and crossbeam.[20] Some say that the *tzurat hapetaḥ* should be at least four *tefaḥim* wide, as four *tefaḥim* is considered to be a significant measurement of space.[21]

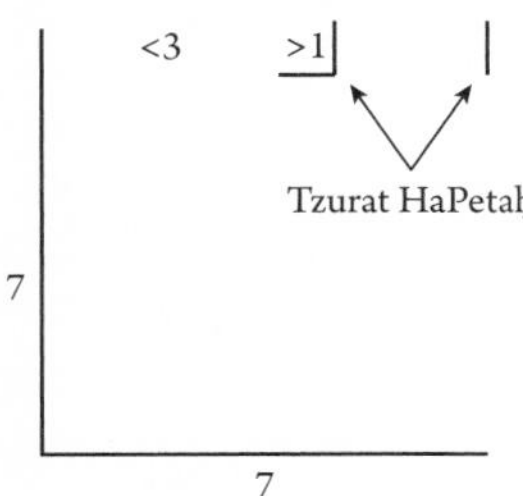

The *Aḥaronim* debate, when the two walls of the *sukka* are more than seven *tefaḥim*, whether this *tzurat hapetaḥ* should extend to the end of the opposite wall, as in the picture above,[22] or whether it must merely extend three additional *tefaḥim*, completing a seven-*tefaḥ* wall composed of a *tzurat hapetaḥ*, a *tefaḥ* of wall, and less than three *tefaḥim* of space:[23]

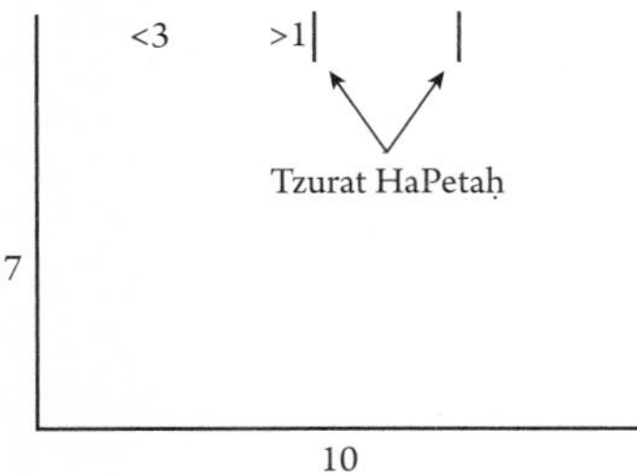

Some require the *tzurat hapetaḥ* to enclose an area of four *tefaḥim* (totaling at least eight *tefaḥim*), as the narrowest doorway is at least four *tefaḥim* wide.

Rema rules that one may count the *sekhakh* that extends from the end of the *tefaḥ*-long wall until the opposite wall as a *tzurat hapetaḥ*. However, the *Mishna Berura* cites *Magen Avraham*, who suggests that one must specifically place a crossbeam for this purpose, and may not rely upon the *sekhakh*. The *Mishna Berura* concludes, however, that one may follow the lenient opinion of Rema.[24] Some *Aḥaronim* insist that this extra doorway is only a rabbinic requirement.[25]

The second scenario described by the Gemara entails two walls parallel to each other, a "*sukka* in the shape of a *mavui* [alleyway]." In this case, the Gemara explains:

> R. Yehuda said: A *sukka* made like an [open] alleyway is valid, and this *tefaḥ* [wall] is placed on whatever side one pleases. R. Shimon, or some say R. Yehoshua b. Levi, says: He makes a strip of slightly more than four [*tefaḥim*] and places it within three handbreadths of the wall, since whatever is less than three handbreadths from the wall is regarded as joined to the wall. But why did you say in the previous case that one "loose *tefaḥ*" suffices, while here you say that there must be a strip of four *tefaḥim*? In the previous instance, where there are two valid walls, a "loose *tefaḥ*" suffices, but here, where there are not two valid walls, if there is a strip of four *tefaḥim* it is valid; otherwise, it is not [valid].... He answered: I accept the other reading of [the statement of] Rava; in addition [to a board of the size of a handbreadth], the form of a doorway is also necessary.

In this case, the two full walls with another *tefaḥ* do not suffice, because the walls are not connected. As a result, one must place a wall slightly more than four *tefaḥim* long and ten *tefaḥim* high within three *tefaḥim* of one the walls, totaling a valid wall of seven *tefaḥim*. In addition, one must construct a *tzurat hapetaḥ*, as in the case above, which extends from the four-*tefaḥ* wall until the third wall:

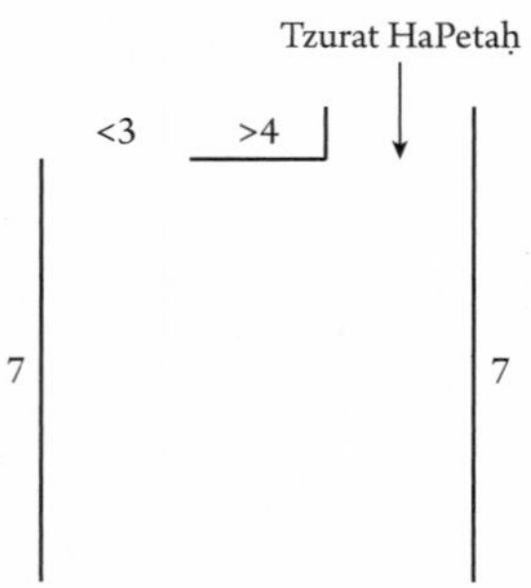

This *tzurat hapetaḥ* joins all three walls together. Although the *Shulḥan Arukh* cites a debate whether this *tzurat hapetaḥ* is necessary, as the combination of the partial wall and the space add up to the length of a valid wall (seven *tefaḥim*),[26] the *Mishna Berura* rules that one should add this *tzurat hapetaḥ*.[27]

While these scenarios may not sound common, one who builds a *sukka* on his balcony may certainly encounter this halakha. Ideally, one who uses a balcony should use all four walls – that is, the three walls of the balcony and the outer house wall – as the walls of the *sukka*. Often, however, one intends to use three walls: the wall parallel to his house, one of the perpendicular walls, and a portion of the house wall and the doorway, which serves as a *tzurat hapetaḥ*.

In such a case, one should be careful that the doorway to the balcony is at least four *tefaḥim* from the perpendicular wall. These four *tefaḥim*, in addition to a *tzurat hapetaḥ*, combine to form the third wall:

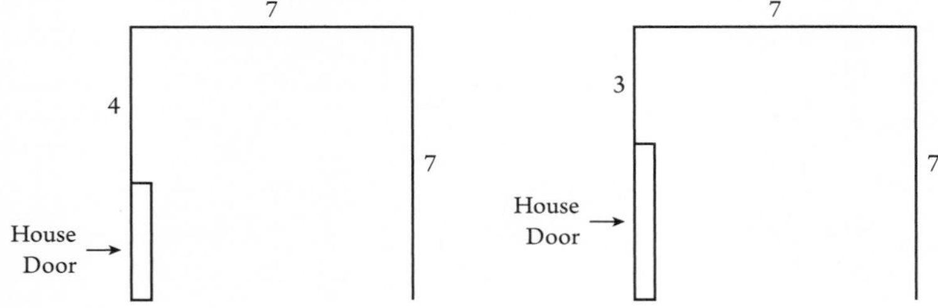

However, if the doorway is toward the edge of the balcony, within four *tefaḥim* of the perpendicular wall, then the *sukka* would be invalid when the door to the balcony is opened; the third wall must have at least four *tefaḥim* of wall, or at least more than a *tefaḥ* of wall joined with less than three *tefaḥim* of space, in order for the added *tzurat hapetaḥ* to complete the third wall. Furthermore, it may be prohibited to open and close the door on Shabbat and Yom Tov in such a *sukka*, as by validating and invalidating the *sukka*, this would violate the *melakhot* of *boneh* (building) and *soter* (destroying).[28]

The *Rishonim* derive from these cases that at least two of the walls of the *sukka* must connect at a perpendicular angle. The *Rishonim* refer to this as "*de'areivan*" – the two walls must be connected.[29] The walls may connect physically or through *lavud* – that is, being within three *tefaḥim* of each other; a *tzurat hapetaḥ* at the corner will not suffice.

HAPARUTZ MERUBEH AL HAOMED

Based upon a passage in the Gemara, the *Rishonim* discuss what percentage of the walls of the *sukka* may be incomplete, consisting of gaps, windows, or doorways. When one constructs the third wall in the manner described above, the third and fourth wall are certainly made up of more empty space than physical wall. This is called "*haomed merubeh al haparutz*" – the area of gaps is larger than the area of wall material.

What about the other two walls? Must the majority of the other two walls be made of solid material? Indeed, many people incorporate windows and doors into their *sukkot*, and others leave gaps in between multiple wooden planks that combine to form a wall. Even if one's wall is more than seven *tefaḥim* long, how much of the wall can be incomplete? The Gemara contrasts the laws of *meḥitzot* (partitions) as they relate to Shabbat and Sukkot:

> And the [law relating to] Shabbat is more [stringent] than that of *sukka*, in that the [wall for purposes of] Shabbat is valid only if its standing portion is more than that which is broken (*haomed merubeh al haparutz*), which is not the case with the *sukka*. (Sukka 7a)

In the laws of Shabbat, a *reshut hayaḥid*, within which one may carry on Shabbat, is defined as an area surrounded by four walls, of which the halakha requires *omed merubeh al haparutz*.[30] In other words, at least half of the sum total of the *meḥitzot* must be composed of solid material. A wall made up of solid strips or wires within three *tefaḥim* of each other (*lavud*) is considered to be entirely solid (*omed*). Nevertheless, although slightly less than half of the partition may be composed of windows, entrances, and holes, a gap of over ten *amot* invalidates the entire partition, and one may not carry within this area. One may, however, close a gap of ten *amot* with a *tzurat hapetaḥ*, consisting of two vertical posts, each ten *tefaḥim* high (*leḥi'im*), and a horizontal beam

should not misinterpret the availability of canvas *sukkot* as an endorsement of their validity.[20]

In recent years, the practice of using horizontal poles or tightly strung strings and relying upon the *halakha* of *lavud* has gained great popularity. As we discussed previously, as long as there are no uninterrupted gaps of more than three *tefaḥim* in a wall the height of ten *tefaḥim*, the walls of the *sukka* are valid, even though the majority of space is not filled with solid matter. Assuming that three *tefaḥim* is minimally 24 cm and ten *tefaḥim* is 80–100 cm, one should place a horizontal pole or string at intervals of approximately 24 cm so that three "walls" of 80–100 cm are constructed. The *Shulḥan Arukh* actually mentions this practice, which originally appeared in the *Hagahot Rabbeinu Peretz* on *Semak*. He writes, "One who wishes to make [his walls with] sheets should preferably weave *meḥitzot* of reeds less than three *tefaḥim* apart."[21] This practice is also relevant for those who construct *sukkot* on their balconies, often using the picketed balcony as the walls.

Not all agree that one can construct a *sukka* from horizontal strings within three *tefaḥim* of one another. *Magen Avraham,*[22] based upon the view of Tosafot,[23] writes that unless one encloses all four walls of a *sukka* with these "walls," one cannot rely upon *lavud*. *Eliya Rabba* writes, however, that one should not be concerned with this view in our case, as the true halakhic wall is the canvas wall, and the *lavud* wall is added as a stringency.

SUPPORTING THE *SEKHAKH* ON A *DAVAR HAMEKABEL TUMA*

The walls of the *sukka* serve two functions. First and foremost, they are the *meḥitzot* of the *sukka*; as we discussed above, a *sukka* must be constructed of at least three walls, or two walls and a small section. Second, the walls may (although not necessarily) support ("*maamid*") the *sekhakh*, which must cover the entire *sukka*. In this second context, the Mishna teaches:

> If a man supports his *sukka* [i.e., the *sekhakh*] with the legs of a bed, it is valid. R. Yehuda said: If it cannot stand by itself, it is invalid. (Sukka 21b)

Why does R. Yehuda prohibit placing the *sekhakh* on the legs of a bed? The Gemara explains:

> What is the reason of R. Yehuda? R. Zeira and R. Abba b. Mamal disagree. One says: It is because the *sukka* has no permanence (*mipnei she'ein la keva*), and the other says: It is because he supports [the *sekhakh*] with something which is *mekabel tuma*.

The *Rishonim* offer different explanations for both interpretations of R. Yehuda, and, as we shall see, differ regarding the final *halakha*.

Why does the fact that "the *sukka* has no permanence" invalidate a *sukka* resting upon the legs of a bed? And in what way does resting the *sekhakh* on the legs of a bed undermine the permanence of a *sukka*? Rashi explains that since the entire *sukka* rests upon the bed and is therefore mobile, it lacks "permanence."[24] Raavad suggests that this *sukka* lacks "permanence" because if the bed is moved, the *sukka* will collapse.[25]

Why would R. Yehuda forbid one to support the *sekhakh* on something that is *mekabel tuma*? Rashi explains:

> Even though we only learned this disqualification regarding *sekhakh*, since [the *maamid*] supports the *sekhakh*, it is as if he used that which is *mekabel tuma* for *sekhakh*.[26]

Rashi implies that by supporting the *sekhakh* with an object that is *mekabel tuma*, it is as if this object was used as the *sekhakh*, and items that are *mekabel tuma* are invalid as *sekhakh*. This interpretation is difficult, not only because Rashi implies that this is a problem *mideoraita*, but also because he views that which supports or enables the *sekhakh* as part of the *sekhakh* itself. Other *Rishonim* explain that the Rabbis prohibited placing *sekhakh* upon a *davar shemekabel tuma* lest one come to use this material as *sekhakh*.[27]

The *Rishonim* differ as to whether the halakha follows the first opinion of the Mishna – that of the *ḥakhamim*, who permit supporting a *sukka* on the leg of a bed – or R. Yehuda. Furthermore, if the halakha follows the opinion of R. Yehuda, is it because such a *sukka* lacks permanence or because the *sekhakh* rests upon a material that is *mekabel tuma*? Rambam,[28] Baal HaMaor,[29] Raavya,[30] Maharil,[31] and others rule like the *ḥakhamim*. Other *Rishonim*, however, rule in accordance with R. Yehuda. Rosh accepts the opinion that explains that R. Yehuda requires that the *sukka* have "permanence,"[32] while Ramban and many other *Rishonim* rule that one may not rest the *sekhakh* upon a *davar shemekabel tuma*.[33] Interestingly, the *Shulḥan Arukh* appears to rule like the *ḥakhamim*, as he validates a *sukka* resting upon the legs of a bed.[34] On the other hand, elsewhere, he explicitly expresses doubt regarding whether one may use a ladder, which is *mekabel tuma*, to support the *sekhakh*.[35]

The *Aḥaronim* disagree regarding how to understand this apparent contradiction in the *Shulḥan Arukh*. *Taz* explains that a ladder is not valid for *sekhakh* because it is more than four *tefaḥim* wide, and the Rabbis prohibited using boards more than four *tefaḥim* wide.[36] The *Shulḥan Arukh* forbade using a ladder to support the *sekhakh* for fear that one might confuse using this ladder to support *sekhakh* and using this actual ladder as *sekhakh* – not because it is *mekabel tuma*.[37] Other *Aḥaronim*, including *Magen Avraham*,[38] insist that the *Shulḥan Arukh* is expressing concern that it may be prohibited to support *sekhakh* on a material that is *mekabel tuma*.

The *Arukh HaShulḥan* asserts that the halakha is in accordance with the lenient opinion; we are not concerned with supporting *sekhakh* upon a material that is *mekabel tuma*.[39] The *Mishna Berura*, however, writes that although the law is really in accordance with the more lenient opinion, one should preferably act stringently regarding this matter.[40]

Interestingly, the *Shulḥan Arukh* implies that all agree that one may rest the *sekhakh* upon a material that is not *mekabel tuma* that is supported by a material that is *mekabel tuma* ("*maamid demaamid*"), permitting one to connect the wooden beams of the *sukka* with metal nails, which are *mekabel tuma*.[41] Many *Aḥaronim* explain that even those who are stringent regarding *maamid al davar shemekabel tuma* certainly permit one to place *sekhakh* on materials that are not *mekabel tuma* but are supported by material that is *mekabel tuma*.[42] *Ḥazon Ish* disagrees,[43] and to this day, his students use only wooden pegs, which are not *mekabel tuma*, in constructing the *sukka*.

In practice, it is customary not to be concerned with *maamid demaamid* and to construct *sukkot* with metal frames. However, many avoid placing *sekhakh* directly upon materials that are *mekabel tuma*. Rather, they place wooden beams above the metal horizontal beams of the frame, and place the *sekhakh* on the wooden beams.

DOFEN AKUMA: USING PART OF THE ROOF AS A WALL

We discussed above the materials and physical viability of the *sukka* walls, as well as their relationship to the *sekhakh*. We will conclude with a brief discussion of a *sukka* wall composed of a wall and part of the roof. The Mishna teaches: "If [the roof of] a house is breached, and he placed a *sukka*-covering over it, if there is a distance of four cubits from the wall to the covering, it is invalid" (Sukka 17a). The Mishna describes a case in which there is a hole in the middle of a house's roof. The person wishes to put *sekhakh* over the hole and rely upon the walls of the house to function as the walls of the *sukka*. Part of the roof, however, still extends from the walls of the house until where the *sekhakh* begins. The Mishna teaches that if the existing roof is larger than four *amot*, the walls of the house cannot be relied upon as walls of a *sukka*. However, if the part of the remaining roof is smaller than four *amot*, then the *sukka* is valid. The Gemara bases this upon the principle of "*dofen akuma*" (literally, "a bent wall") (Sukka 4a, 17a).

The *Rishonim* offer different explanations for this principle. Rashi cites two possibilities. He first suggests that the wall and the roof combine; the end of the roof is considered to be the meeting place of the wall and the *sekhakh*. This is only possible, he claims, where there is a covering of some sort at the edge of the roof, as *sekhakh pasul* can combine and join the wall. Air, however, cannot become part of the wall. Thus, if there is an actual gap of three *tefaḥim* between the wall and the *sekhakh*, the *sukka* is invalid. Rashi then suggests, and rejects, the possibility that we view the wall as slanting at a diagonal angle toward the *sekhakh*. In this image, the wall is moved closer to the *sekhakh*, but the *sekhakh pasul* remains *sekhakh pasul*.[44]

The Gemara, earlier in the tractate, offers another application of *dofen akuma*. It describes an improperly built *sukka* in which the *sekhakh* is over twenty *amot* high. In an attempt to salvage part of the *sukka*, the person builds a platform along the corner-edge of the *sukka*, so that the distance between the *sekhakh* and the elevated platform is less than twenty *amot*. However, only two of the walls join the platform to the *sekhakh*; in order to validate the *sukka*, he needs to somehow make use of the opposite, third wall. The Gemara teaches that if the opposite wall is within four *amot* of the platform, one may apply the principle of *dofen akuma* (Sukka 4a).

Rashi explains that we view the *sekhakh* that is above twenty *amot* as a continuation of the third wall, as though the third wall is bent at a right angle. In other words, the invalid, twenty-*amot*-high *sekhakh* becomes an extension of the wall, meeting the kosher *sekhakh* over the platform at a distance of less than four *amot*.[45] According to this interpretation, although such a *sukka* would be valid, one would only be able to sit under the valid *sekhakh* above the platform; the rest of the *sekhakh* is actually considered to be "wall."

Ritva brings another interpretation,[46] citing an opinion of Rashi that is found in other *Rishonim*[47] but not in our printed Talmud. Rashi explains that the third wall joins with the *sekhakh* and is considered bent diagonally toward the *sekhakh* over the platform. Accordingly, it joins the *sekhakh kasher*, and the entire *sukka* becomes valid. Ritva adds that according to this interpretation, one may even sit under the *sekhakh* that is above twenty *amot*, as it is simply considered *sekhakh pasul* within a valid *sukka*! This opinion is similar to the opinion Rashi rejected previously.

Interestingly, Rambam describes the principle of *dofen akuma* differently when citing the Gemara's different cases. Regarding the case in which the *sukka* was built over twenty *amot* high and one builds a platform to validate it, he writes:

> Should one build the bench in the middle [of the *sukka*], if there are more than four *amot* from the edge of the bench to any of the sides [of the *sukka*],

> it is not acceptable. If there are fewer than four *amot*, it is valid. *It is considered as if the walls touch the bench*, and the distance from the bench to the *sekhakh* is less than twenty *amot*.[48]

Regarding the case in which the roof of the house was breached, he writes:

> Where the substance that is unacceptable as *sekhakh* is at the side, it disqualifies the *sukka* if there are four *amot* of it. [If there is] less than that, the *sukka* is valid. For example, (a) [The roof of] a house which was opened in the center and *sekhakh* placed over the opening; (b) a courtyard surrounded by an exedra which was covered with *sekhakh*; (c) a large *sukka* over which was placed a substance that was not acceptable as *sekhakh* near the sides of its walls. [In all these cases,] if there are four *amot* [or more] from the edge of the kosher *sekhakh* until the wall, it is not acceptable. If there is less than that amount, **we view it as though the wall has been made crooked; that is, the substance that is not acceptable as *sekhakh* is considered part of the wall and it is valid**. This concept is a halakha received by Moshe on Mount Sinai.

In the first case, Rambam describes the walls of the house as if they touch the bench or platform, similar to the position of Rashi as cited by Ritva, or the interpretation Rashi rejected. In the second case, Rambam describes how the *sekhakh pasul* becomes part of the wall, similar to Rashi's first opinion. Rambam seems to accept both understandings of *dofen akuma*!

R. Soloveitchik explains that in the second case, a *halakha leMoshe miSinai* teaches that the *sekhakh pasul* can become part of the wall and "bend" toward the platform, making one long wall. However, in the first case, the *sekhakh pasul* cannot become part of the wall, as it is higher than twenty *amot*, and it therefore must remain *sekhakh pasul*. However, we may view the wall as if on a diagonal angle, as walls are often bent slightly, and thereby validate the *sukka*.[49] The *Shulḥan Arukh* cites both cases of *dofen akuma* and rules that one should not sleep under the *dofen akuma* if it is more than four *tefaḥim* wide.[50]

This principle may be relevant when a *sukka* is built on a semi-enclosed patio. If the patio is enclosed on two sides by walls and an overhang extends from the outer wall of the house over the patio, the wall of the house may be considered the third wall of the *sukka* as long as the overhang is less than four *amot* long. In this case, one may place the *sekhakh* over the patio and the *sukka* is valid, even if the fourth, outer "wall" is entirely open.

CHAPTER 20

The *Sekhakh*

THE CENTRALITY OF THE *SEKHAKH*

In the previous chapter, we discussed the laws pertaining to the walls of the *sukka*, including the material from which they may be fashioned, their physical stability, and the possibility of combining part of the roof and the wall (*dofen akuma*) in order to validate a *sukka*. In this chapter, we will begin our study of the laws of the *sekhakh*.

A careful study of the Gemara and its commentaries points to the centrality of the *sekhakh* in the structure of the *sukka*. While the Gemara and *Rishonim* at times debate the extent to which the walls are also considered to be part of the *sukka*, the importance of the *sekhakh* remains clear. For example, as we discussed previously, the Gemara offers different explanations for the Mishna's assertion that "a *sukka* which is more than twenty *amot* high is not valid":

> From where do we know this? Rabba answered: Scripture says, "That your generations may know that I made the Children of Israel to dwell in *sukkot*." [With a *sukka*] up to twenty *amot* [high], a man "knows" that he is dwelling in a *sukka*, but with one higher than twenty *amot*, he does not "know" that he is dwelling in a *sukka*, since his eye does not see it. R. Zeira replied: From the following verse: "And there shall be a booth for a shadow in the daytime from the heat." [With a *sukka*] up to twenty *amot* [high], a man sits in the

> shade of the *sukka;* but with one higher than twenty *amot,* he does not sit in the shade of the *sukka,* but in the shade of its walls.... Rava replied: [It is derived] from the following verse, "You shall dwell in booths seven days." The Torah declared: For the whole seven days, leave your permanent abode and dwell in a temporary abode. [With a *sukka*] up to twenty *amot* [high], a man makes his abode a temporary one; [in one] higher than twenty *amot,* a man does not make his abode temporary, but permanent. (Sukka 2a)

According to both R. Zeira and Rabba, a *sukka* higher than twenty *amot* is invalid because one cannot properly appreciate or benefit from its *sekhakh.* Indeed, Rashi explains that according to Rabba, "He does not see the *sekhakh,* and the *sukka* is the *sekhakh,* after its name."[1] Even according to Rava, defining a *sukka* as a temporary or permanent abode depends upon the quality and location of the *sekhakh,* not the walls.

Similarly, the Gemara teaches that one may not derive benefit from the "wood of the *sukka*" for the duration of the festival:

> From where do we know that the wood of the *sukka* is forbidden all seven [days of the festival]? From Scripture, which states, "The Festival of Sukkot, seven days to the Lord." And it was taught, R. Yehuda b. Beteira says: Just as the Name of Heaven rests upon the festival offering, so does it rest upon the *sukka,* since it is said, "The Festival of Sukkot, seven days to the Lord" – just as the festival [offering] is "to the Lord," so is the *sukka* also "to the Lord." (Sukka 9a)

While all agree that this prohibition refers to the *sekhakh,* the *Rishonim* disagree as to whether this prohibition applies to the walls as well. Rosh maintains that the prohibition to benefit from the "wood" of the *sukka* applies *only* to the *sekhakh,*[2] while Rambam maintains that it also applies to the walls.[3] R. Soloveitchik suggests that Rosh and Rambam disagree regarding the essential definition of a *sukka.* Rosh believes that the walls are not inherently part of the *sukka,* but merely support the *sekhakh;* the prohibition of benefiting from the *sukka* therefore is not relevant to the walls. Rambam, on the other hand, views both the walls and the *sekhakh* as part of the *sukka,* and the prohibition is therefore relevant to both.[4]

R. Soloveitchik's grandfather, R. Chaim Soloveitchik, reportedly maintained that even Rambam agrees that the walls are not considered part of the *sukka* at all. The reason for the prohibition of deriving benefit from the walls of the *sukka* is instead related to the fulfillment of the mitzva of *yeshiva basukka,* which one fulfills inside the entire *sukka.*

Some relate the question of the importance of the walls to another intriguing debate. The first mishna of Tractate Sukka teaches that a *sukka* "that has more sun than shade [*ḥamata meruba mitzilata*], is not valid." The Gemara records a debate regarding how we measure the ratio of sun to shade:

> Our Rabbis taught: [This applies only when] the sunshine is due to the scanty covering, but not when it is due to [gaps in] the walls, while R. Yoshiya says: Even when it is due to [gaps in] the walls. R. Yemar b. Shelemia said in the name of Abaye: What is the reason of R. Yoshiya? Because it is written: "And you shall cover the ark with the veil" [Exodus 40:3]. Now, since the "veil" was a partition and the divine law nevertheless called it a "covering," it is evident that a wall must be akin to a covering. (Sukka 7b)

While the first opinion clearly limits the halakha of *ḥamata meruba mitzilata* to the *sekhakh,* R. Yoshiya applies it to the walls of the *sukka* as well, implying that the walls themselves form a crucial part of the *sukka.*

Similarly, the *Or Zarua* cites a Yerushalmi that derives from the same verse that one may not construct a *sukka* from materials that are *mekabel tuma* (objects that potentially may become *tamei,* ritually impure) – that is, materials which may not be used for *sekhakh.*[5] Again, this source implies a similarity between the *sekhakh* and the walls.

Despite the dispute regarding the definition of the *sukka* and the roles of the *sekhakh* and the walls, some halakhot of the *sukka* clearly refer to the *sekhakh* alone. For example, the Gemara indicates that the *sukka* must be built "*lishma,*" for the sake of the mitzva. This requirement – or at least the requirement that the *sukka* not be "old" – refers to the *sekhakh* (Sukka 9a). Similarly, the Gemara learns from the verse, "The Holiday of Sukkot you shall make (*taaseh*)" (Deut. 16:13), the principle of "*taaseh – velo min haasui*"; the *sekhakh* must be actively placed on the *sukka.* One should not construct the *sukka* in a manner in which the *sekhakh,* already placed upon the *sukka,* only later becomes valid. These halakhot and others further highlight the primacy of the *sekhakh* in the building of the *sukka*. When the Torah says, "you shall make," it refers to the *sekhakh*. Regardless of whether one focuses upon the transient nature of the *sukka* from a physical or spiritual perspective, as we have discussed previously, one's experience within the *sukka* relates primarily to its *sekhakh*. Thus, as Rashi writes, "the *sukka* was named for the *sekhakh*."

THE DEFINITION OF VALID AND INVALID *SEKHAKH* (*SEKHAKH KASHER* AND *SEKHAKH PASUL*)

The Talmud teaches that only materials that fulfill three conditions may be used for *sekhakh*: they must grow from the ground (*gidulo min haaretz*), they must not be able to contract *tuma* (*eino mekabel tuma*), and they must not be connected to the ground (*eino meḥubar lekarka*):

> This is the general rule: Whatever is susceptible to *tuma* and does not grow from the soil may not be used for *sukka*-covering, but whatever is not susceptible to *tuma* and grows from the soil may be used for *sukka*-covering.... When Ravin came, he said in the name of R. Yoḥanan: Scripture says, "[You shall keep the Feast of Tabernacles seven days] after you have gathered in from your threshing floor and from your wine-press" [Deut. 16:13]. The verse thus speaks of the leavings of the threshing floor and the wine-press. (Sukka 11a–12a)

The Gemara interprets the verse as referring to making *sukkot* "from that which you have gathered in from your threshing floor and from your wine-press."

Regarding *gidulo min haaretz*, some *Rishonim* note that animals, which receive their sustenance from the land, are sometimes considered *gidulei karka*. Me'iri discusses whether leather hides may be used for *sekhakh* (Sukka 11a), but most *Rishonim*, as well as the *Shulḥan Arukh*,[6] rule that one may only use materials that grow from the ground, such as branches, for *sekhakh*.

Items that are *mekabel tuma* include vessels made from metal, as well as some materials that would ordinarily be valid for *sekhakh*, such as wood, that were shaped into a *beit kibul* (a receptacle). Thus, one may not use cartons or boxes for *sekhakh*.

What about wood boxes that were broken and are no longer considered vessels? The Gemara teaches that "If he covered the *sukka* with discarded vessels, it is invalid" (Sukka 15b). In other words, even though the broken vessel is no longer *mekabel tuma*, one may not use it for *sekhakh*. The *Rishonim* dispute the reason for this prohibition. Rashi explains that since these broken vessels were once vessels, the Rabbis prohibited using them for *sekhakh*.[7] Rambam explains that the Rabbis prohibited using broken vessels as *sekhakh* lest one come to use a vessel which is still *mekabel tuma*.[8]

The *Arukh HaShulḥan* writes that according to Rambam, if one intentionally breaks a vessel with the intention of "purifying" it, one may use the pieces for *sekhakh*.[9] *Shevet HaLevi* writes, however, that the halakha is not in accordance with the *Arukh HaShulḥan*.[10] But what if one cannot discern whether the pieces of wood were once a vessel? R. Eliezer Yehuda Waldenberg relates the following story:

> It once happened that a rabbi from *ḥutz laaretz* moved to Israel right before Sukkot. He took apart the wooden crate within which his belongings were packed and made them into thin wooden strips ... and used them as *sekhakh* for his *sukka*. His neighbors mocked him, claiming that his *sukka* is invalid since he used *sekhakh* which came from a vessel, as the crates were considered a *davar hamekabel tuma*. He came to me during Ḥol HaMo'ed to ask if, indeed, they were correct. I answered him that they were.... I saw he was greatly distressed at the embarrassing prospect of having to disassemble his *sukka* and erect a new one on Ḥol HaMo'ed.[11]

R. Waldenberg describes how he showed the man the opinion of the *Arukh HaShulḥan* cited above in an attempt to comfort him. That evening, he discussed the issue with another person, who related that although R. Chaim Berlin also prohibited using these wooden strips for *sekhakh*, R. Shmuel Salant, the former Chief Rabbi of Jerusalem, permitted using these strips if they no longer appeared as if they came from the original wooden vessel.

In addition, some suggest that a "lift" – a wooden moving container which is broken open after use – is not *mekabel tuma*; one may therefore use its pieces for *sekhakh*.[12]

Finally, the *Rishonim* search for the source of the requirement that *sekhakh* be detached from the ground (*talush min hakarka*). Rashi explains that the verse says, "That you have gathered," implying that it is used after being cut from the ground.[13] Ritva suggests that this requirement is related to the principle of *taaseh velo min haasui*; *sekhakh* must be *placed* on the *sukka*.[14]

In addition to the above requirements of valid *sekhakh*, the Rabbis also prohibited certain types of *sekhakh* that would ordinarily have been valid. For example, one may not use *sekhakh* that emits a foul smell or *sekhakh* from which pieces fall into the *sukka*, as this may cause one to leave the *sukka* (Sukka 12b). The Talmud also records rabbinic enactments that disqualify certain types of *sekhakh* even if they fulfill the requirements delineated above. We will discuss one of these types of *sekhakh pasul*, which may have particular relevance.

GEZEIRAT TIKRA

The Mishna cites a debate concerning the use of wooden planks as *sekhakh*: "Planks may be used for the *sekhakh*; these are the words of R. Yehuda. R. Meir forbids them" (Sukka 14a). The Gemara cites a difference of opinion regarding this mishna:

> Rav said the dispute concerns planks that are four [*tefaḥim* wide], in which case R. Meir holds by the preventive measure against [the possible use of] an ordinary roofing (*gezeirat tikra*), while R. Yehuda disregards this preventive measure against [the use of] an ordinary roofing. But in the case of planks that are less than four *tefaḥim* wide, all agree that the *sukka* is valid [as the preventive measure does not apply]. Shmuel, however, says.... If they are four [*tefaḥim* wide], the *sukka* is invalid according to all; if they are less than three, it is valid according to all. What is the reason? Since they are mere sticks. What do they dispute? Regarding [planks that are] from three to four [*tefaḥim* wide].

According to Rav, all agree that one may use thin planks as *sekhakh*; R. Yehuda and R. Meir disagree regarding planks wider than four *tefaḥim*, as they may be prohibited by the "*gezeirat tikra*." Shmuel maintains that they argue even regarding narrow planks between three and four *tefaḥim* wide, while all agree that one may not use planks wider than four *tefaḥim*, as the "*gezeirat tikra*" applies.

The *Rishonim* disagree as to whether we rule in accordance with Shmuel according to R. Yehuda (planks three to four *tefaḥim* wide are valid, but those larger than four *tefaḥim* are not) or Rav according to R. Meir (planks larger than four *tefaḥim* are invalid), the conclusion is the same. The *Shulḥan Arukh* thus rules that one may not use planks for *sekhakh* that are wider than four *tefaḥim*, even if they are placed on their narrow side.[15]

What is the reason behind this enactment, described by the Gemara as the "*gezeirat tikra*," "a preventive measure against [the possible use of] an ordinary roofing"? Rashi explains that since most roofs are constructed from planks of at least four *tefaḥim* wide, one may come to justify sitting in one's house during Sukkot: "What is the difference between using these [planks] for *sekhakh* and sitting under the roof of my house?"[16] In other words, if one is permitted to used planks for *sekhakh* that are similar to the ones used for a roof, one might mistakenly conclude that one could construct a *sukka* under his own roof!

Ritva[17] and Ran[18] question Rashi's assumptions. First, they note that the Gemara elsewhere relates that most roofs are constructed from beams narrower than four *tefaḥim*.[19] Second, the *gezeira* was intended for the observer, not the builder of the *sukka*. They conclude that since beams that are four *tefaḥim* wide, or wider, are generally only used for houses (*dirot keva*), one who observes another sitting in a *sukka* covered by such beams may erroneously conclude that constructing a *sukka* in one's house and sitting under one's roof is acceptable as well.

Interestingly, Ran clarifies Rashi's assertion that the majority of roofs are constructed from beams of at least four *tefaḥim* wide. He explains that Rashi refers to planks that are made of thin boards joined together to form wider boards. Rashi believes that although the planks are composed of narrow boards, one may still not use the larger, composite planks for *sekhakh*. Ritva, on the other hand, apparently focuses upon the actual wooden strips, and therefore only prohibits solid planks that are four *tefaḥim* wide.

Similarly, Rashba discusses whether one may use a lattice board as *sekhakh*, consisting of thin wooden beams held together by metal nails. He relates that "according to one of our teachers," this would be prohibited due to the *gezeirat tikra*. He concludes that this issue is subject to debate, and one should not criticize someone who uses these boards: "Leave [it up] to Israel – if they are not prophets, they are the sons of prophets."[20] While it is difficult to determine Rashba's actual conclusion, *Magen Avraham* rules that narrow wooden strips joined together to form a plank more than four *tefaḥim* wide are invalid as *sekhakh*.[21] *Ḥayei Adam* also questions whether a lattice plank should be prohibited, even if one placed the *sekhakh* on top of it. He concludes that one should not criticize those who are lenient, since he places *sekhakh* on top of it.[22]

Although the *Shulḥan Arukh* does not relate to this particular case, it appears that one should not use lattice planks more than four *tefaḥim* wide for *sekhakh*. This discussion is relevant to the use of *sekhakh* mats, as we will see below.

USING REED MATS FOR *SEKHAKH*

The Mishna cites a debate regarding whether one may use a reed mat for *sekhakh*:

> A large reed mat, if made for reclining upon, is susceptible to *tuma* and is invalid as *sekhakh*. If made for a covering, it may be used for *sekhakh* and is not susceptible to *tuma*. R. Eliezer ruled that whether small or large, if it was made for reclining upon, it is susceptible to *tuma* and is invalid as *sekhakh*; if made for a covering, it is valid as *sekhakh* and is not susceptible to *tuma*. (Sukka 19b)

The Gemara explains the dispute:

> Rather, said R. Papa: With regard to a small [mat], all agree that it is ordinarily intended for reclining upon. What do they dispute? The case of a large one. The first *Tanna* is of the opinion that a large one is ordinarily intended for a covering [and therefore valid], while R. Eliezer is of the opinion that a large one is ordinarily intended for reclining upon as well.

In other words, although both *Tanna'im* agree that a small mat is ordinarily intended for reclining upon and therefore is *mekabel tuma,* they disagree whether one should make the same assumption regarding a large mat (R. Eliezer), or whether one may assume that a large mat is ordinarily made for covering (*Tanna kama*) and is not *mekabel tuma.* The halakha is in accordance with the *Tanna kama.*

Who determines whether a mat is intended for reclining or covering? Rosh cites R. Yishaya Di Trani, an Italian talmudist and author of the *Tosafot Rid*:

> R. Yishaya Di Trani wrote: The mats that the merchants sell, which are generally made for reclining upon... and they are also used for partitions – therefore, we do not follow how they were made, because the artisan simply makes them to be sold to whoever needs them, every person according to his need. Rather, one should follow [the intention at] the time of purchase, and if it was purchased to recline upon, it is *mekabel tuma*.... Therefore, a person may purchase a new mat in order to cover his *sukka,* even though it can also be used for reclining.

Rosh disagrees:

> This does not seem correct to me. Rather, one should follow the custom of the local people.... Therefore, in a place where [people] are accustomed to reclining on [these mats], even if he asked the artisan to prepare a mat for covering the *sukka,* one may not use it for *sekhakh.*[23]

While the *Shulḥan Arukh* implies that we follow the intention of the artisan,[24] Rema cites the view of Rosh, that we follow the custom of the majority of people in that place.[25] The question of whether one may use mats purchased from public markets for *sekhakh* has occupied *posekim* for generations.[26] The *Mishna Berura* concludes that in his region, the majority of mats were made for reclining, and therefore may not be used for *sekhakh.*[27]

Nowadays, while one may certainly not use mats intended for reclining, or even venetian blinds, as they are *mekabel tuma* even after they are no longer used for that purpose,[28] mats produced from reeds or narrow wooden sticks and sold for the purpose of using them for *sekhakh* may be used for *sekhakh*. However, the *posekim* raise two issues concerning the use of mats for *sekhakh*: First, mats made of bamboo reeds or wood strips must not be woven together with a material that is *mekabel tuma* or materials that are not *gidulo min haaretz*, as these materials may not be used as *sekhakh*. One should preferably tie the reeds together with wooden fibers, flax, or other natural materials that were not processed. Some even permit using processed fibers produced from *gidulei karka*, as they are only rabbinically invalid for *sekhakh*.[29] Second, bamboo mats may violate the *gezeirat tikra*. R. Binyanim Zilber (1917–2008) cites the view of R. Yosef Shalom Elyashiv (1910–2012), who prohibits using these mats because the reeds or strips are fastened together closely and strongly, thereby violating the rabbinic prohibition of using boards over four *tefaḥim* wide. He finds precedent for this in the view of Rashba cited above, who reports that some prohibit using narrow boards nailed together so that they are wider than four *tefaḥim*.[30] R. Eliezer Yehuda Waldenberg concurs.[31]

Most *posekim* disagree, however, and permit using mats produced and sold specifically to be used as *sekhakh*.[32] Some argue that these mats are thin and flexible, and therefore do not resemble the planks mentioned by Rashba. Others note that these mats are generally made from bamboo reeds and not wooden planks, and therefore should not be included in the enactment of *gezeirat tikra*.

THE IMPACT OF GAPS AND INVALID *SEKHAKH* ON THE *SUKKA*

Previously, we encountered halakhot pertaining to both *sekhakh pasul* and gaps in the *sekhakh*. The Talmud discusses the extent to which *sekhakh pasul* or air affects the *sukka*, and whether or not one may eat and sleep under them.

We have already learned that if *sekhakh pasul* at the side of one's *sukka* is less than four *amot* wide, we invoke the principle of *dofen akuma*, and the *sukka* is valid. However, when the *sekhakh pasul* is more than four *amot* from the side, the *sukka* is disqualified. What about *sekhakh pasul* in the middle of the *sukka*? The Talmud cites a dispute between Rav and Shmuel:

> In Sura, they taught this decision in the above words; in Nehardea, they taught [as follows]: R. Yehuda said in the name of Shmuel: Invalid *sekhakh* in the middle [of the *sukka*] invalidates if it is four [*tefaḥim* wide]; at the side, only if it is four *amot* wide, while Rav says: Whether in the middle or at the sides, [it invalidates] only if it is four *amot* wide. (Sukka 27a)

Most *Rishonim,* including Rif,[33] Rambam,[34] Rosh,[35] and Ran,[36] rule in accordance with Shmuel and disqualify a *sukka* even if the portion of *sekhakh pasul* is only four *tefaḥim* wide.

Only *sekhakh pasul* that runs the entire length of the *sukka* disqualifies the *sukka,* however. Furthermore, this invalidation only applies to a *sukka* constructed of three walls, when the *sekhakh pasul* begins from the middle wall and extends across the *sukka* to the side without a wall; in that case, neither remaining side has enough walls for a valid *sukka.* However, if a strip of *sekhakh pasul* runs across a *sukka* constructed from four walls, it may simply divide the *sukka* into two separate valid *sukkot,* as long as each has three complete walls of at least seven *tefaḥim* by seven *tefaḥim.*

The Gemara teaches that although one may not sleep under a gap in the *sekhakh,* even one which is under three *tefaḥim* wide, one may sleep under *sekhakh pasul* less than four *tefaḥim* wide (Sukka 19a). Most *Rishonim,* including Baal HaMaor,[37] permit one to sleep under a section of *sekhakh pasul* less than four *tefaḥim* wide. Raavad[38] and Ritva,[39] however, insist that one may only sleep under a portion of *sekhakh pasul* less than three *tefaḥim* wide. The *Shulḥan Arukh* does not cite this distinction,[40] but the *Mishna Berura* cites some *Aḥaronim* who rule that one should preferably be stringent.[41]

Regarding a gap in the *sekhakh* (*avir*), the Mishna teaches, "If one distances the *sekhakh* three *tefaḥim* from the walls, it is invalid" (Sukka 17a). The Gemara discusses whether this principle, which overlooks a gap of less than three *tefaḥim* (*lavud*), applies in all cases:

> This applies only to the side, but as regards the middle, R. Aḥa and Ravina differ. One says that the rule of *lavud* applies in the middle, while the other says that the rule of *lavud* does not apply in the middle. (Sukka 18a)

Rambam,[42] Rosh,[43] and *Shulḥan Arukh*[44] rule that *lavud* applies to a gap both from the side of and in the middle of the *sekhakh*.

A gap in the *sekhakh* differs from *sekhakh pasul* in that *sekhakh pasul* only poses a problem if it is wider than four *tefaḥim*. Furthermore, while one may sleep under *sekhakh pasul* of less than four (or three) *tefaḥim*, the Gemara teaches that one may not sleep under a gap in the *sekhakh* even if it is under three *tefaḥim* wide (Sukka 19a). What is the meaning of this prohibition? Clearly, the Gemara does not intend to insist that the *sekhakh* of one's *sukka* be similar to the roof of a house, without any holes.

Some *Rishonim* explain that one may not sleep under a gap of less than three *tefaḥim* within which one may fit one's head or the majority of one's body.[45] Others, however, disagree, and rule that one may not sleep under a gap of this width that runs the entire length of the *sukka*.[46] Rema cites both opinions;[47] therefore, one should not sleep under a gap that either runs the length of the *sukka* or within which one may fit his head or the majority of his body.[48]

The Gemara concludes that in a large *sukka* of over seven *tefaḥim* by seven *tefaḥim*, *sekhakh pasul* does not combine with air in order to disqualify the *sukka* (Sukka 17a). The *Rishonim* discuss whether a total of four *tefaḥim* of *sekhakh pasul* divided by less than three *tefaḥim* of air disqualifies the *sukka*. Although air cannot combine with *sekhakh pasul* in order disqualify the *sukka*, does it function, in this case, like *sekhakh kasher*, interrupting between the two segments of *sekhakh pasul*?[49] The question remains unresolved.[50]

THICKNESS AND QUALITY OF THE *SEKHAKH*

Tur writes:

> [What is the] ideal place for the *sukka*? It should be constructed under the sky, as it says, "And you shall sit in *sukkot*," and we learn from this – not in a *sukka* under a *sukka*, nor a *sukka* under a house, and not in a *sukka* under a tree.... Just as the *sukka* should be under the sky, and there should not be another *sekhakh* covering it, so too, there should not be another *sekhakh* between him and the *sekhakh*.[51]

Tur explains that there should be no interference between the *sekhakh* and the sky, nor should there be any obstruction between the *sekhakh* and the person sitting in the *sukka*.

THE THICKNESS OF THE *SEKHAKH*: SEEING THE STARS AND PROTECTING FROM RAIN

One of the central themes of the laws pertaining to building a *sukka* relates to defining the difference between a *sukka* and a house. The Gemara discusses in numerous contexts the concern that a *sukka* may be too similar to a *dirat keva* (a permanent abode). As we saw above, the Rabbis prohibited using wooden planks wider than four *tefaḥim,* which would ordinarily have been valid for *sekhakh,* lest one think that he may simply construct a *sukka* in his house and sit under his own roof. As a result of this concern, the Gemara carefully balances the need to construct a viable and sturdy structure that one can live in for the duration of the festival (*teshvu ke'ein taduru*) with the requirement to build a temporary abode (*dirat arai*).

The Mishna discusses the density of the *sekhakh* with which one must cover the *sukka*: "If [the covering] is close-knit like that of a house, it is valid, even though the stars cannot be seen through it" (Sukka 22a). The *Aḥaronim* disagree as to why and to what extent one should be able to see the stars from inside the *sukka*. R. Yosef Teomim (1727–1792) explains in his *Peri Megadim* that by seeing the stars from the *sukka,* one is reminded of "Who created them, and that one is a stranger in this world, as it says [Ps. 8:4], '[When I behold Your heavens, the work of Your fingers,] the moon and the stars, which You have established.'" He rules that it is sufficient to be able to see the stars even from one part of the *sukka*.[52] Alternatively, R. Yaakov Ettlinger argues in his commentary to *Hilkhot Sukka,* the *Bikkurei Yaakov,* that the ability to see the stars is a measurement of the density of the *sekhakh*. Therefore, one should preferably be able to see the stars through the *sekhakh* covering one's entire *sukka,* and one should be careful that a four-*tefaḥ*-wide area through which one cannot see the stars does not run the length of the *sukka,* similar to *sekhakh pasul*.[53] Apparently, these *Aḥaronim* dispute whether the

Mishna refers to one's personal ability to properly experience sitting in a *sukka,* which includes seeing the stars through the *sekhakh,* or whether it offers an objective means of measuring the density of the *sekhakh,* in contrast to a covering which is "like that of a house" (Sukka 22a).

The Gemara teaches that although ideally one should see the stars through the *sekhakh* of the *sukka, bediavad,* "If [the *sekhakh*] is close together like a house, even though the stars cannot be seen through it, it is valid." If the *sekhakh* is arranged densely, like the roof of a house, so that one cannot see the stars, the *sukka* is still valid. The *Hagahot Maimoniyot,* however, records that Rabbeinu Tam disqualified a *sukka* whose *sekhakh* was so thick that the rain could not penetrate the *sukka.* He relates that Rabbeinu Tam's brother-in-law, R. Shimon, built a *sekhakh* from thin planks joined by nails, and Rabbeinu Tam disqualified the *sekhakh,* as it protected the *sukka* from the rain.[54] The *Mordekhai* cites the view of Rabbeinu Tam, but notes that Rashi disagrees. According to Rashi, even if the *sekhakh* protects the inside from rain, the *sukka* is still valid.[55]

Why does Rabbeinu Tam disqualify a sukka because its *sekhakh* is too dense and protects the *sukka* from rain? The *Hagahot Maimoniyot,* as well as the *Mordekhai* and Rosh,[56] explain that a *sukka* that is impervious to rain is similar to a house, and is therefore not a valid *sukka.* The *Shulḥan Arukh* omits the view of Rabbeinu Tam, leading some *Aḥaronim* to assume that he rejects Rabbeinu Tam's view; if the *sekhakh* protects a *sukka* from rain, the *sukka* is still valid. *Peri Megadim* disagrees, however. He observes that the *Shulḥan Arukh* writes that a *sukka* from which one cannot see the stars is valid, implying that if the *sekhakh* is any denser than this, so that it would protect the *sukka* from the rain, the *sukka* is invalid, as Rabbeinu Tam argued.[57] R. Ettlinger asserts that according to Rabbeinu Tam, the *sukka* is only invalid if the *sekhakh* keeps out the rain completely. However, if it merely delays the penetration of rain, the *sukka* is still valid.[58] Many *Aḥaronim,* including *Baḥ,*[59] *Shulḥan Arukh HaRav,*[60] *Ḥayei Adam,*[61] *Arukh HaShulḥan,*[62] and *Mishna Berura,*[63] write that in extenuating circumstances, one may rely upon the lenient opinions and sit in a *sukka* whose *sekhakh* is impervious to rain.

The Gemara teaches that *sukkot* known a *sukkot ganba"k* (an acronym for *sukkot* erected by non-Jews or women and *sukkot* erected for animals) and *sukkot rakba"sh* (an acronym for *sukkot* used by shepherds, field-watchers, city guards, and orchard-keepers) are valid, "provided that they are covered according to the rule." R. Ḥisda explains that this means, "Provided [the *sekhakh*] was made [with the intention of providing] the shade for the *sukka*" (Sukka 8b). Rosh cites Rabbeinu Tam, who explains that as long as the *sukka* was erected to provide shade from the sun and not to protect one from the rain, it is valid.[64]

Baḥ explains that according to Rosh, whether or not a *sukka* is impervious to rain is not a significant measure of thickness of the *sekhakh*. Rather, it reflects the intentions of the person who built the *sukka*. One need not fear that a regular *sukka* impervious to rain is invalid, but a *sukkat ganba"k* or *rakba"sh*, regarding which we are extra careful about the intention of its construction, may be invalid if it is impermeable to rain, lest it was built for that intention and not to provide shade.[65]

ḤAMATA MERUBA MITZILATA

The Mishna teaches that "A *sukka*...which has more sun than shade is not valid" (Sukka 2a). Later in the tractate, the Mishna asserts that "a *sukka*...whose shade is more than its sun is valid" (Sukka 22b). The Gemara asks:

> But if they are equal it is invalid? But have we not learnt in the other chapter, "or whose sun is more than its shade, is invalid," from which it follows that if they are equal it is valid? There is no difficulty, since the former refers to above and the latter to below. R. Papa observed: This bears on what people say, "The size of a *zuz* above becomes the size of an *issar* below."

The first mishna implies that a *sukka* is valid as long as there is not more sun than shade (and even if they are equal), while the second implies that a *sukka* is valid only as long as there is more shade than sun. The Gemara explains that one mishna refers to "above" – that is, the ratio between the amount of *sekhakh* and the amount of air on top of the *sukka* – and one mishna refers to "below" – that is, the amount of sunlight that actually enters the *sukka*. It is not clear, however, which mishna applies "above" and which "below." Rashi explains that even if the ratio of *sekhakh* to air on the top of the *sukka* is equal, more sunlight than shade will enter the *sukka*, and the *sukka* will be disqualified. However, if the ratio of sunlight to shade in the *sukka* is equal, then clearly there is more *sekhakh* than air, and the *sukka* is valid.[66] Thus, a *sukka* that has more shade than sun "above" is valid.

Rabbeinu Tam offers the opposite interpretation. If one views the *sukka* from above and the ratio of *sekhakh* to sunlight appears to be equal, then the *sukka* is valid. However, if from below, the ratio of *sekhakh* to air seems to be equal, then most likely he is mistaken; there is more air than *sekhakh*, and the *sukka* is invalid.[67]

The *Shulḥan Arukh* rules in accordance with Rashi – the shade and sunlight must be equal from inside the *sukka*.[68] The *Shulḥan Arukh* further writes that if the majority of the *sukka* is *tzilata meruba meḥamata* and a minority is *ḥamata meruba mitzilata*, the *sukka* is valid, and one may even sit under the area which has more sunlight.[69] However, Rema writes that in a large *sukka*, if there is an area of seven *tefaḥim* by seven *tefaḥim* (the minimal dimensions of a *sukka*) within which there is more sunlight than shade, one may not sit under that portion, although the rest of the *sukka* is valid.[70]

Based on the above, one should be careful to cover the *sukka* with enough *sekhakh* to ensure that it provides sufficient shade for the *sukka* – that is, that the *sekhakh* is in the majority – and that it is heavy enough or securely fastened so that it will not blow away. However, one should still allow for the possibility of viewing the stars through the *sukka*, and the *sekhakh* should certainly not be so thick that it renders the *sukka* impervious to rain.

A *SUKKA* UNDER A *SUKKA* AND A *SUKKA* UNDER A TREE

The Talmud teaches that not only must the *sukka* be considered to be "under the sky," but one may also not build a *sukka* under another *sukka*, under a tree, or under a house. For example, the Mishna teaches,

"If one *sukka* is erected above another, the upper one is valid but the lower is invalid. R. Yehuda said: If there are no occupants in the upper one, the lower one is valid." The Gemara explains, "Our Rabbis taught, 'You shall dwell in *sukkot'* – but not in a *sukka* under another *sukka,* nor in a *sukka* under a tree, nor in a *sukka* within the house" (Sukka 9b). Minimally, this halakha teaches that there should be no interference between the *sukka* and the sky.

It is not uncommon to find oneself building a *sukka* close to, and at times under, the branches of a tree. The Mishna discusses the impact of the shade from a tree on this principle: "If one made his *sukka* under a tree, it is as if he made it within the house." The Gemara cites Rava, who explains:

> [Our mishna] was taught only in respect to a tree whose shade is greater than the sun [shining through its branches], but if the sun is more than its shade, it is valid.... But even where the sun is more than the shade, what is the advantage, seeing that all invalid covering is joined to a valid one? R. Papa answered: [This is a case] where [the branches of the tree] were pushed down [and interwoven].

The *Rishonim* disagree as to how to properly understand this passage. Rashi explains that if the tree branches provide more shade than sunlight, then certainly the *sukka* underneath the tree is invalid. However, if the tree allows more sunlight than shade, then we must look at the *sukka*. If the *sukka* itself, without the shade provided by the tree, is valid, then we ignore the branches hanging above the *sukka*. However, if the *sekhakh* allows more sunlight than shade and only with the branches of the tree above do they together provide more shade than sunlight, then the *sukka* may be valid as long as one lowers the branches and weaves them into the *sekhakh*.[71]

However, R. Eliezer b. Yoel HaLevi, known as Raavya, writes in his *Avi HaEzri* that even if the *sukka* is perfectly valid (that is, its *sekhakh* ensures *tzilata meruba meḥamata* without the tree), even branches that allow more sunlight than shade invalidate the *sekhakh* located directly below. Therefore, if, in the absence of the *sekhakh* beneath these branches, there is not enough *sekhakh* for a valid *sukka*, the *sukka* is *pasul*.[72]

The *Geonim* and Rabbeinu Tam offer a third interpretation. They claim that the tree branches only disqualify the *sekhakh* located below if the *sukka* is built under the tree. However, if the *sukka* was built properly and the branches then grew over the *sukka,* then the *sekhakh* and *sukka* are valid.[73]

The *Shulḥan Arukh* cites both Rashi and Raavya.[74] *Biur Halakha* notes that when the *Shulḥan Arukh* cites two opinions, both beginning with "*veyesh omrim*" ("and some say"), the halakha is in accordance with the second view – in this case, the view of Raavya.[75] Interestingly, both *Tur* and *Shulḥan Arukh* omit the view of the *Geonim* and Rabbeinu Tam. *Tur* records that based upon the stringent opinion of Raavya, some prohibit the apparently once common practice of removing the bricks from one's roof and building a *sukka* under the wooden beams that support the roof. Rabbeinu Yeḥiel reportedly would raise the *sekhakh* to the height of the roof in order to "mix" the wooden beams with the *sekhakh,* similar to the lowering of the tree branches described above. *Tur* cites Baal HaIttur, who claims that by removing the bricks, one demonstrates that the wooden beams are intended to be part of the *sukka,* and they are not to be considered *sekhakh pasul. Tur* himself disagrees, however, insisting that even if the beams were invalid, there still remains enough *sekhakh kasher* in between the beams to validate the *sukka.*[76] The *Shulḥan Arukh* rejects this stringency entirely and rules that one may build a *sukka* under the horizontal beams of a house after removing the bricks from the roof.[77]

MAKING A *SUKKA* UNDER A BED

The Mishna teaches that "he who sleeps under a bed in the *sukka* has not fulfilled his obligation" (Sukka 20b). Many *Rishonim* explain that just as one may not build his *sukka* under another *sukka,* one similarly may not sleep under a bed.[78] Apparently, they understand that the disqualification of a *sukka* built under another *sukka* teaches that there should be no significant interference between both the *sekhakh* and the sky and the *sekhakh* and the person. Alternatively, some have suggested that one should not sit under "two coverings," but rather under only one, as the verse says, "and you shall sit in *sukkot.*"

Baal HaMaor, however, disagrees. He explains that one who sleeps under a bed inside the *sukka* is akin to one who sleeps in a tent inside a *sukka*. In this case, one does not fulfill his obligation, as one must sleep "under the shade of the *sukka*, and not under the shade of a tent."[79] Ramban rejects this approach, arguing that a significant structure, such as a bed higher than ten *tefaḥim*, negates the *sukka* found above.[80] The Gemara discusses different types of beds and tents under which one may not sleep (Sukka 20b, 10b–11a).

NOY SUKKA: *SUKKA* DECORATIONS

Although one must sit under the shade of the *sukka*, the Talmud allows, and even praises, one who adorns the *sukka*, including the *sekhakh*, with decorations. The Gemara describes how *sukkot* were beautifully adorned:

> If he covered it according to the rule, and adorned it with embroidered hangings and sheets, and hung therein nuts, almonds, peaches, pomegranates, bunches of grapes, wreaths of ears of corn, [phials of] wine, oil, or fine flour, it is forbidden to make use of them. (Sukka 10a)

The Gemara further teaches:

> For it was taught: "This is my God, and I will adorn him" [Ex. 15:2] – adorn yourself before Him in [the fulfillment of] precepts. [Thus:] make a beautiful *sukka* in His honor, a beautiful lulav, a beautiful shofar, beautiful *tzitzit*, and a beautiful *sefer Torah*. (Shabbat 133b)

Furthermore, Rashba explains that not only do *sukka* decorations beautify the mitzva, but they also make one's living in the *sukka* more pleasant. This is especially significant in the mitzva of *sukka*, where we are commanded to transform the *sukka* into our home for the duration of the festival.[81]

The Gemara cites a debate regarding the maximum distance that the *sukka* decorations may be hung from the *sekhakh*:

> It was stated: The adornments of a *sukka* which are removed four [*tefaḥim* from the roof] – R. Naḥman declared valid and R. Ḥisda and Rabba son

> of R. Huna declared invalid. R. Ḥisda and Rabba son of R. Huna once came to the house of the exilarch, and R. Naḥman sheltered them in a *sukka* whose adornments were separated four *tefaḥim* [from the roof]. They were silent and said not a word to him. Said he to them, "Have our Rabbis retracted their teaching?" "We," they answered him, "are on a religious errand, and [therefore] free from the obligation of the *sukka*." (Sukka 10b)

R. Ḥisda and Rabba maintain that if the decorations hang lower than four *tefaḥim* from the roof, then the *sukka* is invalid, but R. Naḥman disagrees.

Assuming the halakha is in accordance with R. Ḥisda and Rabba,[82] why do decorations that hang lower than four *tefaḥim* from the *sekhakh* potentially invalidate the *sukka*? Some *Rishonim* understand that *noy sukka* that hang lower than four *tefaḥim* may create their own sub-area within the *sukka*, similar to a tent within a *sukka*. Me'iri, for example, writes that *noy sukka* hung lower than four *tefaḥim* would only pose a problem if its dimensions are under seven *tefaḥim* by seven *tefaḥim* and if it provides more shade than sunlight, constituting a separate, invalid *sukka* within the *sukka*.[83]

Other *Rishonim* explain that as long as the items hanging from the *sekhakh* were intended for decorative purposes and they hang within four *tefaḥim* of the *sekhakh*, they are considered "*batel*" and ignored. However, *sukka* decorations that hang lower than four *tefaḥim* are considered to be *sekhakh pasul*.[84] Seemingly, like all *sekhakh pasul*, one may sit under *noy sukka* hung lower than four *tefaḥim* from the *sekhakh* as long is it is not four *tefaḥim* wide. These *Rishonim* debate whether we consider *noy sukka* hung lower than four *tefaḥim* to be *sekhakh pasul* even if it allows more sunlight than shade, or only if it provides more shade than sunlight.[85]

Rema writes that one should be careful not to hang any decorations lower than four *tefaḥim* from the *sekhakh*.[86] The *Mishna Berura* concludes that although technically, one may hang *noy sukka* below four *tefaḥim*, as long as they are less than four *tefaḥim* wide, one should refrain from doing so, lest one come to hang many decorations that may add up to four *tefaḥim* in width. He adds that one need not be stringent regarding a light hung above the table, and in fact, it may be preferable to distance it as much as possible from the *sekhakh*.[87]

If it is permissible to hang decorations from the *sekhakh* and they do not disqualify the *sukka*, may one hang items from the *sukka* for other reasons? The Mishna teaches, "If one spreads a sheet over it because of the sun or beneath it because of falling [leaves] ... [the *sukka*] is invalid." The Gemara explains that "R. Ḥisda stated: [Our mishna] speaks only [of a sheet spread] because of falling [leaves], but if [it was spread] in order to beautify [the *sukka*], it is valid." (Sukka 10a)

The Gemara implies that one may only hang a sheet above or below the *sekhakh* in order to beautify the *sukka*. Rashi and Rambam explain that one hangs the sheet in order to protect the table from falling leaves.[88] The *Mordekhai*, citing R. Peretz, adds that since the sheet was hung for the person's sake and not for the *sukka*, it cannot be considered to be *noy sukka*. *Noy sukka* beautify the *sukka*, and are therefore *batel* (nullified) in relation to the *sekhakh*.[89]

Other *Rishonim*, however, limit the case of the Mishna and permit one to hang a non-decorative sheet above or below the *sekhakh* under certain circumstances. The *Geonim*, for example, explain that if the *sukka* was already constructed properly – that is, it provides more shade than sun – one may hang a sheet above or below the *sekhakh* to protect the *sukka* from the falling leaves.[90] Rabbeinu Tam explains that the Gemara prohibits hanging a sheet whose purpose is to prevent the *sekhakh* from drying out and falling; the *sukka* is invalid in this case because the *sekhakh* no longer provides ample shade. In other words, this sheet, according to Rabbeinu Tam, contributes to the validity of the *sukka*, and is therefore *pasul*. However, if one hangs a sheet not in order to maintain the integrity of the *sekhakh*, but rather to protect those sitting in the *sukka* from the sun or the falling leaves, it does not invalidate the *sukka*.[91]

Interestingly, Tosafot and Rosh imply that Rabbeinu Tam believes that if the *sukka* is constructed properly and the *sekhakh* provides more shade than sunlight, the *sukka* is valid, even if afterward, tree branches extend over the *sukka*, or one hangs a sheet above or below the *sekhakh*.[92] *Tur*, however, cites this view only regarding a sheet,[93] and not regarding tree branches.[94] *Beit Yosef* writes that there is apparently a distinction between these two cases.[95] *Baḥ* suggests that a sheet whose purpose is to make one's stay in the *sukka* more pleasant, by protecting the *sukka* from the sun or from falling leaves, may be considered to be *noy sukka,* which does not invalidate the *sukka*. However, the branches cannot, in any way, be considered *noy sukka,* and therefore they disqualify the *sekhakh* found below. Alternatively, *Baḥ* suggests that *Tur* accepts Rabbeinu Tam's leniency in both the case of the sheet and that of the branches, as long as the *sukka* was erected first. *Tur* did not record this opinion in chapter 626 regarding the tree branches, as there, he was referring to branches found more than four *tefaḥim* above the *sekhakh*. If the branches are within four *tefaḥim* of the *sekhakh, Tur* maintains that they would certainly not disqualify the *sekhakh* below.[96]

The *Shulḥan Arukh* cites the view of Rashi and Rambam, and then the view of Rabbeinu Tam.[97] The *Mishna Berura* writes that one should follow the ruling of Rashi and Rambam, who prohibit hanging a sheet for non-decorative purposes. He concludes, however, that in extenuating circumstances, if one cannot sit in the *sukka* due to falling leaves or strong winds (or even rain[98]), it may be preferable to hang a sheet within four *tefaḥim* of the *sekhakh,* but one should not recite the blessing of "*leishev basukka*."[99]

One may not remove or benefit from *noy sukka* for the duration of the festival.[100]

CHAPTER 21

Laws Relating to the Construction of the Sukka

IN ADDITION TO the numerous laws dictating the dimensions and the materials of the *sekhakh* and *sukka,* the Talmud also discusses the manner in which one must construct the *sukka*. In this chapter, we will question whether a *sukka* must be constructed with specific intentions (*kavana*), whether the walls of the *sukka* must be erected before the *sekhakh*, and the laws pertaining to the sanctity of the *sukka*.

SUKKA YESHANA: AN "OLD" *SUKKA*

Does one need proper "intention" when erecting the *sukka*? The Talmud addresses this issue in numerous contexts. For example, the Gemara discusses an "old" *sukka* (*sukka yeshana*), which was not constructed specifically for the present festival. The Mishna teaches:

> *Beit Shammai* declares an "old *sukka*" invalid, but *Beit Hillel* pronounces it valid. What is an "old *sukka*"? One made thirty days before the festival; but if one made it for the purpose of the festival, even at the beginning of the year, it is valid. (Sukka 9a)

According to the Mishna, *Beit Shammai* clearly maintains that a *sukka* must be built with "intent" for the present festival. If it was built within thirty days of the festival, one may assume that it was built with the proper intention. However, if it was built more than thirty days prior to the festival, it is only valid if it was built "for the purpose of the festival." The Gemara explains that this requirement is derived from a verse: "You shall make the Festival of Sukkot for seven days" (Deut. 16:13), which implies that the *sukka* should be made for the sake of the festival.

Although this passage indicates that *Beit Hillel* completely rejects the notion of "intention" for the construction of the *sukka*, the Yerushalmi records that one must "innovate" part of the *sukka* ("*leḥadesh bo davar*"). The Yerushalmi cites two opinions regarding the extent of the necessary *ḥiddush* (innovation) – some say that it should affect a *tefaḥ*, while others say even a small portion, a *kol shehu*, spread across the entire *sukka* suffices (Y. Sukka 1:2).

The *Rishonim* differ as to whether the Yerushalmi disagrees with the Bavli. Some *Rishonim* do not cite the Yerushalmi at all, implying that they view the Yerushalmi as arguing with the Bavli. They rule in accordance with the Talmud Bavli, which implies that *Beit Hillel* validates an "old" *sukka*.[1] Most *Rishoshim*, however, do cite the Yerushalmi, but they disagree regarding whether the Yerushalmi mandates innovating part of the *sukka* or merely records the "*mitzva min hamuvḥar*" (the preferable way of performing the mitzva). R. Yehudai Gaon, for example, maintains that according to the Yerushalmi, *Beit Hillel* demands that at least part of the *sukka* be innovated; if not, the *sukka* is invalid.[2] Ran, however, explicitly describes the Yerushalmi as relating the "*mitzva min hamuvḥar*."[3]

In his *Beit Yosef*, R. Yosef Karo explains that according to all *Rishonim* except for Ran, one must renew part of a *sukka* erected more than thirty days before Sukkot, and if one does not do so, he undermines the validity of the *sukka*.[4] In his *Shulḥan Arukh*, R. Karo also implies that one must innovate part of the *sukka*.[5] *Magen Avraham*,[6] *Taz*,[7] and other *Aḥaronim*,[8] however, rule in accordance with Ran and view the *ḥiddush* as a "*mitzva min hamuvḥar*."[9]

What type of innovation does the Yerushalmi refer to? As we noted above, the Yerushalmi cites two opinions – that the change must affect a *tefaḥ*, or perhaps even a small amount (*kol shehu*) spread over the entire *sukka*. *Tur*[10] and *Shulḥan Arukh*[11] assume that these opinions do not disagree, but rather relate to different scenarios. If one changes one side of the *sukka*, then he must change a full *tefaḥ*. However, if one changes the entire length or width of the *sukka*, then even a small amount suffices.

What kind of change does the Yerushalmi demand? Most *Rishonim* explain that one must change the *sukka* itself.[12] Some *Rishonim* cite *Behag*, who implies that simply bringing chairs into the *sukka* would suffice.[13]

The *Shulḥan Arukh* rules that in the case of a *sukka yeshana* – a *sukka* built more than a month prior to Sukkot without intention or a *sukka* built more than a year before (before the previous Sukkot) – one must renew part of the *sukka* itself (*begufa*) by either adding a square *tefaḥ* to one part of the *sukka*, or a *ḥiddush* across the entire *sukka*, a *kol shehu*. If, however, the *sukka* was built within the past year and one had intention when constructing the *sukka*, it does not require a *ḥiddush*.[14] Where must one innovate in the *sukka*? The *Mishna Berura* writes that one may add to the *sekhakh* or even to one of the necessary walls of the *sukka*.[15]

SUKKOT GANBA"K AND *RAKBA"SH*: *SUKKOT* ERECTED TO PROVIDE SHADE

Although we have demonstrated that a *sukka* need not be built with the specific intention of being a *sukka*, another source implies that it *must* be built in order to provide shade. The Gemara teaches:

> Our Rabbis taught: *Ganba"k* – [an acronym for] a booth of gentiles, women, cattle, or Samaritans – and any other booth is valid, provided that it is covered according to the rule. What is meant by "according to the rule"? R. Ḥisda answered: Provided that [the covering] was made [with the intention of providing] the shade for the *sukka*.
>
> What does "any other booth" include? It includes the booths [whose acronym is] *rakba"sh*, as our Rabbis taught: The booth of shepherds, the booth of field-watchers, the booth of city guards, and the booth of orchard-keepers, and any other booth is valid, provided that it is covered according to the rule. What is meant by "according to the rule"? R. Ḥisda answered: Provided [the covering] was made [with the intention of providing] the shade for the *sukka*. What does "any other booth" include? It includes the booths [whose mnemonic] is *ganba"k*. (Sukka 8b)

The Gemara rules that *sukkot* constructed by a gentile, woman, or Samaritans, and *sukkot* erected for cattle are valid as long as they were built in order to provide shade. Similarly, the more temporary structures built for shepherds, field-watchers, city guards, and orchard-keepers are also valid, again assuming they were built in order to provide shade.

The *Rishonim* offer different explanations of this passage. Rashi, for example, explains that one must build the *sukka* with the intention specifically of providing shade, and not in order to offer privacy.[16] Rabbeinu Tam explains that the Gemara validates a *sukka* constructed for shade, as opposed to a *sukka* constructed in order to protect from rain, which is invalid.[17] Ran argues that if the *sukka* was built to be a living quarters (*dira*) or storage area (*otzar*), it is invalid.[18] The *Shulḥan Arukh* implies that the *sukka* must be built in order to provide shade, and does not cite Ran.[19] The *Arukh HaShulḥan*, however, writes that a *sukka* built for privacy or storage is invalid.[20]

Although a *sukka* may be constructed by a non-Jew, one should be careful to ensure that it is built properly and with the correct intention, as we will see below. The responsa *Binyan Shlomo* suggests that one should preferably always build his own *sukka,* in fulfillment of the dictum "*mitzva bo yoter mibisheluḥo.*"[21]

A number of *Aḥaronim* suggest that one express one's intentions – "*leshem sukka*" or "*leshem tzel*" – while placing the *sekhakh* over the *sukka.*

TAASEH VELO MIN HAASUI

Although one usually constructs the walls of the *sukka* and then places the *sekhakh* on top, at times, one might wish to make the *sukka* in a different manner. For example, the Mishna discusses a case in which one intends to create walls and *sekhakh* by hollowing out a haystack: "If he hollows out a haystack to make for himself a *sukka,* it is not a valid *sukka*" (Sukka 15a). The Gemara explains that this law is based upon the verse, "You shall make (*taaseh*)" – "[which implies] not from that which is made (*taaseh velo min haasui*)." In other words, since the Torah says that one must "make" the *sukka,* we learn that the *sukka* must be made actively, and not "automatically."

The *Rishonim,* however, disagree as to the scope and definition of this halakha. Rambam writes:

> A *sukka* that was made for any purpose whatsoever – even if it was not made for the purpose of [fulfilling] the mitzva – if it was made according to law, it is kosher. However, it must be made for the purpose of shade. Examples of this are *sukkot* made for gentiles, *sukkot* made for animals, and the like.
>
> In contrast, a *sukka* that came about on its own accord is unacceptable, because it was not made for the purpose of shade. Similarly, when a person hollows out a place in a heap of produce and thus makes a *sukka,* it is not considered to be a *sukka,* **because the produce was not piled there for this purpose.** Accordingly, were one to create a space one handbreadth [high] and seven [handbreadths] in area for the purpose of a *sukka,* and afterward hollow it out until it reached ten [handbreadths], it is kosher, **since its *sekhakh* was placed for the purpose of shade.**[22]

Rambam relates the halakha of *taaseh velo min haasui* to our previous discussion regarding whether intention is required during the building of the *sukka*. He writes that since the *sukka* must be constructed with the intention of providing shade, the *sekhakh* must be placed with that intention, or, alternatively, the haystack may be hollowed out further if it already functions as an "*ohel*" – that is, it is at least a *tefaḥ* above the hay below.

Assuming that *taaseh velo min haasui* teaches that the *sekhakh* must be placed with the intention of providing shade, *Hagahot Maimoniyot* adds that one must first construct the walls and only afterward place the *sekhakh*.[23] Rema rules accordingly.[24]

Baḥ disagrees, however. He writes:

> This is quite puzzling. How is this case at all similar to one who hollows out a haystack, regarding which he did not place the haystack for the purpose of providing shade, but rather for storage?! But here [regarding one who places the *sekhakh* before the walls], he placed the *sekhakh* with the intention of being a *sukka*! And if [you will argue that] since there are no walls, [the *sekhakh*] is not considered to be an *ohel* – certainly all we require is that the *sekhakh* be placed for the purpose of providing shade.[25]

Baḥ argues that even if *taaseh velo min haasui* teaches us that the *sekhakh* must be placed with the intention of providing shade, it still constitutes a formal *ohel* if it is suspended before the walls, and the *sekhakh* and *sukka* are still valid. While *Baḥ*, *Magen Avraham*,[26] and *Arukh HaShulḥan*,[27] validate such a *sukka bediavad*, *Levush* and *Taz* disqualify this *sukka*.[28]

In summary, some *Rishonim* understand that *taaseh velo min haasui* teaches that the *sekhakh* must be placed with the intention of providing shade, and the *Aḥaronim* differ as to whether one who suspends the *sekhakh* before erecting the walls has made the *sekhakh* with the intention of shade. Other *Rishonim*, however, understand this halakha differently. They maintain that *taaseh velo min haasui* relates to the *sekhakh* itself – the *sekhakh* must be placed in such a manner that it is inherently valid when placed. If the *sekhakh* is part of a larger haystack and is only distinguished from the walls by hollowing out the haystack, or if the *sekhakh* is placed on the walls while it is still attached to the ground and only afterward detached (Sukka 11a), we invoke the principle of *taaseh velo min haasui.*

Must the *sekhakh* be placed after the walls are erected? The *Rishonim* discuss the practice of erecting a *sukka* underneath a roof from which the bricks were removed. This once-common practice raised numerous questions concerning the validity of the *sukka* and whether one may open and close the roof on Shabbat and Yom Tov. *Beit Yosef* cites different opinions regarding this practice. He first cites the view of Maharam,[29] who writes the following:

> I found written [in the responsa of Maharam]: A *sukka* [erected] under a roof – people say that one may not construct the *sukka* before removing the roof, because of *taaseh velo min haasui.* R. Elḥanan explained that we only apply the principle of *taaseh velo min haasui* to a *sukka yeshana,* but not in this case. As a proof, we say that a *sukka* higher than twenty *amot* should be lowered; in other words, we do not say that he must remove the *sekhakh* first.

According to the first view, because the *sukka* was not actually halakhically valid until after the roof was removed, we consider this case to be a violation of *taaseh velo min haasui.* R. Elḥanan, however, disagrees, and insists that this case does not constitute such a problem. *Beit Yosef* then cites *Orḥot Ḥayim,*[30] who offers another reason to be lenient:

> We may say that those who make their *sukka* inside a house and do not remove the bricks [of the roof] until after the *sekhakh* is placed on the *sukka* – they do not need to shake the *sekhakh* afterward, because of *taaseh velo min haasui,* because removing the bricks and adjusting the beams is the act that validated the *sekhakh* that was placed improperly.[31]

Although R. Elḥanan and *Orḥot Ḥayim* agree practically – the *sukka* described is valid – they fundamentally disagree. R. Elḥanan maintains that placing the *sekhakh* before removing the roof poses no problem whatsoever, while *Orḥot Ḥayim* acknowledges a problem, but views the removing of the bricks as part of the process of placing the *sekhakh,* thereby fulfilling the requirement of *taaseh velo min haasui.*

Apparently, these *Rishonim* disagree as to the nature of the requirement of *taaseh velo min haasui* in the laws of *sukka.* R. Elḥanan must believe that *taaseh velo min haasui* dictates how the *sukka* should be constructed – the *sekhakh* must be placed after the walls in order to provide shade. However, once a valid *sukka* consisting of walls and *sekhakh* is constructed, the *sukka* is valid even if one cannot sit in the *sukka* due to an external factor. The other *Rishonim*, however, believe that whenever a *sukka* is disqualified, even due to external factors, one must repeat the order dictated by the principle of *taaseh velo min haasui*.

Rema rules that one may build a *sukka* under a roof, provided that he removes the bricks of the roof afterward. He adds that one may erect a *sukka* under roofs that are made to open and close, and that they may be closed during the rain and re-opened afterward.[32] Thus, although Rema ruled that one must erect the walls before suspending the *sekhakh*, as we saw above, in this context, he validates a *sukka* built under a roof, and even under a roof that opens and closes. Apparently, the principle of *taaseh velo min haasui* invalidates a *sukka* in which the *sekhakh* is placed in a manner through which it does not function as *sekhakh*. However, when the *sukka* is constructed properly but remains invalid due to an outside factor, the *sukka* is valid.

The *Aḥaronim* disagree regarding the case of a sliding roof. They insist that the *sukka* should be built while the roof is open and that sliding the roof open and shut is not akin to removing the bricks from the roof in order to validate the *sukka*.[33]

THE SANCTITY OF THE *SUKKA*

The Talmud teaches that the wood of the *sukka* is "*assur behanaa*" – it is prohibited to benefit from it.

> R. Sheshet said in the name of R. Akiva: From where do we know that the wood of the *sukka* is forbidden all the seven [days of the festival]? From Scripture, which states, "The Festival of Sukkot, seven days to the Lord," and it was taught: R. Yehuda b. Beteira says: Just as the Name of Heaven rests upon the festival offering (*ḥagiga*), so does it rest upon the *sukka*, since it is said, "The Festival of Sukkot, seven days to the Lord." Just as the festival [offering] is "to the Lord," so is the *sukka* also "to the Lord." (Sukka 9a)

Regarding the nature of this halakha, one must first question the Gemara's comparison of *sukka* to the festival offering (*korban ḥagiga*). Rashi explains that just as the *ḥagiga* is prohibited until after the *haktarat eimurim* (the burning of the parts intended to be offered on the altar), the *sukka* is only prohibited until the conclusion of the festival.[34] Rashi implies that the comparison to the *ḥagiga* does not relate to the type or nature of the *issur,* but rather to its duration.

Alternatively, *Arukh LaNer* implies that the *sukka* has *kedushat haguf* (inherent sanctity), similar to a *korban ḥagiga*. In fact, he explains that had the Gemara not explicitly compared the *sukka* to the *ḥagiga,* one might have naturally equated the *sukka* with *kodshei bedek habayit,* property of the *Mikdash,* which is also holy, but which may be redeemed.[35] Rashba also writes that a *sukka* has *kedushat haguf* for all seven days of the festival. He even suggests that one might distinguish between different *sukkot*. For example, although the *sukkot* of *ganba"k* and *rakba"sh* are valid, they may not have this *kedushat haguf* because they were not built with the intention of being *sukkot*. Rather, they are considered "ordinary *sukkot*" (*sukkot be'alma*).[36]

This discussion was continued by the *Aḥaronim* and led to a number of interesting discussions. For example, exactly what type of "benefit" may one not derive from the *sukka*? *Taz* explains:

> Certainly one should not say that all of the laws which apply to the *ḥagiga* apply to the *sukka,* because if so, we would say that the *sukka* has *kedushat haguf*! Rather, we must say that "And you shall make the Festival of Sukkot for seven days" – that regarding this, the sanctity of the *sukka* should last as long as the festival, **and you should not take from [the *sukka*] for your enjoyment any part which will nullify its *kedusha***; regarding this, they are similar, and no more.[37]

Taz maintains that one may not take from the *sukka* in a manner that will nullify its *kedusha*.

Other *Aḥaronim* disagree. They cite *Tur*'s assertion that one who is exempt from sitting in the *sukka* and yet remains in the *sukka* does not receive reward and is considered to be a fool (*hedyot*).[38] Is it not prohibited to derive benefit from a *sukka* if not for the sake of the mitzva?

R. Raphael Yom Tov Lipman Halperin (Lithuania, 1816–1879) grapples with this question in his responsa *Oneg Yom Tov,* concluding that "*lo nitna Torah lemalakhei hasharet*" [39] – the Torah was not given to celestial angels, and therefore one is not expected to get up and immediately leave the *sukka* once it begins to rain. Fundamentally, however, one should not derive benefit from the *sukka* when not fulfilling the mitzva.[40] Some note that when it rains, the *sukka* may not even be considered to be a *sukka,*[41] as we discuss in chapter 24, and this question would therefore not be relevant. According to *Taz,* the *sukka* is not comparable to other "*issurei hanaa*" from which one may not derive any benefit; one may simply not nullify the *sukka*'s *kedusha.* The *Mishna Berura* rules in accordance with *Taz.*[42]

Rambam applies this prohibition to both the *sekhakh* and the walls of the *sukka.*[43] Tosafot cite Rabbeinu Tam, who claims that, *mideoraita,* the prohibition only applies to the minimum area necessary to validate the *sukka,* but *miderabbanan,* the prohibition applies to the entire *sukka.*[44] Rosh writes that this prohibition applies only to the *sekhakh.*[45] The *Shulḥan Arukh* rules in accordance with Rambam.[46] Rema writes that even if the *sukka* falls, one may not derive benefit from it.[47] The *Aḥaronim* discuss when and whether one may take down a *sukka* on Ḥol HaMo'ed. Some permit taking down a *sukka* in order to erect it elsewhere, certainly if the *sukka* is portable and meant to be built, taken apart, and built again.

The Gemara teaches that in addition to the *sukka* itself, one should not benefit from the *noy sukka* during Sukkot:

> If he covered it according to the rule, and adorned it with embroidered hangings and sheets, and hung therein nuts, almonds, peaches, pomegranates, bunches of grapes, wreaths of ears of corn, [phials of] wine, oil or fine flour, *it is forbidden to make use of them.* (Sukka 10a)

The Talmud discusses this halakha in the context of the prohibition of *bizui mitzva,* treating mitzvot with disrespect, and this law is of rabbinic origin.[48] The *Shulḥan Arukh* rules that one should not benefit from the *noy sukka* even after they fall.[49] Although the Talmud discusses the possibility of making a condition (*tenai*) to prevent the laws of *bizui mitzva* from applying to *noy sukka,* Rema notes that we are not accustomed to making this *tenai* nowadays.[50] Although one should not remove *noy sukka* during the festival in a disrespectful manner, one may certainly remove *noy sukka* if one fears that they will be stolen or ruined by rain.

CHAPTER 22

The Mitzva to Dwell in a Sukka

THE TORAH ISSUES a simple command regarding the Festival of Sukkot: "And you shall dwell in *sukkot* for seven days" (Lev. 23:42). Similarly, Rambam writes in his *Sefer HaMitzvot*, "And He commanded us to dwell in the *sukka* for seven days during the festival."[1] How does one fulfill this broad commandment of "dwelling" in the *sukka*? The Gemara describes the ideal fulfillment of this mitzva:

> "You shall dwell" – similar to [normal] manner of dwelling (*teshvu ke'ein taduru*). From here [the sages] said: Throughout the seven days [of the festival], the *sukka* must be regarded as one's principal abode, and the house merely a temporary residence. How so? If a person has pretty dishes, he brings them up to the *sukka*; attractive linens, he brings them up to the *sukka*; he eats, drinks, and enjoys himself in the *sukka*, and he studies in the *sukka*. (Sukka 28b)

In this chapter, we will discuss the nature and scope of this mitzva. What does dwelling in the *sukka* entail? Furthermore, what is the difference between the obligation on the first night of Sukkot and that of the rest of the festival?

TESHVU KE'EIN TADURU: HOW MANY MEALS MUST ONE EAT IN THE *SUKKA*?

In determining the nature of the mitzva to dwell in the *sukka*, we must first distinguish between the first night and the rest of the festival. The

Gemara cites a debate between R. Eliezer and the sages regarding how often one must eat in the *sukka*:

> R. Eliezer says: A person is obligated to eat fourteen meals in the *sukka*, one during the day and one at night. And the sages say: There is no defined number, except for the first night of the festival.... What is R. Eliezer's reasoning? "You shall dwell" – similar to [normal] manner of dwelling (*teshvu ke'ein taduru*). Just as [during] residence [in the house], [one eats] one [meal] during the day and one at night, so too in the *sukka* – one [meal] during the day and one at night. (Sukka 27a)

R. Eliezer maintains that the principle "*teshvu ke'ein taduru*" dictates that one must eat fourteen meals in the *sukka*, two meals each day of the festival. The Gemara then cites the position of the sages, who disagree:

> And the sages: "Like residence [in the house]" – Just as [during] residence [in the house], if he wishes, he eats, and if he wishes, he does not eat, so too in the *sukka* – if he wishes, he eats, and if he wishes, he does not eat. If so, even the first night of the festival as well! R. Yoḥanan said in the name of R. Shimon b. Yehotzadak: It is stated here, "the fifteenth," and it is stated regarding the festival of unleavened bread, "the fifteenth." Just as in that case, the first night is obligatory and from then on, it is optional, so too here – the first night is obligatory and from then on, it is optional. And from where do we learn the law there? The verse states, "At evening shall you eat unleavened bread" [Ex. 12:18] – Scripture established it as an obligation.

The sages disagree with R. Eliezer on two points. First, they maintain that eating in a *sukka* is obligatory only on the first night of the festival. Second, they apparently interpret the principle of *teshvu ke'ein taduru* differently than R. Eliezer.

The sages derive that one must eat in the *sukka* on the first night through a *gezeira shava*, a textual comparison between the first night of Pesaḥ, which occurs on the fifteenth of Nissan and upon which one is obligated to eat *matza*, and the first night of Sukkot, which is celebrated on the fifteenth of Tishrei. What do we learn from this comparison to the first night of Pesaḥ? We might suggest that just as one must fulfill the mitzva of *matza* – that is, eating *matza* – on the first night of the seven days of Pesaḥ, one similarly must fulfill the mitzva of *sukka* – dwelling in a *sukka* – on the first night of the seven days of Sukkot. Alternatively, the Gemara may be deriving something much more specific: Just as one must fulfill a mitzva of "eating" on the first night of Pesaḥ, so too, one must fulfill a mitzva of "eating" on the first night of Sukkot.

These different understandings are reflected in the views of the *Rishonim*. Ran, for example, questions how much bread one must eat in the *sukka* on the first night of Sukkot:

> And regarding the first day of the Festival of Sukkot, we also learn that one is obligated to eat an amount that obligates eating in the *sukka*. For based on the law of Yom Tov, it would suffice to eat the quantity of an egg in a casual manner (*arai*) outside the *sukka*. And we learn also from the Festival of Pesaḥ that one is obligated to eat an amount that obligates eating in the *sukka*. It seems, therefore, that one is obligated to eat more than the amount of an egg.[2]

Generally, as we will see below, only one who eats an amount slightly more than a *kebeitza* (the volume of an egg) must eat in the *sukka*. Ran suggests that since the *gezeira shava* teaches that one must fulfill the mitzva of *sukka* on the first evening, one must eat an amount that obligates him to eat in the *sukka* – more than a *kebeitza*. Ran then writes:

> But there are those who say as follows: Since we learn from the Festival of Pesaḥ, we learn entirely from it. Just as in that case the size of an olive [is all that is necessary for fulfilling the mitzva], so too, here, the size of an olive [is all that is required]. And even though on the other days of the Festival [of Sukkot] the size of an olive is regarded as haphazard [eating] and it may be eaten outside a *sukka*, nevertheless on the first night, since Scripture established it as an obligation to eat in the *sukka*, it is regarded as a regular meal.

Ran cites those who believe that one must only eat an amount equivalent to the size of a *kezayit* (an olive) in the *sukka* on the first night, similar to the amount of *matza* that one must eat on Pesaḥ. He implies that the *gezeira shava* may actually define the parameters of dwelling in the *sukka* on the first night; the eating in the *sukka* parallels the eating of the *matza*. Indeed, *Tur* explains that just as one must only eat a *kezayit* of bread in the *sukka* on the first night in order to fulfill his obligation, one may not eat a *kezayit* of bread outside of the *sukka*:

> Once he eats in [the *sukka*] grain in the amount of an olive, he has fulfilled his obligation, even though the measure regarding [the prohibition] of eating outside a *sukka* is the amount of an egg. The first night is different, because the obligation is greater, so that even if he wishes to eat only the amount of an olive, he is forbidden to do so outside the *sukka*. Therefore, he fulfills therewith also the obligation of *sukka*.[3]

According to *Tur,* the *gezeira shava* teaches us not only that the mitzva on the first night is fundamentally a mitzva of "*akhila*" (eating), but that this, itself, defines the amount that it is necessary to eat; a *kezayit* of bread is considered an *akhilat keva,* which must not be done outside of the *sukka*.

After citing the view obligating one to eat a *kezayit* of bread in the *sukka* on the first night, Ritva records:

> However, I heard in the name of one of the great scholars of the generation in France, who would obligate one to sleep in the *sukka* on the first night of Sukkot, even in the rain ... as on the first night, the Scripture established that it is obligatory, from the *gezeira shava* which equates the fifteenth [of Nissan to the] fifteenth from *Ḥag HaMatzot*.[4]

Clearly, this stringency implies that the Torah mandated "dwelling" in one's *sukka* on the first night; because "dwelling" is demanded on the first night of Sukkot, just like eating *matza* is required on the first day of Pesaḥ, the exemption of "falling rain" does not apply.The *Shulḥan Arukh* rules that one should eat a *kezayit* of bread in the *sukka* on the first night of Sukkot.[5] The *Mishna Berura,* however, writes that it is "proper" to eat more than a *kebeitza,* in order to fulfill the view of those who are strict regarding this matter.[6]

The *Rishonim* raise other questions that may relate to our issue. For example, the Gemara concludes (Sukka 27a) (and the *Shulḥan Arukh* codifies[7]) that one must sit in a *sukka* when eating a meal of "*minei targima,*" either a cooked grain dish or meat and fish. May one fulfill his obligation by eating such foods in the *sukka* on the first night of

Sukkot, or is only a bread-based meal acceptable? Tosafot[8] maintain that this question is posed by the Talmud Yerushalmi (Y. Sukka 2:7). As we noted, the *Shulḥan Arukh* rules that one must eat a *kezayit* of "*pat*" (bread), but the *Aḥaronim* discuss whether one may even eat a *kezayit* of baked grain products upon which "*borei minei mezonot*" is recited.[9] The *Mishna Berura* rules that one must eat a *kezayit* of actual bread.[10] It seems that the *posekim* debate whether *minei targima* constitute a "meal," and thus can fulfill the obligation, or whether the meal on the first night of Sukkot must be similar to that of the first night of Pesaḥ, and thus entails eating bread.

The *Rishonim* and *Aḥaronim* also discuss whether some of the laws specific to Pesaḥ should apply to the first night of Sukkot as well. Rabbeinu Peretz,[11] for example, is cited by *Hagahot Asheri*[12] as insisting that based upon the *gezeira shava,* one should not eat until it is completely dark, as is the practice on Pesaḥ. Similarly, R. Yaakov b. Yehuda Weil (Germany, fifteenth century) cites his teacher, Maharil, as ruling that one should eat the *kezayit* of bread on the first night of Sukkot before midnight; this is similar to the *matza,* which must be eaten before midnight on the first night of Pesaḥ. Rema cites both of these views.[13]

The *Magen Avraham* discusses whether one may recite the Kiddush of the first night of Sukkot before dark. He first argues that theoretically, even if we are stringent and rule that one must eat after dark, as on Pesaḥ, we should still sanction making Kiddush before dark, and then reciting the blessing of *leishev basukka* and eating a *kezayit* of bread in the *sukka* after dark. He concludes, however, that since it is customary to recite the *Sheheḥeyanu* said with the Kiddush after the blessing of *leishev basukka,* the *Sheheḥeyanu* is apparently said upon the performance of the mitzva of dwelling in the *sukka,* and not only upon the building of the *sukka* and the festival itself. Therefore, one should not even recite Kiddush until dark, when one may properly fulfill the mitzva of *sukka* on the first night.[14] Some suggest that *Taz* does not maintain that Kiddush must be recited after dark.[15] *Biur Halakha* proposes that Rema maintains that outside of Israel, one may eat during *bein hashemashot* on the second night.[16]

Similarly, R. Yosef Teomim writes in his *Peri Megadim* commentary to the *Shulḥan Arukh* that due to the *gezeira shava* comparing the first night of Sukkot and the first night of Pesaḥ, one should not eat *ḥallot* made from fruit juice, so that it will be similar to the *leḥem oni* ("poor man's bread") eaten on Pesaḥ.[17] Many *Aḥaronim* reject this extreme application of the *gezeira shava.*

In addition, the Yerushalmi questions whether one should refrain from eating on the day before Sukkot so as to enter the festival hungry, just as one should refrain from eating on the day before Pesaḥ in order to fulfill the mitzva of *matza* while hungry (Y. Sukka 2:7). Tosafot[18] and Rosh[19] cite this Yerushalmi, and the *Or Zarua* writes that one should act accordingly.[20] Maharil adds that one should not eat from the sixth hour onward on Erev Sukkot, similar to Erev Pesaḥ.[21] *Leket Yosher* relates that his teacher, *Terumat HaDeshen,* would not even sleep in the *sukka* on Erev Sukkot in order to ensure that he still desired sleeping in the *sukka* that evening![22]

Rema cites Maharil's opinion in his commentary to *Tur,* the *Darkhei Moshe,* concluding, "This seems to me to be a stringency without reason." In his comments to the *Shluḥan Arukh* (Rema), however, he writes that one should not eat during the day before Sukkot from noon onward. Some *Aḥaronim* rule that one need only refrain from eating bread from the tenth hour onward,[23] as we learn regarding Pesaḥ.[24]

Finally, the *Rishonim* discuss whether the exemptions from the requirement to sit in a *sukka,* such as *mitzta'er,* apply on the first night of Sukkot as well. Rashba writes that the exemptions derived from the principle of *teshvu ke'ein taduru* apply on the first night as well, and in the event of rain, one is exempt from sitting in the *sukka.*[25] Ran, however, disagrees (Sukka 12b). As we noted previously, Ran (and Ritva, as cited above regarding sleeping in the *sukka*) maintains that the mitzva to dwell in the *sukka* on the first night is absolute and not subject to the exemptions derived from *teshvu ke'ein taduru.*

As we discussed previously, not only should one have in mind to fulfill the mitzva of *sukka* while eating bread the first night,[26] he should also keep in mind the reasons for the mitzva of *sukka* – the booths the Jewish people built for themselves in the desert, and the *ananei hakavod.*[27]

THE MITZVA OF DWELLING IN THE *SUKKA* AFTER THE FIRST NIGHT

As mentioned above, not only do the sages disagree as to whether one must eat fourteen meals or only one meal in the *sukka,* they also seem to understand the principle of *teshvu ke'ein taduru* differently:

> And the sages: Like residence [in the house]. Just as [during] residence [in the house] – if he wishes, he eats, and if he wishes, he does not eat, so too in the *sukka* – if he wishes, he eats, and if he wishes, he does not eat.... Just as there [Pesaḥ] – [eating *matza* on] the first night is obligatory, and from then on it is optional, so too here – the first night is obligatory, from then on it is optional.

The Gemara implies that it is only obligatory to eat in the *sukka* on the first night of Sukkot. Just as there is no specific mitzva to eat *matza* after the first night of Pesaḥ, there is no inherent mitzva to enter a *sukka* during remaining days of the festival unless one wishes to eat (an *akhilat keva*) or sleep (a *sheinat arai*). What is the meaning of the "optional" nature of this mitzva?

In general, we can distinguish between different types of mitzvot. There are some mitzvot that a person is under no obligation to fulfill unless he chooses to engage in a specific activity. For example, if one wishes to wear a four-cornered garment, he must attach *tzitzit* to the corners. This type of mitzva is often referred to as a "*mitzva kiyumit.*" Alternatively, there are mitzvot that one must perform in all circumstances, such as *tefillin.* This type of mitzva is often referred to as a "*mitzva ḥiyuvit.*" The *Minḥat Ḥinukh* explains:

> There are two kinds of positive precepts. One is an obligation upon every man of Israel, such as *tefillin,* etrog, and the eating of *matza.* Such a mitzva – if a person fulfills it, he does the will of the Creator, blessed and exalted be He, because this is what the King, blessed be He, decreed. And if he neglects the mitzva and fails to don *tefillin* or take a lulav, he nullifies the mitzva and acts in opposition to His will, blessed be He, and he will surely be punished. And there are mitzvot that one is not obligated to perform, like *tzitzit,* for the Torah did not obligate a person to wear a four-cornered garment, and if he so desires, he may go about without a four-cornered garment, and this is not against the

> will of the Creator, blessed be He. If, however, he brings himself to obligation, intentionally wearing a four-cornered garment in order to fulfill the mitzva of *tzitzit,* this is the good and righteous path. The rule is that if he fulfills this mitzva, he does the will of the Creator, blessed be He, but if he fails to fulfill the mitzva, he does not violate His will, but merely does not fulfill the mitzva.

Regarding the mitzva of dwelling in the *sukka,* he continues:

> So too, regarding this mitzva, namely *sukka,* there are two parts to the mitzva. That is to say, on the first night of Sukkot, there is a positive precept to eat the measure of an olive in a *sukka,* and a person is obligated to look for a *sukka.* It does not help that he does not want to eat, because he is obligated to eat, as with *matza* or *tefillin.* And if he fails to fulfill the positive precept on the first night, he acts against God's will, blessed be His name. But on the rest of the nights and days, if he does not want [to eat], he may abstain from eating and not sit in a *sukka,* and he is bound by no obligation, as with *tzitzit.* If, however, he eats, there is a positive precept to eat in a *sukka* and he fulfills His will, blessed be He, but if he does not eat, there is no obligation to do so.[28]

The *Minḥat Ḥinukh* clearly views the mitzva of *sukka* as an "optional" mitzva after the first night.

Some take this a step further and argue that while the mitzva of *sukka* mandates that one may not eat outside of a *sukka,* it does not dictate that there is any inherent value of sitting in the *sukka.* R. Yosef Engel (1859–1920), for example, suggests in his *Atvan Deoraita*:

> Eating in the *sukka* is not pleasing and desired in itself, for were that the case, it would not be right to leave that eating to the will of the individual, so that it is optional. Perforce, then, the intention of the mitzva lies exclusively in the negation – that when a person eats, he must not eat outside the *sukka,* and eating outside the *sukka* is what is not pleasing. But eating in the *sukka* in itself is not at all pleasing or desired.[29]

Similarly, R. Avraham Borenstein (1838–1910), the Sochachover Rebbe, writes in his *Avnei Nezer*:

> It follows from this that regarding a *sukka,* we can say that the *sukka* permits eating, enjoyment, and sleep.... And this is the implication of our passage

> that likens *sukka* to *matza*, which is optional for all seven days. It is explicit, then, that it is merely forbidden to eat outside the *sukka*, just as it is forbidden to eat *ḥametz*.[30]

The *Avnei Nezer* also maintains that the *sukka* merely permits a forbidden activity; eating in a *sukka* is not a value in and of itself.

This understanding is, of course, extremely difficult in light of the verse that states quite clearly that one should dwell in a *sukka* for seven days. It also seems to contradict the talmudic passage cited above, which describes how one should relate to the *sukka*:

> Throughout the seven days [of the festival], the *sukka* must be regarded as one's principal abode, and the house merely a temporary residence. How so? If a person has pretty dishes, he brings them up to the *sukka*; attractive linens, he brings them up to the *sukka*; he eats, drinks, and enjoys himself in the *sukka*, and he studies in the *sukka*. (Sukka 28b)

This passage implies that not only must one refrain from eating outside of the *sukka*, one should eat, drink, enjoy himself, and study Torah in the *sukka*. Accordingly, R. Akiva Eiger rejects the approach that attributes no value to eating in the *sukka* during the rest of Sukkot. He explains that one who eats outside of the *sukka* does not violate a commandment, but rather does not fulfill the positive commandment of dwelling in a *sukka*.[31] We thus might formulate our understanding of the "optional" mitzva differently: Whenever one enters a *sukka*, he fulfills the biblical commandment of "And you shall sit in *sukkot*." Furthermore, activities that imply permanence, such as eating meals and sleeping, which are generally done within one's home, must be done in the *sukka*; one who does not eat a meal or sleep in a *sukka* does not fulfill the positive commandment of dwelling in the *sukka*. However, *teshvu ke'ein taduru* dictates that just as activities that one normally does inside of a house must be done inside a *sukka*, activities normally performed outside of one's house may be done outside of the *sukka*.

Some suggest an even more ambitious approach. R. Alexander Susskind of Grodno (d. 1793), for example, writes in his *Sefer Yesod VeShoresh HaAvoda*:

> "And you shall dwell in *sukkot* for seven days" – like your residence. He commanded us, the holy nation, with a positive commandment that every man should eat and drink and enjoy in the *sukka*, and all of these activities one is obligated, through a positive commandment from the Torah, to do in the *sukka*, and not in the house within which he lives throughout the year.... Therefore, one is obligated to be careful not to leave the *sukka* for one's house at all, unless it is truly necessary – for example, if he needs to leave to his house in order to bring a drink.... In that case, he should not stay in the house longer than necessary.[32]

Similarly, R. Engel, cited above, rejects his initial assumption, and concludes:

> The position itself of the aforementioned *Minḥat Ḥinukh*, who writes that *sukka* is exclusively a negative mitzva – it seems, in my humble opinion, that this is not true. Rather, *sukka* is a positive and independent mitzva, for the Torah wants us to live for seven days in a *sukka*, just as we live all year long in the house. As they said, "You shall dwell" – similar to [normal] residence. The reason that if a person wishes, he does not have to eat or sit in a *sukka* is that this is the essence of residence; occasionally, a person goes out or to the market, and only when he wishes to eat, drink, or sleep does he eat, drink, and sleep exclusively in his house. This is the idea of residence in his house, and thus, the Torah wanted us to live for seven days in a *sukka*. Thus, when the Torah demands residence in a *sukka*, it is asking for a desired and positive thing.

R. Engel insists that the positive commandment of dwelling in the *sukka* entails transforming one's *sukka* into one's home and living there for the duration of the festival. However, unlike drinking, studying, and other activities, eating and sleeping are such demonstrative expressions of dwelling that it is actually prohibited to perform these specific activities outside of the *sukka*.

These different understandings of the mitzva of dwelling in the *sukka* may influence how we understand the following passage:

> But if he wishes to be strict with himself, he may do so, and it does not constitute presumption (*yuhara*). And so it also happened that they brought cooked food to R. Yoḥanan b. Zakkai to taste, and two dates and a pail of water to

> R. Gamliel, and they said, "Bring them up to the *sukka*," but when they gave to R. Tzadok food less than the bulk of an egg, he took it in a towel, ate it outside the *sukka*, and did not say the benediction after it. (Sukka 26b–27a)

Rambam cites this halakha:

> It is permissible to drink water and eat fruit outside the *sukka*. However, a person who follows the stringency of not drinking even water outside the *sukka* **is worthy of praise.**[33]

This Gemara teaches that eating an *akhilat arai* in the *sukka* is not to be considered an act of *yuhara*. Based upon the approaches suggested above, we may understand this passage in different ways. One might view eating a snack in the *sukka* as a fulfillment of a mitzva (*mitzva kiyumit*), even though one is technically exempt from doing so; it is therefore not considered to be an unnecessary or presumptuous stringency. However, one might also view eating a snack in a *sukka* as a fulfillment of one's overall obligation to transform the *sukka* into one's permanent residence; therefore, one is encouraged, if not obligated, to eat all foods in the *sukka* whenever possible.

THE BLESSING OF *LEISHEV BASUKKA*

The Gemara teaches that "upon entering [the *sukka*] to dwell in it, one says, '*asher kiddeshanu… leishev basukka*'" (Sukka 45b). The *Rishonim* discuss two central issues regarding this blessing: When should one recite this *berakha*, and why is this *berakha* recited for the duration of the entire Festival of Sukkot, while the blessing over the *matza* is only recited on the first night? The *Rishonim* debate when one should recite this blessing. Rif, citing the Gemara, simply writes, "Upon entering [the *sukka*] to dwell in it, one says, '*asher kiddeshanu… leishev basukka*.'"[34] Rambam concurs, although he implies that one should recite the blessing before sitting down:

> Every time he enters to sit in the *sukka* all seven days, before he sits down, he recites the blessing, "Who has sanctified us with His commandments

> and commanded us to sit in a *sukka*." On the first night of the festival, he recites a blessing over the *sukka*, and afterward, he recites a blessing over the season [*Sheheḥeyanu*], and he arranges the blessings over a cup [of wine]. Thus, he recites the Kiddush standing, recites the blessing "to sit in a *sukka*," sits down, and afterward recites the blessing over the season. This was the custom of my rabbis and the rabbis of Spain, to stand for the recitation of Kiddush on the first night of Sukkot, as we have explained.[35]

Rambam rules that one should recite the blessing "prior to its performance," before sitting down. Although some question Rambam's focus on "sitting,"[36] Rambam most likely believes that "sitting" both reflects the formulation of the *berakha* and constitutes a demonstrative performance of the mitzva.

Rabbeinu Tam disagrees and rules that one should only recite the blessing of *leishev basukka* before eating in the *sukka*, not upon simply entering. Regarding sleeping, Rosh records the following:

> Ri asked Rabbeinu Tam whether one must recite a blessing over sleeping in the *sukka*, for the laws governing sleeping are more stringent than those governing eating, for one is permitted to snack outside the *sukka*, whereas napping outside the *sukka* is forbidden.[37]

Ri suggests that "one does not recite a blessing over sleeping [in the *sukka*] because perhaps he will be unable to fall asleep." In other words, one should theoretically recite the blessing before going to sleep, but we do not do so in practice, lest one fail to fall asleep. Rabbeinu Tam, apparently not troubled with this concern, explains that "[whatever elements of] the mitzva of *sukka* that a person fulfills between one meal and the next – for example, sleep, enjoyment, and study – the blessing 'to dwell in a *sukka*' that he had recited over the meal exempts him from reciting [another] blessing over them."

The position of Rabbeinu Tam remains somewhat enigmatic. Does Rabbeinu Tam believe that the blessing of *leishev basukka* was only instituted to be recited when eating, or does he simply think that it is more appropriate to say the blessing before eating, the primary expression of "dwelling"? Furthermore, the *Shulḥan Arukh* concludes, "It is customary to recite a blessing over the *sukka* only at the time of eating."[38] Does the *Shulḥan Arukh* mean that it is customary to follow the opinion of Rabbeinu Tam or that it is customary to prefer reciting the blessing before one eats?

Taz writes that one who does not intend to eat bread during the day, and certainly one who is fasting, should recite the blessing of *leishev basukka* upon entering the *sukka*.[39] *Taz* apparently maintains that although it may be customary to recite the blessing before eating, the basic halakha remains that one who enters the *sukka* should recite the blessing. The *Mishna Berura*[40] cites *Taz* and quotes *Ḥayei Adam*, who writes, "When one leaves the *sukka* completely after eating and then returns to the *sukka*, but will not eat until the evening… in this case all would agree that he should recite the blessing."[41] According to this interpretation, Rabbeinu Tam only intended to restrict the blessing to eating *lekhatḥila*, as eating is the most demonstrative form of dwelling. However, one who does not intend to eat should certainly still recite the blessing.

R. Mordechai Karmi disagrees in his commentary to the *Shulḥan Arukh*, the *Maamar Mordekhai*.[42] He explains that Rabbeinu Tam maintains that the blessing was only instituted upon eating, and one *may not* recite the blessing over any other activities. When the *Shulḥan Arukh* writes, "It is customary to," it means that it is customary to follow the opinion of Rabbeinu Tam, who held that the blessing *must* be recited upon eating.

Due to this debate, it is customary to eat an item in the *sukka* upon which one recites the blessing "*borei minei mezonot*" in order to be able to recite *leishev basukka* according to all opinions.[43] Some *Aḥaronim*, however, including R. Shlomo Zalman Auerbach[44] and *Ḥazon Ish*,[45] were accustomed to recite the blessing of *leishev basukka* upon sitting or sleeping in the *sukka*, even without eating.

Although the *Shulḥan Arukh* concludes that it is customary to recite *leishev basukka* only upon eating in the *sukka*, Ritva brings two other opinions regarding the proper time to recite the blessing, which are worth noting even though they are not accepted as the halakha.[46] First, he cites the *Ḥakhmei Tzarfat* (Scholars of France), who assert that one should recite the blessing upon performing any of the activities mentioned in the Gemara, such as eating, drinking, learning, etc. Apparently, they maintain that the blessing was instituted upon any obvious act of dwelling, somewhat similar to the view of Rabbeinu Tam. Ritva also relates that some maintain that one should recite the blessing once each day upon entering the *sukka*.

Rosh records that Maharam of Rothenburg would say *leishev basukka* before reciting the blessing on the bread.[47] Me'iri attributes this practice to fear of interrupting between the blessing over the food and the act of eating.[48] Rosh explains this custom in accordance with the view that one should really say *leishev basukka* immediately upon entering the *sukka*. The *Shulḥan Arukh* rules in accordance with the majority of *Rishonim*, who maintain that it is customary to recite the blessing of *leishev basukka* after saying *hamotzi* (or *borei minei mezonot*) and before eating.[49]

THE DIFFERENCE BETWEEN *MATZA* AND *SUKKA*

The Talmud records a difference of opinion regarding the blessing of *leishev basukka*:

> R. Yehuda citing Shmuel stated: [The blessing is recited over] the lulav for seven [days] and over the *sukka* only on one day. What is the reason? In the case of the lulav, where the nights form breaks between the days, each day involves a separate commandment. In the case of the *sukka*, where the nights do not form breaks between the days, all seven days are regarded as one long day. Rabba b. Bar Ḥana, however, stated in the name of R. Yoḥanan: [The blessing is recited over] the *sukka* for seven days and over the lulav but one day. What is the reason? For the *sukka*, which is a biblical commandment, [the benediction must be recited all the] seven [days]; in the case of the lulav, which is but a rabbinical enactment [in our day], [a blessing on] one day suffices. When Ravin came, he stated in the name of R. Yoḥanan: [The blessing is recited over] the one as well as the other [all] seven [days]. R. Yosef ruled: Hold fast to the decision of Rabba b. Bar Ḥana, since with regard to *sukka*, all the *Amora'im* adopt the same position as he. (Sukka 45b)

While R. Yehuda believes that the blessing of *leishev basukka* should be recited only on the first day of Sukkot, the Gemara concludes, in accordance with Rabba b. Bar Ḥana, that one should recite the *berakha* on all seven days.

This, of course, must be understood in light of the gemara that we studied above, which teaches that "Just as there [Pesaḥ] the first night is obligatory and from then on it is optional, so too here [Sukkot] the first night is obligatory and from then on it is optional" (Sukka 27a). The passage equates eating *matza* and dwelling in the *sukka*; although the mitzva of the first night is obligatory, afterward it is optional.

We discussed above how to understand the mitzva of *sukka* in light of this passage. Is sitting in the *sukka* merely a means of avoiding eating a meal outside of the *sukka*? Does eating in the *sukka* constitute a *mitzva kiyumit*? Or is one truly obligated to carry out most of one's daily activities in the *sukka*? We must now discuss how this question affects our understanding of the halakha that demands that one recite the blessing of *leishev basukka* throughout the week. If the mitzva of *matza* parallels that of *sukka*, why do we not recite the *berakha* of *al akhilat matza* upon eating *matza* throughout Pesaḥ? Why should the blessing recited upon sitting in the *sukka* be recited all seven days of the festival, while the blessing over *matza* is only recited on the first night of Pesaḥ?

Some *Rishonim* explain that while there is no mitzva to eat *matza* after the first night, one who sits in the *sukka* fulfills a mitzva. Maharil explains that one who eats *matza* does not fulfill a mitzva, but "regarding *sukka*, every moment that one sits [in a *sukka*], he fulfills 'and you shall dwell in *sukkot* for seven days.'"[50] One therefore recites a blessing over dwelling in the *sukka* for all seven days, and not before eating *matza* on the other days of the holiday.[51] A number of Provençal *Rishonim* cite R. Shmuel Shakili:

> Rabbeinu Shmuel b. Shlomo ztz"l answered that *matza* is different, because eating it on the other days is not for the sake of the mitzva of *matza*, but for the sake of his body to satisfy his hunger, because he cannot fill himself with *ḥametz*. It is like someone who fills himself with the meat of a kosher animal because he is unable to eat the meat of a non-kosher animal, but does not recite a blessing, "Who has sanctified us with His commandments and commanded us to eat kosher meat." But a person certainly does not dwell in

> a *sukka* for the sake of his body or to satisfy his hunger, but only to fulfill the mitzva, and therefore he must recite a blessing.[52]

Matza after the first night is viewed as no more than food consumed to satiate one's hunger, while we view dwelling in a *sukka* as a mitzva every night of Sukkot. Since dwelling in the *sukka* during the latter days of Sukkot constitutes a *mitzva kiyumit,* while eating *matza* on the latter days of Pesaḥ does not, a blessing is recited upon dwelling in the *sukka* throughout the holiday, while no blessing is recited upon eating *matza*.

Others insist that even one who eats *matza* after the first night does, in fact, fulfill a mitzva. Ibn Ezra, for example, insists that the "*peshat*" of the verse, "And you shall eat *matzot* for seven days," implies that there is an obligation to eat *matzot* for the entire festival.[53] Although *Ḥizkuni* (thirteenth century) does not suggest that one is "obligated" to eat *matzot* for the entire festival, he explains that "if one ate *matzot* for all seven days, he fulfills this verse."[54]

Possible support for this position can be found in the view of the *Geonim,*[55] who explain that one need not lay *tefillin* during Ḥol HaMo'ed because Ḥol H-Mo'ed is itself an "*ot*"; one need not don the "*ot*" of *tefillin* because we dwell in the *sukka* and eat *matza* on Ḥol HaMo'ed.[56] Reportedly, Gra,[57] as well as Ḥatam Sofer,[58] explained that *matza* is viewed as a "*reshut*" on the later days in relation to the obligation of the first night, but it is certainly still a biblical mitzva. The *Arukh HaShulḥan* concludes:

> And you should know that I received the tradition that even though there is no obligation of *matza* except for the first night, there is a mitzva to eat *matza* for all of the days of Pesaḥ, as it says, "For seven days you shall eat *matzot*."[59]

According to this approach, there is a *mitzva kiyumit* to dwell in the sukka throughout Sukkot, as well as one to eat *matza* throughout Pesaḥ. We must thus find another way to distinguish between Sukkot and Pesaḥ to explain why the *berakhot* over the mitzvot are treated differently.

Baal HaMaor, for example, explains:

> It may be answered: Because on the other days [of Pesaḥ], a person can go without eating *matza* and sustain himself on rice and millet and all kinds

> of fruit. This is not the case regarding a *sukka*, for a person cannot go for three days without sleep, and so he must sleep in the *sukka* and enjoy himself there.... This is the reason that we recite a blessing over the *sukka* all seven days, but we do not recite a blessing over *matza* all seven days.[60]

According to Baal HaMaor, since one must, inevitably, dwell in the *sukka* throughout the festival, the Rabbis instituted the blessing of *leishev basukka* for the entire week. *Avnei Nezer* understands that Baal HaMaor must certainly believe that one fulfills a mitzva by eating *matza*, and therefore the distinction between *sukka* and *matza* lies in the inevitability that one will dwell in the *sukka* throughout the week.[61]

Interestingly, even if one views eating *matza* after the first night as a mitzva, one might view dwelling in a *sukka* as a more obligatory one – a mitzva *ḥiyuvit* that one must perform, and it is therefore worthy of a blessing. Ḥatam Sofer writes in his comments to the *Shulḥan Arukh*:

> One is obligated to sit and to live in the *sukka* each day, but eating in the *sukka* [is not obligatory] except for the first night.... But there is an obligation to dwell and to live in the *sukka* for all seven days.[62]

If so, the distinction, according to Ḥatam Sofer, is between a mitzva that one *may* fulfill (*matza*) and a mitzva that one *must* fulfill (*sukka*).

THE DIFFERENCE BETWEEN PESAḤ AND SUKKOT

Our discussion regarding the mitzvot of *sukka* and *matza* leads us to the conclusion that while the focus of Pesaḥ is the first day, Sukkot is more evenly celebrated throughout the seven days. The Talmud elsewhere also seems to arrive at this conclusion. In enumerating the days upon which one says Hallel, the Gemara states that one recites the full Hallel on all of the days of Sukkot, whereas on Pesaḥ, the full Hallel is only recited on the first day. The Gemara explains:

> Why this difference, that on the Sukkot we complete Hallel on all the days, and on the Passover Festival we do not do so on all of its days? The days of Sukkot are differentiated from one another in respect of the sacrifices due

> thereon, whereas the days of Pesaḥ, [the days] are not differentiated from one another in respect of their sacrifices. (Arakhin 10b)

In other words, the *musaf* offering remains the same for the entire week of Pesaḥ, while it changes each day during Sukkot. This daily change somehow generates a new obligation to recite Hallel every day, in contrast to the other festivals, when one full Hallel is sufficient.

This distinction between Pesaḥ and Sukkot may actually be indicated by the Torah itself. The Torah teaches this regarding Pesaḥ: "And on the fifteenth day of this month shall be a feast; seven days shall *matzot* be eaten" (Num. 28:17). Concerning Sukkot, the same section relates:

> And on the fifteenth day of the seventh month you shall have a holy convocation; you shall do no manner of servile work, and you shall keep a feast unto the Lord seven days. (Num. 29:12)

The Festival of Pesaḥ, as described by the Torah, is observed on the night of the fifteenth of Nissan, while *matzot* are eaten for seven days. The Festival of Sukkot, however, is celebrated for seven days. This distinction emerges again in Deuteronomy (16:3, 13) and earlier in Leviticus (23:6, 33–40). In fact, R. Naftali Tzvi Yehuda Berlin explains in his *Haamek Davar* that "*Ḥag HaMatzot*, in the language of the Torah, refers only to the first day, unlike *Ḥag HaSukkot*, which, in the language of the Torah, lasts for seven days."[63]

It seems that one can describe Pesaḥ as having one focal point: the evening of the fifteenth of Nissan. Although the Festival of Pesaḥ is observed for seven days, the remaining days appear as the "wake" of the first day. Sukkot, however, is one long festival of seven days, reflected both in the mitzva of *sukka*, which is observed for the entire week, and the different *korbanot* offered each day, reflecting an additional new day of the festival.

To what can we attribute this distinction? Seemingly, Pesaḥ commemorates a one-time historic event, which occurred and is commemorated on the fifteenth of Nissan. All Pesaḥ rituals are performed on the night of the fifteenth of Nissan, the night that the Jewish people left Egypt. Sukkot, however, commemorates the day-to-day providence bestowed upon the Jewish people during their travels in the desert[64] and the continued divine protection of the Jewish people, who leave their secure homes and live outside, exposed to the elements. Therefore, the entire festival, day after day, is observed as if each day is another new day of the festival.

CHAPTER 23

Eating, Drinking, and Sleeping in the Sukka

EATING IN THE *SUKKA*: DISTINGUISHING BETWEEN *AKHILAT ARAI* AND *AKHILAT KEVA*

In the previous chapter, we contrasted the mitzva to eat in the *sukka* on the first night of Sukkot with the general mitzva of dwelling in the *sukka* for the remaining days. During the remaining days of Sukkot, while ideally one should transform one's *sukka* into his home, and perform most of his daily activities in the *sukka*, the Gemara specifies which foods one *must* eat in the *sukka* and which foods may be eaten outside.

The Mishna distinguishes between one who eats an "*akhilat keva*," loosely translated as a "meal," and one who eats an "*akhilat arai*," a "snack" (Sukka 25a). The *Rishonim* explain that since one ordinarily eats small quantities or snack food outside of one's home, eating an "*akhilat arai*" outside of the *sukka* does not violate the principle of "*teshvu ke'ein taduru*," which demands that one perform those activities that one ordinarily does in one's home in the *sukka*.[1]

The Gemara's discussion regarding eating outside of the *sukka* relates to two foods: bread and fruits. One who eats a significant quantity of bread must eat in the *sukka*, as the Gemara relates:

> Casual eating and drinking are permitted outside the *sukka*. What constitutes a casual meal? R. Yosef said: [The volume of] two or three eggs. Abaye said to him: But sometimes this suffices for [a whole meal for] a man. Why, then, should this not constitute a set meal? Rather, said Abaye: [A small quantity;] only as much as a student tastes before proceeding to the college assembly. (Sukka 26a)

The *Rishonim* all rule in accordance with Abaye, yet they differ as to the precise amount that constitutes an *akhilat arai*.[2] The *Shulḥan Arukh* rules that a quantity of bread the size of a *kebeitza* (an egg) constitutes an *akhilat arai*;[3] therefore, one may not eat more than a *kebeitza* of bread outside of a *sukka*.[4]

The Gemara elsewhere implies that the *Amora'im* disagree as to whether fruit must be eaten in the *sukka* (Yoma 79b). Rosh understands that even the opinion that requires one to eat fruit in the *sukka* refers to a case in which one bases his meal ("*kove'a*") upon the fruit. Furthermore, he records that Maharam of Rothenburg refrained from eating fruits outside of the *sukka*, in deference to the opinion cited in the Gemara.[5] The *Rishonim*, however, rule in accordance with the view that maintains that fruit does not need to be eaten in the *sukka*.[6] The *Shulḥan Arukh* explicitly permits eating fruit outside of the *sukka*,[7] and Rema writes that even one who bases his meal on fruit may eat outside of the *sukka*.[8]

Aside from bread, the Gemara also implies that other foods, known as "*minei targima*," may constitute an *akhilat keva* (Sukka 27a). Although some *Rishinom* explain that *targima* refers to meat, fish, and even cheese,[9] most understand that *targima* refers to a cooked food made from one of the five grains, upon which one recites the blessing of *borei minei mezonot*.[10] The *Shulḥan Arukh* rules in accordance with those who define *targima* as a dish made from grains: "A cooked dish made from the five grains, if one bases a meal upon it (*kove'a alav seuda*), needs [to be eaten in] a *sukka*."[11] Here, too, the *Aḥaronim* discuss whether everyone who eats *targima* must eat in a *sukka*, or only if one is *kove'a alav seuda*.[12] The *Mishna Berura* records that some rule that one should not recite the blessing of *leishev basukka* unless one eats this cooked dish as a meal, and concludes that when reciting the blessing, one should have in mind the additional time one sits in the *sukka* as well.[13]

The *Aḥaronim* also disagree regarding *pat habaa bekisnin* (baked goods), upon which one recites *borei minei mezonot*. While some insist that their status is similar to bread, and therefore one who eats the volume of a *kebeitza* must eat in the *sukka* and recite the blessing *leishev basukka*, others explain that one should only recite *leishev basukka* if he is *kove'a alav seuda*. The *Mishna Berura* concludes, in accordance with *Shaarei Teshuva*, that although one should theoretically omit the blessing of *leishev basukka* when eating *pat habaa bekisnin* as a snack due to the principle of *safek berakhot lehakel* (one who is in doubt whether to say a certain blessing should omit it), it is customary to say *leishev basukka* on all baked goods.[14]

Although, as mentioned above, we generally assume that *targima* refers to foods cooked from the five grains, R. Yoel Sirkis writes that one should be stringent and not eat meat or cheese outside of a *sukka* when one eats them as a meal.[15] The *Eliya Rabba* concurs.[16] Although *Ḥayei Adam* also writes that one who eats more than a *kebeitza* of meat or fish and bases a meal on them (*kava aleihem*) should eat in the *sukka*,[17] the custom is not to be strict regarding meat, fish, and cheese.

DRINKING IN THE *SUKKA*

The Gemara (Sukka 28b)[18] implies that drinking in the *sukka* constitutes a fulfillment of the mitzva of dwelling in the *sukka*. Furthermore, the Mishna teaches that "casual eating and drinking are permitted outside the *sukka*" (Sukka 25b), implying that *shetiyat keva*, similar to an *akhilat keva*, must be performed in a *sukka*. What, if any, type of drinking must one do in the *sukka*?

Some *Rishonim* maintain that drinking a *revi'it* of wine,[19] sitting down to drink wine with other people,[20] or drinking wine with one's meal are considered to be a *shetiyat keva*. Others maintain that even drinking wine is considered to be a *shetiyat arai*.[21] The *Shulḥan Arukh*, however, rules explicitly that one may drink both water and wine outside of the *sukka*.[22] Rema adds that even if one wishes to be "*kava aleihu*," to drink in a set, formal manner, he may still drink outside of the *sukka*.[23] Many *Aḥaronim*, however, insist that one who drinks wine in a formal manner should do so in the *sukka*.[24]

SLEEPING IN THE *SUKKA*

The Gemara teaches that although one may eat a snack (*akhilat arai*) outside of the *sukka*, one may not nap (*sheinat arai*) outside of the *sukka*:

> Our Rabbis taught: Casual eating is permitted outside the *sukka*, but not casual sleeping. What is the reason? R. Ashi said: We fear lest the person fall into a deep slumber.... Rava said: [In the case of *sukka*, the question of] regularity in sleep does not arise. (Sukka 26a)

While according to R. Ashi, it seems that the prohibition of *sheinat arai* is a rabbinic enactment lest one fall into a deep slumber, Rava simply does not recognize a difference between a *sheinat arai* and a *sheinat keva* – both must take place within the *sukka*. The Talmud Yerushalmi cites a similar debate:

> R. Lazar said: Casual eating is permitted; casual sleeping is prohibited. His colleagues explained that a person may fall into a deep sleep. R. Illa explained that a person may sleep even a bit and that may be sufficient. What is the difference between these two opinions? A person who appointed another [to wake him up]. According to his colleagues, this would be permitted. According to R. Illa, it would be prohibited. (Y. Sukka 2:5)

The Shulḥan Arukh rules in accordance with Rava, that all sleep outside of the sukka is prohibited.[25] Some *Aḥaronim* note that one does not need to avoid dozing off while learning or traveling, since one would not ordinarily go home to sleep in this situation (*teshvu ke'ein taduru*).[26] Interestingly, *Tosefet Maase Rav* records that once, when the Vilna Gaon was imprisoned during Sukkot, "he would run from place to place, he would grab his eyelashes and do all sorts of tricks in order not to fall asleep outside of the *sukka*."[27]

Despite the very clear prohibition of sleeping outside of the *sukka*, many *Rishonim* observed that in their communities, it was not customary for men to sleep in their *sukkot*. The *posekim* bring numerous justifications for this practice. Some *Rishonim* explain that in the regions in which they lived, it was simply too cold to sleep outside.[28] Rema, for example, writes:

> Regarding the contemporary leniency regarding sleep, that people do not sleep in the *sukka* except for those who are careful about mitzvot – some say it is because of the extreme cold, since it is uncomfortable to sleep in cold places.[29]

In his commentary to *Tur*, the *Darkhei Moshe*, Rema claims that although this is probably the source for this practice, "in most of our places, it is not that cold, and they could sleep in the *sukka* with blankets and sheets."[30] Others suggest that one who fears thieves or "non-Jews" may sleep inside.[31] Rema insists that this exception only applies if one is concerned for his physical safety, and not for his material belongings.[32]

These concerns, however, raises another problem. Rema, citing *Yerei'im*,[33] writes:

> If one made [the *sukka*] in a place in which one would be uncomfortable to eat, drink, or sleep or where he cannot perform one of the above acts because of the fear of robbers, one does not fulfill [the mitzva] with that *sukka* at all, even when those actions are not uncomfortable, because it is not similar to living-dwelling [in a house] where one can perform all his needs.[34]

If one cannot sleep in the *sukka* due to the cold weather, or due to fear of robbers, then according to Rema, his *sukka* should be considered invalid, and one may not eat in this *sukka* even during the day!

The *Aḥaronim* offer numerous solutions to this problem, which could conceivably invalidate many *sukkot*. The *Mishna Berura*, for example, offers one:

> In the cold places, one fulfills his obligation with eating even though he is unable to sleep there, since it is impossible [to sleep warmly] anyhow, and also since [a *sukka* in a cold place] is considered fit for sleeping if one has sufficient blankets and sheets.[35]

Since there was no option of building a *sukka* in a warmer place, and one can overcome the cold if one has blankets and sheets, this *sukka* is not considered to be invalid. *Yerei'im* only invalidated a *sukka* that was deliberately built in a place that was dangerous when it could have been built elsewhere.

After suggesting that people do not sleep in their *sukkot* due to the inclement weather, Rema offers another justification:

> It seems to me that because the mitzva is for a man to sleep together with his wife the way he does the rest of the year, and in a situation where that is not possible, since they do not have a private *sukka*, he is exempt.

Since one's dwelling in his *sukka* should be akin to dwelling in his home (*teshvu ke'ein taduru*), in a situation in which a man cannot sleep together with his wife, he is exempt from the mitzva.

The notion that *teshvu ke'ein taduru* also includes living together with one's wife in the *sukka* in a similar fashion to the way he lives with his wife during the year appears in the Gemara itself (Arakhin 13b; Sukka 28b). Some *Aḥaronim* explain that one who must sleep apart from his wife is considered to be a *mitzta'er,* one who is uncomfortable in the *sukka,* and he is therefore exempt.[36] *Taz* suggests that just as those who travel to perform a mitzva are exempt from the *sukka* (Sukka 25a), a man, who is obligated to bring happiness to his wife during the festival, is similarly exempt from the *sukka.* [37] He fulfills this obligation of bringing his wife happinness, *Taz* explains, regardless of whether or not he actually has relations with her. Others restrict such an exemption to one who has relations with his wife, fulfilling the mitzva of "*ona,*" who need not return to the *sukka* afterward.[38]

Despite the various justifications cited above, it is preferable to sleep in one's *sukka* if possible. This is certainly true in Israel, where the weather is more conducive to sleeping outside.

SOCIALIZING AND PLAYING IN THE *SUKKA*

In addition to eating, drinking, and sleeping, the Gemara enumerates other activities that should preferably be performed in the *sukka*:

> From what our Rabbis have taught: "You shall dwell" implies – in the same manner as you ordinarily live. Hence they said: All the seven days one

> should make his *sukka* his permanent abode, and his house his temporary abode. In what manner? If he has beautiful vessels, he should bring them up into the *sukka*; beautiful divans, he should bring them up into the *sukka*; he should eat and drink and pass his leisure (*metayel*) in the *sukka*; he should also engage in profound study in the *sukka*. (Sukka 28b)

The *Rishonim* note that one should perform most of his activities in the *sukka*. For example, *Darkhei Moshe* cites Maharil, who rules that "if one wishes to discuss matters with his friend, they should enter the *sukka*." He also quotes Mahari Weil, who writes that "one who wishes to play with blocks or similar [games] should play in the *sukka*."[39]

CHAPTER 24

Those Who are Exempt from the Mitzva of Sukka

In the previous chapter, we learned that although one should ideally transform his *sukka* into his home, spending time and performing various activities in the *sukka*, the technical definition of the obligation is that one is not permitted to eat more than a *kebeitza* of grain products – an "*akhilat keva*" – outside of the *sukka*. In addition, one may not sleep, even for a short time (a *sheinat arai*), outside of the *sukka*.

The Gemara presents numerous scenarios in which one is not required to eat or sleep in the *sukka*. Some of these exemptions are particular to the laws of dwelling in the *sukka* and emerge from the principle of "*teshvu ke'ein taduru*" – one must dwell in the *sukka* in a manner similar to which one dwells in his home. Another type of exemption may be described as external, or even universal: "*Haosek bemitzva patur min hamitzva*" – one who is engaged in the performance of one mitzva is exempt from another. In this chapter, we will study these exemptions from the mitzva of *sukka*.

TESHVU KE'EIN TADURU: THE EXEMPTION OF TRAVELERS

The Talmud teaches that *holkhei derakhim*, travelers, are exempt from the mitzva of *sukka*:

> Our Rabbis taught: Day travelers are free from the obligation of *sukka* by day, but are bound to it at night. Night travelers are free from the obligation of *sukka* at night, but are bound to it by day. Travelers by day and night are free from the obligation both day and night. (Sukka 26a)

Rashi explains:

> It says, "You shall dwell in *sukkot*" – like the dwelling in one's house (*teshvu ke'ein taduru*). Just as during the year one does not refrain from traveling for business purposes, also during the days of the festival that are not Yom Tov, the Torah did not require that one refrain [from traveling].[1]

According to Rashi, this exemption emerges from the basic obligation of *sukka* – one must live in his *sukka* as he would live in his own home. Normally, one might leave his home in order to travel, and he may similarly leave his home during Sukkot, even if he will not be able to sit in a *sukka* during his travels. Rashba also questions how one can be exempt from the biblical obligation of *sukka* in order engage in noncompulsory activities, such as traveling. Like Rashi and Tosafot, he explains that "the Torah established [the obligation] in a place in which a person resides, as it says, 'you shall dwell' – in the manner in which you dwell – and on the road, there is no dwelling."[2]

Interestingly, Ritva, citing Ramban,[3] offers a slightly different approach:

> The question may be raised: Why is the "home-born" ["*ezraḥ*" – Lev. 23:42] mentioned? I heard in the name of our great teacher, Ramban, of blessed memory, that it comes to teach that the obligation of *sukka* applies only to one who is "like a green tree (*ezraḥ raanan*) in its native soil" [Ps. 37:35], to the exclusion of wayfarers (*holkhei derakhim*), produce watchmen (*shomrim*), and one who suffers discomfort (*mitzta'er*), and the like. And that which we say in many places, "'You shall dwell' – similar to [normal] residence" – is derived from here. For this verse clarifies that when it says,

> "you shall dwell," it is not any dwelling, but dwelling similar to normal residence, as in, "And Yaakov dwelt (*vayeshev*) in the land in which his father had sojourned" [Gen. 37:1] and other verses.[4]

Ramban maintains that the principle of *teshvu ke'ein taduru* is derived from the verse, "All that are home-born (*ezraḥ*) in Israel shall dwell in booths"; a person need only dwell in the *sukka* when he is like an "*ezraḥ raanan*" – a green tree planted in its home. Ramban attributes the exemptions of *holkhei derakhim*, *shomrim*, and *mitzta'er* to this verse.

We discussed previously whether the principle of *teshvu ke'ein taduru* applies on the first night of Sukkot. Some *Rishonim* insist that those exceptions that are due to the principle of *teshvu ke'ein taduru* do not apply on the first night,[5] as the Gemara strongly implies (Sukka 27b). Other *Rishonim* differ.[6] The *Aḥaronim* also disagree as to whether the exemption for travelers applies to one traveling on the first night of Sukkot[7] or whether even a traveler would be required to find a *sukka* on the first night of the festival,[8] just as we eat in the *sukka* on the first night even if it rains.

VACATIONS AND *TIYULIM* DURING SUKKOT

May one travel for pleasure during Sukkot and eat outside of the *sukka*, relying upon the exemption of *holkhei derakhim*? This question is especially relevant for those who may only take a vacation from work during Ḥol HaMo'ed, or for youth groups, especially in Israel, who wish to offer overnight *tiyulim* during Sukkot.

Some question whether the Gemara only permits one to travel and thereby exempt himself from the mitzva of *sukka* for great necessity. R. Moshe Feinstein, for example, based upon the Rashi cited above, insists that the entire exemption of *holkhei derakhim* only applies to those who must travel for business reasons ("*seḥora*"), and not to those who travel for pleasure.[9] R. Ovadia Yosef also argues that one may only exempt oneself from the mitzva of *sukka* for a pressing need, such as traveling for *parnassa* (earning a living).[10] Many *Aḥaronim* disagree, arguing that other *Rishonim* do not indicate that *holkhei derakhim* refers only to one who must travel for business reasons.[11] Some suggest that while "*tiyulim*" outside of Israel may have no inherent value, touring the Land of Israel may constitute a mitzva of sorts, and therefore may justify employing the exemption of *holkhei derakhim*.

Others object to intentionally traveling during the festival and deliberately avoiding fulfilling the mitzva of *sukka* (Shabbat 19b). This concern may, in fact, be universal, and not particular to Sukkot, as the Gemara rules that one should not embark on a ship within three days of Shabbat except for the sake of a mitzva. Some *Rishonim* explain that the Gemara prohibits entering a potentially life-threatening situation in close proximity to Shabbat, as one will inevitably need to violate the Sabbath.[12] Other *Rishonim* express concern that this journey will most likely detract from one's enjoyment of Shabbat (*oneg Shabbat*).[13] This general prohibition might concern us here as well.

Regarding Sukkot more specifically, *Or Zarua* records:

> There are some who, after they let blood during the holiday, eat outside the *sukka*. They say they are no different than those who feel pain in their eyes or have headaches [and, as sick people, are exempt from eating in the *sukka*]. They are mistaken, for one who lets blood is not sick; on the contrary, he is happy and eats and drinks much. Furthermore, he did not have to choose to let blood during the holiday. Even with regard to a mourner, whose suffering is due to causes outside his control, we say that he must calm himself and fulfill the mitzva [of *sukka*]. Certainly, the same should apply to these [who let blood], for they should not have chosen to let during the holiday.[14]

The *Or Zarua* objects to blood-letting purposely during the festival, a practice which may be equated, in this case, to an elective medical procedure, and then claiming an exemption from *sukka* due to discomfort (*mitzta'er*). Based upon this view, cited by Rema,[15] *Magen Avraham* writes:

> According to this reason, one who drinks a laxative is still obligated in *sukka*, even though he is in great pain, for he should have done this before the holiday or afterward. Therefore, he should not time this for the holiday.[16]

Magen Avraham objects to one who deliberately schedules an elective procedure during Sukkot and then claims an exemption from the *sukka* due to discomfort. The *Aḥaronim* explain that in this case, one is bloodletting for "pleasure," and not for an urgent medical need. Some suggest that just as one should not deliberately create a medical reason that will exempt one from *sukka,* certainly one should not intentionally plan a trip during Sukkot that will inevitably lead to the inability to fulfill the mitzva of *sukka.*

We should note, however, that there are clearly instances in which one may be exempt from the obligation of *sukka.* For example, the Gemara relates how R. Ḥisda and Rabba b. R. Huna would travel to their teacher on the festival, overriding their obligation to sit in the *sukka,* in order to perform the mitzva of visiting one's teacher on the festival (Sukka 26a).

Some authorities insist that we must investigate the extent to which travelers are exempt. Is the travelers' exemption absolute, or are they required to expend time and energy finding a *sukka*? Does the travelers' exemption assume that it is simply not possible to find a *sukka* and fulfill the mitzva? The Gemara cited above, for example, teaches that day travelers are obligated in *sukka* at night. Tosafot explain that one is only obligated in *sukka* at night if he sleeps in a town, presumably where there is a *sukka.* However, if there is no available *sukka* at night, his status as a "traveler" exempts him at night as well.[17] Me'iri cites an opinion that requires one to construct a *sukka* where one sleeps, but he rejects this understanding.[18]

The debate regarding whether the traveler is completely exempt only while actively traveling or even at night is also found among the *Aḥaronim.* Rema writes that the traveler is obligated at night only if he can find a *sukka*; if he is unable to find a *sukka,* he may continue traveling and eat and sleep outside of a *sukka* by day and night.[19] *Magen Avraham,* however, understands Tosafot differently. He argues that one must erect a *sukka* where he spends the night, and insists that even Tosafot maintain that when one reaches a town, he must erect a *sukka.*[20] Most *Aḥaronim* rule that one is not obligated to erect a *sukka* at night if he does not find one where he sleeps.[21]

Despite ruling that a traveler does not need to erect a *sukka* where he sleeps, Rema also cites *Orḥot Ḥayim,* who writes:

> Since day travelers are obligated in *sukka* at night, we suggest that those who travel to villages collecting debts on Ḥol HaMo'ed must return home at night to eat in the *sukka* if the village does not have one. Even though one can maintain otherwise, one who follows this stringency will be blessed.[22]

Rema writes that one should preferably be stringent and return home in order to eat in the *sukka*.[23]

Furthermore, although a traveler is technically exempt from eating and sleeping in the *sukka* even at night, many *Aḥaronim* write that although one does not need to delay eating in order to find a *sukka* while traveling, one who is able to should ideally eat in a *sukka*.[24] What clearly emerges is a discomfort with the blanket exemption of *holkhei derakhim*, and a recommendation to seek out a *sukka*, even when legitimately exempt.

In conclusion, one may find justification for the practice of those who travel during Sukkot and invoke the exemption of *holkhei derakhim*, especially those engaged in educational activities, as Ḥol HaMo'ed may, indeed, be the only opportunity to organize such a *tiyul*. However, it seems that given the ease with which one may find a *sukka* in our day and age, one should be strict and plan to eat those meals that require a *sukka* in a *sukka*.

R. Aharon Lichtenstein raises broader concerns. He argues that "one should be firmly and sharply opposed – both educationally and from the perspective of Jewish beliefs and values – to *tiyulim* or activities organized in a way that involves not observing the mitzva of *sukka*."[25] He cites Rambam, who writes the following regarding *tzitzit*, which technically one must only attach while wearing a four-cornered garment:

> Even though a person is not obligated to purchase a *tallit* and wrap himself in it so that he must attach *tzitzit* to it, it is not proper for a person to release himself from this commandment. Instead, he should always try to be wrapped in a garment that requires *tzitzit* so that he will fulfill this mitzva.[26]

So, too, argues R. Lichtenstein, from an educational perspective, as well as a broader spiritual outlook, it is improper to intentionally remove oneself from the obligation of *sukka*.

ḤOLIM: THE EXEMPTION OF THE SICK

The Mishna teaches that "the sick and their attendants are free from the obligation of *sukka*" (Sukka 25b). The Tosefta, cited by the Gemara, explains:

> Our Rabbis taught: The sick spoken of here is not [only] a sick person who is in danger, but also one who is not in danger, even one who suffers from eye ache or headache. R. Shimon b. Gamliel said: On one occasion, I was suffering with my eyes in Caesarea and R. Yose beRebbe permitted me and my attendants to sleep outside the *sukka*. (Sukka 26a)

The *Rishonim* explain that the sick are exempt from dwelling in the *sukka* because of the principle of "*teshvu ke'ein taduru*," as a sick person might even leave his own home in order to find a more comfortable place.[27] Many *Aḥaronim* therefore assume that this exemption only applies to one who can seek relief outside of the *sukka*.[28]

Taz, however, maintains that the exemption for the sick and of the "*mitzta'er*" in the *sukka* is due to one's inability to properly concentrate on the mitzva of *sukka* while experiencing discomfort. Therefore, regardless of whether one's discomfort will be alleviated upon leaving the *sukka*, such a person is exempt from the mitzva of *sukka*.[29]

The *Aḥaronim* disagree as to the reason for the exemption of the "attendants" (*meshamsheihen*). Some explain that the attendants are exempt due to the principle of "*haosek bemitzva patur min hamitzva*," one who is engaged in the performance of one mitzva is exempt from another.[30] The *Arukh HaShulḥan* argues that the exemption of the attendants is also based upon *teshvu ke'ein taduru*, as one who serves a sick person will also leave one's house when necessary.[31] R. Yaakov Reischer (1661–1733) argues in his *Shevut Yaakov* that the attendants are exempt because they are "*mitzta'er*," as they feel the pain of the sick to whom they are attending.[32] The *Shulḥan Arukh* rules that those who are sick, even those who suffer from a headache, are exempt from the *sukka*, while their attendants are only excused when they are needed.[33]

MITZTA'ER: ONE WHO EXPERIENCES DISCOMFORT IN THE *SUKKA*

The Gemara teaches:

> Rav permitted R. Aḥa Bardela to sleep in an enclosed bed in a *sukka* in order [to shut out] the gnats. Rava permitted R. Aḥa b. Adda to sleep outside the *sukka* on account of the odor of the day. Rava is here consistent, since Rava said: He who is in discomfort is free from the obligation of *sukka*. (Sukka 26a)

One who suffers discomfort, according to the Gemara, is exempt from the *sukka*. The *Rishonim* debate the halakhic significance of this discomfort, as well as the type of discomfort that may exempt one from the *sukka*.

As mentioned above, most *Rishonim* view *teshvu ke'ein taduru* as the source of this exemption – just as one would not remain in one's house when feeling discomfort, so too, one may leave the *sukka* upon experiencing discomfort. Some, however, exempt one experiencing discomfort for different reasons. As we saw above, Ramban understands that "the obligation of *sukka* applies only to one who is 'like a green tree (*ezraḥ raanan*) in its native soil' (Ps. 37:35) – to the exclusion of wayfarers, produce watchmen, and one who suffers discomfort."[34] Similarly, *Taz* maintains that the exemption of the "*mitzta'er*" is due to his inability to properly concentrate on the mitzva of *sukka* while experiencing discomfort.[35] This is consistent with the position of *Baḥ*, *Taz*'s father-in-law, who rules that one must keep in mind the intention of the mitzva of *sukka*, as the verse (Lev. 23:42) says, "that your generations may know."[36] Therefore, regardless of whether one's discomfort will be alleviated upon leaving the *sukka*, such a person is exempt from the mitzva of *sukka*. Rema rules that one is only exempt if leaving the *sukka* will relieve his discomfort.[37]

What are considered legitimate sources of discomfort? In addition to gnats and foul odors, the Gemara relates that if strong winds cause small pieces of *sekhakh* to fall into the *sukka*, causing discomfort, one is exempt (Sukka 29a). The Yerushalmi mentions extreme heat and mosquitoes as causes to leave the *sukka* as well (Y. Sukka 2:1).

Terumat HaDeshen rules that if one's light is extinguished during the Shabbat meal and there is light in the house, one may leave the *sukka* and eat in the house. Furthermore, one need not exert much effort to bring one's meal to another's *sukka,* as this is also considered to be "uncomfortable."[38] The *Shulḥan Arukh* mentions winds, flies, and foul odors,[39] and Rema cites *Terumat HaDeshen.*[40]

Is there an objective level of discomfort, at which point one is exempt from the *sukka*? *Tur* writes:

> It seems that an individual person cannot say, "I am uncomfortable" in order to be exempt from the *sukka*. Rather, [one is only exempt] with a situation which people ordinarily find uncomfortable.[41]

In other words, *Tur* maintains that there must be some sort of "objective" criterion for *mitzta'er*. *Biur Halakha*[42] notes that Ran[43] most likely disagrees, but Rema rules in accordance with *Tur.*[44]

The *Aḥaronim* question the validity of this ruling, as the Gemara brings the case of R. Yosef, who wished to leave the *sukka* when it began to rain, before his "porridge spoiled," as the Mishna prescribes (Sukka 28b). He said, "For me, as I am fastidious, this is like the porridge becoming spoiled" (Sukka 29a). R. Yosef apparently maintains that an *istenis,* an especially sensitive person (*aninei hadaat*), may be exempt before others. This seems to imply that the standards of *mitzta'er* are subjective, and not objective. *Taz* explains that since all those who fall under the classification of *istenis* would experience discomfort in such a situation, this constitutes an objective level of discomfort for them.[45]

BUILDING A *SUKKA* IN A PLACE OF DISCOMFORT

The Yerushalmi cited above mentions excessive heat as a reason to deem one *mitzta'er,* and it would seem that extreme cold should also be reason to exempt one from sitting in the *sukka*. Rashi, in fact, mentions cold as a source of discomfort,[46] and Rema writes that "people do not sleep in the *sukka,* except for those who are careful about mitzvot, because of the extreme cold, since it is uncomfortable to sleep in cold places."[47]

Rema, citing *Yerei'im,*[48] raises a new and serious concern, however:

> If one made [the *sukka*] in a place in which one would be uncomfortable to eat, drink, or sleep, or where he cannot perform one of the above acts because of the fear of robbers, one does not fulfill [the mitzva] with that *sukka* at all, even when those actions are not uncomfortable, because it is not similar to living-dwelling [in a house] where one can perform all his needs.[49]

According to this position, if one cannot sleep in the *sukka* due to the cold, then the *sukka* may be entirely invalid, and one may not even eat in the *sukka* during the day!

R. Tzvi Hirsch b. Yaakov Ashkenazi, *Ḥakham Tzvi,* disagrees with *Yerei'im* in his responsa, ruling that one may erect one *sukka* intended for eating and another for sleeping.[50] What is the basis of this debate? *Yerei'im* must maintain that a *sukka* in which one cannot sleep is simply not considered a *sukka*; in other words, the *sukka* itself is disqualified. *Ḥakham Tzvi* argues, on the other hand, that the principle of *teshvu ke'ein taduru,* from which the exemption of *mitzta'er* is derived, relates to the person's personal obligation, and not to the validity of the *sukka*.[51]

Assuming that we accept the position of *Yerei'im,* the *Aḥaronim* question how one may ever build a *sukka* in a cold or hot climate, or in any place in which one cannot reside in the *sukka* both day and night. They offer numerous justifications. The *Mishna Berura,* for example, cites those who explain that even a *sukka* built in a cold place may be considered "fit for sleeping" if one has sufficient blankets and sheets.[52]

However, we might suggest an entirely different understanding of *Yerei'im*. While the *Ḥakham Tzvi* understands that only a *sukka* that is unfit for both sleeping and eating is invalid, *Yerei'im* may maintain that one's obligation to "dwell" in a *sukka* entails ensuring that one can both eat and sleep in a *sukka*, just as one can both eat and sleep in one's house. If, however, one were to build one *sukka* for eating and another for sleeping, that would seemingly also suffice.

Furthermore, if one is simply unable to construct a *sukka* in which he can sleep, this is possibly also sufficient, as one has ensured that he may live in a *sukka* to the best of his abilities, and thus fulfilled "and you shall dwell." Similarly, *Peri Megadim* writes that if it is impossible to build a *sukka* in a place where he can sleep, "this is considered to be *ke'ein taduru*."[53] The *Aḥaronim* write that *bediavad*, one may eat in a *sukka* constructed in a place in which one cannot sleep.[54]

Finally, as mentioned above, the *Rishonim* debate whether a *mitzta'er* is exempt from the *sukka* on the first night as well. Rema writes that on the first night of Sukkot, a *mitzta'er* is obligated to eat in the *sukka*.[55] The *Mishna Berura* rules that since one sits in the *sukka* out of doubt in this case, one should not say the blessing "*leishev basukka*."[56]

RAIN: THE EXEMPTION OF *YARDU GESHAMIM*

The Talmud teaches that one who is sitting in the *sukka* when it begins to rain may leave the *sukka*:

> All the seven days [of the festival], a man must make the *sukka* his permanent abode and his house his temporary abode. If rain fell, when may one be permitted to leave it? When the porridge would become spoiled. They propounded a parable. To what can this be compared? To a slave who comes to fill the cup for his master, and he poured a pitcher over his face. (Sukka 28b)

The Gemara explains the parable: "The master poured the pitcher over his face and said, 'I have no desire for your service.'" As Rema writes, "One who leaves the *sukka* because of rain should not leave in a contemptuous manner, but rather he should humbly leave like a servant who poured a drink for his master, who then poured it on his head."[57]

The Mishna implies that the ideal fulfillment of the mitzva of *sukka* – "*teshvu*" – entails "making the *sukka* his permanent abode." Most *Rishonim* assume that one may therefore leave the *sukka* when it rains, just as anyone who experiences discomfort in the *sukka* may seek relief in one's house.[58] If so, then we must understand why the Mishna specifies an objective "*shiur*" at which point one may leave the *sukka*.

According to *Tur*, who maintains that there must be a somewhat objective level of discomfort in order to leave the *sukka*, the Mishna simply spells out this objective level.[59] Interestingly, Ran, who, as we saw above, may maintain that the level of discomfort that frees one from the obligation is subjective, offers a different interpretation of our mishna. He explains that one who experiences discomfort from the rain certainly does not need to enter the *sukka* in the first place. The Mishna, however, relates to another concern – one who leaves the *sukka* in the middle of his meal may appear to be "rejecting the *sukka*" (*kemeva'et besukka*), and therefore may only leave the *sukka* after his food has spoiled. He concludes, however, that he personally does not rely upon this leniency, as it cannot be supported by other sources.[60]

Must one start a meal in the *sukka* when it appears that it will begin raining shortly? Ritva writes that if one sees that it is about to rain, one is already exempt from the *sukka*. Seemingly, one would not begin eating a meal in one's house, with all the necessary preparations, if he knows that he will have to stop in the middle and continue eating elsewhere (*teshvu ke'ein taduru*).[61] Radbaz disagrees,[62] and the *Shulḥan Arukh* implies that the rain exemption only applies once one has begun to eat in the *sukka*.[63]

Some understand the exemption due to rain in a completely different manner. They suggest that while one who experiences discomfort may be not be required to remain in the *sukka*, a *sukka* which cannot protect those sitting in it from rain cannot be considered a home at all! Indeed, the verse says, "And there shall be a pavilion (*sukka*) for a shadow in the daytime from the heat, and for a refuge and for a covert from storm and from rain."[64] A *sukka* that cannot provide shelter from the rain cannot be considered a *sukka*.[65]

Whether we view this halakha as a "*petur gavra*" (a personal exemption) or a "*pesul beḥeftza*" (a disqualification of the *sukka*) may yield numerous differences. For example, as we discussed previously, the *Rishonim* debate whether *teshvu ke'ein taduru* and the exemption of one who experiences discomfort applies on the first night of Sukkot. Some *Rishonim* cite a view that maintains that one must eat in the *sukka* on the first night even if it rains.[66] Others insist that the Gemara did not distinguish between the first night and other nights; one may always leave the *sukka* when it begins to rain.[67]

Rema rules that on the first night, one should eat at least a *kezayit* in the *sukka,* even if it is raining.[68] The *Aḥaronim* debate whether, in this case, one should eat without the blessing of "*leishev basukka,*" as Rema may only require one to eat in the *sukka* as a stringency,[69] or whether one should say the *berakha,* in accordance with those *Rishonim* who maintain that one must eat in the *sukka* on the first night, even in the rain.[70] Practically, if it rains on the first night of Sukkot, it is customary to eat a *kezayit* of bread in the *sukka* without the *berakha,* and if the rain stops, to return to the *sukka* and eat a *kebeitza* of bread with the blessing.

Gra writes that those who maintain that one is exempt from eating in the *sukka* on the first night in the rain believe that "*ein shem sukka alav*" – the *sukka* is not considered to be a valid *sukka.*[71] *Sefer Maase Rav* records that Gra ruled that one should not eat in the *sukka* in the rain on the first night, because the *sukka* is not considered to be a *sukka* at all. However, he held that one should stay up all night, waiting for the rain to stop, in order to eat in the *sukka.*[72] Gra apparently agreed that *teshvu ke'ein taduru* does not exempt one from eating in the *sukka* on the first night, but until it stops raining, there is no *sukka* to eat in!

The *Aḥaronim* debate whether one may rely upon the lenient opinion and eat in one's home if it rains on the second night of Yom Tov outside of Israel or whether one must recite Kiddush and eat a *kezayit* in the *sukka,* and then conclude the meal his home.[73] The *Mishna Berura* writes that one may recite Kiddush and *Sheheḥeyanu* and eat the entire meal in his home, afterward eat a *kezayit* of bread in the *sukka,* and then recite *Birkat HaMazon* in the house.[74]

What should one do when the rain stops after leaving the *sukka*? The Gemara cites a tosefta, which teaches this:

> Our Rabbis taught: If he was eating in the *sukka* and rain fell and he left [the *sukka*], he need not trouble to return there until he has finished his meal. (Sukka 29a)

The *Aḥaronim* explain that the effort expended to return to the *sukka* may constitute a sort of *mitzta'er,*[75] and changing location in the middle of a meal is certainly not "*ke'ein taduru.*"[76] Similarly, one who is sleeping is the *sukka* when it begins to rain may leave the *sukka,* and does not need to return after the rain stops.

> If he was sleeping in the *sukka* and rain fell and he left, he need not trouble to return until it is dawn. They asked them: [Is the reading] "*sheyeor*" [until he awakens] or "*sheyeor*" [until it is dawn]? Come and hear: [It has been taught]: Until he awakens and the morning star appears. (Sukka 29a)

One does not need to return to the *sukka* until one awakens the next morning.[77]

ONE WHO IS FULFILLING A DIFFERENT MITZVA: *OSEK BEMITZVA PATUR MIN HAMITZVA*

We discussed above those who are exempt due to the principle of *teshvu ke'ein taduru.* As we saw, travelers, guards, watchmen, the sick, and those experiencing discomfort are not obligated to dwell in the *sukka,* as each of them would not normally hesitate to leave his home in the given situation. Interestingly, the Mishna begins its discussion of those who are released from the mitzva of *sukka* with a universal exemption: *osek bemitzva patur min hamitzva* (Sukka 25b). The Gemara teaches:

> Those who are engaged on a religious errand (*sheluḥei mitzva*) are free from [the obligations of] *sukka.*
>
> It has been taught: R. Ḥanania b. Akavya said: Scribes of books of the Law, *tefillin,* and mezuzot, their agents, and their agents' agents, and all who are engaged in holy work, including sellers of *tekhelet,* are free from the obligation of prayer and *tefillin* and all the commandments mentioned in the Torah. This confirms the words of R. Yose the Galilean, who established: One who is occupied with the performance of a religious duty is [at that time] free from the fulfillment of other religious duties.

The Gemara also relates a story about R. Ḥisda and Rabba son of R. Huna, "who, when visiting on the Sabbath of the festival the house of the Exilarch, slept on the river bank of Sura, saying, 'We are engaged on a religious errand and are [therefore] free [from the obligation of *sukka*].'" Traveling to greet the Exilarch constitutes a religious duty,[78] a mitzva, which would suffice to exempt one from sitting in the *sukka.*

The *Rishonim* debate whether one is only exempt from the second mitzva if its performance would hinder the fulfillment of the first[79] or whether even one who can fulfill both mitzvot is exempt as long as he is actively engaged in the fulfillment of the first.[80] Apparently, these *Rishonim* disagree as to whether one is essentially obligated in both mitzvot, but excused from one if its performance will hinder the fulfillment of the other, or whether fundamentally one cannot be obligated to actively fulfill two mitzvot simultaneously. These approaches may yield different halakhic conclusions.

For example, in general, one who misses one of the three obligatory daily prayers should recite the next prayer twice (*tashlumin*, a "make-up" prayer). One who did not recite the morning *Shemoneh Esreh*, for example, should recite the *Shemoneh Esreh* of Minḥa a second time. The *Aḥaronim* debate whether one who missed a prayer because he was involved in the performance of another mitzva, such as one who was involved in communal needs (*tzarkhei tzibbur*), should recite a *tefillat tashlumin*. *Derisha* writes that since he was exempt from prayer at the time, as he was *osek bemitzva*, he does not need to recite a *tefillat tashlumin*.[81] *Taz* disagrees, however, and writes that one who is involved in the performance of a mitzva is no different from one who is sick and unintentionally, or because of reasons beyond his control, could not pray, in which case one prays the next *Shemoneh Esreh* twice.[82]

Derisha and *Taz* clearly disagree as to whether one who is engaged in the fulfillment of a mitzva is completely exempt from the second mitzva or simply excused from it. Similarly, the *Aḥaronim* question whether one who does fulfill both mitzvot should recite a blessing on the second mitzva.[83]

Rema rules in accordance with Tosafot,[84] and the *Shulḥan Arukh* rules that *sheluḥei mitzva*, including those traveling to greet their teacher on the festival, to learn Torah, or to redeem captives, are exempt from the *sukka*.[85] Some suggest that one may visit one's parents on the festival, a fulfillment of the mitzva of *kibbud av va'em* (honoring one's parents), even if he will not have a *sukka* within which to sleep.[86]

CHAPTER 25

The Mitzva to Take the *Arba Minim*

THE TORAH COMMANDS that one take the "*arba minim*," the "four species," on the Festival of Sukkot and "rejoice before God" for seven days:

> And you shall take for yourselves on the first day the fruit of goodly trees [etrog], branches of palm-trees [lulav], and boughs of thick trees [*hadassim*], and willows of the brook [*aravot*], and you shall rejoice before the Lord your God seven days. (Lev. 23:40)

The Mishna records that in the *Beit HaMikdash*, the *arba minim* were taken all seven days of Sukkot, while outside of the *Mikdash*, they were taken only on the first day (Sukka 41a). Rashi[1] cites the Sifra,[2] which explains the phrase "before the Lord" as referring to the *Beit HaMikdash*. The Gemara continues to explain that after the destruction of the *Beit HaMikdash*, R. Yoḥanan b. Zakkai instituted a rabbinic enactment that the *arba minim* should be taken for all seven days in remembrance of the Temple (*zekher laMikdash*). In this chapter, we will discuss the nature and scope of the biblical and rabbinic obligation to take the *arba minim*, and then we will begin our study of the laws pertinent to the performance of the mitzva.

RELATIONSHIP BETWEEN THE BIBLICAL MITZVOT

R. Soloveitchik poses the following question:[3] How is one to understand the relationship between the beginning of the verse, "And you shall take for yourselves on the *first day*" and the conclusion of the verse, "And you shall rejoice before the Lord your God *seven days*" – which are understood to refer to the taking of the *arba minim* outside and inside of the *Beit HaMikdash*, respectively? On the one hand, we may suggest that the difference is quantitative – the same mitzva, which is performed for one day outside of the Temple, is performed for an entire seven days inside the Temple. On the other hand, one might understand that the verse points to two separate and qualitatively distinct mitzvot – one which is observed in the Temple for seven days, and the other which is observed outside of the Temple, on the first day of Sukkot.

R. Soloveitchik identifies numerous *Rishonim* who relate to this question. Rashi,[4] Tosafot,[5] and Rosh[6] agree that the mitzva of *netilat lulav* in the *Mikdash* shares *the same* characteristics and standards as the mitzva to take the *arba minim* outside of the Temple. As a result, the requirements of "*lakhem*" (ownership) and "*hadar*" (beauty), which we will discuss below, apply to both situations. Rambam, however, disagrees:

> All the species that we categorized as unacceptable because of the blemishes we described or because they were stolen or taken by force are [disqualified for use] only on the first day of the festival. On the second day of the festival and on the other days, they are all kosher.[7]

Rambam implies that the requirements of ownership and of "*hadar*" apply only on the first day, even in the *Beit HaMikdash*!

R. Soloveitchik explains that Rashi and Tosafot view the mitzva to take the *arba minim* in the *Mikdash* all seven days as an extension of the original mitzva, and all of the details that apply on the first day therefore apply throughout the week. Rambam disagrees and apparently maintains that while the mitzva on the first day is one of "*lekiḥa*" (taking) – as the verse says, "and you shall take" – the mitzva in the *Mikdash* is one of "*simḥa*" (to rejoice) – as the verse says, "and you shall rejoice." Therefore, although certain "*pesulim*" that disqualify the *arba minim* themselves do apply all week (such as a lulav or etrog that must be burned due to its involvement in pagan worship, "*ketutei mikhtat shiurei*"), the external details, such as the laws of *hadar* (beauty) and *ḥaser* (incomplete), do not apply during the extended mitzva in the *Mikdash*.

Ramban offers a third approach. He insists that although one may use a borrowed lulav in the *Mikdash* after the first day, as the requirement of owning ("*lakhem*") the *arba minim* only applies on the first day, the other *pesulim* (*hadar* and *ḥaser*) apply in the *Mikdash* during the entire week.[8] R. Soloveitchik explains that Ramban agrees with Rambam, distinguishing between the mitzva in the *Mikdash* on the first day and during the rest of the week. However, he views *hadar* and *ḥaser* as integral to the fulfillment of the mitzva of *arba minim,* and they therefore would invalidate the *arba minim* throughout the week.[9] Alternatively, Ramban views *hadar* and *ḥaser* as integral to the definition of the species of the *arba minim.* Thus, although the mitzva during the rest of the week differs from the mitzva of the first night, one must still adhere to certain basic standards of the *arba minim.*

The *Aḥaronim* discuss whether the fulfillment in the *Mikdash* on the first day is strictly one of rejoicing or also one of taking. Theoretically, they suggest, one who takes the *arba minim* at home on the first day and then arrives at the *Mikdash* might be obligated to take the *arba minim* again in order to fulfill the additional requirement of "and you shall rejoice." Although this latter debate may seem somewhat theoretical, the question of whether we apply the *pesulim* of *hadar* and *ḥaser* after the first day is of extreme practical importance. We will devote the next section to a brief overview of when the various *pesulim* are applied.

OVERVIEW OF WHEN EACH *PESUL* INVALIDATES THE *ARBA MINIM*

As mentioned above, outside of the *Mikdash,* on the first day of Sukkot, one fulfills the biblical obligation of "and you shall take for yourselves on the first day"; during the rest of the week, the obligation is rabbinic, "*zekher laMikdash.*" The Gemara distinguishes between different types of characteristics of the *arba minim* – those necessary for the entire festival and those which apply only on the first day.

For example, the measurements of the *arba minim* (etrog – larger than an egg; *hadassim* and *aravot* – three *tefaḥim*; lulav – four *tefaḥim*) must be observed for all seven days of Sukkot. Furthermore, the invalidating characteristics inherent to each specific species, such as a grafted etrog, a *hadas shoteh* whose leaves are uneven (Sukka 32b), or an *arava* that is a "*tzaftzafa*" (Sukka 34a), apply during the entire week. Finally, as mentioned above, at times one may not discharge one's obligation with the *arba minim* because they must be burned or because they were acquired through "illegal" means (*mitzva habaa be'aveira*).

In addition, the Talmud speaks of three other requirements: "*lakhem*," "*hadar*," and "*ḥaser*." "*Lakhem*," derived from the verse "*ulekaḥtem lakhem*" (and you shall take for yourselves), teaches that the *arba minim* must belong to the person "taking" them. "*Hadar*," derived from the Torah's description of the etrog as a "*peri etz hadar*," requires that each species must maintain a defined level of beauty, expressed in different physical characteristics for each species. Finally, the *arba minim* must be whole and cannot be "*ḥaser*," physically incomplete. The physical expression of *hadar* and *ḥaser* differs from species to species.

Which of these *pesulim* apply on the first day, upon which one fulfills the mitzva *mideoraita* of *arba minim*, and which apply throughout the week? On the first day, upon which one is biblically obligated to take the *arba minim*, one must ensure that the lulav belongs to the person fulfilling the mitzva, as the verse says, "And you shall take for yourselves (*ulekaḥtem lakhem*)." Thus, one may not use a borrowed, and certainly a stolen, lulav to fulfill the mitzva of *arba minim* on the first day of Sukkot.[10]

Although nowadays, it is customary for each person to have own his own set of *arba minim* (although often one's wife and children may not have their own set), this was not common until recently. How is one who does not own his own set of *arba minim* to fulfill the mitzva on the first day of Sukkot? The Gemara reports:

> And it once happened that when R. Gamliel, R. Yehoshua, R. Elazar b. Azaria, and R. Akiva were traveling on a ship and R. Gamliel alone had a lulav, which he had bought for one thousand *zuz*. R. Gamliel took it and fulfilled his obligation with it; then he gave it as a gift to R. Yehoshua, who took it, fulfilled his obligation with it, and gave it as a gift to R. Elazar b. Azaria, who took it, fulfilled his obligation with it, and gave it as a gift to R. Akiva, who took it, fulfilled his obligation with it, and then returned it to R. Gamliel. Why does he need mention that he returned it? He teaches us something incidentally – that a gift made on condition that it be returned constitutes a valid gift. (Sukka 41b)

Accordingly, one may give his friend his *arba minim* as a "*matana al menat lehaḥzir*," a gift given on the condition that it is returned. As long as the *arba minim* are returned, this is considered to be ownership, and the recipient fulfills the mitzva of *arba minim*. Furthermore, the *Shulḥan Arukh* records that it was customary for an entire community to purchase one etrog under the assumption that each "partner" gives his portion to the person taking the *arba minim* as a "*matana al menat lehaḥzir*."[11]

Rema[12] cites *Terumat HaDeshen*,[13] who rules that after the first day, one may even take another person's lulav without permission if necessary, and it is considered to be "borrowed." We can assume that the owner would willingly give permission for one to fulfill a mitzva with his money.

The *Rishonim* disagree regarding whether the requirement of "*hadar*" – expressed differently in each of the four *minim* – applies all week or only on the first day. Most *Rishonim*[14] assume that "*hadar*" applies the entire week, as the Gemara implies (Sukka 29b). Rambam, however, disagrees.[15] Although the *Shulḥan Arukh* quotes Rambam and rules that these halakhot do not apply after the first day,[16] Rema implies that he accepts the more stringent approach.[17]

The Gemara teaches that an etrog that is "*ḥaser*" – incomplete – is valid after the first day. The Gemara even relates that "R. Ḥanina tasted a part [of an etrog] and fulfilled his obligation [with the remainder]," explaining that this passage refers to the rest of the days (Sukka 36a). Therefore, an etrog that was cracked (*nisdak*) or punctured (*nikav*), or whose "*oketz*" (the bottom tip) fell off, is valid after the first day. Rema rules that even an etrog whose *pitom* has fallen off is valid after the first day, assuming that an etrog whose *pitom* falls off is disqualified on the first day due to the *pesul* of *ḥaser*.[18]

The *Rishonim* disagree as to why an etrog that is "*ḥaser*" is invalid on the first day. Some *Rishonim* relate this to another category: *lekiḥa tama*. The Gemara teaches regarding other halakhot that one's "taking" must be whole and complete – *tama* – and therefore, these *Rishonim* argue, if the etrog is incomplete, so is one's "taking."[19] Others insist that "*ḥaser*" is invalid because it is not considered to be "*hadar*."[20]

Interestingly, the *Rishonim* discuss whether the *arba minim* standards of Yom Tov Rishon, the first day of Sukkot, should apply equally on Yom Tov Sheni, the second day of the festival, observed as a Yom Tov outside of Israel. While Rambam implies that the second day should be similar to Ḥol HaMo'ed,[21] Ritva disagrees.[22] The *Shulḥan Arukh* rules that if necessary, one may, on the second day, take *arba minim* that are generally invalid on the first day, but without a blessing.[23]

RELATIONSHIP BETWEEN THE *ARBA MINIM*

The Talmud discusses, in different contexts, the relationship between the four *minim* to one another. After all, the notion of one mitzva composed of four separate parts is a rare halakhic phenomenon. We will first discuss whether the lulav, *hadassim*, and *aravot* must be taken together, tied together in one bundle, or whether tying the *minim* together is merely a "*hiddur mitzva*," a beautification of the mitzva. We will then discuss whether the four *minim* must be taken together or whether they may even be taken separately, one after the other.

Egged: Binding The Arba Minim

The Talmud cites a debate between R. Yehuda and the *ḥakhamim* regarding the relationship between each *min* of the four species. R. Yehuda maintains that "*lulav tzarikh egged*" – the lulav must be tied together with the *hadassim* and *aravot* in order to fulfill the mitzva. The *ḥakhamim* disagree – they hold that the *arba minim* do not need to be taken together. Seemingly, R. Yehuda, who believes that "*lulav tzarikh egged*," maintains that not only must all four species be taken together at the same time, but they must also be tied together. The *ḥakhamim* disagree, rejecting the second assumption – the four species do not have to be tied together. Ritva, however, cites (and rejects) the view of his teacher, Raa, who understands that R. Yehuda only requires that the *minim* be held together, and the *ḥakhamim* reject even this.[24]

Interestingly, the Gemara concludes that "it is a pious deed to bind the lulav, but [even] if he did not bind it, it is valid… [and] the pious deed spoken of is due to 'This is my God and I will glorify Him'" (Sukka 11b). The Gemara maintains that even the *ḥakhamim* prefer that one bind the species together, in accordance with the universal principle of *hiddur mitzva* (beautifying a mitzva), derived from the verse, "This is my God and I will glorify Him" (*zeh Keli ve'anvehu*).

Although one may bind the lulav, *hadassim,* and *aravot* together with any material, it is customary to tie them together with a leaf of the lulav.[25] Furthermore, R. Eliezer of Metz rules that this *egged* must follow the Torah's standard of a knot, as defined in the laws of the Sabbath. Therefore, one should bind the *arba minim* with a double knot.[26] The *Shulḥan Arukh* cites this position and adds that if one forgot to bind his *arba minim* together before Yom Tov, or if the knot became undone, he should tie them with a bow, since tying a double knot is prohibited on Yom Tov.[27] Rema cites *Tur,*[28] who rules that on Yom Tov, one should make a loop around the lulav, *hadassim,* and *aravot,* and then put the head of the string through the loop and tighten it. Rema adds that it is customary to tie this way during the week as well.[29] *Peri Megadim* cites a similar custom, and he records that this was his practice.[30]

Nowadays, it is common practice to bind the *arba minim* with rings and with a small basket made from lulav leaves, known as "*koishikleḥ,*" which hold the *hadassim, aravot,* and lulav together. The *Mishna Berura* cites the responsa *Agura BeOhalekha,* who justifies this practice despite the fact that these "*koishikleḥ*" do not seem to qualify as a double knot.[31] The *Arukh HaShulḥan* also records that it was customary to use these baskets and then to bind them with additional rings; he explains that this is simply "nicer" (*na'eh yoter*).[32] Some *Aḥaronim* criticize this practice, and suggest tying at least one double knot at the bottom of the four *minim.*[33] In addition, those who maintain that one must tie the *arba minim* with a double knot also insist that they be tied in a manner in which one cannot remove one of the species on Yom Tov. Therefore, one would not be able to replace one's *hadassim,* as some do, on Yom Tov.

Preferably, one should prepare his *egged* before Yom Tov. What should one who forgot to prepare and bind the four *minim* do on

Yom Tov? Some *Aḥaronim* insist that one may rip off a leaf from a lulav on Yom Tov, as the labor of "*tolesh*" does not apply to items that have already been separated from the ground.[34] *Shaarei Teshuva* records that although it is customary to be stringent, one may cut the leaves of the lulav with one's teeth, which is considered to be a "*shinui*" (a *melakha* done in an abnormal manner), which would be permitted for the sake of a mitzva. However, one should only do so in private.[35]

There are a number of divergent customs regarding the number of knots tied around the *arba minim*. Rema,[36] citing the *Mordekhai*, writes that one should bind the lulav, *hadassim*, and *aravot* with three knots. *Magen Avraham* explains that the three knots correspond to our three forefathers.[37] Some tie one knot around all of the species and another two around the lulav;[38] others tie three knots around the lulav, aside from an additional knot around the three species.[39] R. Shalom Shachneh Tsherniak writes that one should tie three knots around the three species and another two, above them, around the lulav.[40] *Kaf HaḤayim* records that Arizal would tie eighteen knots around his *arba minim*.[41] Regardless of one's personal custom, one should tie the four *minim* together at least once.

Taking Each Species Separately: Four Parts of A Whole

Unlike *tefillin* – a mitzva composed of two distinct parts (the *tefillin shel rosh,* worn on one's head, and the *tefillin shel yad,* worn on one's upper arm) – which most *Rishonim* count as two separate mitzvot,[42] all seem to agree that the *arba minim* together make up one single mitzva. How, then, are we to understand this mitzva and the relationship between the four species?

The Talmud teaches that all four species must be taken; if not, it seems that one has not fulfilled the mitzva:

> And from where do we know that they are a hindrance to one another [i.e., that one cannot fulfill the mitzva without taking all four]? Scripture teaches: "And you shall take" – [implying] that the taking must be complete (*lekiḥa tama*). (Sukka 36b)

Elsewhere, the Gemara asserts that "this was taught only in the case in which he did not have them at all, but when he had them all (*yesh lo*), one does not invalidate the other" (Menaḥot 27a). The *Rishonim* disagree regarding how to understand this passage.

Behag, cited by Tosafot and Rif,[43] accepts the simple understanding of the Gemara: One who takes all four *minim*, even consecutively, has fulfilled his obligation. The *Rishonim* differ as to how to understand *Behag*'s position. Some *Rishonim* insist that the four *minim* must all be in one's possession in order to fulfill the mitzva. Ritva, for example, explains that as long as he has all four species in his possession, he fulfills the mitzva even if he takes one species after another. If, however, he does not have all four species in his possession, then he cannot fulfill the mitzva in this manner.[44] While Ritva implies that the *arba minim* must merely be in his possession, Rosh writes that the four species should be "*munaḥin kol arebaatan lefanav*" – physically present, in front of him.[45] Interestingly, Rambam explains that the four species must be "*metzuyin etzlo*"[46] – which may imply that they must be "in one's possession," like Ritva's interpretation, or that the four species must be present physically in front of him, like Rosh argued. Ran cites Ramban, who explains that even one who does not have all four *minim* in his possession should take each one as he receives it, and after taking all four, he fulfills his obligation. The Gemara only intended to exclude a case in which a person did not take all four species.[47]

Rabbeinu Tam rejects this understanding of the Gemara, and wonders how one can fulfill the mitzva of *arba minim* when the four species are taken at different times, if taking the *arba minim* is considered to be one single mitzva. He therefore suggests that the correct text should read, "However, if he has them, even though he did not bind them together…" In other words, this passage simply supports that position of the *ḥakhamim*, that the four species need not be bound together. However, the *arba minim* certainly must be taken together.[48]

How are we to understand the requirement of *lekiḥa tama* according to these different views? Rabbeinu Tam must believe that had the Torah not required a "*lekiḥa tama*," one may have been able to take the four species consecutively. *Lekiḥa tama* teaches that the *arba minim* are to be viewed as one mitzva, which, logic dictates, must be taken at once. The other *Rishonim* (Ritva, Rosh, and Rambam), however, may maintain that without the *lekiḥa tama,* one might have viewed the four species as four separate mitzvot; one who takes even one or two of the species fulfills a mitzva. Indeed, some *Rishonim* record that since "*lekiḥa tama*" only applies on the first day, as we saw regarding *ḥaser,* one who does not have all four species on Ḥol HaMo'ed may still take some of them and recite a blessing![49] These *Rishonim* maintain that *lekiḥa tama* requires that all four *minim* be taken together on the first day, and they simply disagree as to what constitutes "together." Ramban, however, insists that the *lekiḥa tama* merely requires that one take all four *minim,* and not that they must be taken – in any way – "together."[50]

The *Shulḥan Arukh* rules in accordance with Rambam; one need not take all four species together in order to fulfill the mitzva, but rather, as long as they are "*metzuyin etzlo,*" he discharges his obligation. If, however, one species is missing, he should take the rest as a "*zekher be'alma*" (a remembrance).[51] Rema adds that the four *minim* should be "*lefanav*" – physically in front of him – and that one should first take the lulav and recite the blessing "*al netilat lulav.*" If he talks in between taking any of the four *minim,* he should recite a separate blessing on each remaining species.[52] *Magen Avraham* disagrees.[53] Although the halakha permits one to take the four *minim* individually, but consecutively, it remains unclear whether one fulfills the mitzva only after all four *minim* have been taken or whether there is an inherent fulfillment of a mitzva each time one of the *minim* is taken.[54]

THE PROPER MANNER OF RECITING THE BLESSING OVER THE *ARBA MINIM*

In numerous contexts, the Talmud discusses the blessings recited before performing mitzvot. The Gemara and *Rishonim* grapple with questions such as the proper text or formula for a blessing and interruptions between the blessing and the performance of a mitzva.

One of the central issues relevant to the laws of these *berakhot* relates to the proper time and manner of reciting a *birkat hamitzva*. The

Gemara teaches that "one should recite the blessing before performing a mitzva" (*kol haberakhot mevarekh aleihen over le'asiyatan*) (Pesaḥim 7a). Although the Gemara implies that the blessing must be recited before the mitzva, and some *Rishonim*, such as a Rambam,[55] rule that one may not recite the blessing after one has already fulfilled the mitzva, the *Or Zarua* writes that if one forgets to recite the blessing before the mitzva, one may recite it after performing the mitzva.[56]

What is the reason that the blessing must precede the mitzva? This question may relate to a broader and more fundamental question: Why did the Rabbis insist that one recite a blessing upon performing a mitzva at all? Seemingly, one might suggest that the blessings recited before doing a mitzva are similar to *birkot hashevaḥ*, blessings of praise recited after experiencing an occurrence worthy of giving praise. Alternatively, we might suggest that reciting the *berakha* prepares us for the performance of the mitzva, similar to the practice of those who say "*hineni mukhan…*" before doing a mitzva. One may even attempt to equate the *birkot hamitzva* with *birkot hanehenin*, blessings that permit one to eat.[57] R. Soloveitchik suggested, based on Rambam's comments regarding *birkot hanehenin*, that just as one must ask "permission" to eat by reciting a blessing, one must ask "permission" to perform a mitzva.

The debate regarding one who forgot to say the blessing before the mitzva may reflect different approaches to, and alternate understandings of *birkot hamitzva*. *Or Zarua* must view the *birkot hamitzva* as a type of *birkot hashevaḥ*, which thus can be recited after the mitzva. The other *Rishonim*, however, including Rambam, must view the *birkot hamitzvot* as preparation for the mitzva, or possibly as a type of permission taken before doing a mitzva. The well-known debate recorded by the Talmud Yerushalmi regarding whether one should recite the blessing before fulfilling the mitzva or during its performance may also be relevant to our question (Y. Berakhot 9:3).

The Gemara presents one exception to the rule of "*over le'asiyatan*": *tevila*. The *Rishonim* debate whether this gemara refers to the immersion of a convert, who cannot recite a blessing before his immersion because he is not yet Jewish, or to other immersions, including *tevilat nidda* and even the *netilat yadayim* performed before eating bread.[58]

The *Rishonim* discuss the proper time for reciting the blessing upon taking the *arba minim*. On the one hand, one should recite a blessing over a mitzva while holding the mitzva object; for this reason, one says the blessing over *tefillin* after putting them on his arm, but before tightening the knot (Menaḥot 35b). On the other hand, the Gemara teaches that "as soon as one has lifted them [the *arba minim*], he has fulfilled his obligation" (Sukka 42a). Thus, saying the blessing after picking up the *arba minim* may be too late!

Tosafot offer three solutions. First, they suggest that one take the lulav, but leave the etrog on the table, and then recite the blessing before taking the etrog. They then propose that one hold the lulav upright and the etrog upside down, recite the *berakha*, and then flip the etrog; since the *arba minim* must be taken "*kederekh gedilatan*," in the manner in which they grew (Sukka 45b), one has not fulfilled the mitzva until one turns the etrog over. Finally, Tosafot advise taking all four *minim*, but having in mind not to fulfill the mitzva until after reciting the blessing.[59]

Interestingly, some *Rishonim* do not seem troubled by this question. Rambam, for example, writes that one recites the blessing and then picks up the bundle of the *arba minim* off the table.[60] Alternatively, Tosafot suggest that although one has already fulfilled the mitzva as soon as one lifts the *minim*, since one has not "completely finished the mitzva," as the shaking of the *lulav* (*naanua*) is part of the mitzva, one may still recite the blessing.[61] Gra writes that it is simply impossible to recite the blessing before this mitzva, and the blessing is therefore recited immediately after taking the *arba minim*.[62] Each of these answers deserves extensive analysis, and raises fascinating issues relating to the laws of *berakhot* and the *arba minim*, as well as the role of *kavana* in the performance of a mitzva.

Finally, R. Yoel Sirkis asks a fascinating question in his commentary to *Tur*. He observes that the suggestion of taking the *arba minim* in an abnormal manner, such as turning over the etrog before the blessing, seems to contradict what we learned previously – that one may take the four *minim* separately. If so, then once one has taken even one of the *minim* properly, he has partially fulfilled the mitzva, and the blessing is no longer considered to have been recited "*over le'asiyatan*," before performing the mitzva! He suggests that even though one may take all four *minim* separately, the mitzva is only fulfilled, retroactively, after having taken all four *minim*. There is no inherent value in taking each species alone. This question may further depend upon the debate we saw above concerning whether individual blessings may be recited upon the individual species.[63]

Practically, the *Shulḥan Arukh* rules that one should recite the blessing before taking the etrog or while holding the etrog upside down.[64] Although Gra writes that it may be preferable to take all four species in a normal manner and to have in mind not to fulfill the mitzva until after the blessing,[65] it is customary to recite the blessing when holding all four *minim* while the etrog is upside down.

THE WAVING OF THE LULAV (*NAANUIM*) AND THE RECITATION OF HALLEL

As we mentioned above, some *Rishonim* maintain that reciting the blessing before waving the lulav (*naanua*) is still considered to be "*over le'asiyatan*." Indeed, the Talmud elsewhere indicates that waving the lulav is considered to be part of the mitzva. For example, a child is obligated in the mitzva of lulav from the age that he "knows how to wave" (Sukka 42a). Furthermore, the Gemara teaches that a lulav must be at least four *tefaḥim* long in order for there to be a *tefaḥ* above the other species "to wave" (Sukka 29b, 32b). What is the significance of waving the lulav?

Some *Rishonim* use the term "*sheyarei mitzva*" to describe the *naanuim*,[66] which may imply that waving is a significant part of the mitzva.[67] Tosafot describe the waving as "*makhshirei mitzva*,"[68] possibly minimizing the significance of the *naanuim*.[69] Interestingly, Rambam describes two levels of the mitzva of taking the *arba minim*:

> Once one lifts these four species ... he has fulfilled his obligation, so long as he lifts them in the manner in which they grow [i.e., upright] .... The proper performance of the mitzva is to lift a bundle of the three species in one's right hand and the etrog in the left, and then thrust them forward, bring them back, lift them upward, and lower them, and wave the lulav three times in every direction.[70]

While minimally, one should "lift" the four species, the "proper performance" entails shaking the lulav three times in each direction.

What is the role of these *naanuim*? The Talmud describes how one waves the lulav during the recitation of Hallel (Ps. 118):

> And where is [the lulav] waved? At the commencement and the conclusion of the psalm, "O give thanks unto the Lord" and at "Save now, we beseech thee, O Lord." These are the words of *Beit Hillel*. *Beit Shammai* says: Also at "O Lord we beseech thee, send now prosperity." R. Akiva stated: I watched R. Gamliel and R. Yehoshua, and while all the people were waving their lulavs [at other verses], they waved them only at, "Save now, we beseech thee, O Lord." (Sukka 37b)

The *Rishonim* question why the Gemara describes the waving of the *arba minim* only in the context of Hallel. Should one wave the lulav after reciting the *berakha* as well?

On the one hand, some *Rishonim* insist that the Mishna never intended to exclude the waving of the *arba minim* after saying the blessing over the lulav, which are, in fact, the main *naanuim*. For example, Rosh notes that the Gemara obligates a "child who knows how to wave" the lulav, even though he does not know how to recite Hallel. Furthermore, the Gemara discusses one who must wake up early and pray and who is given a lulav to wave (Berakhot 30a); this gemara does not imply that Hallel is recited at the time. Rosh also cites Raavya, who supports his assertion and who brings passages from the Yerushalmi and Bavli that imply that the *naanuim* "ward off the *Satan*" or express our wish that the "winds be restrained." He describes the waving of the lulav during Hallel as "*naanua be'alma*" (mere shaking), and no more.[71] Me'iri also agrees that the main *naanuim* occur when the *berakha* is recited, but he describes the shaking during Hallel as "arousing one to joy" (*hitorerut lesimḥa*).[72] Some cite Rashi, who implies that even during Hallel, one shakes the lulav in order to "restrain harmful winds and harmful dews" – in other words, to pray for the proper weather.[73] According to these opinions, waving the lulav does not seem to be an inherent part of Hallel.

On the other hand, other *Rishonim* indicate that the *naanuim* need not be performed while saying the blessing, and are central to the recitation of Hallel.[74] Furthermore, Tosafot explain that according to *Beit Hillel,* one waves the lulav during Hallel as a fulfillment of the verse, "Then shall the trees of the wood sing for joy, before the Lord," which precedes, "O give thanks unto the Lord; for He is good."[75] Shaking the lulav is an expression of praise for God, which should be performed specifically while reciting Hallel.[76] Indeed, Rosh cites a beautiful midrash, which explains that one "rejoices with one's lulav like a person who was declared innocent by the judge and is happy, as it says, 'Then shall the trees of the wood sing for joy' – when they leave God innocent after the world is judged. And how should they express their joy? With *Hodu* and *Hoshia na.*"[77] On Sukkot, we express our happiness after being judged on Yom Kippur, most specifically through the taking, and shaking, of the lulav.[78]

Similarly, after describing how the "preferred" mitzva is to pick up the *arba minim* and shake them, Rambam writes:

> What does the above entail? One passes the lulav forward and shakes the top of the lulav three times, brings it back and shakes the top of the lulav three times. One follows this same pattern when lifting it up and down. At what point [in prayer] does one pass the lulav back and forth? *During the reading of the Hallel.*[79]

Rambam implies that the preferred performance of the mitzva entails shaking the lulav while reciting Hallel.

These different understandings of the *naanuim* may impact upon when one should perform the mitzva. The *Aḥaronim* debate whether one should take the lulav and recite the blessing in one's *sukka,* before coming to synagogue, or during the service, before reciting Hallel. The *Shulḥan Arukh* writes that the "*ikkar mitzva*" of lulav is during the recitation of Hallel, which would lead one to conclude that one should recite the blessing before Hallel.[80] *Magen Avraham,* however, cites *Shela,* who writes that one should take the *arba minim* in one's *sukka* before going to synagogue.[81] The *Aḥaronim* attribute this practice to Arizal.[82] *Sefer Piskei Teshuvot* cites sources that attest that great scholars, such as *Ḥakham Tzvi,* R. Ḥayim of Volozhin, and Ḥatam Sofer, took the *arba minim* in their *sukkot* before prayers.[83]

We mentioned above that the *Rishonim* offer different suggestions as to how one can properly recite the blessing upon taking the four *minim over le'asiyatan?* Tosafot[84] cite the following gemara:

> This was the custom of the men of Jerusalem: When a man left his house he carried his lulav in his hand; when he went to the synagogue, his lulav was in his hand; when he read the *Shema* and his prayers, his lulav was still in his hand. But when he read in the Law or recited the priestly benediction, he would lay it on the ground. If he went to visit the sick or to comfort mourners, he would go with his lulav in his hand, but when he entered the House of Study, he would send his lulav by the hand of his son, his slave, or his messenger. What does this teach us? It serves to inform you how zealous they were in the performance of religious duties. (Sukka 41b)

Tosafot explain that since continuous holding of the lulav is considered a "*mitzva min hamuvḥar*," a blessing recited after picking up the *arba minim* is viewed as "*over le'asiyatan.*"

Are we to understand from this passage that even *naanuim* performed separately from or long after the taking of the four *minim* may be considered to be a mitzva? What if one forgot to recite the blessing over the *arba minim* and remembers only before or during Hallel? While some[85] rule that one may still say the *berakha,* as the "shaking is still part of the mitzva," others insist that one may even say the *berakha* **after** shaking the lulav during Hallel.[86] The *Arukh HaShulḥan* goes even further, writing that as long as one is still holding the *arba minim,* he may recite the blessing.[87] These opinions clearly disagree regarding the the significance of the *naanuim,* especially when done after the performance of the mitzva and the recitation of Hallel.

In addition to circling the altar, the Gemara refers to a mysterious ritual called "*ḥibbut arava.*" The Gemara elsewhere, describing the taking of the *arava* outside of the *Beit HaMikdash,* relates that "a man brought a willow-branch… and he took it and '*ḥabbeit ḥabbeiit*' without reciting any blessing" (Sukka 44b). What was this "*ḥibbut arava,*" which was performed on the seventh day? Most *Rishonim,* including Rambam,[21] explain that one should beat the *arava* on the ground or on a vessel. Rashi, however, explains that the *arava* was waved (*naanua*).[22]

What is the significance of the "*ḥibbut arava*"? Seemingly, if "*ḥibbut arava*" refers to waving the *arava,* then the waving of the *arava* should be similar to the *naanuim* of the *arba minim* – just as the *arba minim* serve as an object that one uses to praise God, the "*arvei naḥal*" serve as an instrument for petitioning God for rain. If, however, as most *Rishonim* understand, the "*ḥibbut arava*" refers to beating the *aravot* on the ground or on a vessel, there must be some other significance to the practice. We can identify two broad approaches to *ḥibbut arava.*

On the one hand, one may view the *ḥibbut arava* as a prayer for rain, among the other prayers for rain recited on Hoshana Rabba, since the world's supply of rain is decided on the Festival of Sukkot (Rosh HaShana 2a). Beating the *aravot* on the ground may symbolize surrender or prostration. It may also demonstrate how desperately we need rain to hit and penetrate the earth. Why are *aravot* used for this purpose? The *aravot,* or "*arvei naḥal,*" grow on the water and depend on water for their sustenance. Furthermore, *Ḥazal* suggest that all four *minim* correspond to the parts of the body – the lulav parallels the spine, the etrog the heart, the *hadassim* the eyes, and the *aravot* resemble the mouth – as all parts of the body are used to praise God.[23] Therefore, the *aravot* may be the most appropriate instrument used for our prayers for rain, as they resemble the mouth, the vessel of prayer.[24]

Interestingly, R. Avraham Yitzchak HaKohen Kook, as cited by R. Moshe Tzvi Neria,[25] offers a different explanation. The Midrash explains how each of the four *minim* correspond to a different type of Jew. The etrog, with its smell and taste, represents a Jew with "Torah and good deeds," the *hadassim* and lulav represent Jews with good deeds but no Torah or no Torah but good deeds, and the *arava,* which has neither a nice smell nor a good taste, represents those Jews who have no Torah or good deeds.[26] This beautiful midrash explains that when taken together, "they atone one for the other." R. Kook, however, understood the role of the *arava* slightly differently. The *arava* represents the "*am haaretz*" – the simple Jew, who often demonstrates intuitive, healthy, and natural religious instincts.[27] On Hoshana Rabba, R. Kook explains, we do not "beat the *aravot*," but "beat *with* the *aravot*," invoking that simple religious fervor in our pleas for rain.

On the other hand, beating the *aravot* may indeed symbolize "beating," in the negative sense. R. Tzemaḥ Gaon,[28] for example, in response to a query regarding the reason for this practice, cites those who explain, "During the preceding holidays [Rosh HaShana and Yom Kippur], Satan incites, and the Jewish people, with all of their mitzvot, repel him. From now onward, anyone who rises against us will not be able to control us, and will fall to the ground." Some kabbalistic sources speak of beating the strict attribute of Justice (*midat hadin*).

Some understand this custom to refer to our relationship to other Jews. For example, R. Moshe Sternbach, in a somewhat shocking essay, writes,

> It is well known that the *arava*, which has no taste and no smell, is pleasant to us only when bound together with the lulav, etrog and *hadassim*. This hints to the sinners of Israel, who have no taste or smell.... When the *arava* is taken alone, we are obligated to beat it on the ground, to hint to us that those sinners who separated into their own groups, such as the Reform, Conservative, Nationalists (*leumi'im*), and the like, since they come by themselves, we are obligated to "beat them" until they surrender and are lowered, and not to bring them closer at all, and certainly not to bind ourselves to them.[29]

R. Kook's explanation, cited above, stands in sharp contrast to these harsh words.

HOSHANA RABBA OUTSIDE OF THE *BEIT HAMIKDASH*

The Gemara explains that outside of the *Beit HaMikdash*, the mitzva of *arava* was observed for one day – on the seventh day, Hoshana Rabba

(Sukka 44a–44b). The *Amora'im* disagree as to whether this practice is considered a "*yesod nevi'im*" (actual legislation of the later prophets) or a "*minhag nevi'im*" (a custom of the prophets):

> It was stated: R. Yoḥanan and R. Yehoshua b. Levi differ. One holds that the rite of the willow-branch is a "*yesod nevi'im,*" and the other holds that the willow-branch is a "*minhag nevi'im.*" It can be concluded that it was R. Yoḥanan who said that it is a "*yesod nevi'im,*" since R. Abbahu stated in the name of R. Yoḥanan: The rite of the willow-branch is a "*yesod nevi'im.*" This is conclusive.

The *Rishonim* explain that while one may recite a blessing over a "*yesod nevi'im,*" similar to a rabbinic enactment, one may not say a blessing over a "*minhag nevi'im.*"[30] *Tur* cites R. Shmuel b. Ḥofni, who rules that outside of the *Beit HaMikdash, arava* is a *yesod nevi'im* and a blessing is therefore recited.[31] Most *Rishonim,*[32] however, as well as the *Shulḥan Arukh,*[33] rule that *arava* outside of the *Beit HaMikdash* is a *minhag nevi'im,* and therefore no *berakha* is recited.

Incidentally, the *Rishonim* disagree as to whether one may derive from this gemara that a blessing is never recited over a custom[34] or that there are certain customs, such as the recitation of Hallel on Rosh Ḥodesh,[35] upon which one may say a *berakha.*[36]

The Talmud further discusses whether the *arava* taken on Hoshana Rabba must be taken separately, or whether one can use the *arava* taken with the lulav. Some *Rishonim* rule in accordance with R. Ḥisda, who permits one to take the *arba minim* a second time in order to fulfill the mitzva of *arava,*[37] but others rule that one must take the *arava* separately.[38] The *Shulḥan Arukh* cites both opinions.[39] The *Mishna Berura*[40] cites the *Bikkurei Yaakov,* who writes that if one takes the *arba minim* and then unbinds them, removes the *aravot,* and takes them separately, he fulfills his obligation.

The Gemara also relates the minimum physical characteristics of the *arava*:

> What is its prescribed minimum? R. Naḥman said: Three fresh twigs with leaves. R. Sheshet, however, said: Even one leaf and one twig. One leaf and one twig! Can such a rule be imagined? Say rather: Even one leaf on one twig.

Tur[41] cites R. Hai Gaon, who writes that although the Gemara validates an *arava* branch with only one leaf, it is "*mekhuar*" (repulsive) to use such a branch for the mitzva. Therefore, Rema writes, one should take a bundle of *aravot*, known as "*Hoshanot*," in order to fulfill the principle of "This is my God, and I beautify Him" (*hiddur mitzva*).[42] The *Mishna Berura* writes that one should have at least three, if not five *aravot*, in accordance with the custom of Arizal.[43] The *Mishna Berura* also writes that these *aravot* should be tied together.[44]

Rashi implies that the *arava* may be shorter than three *tefaḥim*, the minimum length required for *aravot* when taken with the *arba minim*.[45] Ran, however, disagrees, and argues that all agree that the *arava* branch must be at least three *tefaḥim* long.[46] The *Shulḥan Arukh* rules in accordance with Ran; although one may take one branch with one leaf to fulfill the mitzva of *arava* outside of the *Beit HaMikdash*, the branch must be at least three *tefaḥim* long.[47]

The *Rishonim* debate whether on Hoshana Rabba, one encircles the *bima* while holding the lulav or also the *arava*. The *Shulḥan Arukh* records that it was customary to take the *arava* as well.[48] Rema, however, writes that one should preferably not take the *arava* with the lulav at all.[49] The *Mishna Berura* cites Arizal, who opposed taking the *arava* with the lulav.[50] The *Mishna Berura* relates that nowadays, it is customary to take the lulav alone, put it down when one reaches the prayer "*Taaneh Emunim*," and only afterward to take the bundle of *aravot*.[51] Some follow the practice of Arizal and do not put down the lulav until after the full Kaddish, and then take the *aravot* and beat them.

What should one do with his "*Hoshanot*" (bundle of *aravot*)? As we mentioned above, the Gemara describes a ritual called "*ḥibbut arava*," which was performed both in the *Beit HaMikdash* and, according to the story related in the Gemara, after its destruction as well (Sukka 44b). The *Rishonim* disagree as to whether *ḥibbut* refers to "beating" the *arava* or shaking it. The *Shulḥan Arukh* cites Rambam and rules that one should beat the *arava* on the ground or on a vessel two or three times.[52] Rema, however, writes that it is customary to shake and then beat the *arava*.[53] The *Mishna Berura*, citing the practice of Arizal, writes that one should beat the *arava* on the ground five times, and then beat it on a vessel in order to remove some of the leaves. *Arukh HaShulḥan* records that he has not heard of this custom, but does recommend "shaking it a bit" before beating it.[54]

THE SIGNIFICANCE OF HOSHANA RABBA

In the Talmud, Hoshana Rabba is simply known as "the seventh day of the *arava*" (Sukka 42b); the phrase "Hoshana" or "Hoshana Rabba" appears in the Midrash.[55] Although the *arava* ritual described above indicates that the seventh day of Sukkot is unique, its significance is not discussed by the Talmud.

The Yerushalmi teaches, "Yet they seek Me daily (*yom yom*)[56] – this refers to the *tekia* [shofar] and the *arava*" (Rosh HaShana 5:8) – implying that Hoshana Rabba is similar to Rosh HaShana, as they are both days in which objects are employed as instruments of prayer. The Zohar adds that Hoshana Rabba is a day of judgment: "This [Hoshana Rabba] is the final day of judgment for water, source of all blessings. On the seventh day of Sukkot, the judgment of the world is finalized and the edicts (*pitkin*) are sent forth from the King."[57]

The *Rishonim* expand on this idea, explaining that Hoshana Rabba is the final day of the period of judgment, which began on Rosh HaShana.[58] Indeed, as *Tur* reminds us, the world's water supply is judged on Sukkot, and therefore we lengthen our prayers on Hoshana Rabba, like on Yom Tov.[59]

Based upon this view of Hoshana Rabba, many customs developed. Some are accustomed to learn the entire night of Hoshana Rabba.[60] Others read the entire Book of Deuteronomy, which emphasizes the love and fear of God, on the night of Hoshana Rabba.[61] In addition, the *Aḥaronim* record that it is customary for the *sheliaḥ tzibbur* to wear a *kittel* and to recite the long *Pesukei DeZimra* of Yom Tov (except for *Nishmat* and *Shokhen Ad*).[62] Based upon the Zohar cited above, it is customary to greet one another with the salutation, "*pitka tova*," wishing a "good edict."

THE CONCLUSION OF SUKKOT: LEAVING THE *SUKKA*

Toward the end of Hoshana Rabba, we begin our transition from the Festival of Sukkot to Shemini Atzeret. The Mishna describes:

> When a man has finished his [last] meal, he may not dismantle his *sukka*. He may, however, remove its furniture from the afternoon onward in honor of the last day of the festival. (Sukka 48a)

Many have the custom of eating a bit in the *sukka* before the end of the day, and declaring, "It should be His will that we will merit to sit in the *sukka* of the Leviathan."[63]

CHAPTER 27

Shemini Atzeret and Simḥat Torah

After celebrating the Festival of Sukkot for seven days, dwelling in one's *sukka* and taking the *arba minim* each day, the Torah instructs that the eighth day, known as "Shemini Atzeret," should be observed as a Yom Tov (Num. 29:35–38). Unlike Pesaḥ, which is celebrated for seven days, the Festival of Sukkot is extended an additional day, and Shemini Atzeret is observed on the eighth day. Why is there an "extra" day of Sukkot? What is the nature of this additional day?

The Talmud suggests that the different *korbanot* offered on Sukkot and Shemini Atzeret may explain the difference between these two days. On the one hand, the "*parei haḥag*," the seventy bulls brought on Sukkot, which correspond to the seventy nations of the world, highlight the universal theme of Sukkot.[1] On the other hand, the single bull brought as a *korban* on Shemini Atzeret points to a more particular theme. This led the Gemara to teach the following parable:

> R. Elazar taught: The seventy cows [of Sukkot] correspond to the seventy nations of the world. What is the purpose of the lone cow [of Shemini Atzeret]? It corresponds to the lone nation. It is like a parable of a king who said to his servants, "Make for me a great feast." On the last day, he said to his lover, "Make for me a small feast so that I may derive pleasure from you." (Sukka 55b)

Rashi offers a similar understanding:

> This is language of affection, like children departing from their father. He says, "Your departure is difficult for me. Delay it one more day."[2]

Ḥizkuni also views Shemini Atzeret as a celebration of the relationship between God and the Jewish people, adding:

> This is a parable to a king whose children came to visit him. The first time the king asked, "When will you return to me?" They told him, "In fifty days." He said, "Go in peace." The second time he asked, "When will you return?" They said in four months, and he told them, "Go in peace." The third time, they told him, "We cannot return for seven months." The king said, "If that is the case, please stay with me one more day so I can enjoy your company, since you will be so delayed for so long." For this reason, there is no *atzeret* for the Jews on Pesaḥ, for they return on Shavuot. And there is no *atzeret* on Shavuot, for they will return on Sukkot. But on Sukkot, when they will not return again until Pesaḥ, God delays them one day.[3]

God wishes to spend one final day, before the long winter void of festivals, alone with His nation.

Shemini Atzeret emphasizes the specific, particular relationship between God and the Jewish people, beyond the universal relationship between God and the nations of the world. These sources portray Shemini Atzeret as a beautiful celebration of the loving relationship between God and Am Yisrael.

THE NATURE OF SHEMINI ATZERET AND ITS RELATIONSHIP TO SUKKOT

The Talmud enumerates six ways in which Shemini Atzeret differs from the previous seven days, the Festival of Sukkot:

> It has been taught in agreement with R. Naḥman: Shemini Atzeret is a separate festival (*regel bifnei atzmo*) with regard to PZ"R KSH"B – that is with regard to "***payis***" [balloting][4] it is a separate festival, with regard to the "***z****eman*" [*birkat sheheḥeyanu*][5] it is a separate festival, with regard to "***regel***" [the nature of the festival][6] it is a separate festival, with regard to "***k****orban*" [its sacrifice][7] it is a separate festival, with regard to "***sh****ir*" [its psalm][8] it is a separate festival, and with regard to its "***b****erakha*"[9] it is a separate festival. (Sukka 48a)

The *Aḥaronim* discuss whether these differences imply that Shemini Atzeret should actually be perceived as a separate festival, or simply as the eighth day of the Sukkot festival, whose halakhot differ somewhat from the seven previous days. Some attempt to relate this to an interesting question regarding the proper formula for the Shemini Atzeret insertion in one's prayers. The *Rishonim* write that one inserts "*yom shemini Ḥag HaAtzeret hazeh*" into the *Shemoneh Esreh* and *Birkat HaMazon*,[10] and the *Shulḥan Arukh* records this formula.[11] Rema writes, however, that it is customary to say "*yom shemini HaAtzeret hazeh*," and not to mention the word "*ḥag*" at all, as "we do not find that [Shemini Atzeret] is called a *ḥag*."[12] Maharshal[13] and *Taz*[14] conclude that one should say "*yom Shemini Atzeret haḥag hazeh*," as the "*ḥag*" refers to Sukkot, and not to Shemini Atzeret. The *Arukh HaShulḥan* records that this is the "*minhag haolam*," the accepted practice.[15] R. Chaim Yosef David Azulai, however, insists that the majority of *Rishonim* and *Aḥaronim* held that one should insert "*yom shemini ḥag HaAtzeret hazeh*."[16] This discussion highlights the different approaches regarding whether to view Shemini Atzeret as the conclusion of Sukkot, or as an independent festival.

What if one were to forget to mention Shemini Atzeret, and simply inserted "*yom Ḥag HaSukkot hazeh*," as he did for the previous seven days? *Shaarei Teshuva* cites numerous opinions on this matter.[17] *Ḥayei Adam*,[18] *Arukh HaShulḥan*,[19] and R. Moshe Feinstein[20] rule that one should not repeat his prayer in this case. *Birkei Yosef*, however, rules that if one has already taken three steps backward when he recalls his error, he should repeat his prayer.[21] Some suggest that on Shemini Atzeret outside of Israel (that is, the eighth day, but not the ninth day), one need not repeat his prayer, as the eighth day is considered to be a "doubt" if it is really the seventh day and therefore still Sukkot.[22]

One might suggest that those who maintain that one must repeat his prayer must certainly view Shemini Atzeret as a completely different festival, while those who say that one need not repeat his prayer believe that Shemini Atzeret is fundamentally the eighth day of Sukkot, and not a completely separate festival.[23]

ACCEPTING SHEMINI ATZERET EARLY

As mentioned above, Shemini Atzeret differs from Sukkot in that one does not dwell in the *sukka*, nor does one take the *arba minim*. Therefore, in Israel, where there is no doubt regarding the calendar, one does not eat in the *sukka* on the night of Shemini Atzeret. Furthermore, the Talmud discusses whether one who sits in the *sukka* on Shemini Atzeret with the intention of fulfilling the mitzva violates the prohibition of "*bal tosef*," adding to the mitzvot of the Torah.[24]

Interestingly, the *Aḥaronim* debate whether one who accepts Shemini Atzeret early must eat his evening meal in the *sukka*. On the one hand, as there is still light outside, one may argue that it is still Sukkot and that one must therefore still eat in the *sukka*. On the other hand, as one has already accepted upon himself the new day of Shemini Atzeret, on which one does not sit in the *sukka*, it seems that one need not eat in the *sukka*.

Maharshal argues that one who accepts Shemini Atzeret early should not eat before dark. He insists that although one may accept Shemini Atzeret early, along with the laws related to *kedushat Yom Tov*, the day still formally remains Sukkot, and it is therefore forbidden to eat outside of the *sukka* until dark. In order to avoid being required to eat in the *sukka* and to recite the blessing of *leishev basukka*, one should wait until dark before eating.[25] *Taz* disagrees and argues that *tosefet Yom Tov*, the time period added on to Yom Tov, may actually uproot the previous day's obligations as well; one who accepts Shemini Atzeret early would therefore no longer be obligated to eat in the *sukka*.[26] It is customary, however, to wait until dark before eating on the evening of Shemini Atzeret.

EATING AND SLEEPING IN THE *SUKKA* ON SHEMINI ATZERET

We have previously discussed the institution of Yom Tov Sheni outside of Israel. Since the communities outside of Israel did not know the exact date of the month, they would observe two days of Yom Tov out of doubt. This custom continued even after the establishment of a set calendar. Therefore, outside of Israel, one observes two days of Yom Tov at the beginning of Sukkot, and two days of Shemini Atzeret at the end.

Because of the doubt, the "eighth day" – Shemini Atzeret – may actually be the seventh day of Sukkot, at least in theory. Should someone outside of Israel therefore sit in the *sukka* on Shemini Atzeret? The Talmud cites a debate on this matter, recording that some maintain that one does not sit in the *sukka* at all, others maintain that one sits in the *sukka* and recites a blessing over the *sukka,* and still others are accustomed to sit in the *sukka* but not recite the blessing of *leishev basukka.* The Gemara concludes: "And the law is that we must, indeed, sit in the *sukka,* but may not recite the benediction."[27] The *Rishonim* offer different interpretations of this conclusion.

Rambam, in a responsum written to Ḥakhmei Lunel, focuses on the inability to recite the blessing. He derives from this passage that one does not recite a *birkat hamitzva* when in doubt whether or not he is actually obligated in the mitzva. Accordingly, he concludes, one should not recite a blessing over the circumcision of an androgynous infant, as it is not certain that this *mila* is actually required.[28] Alternatively, Rif offers a different explanation:

> Since it is Shemini Atzeret, making a *berakha* would lead to a contradiction: If it is a day of [sitting in the] *sukka,* then it is not Shemini Atzeret, and if it is Shemini Atzeret, then it is not a day of [sitting in the] *sukka*! Since we are in doubt, we act stringently on both counts. We eat in the *sukka,* but make no *berakha* and treat the day as *ḥag* [i.e., Shemini Atzeret].[29]

Rif insists that sitting in the *sukka* and reciting the blessing on Shemini Atzeret constitutes an inherent contradiction. The *Ḥinukh* attempts to explain this contradiction:

> The Rabbis commanded us to sit in the *sukka* to fulfill the obligation [of Jews outside Israel] to add one day to every holiday; hence, we add a day to Sukkot and make it eight days, but we do not make a *berakha* on the *sukka* on that day because it is really a different holiday altogether. Since nowadays we know the calculation of the calendar and hence the true date, it is more appropriate to make *berakhot* relating to the true character of the day rather than to the aspect of the day instituted by *Ḥazal.* One may ask: Why do we not mention both Sukkot and Shemini Atzeret in our blessings, as we do with regard to Shabbat and Yom Tov when they coincide? [The answer is] we find that it is possible for Shabbat and Yom Tov to occur on the same day, but *two different holidays cannot occur at the same time,* and hence we should not recite such a *berakha.* But it is perfectly appropriate to sit in the *sukka* on Shemini Atzeret, *since this does not detract from the holiday of Shemini Atzeret at all.*[30]

The *Ḥinukh* explains that although sitting in the *sukka* does not contradict the day of Shemini Atzeret,[31] per se, it is not possible to recite blessings for two different festivals on the same day. It is this inherent contradiction that led the Rabbis to rule that one should sit in the *sukka* on Shemini Atzeret outside of Israel, but not recite the *berakha.*

Ran offers another explanation, which he believes is the proper understanding of Rif. He writes that we do not recite the *berakha* of *leishev basukka* on Shemini Atzeret "so that we do not come to treat Yom Tov lightly" (*lezalzulei beYom Tov*). On a normal Yom Tov Sheni, we recite the Yom Tov Kiddush and prayers in order to ensure that one does not treat the second day of Yom Tov lightly.[32] In our case, we fear that one might treat the first day of Yom Tov lightly if we emphasize that it may "only" be the seventh day of Sukkot.[33]

Must one also sleep in the *sukka* on Shemini Atzeret? The *Mordekhai* cites Raavya, who explains that merely sitting in the *sukka* without reciting a *berakha* does not appear similar enough to the mitzva of dwelling in the *sukka* to violate the prohibition of "*bal tosef,*" adding to the mitzvot. However, he adds, one may not sleep in the *sukka* on Shemini Atzeret; since one does not ordinarily recite a blessing before sleeping in the *sukka,* this would appear no different than sleeping in the *sukka* on Sukkot, and it is therefore prohibited because of "*bal tosef.*"[34] Although *Beit Yosef* argues on this point, noting that the *Rishonim* did not distinguish between sleeping and eating in the *sukka* on Shemini Atzeret,[35] Rema records in the *Darkhei Moshe HaArukh* that the custom is in accordance with Raavya.[36] The *Mishna Berura* writes that although many *Aḥaronim,* including Gra,[37] do not distinguish between eating and sleeping in the *sukka,* it is customary not to sleep in the *sukka* on Shemini Atzeret.[38]

The Gemara concludes, and the *Shulḥan Arukh* rules,[39] that outside of Israel, one should eat in the *sukka,* but not recite the blessing of *leishev basukka.* Many communities, however, are accustomed to eat in their homes on Shemini Atzeret, and at most, recite Kiddush and eat a bit in their *sukka.* Although this practice is often attributed to hasidic communities, it already appears in the *Rishonim.*[40] What is the basis for this practice, which seemingly contradicts the explicit ruling of the Talmud?

Many *Aḥaronim*[41] base this custom on the words of R. Netanel Weil in his notes on Rosh, *Korban Netanel.*[42] *Korban Netanel* notes that Tosafot explain that sitting in the *sukka* on Shemini Atzeret does not violate the prohibition of *bal tosef* because sitting outside in the *sukka* is pleasant; one might do so even if it were not Sukkot.[43] But, *Korban Netanel* notes, "if on that day it is cold, or if there is wind or another change in the weather, it would be inappropriate to sit in the *sukka* on the eighth day," as then it would be clear that one is sitting the *sukka* for mitzva purposes, and this would be *bal tosef.*

The *Aḥaronim* explain that in Western and Northern Europe, where it was cold and windy on Sukkot, one who sat in the *sukka* on Shemini Atzeret was clearly sitting there in order to fulfill the mitzva. It therefore became customary to eat only the day meal in the *sukka,*[44] to make Kiddush in the *sukka* and then to eat inside, or not to eat in the *sukka* at all.[45]

We discussed previously whether a visitor to Israel must keep one or two days of Yom Tov. According to those who rule that this visitor must observe two days, should he eat in the *sukka* on Shemini Atzeret even in Israel? R. Shlomo Zalman Auerbach rules that a visitor to Israel keeping two days of Yom Tov should not eat in the *sukka* on Shemini Atzeret.[46] R. Ovadia Yosef writes, however, that although a guest at someone else's home should eat with his host inside the house, one who is celebrating Yom Tov on his own or in a hotel should eat in a *sukka* on Shemini Atzeret.[47] Others insist that a visitor should eat in a *sukka* on Shemini Atzeret, even in Israel.[48]

SIMḤAT TORAH

The final day of Sukkot, the ninth day in the Diaspora and the eighth day in Eretz Yisrael, is known as Simḥat Torah.[49] On Simḥat Torah, the final *parasha* of the Torah, *VeZot HaBerakha*, is read, and the congregation celebrates the completion of another Torah cycle. After dancing with the *sifrei Torah* for the seven *hakafot*, the Torah is read at night and again during the day. The Torah is completed during the *aliya* of the *Ḥatan Torah*, and then begun anew during the *aliya* of the *Ḥatan Bereishit*.

This practice developed toward the end of the geonic period. Until the early Middle Ages, there were two ancient customs of reading the Torah each Shabbat. In Israel, the Torah was divided into either 155 portions and completed once every three years (Megilla 29b), or into 175 portions and completed every three and a half years (Soferim 16:8). Benjamin of Tudela (1130–1173) records that in twelfth-century Cairo, there were still "men of the Land of Israel" who finished the Torah every three years. He relates, however, that on Simḥat Torah, they would join the other community and celebrate Simḥat Torah with the entire Jewish community.[50] Similarly, Rambam mentions the annual celebration as a custom, but not the prominent practice.[51] In fact, while Babylonian communities celebrated Simḥat Torah every year, in Eretz Yisrael, Simḥat Torah was only observed every three years.[52] With the acceptance of the Babylonian custom of completing the reading of the Torah each year, Simḥat Torah became universally observed on the last day of Sukkot.

We find numerous customs which developed as early as the geonic period. For example, the *Geonim* were asked whether one may burn incense in the synagogue on Simḥat Torah[53] and whether one may dance for the Torah despite the rabbinic prohibition of dancing on Yom Tov.[54]

Although the *Geonim* do not explain why the final *parasha* of the Torah is read on Shemini Atzeret specifically, some *Rishonim*[55] explain that the blessings of Moshe, which appear in *Parashat VeZot HaBerakha*, are purposely read on the day on which we read how Shlomo HaMelekh blessed the people on the eighth day of Sukkot (I Kings, chap. 8). The *Maḥzor Vitry* adds that Simḥat Torah was intentionally observed on Sukkot,[56] regarding which the Torah mentions the commandment of "*simḥa*" twice.[57]

R. Yitzchak Abrabanel (1437–1508) suggests that the celebration of Simḥat Torah on Sukkot is rooted in the mitzva of *hak'hel* (Deut. 31:11–12), during which the king would read the Torah to the nation upon the completion of the *Shemitta* year.[58] Although some scholars also accepted this theory, Avraham Yaari rejects it out of hand.[59] Others attempt to relate Simḥat Torah to the ancient celebration of the *Simḥat Beit HaSho'eva*, Hoshana Rabba, and even to Yom Kippur, upon which, according to tradition, the second Tablets were given to Moshe.

In the Diaspora, Shemini Atzeret and Simḥat Torah are observed on separate days, but in Israel, where one day of Yom Tov is observed, Simḥat Torah and Shemini Atzeret are observed on the same day. Therefore, the festive *hakafot* are followed by the serious prayer of *Tefillat Geshem*. At times, one feels that the identity of Shemini Atzeret, as described above, is lost due to the festivities of Simḥat Torah. However, it seems that if Shemini Atzeret commemorates the unique, particular relationship between God and the Jewish people, then there is no better time than Shemini Atzeret to celebrate the Torah, God's gift to the Jewish people, and its completion.

Ḥanukka

CHAPTER 28

Ḥanukka in Custom and Prayer

THE MIRACLE OF ḤANUKKA AND ITS COMMEMORATION

Ḥanukka commemorates the events that took place during the Hasmonean rebellion against Antiochus IV Epiphanes, the Seleucid king of Syria, in 265 BCE. In the *Al HaNissim* prayer inserted in the *Shemoneh Esreh* and *Birkat HaMazon* throughout the holiday, we relate,

> In the days of the Hasmonean Matityahu, son of Yoḥanan the High Priest, and his sons, when the iniquitous Greco-Syrian kingdom arose against Your people Israel to make them forget Your Torah and to turn them away from the ordinances of Your will – in Your abundant mercy, You arose for them in their time of distress, waged their battle, executed judgment, avenged their wrong, and delivered the strong into the hands of the weak, the many into the hands of few, the impure into the hands of the pure, the wicked into the hands of the righteous, and insolent ones into the hands of those occupied with Your Torah. Both unto Yourself did You make a great and holy name in Your world, and unto Your people did You achieve a great deliverance and redemption.

We go on to recount the rededication of the *Beit HaMikdash*.

> Thereupon, Your children entered the sanctuary of Your abode, cleansed Your Temple, purified Your sanctuary, kindled lights in Your holy courts, and established these eight days of Ḥanukka in order to give thanks and praises unto Your holy name.

The *Al HaNissim* insertion clearly focuses upon the military victory and the subsequent rededication of the Temple.

The battle commemorated by Ḥanukka, however, was clearly not considered a standard military victory. Interestingly, many quasi-festivals were instituted throughout the Second Temple period, during which it is prohibited to eulogize and fast. Many of these days, as they are recorded in *Megillat Taanit,* relate to the various victories of the Hasmoneans. However, although after the destruction of the Second Temple the days mentioned in the *Megillat Taanit* are no longer commemorated ("*batla Megillat Taanit*"), the holiday of Ḥanukka, due to the mitzva of "*hadlakat neirot*" and their importance in publicizing of the miracle, remained intact (Rosh HaShana 18b).

Apparently, since its conception, Ḥanukka was perceived and treated as no ordinary military victory. Ḥanukka signified the successful culmination of the Hasmonean revolt, and therefore deserved special celebration. Although the Hasmonean dynasty later tragically strayed from the spiritual legacy of Matityahu, and was in fact eliminated entirely by the time Herod rose to power,[1] the establishment of the dynasty, which began with the Ḥanukka victory, is nevertheless cause for great celebration. Indeed, Rambam writes:

> In the time of the Second Temple, when the Greeks ruled over Israel, they issued evil decrees against them, banning their religion and forbidding them to study the Law and to fulfill the commandments.... And Israel was in sore straits in consequence thereof and suffered great persecution – until the God of our fathers took pity on them and saved and delivered them from the Greeks.... *They set up a king from among the Priests and restored Israel's kingdom for a period of more than two hundred years, until the destruction of the Second Temple.*[2]

Some suggest that Rambam's emphasis upon the two hundred years of Hasmonean autonomy, despite their corrupt reign and tragic end, was intended to note the uniqueness of this victory; it resulted in political autonomy that endured for over two centuries. The Talmud, however, focuses on a different aspect of the Hasmonean victory:

> What is [the reason for] Ḥanukka? For our Rabbis taught: On the twenty-fifth of Kislev the days of Ḥanukka [commence] – eight days during which eulogizing the dead and fasting are forbidden. For when the Greeks entered

> the Temple, they defiled all the oils therein, and when the Hasmonean dynasty prevailed against them and defeated them, they searched and found only one cruse of oil which lay with the seal of the High Priest, but which contained sufficient oil for only one day's lighting. Yet, a miracle occurred and they lit [the Menora] with the oil for eight days. The following year, these [days] were designated as a festival, with [the recital of] Hallel and thanksgiving. (Shabbat 21b)

This passage focuses upon a miracle related to the rededication of the Temple, and not on the victory itself. Indeed, the length of the festival, which clearly relates to the miracle of the flask of oil, also attests to the centrality of the post-victory events.

This centrality is underscored by a comment of *Peri Ḥadash,* who sought to resolve *Beit Yosef*'s famous question: why is Ḥanukka observed for eight days if the flask contained enough oil for one day? The miracle really lasted only seven days, not eight! *Peri Ḥadash* answered that on the first day of Ḥanukka, we commemorate the miraculous military victory, whereas the subsequent seven days celebrate the miracle of the oil.[3] This answer reflects the perspective that views the events *following* the victory as the primary cause of our celebration.

Why did the Hasmoneans' successful efforts to rededicate the Temple after the revolt deserve special celebration? This question is strengthened when we consider that the entire miracle of the flask of oil appears to have been entirely unnecessary. A number of *Aḥaronim* note that the halakhic principle of "*tuma hutra betzibbur*" (Yoma 6b), which allows national Temple rituals to be performed even in a state of ritual defilement, should have deemed the miracle superfluous. Defiled oil would also have been suitable for use in kindling the Menora.

To answer this question, R. Michael Rosensweig[4] notes that the Gemara discusses various levels of observance of the mitzva of candle lighting. Unlike other mitzvot, in which higher levels are not expected of everyone, it appears from the Gemara that the optimal level of observance of candle lighting, "*mehadrin min hamehadrin,*" is expected from everyone; indeed, the universally accepted practice is to adhere to that standard.

R. Rosensweig explains that Antiochus did not wish to annihilate the Jewish people (in contrast to other instances of persecution, such as Haman's decree). Rather, he wished to reduce their halakhic observance and spiritual expression to a private matter, performed in a "*bediavad*" manner. The Hasmonean revolt rejected this attempt to institutionalize "spiritual mediocrity." Just as under certain circumstances a Jew's response to persecution must be "*yehareg ve'al yaavor*," to die in affirmation of one's commitment to Torah, the Jewish people at the time of Ḥanukka risked their lives to be able to live and practice a complete and optimal spiritual lifestyle.

While the miracle of the flask of oil may, indeed, have been superfluous, relying on leniencies would have undermined the entire message of the revolt. For the same reason, the observance of Ḥanukka is unique in its focus upon "*hiddur*"; although one may fulfill the basic mitzva of "*ner ish uveito*," one candle per home, he is expected to fulfill the mitzva in its most ambitious and ideal form. In fact, the *Shulḥan Arukh* does not even mention the possibility of lighting "*ner ish uveito*"! Thus, R. Rosensweig suggests, the fundamental reason for the revolt, and more importantly, the Jewish people's response to the miraculous events, were worthy of a permanent celebration.

THE NATURE OF THE MITZVOT OF ḤANUKKA

Rambam begins each section of his *Mishneh Torah* by listing the biblical and rabbinic mitzvot addressed within that section. In his introduction to the laws of Purim and Ḥanukka, he writes, "Contained within are two positive rabbinic mitzvot (*mitzvot aseh miderabbanan*)." This statement appears strange. Don't the observances of Purim and Ḥanukka contain more than just two mitzvot? On Purim alone, one is obligated to read the Megilla twice, send *matanot la'evyonim* (gifts for the poor) and *mishlo'aḥ manot* (gifts to fellow Jews), and eat a festive meal. On Ḥanukka, we light candles and recite Hallel for eight days. How, then, does Rambam arrive at a total of only two mitzvot?

Apparently, Rambam believes that the numerous actions performed on both Purim and Ḥanukka still only make up one single mitzva – the obligation of "*shevaḥ vehodaa*," praise and thanksgiving to God. Indeed, the *Al HaNissim* prayer concludes, "and established these eight days of Ḥanukka *in order to give thanks and praises unto Your holy name*." This mitzva of *shevaḥ vehodaa* is fulfilled through various activities, such as publicizing the miracle (*pirsumei nissa*) through reading the Megilla and lighting the *neirot Ḥanukka*, sending *matanot la'evyonim* and *mishlo'aḥ manot*, participating in a festive thanksgiving meal, and certainly through the recitation of Hallel.

Interestingly, Rambam discusses the laws of Hallel in the first of the two chapters dedicated to the laws of Ḥanukka (*Hilkhot Megilla VeḤanukka*, chap. 3), rather than among the laws of prayer or Yom Tov. Rambam chose *hilkhot Ḥanukka* as the most suitable context for the laws of Hallel because the laws of Ḥanukka are essentially the laws of "*shevaḥ vehodaa*."

HALLEL ON ḤANUKKA

The Talmud lists the eight days of Ḥanukka among the eighteen days (twenty-one days in the Diaspora) on which we recite the full Hallel (Arakhin 10a). The Gemara continues to determine the criteria for the Hallel obligation:

> As R. Yoḥanan said in the name of R. Shimon b. Yehotzadak: There are eighteen days on which an individual must recite the entire Hallel: the eight days of Sukkot, the eight days of Ḥanukka, the first Yom Tov of Pesaḥ, and the Yom Tov of Shavuot.... On Shabbat, which is distinct in its sacrifices, let us recite [Hallel]? It is not called a *mo'ed* (festival). On Rosh Ḥodesh, which is called a *mo'ed*, let us recite [Hallel]? It is not sanctified with regard to the performance of *melakha* (activity forbidden on Shabbat and Yom Tov).

The Gemara seems to indicate that in order for a day to require the recitation of Hallel, it must be distinguished by a unique *korban*, be called a *mo'ed*, and feature a prohibition of *melakha*. Ḥanukka, of course, does not meet any of these criteria. The Gemara raises this question and responds, "Because of the miracle." The obligation to recognize the miracle of Ḥanukka itself generates the requirement to recite Hallel.

Indeed, as we declare during the *HaNeirot HaLalu* prayer after candle lighting, the days of Ḥanukka were established "in order to thank and praise [God] for the miracles."

The Gemara thus draws a distinction between two types of Hallel: Hallel that is recited on the festivals and Hallel that is recited in response to a miracle. This distinction similarly emerges from the Gemara's discussion in Pesaḥim:

> Who recited this Hallel? The prophets among them instituted that Israel should recite it for every season [on every special occasion], and for every crisis that might come upon them – when they are redeemed from it, they recite it over their redemption. (Pesaḥim 117a)

Interestingly, both *Maggid Mishneh* and Ḥatam Sofer suggest that the Hallel of Ḥanukka may actually be a greater obligation than the Hallel recited on the festivals. Based on the passage in Pesaḥim, *Maggid Mishneh* suggests that the obligation to recite Hallel in response to divine salvation originates "*midivrei kabbala*," the words of the prophets.[5] Ḥatam Sofer goes so far as to suggest that while Hallel on the festivals may be a rabbinic obligation, the Hallel of Ḥanukka may apply *mideoraita* – on the level of biblical obligation![6] Indeed, R. Avraham b. HaRambam[7] (1186–1237) records that a contemporary and critic of his father, R. Daniel HaBavli, held that Hallel of Ḥanukka is certainly of biblical origin, as one is biblically obligated to recite praise upon being miraculously delivered from harm. Most authorities, however, disagree, insisting that Hallel on Ḥanukka, and possibly all occasions, is of rabbinic origin.[8]

If we assume that Hallel on Ḥanukka is of rabbinic origin, we may conclude that women are obligated to recite it. Women are included in the mitzva of lighting Ḥanukka candles, despite the fact that it is a time-bound commandment, because of the principle of "*af hen hayu beoto ha'nes*" – "they were also in the miracle" (Shabbat 23a). (This is similarly the case regarding Megilla reading [Megilla 4a], *matanot la'evyonim*, and *mishlo'aḥ manot* on Purim.[9]) It would seem that women should be obligated to recite Hallel on each of the eight days of Ḥanukka for the same reason. Indeed, Tosafot offers a similar argument regarding Hallel of the night of Pesaḥ (Sukka 38a).

The *Aḥaronim* debate this issue. R. Shimon Sofer (1850–1944), son of *Ketav Sofer* and grandson of Ḥatam Sofer, writes in his responsa *Hitorerut Teshuva* that based upon the Tosafot cited above, women are obligated to recite Hallel all eight days of Ḥanukka. Others infer from Rambam,[10] however, that women are exempt.[11]

AL HANISSIM

During the eight days of Ḥanukka, we add the *Al HaNissim* prayer in both *Shemoneh Esreh* (after *Modim*) and *Birkat HaMazon* (during the second blessing). One who recites the blessing and realizes that he forgot to insert *Al HaNissim* does not return to the point where it should be recited; he simply continues the *Shemoneh Esreh* or *Birkat HaMazon*.

The *Rishonim* debate whether one adds a text about the uniqueness of the day, "*me'ein hameora*," in the *Birkat Me'ein Shalosh*, known as *Al HaMiḥya*.[12] Rambam rules that one should mention special occasions in the *Birkat Me'ein Shalosh*,[13] but *Hagahot Maimoniyot* notes that this applies only to Shabbat and Yom Tov;[14] we do not mention Purim or Ḥanukka in *Al HaMiḥya*.

Why do Purim and Ḥanukka differ from Shabbat and Yom Tov in this regard? Why shouldn't we mention the special occasion in *Al HaMiḥya*, just as we do on Shabbat and Yom Tov? R. Mordekhai Yoffe, known as *Levush*, after his commentary on the *Shulḥan Arukh*, explains that *Al HaNissim* is fundamentally a prayer of thanksgiving, and we therefore insert it in the blessings of thanksgiving in the *Shemoneh Esreh* and *Birkat HaMazon*. The blessing of *Al HaMiḥya*, however, does not contain a section dedicated to thanking God, and therefore *Al HaNissim* is simply thematically inconsistent with *Al HaMiḥya*.[15]

R. Yosef Dov Soloveitchik offers a different explanation.[16] He contends that the paragraph of *Retzei*, which we recite on Shabbat, and that of *Yaale VeYavo*, which we recite on Yom Tov and Rosh Ḥodesh, should be viewed as independent *berakhot*, and not as mere insertions into the text of *Birkat HaMazon*. He proves this theory via the halakha that requires that one who omits *Retzei* or *Yaale VeYavo* recite a separate blessing that expresses the same idea, such as "*shenatan Shabbatot limenuḥa le'amo Yisrael.*"[17] The fact that the omission of *Retzei* and *Yaale VeYavo* warrants a separate blessing and requires that one repeat *Shemoneh Esreh* indicates that they are not mere insertions, but rather independent prayers. These prayers must be recited either during the *berakha* of *Boneh Yerushalayim* or, when forgotten, as a separate blessing afterward. The omission of *Al HaNissim,* on the other hand, does not necessitate the repetition of *Shemoneh Esreh* or *Birkat HaMazon. Al HaNissim* does not constitute a separate prayer, but rather a mere "*hazkara,*" a text inserted into our prayers. The *berakha* of *Me'ein Shalosh* serves as an abridged version of the *Birkat HaMazon,* and is thus composed of passages that are integral to the *Birkat HaMazon.* Passages that are not essential enough to warrant repetition or the insertion of a separate blessing if they are omitted are not mentioned. Therefore, Purim and Ḥanukka are not mentioned in *Al HaMiḥya.*

The question remains, however, why *Al HaNissim* differs from *Retzei* and *Yaale VeYavo* in this regard. Why did *Ḥazal* establish *Retzei* and *Yaale VeYavo* as independent *berakhot,* while *Al HaNissim* is only considered an insertion within a *berakha*? R. Soloveitchik explains that the difference lies in the formal *kedushat hayom* (sanctity of the day) with which Shabbat and Yom Tov are endowed. This special status mandates inserting a separate and independent prayer mentioning these days in the *Shemoneh Esreh* and *Birkat HaMazon.* Purim and Ḥanukka, however, do not have *kedushat hayom.* One therefore merely mentions the miracles of these days during the prayers, but this does not constitute a separate prayer.[18]

LAWS AND CUSTOMS OF THE DAYS OF ḤANUKKA

As mentioned above, the Gemara relates that Ḥanukka was included in *Megillat Taanit,* the list of festive days upon which it is prohibited to fast and eulogize (Rosh HaShana 18b). Unlike the other days mentioned in *Megillat Taanit,* whose observance was canceled with the fall of the Second Commonwealth, the celebrations of Ḥanukka and Purim remain. As such, eulogies are not delivered on Ḥanukka, nor may one fast on any of the eight days of this holiday (Shabbat 21b).

The Rabbis did not institute a mandatory festive meal (*seuda*) on Ḥanukka, as they did on Purim. *Levush* explains that because the threat and deliverance of Purim related to the physical existence of the Jewish people, our celebration is expressed in a physical manner – through food and festivities. On Ḥanukka, however, the threat and deliverance related to spiritual survival, and the celebratory response is therefore spiritual, in the form of *hadlakat neirot*.[19] *Taz* disagrees with *Levush*'s explanation,[20] arguing that causing another to sin may be an even greater offense than murder. He explains that since the miracle of Ḥanukka is less apparent than that of Purim, the primary mitzva of the day is to publicize the miracle. Since the miraculous deliverance of Purim was apparent to all, the celebration can focus upon physical enjoyment in the form of a celebratory meal.

Rema writes that there is a "slight mitzva" ("*ketzat mitzva*") to eat festive meals on Ḥanukka and that meals during which one sings and praises God are certainly considered *seudot mitzva*.[21] Indeed, Rambam describes Ḥanukka as "days of *simḥa vehallel*," rejoicing and praise.[22] Rema also cites opinions that encourage eating dairy foods during these meals in commemoration of the dairy food Judith fed to the Greek general, which caused him to fall asleep and allowed her to assassinate him.[23] Rambam's father, R. Maimon, in his Arabic commentary on the prayers,[24] records the custom to eat dough fried in oil on Ḥanukka in remembrance of the miracle of the oil, insisting that one should not treat such *minhagim* lightly.

Tur cites the custom of women to refrain from *melakha* while the Ḥanukka candles are burning.[25] While some criticize this custom,[26] other *Aḥaronim* approvingly record the custom for women to refrain from *melakha* until midnight or for the entire first and eighth days.[27] The *Aḥaronim* offer different reasons for the common custom for women to refrain from *melakha* while the candles are burning. Some suggest that it serves as a reminder not to derive benefit from the Ḥanukka lights. According to this reason, the *Mishna Berura* suggests that women should refrain from *melakha* only during the first half-hour, after which, strictly speaking, halakha permits deriving benefit from the lights.[28] Alternatively, *Levush* suggests that the custom underscores the fact that the days of Ḥanukka were established as festive days, similar to Rosh Ḥodesh and Ḥol HaMo'ed. Women, who were responsible for bringing about the miracle of Ḥanukka, as discussed in the next chapter, therefore refrain from *melakha* while the lights are burning.[29] It would appear that according to this theory, women should refrain from *melakha* as long as the lights burn, and not merely within the first half-hour. The accepted custom is for women to refrain from labors prohibited on Ḥol HaMo'ed (such as laundry and sewing) for the first half-hour after the candles are lit. Other chores, such as cooking (and frying), are permitted.

CHAPTER 29

Women and Ḥanukka Candles

WOMEN AND ḤANUKKA CANDLES

The Gemara teaches that despite their broad exemption from time-bound commandments (*mitzvot aseh shehazeman geraman*), women are obligated to fulfill the mitzva of lighting Ḥanukka lights:

> Women certainly light, as R. Yehoshua b. Levi taught: Women are obligated in *ner Ḥanukka*, as they were also in the miracle. (Shabbat 23a)

Elsewhere, the Gemara obligates women to fulfill the mitzvot of *mikra Megilla* on Purim (Megilla 4a) and *arba kosot* on Pesaḥ (Pesaḥim 108a), which are also time-bound commandments, for the same reason – "*af hen hayu beoto ha'nes.*"

The *Rishonim* discuss the precise meaning of the phrase "*af hen hayu beoto ha'nes,*" "they were also in the miracle." In the context of Megilla reading, Rashi explains that the decree of annihilation included both men and women, and hence, the mitzvot enacted to commemorate the nation's deliverance naturally apply to men and women alike.[1] Rashbam disagrees, explaining that in all three instances of salvation – in Persia (Purim), in Egypt (Pesaḥ), and during the Greek persecution (Ḥanukka) – women played a crucial role in Am Yisrael's salvation.[2] Esther brought about the deliverance of the Jewish people during the time of Aḥashveirosh, and the sages comment that "in the merit of righteous women, the Children of Israel were redeemed from Egypt" (Sota 11b). As for the Ḥanukka miracle, Rashbam claims that this miracle was facilitated by Judith, a beautiful Jewish widow known to us through the apocryphal Book of Judith. Judith ingratiated herself to the enemy general, Holofernes, and eventually decapitated him while he slept in a drunken stupor. The Seleucids fled, having lost their leader, and the Jewish people were saved.

Aside from the questionable historicity of this story, Tosafot note that the phrase, "they were *also* in the miracle," indicates that the women were *also* saved, or, as the Talmud Yerushalmi puts it, they were "also in the same danger," and not that they were responsible for the miraculous deliverance in each episode.

The *Rishonim* also discuss the scope and nature of this halakha. Tosafot, for example, question why women are exempt from the commandment to dwell in *sukkot* given that they, too, benefited from God's miraculous protection in the wilderness.[3] Elsewhere, Tosafot ask why the Talmud does not invoke the rule of *af hen hayu* as the basis for women's inclusion in the mitzva of *matza*, resorting instead to a different source.[4] Similarly, Ḥatam Sofer asks why the Talmud did not obligate women to wear *tefillin*, which also serve as a reminder for the Exodus from Egypt.[5]

Tosafot suggest that the principle of *af hen hayu* refers only to women's obligation to perform mitzvot that are of rabbinic origin (*miderabbanan*). As such, this rule cannot be applied to *sukka* or *matza*. Furthermore, *af hen hayu* is effective only in obligating women on a rabbinic level; it cannot mandate the performance of a mitzva on the level of Torah obligation (*mideoraita*).[6] According to Tosafot, the principle of *af hen hayu beoto ha'nes* may theoreticaly obligate women to perform any mitzva of rabbinic origin instituted to commemorate a miracle experienced equally by women. Thus, for example, we might consider applying this rule to the obligation of *shalosh seudot,* to eat three meals on Shabbat. The Talmud (Shabbat 117b) infers this requirement from the Torah's threefold use of the word "today" (*hayom*) in reference to the manna: "And Moshe said: Eat it [the manna] today, for today is Shabbat to God; today you will not find it in the field" (Ex. 16:25). While according to most opinions, the obligation to eat three meals on Shabbat is of rabbinic origin, the Gemara clearly relates its performance to the miracle of the manna. Rabbeinu Tam insists that women are included in this obligation, as they also benefited from the miracle of the manna that the three Shabbat meals are intended to commemorate.[7] The *Shulḥan Arukh* codifies this position,[8] although his ruling results from other factors and does not necessarily stem from Rabbeinu Tam's contention.[9]

Alternatively, R. Yosef Dov Soloveitchik often cited his father, R. Moshe Soloveitchik, as suggesting a distinction between a mitzva intended to publicize a miracle (*pirsumei nissa*) and a mitzva that we perform merely to recall a miracle. The three mitzvot to which the Talmud applies the rule of *af hen hayu* – *ner Ḥanukka, mikra Megilla,* and *arba kosot* – are intended for *pirsumei nissa,* to publicize the respective miracles. This is not the case with the other mitzvot mentioned above. Although by sitting in a *sukka* one recalls God's protection of the Jewish people in the desert and the three Shabbat meals commemorate the miracle of the manna, their primary function is not to publicize those miracles. Since "*af hen hayu beoto ha'nes*" applies only to mitzvot of *pirsumei nissa,* it does not apply to mitzvot such as *sukka, tefillin,* and *shalosh seudot.* This approach clearly underscores the special quality of *ner Ḥanukka* as a mitzva defined and dictated by its ability to publicize the miracle.

WOMEN AND *MEHADRIN MIN HAMEHADRIN*

The basic mitzva of *ner Ḥanukka* is "*ner ish uveito*" (Shabbat 21b), that a single light be kindled in the home each night of Ḥanukka. Rema rules that the higher level of performance, or "*mehadrin,*" requires that each member of the household light Ḥanukka candles. Should women, especially married women, kindle their own lights like the other members of the household, or should they fulfill their obligation through their husbands' lighting, or via other family members?[10]

Maharshal writes that one candle suffices for both husband and wife.[11] *Eliya Rabba,*[12] and later the *Mishna Berura,*[13] explain that married women do not light because of the halakhic concept of "*ishto kegufo*" ("a man's wife is like himself"), even to fulfill the level of "*mehadrin.*" R. Moshe Feinstein notes that according to this rationale, if the wife had lit Ḥanukka candles, the husband should not light, unless he specifically had in mind not to fulfill his obligation through his wife's lighting.[14] Furthermore, it would seem that according to the *Eliya Rabba,* there is no inherent preference for the husband to light instead of the wife, and they may even take turns if they so desire. Accordingly, the practice among many married women is not to light Ḥanukka candles. As noted by many *Aḥaronim,* this custom is valid only with regard to married women; it would seem that unmarried women and women whose husbands are not currently at home must certainly light Ḥanukka candles.

Nevertheless, in many communities, it is customary even for single women not to light Ḥanukka candles. Some have suggested that since this lighting should preferably take place outside and imposing such a requirement upon an unmarried girl would violate her "modesty," the custom developed for unmarried women not to light at all.[15] Others explain that it would be disrespectful for a girl to light given that her married mother does not.[16] Yet a third theory claims that since a girl will not light after her marriage, there is no reason to encourage her to light while still single. Clearly, however, a woman living alone must light *neirot Ḥanukka.*

R. Soloveitchik, as recorded by R. Hershel Schachter, found it difficult to apply the principle of *ishto kegufo* to this mitzva, and therefore ruled that even married women, and of course unmarried women, should kindle their own Ḥanukka lights.[17] Similarly, R. Moshe Harari cites previously unpublished comments of R. Moshe Feinstein recalling that women in his hometown in Europe did, in fact, light *neirot Ḥanukka* with a *berakha,* contrary to the impression given by the *Mishna Berura.*[18] R. Feinstein's wife, however, was not accustomed to lighting *neirot Ḥanukka,* and R. Feinstein did not impose his customs on his wife. In any event, R. Feinstein observed that women in America are not accustomed to lighting *ner Ḥanukka.*

Since women are equally obligated in the mitzva of *ner Ḥanukka,* a woman may fulfill her family's obligation to light. In chapter 31, we will discuss whether it is preferable for a man who cannot be home during the optimal time to light (after sunset) to have his wife light for him or whether he should light upon returning home at a later hour.

CHAPTER 30

The Mitzva of Lighting Ḥanukka Candles

NER ISH UVEITO: HOW MANY CANDLES MUST ONE LIGHT?

One of the great difficulties in understanding the mitzva of *ner Ḥanukka* relates to the following talmudic passage:

> Our Rabbis taught: The precept of Ḥanukka [demands] one light for a man and his household (*ner ish uveito*); the zealous (*mehadrin*) [kindle] a light for each member [of the household]; and the extremely zealous (*mehadrin min hamehadrin*) – *Beit Shammai* maintains: On the first day, eight lights are lit, and thereafter, they are gradually reduced; but *Beit Hillel* says: On the first day, one is lit, and thereafter, they are progressively increased. (Shabbat 21b)

As we noted previously, the Talmud presents an unprecedented three-tiered description of this mitzva's performance: *ner ish uveito, mehadrin,* and *mehadrin min hamehadrin.* This, itself, requires some explanation, as we have noted above. Moreover, the relationship between the levels of *mehadrin* and *mehadrin min hamehadrin* is unclear and subject to considerable debate, as we shall see.

There is, however, a more basic question about the obligation of *neirot Ḥanukka* that lies at the root of many other halakhic issues on this topic, such as how many candles one lights, where one should light, whether and how a guest should light, and whether a traveler or someone with no home should light: Should we view the mitzva as a personal obligation (*ḥovat gavra*) that one performs (perhaps only preferably) at the entrance of his house, or rather as an obligation upon a house itself (*ḥovat habayit*), similar to the mitzva of affixing a mezuza?

The Gemara mentions an obligation imposed upon a person (*ish*) and his household (*beito*). On the one hand, the Gemara may be instructing us that one fulfills his personal obligation by lighting a candle at the entrance to the house. The fact that the lighting should take place in the context of one's home, according to this perspective, is but one detail of the mitzva, which is defined essentially as a personal obligation. Conceivably, if we accept this approach, we may even allow the fulfillment of this mitzva in the absence of a house, since the house is not essential to the basic definition of the obligation. Furthermore, if the obligation is personal, one might be required to light even when not in his own home.

On the other hand, we might suggest that the mitzva is essentially defined as requiring candle lighting in one's home. Rambam, for example, writes, "The mitzva is such that *each and every house should light one candle,* regardless of whether the inhabitants of the house are many, or even just one…"[1] Rambam describes the mitzva as a requirement incumbent upon the house, rather than an obligation upon individuals. Similarly, Ran understood a comment in the Gemara as proposing that guests are entirely exempt from *ner Ḥanukka,* just as a guest is not obligated to affix his own mezuza in someone else's house.[2] This notion certainly reflects a perspective that views the mitzva as essentially defined as an obligation upon the home. This question may also affect our understanding of the *mehadrin* and *mehadrin min hamehadrin* levels of *ner Ḥanukka*.

MEHADRIN AND *MEHADRIN MIN HAMEHADRIN*

The Gemara establishes that there are two higher levels at which this mitzva may be performed beyond the basic obligation of *ner ish uveito*:

mehadrin and *mehadrin min hamehadrin,* the latter of which is subject to a debate between *Beit Shammai* and *Beit Hillel* (Shabbat 21b). The Gemara teaches that "the zealous (*hamehadrin*) [kindle] a light for each member [of the household] ..." This implies that the *baal habayit* (head of the household) lights, on each night, the number of candles corresponding to the members of the household. It is possible that this attention to the number of individuals in the home is evidence of a *ḥovat gavra;* each person has an obligation to have a candle lit on his behalf. Alternatively, it is possible that a "*mehadrin* house" must also reflect the number of its inhabitants.

The Gemara continues to describe the dispute between *Beit Hillel* and *Beit Shammai*:

> Ulla said: Two *Amora'im* in the West [Israel], R. Yose b. Abin and R. Yose b. Zebida, differ [regarding the basis of the debate]. One maintains that *Beit Shammai*'s reason is that it shall correspond to the days still to come, and that of *Beit Hillel* is that it shall correspond to the days that have passed; but the other maintains that *Beit Shammai*'s reason is that it shall correspond to the bullocks of the festival [Sukkot], whilst *Beit Hillel*'s reason is that we advance in [matters of] sanctity, but do not reduce (*maalin bakodesh ve'ein moridin*).

The *Rishonim* differ as to how to understand the *mehadrin min hamehadrin* standard. Tosafot,[3] Raa,[4] and others understood that the Gemara establishes two types of *hiddur* ("enhancement"). The first, "*mehadrin,*" dictates lighting in a manner which reflects the number of *inhabitants* of the house, while the other, "*mehadrin min hamehadrin,*" requires lighting in a manner that reflects the ascending or descending *days* of Ḥanukka. In other words, *mehadrin min hamehadrin* is not an extension of *mehadrin;* rather, it stands independently of the *mehadrin* and expands the basic mitzva of "*ner ish uveito.*"

Tosafot note that if *mehadrin min hamehadrin* were actually an expansion of *mehadrin,* the entire purpose of these higher standards would be undermined. Since the number of candles would correspond to both the members of the household and the number of days that have passed, observers would be unable to determine the number of members of the household or the number of days that have passed!

Tosafot therefore maintain that the *mehadrin min hamehadrin* standard is intended to reflect the number of days *instead of* (and not in addition to) the members of the household. Representing the number of days emphasizes the enormity of the miracle of the oil, and is thus a greater form of *pirsum ha'nes*, publicizing the miracle. It would seem, however, that Tosafot would agree that if one could light in a manner that would accurately reflect the amount of days as well as the number of residents, that would certainly be preferable. We will return to this point shortly.

Rambam records the following as "the simple custom in all our cities in Sepharad":

> All the members of the house light one candle on the first night, and they continually add a candle each night until they have lit eight lights, regardless of whether the members of the household are numerous, or even one.[5]

This custom corresponds with Tosafot's view that *mehadrin min hamehadrin* does not include the *mehadrin*; each household – and not each person – lights the number of candles corresponding with the number of the day. *Hadlakat neirot*, according to this view, would appear to be a *ḥovat habayit*, not a *ḥovat gavra*.

Rambam himself,[6] however, as well as R. Yonatan of Lunel[7] and Ritva,[8] disagree with this practice. Rambam explains that the *mehader et hamitzvot*, one who performs the mitzvot in a beautified manner, lights the number of candles corresponding to the number of household members, while one who wishes to beautify the mitzvot even more and fulfill the mitzva in the optimal way *also* takes into consideration which night of Ḥanukka it is. Therefore, he concludes, if there are ten members of the household, the *baal habayit* lights ten candles on the first night and eighty on the eighth night. Tosafot, as we noted above, rejects this option, as one who sees these lights cannot readily discern between the number of household members and the number of nights. In summary, while Tosafot prefer to publicize that the miracle lasted for eight days, Rambam views the additional lights reflecting both multiple nights and household members as the *hiddur*.

Maharil records the prevalent custom – presumably among German communities – of each individual lighting *neirot Ḥanukka.*[9] This practice seems to imply that the mitzva of *ner Ḥanukka,* or at least the *mehadrin min hamehadrin* standard, focuses upon the lighting of the individual, or what we referred to as a *ḥovat gavra.*

PRACTICAL HALAKHA

The *Shulḥan Arukh* rules in accordance with the position of Tosafot and the practice documented by Rambam: the *baal habayit* alone should light one candle each night, corresponding to the number of nights, concluding with eight candles on the eighth night.[10] Rema, however, writes:

> Some say that each member of the house should light, and that is the common custom. [But] each person should be careful to place his lights in a designated place, so that it should be clear how many candles are being lit.[11]

Some *Aḥaronim* question why the *Shulḥan Arukh,* who represents the Sephardic tradition, rules in accordance with Tosafot, while Rema, the voice of Ashkenzic practice, seems to favor Rambam's position.[12] In truth, the *Shulḥan Arukh*'s ruling follows the prevalent custom of the cities of Sepharad as recorded by Rambam, and it should therefore come as no surprise. As a result of this ruling, some authorities maintain that unmarried Sephardic men, such as soldiers or students away from home, fulfill their obligation through the lighting in their homes, as the obligation falls on the household of which they are still a part.[13] Others, however, maintain that single soldiers and students (after high school) are considered independent and must light on their own.[14]

Rema, who rules that the number of lights should correspond to the number of residents as well as to the number of days, indeed seems to accept Rambam's ruling over that of Tosafot, in contrast to Rema's usual procedure of codifying the Ashkenazic custom. A closer examination of Rema's ruling, however, reveals that it does not, in fact, reflect the view of Rambam. While Rambam rules that the *baal habayit* lights all of the candles for his household, Rema insists that each individual light in his own separate place. In his earlier work, the *Darkhei Moshe* (a commentary on *Tur*), Rema cites the Maharal of Prague as commenting that since the majority of us no longer light outside, it is possible for each person to light in a separate area, such that both the number of days and number of residents can be indicated through the lighting. In other words, Rema actually rules according to Tosafot, who would agree that when possible, one should fulfill *both* types of *hiddur*, reflecting the number of inhabitants as well as the number of days. He therefore rules that nowadays, when this dual *hiddur* is attainable, it is the ideal arrangement for lighting. Rema's interpretation of Tosafot strongly suggests an emphasis upon the *ḥovat gavra*, as opposed to an obligation upon the household.

The *Aḥaronim* raise a serious objection to Rema's ruling. According to Rema, once one person has lit and all the members of the household have fulfilled the basic obligation of *ner ish uveito*, how is it possible for other members of the household to light with a *berakha*? Some suggest that one should have in mind not to fulfill the mitzva through another person's lighting.[15] Others disagree, and must therefore explain how one can recite a blessing on the additional level of *mehadrin min hamehadrin*.

R. Yitzchak Ze'ev Soloveitchik (1886–1959), for example, explains that although the *mehadrin* performance of the mitzva is only a *hiddur mitzva*, Rema maintains that one may recite a blessing upon performing a *hiddur* mitzva, even when performed separately from the mitzva itself.[16] Alternatively, some suggest that the Talmud here establishes three distinct ways to perform the mitzva, such that one who fulfills the *mehadrin min hamehadrin* standard has not simply "glorified" the mitzva, but has rather fulfilled a different mitzva of reflecting the number of days and the house's residents through the number of lights. Since he fulfills an entirely new mitzva by lighting the extra candles, he recites a *berakha* despite the fact that he has already fulfilled the basic obligation.[17]

The *Aḥaronim* raise a number of interesting questions that may relate to this issue. For example, may one who began lighting without reciting the *berakha* subsequently recite the *berakha* and continue lighting?[18] Do the halakhot regarding personal use of the light of the *ner Ḥanukka* apply to the *mehadrin min hamehadrin* candles as well? These questions may relate to whether we view the extra candles as integral to the basic obligation or as fulfilling a separate mitzva.

"*HADLAKA OSA MITZVA*"

The Gemara raises the fundamental question of whether one fulfills the mitzva of *ner Ḥanukka* through the *hadlaka* – by lighting the *neirot* – or through *hanaḥa* – by putting them in their proper place after they are lit:

> For the scholars propounded: Does the kindling (*hadlaka*) or the placing (*hanaḥa*) constitute the precept? Come and hear: For Rabba said: If one was standing and holding the Ḥanukka lamp, he has done nothing; this proves that the placing constitutes the precept! [This is not so:] There, an observer may think that he is holding it for his own purposes [and the sages therefore required putting the lamp down]. Come and hear: For Rabba said: If one lights it inside and then takes it outside, he has done nothing. Now, it is well if you say that the kindling constitutes the precept; [for this reason] we require the kindling to be [done] in its proper place, [and] therefore he has done nothing [if he lit inside]. But if you say that the placing constitutes the precept, why has he done nothing? [This also does not follow:] There, too, an observer may think that he lit it for his own purposes.

The Gemara attempted to resolve this question on the basis of the halakhot relevant to one who stands holding a candle and one who lit inside (the improper place to light) and then brought the candle outside. But the Gemara dismisses these proofs and then attempts another:

> Come and hear: For R. Yehoshua b. Levi said: With regard to a lantern that was burning the whole day [of Shabbat], at the conclusion of Shabbat it is extinguished and then relit [for the purpose of lighting Ḥanukka candles]. Now, it is well if you say that the kindling constitutes the precept; then it is correct. But if you say that the placing constitutes the precept, is this "extinguished and [re-]lit" [all that is required]? Surely it should [have stated]: "It must be extinguished, lifted up, replaced, and then relit"!

The Gemara asserts that if one must merely extinguish and relight a pre-existing flame in order to fulfill the mitzva, rather than also lifting it and replacing it, then evidently the obligation focuses on the *hadlaka*, and not the *hanaḥa*. The Gemara concludes:

> Moreover, since we recite the *berakha*, "Who sanctified us by His commandments and commanded us to *kindle* the lamp of Ḥanukka," it proves that the kindling constitutes the precept.

The Gemara further notes that since the *hadlaka* constitutes the essential obligation, a "*ḥeiresh, shoteh, vekatan*" (deaf-mute, mentally impaired person, or a minor) may not light the Ḥanukka candles on behalf of an adult. Since these groups of people are exempt from the mitzva, which is fulfilled through the act of lighting, their lighting does not satisfy the obligation.

REKINDLING AN EXTINGUISHED FLAME: "*KAVTA ZAKUK/LO ZAKUK LA*"

In the midst of a discussion regarding the disqualification of certain oils and wicks for use as Shabbat lights due to the inferior quality of the flame they produce (Shabbat 21a), the Gemara cites a debate regarding whether such wicks and oils may be used for Ḥanukka lights. According to R. Huna, wicks and oils that are disqualified for Shabbat lights are similarly invalid for use as Ḥanukka lights. R. Ḥisda and Rav, however, maintain that they may be used for Ḥanukka lights. The Gemara explains:

> What is R. Huna's reason? He holds that if it [the Ḥanukka lamp] is extinguished, one must attend thereto (*kavta zakuk la*).... R. Ḥisda maintained:... If it is extinguished, it does not require attention (*kavta lo zakuk la*).... R. Yirmiyahu said: What is Rav's reason? He holds that if it is extinguished, it does not require attention.

The Gemara concludes that extinguished lights do not, in fact, require rekindling – *kavta lo zakuk la*.[19]

It is possible to relate this question to our previous discussion regarding whether or not the mitzva focuses specifically on the act of lighting. Perhaps since "*hadlaka osa mitzva*," the mitzva is fulfilled even if the light is subsequently extinguished.[20] If, however, the focus of the mitzva lies in its "placement," then it stands to reason that one must ensure that the candles achieve the objective of *pirsumei nissa* throughout the designated time frame. Indeed, the *Shulḥan Arukh* writes, "The mitzva is fulfilled through the lighting; *therefore*, if the light is extinguished [even] before its time has passed, one need not rekindle it."[21] This passage certainly indicates a direct correlation between the two issues.

However, the Talmud itself did *not* point to a relationship between *hadlaka osa mitzva* and *kavta lo zakuk la*. *Taz* therefore remarks:

> I do not understand how these two laws are connected.... Why didn't the Gemara bring [the fact that *hadlaka osa mitzva*] as proof that we rule that if the light is extinguished it need not be rekindled!?[22]

Taz concludes that the *Shulḥan Arukh* should not be read literally; rather, the *Shulḥan Arukh* meant that since one fulfills the mitzva immediately upon lighting, it is unnecessary to rekindle the flame if it is extinguished. According to *Taz*, the two *sugyot* address different questions. First, the Gemara questions whether the lighting constitutes a mere preparation for the *maase mitzva* of *hanaḥa*, at which point the lights are potentially poised to publicize the miracle, or whether the potential to publicize the miracle must also be incorporated into the lighting (*hadlaka*) itself. R. Huna and R. Ḥisda, however, question whether even after performing the mitzva one must still ensure that the lights remain lit in order to maximize their *pirsumei nissa*.

While in practice we rule that *kavta lo zakuk la*, the candles need not be relit, the Gemara does teach that the *potential* to successfully publicize the miracle contributes to the definition of the *hadlaka*. The lights must therefore be lit at a certain time, and must also be able to remain lit for a specific amount of time, as we shall learn in the next chapter.

CHAPTER 31

The Proper Time for Lighting

INTRODUCTION

In addressing the view that one need not rekindle an extinguished flame (*kavta lo zakuk la*), the Gemara asks:

> Now, if it is extinguished, does it not require attention [i.e., must it be rekindled]? But the following [*baraita*] contradicts it: Its observance is from sunset until there is no wayfarer in the street (*ad shetikhle regel min hashuk*). Does that not mean that if it is extinguished [within that period] it must be relit?

This *baraita* implies that the flame must remain lit until there are no longer any people in the street; therefore, by extension, if the light is extinguished, it must be relit. The Gemara responds by offering the following interpretation of the *baraita*: "If one has not yet lit, he must light it [during this period]; or, [it refers] to the statutory period [during which the candles must burn]." In other words, *ad shetikhle regel min hashuk* refers either to the time period during which one may light the Ḥanukka lights, or to the amount time which the Ḥanukka lights must remain lit.

This gemara raises a number of practical questions. What is the earliest time that one may light Ḥanukka lights? Must one light at sunset, or may one light even later? How long must the lights remain lit? Does this impact upon the minimum required amount of oil? Finally, are these requirements different if the Ḥanukka lights are kindled indoors?

THE EARLIEST TIME FOR LIGHTING ḤANUKKA CANDLES

The Gemara teaches that "its observance is from *mishetishka haḥama* until there is no wayfarer in the street." The *Rishonim* debate the precise definition of "*mishetishka haḥama.*" In part, this discussion depends upon our calculation of the halakhic times of nightfall. A brief review of these opinions will be helpful in determining the proper time for lighting *neirot Ḥanukka.*

The *Rishonim* offer two different approaches to understanding the halakhically significant evening times based upon two seemingly contradictory passages in the Talmud (Shabbat 34b–35a and Pesaḥim 94a).

On the one hand, Rabbeinu Tam asserts that there are actually two phenomena called "*shekia*" (sunset).[1] The first *shekia*, the astronomical sunset, begins as the sun disappears below the horizon. The second *shekia* occurs much later, when the sky is completely dark except for its western extremity, which glows red from the sun beneath the horizon. This second *shekia*, which the Gemara describes in Tractate Shabbat, ends when the entire sky becomes completely dark – *tzeit hakokhavim*. *Tzeit hakokhavim* occurs ¾ of a *mil* after the second sunset, as described in Shabbat, and 4 *millin* after the first sunset, as described in Pesaḥim. A *mil* is technically a unit of distance approximately equal to a kilometer. In this context, the Talmud uses the term to refer to the amount of time it takes for the average person to walk a *mil*. The *Terumat HaDeshen,*[2] *Shulḥan Arukh,*[3] and Rema[4] define a *mil* as eighteen minutes. According to Rabbeinu Tam, some halakhot depend upon the second *shekia*. Shabbat, for example, begins with the second *shekia*. Therefore, prohibited labors may be performed on Friday until 3¼ *millin* after the first *shekia* – approximately an hour after the astronomical sunset. Shabbat ends with *tzeit hakokhavim*, 72 minutes after the astronomical sunset.

On the other hand, the *Geonim*[5] and Gra[6] disagree with Rabbeinu Tam's calculation. They explain, based on the Gemara in Shabbat, that the period between sunset (*shekia*) and nightfall (*tzeit hakokhavim*), referred to as "*bein hashemashot*," spans ¾ of a *mil*. Gra objects to Rabbeinu Tam's opinion not only on textual grounds, but also because "*haḥush makhḥish*" – empirical evidence contradicts Rabbeinu Tam's position. The skies are already entirely dark during the time that Rabbeinu Tam considers daytime! Therefore, *tzeit hakokhavim*, as defined by the *Geonim*, occurs 13.5 minutes after the astronomical sunset. Gra acknowledges that the time spans mentioned in the Gemara – ¾ of a *mil* and 4 *millin* – apply only to the latitude of Israel and Babylonia during the times of the fall and spring equinox. In other regions, such as Northern Europe, *bein hashemashot* and *tzeit hakokhavim* occur much later. Since the season, latitude, and altitude impact upon the visibility of the stars, the *Aḥaronim* debate when one may actually recite the evening *Shema* or end Shabbat according to this approach. With this background information in mind, let us now examine the various views among the *Rishonim* concerning the proper time for lighting *neirot Ḥanukka*. There are three views in the *Rishonim* regarding the proper time to light:

(1) Rambam writes that one should light "with the sunset, neither later nor earlier," implying that the mitzva should be performed as the sun dips below the horizon.[7] Maharam of Rothenburg also maintains this position,[8] noting that by lighting the Ḥanukka candles at sunset, when there is still some daylight, one makes it clear that he lights for the sake of publicizing the miracle, and not because he needs the light.

(2) Some *Rishonim* imply that one should light at the second *shekia,* the beginning of *bein hashemashot* as defined by Rabbeinu Tam, which begins about one hour after the astronomical sunset.[9]

(3) Rabbeinu Tam[10] and Rosh[11] maintain that one should not light until "*sof hashekia,*" or *tzeit hakokhavim,* which, according to Rabbeinu Tam, occurs no earlier than 72 minutes after the astronomical sunset.

The *Shulḥan Arukh* rules that one should light at the "end of the sunset," referring to Rabbeinu Tam's *tzeit hakokhavim,* which occurs no earlier than 72 minutes after sunset.[12] The Vilna Gaon, however, rules that one should preferably light at the astronomical sunset, in accordance with his general view regarding the evening times.[13] The *Mishna Berura* seems to concur with Gra's approach.[14] In the *Biur Halakha,* he writes that one should preferably light at sunset, before reciting the Maariv service. This was, indeed, the practice of the Vilna Gaon's students who moved to Jerusalem, as well as that of R. Yitzchak Ze'ev Soloveitchik, the "Brisker Rav."[15] Later *Aḥaronim* advise that those who light at the astronomical sunset should use enough oil to sustain the candle for at least a half-hour after *tzeit hakokhavim.*[16]

Although most communities do not adopt Rabbeinu Tam's definition of *tzeit hakokhavim* for the determination of the beginning and conclusion of Shabbat, many follow his practice of lighting *neirot Ḥanukka* at *tzeit hakokhavim,* but as defined by the *Geonim.*[17] This is approximately fifteen to twenty minutes after sunset in Israel.[18] The *Ḥazon Ish* lit twenty minutes after sunset.[19]

In America and Europe, where there is more time between sunset and *tzeit hakokhavim* than in Israel, R. Moshe Feinstein recommended lighting approximately ten minutes after sunset and using enough oil to sustain the flame for at least an hour, meaning until a half-hour after *tzeit hakokhavim.*[20] R. Shimon Eider reports that R. Aharon Kotler would light Ḥanukka candles twenty-five to thirty minutes after sunset.[21]

TEFILLAT MAARIV FOR ONE WHO LIGHTS AT *TZEIT HAKOKHAVIM*

One who lights before *tzeit hakokhavim* should recite the Maariv prayer only after candle lighting, as noted by the *Biur Halakha.* When should those who light at *tzeit hakokhavim* recite Maariv? On the one hand, we might require them to light immediately at *tzeit hakokhavim,* before reciting Maariv, so that they may fulfill the mitzva of *hadlakat neirot* at the proper time, in accordance with the precept of "*zerizin makdimin lemitzvot*" – the zealous perform mitzvot as early as possible. Furthermore, as *Peri Megadim* notes,[22] according to one reading of the Gemara, the *neirot Ḥanukka* must be lit at the point of "*mishetishka haḥama,*" and reciting Maariv first might jeopardize the proper fulfillment of the mitzva. On the other hand, the Maariv service includes the recitation of the *Shema,* a biblical commandment, whose performance generally takes precedence over mitzvot enacted by *Ḥazal.* Moreover, a frequent mitzva generally takes precedence over an infrequent mitzva ("*tadir veshe'eino tadir, tadir kodem*").

Magen Avraham writes that one who has not yet recited Maariv should first light the Ḥanukka candles, as he is unlikely to forget to pray due to lighting *neirot Ḥanukka.*[23] R. Yaakov Reischer, however, disagrees.[24] The *Ḥayei Adam* rules that one should first recite Maariv, as long as he will not miss the proper time for lighting as a result.[25] The *Arukh HaShulḥan* similarly records that it is customary to light Ḥanukka candles only after reciting Maariv.[26]

One who feels unsure as to how to practice may find comfort in the knowledge that he is in good company. R. Chaim Benveniste, in his *Shiyurei Knesset HaGedola,* relates that during his childhood years, he would light after praying Maariv, in accordance with his father's custom. At some point, however, he changed his custom and began lighting before Maariv. Later, upon learning a passage in *Baḥ,* who insists that the majority of *Aḥaronim* advocate reciting Maariv first, he returned to his original family custom to light after Maariv.

LIGHTING EARLIER THAN SUNSET

May one, under extenuating circumstances, light Ḥanukka lights earlier than the prescribed time of *mishetishka haḥama*? As we saw above, Rambam writes that one should light "with the sunset, neither later nor earlier,"[27] clearly disqualifying candle lighting before sundown. Similarly, *Behag,* as cited by Rashba and Ran,[28] implies that one should not light before sunset. Rashba and Ran, however, disagree. They comment that although the Gemara requires lighting "from sunset until there is no wayfarer in the street," it is certainly acceptable to light earlier than sunset, just as one lights before sunset on Erev Shabbat.

Furthermore, the *Orḥot Ḥayim*[29] cites Mahari Abuhav as allowing "one who is busy" to light *neirot Ḥanukka* as early as *pelag haMinḥa,* 1¼ halakhic hours before sundown, as long as he provides enough oil to sustain the flame until at least a half-hour after *tzeit hakokhavim.* The *Shulḥan Arukh* codifies this ruling of the *Orḥot Ḥayim.* While a minority of *posekim* rule that one who lights before sundown on a weekday (as opposed to Erev Shabbat) should not recite the *berakha,*[30] most permit reciting the *berakha* in such a circumstance.[31]

THE DURATION OF AND LATEST TIME FOR CANDLE LIGHTING

In explaining the *baraita*'s comment that the mitzva of *ner Ḥanukka* extends "from sunset until there is no wayfarer in the street," the Talmud states, "if one has not yet lit, he must light it; *or*, [it refers] to the statutory period [during which the candles must burn]." The *Rishonim* take different approaches in interpreting this passage.

Some *Rishonim*[32] explain that the Gemara offers two different and independent readings of the *baraita*. The first reading interprets "its observance is from sunset until there is no wayfarer in the street" to mean that one may light until the point when there are no wayfarers in the street, but not afterward. Accordingly, the candle must remain lit only until the streets are empty. According to the second reading, one may theoretically light the entire night, but the candles must remain lit for the amount of time described by the Gemara, "from sunset until there is no wayfarer in the street" – that is, approximately a half-hour. Other *Rishonim* explain that the Gemara's two explanations are complementary, and not contradictory. Therefore, one may light until there "are no wayfarers in the street," but he must ensure that the candle remains lit for the prescribed *shiur*.

Rambam[33] and one opinion in Tosafot[34] accept the first understanding, and rule that one may not light after the point designated by the Gemara, when "there is no wayfarer in the street." Others maintain that since the Gemara does not explicitly rule in accordance with either of the two readings of the *baraita*, one may, out of doubt, light even after the prescribed time.[35] Seemingly, according to this view, one would not recite a *berakha* upon this lighting. Rashba, however, rules that the Gemara never intended to exclude lighting after the proper time,[36] as "any mitzva whose time is at night may be performed the entire night."[37] One who lights later has simply not fulfilled the mitzva in its optimal form. The *Shulḥan Arukh* rules:

> One who forgot or intentionally did not light with the sunset may light until there are no longer wayfarers in the street, meaning approximately a half-hour [after sunset], as during that time people still roam the streets, and the miracle can still be publicized. However, this is only the optimal

While the element of lighting may be fulfilled through a *shaliaḥ*, the other component of the mitzva, viewing the lights, must be fulfilled by the individual himself, and therefore the appropriate formula for the blessing is "*lehadlik*." Second, Ramban suggests that "the lighting is the mitzva – which achieves the mitzva." In other words, one does not fulfill the mitzva through the act of lighting itself; rather, the mitzva is fulfilled as a *result* of the fact that the candles burn. Ostensibly, Ramban is suggesting that unlike most other mitzvot, the focus of the *neirot Ḥanukka* obligation is not the act of lighting, but rather the result of having a *ner Ḥanukka* burning in one's house.

In light of Ramban's comments, we must reevaluate the possiblity of assigning a *shaliaḥ* to light Ḥanukka candles on one's behalf. The agent's lighting may not constitute classic *sheliḥut*, whereby the agent's action is attributed to the person who appointed him. Rather, one fulfills the mitzva through the very fact that a candle is lit in one's house, regardless of who lit it.

In any event, once we have established that one may assign someone else to light on his behalf, the question arises as to whether it is preferable to light through an agent at the optimal time or to light personally, earlier or later.

LIGHTING AFTER *PELAG HAMINḤA* VERSUS LIGHTING LATE

Although, as mentioned above, the *Shulḥan Arukh* does permit lighting after *pelag haMinḥa*, most *posekim* rule that one should preferably light upon returning home.[61] R. Shmuel Wosner rules that it is even preferable to appoint an agent to light later at night, rather than to light oneself after *pelag haMinḥa*.[62]

LIGHTING VIA A *SHALIAḤ* VERSUS LIGHTING LATE

When one must choose between appointing a *shaliaḥ* to light on time or lighting personally, but later at night, he faces the more complex question of whether the punctual fulfillment of the mitzva through a *shaliaḥ* is preferable to personal fulfillment. Essentially, he must choose between the values of "*zerizin makdimin lemitzvot*" – performing mitzvot as early as possible – and "*mitzva bo yoter mibisheluḥo*" – the preference of personal performance over assigning a *shaliaḥ*. In addition, lighting immediately after *shekia* may be preferable not only because of "*zerizin makdimin*," but also because that is intrinsically the ideal time for performing the mitzva.

Some authorities recommend appointing a *shaliaḥ*, such as a friend, spouse, or other family member, to light at the proper time.[63] Others, however, prefer that one light personally, even later in the evening.[64] Presumably, those who maintain that one who lights after there is no longer any *pirsumei nissa* should not recite a *berakha* would prefer appointing a *shaliaḥ* over lighting personally late at night.

There are, however, other factors worth considering. Is it, for example, preferable for one who must consistently work late to always fulfill the mitzva through an agent and never fulfill the mitzva himself? Furthermore, lighting through a *shaliaḥ* or not waiting for other family members to return home may adversely affect *shalom bayit*, domestic harmony, which is certainly also an important value. The Gemara itself teaches that if one must choose between *ner Ḥanukka* and *ner beito*, the Shabbat lights, one should choose *ner beito* in the interest of *shalom bayit* (Shabbat 23b). Indeed, R. Shlomo Zalman Auerbach permits the wife of a shopkeeper who returns late at night to wait for her husband if lighting without him would affect their marital harmony.[65] Similarly, R. Moshe Feinstein instructs a man who usually lights with his family to delay lighting until his family arrives.[66]

Is learning Torah a sufficient reason to delay lighting *neirot Ḥanukka*? Maharshal writes that one should not eat or even learn before lighting *neirot Ḥanukka*.[67] R. Herschel Schachter records,[68] however, that when the afternoon Kollel was first established in Yeshiva University in 1962, R. Aharon Lichtenstein, then the Rosh Kollel, asked R. Soloveitchik whether the students should interrupt their studies to light Ḥanukka candles at the proper time. R. Soloveitchik cited Me'iri, who relates that the *benei yeshiva* would light after returning from the *beit midrash*.[69] This is indeed the practice of the Yeshiva University Kollel to this day. It is customary in most yeshivas and Kollels in Israel, however, including in R. Lichtenstein's Yeshivat Har Etzion, to interrupt their learning to light Ḥanukka candles at the preferred time. In fact, R. Shlomo Zalman Auerbach reportedly criticized those who suggested that full-time students should remain in yeshiva and appoint their wives to light on their behalf.[70]

EATING BEFORE *HADLAKAT NEIROT*

May one eat or drink before fulfilling the mitzva of *hadlakat neirot*? As noted above, Maharshal writes that once the time for performing the mitzva arrives, one should refrain from eating and even Torah learning.[71] Some suggest that one should refrain from eating already a half-hour before the time for lighting.[72] Some *Aḥaronim* note that drinking and eating less than a *kebeitza* of bread is permitted before lighting.[73]

CHAPTER 32

The Proper Place for Lighting

THE GEMARA DISCUSSES three places where one may, under different circumstances, light *neirot Ḥanukka*:

> The mitzva is to place the Ḥanukka lights at the entrance to one's house, outside. If one lives in a loft, he should place [them] in a window adjacent to the public thoroughfare (*reshut harabbim*). And in times of danger, he should place [them] on his table [inside], and that suffices. (Shabbat 21b)

LIGHTING AT THE ENTRANCE TO ONE'S HOUSE

The Gemara clearly prefers that one light at the entrance to one's house. This preference appears in a later source as well: "The mitzva is to place the Ḥanukka lights at the entrance **adjacent to the public**

thoroughfare (*reshut harabbim*)" (Masekhet Soferim 20:5). Rashi explains that the lights should be placed at the entrance of the house in order to publicize the miracle (*pirsumei nissa*). According to Rashi, the Gemara refers to a situation in which the house's entrance faces outward into the *ḥatzer*, the courtyard. Even though the lights are not visible to the passersby in the *reshut harabbim*, Rashi maintains that one should light at the entrance to one's house, rather than the entrance to the courtyard.[1] Tosafot disagree, explaining that the Gemara speaks of a case in which the entrance to the house faces the *reshut harabbim* itself. If the entrance were to face the courtyard, one should light at the entrance to the courtyard, facing the *reshut harabbim*.[2]

At first glance, Tosafot's view appears more compelling. Since the purpose of *hadlakat neirot* is ultimately to publicize the miracle, it stands to reason that one should light as close to the *reshut harabbim* as possible. Rashi's insistence that one light at the entrance to the house requires clarification. It appears that Rashi's interpretation assumes an intrinsic relationship between *hadlakat neirot* and the house. As we noted previously, some *Rishonim* understand the obligation to light *neirot Ḥanukka* as a "*ḥovat bayit*," an obligation upon the house. Indeed, Rambam formulates the mitzva as such: "The mitzva is for each and every *house* to light."[3] Rif,[4] Rambam,[5] and Rosh[6] cite the Gemara's statement verbatim, implying that they, like Rashi, draw no distinction between an entrance that faces a courtyard and an entrance that faces a *reshut harabbim*. The *Shulḥan Arukh*, however, rules in accordance with Tosafot.[7]

The *Aḥaronim* debate the applicability of this halakha to modern-day courtyards. *Ḥazon Ish* distinguishes between modern-day *ḥatzerot*, which are external to one's house, and the courtyards of old, where most of the housework was performed. The *ḥatzer* was then considered part of the house itself. *Ḥazon Ish* thus contends that nowadays, even the *Shulḥan Arukh* would require lighting at the entrance to one's house, and not at the entrance to the courtyard.[8] Others, however, disagree, arguing that today's courtyards are no different from ancient *ḥatzerot* as far as this halakha is concerned. These authorities differ, however, as to whether one may light at an entrance to a courtyard that has no formal "doorway" requiring a mezuza. According to R. Yitzchak Ze'ev Soloveitchik, one should not light at the entrance of a courtyard that does not have a lintel.[9] Others cite R. Shlomo Zalman Auerbach and R. Shalom Yosef Elyashiv as ruling that one should light at the entrance to one's courtyard, even if it has no doorway.[10] Some suggest that if one's doorway is visible through a courtyard from the *reshut harabbim,* he should light at the doorway, thereby fulfilling the views of both Rashi and Tosafot.[11]

LIGHTING IN THE WINDOW

The Gemara presents a second scenario:

> If one lives in a loft, he should place [the candles] in a window adjacent to the public thoroughfare (*reshut harabbim*). (Shabbat 21b)

Rashi explains that the window is used "because he has no place in the courtyard to place them." As we saw earlier, Rashi insists that one should always light at the entrance to the house. He thus interprets the window scenario as referring to one who has no entrance to his loft from the courtyard, but rather enters the loft through the house. He cannot light by the entrance to the house, since the "house" is not his residence. Therefore, as lighting inside the house at the entrance to his loft does not appear to be a desirable option, he lights by the window that opens to the *reshut harabbim.*

According to Tosafot, who maintain that one may light at the entrance to the courtyard from the *reshut harabbim,* why should one light at his window? *Beit Yosef* explains that the resident of a loft should light by his window so that observers will be able to identify his candles as belonging to him. Were he to light at the entrance to the courtyard, or even at the entrance to the house, it would not be apparent that those lights belong to an inhabitant of the loft. The loft resident should light by his window so that observers will immediately recognize that he, the occupant of the loft, has lit Ḥanukka candles. One whose doorway faces the *reshut harabbim,* however, should certainly light at the entrance.[12]

LIGHTING INSIDE ONE'S HOUSE

The Gemara teaches that "in times of danger, one places [the lights] on the table, and that suffices" (Shabbat 21b). The *Rishonim* disagree whether the "danger" of which the Gemara speaks refers to a specific edict prohibiting lighting candles except in pagan houses of worship, a general ban on mitzva observance, or a specific ban on *neirot Ḥanukka*.[13] Others explain that the Gemara refers to an environment of general animosity between Jews and non-Jews, and some even extend this leniency to areas of inclement weather.[14]

Many *Rishonim* testify to a widespread custom to light indoors. In fact, the *Or Zarua* questions why it is not customary to light outdoors.[15] *Shibbolei HaLeket* suggests that once Jews had grown accustomed to lighting indoors because of danger, they continued doing so even in peaceful times.[16]

Many *Aḥaronim* note the nearly universal practice in the Diaspora to light indoors, attributing this practice to the fact that Jews live amongst non-Jews or to inclement winter weather.[17] Some maintain that one should still ideally light by one's window, facing the *reshut harabbim*.[18] Others, however, still insist that one should try to light outdoors in glass boxes that protect the flames from the elements.[19] In Israel, the majority of *posekim* strongly encourage lighting outdoors, and this has been the practice of the great rabbinical figures of Jerusalem since the students of the Vilna Gaon arrived in Israel.

R. Yitzchak Yaakov Weiss (1902–1989), however, defends the widespread practice of lighting inside.[20] R. Yehoshua Ehrenberg goes so far as to suggest that once the Rabbis instituted lighting inside during times of danger, one who lights outside has not fulfilled his obligation![21] Sephardic authorities also justify the widespread custom of lighting indoors and condemn the authorities who censure those who light indoors.[22]

In Israel, it is customary that those who light outside use glass boxes, as described by R. Yaakov Emden. R. Tzvi Pesach Frank (1874–1960), the former Chief Rabbi of Jerusalem, records that this was the custom of the Jerusalemites of his time.[23] Interestingly, he relates that

R. Yehoshua Yehuda Leib Diskin (Maharil Diskin) questioned whether one fulfills his obligation by lighting in a glass box. At the moment when one lights the candles inside the box, they are in a position in which they cannot possibly remain lit for an extended period due to the wind. It is only once one closes the box immediately after lighting that the flames are secure. As we have seen previously, we follow the view that "*hadlaka osa mitzva*," one fulfills the mitzva through the act of lighting, and not by placing a lit candle in its proper location. One must therefore ensure that at the time of lighting the candles have the potential to remain lit for the minimum required duration. Thus, one who lights in a glass box does not fulfill the obligation of *neirot Ḥanukka*, since at the moment of kindling, the lights have virtually no chance of burning for a half-hour. To avoid this concern, R. Diskin prepared a special box with a hole in the bottom. He lit the candles through that hole and left it open throughout the time the candles burned. R. Frank, as well as R. Binyamin Zilber[24] and R. Shlomo Zalman Auerbach,[25] defend the widespread custom to light in glass boxes.

As we noted previously, the issue of where one lights may impact upon the questions of when one lights and for how long the candles must burn. Many *Rishonim*, as well as Rema,[26] assert that those accustomed to lighting inside may not have to light at sundown. Since the lighting in this case is directed inward, toward the residents of the home, the presence of pedestrian traffic has no bearing on when the candles are lit. It might therefore be unnecessary to light at the time when people walk the streets.

Where should apartment building residents light Ḥanukka candles? Theoretically, four possibilities present themselves: by one's window, anywhere in the apartment (such as on one's table), outside the door to the hallway, or at the entrance to the building.

Some argue that the case of an apartment building resembles the situation of the loft discussed in the Gemara. As we saw, *Beit Yosef* explains that one who does not have a private entrance from the courtyard should light at his window so that his lighting will be clearly identifiable. Analogously, perhaps one who lives in an apartment building should light at his window, as the number of entrances to the individual apartments is not obvious to the public. According to those who advocate lighting at a window, one may also light on his balcony or porch. If one's window is above twenty *amot* (9.5–11.5 meters) from the ground, some authorities assert that it is better to light at the doorway, since lights at the window would not be noticeable to pedestrians below.[27] Others suggest that one may light at a window even in such a case as long as it faces adjacent buildings. Moreover, the fact that the apartment's residents can themselves see the lights may suffice, even if no one outside can view them.

Alternatively, one might suggest lighting at the entrance to the building, or the entrance to the stairwell. This, however, may depend upon the debate between Rashi and Tosafot cited above. Rashi, as already noted, requires lighting by the entrance to the home, and not the entrance to the courtyard, and thus would certainly not sanction lighting at the entrance to one's apartment building. Some light outside the door to the apartment, facing those who walk through the hallway. They view this practice as fulfilling the obligation to light at the "entrance of one's house facing the courtyard." Tosafot, on the other hand, might suggest lighting at the entrance to the stairwell, as the stairwell may be considered one's "courtyard" in such a case. Indeed, as we saw above, R. Shlomo Zalman Auerbach ruled that one may light at the entrance to his building, or even at the end of a path facing toward the *reshut harabbim* (in opposition to the view of the *Ḥazon Ish*[28]).

R. Moshe Feinstein concludes that the guiding principle in choosing where to light should be the maximization of *pirsumei nissa*. He attests that he personally lit at his window, which was visible to passersby, for this very reason.

PLACEMENT AND HEIGHT OF THE ḤANUKKA CANDLES

After establishing that the *neirot Ḥanukka* should ideally be lit at the entrance to one's house (or courtyard), the Gemara describes in greater detail where the lights should be kindled:

> Rabba said: The Ḥanukka lamp should be placed within the *tefaḥ* [a handbreadth; approximately 8 cm] nearest the door. And where is it placed?

> R. Aḥa son of Rabba said: On the right hand side. R. Shmuel of Difti said: On the left hand side. And the law is – on the left, so that the Ḥanukka lamp shall be on the left and the mezuza on the right. (Shabbat 21b)

The *Rishonim* explain that one should light within a *tefaḥ* of the doorway in order to make it clear that the lights were placed there by the home's inhabitants.[29] The *Shulḥan Arukh* rules that one should preferably light within a handbreadth of the left side of the doorway, so that the mezuza is on the right side and the *ner Ḥanukka* is on the left.[30] The *Shulḥan Arukh* also writes – following the view of most *Rishonim* – that when there is no mezuza, one should light on the right side of the doorway,[31] as "regarding mitzvot, the right side is preferable."[32]

The *Aḥaronim* address the question of whether one who lights indoors should preferably light at his window or within a *tefaḥ* of the doorway. Although many of the hasidic *gedolim* apparently lit at the doorway within a *tefaḥ* of the entrance,[33] most *posekim* recommend lighting at the window when possible.[34]

The Talmud also discusses the optimal and maximum height of the *neirot Ḥanukka*. Regarding the optimal height, the Talmud states:

> If a camel laden with flax passes through a street, and the flax overflows into a shop, catches fire at the shopkeeper's lamp, and sets the building alight, the camel owner is liable; but if the shopkeeper placed the light outside, the shopkeeper is liable. R. Yehuda said: In the case of a Ḥanukka lamp, he is exempt.
>
> Ravina said in Rava's name: This proves that the Ḥanukka lamp should [optimally] be placed within ten *tefaḥim* [of the ground]. For should you think [it is acceptable to place it] above ten, let him [the camel owner] say to him [the shopkeeper], "You ought to have placed it higher than a camel and his rider." [The Gemara then refutes this claim:] Perhaps if he is put to too much trouble, he may refrain from the [observance of the] precept.

According to Ravina, the Ḥanukka lights should be placed within ten *tefaḥim* (approximately 80 cm) of the ground. Rosh explains that lights kindled below ten *tefaḥim* provide greater *pirsumei nissa,* as it is clear that they are not intended for personal use; one who wanted use the light for his own needs would certainly light a lamp much higher.[35]

The Gemara, however, refutes Ravina's inference, and the *Rishonim* disagree as to whether the halakha nevertheless follows Ravina. Many, including Rif and Rambam, omit this height requirement entirely. R. Menachem Me'iri not only omits Ravina's requirement, he claims that one should actually light the Ḥanukka candles higher than ten *tefaḥim* in order to maximize the *pirsumei nissa*. Furthermore, Ritva records the common practice of lighting above ten *tefaḥim*. This was done possibly because people generally lit inside, and the halakhic details intended to increase *pirsumei nissa* were not generally applicable.[36] Others, at the opposite extreme, cite Ravina's ruling and hold that the lights should preferably be situated below the height of ten *tefaḥim*.

Beit Yosef and *Darkhei Moshe* note that those who were "meticulous" (*hamedakdekim*) in their day kindled the lights between three to ten *tefaḥim* above the ground. The *Shulḥan Arukh* rules in accordance with Ravina – it is a "mitzva" to light one's candles within ten *tefaḥim* of the ground.[37] R. Eliyahu b. R. Binyamin Wolf Shapiro, in his *Eliya Rabba*, reports that the custom in his day was to light above ten *tefaḥim*. He infers from the fact that *Beit Yosef* and *Darkhei Moshe* refer to those who lit below ten *tefaḥim* as "meticulous" that the popular custom was actually to light higher than ten *tefaḥim*.

Regarding the lowest acceptable height for lighting, the *Mordekhai* relates that his teacher, R. Meir of Rothenburg (1215–1293), would light his candles at least three *tefaḥim* (approximately 24 cm) above the ground and below ten *tefaḥim*.[38] The *Shulḥan Arukh* rules in accordance with this view.[39] The *Mishna Berura*[40] cites *Peri Ḥadash*,[41] who rules that one who lights below three *tefaḥim* has nevertheless fulfilled his obligation, and need not light again.

The Talmud also discusses the maximum height allowed for Ḥanukka candles:

> R. Kahana said: R. Natan b. Minyomi expounded in R. Tanḥum's name: If a Ḥanukka lamp is placed above twenty cubits [from the ground], it is unfit. (Shabbat 22a)

The *Shulḥan Arukh* rules in accordance with the passage. However, as noted above, some *Aḥaronim* allow apartment building residents to light at a window in the apartment, even above the height of twenty *amot* from the ground.

AN *AKHSANAI*

The Gemara teaches:

> R. Sheshet said: A lodger (*akhsanai*) is obligated in *ner Ḥanukka*. R. Zeira said: At first, when I would visit the house of Rav, I would share the costs with the host. After I was married, I concluded that now I certainly don't need [to light when a guest elsewhere], as [my wife] is lighting for me at my home. (Shabbat 23a)

Two halakhot emerge from this passage: (1) A traveler may fulfill his obligation through the lighting performed by someone else in his home. (2) A guest may fulfill his obligation by sharing the costs of the Ḥanukka lights with the host.

Ran explains that R. Sheshet initially compared the obligation of *hadlakat neirot* with that of mezuza. The mitzva of mezuza is purely a *ḥovat bayit*, an obligation on the house, as opposed to a personal obligation. Similarly, R. Sheshet thought, a guest would not be obligated to light *neirot Ḥanukka*, as the obligation is on the house and not each individual. He ultimately concluded, however, that a guest is, in fact, obligated. It remains unclear which aspect of his initial assumption he rejected. Perhaps he concluded that *hadlakat neirot* is actually a *ḥovat gavra* (personal obligation), and that it therefore remains binding even if one resides in another person's home. Alternatively, he may have accepted the classification of *ner Ḥanukka* as a *ḥovat bayit*, but maintained that it applies to a traveler nevertheless. A guest must thus participate in his host's expenses in order to fulfill this mitzva.[42]

The *Shulḥan Arukh* rules in accordance with this gemara, stating that a guest who has no one to light for him at his own home and who does not have a separate entrance where he lodges should fulfill his obligation by sharing in the host's expenses for the oil.[43] The *Aḥaronim* discuss whether or not the host must actually add some oil to serve as the guest's share. *Magen Avraham* notes that the while the guest may pay for the additional oil, the host may give him a portion as a gift.[44] R. Yaakov Chaim Sofer (1870–1939) writes that the guest should explicitly state that he is giving the money to the host to acquire a share in the costs of the lights. The host should then respond that he transfers a portion of the lights in exchange for the money he received.[45]

Nowadays, it is customary among Ashkenazim to kindle their own Ḥanukka lights rather than rely upon the lighting of the *baal habayit* (host). It is possible that this practice is rooted in the general observance of the *mehadrin min hamehadrin* standard, which requires each member of the household to light. Even if a guest fulfills his basic obligation through the host's lighting, the higher standard of *mehadrin min hamehadrin* might require him to light his own candles. Interestingly, R. Yaakov b. Moshe Moelin, Maharil, records the custom among guests in his day (the fourteenth century) not to share the costs of the host's lights, but rather to light personally. Instead of explaining this practice as an attempt to fulfill the *mehadrin min hamehadrin* standard, he attributes it to the concern that others might suspect that he did not light.[46] Others imply that despite this prevalent practice, one may still share the costs with the host and need not be concerned with the possibility of suspicion.[47]

The *Mishna Berura* cites the view requiring guests to kindle their own lights in order to avoid suspicion, but he then dismisses this argument.[48] He rules in accordance with the view of *Magen Avraham* that only guests who stay in quarters with a separate entrance must light their own lights.[49] Nevertheless, the *Mishna Berura* concludes that whenever possible, a guest should kindle his own lights in order to fulfill the *mehadrin min hamehadrin* standard.

Although this is indeed the common practice, R. Eliyahu Schlesinger suggests that a lodger's lighting might be halakhically meaningless if he does not formally join his host's household. The obligation of *ner Ḥanukka* requires lighting in one's *bayit*, his home, and a guest does not have a "home" in which to light unless he becomes part of his host's household. R. Schlesinger therefore suggests, in contrast to the *Mishna Berura*'s position, that a lodger *must* share the costs of the lights in order to fulfill the mitzva at all.[50]

R. Sheshet noted that a married traveler need not be concerned with participating in his host's lighting, as his wife lights for him at home. May a traveler whose wife lights for him still light his own candles where he sleeps? *Terumat HaDeshen* cites two opinions regarding whether the guest may kindle his own lights with the *berakhot* in this situation.[51] Maharil observed that most guests in his time lit on their own even in such situations, and he maintained that a guest may even recite the *berakhot* in this case, as he presumably has in mind not to fulfill his obligation through his wife's lighting.[52] *Beit Yosef*, however, disagrees, rendering such a *berakha* a *berakha levatala* (a blessing in vain).[53] The *Eliya Rabba* cites *Shaar Efraim*, who suggests that this debate relates to the definition of *mehadrin min hamehadrin*. According to the Sephardic tradition, which demands that only the head of the household light, once one's wife lights at home, the husband has no reason to light his own candles. According to the Ashkenzic tradition, however, which mandates that each and every member of the household light, even if one's wife lit at home, he should still ideally light his own *neirot Ḥanukka*. *Eliya Rabba*[54] himself, however, rejects this reasoning, suggesting that even according to Ashkenazic tradition, a traveler whose wife lights for him at home is not encouraged to light his own candles.

Rema rules that a traveler whose family lights for him back home may still light with the *berakhot*.[55] *Levush*,[56] *Taz*,[57] *Magen Avraham*,[58] and other *Aḥaronim* rule in accordance with Rema, whereas Maharshal and *Peri Ḥadash* disagree. Given the difference of opinion among the authorities in this regard, the *Mishna Berura* suggests that one should preferably listen to someone else's *berakhot* rather than recite them personally, although he does not censure those who do recite the *berakhot* in such a case.[59]

DEFINING ONE'S HOME: ONE WHO EATS AND SLEEPS IN DIFFERENT PLACES

Clearly, one who eats and sleeps at home should light *neirot Ḥanukka* at his own home. *Taz* criticizes the mistaken practice of dinner guests who light in their hosts' homes instead of their own, for "this is no different than if they had been standing in the street during candle lighting, where lighting is certainly not applicable."[60] (We will later discuss the case of one who has no home.) Thus, if one visits friends or family for dinner and plans to return home, he must light Ḥanukka candles at home, and not with his hosts.

A more complex question involves guests who sleep in one place and eat somewhere else. *Tur* cites his father, Rosh, as ruling that a person in this situation should light in the place where he *sleeps,* for if he lights in the house where he eats, people might suspect that he did not light *neirot Ḥanukka* at all.[61] In his *Darkhei Moshe* commentary on the *Tur,* Rema notes that Rashba disagrees with this conclusion, ruling that one who eats in someone else's house must share in the host's lighting expenses even if he sleeps elsewhere.[62] In other words, Rashba assumes that the place where one *eats* determines his status regarding the obligation of *hadlakat neirot.*

R. Yosef Karo rules in the *Shulḥan Arukh* that one who has a private entrance to his residence should light there, even if he regularly eats elsewhere.[63] Rema disagrees, once again citing Rashba, and writes, "Some say that nowadays, when we light inside the house, one should light in the place where he *eats,* and such is the custom."[64]

This debate between Rosh and Rashba affects one who stays at a hotel during Ḥanukka, sleeping in his room but eating in the hotel's dining hall. According to Rosh, he should light in the room where he sleeps. Rashba, however, would seemingly rule that one should light in the dining room. However, since the entrance to the building might be considered the "entrance of one's courtyard adjacent to the *reshut harabbim,*" it may be the preferred location for lighting. This indeed seems to be the custom in many hotels, especially due to fire safety concerns.[65]

A similar question arises when one travels for just one night. When one goes away for Shabbat, for example, and returns home on Saturday night, where should he light Ḥanukka candles that night? Is his status determined by the place where he slept the night before or the place where he intends to sleep that night? Some suggest that if one can return home in time to light while there are still people outside, he should quickly return home after Shabbat and light there.[66] Others, however, maintain that one may light in his host's house before returning home, particularly if he will be returning home late.[67]

DORMITORY STUDENTS

Much has been written regarding the question of where yeshiva students should light Ḥanukka candles. As we have already discussed, since Sephardic authorities maintain that only one person per household must light, Sephardic students must establish if they are considered independent in determining whether they should personally light or if their obligation is fulfilled through their families' lighting at home. Students of Ashkenazic descent should certainly light, as according to Ashkenazic authorities, every member of the family lights in order to fulfill the *mehadrin min hamehadrin* standard. In addition, since they essentially live independently from their parents, it is possible that they must light even to fulfill the basic mitzva of *ner ish uveito*, which they likely no longer fulfill through their parents' lighting.

Students in school or yeshiva often eat and sleep in different rooms, and even in different buildings if the cafeteria and dormitory are situated in different places on the campus. Where should one light in such a situation? R. Moshe Feinstein maintains that students should light where they sleep, as the dining room is communal and not designated specifically for any particular student. He advises that students "draw lots" to determine who should stay and watch the lights to prevent a fire.[68] R. Yitzchak Weiss,[69] R. Binyamin Zilber,[70] and R. Shmuel Wosner[71] concur. Some suggest that one who lights in a dormitory room should light at the door facing toward the hallway, while others prefer lighting at the window.[72] In contrast, *Ḥazon Ish*[73] and R. Aharon Kotler[74] rule that one should light where he eats, in accordance with Rema's ruling noted above.

R. Moshe Harari cites R. Shlomo Zalman Auerbach as commenting in a personal conversation that students may light *neirot Ḥanukka* either in the entrance to their dormitory building or in the cafeteria – but not in their rooms, due to safety concerns.[75] This is, in fact, the custom in

R. Auerbach's yeshiva, Kol Torah, in Jerusalem. Students at Yeshiva University also light at the entrance to their dormitory buildings.

ON THE ROAD: ONE WHO TRAVELS WITHOUT A HOME

May one fulfill the mitzva of *ner Ḥanukka* outside of a house?[76] For example, may one traveling on a train or camping in an open field light *neirot Ḥanukka*? We have previously questioned whether we should define the mitzva of *ner Ḥanukka* as a *ḥovat bayit* – an obligation upon the house, similar to mezuza – or a *ḥovat gavra* – a personal mitzva that happens to be performed in the home. Clearly, one who views the obligation as a *ḥovat bayit* would not require lighting in the situations mentioned, just as one is obviously not obligated in mezuza if he has no home. If, however, we view the obligation as a *ḥovat gavra,* then the question arises as to whether the obligation remains applicable even in the absence of a home.

Although the *Rishonim* do not explicitly address this question, later authorities inferred from a number of sources that the obligation of *ner Ḥanukka* requires a house. For example, Tosafot explain that the *berakha* of "*she'asa nissim*" upon viewing Ḥanukka lights was instituted to enable "those who do not have houses and who are unable to fulfill the mitzva" to participate in the mitzva of Ḥanukka.[77] This comment assumes that people without homes do not light Ḥanukka candles. Similarly, Rashi explains that this *berakha* is intended for one who has not yet lit in his house and for one traveling by boat, who does not light.[78] (Rashi does not explain, however, why a boat is not considered a house.) Furthermore, Rambam writes that "the mitzva [of Ḥanukka] entails that each and every house light,"[79] implying that the mitzva must be performed in (or by) a house. In contrast, Ran cited earlier seems to understand the Gemara as establishing that the mitzva is not a *ḥovat bayit,* but rather a personal obligation.[80] Finally, above we cited *Taz,* who criticizes the mistaken practice of dinner guests who light in their hosts' homes instead of their own, noting that "this is no different than if they had been standing in the street during candle lighting, where lighting is certainly not applicable."[81] This clearly implies that one without a house may not light Ḥanukka candles. R. Moshe Feinstein[82] and R. Shlomo Zalman Auerbach[83] rule accordingly.

Other *Aḥaronim* maintain that although one must light in a "house," even a temporary residence may be considered a "house" in this respect. For example, R. Shalom Mordechai Schwadron (Maharsham, 1835–1911) writes that one may light while traveling on a train, as he in effect "rents" his cabin.[84] The *Arukh HaShulḥan* concurs.[85] Interestingly, R. Aharon Lichtenstein accepts the assumption that one may light only in a "*bayit*," yet questions whether a "*bayit*" must, by definition, be a roofed enclosure or if any fixed dwelling place, even without a roof, would suffice. If such a structure may plausibly be considered a *bayit*, one must have dwelled there for a minimum amount of time, either a week or even thirty days, in order for it to be considered one's home. Therefore, campers who sleep in a certain place for less than a week should not light *neirot Ḥanukka*, but should rather rely on the lighting performed in their homes.[86] R. Auerbach apparently also shared this doubt, as he ruled that while soldiers who sleep in the open fields should not light, those sleeping in trenches should light without reciting the *berakhot*.

Others maintain that the requirement of "*bayit*" is optimal, but not mandatory, and one may therefore light even without a house. R. Eliezer Waldenberg, for example defines the mitzva as one which is incumbent "*akarkafta degavra*," upon each and every head, and thus does not depend upon a house at all.[87] R. Binyamin Zilber concurs.[88] R. Waldenberg therefore maintains that soldiers should light next to their beds and with the *berakhot*.[89] R. Tzvi Pesach Frank ruled in 1974 that while soldiers who sleep in tents that protect them from the rain may light *neirot Ḥanukka*, those who sleep in open fields should not.[90] R. Ovadia Yosef rules that soldiers sleeping outside should light without reciting the *berakhot*.[91]

LIGHTING IN SYNAGOGUES AND OTHER PUBLIC PLACES

The custom to light Ḥanukka candles in the synagogue is mentioned already by the *Rishonim*. R. Yitzchak b. Abba Mari (France, twelfth century), for example, discusses this practice and cites different customs regarding whether the lights are kindled in the center of the synagogue or at the entrance.[92]

The *Rishonim* suggest numerous reasons for this practice. R. Avraham b. R. Natan (Provence, twelfth century) explains that we light in the "mini-*Mikdash*"[93] to publicize the miracle that occurred in the *Beit HaMikdash*. Ritva explains that we light in the synagogue "to publicize the miracle in a public place" (Shabbat 23a). Similarly, Rivash suggests that once it became customary to light *neirot Ḥanukka* indoors out of fear of the surrounding non-Jews, the authorities enacted that communities should light in their synagogues in order to properly publicize the miracles of Ḥanukka.[94] Some *Rishonim* suggest that the synagogue lighting enables those who have no house to at least recite the *berakhot* upon seeing the lights, just as Kiddush is recited in the synagogue for the sake of those who will not recite it on their own.[95]

R. Tzedkia b. Avraham HaRofeh asserts that lighting in the synagogue is halakhically superfluous, and he therefore questions whether the *berakhot* should be recited upon this lighting.[96] The *Shulḥan Arukh,* however, codifies the practice of lighting in the synagogue with the *berakhot,* explaining that this lighting serves the purpose of *pirsumei nissa.*[97] Rema adds that these candles are lit between the Minḥa and Maariv prayers.[98]

Some *Aḥaronim* write that the one who lights in the synagogue repeats all the *berakhot* – including *she'asa nissim* and *Sheheḥeyanu* – upon kindling his own lights at home.[99] Others rule that he should omit these two *berakhot,* unless he recites them for his family.[100]

In some communities, it is customary to kindle Ḥanukka lights with the *berakhot* in all public places. This issue seemingly depends upon the reason for the synagogue lighting. If we light in the synagogue to commemorate the lighting in the *Beit HaMikdash* or for the sake of those with no home, there is no reason to light with *berakhot* in other public settings. Ritva's explanation that we light in a synagogue to publicize the miracle, however, might apply to other public areas as well.

Minḥat Yitzḥak[101] and *Tzitz Eliezer*[102] object to this practice, while R. Binyamin Zilber supports the custom.[103] R. Ovadia Yosef defends the practice, although he recommends praying at the site of the lighting to lend it the status of a "synagogue" in this respect.[104] The previous Lubavitcher Rebbe, R. Menachem Mendel Schneerson (1902–1994), encouraged his followers to light in public places in order to publicize the miracles of Ḥanukka, in line with the reasoning of Ritva. It is customary to light at the Western Wall, as it functions as a synagogue year-round.[105]

CHAPTER 33

The Order and Manner of Lighting

THE *BERAKHOT* RECITED BEFORE CANDLE LIGHTING

Like most mitzvot, the mitzva of *hadlakat neirot* is preceded by a *birkat hamitzva*. However, the precise text of this *berakha* is subject to some debate. Most *Rishonim* record the text as "*lehadlik ner shel Ḥanukka*" ("to kindle the light of Ḥanukka"), but some omit the word "*shel*." The *Shulḥan Arukh* rules that one should say "*lehadlik ner Ḥanukka*," in accordance with Sephardic practice.[1] Ashkenazic authorities differ as to whether one should omit[2] or include[3] the word "*shel*." Interestingly, according to the Talmud Yerushalmi, the correct text is actually, "*al mitzvat hadlakat ner Ḥanukka*" ("upon the commandment of lighting the light of Ḥanukka") (Y. Sukka 3:4). The Yerushalmi's formulation of the *berakha* is not accepted.

Regarding the second *berakha* recited over the Ḥanukka lights, "*she'asa nissim*," the Talmud teaches:

> R. Ḥiyya b. Ashi said: One who *lights* the lamp must recite a *berakha*; while R. Yirmiyahu said: One who *sees* the Ḥanukka lamp must recite a *berakha*. R. Yehuda said: On the first day, one who sees must recite two *berakhot*, and one who lights must recite three *berakhot*; thereafter, one who lights recites two *berakhot*, and one who sees recites one *berakha*. What is omitted? The

> "season" [*Sheheḥeyanu*] is omitted. Why not let the "miracle" [*she'asa nissim*] be omitted [as well]? The miracle is relevant every day. (Shabbat 23a)

According to the Gemara, one recites the *berakha* of *she'asa nissim* in two situations: upon lighting and upon seeing *neirot Ḥanukka*.

The *Rishonim* discuss the circumstances under which one recites *she'asa nissim* upon seeing Ḥanukka candles, and they also address the nature of this *berakha* and its relationship to the *berakhot* recited upon lighting the *neirot Ḥanukka*.

Some *Rishonim* explain that one who has yet to light his own candles recites *she'asa nissim* upon seeing another person's lights.[4] Some suggest that one may even recite the *berakha* upon seeing *neirot Ḥanukka* and then say the *berakha* again upon lighting his own candles.[5] Others maintain that one who intends to light later should preferably wait to recite *she'asa nissim* upon lighting his own candles.[6] In their view, only one who will not light his own candles later that evening recites *she'asa nissim* upon seeing someone else's Ḥanukka lights. The *Mordekhai*[7] and Maharshal[8] maintain that even one who is away from home and fulfills his obligation through the lighting performed by his family members should recite *she'asa nissim* upon seeing Ḥanukka lights.

R. Yoel Sirkis offers an explanation for these opinions, which maintain that even one who fulfills the mitzva of Ḥanukka lights may still, under certain circumstances, say the blessing of "*she'asa nissim*." He explains that there are actually two mitzvot fulfilled through *ner Ḥanukka*: the obligation of ***hadlaka*** (lighting) and an obligation of ***hodaa*** (thanking God for the miracle). One who has somebody lighting for him at his home fulfills his obligation to light, but does not fulfill his personal obligation of *hodaa*, which one fulfills through reciting the *berakha* of *she'asa nissim* upon seeing lit Ḥanukka candles.[9]

Other *Rishonim*[10] disagree, ruling that only one who will not light and who has no one at home lighting on his behalf should recite this *berakha*. This is also the implication of Tosafot, who explain that the *berakha* upon "seeing" was instituted for *neirot Ḥanukka*, and not other mitzvot, because people without a home are unable to fulfill the mitzva of *hadlakat neirot*. *Ḥazal* therefore instituted a special *berakha* to include them in the mitzva.[11] This certainly implies that the *birkat haro'e* was intended for those who do not fulfill the mitzva at all. The *Shulḥan Arukh,*[12] and subsequently *Taz*[13] and *Magen Avraham,*[14] rule that one recites this *berakha* only if he will not light and has no one lighting for him at home.

The *Rishonim* discuss the timing as well as the nature of the *berakha* of *she'asa nissim* recited upon lighting the *neirot Ḥanukka.*[15] Some maintain that one should recite the *berakha* before lighting the candles, as one always recites *berakhot* immediately before their performance. Others insist that one should first recite the *berakha* of "*lehadlik ner,*" light the candles, and then say "*she'asa nissim*" upon seeing the lit candles.[16] These views likely disagree as to whether the *berakha* of *she'asa nissim* functions as a "*birkat hamitzva,*" which must always be recited before the mitzva's performance, or exclusively as a "*birkat hashevaḥ,*" which one generally recites after observing a specific phenomenon.

Rema, citing Maharil, rules that one should recite all the *berakhot* – including *she'asa nissim* – before lighting the candles.[17] R. Soloveitchik reported that his father would attempt to fulfill both opinions after the first night. He would first recite the *birkat hamitzva,* light the first candle, recite *she'asa nissim,* and then light the remaining candles.[18]

As we saw above, the Talmud teaches that one should recite the *berakha* of *Sheheḥeyanu* on the first night of Ḥanukka, regardless of whether he personally lights or merely observes the candles lit. Interestingly, Me'iri cites those who assert that one who will neither light nor see *neirot Ḥanukka* should nevertheless recite the *berakha* of *Sheheḥeyanu* upon the occasion of Ḥanukka.[19] Ḥafetz Ḥayim writes this in his *Shaar HaTziyun* notes to the *Mishna Berura*:

> It is possible that just as we maintain in general that the *berakha* of *Sheheḥeyanu* may be recited [on Yom Tov] even in the marketplace, because it relates to the special quality of the festival itself, here too, it relates to the special quality of Ḥanukka, at which time miracles and wonders were performed [for us], though ideally [the Rabbis] adjoined it to the time of lighting. A similar argument is found in the Me'iri.[20]

Similarly, in his *Biur Halakha,* Ḥafetz Ḥayim cites a debate among the *Aḥaronim* as to whether one who is unable to read the Megilla on Purim should nevertheless recite the *birkat Sheheḥiyanu.*[21] Practically, *Peri Ḥadash,*[22] R. Moshe Feinstein,[23] and R. Ovadia Yosef[24] conclude that one does not recite *Sheheḥeyanu* on the occasion of Ḥanukka itself if he does not light candles.

HANEIROT HALALU

The *HaNeirot HaLalu* prayer, which is traditionally recited after the Ḥanukka candles have been lit, appears in the eighth-century minor tractate of Soferim.[25] Centuries later, this prayer appears in the writings of Maharam of Rothenberg and his student Rosh.[26] *Tur* testifies that his father, Rosh, as well as Maharam, would recite this prayer upon lighting the *neirot Ḥanukka.*[27]

The formulation of the Mishna in Masekhet Soferim strongly implies that one should recite the *birkat hamitzva,* recite *HaNeirot HaLalu,* and only then conclude with *Sheheḥeyanu* and *she'asa nissim.* This sequence is quite puzzling, as the recitation of *HaNeirot HaLalu* would seemingly constitute an interruption between the first *berakha* and the second and third!

R. Soloveitchik, as cited by R. Hershel Schachter, explains that *HaNeirot HaLalu* is not simply a liturgical poem. Rather, just as the *pirsumei nissa* of Pesaḥ and Purim require a text to properly publicize the miracle (the Haggada and the Megilla, respectively), we similarly recite *HaNeirot HaLalu* as the text through which our lighting properly publicizes the miracle of Ḥanukka. Thus, one should integrate the text of the *pirsumei nissa, HaNeirot HaLalu,* within the fulfillment of the mitzva, as Masekhet Soferim apparently maintains.[28] Rema, however, as we learned above, cites Maharil as requiring one to first recite all three *berakhot,* and only then recite *HaNeirot HaLalu.*[29] The *Shulḥan Arukh* likewise rules that one should recite *HaNeirot HaLalu* after lighting.[30]

Should one recite *HaNeirot HaLalu* after lighting *all* the candles or immediately after kindling the first light? Maharshal writes that one should recite *HaNeirot HaLalu* immediately after lighting the first candle, while lighting the remaining candles.[31] Others recite it only after lighting all the candles.[32] The *Mishna Berura* cites both opinions, although he seems partial to the first practice.[33]

R. Yosef b. Moshe records the custom of reciting the famous *Maoz Tzur* hymn. He relates that his teacher, *Terumat HaDeshen,* would "play" (*menagen*) this poem after reciting *HaNeirot HaLalu.* On Shabbat, however, he would recite it during the meal, along with the other *mizmorim.*[34] *Shela* records the final stanza of the hymn ("*Ḥasof zero'a kodshekha*"), in which we pray for the redemption from our current exile. This stanza does not appear in the earlier versions of *Maoz Tzur.*

THE PLACEMENT OF THE LIGHTS: *ḤANUKIYOT*

The Talmud teaches:

> Rava said: If one fills a dish with oil, surrounds it with wicks, and places a vessel over it, it is credited to many people; if he does not place a vessel over it, he turns it into a kind of "*medura*" (fire), and is not credited even to one. (Shabbat 23b)

This passage teaches two halakhot. First, each person's lights must appear separate and distinct from that of others. Second, one must light a ***ner*** *Ḥanukka* (Ḥanukka **flame**), and not what appears as a large fire (*medura*). Nowadays, people customarily light separate candles or cups of oil, which are often held in place by the "*ḥanukiya.*"

Rema rules that one should place the lights in a row, and not in a circle, which would give the appearance of a *medura.*[35] However, the *Ben Ish Ḥai,* R. Yosef Ḥayim b. Eliyahu al-Ḥakham (Baghdad, 1835–1909), suggests that while the lights should preferably be arranged in a straight line, similar to the Menora of the *Beit HaMikdash,* our lights, which are generally separate and distinct candles, may be arranged in a circle.[36] Similarly, R. Ḥezekiah da Silva (1659–1698) rules that one need not be concerned with Rema's ruling as long as the candles are separate from each other,[37] similar to one who "fills a dish with oil and surrounds it with wicks, and places a vessel over it." It seems, however, that common practice follows Rema's ruling.

Magen Avraham cites Maharil as opposing lighting the candles in a jagged line (one in, one out).[38] The *Mishna Berura* cites this ruling as well, commenting that it is not "worthwhile" to arrange the candles in this manner, as it may lead one to place the candles in a circular pattern.[39]

THE ORDER FOR LIGHTING ḤANUKKA CANDLES

From which direction should one kindle the Ḥanukka lights? The *Mordekhai* reports that his teacher, Maharam of Rothenburg, would begin lighting from the left and continue lighting the remaining candles while moving toward the right.[40] As proof, he cites the Talmud's comment regarding the Yom Kippur sacrificial service that "all of your turns should be toward the right" (Yoma 58b). Similarly, Maharil would begin lighting from the leftmost candle, and complete the lighting while facing toward the right.[41] R. Yosef Colon, Maharik (1420–1480), a disciple of Maharil, adds that on each night, one should recite the *berakha* over the newest candle, added on the left, in order to highlight the miracle wrought on each additional day of Ḥanukka.[42]

Terumat HaDeshen cites two customs in this regard. While the Western Rhine communities would begin lighting from the left side, in accordance with Maharam and Maharik, the Eastern communities of Austria and its environs would light from the right side.[43] *Levush*[44] and the Vilna Gaon[45] also rule that one should begin from the right. In his comments to the *Shulḥan Arukh,* however, the Vilna Gaon writes that one should always begin with the candle closest to the door.[46] The *Shulḥan Arukh* rules in accordance with Maharam, writing that on the first night one should light on the right side, and on subsequent nights, one should begin from the left and continue rightward.[47] Common custom follows this view.[48]

CHAPTER 34

The Oils and Wicks for Ḥanukka Candles; Deriving Benefit from the Ḥanukka Lights

THE PROPER OILS FOR ḤANUKKA CANDLES, AND ELECTRIC *ḤANUKIYOT*

The Talmud concludes that all wicks and oils, even those which may not be used for *neirot Shabbat,* may be used for *neirot Ḥanukka* (Shabbat 21b). The Gemara does, however, express a preference for olive oil:

> R. Yehoshua b. Levi said: All oils are fit for the Ḥanukka lamp, but olive oil is the most preferred. Abaye said: At first the Master [Rabba] used to seek poppy-seed oil, saying: The light of this lasts longer; but when he heard this [dictum] of R. Yehoshua b. Levi, he was particular for olive oil, saying: This yields a clearer light. (Shabbat 23a)

Many *Rishonim* interpret the anecdote about Rabba as referring to *ner Ḥanukka,* and thus express preference for olive oil due to its clear flame.[1] Others prefer olive oil because the miracle of the flask of oil occurred with olive oil.[2] Some *Rishonim,* however, record no preference.[3]

Rema writes that while it is preferable to light with olive oil, it is customary to light with wax candles, because they, like oil, produce a clear flame.[4] Some *Aḥaronim* write that one should preferably light with olive oil in remembrance of the miracle. Interestingly, R. Yehuda b. Betzalel Loew, Maharal of Prague, prohibited lighting with wax candles.[5] His grandson records that Maharal instituted a communal ban on lighting with wax, and even forced his synagogue to change their menora to accommodate lighting with oil.[6]

In recent years, *posekim* have addressed the question of whether one may use electric lights for *neirot Ḥanukka.* A minority of authorities have sanctioned using electric *ḥanukiyot* to fulfill one's obligation.

For example, R. Yosef Mashash (1892–1974), the former Chief Rabbi of Haifa, rules that one may use electric, incandescent lights for *neirot Ḥanukka*.[7] He insists that that the metal filament of the lightbulb fulfills the requirement for a "wick." Furthermore, he argues that since Ashkenazic Jews traditionally used wax candles for *hadlakat neirot,* as Rema records, there seems to be no actual requirement to use oil. The act of turning the light off and on should also satisfy the requirement of *hadlaka*. Indeed, in his work on the laws of Ḥanukka, he shockingly asserts:

> And I say more, that it is simple and clear that if the electrical light existed in the time of the Temple, certainly with it they would have lit the Menora, since it is impossible that we would fill our everyday homes with these great lights of the precious electrical light…and in the House of Our Holy Lord we would light with olive oil, which even the extremely poor are disgusted by at this time! And it is simple that from it [electrical light] we will light in the last House [Temple] that will be built speedily in our days, Amen![8]

However, most authorities object to using electric lights for *neirot Ḥanukka* for a number of reasons. First, the light produced by an electric light may not satisfy the halakhic requirement of "*esh*" (fire). Most *posekim* agree, based on Rambam,[9] that heating the filament of an incandescent light bulb, thereby causing it to glow, violates the *melakha* of *mav'ir* (kindling a flame) on Shabbat, as the hot, glowing metal is considered "*esh*." Fluorescent, neon, and LED displays, however, do not create light through the heating of a metal filament, and are thus not considered "*esh*" in the context of Shabbat.

Assuming that the mitzva of *neirot Ḥanukka* requires "*esh*," one certainly cannot light a fluorescent light or LED display in order to fulfill the mitzva. At first glance, it would seem that the (possible) requirement of *esh* for *neirot Ḥanukka* should be comparable to the definition of *esh* on Shabbat, thus allowing for the use of incandescent bulbs. Some authorities, however, nevertheless disqualify the use of an incandescent bulb, claiming that even if it contains *esh,* it does not constitute a "*ner*," a burning flame. Along these lines, R. Tzvi Pesach Frank cites R. Yosef Rosen, the Rogatchover Gaon (1858–1936), as permitting the use of an incandescent bulb for Havdala, as such a bulb qualifies for the necessary "*esh*," but not for Shabbat candle lighting, as it does not qualify as a the necessary "*ner*."[10] Furthermore, some authorities claim that a bulb produces too much light, rendering it similar to a *medura*, the large fire invalidated by the Gemara.

R. Yaakov Chaim Sofer contends that a bulb is not acceptable for an entirely different reason – it differs too dramatically from the miracle that occurred in the *Beit HaMikdash*.[11] Additionally, some authorities argue that, by definition, *ner Ḥanukka* requires a source of fuel, either oil or wax, and a wick, both of which are absent from electric lights. Some authorities similarly disqualified the use of electric bulbs because of the requirement to light candles containing at least enough wax or oil to burn for a half-hour. Since an electric bulb has no fuel, it cannot be used. One could argue, however, that the use of a battery suffices as an adequate source of "fuel" in this regard.

While most *posekim* do not accept the use of electric lights for *neirot Ḥanukka*, some suggest that under extenuating circumstances, one should light an electric light without reciting a *berakha*, in order to satisfy the minority opinion.[12]

DERIVING BENEFIT FROM THE ḤANUKKA LIGHTS

The Talmud teaches:

> R. Huna said: The wicks and oils about which the sages said that one must not light therewith on Shabbat, one may not light therewith on Ḥanukka, neither on Shabbat nor on weekdays. Rabba said: What is R. Huna's reason? He holds that if it [the Ḥanukka lamp] goes out, one must attend thereto, *and one may make use of its light*.... R. Zeira said in R. Mattena's name, and others state that R. Zeira said in Rav's name: Regarding the wicks and oils about which the sages said that one must not light therewith on Shabbat, one may light therewith on Ḥanukka, both on weekdays and on Shabbat. R. Yirmiyahu said: What is Rav's reason? He holds that if it goes out, it does not require attention, *and one may not make use of its light*. (Shabbat 21a–b)

The Talmud teaches that wicks and oils that do not produce a steady flame may not be used for lighting the Shabbat lights, due to the concern that one might adjust the flame in violation of Shabbat. The Talmud cites different opinions as to whether these wicks and oils may be used for the Ḥanukka lights. The debate hinges on the question of whether one may derive benefit from the Ḥanukka lights. R. Huna permits one to derive benefit from the Ḥanukka lights; therefore, these inferior wicks and oils may *not* be used on Shabbat Ḥanukka, as one might adjust the faltering flame in the course of using its light. However, Rav maintains that one may not benefit from the flame of the Ḥanukka lights; therefore, these wicks and oils may be used on Shabbat Ḥanukka, as there is no fear that one will adjust the flame. The Gemara concludes that the halakha follows Rav's position.

The *Rishonim* debate the question of why Rav prohibits deriving benefit from the Ḥanukka lights. Rashi[13] and Rosh (Shabbat 2:6) explain that if one makes use of the lights, it may not be noticeable that he lit them for the purpose of the mitzva. Ran,[14] Rashba,[15] and Baal HaMaor[16] explain that the Rabbis modeled the mitzva of *hadlakat neirot* after the Menora of the Temple, through which the original miracle occurred. Therefore, just as no one derives personal benefit from the light of the Menora, which stands in the inner sanctuary of the *Mikdash*, one similarly should not derive benefit from the light of the *neirot Ḥanukka*. These *Rishonim* argue as to whether the prohibition is rooted in the need to maximize *pirsumei nissa* by not confusing lighting for one's personal needs with lighting for the sake of a mitzva, or in the inherent sanctity extended to the Ḥanukka lights, which are similar to the lights of the Menora in the *Beit HaMikdash*.

This debate impacts our understanding of the continuation of the gemara:

> R. Yehuda said in R. Assi's name: One must not count money by the Ḥanukka light. When I stated this before Shmuel, he said to me: Has then the lamp sanctity? R. Yosef demurred: Does blood possess sanctity? For it was taught, "He shall pour out [the blood thereof], and cover it [with dust]" – wherewith he pours out, he must cover – that is, he must not cover it with his foot, so that precepts may not appear contemptible to him. Here, too, it is so that precepts may not appear contemptible to him.

What is the connection between Rav's statement that one may not derive benefit from the Ḥanukka lights and R. Assi's remark that one should not count money by the Ḥanukka light due to the concern of "*bizui mitzva*," showing contempt for the mitzvot?

Baal HaMaor suggests that Rav and R. Assi debate the reason and scope of the prohibition against deriving benefit from the light. Rav bases this halakha on the absolute prohibition to benefit from the holy light of the Menora, and thus prohibits *all* benefit from the Ḥanukka lights. R. Assi, in contrast, who relates this prohibition to the more universal concern of "*bizui mitzva*," only prohibits mundane uses of the *neirot Ḥanukka*, such as counting money. Therefore, one may, according to R. Assi, use the light of the *neirot Ḥanukka* for sacred purposes, as using the Ḥanukka lights for such purposes is not degrading to the mitzva.[17] Indeed, *Tur* cites Baal Ittur as permitting using the Ḥanukka lights for a "sacred purpose,"[18] and *Shibbolei HaLeket* likewise permits learning Torah by the light of the *ner Ḥanukka*.[19]

Others explain that, to the contrary, R. Assi is more stringent than Rav. As we saw above, Rosh claims that Rav prohibits benefiting from the Ḥanukka lights so that one's lighting should be clearly perceived as being for the sake of the mitzva. Therefore, Rav only prohibited "permanent" uses of the Ḥanukka lights. R. Assi, however, adds that even a temporary use of the light, which may not create a misimpression regarding the person's intentions, still degrades the mitzva and violates the universal principle of "*bizui mitzva*."[20] The *Shulḥan Arukh* rules:

> It is prohibited to use the Ḥanukka light, both on Shabbat and on a weekday. Even to examine coins or to count them by their light is prohibited; even a sacred use, such as to learn by its light, is prohibited. Some permit a sacred use.[21]

Magen Avraham[22] and *Taz*[23] attest that it was customary to refrain from using the Ḥanukka lights for any benefit.

Interestingly, Ritva records that his teacher prohibited even speaking with one's friend by the light of the *neirot Ḥanukka*.[24] Me'iri also records that he would light another candle when he wished to talk to someone near the light of the *neirot Ḥanukka*.[25] The *Aḥaronim* apparently disagree with this stringent position, ruling that one may sit in a room lit by the Ḥanukka lights, as this type of indirect benefit is not prohibited.[26]

May one derive benefit from the light after the candles have burned for the minimum required duration? The *Shulḥan Arukh*[27] rules in accordance with Rif[28] who permits one to benefit from the *neirot Ḥanukka* after the passage of the minimum required time (a half-hour). The *Mishna Berura*,[29] however, cites Maharshal, who forbids benefiting from the light while the candles are still lit, even after a half-hour has passed, as onlookers might suspect him of benefiting from the *neirot Ḥanukka* used to fulfill the mitzva.[30]

LIGHTING ONE CANDLE FROM ANOTHER

Occasionally, one of the Ḥanukka lights is extinguished and one wishes to rekindle it. May he light it from the adjacent candle, which is still burning, or must he light it from an outside source? The Gemara teaches: "Rav said: One must not light from lamp to lamp; but Shmuel maintained: One may light from lamp to lamp" (Shabbat 22a–b). The Gemara concludes that even Rav prohibits lighting one candle from another by means of a "*kisam*," a wooden chip, as it "denigrates" the mitzva. One may, however, light one Ḥanukka candle directly from another ("*misheraga lesheraga*"), even according to Rav. Shmuel, however, permits lighting one candle from another even through the use of a "*kisam*."

Tosafot record that it is customary not to light one candle from another, even directly, despite the fact that this is, technically speaking, permissible.[31] *Tur* cites two opinions as to whether halakha follows the lenient position of Shmuel or the stricter opinion of Rav.[32] The *Shulḥan Arukh* cites both opinions brought in *Tur*.[33] Rema, citing Tosafot, records that it is customary not to light one candle from another, neither directly nor through the use of a "*kisam*." He explains that since the mitzva is technically fulfilled after lighting the first light (*ner ish uveito*), lighting the other candles is considered to be *reshut* (optional), a *hiddur mitzva*, and one should therefore not light them from a *ner Ḥanukka.*[34] Rema concludes that one may certainly light from the Ḥanukka candles after the minimum time of the mitzva has passed (thirty minutes). The *Mishna Berura* notes that although it is customary not to benefit from the *neirot Ḥanukka* even after the minimum time has passed, as we saw above, in this case, one may certainly light for the sake of a mitzva after the candles have been lit for thirty minutes.[35]

THE *SHAMASH*

The Talmud teaches:

> The Rabbis taught: The Ḥanukka candle – the mitzva is to place it at the entrance of one's home, outside. If one lives in a loft, he places it in the window adjacent to the public domain. During times of danger, one places it on his table, and this suffices.
>
> Rava said: One requires another candle to use its light. If there is a fire, he does not need [the extra candle]; if he is a prominent person, then even though there is a fire, he needs another candle. (Shabbat 21b)

The Gemara requires another light, in addition to those used to fulfill the mitzva. What is the reason for this extra light, and why does the Gemara juxtapose this requirement to its discussion of the different places in which one may light *neirot Ḥanukka*?

Some *Rishonim* explain that one who lights on the table in his home due to danger must light an additional light in order to clarify that the *neirot Ḥanukka* were lit for the purpose of the mitzva, and not merely to provide light.[36] Accordingly, one who lights inside his home must light an additional light in order to avoid misconceptions, regardless of whether he rules in accordance with R. Huna or Rav regarding benefiting from the Ḥanukka lights. Others, however, explain that one must light an additional candle due to the prohibition to benefit from the Ḥanukka lights.[37] When the *neirot Ḥanukka* are the only lights in the house, one should provide another light, a *shamash,* from which one may derive benefit. If, however, there is another fire (*medura*) in the room, one need not light a *shamash.*

What if one lit in a place where he will not likely make use of the light? Must he still light the *shamash*? Me'iri writes the following in the name of "*miktzat rabbanim*" ("a few rabbis"):

> Nevertheless, it appears to me in light of the *sugya* that they required another candle only when one places it on his table. But if he places it near his entrance, he does not need another candle, even though it stands there for him, since he will not come to use specifically its light for some purpose. Indeed, I have seen a few rabbis who had the practice of standing there and speaking to their colleagues without another candle.

However, he concludes: "But in practice I customarily light another candle [that is] not for the sake of the mitzva, and the custom of our forefathers is in our hands." The *Shulḥan Arukh* mentions the requirement to light an additional candle in two contexts. In one place, he writes:

> The Ḥanukka candle is placed at the entrance near the public domain, outside.... In times of danger...one places it on his table, and this suffices. One must have an additional candle to make use of its light. If there is a fire, one does not need a different candle. If he is a prominent person, who does not customarily use the light of a fire, he requires a different candle.[38]

Elsewhere, he writes:

> It is forbidden to make use of the Ḥanukka candles.... It is forbidden even to check or count money by their light.... The custom is to light an additional candle so that if he makes use of its light, it will have been from the additional light, which was lit last. One places it somewhat distant from the other candles used for the mitzva.[39]

Seemingly, the *Shulḥan Arukh* rules in accordance with both explanations, requiring an additional candle to help distinguish between the *neirot Ḥanukka* and other lights (in the first halakha), and to prevent one from benefiting directly from the Ḥanukka lights (in the second halakha).

The *Rishonim* discuss where the *shamash* should placed.[40] While the *Shulḥan Arukh* writes that the *shamash* should be placed separate from the other candles,[41] Rema adds: "In these countries, the practice is not to add [another candle], but rather to place next to them the *shamash* from which one lights the candles, and this is preferable."[42] According to Rema, it is preferable not to add a candle, but rather to place the light used to kindle the *neirot Ḥanukka* (the *shamash*) next to the *ḥanukiya*. Apparently, this is so that the candle used to kindle the others will not be confused with one of the mandatory Ḥanukka lights. In fact, the *Arukh HaShulḥan* insists that the *shamash* should be placed with the other lights, as everyone knows that it is customary to light an additional light for the *shamash*.[43] Some *Aḥaronim*, however, record that it is customary to place the *shamash* above the other lights.[44]

Purim

CHAPTER 35

Parashat Shekalim and *Parashat Zakhor*

THE MONTH OF ADAR

The Talmud teaches:

> Our sages taught: Just as our joy is reduced when the month of Av begins, so is our joy increased when the month of Adar begins. R. Papa said: Therefore, a Jew who is involved in litigation with a non-Jew should avoid him during Av, for it is a time of ill omen for him. And he should attempt to meet him in court in Adar, for it is a time of good omen for him. (Taanit 29a)

The *Rishonim*[1] raise the question of how this comment can be reconciled with the well-known principle that "*ein mazal leYisrael*" (Shabbat 156a) – the Jewish experience is not determined by astrological forces. Some interpret R. Papa's comment to mean that the months of Adar and Av are subject to different terms of divine providence. Others simply minimize the theological importance of these statements, reducing the phrase "ill omen" to a description of the rabbinic legislation, as opposed to an astrological reference.

Alternatively, we might suggest viewing our behavior during these two months as reflecting different aspects of our relationship with God. During Adar, we express our confidence in our special relationship with the Almighty, which at times grants us divine shelter and protection, and which we commemorate on the holiday of Purim. During Av, however, we express the reality of our particularly precarious existence and our being unworthy of divine protection, which we feel most intensely on Tisha B'Av. Interestingly, Rambam, as well as the *Shulḥan Arukh*, omit this passage in their presentation of the laws of Purim.[2]

THE *ARBA PARASHOT*: FOUR SPECIAL TORAH READINGS

The Mishna (Megilla 29a) and Tosefta (Megilla 3:1–3) enumerate the four Torah sections read during the months of Adar and Nissan:

> If Rosh Ḥodesh Adar falls on Shabbat, we read *Parashat Shekalim*. If it falls during the week, then we read *Shekalim* on the Shabbat preceding it.... On the second [week of the month of Adar], we read [*Parashat*[*Zakhor*; on the third [week, we read *Parashat*] *Para Aduma*, and on the fourth, "*HaḤodesh*."

The Talmud records a debate between R. Ami and R. Yirmiya as to whether these sections are read in place of the regular Torah reading or only as the *maftir* section added on to the scheduled reading (Megilla 30b).[3] Rambam[4] and the *Shulḥan Arukh*[5] follow the second view. According to our custom[6] that the *maftir* is read in addition to the seven *aliyot* of the *parasha*, these four sections are read as the *maftir* on these four Shabbatot.

PARASHAT SHEKALIM

As the Mishna teaches, we read *Parashat Shekalim* and *Parashat Zakhor* before Purim. *Parashat Shekalim* (Ex. 30:11–16), according to Shmuel (Megilla 29b), is read in commemoration of the *maḥatzit hashekel*, the half-shekel that was donated annually for the sacrificial service. The verses note the uniformity of the donation ("the wealthy shall not add, nor shall the impoverished detract"; Ex. 30:15), as well the "atonement" it provided ("to atone for your souls"; ibid.). Apparently, the equal participation of all Jews in the communal sacrifices emphasizes the unity of the Jewish people and their shared aspiration to serve God, which ultimately renders them worthy of divine forgiveness.

Why do we read this *parasha* before Purim? Rashi (Megilla 29a) associates this reading with the Mishna's comment (Shekalim 1:1) that on the first of Adar, the High Court "announced" the mitzva of the half-shekel. Starting from Nissan, sacrifices must be purchased from new donations, and the half-shekel collection thus commenced each year on Rosh Ḥodesh Adar to ensure the availability of new funds by Rosh Ḥodesh Nissan. Rashi apparently maintains that the reading of *Parashat Shekalim* predates the destruction of the *Beit HaMikdash* and served as a public announcement to bring the *maḥatzit hashekel.*

The *Mishna Berura*[7] cites *Levush* as explaining that we read *Parashat Shekalim* in fulfillment of the verse, "and we will offer our lips [in place of] bulls" (Hos. 14:3). In other words, the Rabbis instituted the reading of *Parashat Shekalim* after the destruction of the Temple as a commemoration of the *maḥatzit hashekel,* so that we can fulfill this mitzva on some level through this reading. Similarly, the *Sefer HaḤinukh*[8] explains that the reading of *Parashat Shekalim* serves to remind us of the mitzva of *maḥatzit hashekel,* which we unfortunately can no longer observe due to the absence of the *Mikdash.*

While the *posekim* cited above do not draw any connection between *Parashat Shekalim* and Purim, the Talmud points to such a connection:

> It was revealed and clear before the Holy One, Blessed be He, that in the future, Haman would exact *shekalim* from Israel; He therefore preceded their *shekalim* to his, as it says, "and they would announce the *shekalim*... on the first of Adar." (Megilla 13b)

Similarly, the Yerushalmi suggests that the merit of the Jews' communal participation in the sacrificial service through the donation of the *maḥatzit hashekel* protected them from Haman's edict, which included a payment of money ("*eshkol*"; Est. 3:9) to the royal treasury. Why did the merit of the *maḥatzit hashekel* protect the Jews from Haman's decree? A deeper understanding of the mitzva of *maḥatzit hashekel* may help us to understand this Yerushalmi.

R. Moshe Alshikh explains in his Torah commentary that the commandment to donate specifically a half-*shekel* (as opposed to a complete *shekel*) demonstrates how all members of the nation combine to make a single, organic whole. No Jew can feel complete as a lone individual, separated from the nation; it is only when each person participates with the rest of Am Yisrael, by contributing his share, that he – and the nation – become whole (Ex. 30:11).

This insight may shed light on the Yerushalmi's comment cited above. The unity of the Jewish people as demonstrated through the *maḥatzit hashekel* donation counters Haman's accusation that the Jews are "a certain people scattered abroad and dispersed among the peoples" (Est. 3:8). When each member of the Jewish people recognizes that he is but a "half," one part of the greater whole, thus engendering a sense of unity among the nation, they then become worthy of forgiveness and immune to Haman's plans. As the Yerushalmi adds, "Therefore, we precede and read the section regarding *shekalim*" (Megilla 1:5). The Rabbis instituted that we remember and internalize the true reason behind the salvation from Haman in preparation for our festive observance of Purim.

ZEKHER LEMAḤATZIT HASHEKEL

Besides reading the section of *Shekalim*, it is also customary before Purim to donate money to charity "*zekher lemaḥatzit hashekel*" – in commemoration of the *maḥatzit hashekel*. The *Mordekhai* records a custom to donate three "half coins" before Purim, corresponding to the three instances of the word "*teruma*" (donation) in the *Shekalim* section in the Torah.[9] Although this custom is not mentioned by other *Rishonim*, Rema writes, "Some say that before Purim, one should give a half of the current currency of that time and place, in commemoration of the *maḥatzit hashekel*."[10]

In order to understand some of the details pertinent to this custom, let us briefly review the laws of the original *maḥatzit hashekel* donation. Rambam writes that "there is a positive commandment for each Jewish male to give half of a shekel each year."[11] This mitzva, however, "applies only during the time of the Temple, and during the time of the Temple, the *shekalim* are given in Israel as well as in the Diaspora;[12] and when the Temple is destroyed, [the mitzva] does not apply even in the Land of Israel."

Furthermore, Rambam[13] rules, in accordance with the Mishna (Shekalim 1:3), that women and children are exempt from the obligation of *maḥatzit hashekel*. R. Ovadia Bartenura (fifteenth century) explains that "children" in this context refers to males under twenty years old.[14] In contrast, R. Yom Tov Lipman Heller[15] and Ramban (Ex. 30:12) rule that this obligation is no different from any other commandment, in which a male becomes obligated already at the age of thirteen.

The *Aḥaronim* discuss a number of issues related to the commemoration of *maḥatzit hashekel* observed nowadays, at least some of which appear to depend upon the extent to which this custom is modeled after the original mitzva. For example, *Magen Avraham* cites those who obligate women and minors in *zekher lemaḥatzit hashekel* and questions the basis and rationale for such a position.[16] R. Barukh HaLevi Epstein, author of the *Torah Temima*, explains that the half-*shekel* donation served different roles in different contexts. During Benei Yisrael's sojourn in the wilderness, the donation served to count the males eligible for military service. The custom to give charity before Purim, however, simply commemorates the miracles of Purim, which women and children certainly experienced no less than men, and they are therefore included in this commemoration.[17] Furthermore, R. Yaakov Ḥayim Sofer explains in his *Kaf HaḤayim*[18] that women and children participate in this custom despite their exemption from the original *maḥatzit hashekel* obligation because this mitzva serves "to atone for their souls," and women and children also require atonement.

Regarding the age from which one should give the *maḥatzit hashekel*, Rema writes that "only one who is twenty years old must give." As we have seen, however, some authorities rule that the original obligation begins at the age of thirteen, just like other mitzvot. The *Mishna Berura*[19] records that it is customary to give the *maḥatzit hashekel* even on behalf of one's children and for pregnant women to donate on behalf of the unborn child.

As for the amount that one is required to donate, *Kaf HaḤayim*[20] writes that ideally, one who has the financial means should give an amount corresponding to the amount of the original *maḥatzit hashekel*, namely, three dram, or approximately nine grams of pure silver. Rema, however, codifies the practice recorded in the *Mordekhai*, which we cited earlier:

> Some say that before Purim, one should give a half of the current currency in that time and place, in commemoration of the *maḥatzit hashekel*. Since the word "*teruma*" (donation) appears three times in the *parasha*, one should give three [coins].[21]

Must one give specifically "half coins"? R. Eliezer Waldenberg rules in his *Tzitz Eliezer* that one who forgot to prepare "half coins" may give his donation together with another person, or simply give "whole coins," intending that the halves should serve to fulfill the custom of *zekher lemaḥatzit hashekel* and the rest should simply count as *tzedaka*.[22]

Kaf HaḤayim,[23] as well as the Vilna Gaon,[24] disputes Rema's ruling that one must donate three half coins and maintains that one may simply give one half coin. Furthermore, some *Aḥaronim*[25] emphasize that the *zekher lemaḥatzit hashekel* is merely a custom, and it is sufficient to give any sum of charity, and even bills or checks.

Regarding the proper time to fulfill this custom, the Mishna states that one should give the donation before *Shabbat Zakhor* (the Shabbat before Purim) (Masekhet Soferim 21:3). Rema, however, writes, "Some give it on the eve of Purim, before reciting Minḥa, and that is the custom in these lands."[26] *Magen Avraham* records that it was customary to fulfill this *minhag* on Purim morning, before the Megilla reading.[27]

To whom should the *zekher lemaḥatzit hashekel* funds be given? Masekhet Soferim teaches that the funds should be used "to provide water and food for our impoverished brethren" (Masekhet Soferim 21:3). Others insist that they should be used to support Torah learning.[28]

The *Shulḥan Arukh* discusses the obligation – or the custom, according to some – of setting aside a percentage of one's income for *tzedaka*, known as "*maaser kesafim*."[29] Generally, one should not use these funds to pay one's debts or obligations, and therefore, *Magen Avraham* writes that one should not use one's *maaser kesafim* funds to fulfill the custom of *zekher lemaḥatzit hashekel*.[30] We will discuss this issue in greater depth when we study the laws of *matanot la'evyonim*.

PARASHAT ZAKHOR

The second of the "four *parashot*," *Parashat Zakhor*, is read on the Shabbat before Purim. Through this reading, which recounts Amalek's attack against Benei Yisrael in the wilderness, we fulfill the command of "*zekhirat Amalek*" – remembering Amalek's hostility:

> Remember (*Zakhor*) what Amalek did to you along the way as you left Egypt; how he confronted you along the way and smote the hindmost among you, all that were enfeebled, when you were faint and weary; and he did not fear God. Therefore, it shall be that when the Lord your God gives you rest from all your enemies around you, in the land which the Lord your God gives you as an inheritance to possess, you shall erase the memory of Amalek from under the heavens; you shall not forget. (Deut. 25:17–19)

The Torah here issues three commandments relevant to Amalek: to *remember, not to forget,* and to *erase* the memory of Amalek.

What is the relationship between the mitzva to remember Amalek and the mitzva to eradicate Amalek? On the one hand, one might view the mitzva to remember and the commandment not to forget Amalek as part of the larger objective of waging war against this nation. Rambam writes:

> We are commanded to remember that which Amalek did to us... and that we should repeat this from time to time and our souls should be aroused through its recitation to fight against them, and we should encourage the nation to hate them.[31]

On the other hand, one might view the commandment to remember Amalek as conveying and expressing independent, broader religious messages, not necessarily directly related to war. Indeed, the Torah introduces this mitzva immediately following the admonition to refrain from using or even owning false weights:

> You shall not have in you bag diverse weights, a large and a small. You shall not have in your house diverse measures, a large and a small. You shall have a perfect and just weight; you shall have a perfect and just measure, so that your days upon the land which the Lord your God gives you shall be

> prolonged. For all that do such things, even all that act dishonestly, are an abomination unto the Lord your God. (Deut. 25:13–16)

The juxtaposition of these two *parashot* may imply a more universal message, beyond the specific commandment to destroy the nation of Amalek. We are commanded to remember Amalek not because they attacked the Jewish people, but rather because their behavior typifies immoral conduct, an "abomination" before God.

R. Soloveitchik suggested that the issue of whether the mitzva to remember Amalek is related to, or dependent upon, the mitzva to eradicate it, may affect a number of halakhic questions, including whether women are obligated in the obligation of *zekhirat Amalek* and which *parasha* one may read to fulfill the mitzva, as we shall discuss below.[32]

HOW AND WHEN TO FULFILL THE MITZVA OF REMEMBERING AMALEK

Interestingly, the Gemara does not discuss when and how we are to fulfill the mitzva of *zekhirat Amalek*. Regarding the proper time to fulfill this mitzva, the *Sefer HaḤinukh* writes,

> Regarding this *zekhira* in one's heart and mouth, we do not know of a set time in the year, or a day.... It is sufficient to remember this once a year, or once every two or three years.[33]

R. Yosef Ben Moshe Babad, in his *Minḥat Ḥinukh* commentary to the *Sefer HaḤinukh*, infers from the *Ḥinukh*'s comments that a person may fulfill the biblical obligation by remembering Amalek once during his lifetime.[34]

Ḥatam Sofer suggests that one should fulfill this mitzva once each year.[35] He notes that in the discussion concerning the *berakha* of *Meḥayei Hameitim*, which one recites upon seeing someone whom he has not seen in twelve months, the Gemara asserts that certain memories are forgotten after twelve months have passed (Berakhot 58b). Ḥatam Sofer thus concludes that perpetuating the memory of Amalek requires recalling the event at least once every year. He then questions

depend upon the relationship between the commandment to remember Amalek and the mitzva to destroy Amalek.

R. Yitzchak Yaakov Weiss, former head of the rabbinical court of the Eida Ḥaredit in Jerusalem and author of the multivolume *Minḥat Yitzchak,* follows the view of R. Natan Adler (the teacher of R. Moshe Sofer), who held that women are, indeed, obligated and that their mitzva should be fulfilled through the public Torah reading. It is customary for women to hear the reading of *Parashat Zakhor,* and many communities arrange readings later in the day to accommodate those who cannot attend synagogue services on the morning of *Shabbat Zakhor.*[60]

R. Shneur Zalman Fradkin of Lublin (1830–1902), a student of the *Tzemaḥ Tzedek* and a well-known Chabad *posek,* presents a third view on this issue. In his work *Torat Ḥesed,*[61] he writes that women are, indeed, obligated to fulfill the Torah obligation of *zekhirat Amalek,* which is not a time-bound mitzva, but they are exempt from the rabbinic obligation to hear *Parashat Zakhor.* They may therefore fulfill the obligation of *zekhirat Amalek* by reading the *parasha* to themselves, without hearing the formal Torah reading. On this basis, R. Shneur Zalman explains why it was unheard of in his community for women to attend the *Zakhor* reading. R. Aaron Felder, in his *Mo'adei Yeshurun,*[62] records that R. Moshe Feinstein likewise held that women may fulfill their obligation by reading the *parasha* from a printed *Ḥumash.*

CHAPTER 36

Taanit Esther and the Dual Nature of Purim

TAANIT ESTHER

Unlike the other "minor" fasts that are enumerated and discussed by the Talmud (Taanit 29a), *Taanit Esther* is not mentioned anywhere in the Mishna or Talmud. In fact, the earliest reference to *Taanit Esther* appears in the eighth-century geonic work *She'iltot DeRav Aḥai,*[1] authored by R. Aḥai Gaon. Nevertheless, the fast is discussed by the *Rishonim,* codified by the *Shulḥan Arukh,*[2] and universally observed.

What is the source and nature of this fast, and how should we understand its relationship to Purim? The *Shibbolei HaLeket* cites Rashi as explaining that *Taanit Esther* commemorates the three-day fast observed by the Jews of Shushan at Esther's behest during the month of Nissan, before she approached Aḥashveirosh to invite him to the feast. Before approaching the king, Esther told Mordekhai:

> Go, gather together all the Jews that are present in Shushan, and fast for me, and neither eat nor drink, for three days, night and day. My maidens and I, too, will fast in like manner; and so will I go in unto the king, which is not according to the law; and if I perish, I perish. (Est. 4:16)

Rashi describes this fast as a "mere custom" (*minhag be'alma*), and criticizes those who treat it with unnecessary stringency.[3]

Rabbeinu Tam, on the other hand, as cited by Rosh, suggests that *Taanit Esther* is a rabbinic obligation alluded to in the Talmud (Megilla 2a), and it commemorates the day upon which the Jews gathered to fight those who sought to destroy them (the thirteenth of Adar). Rosh writes:

> "It is a day of gathering for everyone" – that everyone gathers together for the Fast of Esther. The rural population comes to the cities to recite *Seliḥot* and supplications, just as on this day the Jews gathered together to defend themselves and thus required divine mercy. Likewise, we find that Moshe declared a fast when they [Benei Yisrael] fought against Amalek, as it is written, "And Moshe, Aharon, and Ḥur ascended to the top of the mountain" [Exodus 17:10], and Tractate Taanit derives from here that "three [authorities] are required [to declare] a public fast." Rabbeinu Tam brought proof from here for our observance of *Taanit Esther,* which we commemorate as they did in the days of Mordekhai and Esther when the Jews gathered to defend themselves. We find no other proof for [the practice of *Taanit Esther*] other than here.[4]

Raavad offers yet a third explanation:

> The thirteenth is not similar to the other fasts, as it commemorates the miracle that occurred [on that day]. In addition, we have a written reference to it, as it says [Esther 9:31]: "To confirm these days of Purim in their appointed times, as Mordekhai the Jew and Queen Esther had enjoined them, and as they had ordained for themselves and for their seed, the matters of the *fastings* and their cry..." – in other words, to observe this fast each and every year.[5]

According to Raavad, the Fast of Esther was actually instituted as part of the original Purim edict. Our celebration includes reenacting the fast that preceded the war, during which the Jewish people experienced a miraculous redemption. Incidentally, Rambam also identifies this verse as the source for *Taanit Esther*, although he refers to it as simply a "custom."[6]

We have thus identified three possible sources for this fast, which reflect three different levels of possible obligation. It would seem that the lower the obligation entailed by the fast, the more readily we will permit a person to eat in certain situations. Indeed, the *Shulḥan Arukh* states, "This fast is not an obligation; therefore, we may be lenient regarding the fast in cases of need, such as a pregnant or nursing woman or a sick patient."[7]

A second question arises concerning the nature and character of this fast. While the other fast days express our sorrow over the loss of the *Beit HaMikdash*, it remains unclear whether *Taanit Esther* shares the mournful qualities of the other fasts. Indeed, the quotation from Raavad cited above describes the fast in almost festive terms.

R. Soloveitchik noted a number of practical ramifications of this question.[8] For example, would Rambam's ruling advocating that one refrain from "*idunim*" (entertainment or physical delights) on fast days[9] apply on *Taanit Esther* as well? If we place *Taanit Esther* in a separate category from the other fasts and consider it a festive, rather than mournful, occasion, then we would likely permit such activities. Indeed, *Piskei Teshuvot* rules that on *Taanit Esther*, one may listen to music and prepare new clothing, activities that are generally discouraged on other fast days.[10] Furthermore, R. Soloveitchik suggested that Rambam's assertion that the fast days will not be observed in the messianic era[11] might not apply to *Taanit Esther*, which is an integral part of the Purim celebration.[12]

While questioning the character of the day, one might also explore whether *Taanit Esther* is a separate custom or obligation, or whether it is integrally connected to the observance of Purim. For example, Rambam[13] and *Shulḥan Arukh*[14] rule that when Purim falls on Sunday, in which case we cannot fast on the day immediately preceding Purim (Shabbat), we fast on the previous Thursday. However, R. Aharon b. Yaakov of Lunel rules in his *Kol Bo* that one should fast on Friday, a practice that we generally avoid, so that the fast is juxtaposed to Purim as closely as possible.[15] He apparently views the fast as an integral part of Purim, which should therefore be observed as close to Purim as possible, even at the price of fasting on Friday.

Based on what we have seen, we must ask a deeper question regarding the nature of *Taanit Esther*: In what way, if at all, does the fast contribute to the Purim celebration? Some of the aforementioned sources indicate that while the fast may be commemorative, it is hardly integral to the Purim celebration. Furthermore, according to some views, *Taanit Esther* does not even accurately commemorate the events portrayed by the Megilla. Moreover, it does not conform to the rules of other fast days, as we demonstrated above. These discrepancies seem to indicate that *Taanit Esther* does not commemorate a tragic event – or any event – at all. Rather, it may simply be another, yet different, day of Purim.

R. Soloveitchik suggested that Purim and *Taanit Esther* commemorate two distinct themes of Purim, which are rooted in the different themes of the Megilla itself.[16] In this context, he notes the Gemara's discussion concerning the requirement to read the Megilla twice, both by night and during the day (Megilla 3b). The Gemara cites two scriptural sources for this halakha. In both verses, man is commanded to repeat his call to God. The first source, "My God, I call out to You during the day, but You do not answer, and in the night, as well, I am not silent" (Ps. 22:3), compares the Megilla reading to a desperate cry for help. The second source, "So that my glory may sing praise to You and not be silent, Hashem, my God, I continuously thank You" (Ps. 30:13), equates *mikra Megilla* with a song of praise for God.

R. Soloveitchik suggests that both themes accurately capture the nature of Purim. During most of the Purim story, the Jewish people were threatened and pursued; the redemption surfaces only toward the end of the Megilla. In other words, the story of Purim and its subsequent celebration involves two parts: an acknowledgment of the crisis and "what could have been" as well as thanksgiving for the redemption.

Taanit Esther and Purim, therefore, reflect two aspects of the Purim celebration, and each is incomplete without the other. One cannot truly appreciate Purim without having fasted on *Taanit Esther*, and *Taanit Esther* alone certainly does not capture the totality of the Purim story. Interestingly, *Shibbolei HaLeket* cites R. Amram Gaon as recording the custom of the *Tanna'im* and *Amora'im*, as well as the "house of the courts," to recite supplications and solemn prayers on Purim day itself![17] This custom attempts to integrate both themes into the day of Purim. This dialectic, of course, not only portrays the different components of the Purim story, but accurately reflects the precarious existence of the Jewish people since the destruction of the Temples, during which time the story of Purim occurred.

CHAPTER 37

The Megilla Reading

READING THE MEGILLA WITH A *MINYAN*

The Gemara discusses whether the Megilla may be read privately, without a *minyan*.

> Rav said: The Megilla, when read in its proper time, may be read even by an individual; when read at a different time [on 11–13 Adar[1]], it must be read in the presence of ten. R. Assi said: Regardless of whether it is read in its proper time or not, it must be read in the presence of ten. (Megilla 5a)

Some *Rishonim* rule in accordance with R. Assi and maintain that one who reads the Megilla alone should not even recite the *berakhot* before the Megilla.[2] Most *Rishonim*, however, adopt Rav's lenient view, and this is the position codified in the *Shulḥan Arukh*.[3]

Another question arises concerning the scope of the debate between Rav and R. Assi. Do Rav and R. Assi both agree that *bediavad* (after the fact) one who reads the Megilla alone has fulfilled his obligation, disagreeing only as to whether there is a preference to read the Megilla in a quorum? Or do they disagree on the level of *bediavad*, such that according to R. Assi, one who reads without a quorum has not fulfilled his obligation at all? *Beit Yosef*[4] cites Rashi[5] and Rosh,[6] who explain that R. Assi stated his opinion only on the level of *lekhatḥila* (the preferred standard). Accordingly, in Rav's opinion, there is not even any preference to read the Megilla with a quorum. This is also the view of Baal HaMaor.[7] *Behag*, however, disagrees, explaining that R. Assi, in fact, disqualifies a Megilla reading conducted privately, while Rav maintains that one should preferably read with a quorum. Some attribute this understanding to Rif[8] and Rambam[9] as well.

Apparently, R. Assi held that one must actively create a proper environment of *pirsumei nissa* (publicizing the miracle) by reading the Megilla with a quorum, at least *lekhatḥila* (Rashi, Rosh, Baal HaMaor), and perhaps even *bediavad* (*Behag*, and possibly Rif and Rambam). Rav, however, maintained that reading on the proper day, when everyone else reads, provides sufficient *pirsumei nissa* to justify reading alone, perhaps even *lekhatḥila*.

Interestingly, *Orḥot Ḥayim*[10] cites Raavad as ruling that while one should preferably read the Megilla in the presence of ten, he may read it alone if others have already heard the reading. Raavad explains that one may read privately in this case because "there was already a publicizing in the city through the public reading." In other words, while the day of Purim itself does not generate enough *pirsumei nissa* to justify reading the Megilla privately (*lekhatḥila*), once the Megilla has been publicly read in the city, the desired *pirsumei nissa* has been achieved and one may then read alone.

To what extent, and at what cost, should one maximize the *pirsumei nissa* aspect of one's Megilla reading? The *Arukh HaShulḥan* writes that it is customary to make an effort to hear the Megilla read with a quorum, and "the larger the congregation, the greater the *hiddur* [enhancement of the mitzva], as 'the glory of the King is in the multitude of the people' ('*berov am hadrat Melekh*')." He notes, however, that if one cannot hear the Megilla properly in the synagogue because of the noise, then it may be preferable to gather ten people and read the Megilla at home.[11] We will return to this point when we discuss the custom to make noise upon hearing Haman's name.

THE TIMES FOR MEGILLA READING

The Gemara teaches that one must read the Megilla both at night and during the day:

> R. Yehoshua b. Levi said: A person is obligated to read the Megilla at night and to read it again (*veleshanota*) during the day, as the verse states [Ps. 22:3], "My Lord, I cry by day, but You do not answer, and by night, but have no respite." It was similarly stated by R. Ḥelbo in the name of Ulla of Bira: A person is obligated to read the Megilla at night and to read it again during the day, as the verse states [Ps. 30:13], "In order that my soul may sing praises to You and not be silent; Hashem, my Lord, I will forever be grateful to You." (Megilla 4a)

One might question the nature of these two readings and their relationship to one another. Are these two readings identical in nature, with the Gemara simply teaching that one should perform the same mitzva twice? Indeed, in presenting this halakha, the Gemara employs the term "*veleshanota*," which literally means "to repeat," perhaps indicating that these two readings are identical. Alternatively, are they two distinct obligations, each with its own source and nature?

A clue to the answer may be found in a debate among the *Rishonim* regarding whether the *berakha* of *Sheheḥeyanu* should be repeated before the daytime reading. Rabbeinu Tam[12] and Ri[13] rule that *Sheheḥeyanu* should be repeated during the day, while Rambam[14] and Rashbam[15] disagree and rule that one should recite *Sheheḥeyanu* only before the nighttime reading. It seems that Rambam and Rashbam maintain that although one reads the Megilla twice, the second reading simply repeats the first mitzva, and therefore does not warrant an additional recitation of *Sheheḥeyanu*. Rabbeinu Tam and Ri, on the other hand, apparently maintain that the second reading deserves its own *berakha* because it is something more than a "repeat performance" of the first reading.

According to this view of Rabbeinu Tam and Ri, why and how does the daytime reading differ from the nighttime reading? Some suggest that the daytime reading contains an additional dimension that is lacking in the nighttime reading. Tosafot, for example, write:

> Even though one has recited *zeman* [the *berakha* of *Sheheḥeyanu*] at night, he repeats the *berakha* during the day because the primary expression of *pirsumei nissa* (publicizing of the miracle) occurs at the daytime reading. The verse [cited as indication of the double reading] implies this as well, as it says, "by night, but have no respite" – in other words, even though one reads during the day, he must still read at night. The primary reading is during the day, as the main festive meal is during the day.[16]

According to Tosafot, the additional focus upon *pirsumei nissa* adds a special dimension to the daytime reading, which is, in fact, the primary reading. Rosh adds that "the primary *pirsumei nissa* occurs during the day, during the time of the festive meal, as well as the *matanot la'evyonim* and *mishlo'aḥ manot*." Since the other mitzvot of Purim all occur by day, the *pirsumei nissa* is most effectively expressed during the day of Purim and is characteristic specifically of the daytime reading of the Megilla.

Others note that the nighttime and daytime readings of the Megilla may originate from different sources. R. Yechezkel Landau, for example, suggests in his *Noda BiYehuda* that while the morning reading was established by the prophets, and is therefore categorized as "*divrei kabbala*," the nighttime reading was enacted later by the sages.[17]

Some authorities further distinguish between the daytime and nighttime readings based on their content or level of obligation. For example, R. Tzvi Pesach Frank suggests that even according to the opinions that maintain that a woman's level of obligation in Megilla is lower than that of a man,[18] there may be a difference between the nighttime and daytime readings. On Purim night, Megilla reading constitutes only a rabbinic obligation for men as well, and a woman should therefore be able to read the Megilla for men at night.[19]

R. Ḥanokh Henikh Agus posits in his *Marḥeshet* that one fulfills two mitzvot through the Megilla reading – *pirsumei nissa* and Hallel. The Hallel component of Megilla most likely applies only by day, when Hallel is generally read. This distinction also has implications for the level of women's obligation in the respective readings, as women are not obligated to recite Hallel.[20]

Another possible indication of the different levels of obligation between the nighttime and daytime readings appears in Ran.[21] The Gemara relates that the residents of the small villages would come to the cities on Mondays and Thursdays, the market days, and were allowed to hear the Megilla reading there even a few days before Purim (Megilla 2a). According to Ran, the villagers would only hear the morning reading, but not the evening reading. We might suggest that the primacy given to the morning reading was due to either the heightened *pirsumei nissa*, as described by Tosafot and Rosh, or the nighttime reading's fundamentally lower level of obligation, as discussed by the *Marḥeshet* and *Turei Even*.

The *Shulḥan Arukh* rules in accordance with Rambam, that one should not recite *Sheheḥeyanu* before the daytime reading,[22] and this is the practice of Sephardim. Ashkenazim, however, follow the ruling of Rema,[23] who rules in accordance with Rabbeinu Tam and Ri, that one should repeat the *berakha* during the day.

Magen Avraham cites *Shela* as recommending that an announcement be made before the reader recites the *berakhot* that everyone should have the Purim meal and *mishlo'aḥ manot* in mind when reciting or hearing *Sheheḥeyanu*.[24] Sephardim, who recite *Sheheḥeyanu* only before the evening reading, should have this in mind at night, while Ashkenazim, who repeat this *berakha* before the morning reading, should have this in mind during the recitation of *Sheheḥeyanu* before the morning reading.

Regarding the proper time for the evening reading, it is certainly preferable to wait until nightfall (*tzeit hakokhavim*) to read the Megilla. However, Raavad records the custom in Narbonne to read the Megilla before dark, on the thirteenth of Adar, out of consideration for those who experienced difficulty fasting until nightfall.[25] Several other *Rishonim* cite this Raavad.[26] *Terumat HaDeshen* rules that one who cannot complete the fast may even read the Megilla as early as *pelag haMinḥa* (one and a quarter halakhic hours before nightfall), based upon Rabbeinu Tam's view that even the nighttime *Shema* may be recited as early as *pelag haMinḥa*.[27] Based on these *Rishonim*, the *Shulḥan Arukh* rules that one who is unable to hear the Megilla at night may read it with its *berakhot* already beginning at *pelag haMinḥa*.[28] *Peri Ḥadash* disagrees and insists that one who reads the Megilla before *tzeit hakokhavim* should repeat it after nightfall – with the *berakhot*![29]

This question is far from academic and at times was actually quite relevant. R. Ovadia Yosef, in a responsum written in Adar of 1947, records that during the period of the British Mandate, before the establishment of the State of Israel, the Mandatory authorities imposed a dusk-to-dawn curfew, violators of which were liable to execution. R. Yosef was asked whether people who were unable to hear the Megilla after *tzeit hakokhavim* due to the curfew could read it during the previous day. He concludes that the extenuating circumstances warranted acting leniently, and thus communities should hold public readings on the thirteenth of Adar, before dark, and read the Megilla with its *berakhot*.[30]

One may not eat on Purim night or on Purim morning before fulfilling the mitzva of Megilla reading.[31] This halakha may pose some difficulty on Purim night, which follows the fast of *Taanit Esther*. Moreover, many women are unable to hear the Megilla reading immediately at nightfall and fulfill the mitzva after their husbands return from synagogue, and they may have difficulty fasting until after hearing the Megilla.

Magen Avraham writes that fundamentally, the halakha forbids only eating a substantial quantity (a "*kebeitza*") of bread or cake before Megilla reading. When necessary, therefore, one may be lenient and partake of drinks, foods other than bread and cake, or less than a *kebeitza* of cake before hearing the Megilla.[32] The *Aḥaronim* write that one who has great difficulty fasting should certainly eat and drink in small quantities before Megilla reading, rather than read the Megilla before nightfall. If a small amount does not suffice, one should eat a meal and ask a friend to remind him to attend the Megilla reading.[33]

Regarding the daytime reading of the Megilla, one should preferably read the Megilla only after sunrise (*hanetz haḥama*), but one who reads after dawn (*alot hashaḥar*) has fulfilled his obligation.

THE BLESSINGS RECITED BEFORE AND AFTER MEGILLA READING

The authorities note that the Megilla scroll should preferably not be read in the same manner as the Torah, which one rolls as he goes along. R. Hai Gaon, as cited by numerous *Rishonim*, records the custom to fold the Megilla like a letter, reminding us of the Purim story, which featured the sending of letters throughout the Persian Empire. Some explain this to mean that one should first open the entire Megilla in front of him like a letter and then read it.[34] Others, however, record the custom to unfold the Megilla as one reads it, and then to refold it before reciting the *berakha* after the reading;[35] this is the practice codified in the *Shulḥan Arukh*.[36] The *Mishna Berura* concludes that before reciting the *berakhot*, one should unroll the entire Megilla, and then fold it over, page over page, ensuring that it does not hang over the *bima* and touch the floor.[37] He also cites those who maintain that only the reader, and not the listeners, should fold the Megilla like a letter, although he notes in his *Shaar HaTziyun* that *Peri Megadim* observed the custom that even the listeners fold the Megilla.[38]

The Megilla reading is preceded by three *berakhot*: the *birkat hamitzva* ("*al mikra Megilla*"), the *birkat hanissim* ("*she'asa nissim*"), and the *birkat hazeman* ("*Sheheḥeyanu*"). The Gemara relates that the recitation of the final *berakha* of "*Harav et riveinu*" after the reading of the Megilla is dependent upon communal custom (Megilla 21a). What is the nature of this *berakha*? Some assert that *Harav et riveinu* was instituted not for the Megilla reading, but rather as a *birkat hashevaḥ* – a *berakha* of praise – for the Purim miracle. Ran explains that for this reason, the *berakha* begins with "*barukh*," despite the fact that it is a "*berakha hasemukha laḥaverta*" – a *berakha* adjacent to the blessings that precede the Megilla reading – which generally do not open with "*barukh*."[39] Because the *berakha* of *Harav et riveinu* stands on its own and was not instituted to be recited specifically after the Megilla reading, it therefore requires its own introductory "*barukh*."

Ritva cites this view, but subsequently rejects it (Megilla 21b). *Abudraham* similarly dismisses Ran's theory and advances another:

> The reason why they established a *berakha* after all mitzvot fulfilled through reading –readings required by Torah law, such as the *Shema* reading, as well as readings ordained by the sages, such as reading the Megilla, Hallel, the *haftara*, and *Pesukei DeZimra* – more than other mitzvot, is because we learned that the public reading of the Torah must be followed by a *berakha* through a "*kal vaḥomer*" (a fortiori deduction) from *Birkat HaMazon*, and they therefore established that *all* mitzvot fulfilled through reading should be followed by a *berakha*, like the public Torah reading.[40]

According to *Abudraham*, *Harav et riveinu* indeed relates to the Megilla reading; the sages specifically instituted that this *berakha* be recited at the conclusion of the reading to parallel the Torah reading. The *Arukh HaShulḥan* explains that this *berakha* is not related to the reading of the Megilla per se, but rather is a *berakha* of *pirsumei nissa*, and should therefore be recited publicly.[41]

We have thus identified two approaches to the *berakha* of *Harav et riveinu*: Some view it as an independent *berakha* commemorating the miraculous events of Purim, while others explain that it was instituted to conclude the reading of the Megilla, just as we conclude Hallel, *haftarot*, and *Pesukei DeZimra* with a *berakha*. These two approaches yield some interesting practical ramifications.

The *Shulḥan Arukh* writes that upon completing the Megilla reading, one should roll the Megilla and then recite the *berakha* of *Harav et riveinu*.[42] Maharil explains that it is disrespectful to leave the Megilla open unnecessarily, and he even criticizes a reader who began reciting the *berakha* before rolling the Megilla.[43] *Magen Avraham* offers a different reason for this order, distinguishing between this *berakha* and the *berakhot* recited after the *haftara* reading,[44] which one should recite specifically while the *haftara* scroll is still open.[45] He explains that since the *berakha* of *Harav et riveinu* was not instituted upon the reading of the Megilla, one may, or even should, roll up the Megilla before reciting it. He concludes that one may, if he wishes, recite the *berakha* first, and then afterward roll the Megilla.[46]

Eishel Avraham (Buczacz) writes that only the reader should roll the Megilla before reciting *Harav et riveinu*; the listeners may recite the *berakha* and then roll their scrolls. (Of course, this assumes that even the listeners recited *Harav et riveinu* individually, as opposed to the common practice that only the reader recites this *berakha*.) *Eishel Avraham* comments that it may be preferable for the listeners to recite the *berakha* before rolling their scrolls so that the *berakha* immediately follows the reading. Seemingly, these *Aḥaronim* disagree regarding whether the *berakha* relates to the Megilla reading or if it functions as an independent *berakha* praising God for the miracles of Purim (*Magen Avraham*).

Similarly, the authorities debate whether one may speak between the reading of the Megilla and the recitation of *Harav et riveinu*. *Tur* cites Baal HaIttur's comment that "since the final *berakha* is dependent upon local custom, one should not criticize one who talks between the reading [and the *berakha*]." *Beit Yosef* and *Baḥ* explain that according to Baal HaIttur, since the *berakha* was instituted over the miracle of Purim, and not the reading of the Megilla, interruptions are allowed in between the reading and the *berakha*.

Tur, however, disagrees, arguing that if one recites *Harav et riveinu*, he should not interrupt between the reading and the *berakha*. *Baḥ* explains that *Tur* viewed *Harav et riveinu* as a *berakha* that concludes the reading of the Megilla, similar to the *berakha* of *Yishtabaḥ*, which concludes *Pesukei DeZimra*. Therefore, one should not interrupt between the Megilla reading and the *berakha*.[47]

May one recite the *berakha* of *Harav et riveinu* without a quorum? *Beit Yosef*[48] cites *Orḥot Ḥayim*,[49] who asserts that according to the

Talmud Yerushalmi (Y. Megilla 4:1), one should recite this *berakha* only "*betzibbur*" – in the presence of a quorum. Rema cites this view as well.[50]

Eliya Rabba cites numerous authorities who disagree with the *Orḥot Ḥayim*'s position, and he rules that even an individual may recite *Harav et riveinu*.[51] *Biur Halakha*, however, concludes that since reciting the *berakha* is in any event only a custom, and generally we follow the rule of *safek berakhot lehakel* (we refrain from reciting *berakhot* in situations of doubt), an individual should not recite this *berakha*.

We might suggest that if the *berakha* merely concludes the reading of the Megilla, then just as the Megilla may be read without a quorum (when it is read in the proper time), *Harav et riveinu* may, similarly, be recited privately. On the other hand, if the *berakha* was instituted in order to publicize the miracle, then we should likely limit its recitation to public forums, where the miracle is properly publicized. The *Arukh HaShulḥan*, indeed, explains Rema in this manner.[52]

It is possible to dispute this reasoning, however. Perhaps the *berakha* was instituted specifically as the conclusion of a public Megilla reading, which may differ qualitatively from a private reading. Conversely, even if the *berakha* was instituted to publicize the miracle and to offer thanksgiving, one may still be able to recite it privately.

The *Arukh HaShulḥan* permits reciting the *berakha* even privately.[53] For one thing, he writes, he was unable to locate the passage in the Yerushalmi that was cited as the source for this halakha (possibly because the Yerushalmi may not have referred to *Harav et riveinu* at all, as noted by the Vilna Gaon). Additionally, the requirement of a quorum for the *berakha* of *Harav et riveinu* does not appear in the writings of any other *Rishonim*. Finally, the custom was to recite the *berakha* even without a quorum.

As we will discuss more extensively below, it is questionable whether the "quorum" preferable or even required in certain circumstances refers to a "*minyan*," which generally consists of ten males, or even of ten women, who may join together to make a "community." This question would impact upon the issue of whether *Harav et riveinu* should be recited at a reading for women (regardless of whether the

Megilla is read by a man or a woman). The *Shulḥan Arukh* records that nowadays, it is customary for all communities to recite this *berakha.*[54]

THE READING OF THE MEGILLA: LAW AND CUSTOM

Let us briefly review a number of the practical halakhot relevant to the reading of the Megilla. In general, one who fulfills a mitzva through the reading of a text, such as *Keriat Shema,* should preferably hear his recitation; although, *bediavad* (after the fact), one nevertheless fulfills his obligation if he did not hear what he recited. With regard to the Megilla reading, however, *Beit Yosef* cites Rif, Rambam, and Rosh as maintaining that one who did not hear his reading has not fulfilled his obligation even *bediavad.* Although *Beit Yosef* is inclined to reject this view, he suggests that these *Rishonim* require the reader to hear his reading in order to achieve maximum *pirsumei nissa,* a factor that does not play a role in the mitzva of *Shema.*[55] In any event, one who reads the Megilla should preferably do so audibly such that he can hear his reading.

The Mishna teaches that one who reads the verses of the Megilla out of order has not fulfilled his obligation (Megilla 17a), and this halakha is codified in the *Shulḥan Arukh.*[56] Therefore, one who arrives late to a Megilla reading should not simply listen until the end and then read the part that he missed. Rather, he should recite the *berakhot* and then read from a printed Tanakh until he catches up to the reader, at which point he should listen to the reader. Assuming he catches up before the reader has read more than half the Megilla, he fulfills his obligation despite having read part of the Megilla from a printed text.

Tur,[57] citing the Talmud Yerushalmi (Y. Megilla 2:2), teaches that we do not correct the reader for certain mistakes. Ran explains that if the mistake changes the meaning of the word, such as if one reads "*yosheiv*" ("sitting," Esther 2:21) as "*yashav*" ("sat"), or "*nofel*" ("falling," Esther 7:8) as "*nafal*" ("fell"), he must reread the word in its proper order.[58]

Rashba[59] and Ran[60] write that one must hear every word of the Megilla. Riaz disagrees, insisting that only if one misses a word that alters the text's meaning does he fail to fulfill the mitzva.[61] The *Aḥaronim* rule in accordance with Rashba;[62] therefore, as mentioned above, one who misses a verse should read it from a printed Tanakh and then catch up to the reader. Preferably, one should not speak at all throughout the entire Megilla reading. One who interrupted should read the verses that he missed from a Tanakh, as described above.

The Gemara teaches that one should read the names of Haman's sons (Est. 9:7–10) in a single breath in order to demonstrate that they were all killed together (Megilla 16b).[63] It is customary to begin the breath from the words "*ḥamesh meot ish*" and to conclude with the word "*aseret*." Tosafot note that one who did not read these verses in a single breath has nevertheless fulfilled his obligation.

It is customary for the congregation to read the "four verses of redemption" (Est. 2:4, 8:15, 8:16, 10:3) aloud, and then for the reader to repeat them.[64] It is also customary for the reader, when reciting the verse "*balayla hahu*" (Est. 6:1), which relates how the "king" could not sleep, to raise his voice, hinting to the dual meaning of the word "*hamelekh*" ("the king"). Some also gently raise or shake the Megilla when reading the words "*ha'igerret hazot*" (9:26).

There are some phrases that the reader repeats with slight changes in consideration of divergent texts (Est. 8:11, 9:2). Some repeat the entire verse instead of just the phrase in question.

One of the customs most prominently associated with the reading of the Megilla is the custom to make noise upon hearing Haman's name, which appears fifty-four times in Megillat Esther. This practice appears as early as the twelfth century. R. Avraham b. Natan HaYarḥi writes in his *Sefer HaManhig*[65] that

> The custom of the children in France and Provence is to take two stones, to write upon them the name of Haman, and to hit them against each other when the reader mentions Haman and his evil [deeds], and [say], "Let the names of the wicked rot." (Prov. 10:7)

This practice met with considerable opposition. Some expressed concern that the noise would prevent the congregants from fulfilling their obligation to hear every word of the Megilla. Others objected to the apparent violation of synagogue decorum. Many note that Maharil reportedly did not make noise during the reading of Haman's name.[66] In 1783, a riot nearly erupted in London when the community leaders of the Beit Knesset HaSepharadi HaMerkazi summoned the police to forcefully expel members who made noise during the reading of Haman![67] Rema records this custom, and concludes, "One should not mock this custom, as it was not established without reason."[68]

Some have accepted additional "stringencies" upon themselves, and attempt to drown out other phrases in the Megilla besides Haman. There are those who jokingly jeer upon hearing the word "*mas*" ("taxes"; Est. 10:1), and there are reports of certain anti-Zionist sects who make noise when the reader reads the word "*medina*" ("state")! Each community must find a proper balance between the desire to retain this ancient custom and the concern that the congregation properly fulfills the mitzva of Megilla reading.

CHAPTER 38

The Obligation of Women in *Mikra Megilla*

THE TALMUD EXPLICITLY establishes that women are included in the obligation of *mikra Megilla*, despite the general rule exempting women from time-bound commandments (*mitzvot aseh shehazeman geraman*): "R. Yehoshua b. Levi said: Women are obligated in the reading of the Megilla, as they, too, were included in the miracle (*af hein hayu beoto ha'nes*)" (Megilla 4a). Similarly, the Talmud Yerushalmi states:

> Bar Kappara said: One must read the Megilla before women and minors, for they, too, were involved in the doubt [i.e., danger] ("*she'af otam hivu basafek*"). R. Yehoshua b. Levi acted accordingly; he gathered his sons and the members of his household and read [the Megilla] in their presence. (Y. Megilla 2:5)

The *Rishonim* elaborate on this halakha and discuss the issue of whether a woman may read the Megilla for a man in order to fulfill his obligation.

The Talmud states, "All are qualified to read the Megilla… [this comes] to include women" (Arakhin 3a). Accordingly, most *Rishonim* maintain that men and women share an equal obligation in *mikra Megilla.*[1] In their view, a woman may certainly read the Megilla for a man. Some, however, insist that a woman may not read the Megilla for a man based upon a comment in the Tosefta:

> All are obligated to read the Megilla: Priests, Levites and Israelites… [but] women are exempt and do not enable the many [i.e., men] to fulfill their obligation.[2]

Baal Halakhot Gedolot (*Behag*), for example, writes that although women are obligated because of "*af hein hayu beoto ha'nes*," they still may not fulfill the obligation on behalf of a man.[3]

The *Rishonim* and *Aḥaronim* question why a woman cannot fulfill a man's obligation according to this view, given that she is also obligated in the mitzva. According to one approach,[4] although men and women indeed share an equal level of obligation, a woman should not read for men due to external considerations, such as *kevod hatzibbur* (the honor of the congregation)[5] or *zila behu milta* (impropriety). Tosafot, for example, write:

> Because we are dealing with a community, it would be a breach of propriety (*zila behu milta*) were a woman to assist the masses in fulfilling their obligation. Thus, women are obligated in Megilla reading, but Baal Halakhot Gedolot rules that women cannot assist the masses in fulfilling their Megilla obligation.[6]

Kol Bo cites *Sefer HaIttur* as prohibiting a woman from reading for a man for a different reason:

> The author of *Aseret HaDibberot* wrote that when reading [the Megilla], women do not enable men to fulfill their obligation; the reason is *kol be'isha erva* [their voice is considered like "nakedness"].[7]

According to this view, a woman should not read the Megilla for men because this would violate the law that forbids men from listening to a woman singing.

It is important to note, however, that although the *Shulḥan Arukh* rules (based on the Rosh and Rambam) that men should refrain from listening to a woman's singing voice,[8] especially during the recitation of *Keriat Shema,*[9] most *posekim* maintain that a woman reading the Megilla would not violate this halakha. They note that the Mishna implies that a woman would even be permitted to publicly read the Torah, were it not for the consideration of *kevod hatzibbur* (Megilla 23b).

Other *Rishonim* explain that the reason a woman cannot read the Megilla for a man is not due to external factors, but rather because women's obligation in *mikra Megilla* differs fundamentally from that of men. Rosh, for example, writes,

> And Baal HaHalakhot ruled that women are only obligated to *hear* the Megilla; however, her reading [of the Megilla] cannot assist the men in fulfilling their obligation. For the men are obligated to *read* [and do not fulfill their obligation] until they hear the Megilla read by men, who are obligated in *reading* like them. Hearing [the reading] from women is not equivalent to the men's reading for themselves [but rather a lower level of obligation].... And according to the *Halakhot Gedolot* and Tosefta, the statement in Arakhin, "All are qualified to read the Megilla...to include women," must be explained [as follows]: not that women are qualified to read for men, but [rather that they are qualified to read] only for women. [The significance of this statement is] that one should not suggest that women cannot fulfill their obligation until they hear an important [high-level-obligation] reading of men. [Rather, the Gemara] teaches us that a woman can, indeed, assist her fellow [woman in fulfilling her obligation].[10]

According to *Behag,* a woman's obligation in Megilla reading is of a different nature than a man's, and for this reason, a woman's reading does not suffice to fulfill a man's obligation. The *Mordekhai,* in fact, claims that *Behag* had a different text of the Gemara, which read, "Women are obligated in hearing the Megilla (*mashma Megilla*)."[11]

The *Aḥaronim* offer additional possible reasons for why a man's obligation may differ from that of a woman. Some claim that a man's obligation is either fundamentally broader or stems from a higher level of obligation than the women's requirement. For example, R. Ḥanokh Henikh Agus explains in his *Marḥeshet*[12] that by reading the Megilla, one fulfills two separate mitzvot: *pirsumei nissa* (publicizing the miracle) and Hallel.[13] While men and women share the obligation of *pirsumei nissa* equally, women are exempt from Hallel. Therefore, he concludes, a woman cannot discharge a man's obligation in Megilla reading, as she is not obligated in all of its components.

Incidentally, *Marḥeshet* proposes a possible distinction in this regard between the nighttime reading and the daytime reading, as the Hallel component of the Megilla likely applies only by day.[14] Theoretically, therefore, according to *Behag*, a woman should be able to read for a man on Purim night, but not on Purim day.

Similarly, R. Aryeh Leib Gunzburg argues in his *Turei Even*[15] that while a man's obligation in Megilla originates from *divrei kabbala* (prophetic revelation), a woman's obligation is rabbinic in origin, as it is based upon the principle of *af hen hayu beoto ha'nes*, and is thus a lower level of obligation. For this reason, he explains, a woman cannot discharge the higher obligation of a man.

Interestingly, this theory may also result in a distinction between the nighttime and daytime readings, although the *Turei Even* does not mention it himself. Some *posekim* view the daytime reading as the primary mitzva of *mikra Megilla* and the nighttime reading as an additional reading ordained later by *Ḥazal*. It would thus stand to reason that men and women share the same level of obligation on Purim night, such that a woman would be able to read the Megilla for men at night.

R. Tzvi Pesach Frank proposes a similar theory regarding the situation when Shushan Purim falls on Shabbat, in which case Jerusalem residents read the Megilla on Friday, the fourteenth of Adar, by force of rabbinic enactment. Since this reading is required only *miderabbanan*, a woman might possibly be permitted to read for a man in such a case.[16]

WOMEN'S OBLIGATION: THE HALAKHA

The *Shulḥan Arukh* cites two views on this issue:

> All are obligated in the reading of the Megilla: men, women, and freed slaves. Children, too, are educated to read it. Both one who reads [the Megilla] and one who hears it read by another have fulfilled their obligation, provided that one hears it from someone who is obligated to read it.... And there are those who maintain that women cannot assist men in fulfilling their obligation.[17]

As we might expect, the *Shulḥan Arukh*'s ambiguity has generated much debate. Some Sephardic authorities claim that the halakha follows the second, stringent opinion recorded in the *Shulḥan Arukh*.[18] R. Ovadia Yosef, however, claims that whenever the *Shulḥan Arukh* cites a view without attribution followed by another opinion attributed to "those who maintain" ("*stam ve'aḥar kakh yesh omrim*"), the halakha follows the first view cited. Nevertheless, R. Yosef adds, it is preferable to satisfy all views and not allow a woman to read for men except in extenuating circumstances.[19]

Rema, who to a large extent represents Ashkenazic tradition and practice, appears to rule in accordance with the stringent view of *Behag*: "And there are those who maintain that if a woman reads for herself, she should recite the blessing, '*lishmo'a* (to hear) *Megilla*,' for she is not obligated to read it."[20] Accordingly, it would seem that Ashkenazim should follow this stringent position.[21]

WOMEN'S MEGILLA READINGS

Until this point, we have discussed the debate regarding whether a woman may discharge the obligation of a man. The Gemara quite clearly implies that it would be perfectly acceptable for a woman to read the Megilla for other women (Arakhin 3a). Indeed, the Tosefta cited above only restricts a woman from reading for a man, but not for other women.[22]

R. Netanel Weil, however, in his comments to Rosh, the *Korban Netanel*, asserts that *Behag* even restricts women from fulfilling the obligation of other women. He bases this position on the comments of Tosafot,[23] who mention the consideration of "*zila behu milta*." *Korban Netanel* writes:

> That which the Tosafot wrote in Sukka 38a, "Or else [women cannot recite *Birkat haMazon* for men] because it is dishonorable for the many, for it is [like] Megilla, in which women are obligated [but] the *Halakhot Gedolot* explained that women do not enable the many to fulfill their obligation in Megilla" – that is to say, a woman may not enable many women to fulfill their obligation because it is dishonorable for them [to have the Megilla read to them by a woman]. But as far as reading for men, even without this reason they cannot do so, not even one woman for one man, because they are not obligated [to read].[24]

The *Korban Netanel* asserts that two factors limit a woman's ability to fulfill another's obligation. First, she may not discharge a man's obligation because her obligation is fundamentally different from his; second, Tosafot maintain that due to reasons of impropriety, women may not even fulfill the obligation of other women in a public setting.

R. Yehuda Henkin notes that the Tosafot Rosh, who often restates and clarifies the words of the Tosafot, clearly indicates that Tosafot referred to a case of women reading for men, and not for other women, as violating the boundries of propriety.[25] R. Henkin therefore contends that although later halakhic works such as the *Mishna Berura*[26] cite the *Korban Netanel*'s ruling, his interpretation should be disregarded.[27] In any case, the *Korban Netanel*'s position is certainly a minority view, for which there is little support in other sources. Another basis for objecting to women's reading for other women may be found in the *Magen Avraham*,[28] who cites a comment in the *Midrash HaNe'elam* (a section of the Zohar) forbidding a woman from reading for other women, and even for herself.

Although the conventional interpretation of *Behag*'s ruling would allow women to read the Megilla for other women, some note that since it is preferable to hear the Megilla reading in the presence of a *minyan*, women should preferably attend the synagogue reading rather than conduct a separate women's Megilla reading.[29] However, many women are compelled in any case to miss the synagogue reading due to family responsibilities, and therefore attend later readings held without a *minyan*. Furthermore, some women simply find it difficult to hear from the women's section, as the *Mishna Berura* observes.[30] Therefore, while there may be certain halakhic advantages to hearing the Megilla read by a man, in some communities women hear the Megilla read by other women. These readings have, in certain contexts, gained the approval of such figures as R. Aharon Lichtenstein and R. Yehuda Herzl Henkin.[31] In fact, R. Ovadia Yosef goes so far as to encourage this practice: "The custom of women who make a *minyan* by themselves for Megilla reading... should be encouraged."[32]

Which *berakha* should a woman recite before she reads the Megilla? This issue hinges on the question of whether or not men and women share the same obligation in Megilla reading. Those who equate women's obligation with that of men, either practically or fundamentally, would certainly require women to recite the standard *berakha* of "*al mikra Megilla*." Those who follow *Behag*, by contrast, and distinguish between the obligations of men and women regarding Megilla reading, would require a different blessing.

As noted above, the *Mordekhai*,[33] citing Raavya,[34] understood *Behag* to mean that a woman's obligation requires "hearing," rather than "reading," the Megilla, and they should therefore recite the *berakha* of "*al mashma Megilla*." Along these lines, Rema writes, "There are those who say that if a woman reads for herself, she recites the blessing '*lishmo'a Megilla*' ('to hear the Megilla'), since she is not obligated to read it."[35]

Many *Aḥaronim*, however, dispute Rema's ruling, arguing that the original *berakha* of "*al mikra Megilla*" was intended for both men and women. This is the view of *Peri Ḥadash*[36] and the Vilna Gaon.[37] Others also note that most *Rishonim* view a woman's obligation as similar to a man's, and therefore mandate that they recite the same *berakha*.[38]

This question applies as well to a man who has already heard the Megilla and now reads for women who have yet to fulfill their mitzva. The *Aḥaronim* further discuss whether it is preferable for the listeners in this case to recite their own *berakha* or for the reader to recite the *berakha.* Many rule that the listeners should recite the blessing, although they acknowledge that common practice indicates otherwise.[39]

COUNTING WOMEN TOWARD A QUORUM FOR MEGILLA READING

A final issue relevant to this discussion is whether women may be counted toward a "quorum" for the reading of the Megilla. The concept of a required quorum for Megilla reading initially arises in the context of one who reads the Megilla before Purim (on 11, 12, or 13 Adar). The Gemara allows reading on these days under certain extenuating circumstances, but this reading must be done in the presence of a *minyan* (Megilla 2a). Apparently, one who reads on a day other than Purim must create his own environment of *pirsumei nissa* by reading the Megilla publicly. On Purim itself, however, one may, strictly speaking, read the Megilla privately. Nevertheless, the *Shulḥan Arukh* writes that one should endeavor even on Purim day to read the Megilla in the presence of a quorum of ten men. If this is not possible, the *Shulḥan Arukh* adds, then one may read the Megilla alone.[40] The *Aḥaronim* explain that a public Megilla reading amplifies the *pirsumei nissa* and fulfills the dictum of "*berov am hadrat Melekh*" (public performance of mitzvot brings honor to the Almighty).

The question then arises as to whether this requirement or preference for a "quorum" refers to a halakhic "*minyan*," which is defined as ten adult males, or even to ten women, or men and women. Rema, in discussing the preference to read with a quorum, writes, "One may question whether women combine to form [a quorum of] ten,"[41] thus leaving the issue as an open question. Many *Aḥaronim* claim that Rema's uncertainty relates only to the question of whether women can be counted together with men to form a *minyan* for Megilla reading. A group of ten women, however, certainly constitutes a "*minyan*" for this purpose.[42]

An interesting ramification of this question relates to the situation when the fifteenth of Adar falls on Shabbat. In such a case, Jerusalem residents read the Megilla on Friday (the fourteenth of Adar), insert

Al HaNissim in their prayers on Shabbat, and hold the festive Purim meal on Sunday. (This situation is called "*Purim Meshulash*," or "the triple Purim," as the Purim observance is spread over three days.) The *Aḥaronim* discuss the question of whether the Jerusalemites' reading on Friday should be considered a "*keria bizemana*," reading on Purim day itself, in which case they may read even without a quorum, or if this reading constitutes a reading "*shelo bizemana*," at a time other than Purim, such that a quorum is required. The *Mishna Berura*[43] and *Peri Ḥadash*[44] rule that in such a case, one must, indeed, hear the Megilla in the presence of a *minyan*, but others disagree.[45] According to the first view, we might require all women, even those who cannot attend the earlier reading due to family responsibilities, to hear the Megilla with a *minyan* on the Friday of a *Purim Meshulash*.

It appears that the common custom in Jerusalem is not to require a *minyan* for Megilla reading in Jerusalem on the Friday of a *Purim Meshulash*. Nevertheless, when R. Aharon Lichtenstein originally sanctioned the "women's Megilla reading" in Jerusalem's Midreshet Lindenbaum (a practice that has since been adopted by numerous seminaries and communities), he ruled that they should not hold such a reading on the Friday of a *Purim Meshulash* so that the women could read with a quorum. This ruling is based upon two stringencies: first, that the Jerusalemites' reading on Friday of a *Purim Meshulash* constitutes a *keria shelo bizemana*, and second, that women do not count toward a quorum for a *keria shelo bizemana*. As noted, however, it seems to be customary among Jerusalem residents to permit private readings for women, especially when more than ten women are present.

CHAPTER 39

The Unique Status of a Walled City; Traveling on Purim

One of the unique aspects of Purim relates to the different times and places in which it is celebrated. The Megilla describes how the Jewish people gathered in the cities throughout the Persian Empire and waged battle against their enemies on the thirteenth of Adar. Esther then requested that the Jews of Shushan be granted an additional day to fight, and they continued their battle on the fourteenth of Adar. The Megilla then relates:

> On the thirteenth day of the month Adar, and on the fourteenth day of the same, they rested, and made it a day of feasting and gladness. But the Jews that were in Shushan assembled together on the thirteenth day thereof, and on the fourteenth thereof; and on the fifteenth day of the same they rested and made it a day of feasting and gladness. Therefore do the Jews of the villages, that dwell in the *unwalled* towns, make the fourteenth day of the month Adar a day of gladness and feasting, and a good day, and of sending portions one to another. And Mordekhai wrote these things, and sent letters unto all the Jews that were in all the provinces of the king Aḥashveirosh, both near and far, to enjoin them that they should keep the fourteenth day of the month Adar, and the fifteenth day of the same, yearly, the days wherein the Jews had rest from their enemies, and the month which was turned unto them from sorrow to gladness, and from mourning into a good day; that they should make them days of feasting and gladness, and of sending portions one to another, and gifts to the poor. (Est. 9:17–22)

While throughout the Empire, the Jews designated the fourteenth of Adar as a day of celebration, in Shushan, they celebrated on the fifteenth of Adar, commemorating the day on which they rested. Accordingly, the Mishna teaches: "Walled cities from the days of Yehoshua ben Nun read on the fifteenth, and villages and large cities read on the fourteenth" (Megilla 2a). According to the Mishna, the Rabbis instituted that not only residents of Shushan, but residents of other walled cities as well should read on the fifteenth. The Talmud derives this from the verses, "Therefore do the Jews of the villages, that dwell in the unwalled towns, make the fourteenth day of the month Adar a day of gladness and feasting, and a good day, and of sending portions one to another." The Megilla emphasizes that the Jews in unwalled cities observe Purim on the fourteenth, suggesting that Jews of walled cities observe the holiday on the fifteenth (Megilla 2b).

R. Yehoshua b. Korḥa asserts that only cities that were surrounded by walls during the days of Aḥashveirosh read the Megilla on the fifteenth (Megilla 2b). The Mishna, however, rules that the observance on the fifteenth is restricted to cities that were walled already during the time of Yehoshua ben Nun, when Benei Yisrael first conquered the Land of Israel. The halakha follows the opinion of the Mishna.

Notwithstanding the historical basis for celebrating the victory over Haman on different days, some *Rishonim* note the seeming peculiarity in the institution of a holiday celebrated in different locations on different days. Furthermore, they question why the distinction is drawn between walled and unwalled cities and why a city's status is determined based upon its condition specifically at the time of Yehoshua ben Nun.

Ramban writes that the different celebrations during the year of the miracle itself do not suffice to explain why two different days were established. Even in Shushan, he notes, the holiday should theoretically be observed on the fourteenth of Adar, the day when the nation as a whole was spared the fate of Haman's decree.[1] In order to explain this unique halakhic phenomenon of two different days of celebration, Ramban resorts to historical and exegetical conjecture. He explains that in response to the miracle of Purim, the Jews who resided in villages and cities independently began to celebrate annually on the fourteenth of Adar, as they felt most vulnerable to the threat of Aḥashveirosh then. However, the residents of the walled cities did not celebrate in future years, as they had felt secure in their fortified cities during the events of Purim and therefore did not view their survival as a miraculous salvation. For this reason, the Megilla speaks only of the celebrations instituted in the unwalled cities (Est. 9:19), and makes no mention of celebration in the walled cites. Even in Shushan, Ramban contends, the Jews only celebrated during the first year, as the Megilla relates.

Later, Mordekhai and the sages, following the lead of the inhabitants of the villages and cities, instituted a holiday to commemorate the salvation of Purim.[2] Since these Jews had already grown accustomed to celebrating on the fourteenth, the Rabbis established their day of celebration on the fourteenth. In addition, they established that even the Jews in walled cities, who felt less vulnerable to Haman's threat, should celebrate Purim, as the Purim miracle, in reality, saved them as well. These communities, however, should celebrate on the fifteenth, the day upon which the inhabitants of Shushan initially rested and celebrated their victory.

Ramban continues to explain that at the time of the Purim story, the majority of the Jewish people had already returned to Israel from the Babylonian exile, and therefore most of the Jews affected by this miracle lived in Israel. However, the Land of Israel was still in ruins as a result of the Babylonian conquest and ensuing exile, and the cities and their walls had yet to be rebuilt. Had the sages made the celebration in walled cities dependent upon the presence of a wall during Aḥashveirosh's time, this would have highlighted the state of ruin that prevailed in the Land of Israel at that time. Ramban cites in this context the comment in the Talmud Yerushalmi, "They afforded honor to Eretz Yisrael, which was desolate at that time, and they [made the date for the reading of the Megilla] dependent upon the days of Yehoshua ben Nun" (Y. Megilla 1:1). In other words, Ramban explains, the Rabbis made the distinction between the celebrations on the fourteenth and fifteenth dependent upon the state of the cities in the days of Yehoshua ben Nun in order to give honor to the Land of Israel.

Ran challenges Ramban's theory.[3] First, he claims that the majority of the Jewish people still lived in Persia, not the Land of Israel, during the time of the Purim events. Furthermore, he disagrees with Ramban's assumption that those in walled cities were more secure and hence less "traumatized" by the threat of Haman. Jews and gentiles lived together in the walled cities, Ran notes, and the Jewish population there, therefore, faced no less danger than those in other cities. To the contrary, the primary miracle occurred in Shushan, and it is for that reason that other walled cities commemorate Purim on the fifteenth – to emphasize the miracle that took place in Shushan.

Ran therefore attributes the two days of celebration to the original events, during which the residents of the villages and cities celebrated on the fourteenth and the residents of Shushan celebrated on the fifteenth. He agrees with Ramban and the Talmud Yerushalmi that the provision determining a city's status based on whether it was walled at the time of Yehoshua ben Nun was enacted to avoid "embarrassing" the Land of Israel, which lay in ruins during the time of Aḥashveirosh. In the pages that follow, we will attempt to define more precisely a "walled city" for the purpose of this halakha and discuss the situation of those who travel from a walled city to an unwalled city and vice versa.

DEFINITION OF A WALLED AND UNWALLED CITY

The *Rishonim* disagree regarding the definition of the term "*kerakh*" ("walled city") in this context. Later scholars, and, in particular the *posekim* of the last century, struggled to determine whether there are "walled cities" in Israel besides Jerusalem (such as Akko, Bet El, Tiberias, Lod, Shilo, and Tzefat), or even outside of Israel (such as Damascus, Istanbul, and Prague), which must read on the fifteenth of Adar. Indeed, there are some cities in Israel in which some individuals read on both the fourteenth and fifteenth of Adar to satisfy all opinions. This issue lies beyond the scope of our discussion; for our purposes, we will assume that Jerusalem is the only city that definitely observes Purim on the fifteenth of Adar.

The Talmud establishes that not only do residents of a walled city observe Purim on the fifteenth, but residents of some "satellite" villages and towns also observe the holiday on this date:

> A walled city – and that which is near it (*samukh lo*) or seen with it (*nireh imo*) is akin to the walled city.... Near, even though it is not seen, or seen, even though it is not near. It makes sense that a city can be seen even though it is not near – for example, if it sits atop a hill. However, how is it possible

> to be "near, yet not seen"? R. Yirmiya said: If it is situated in the valley. (Megilla 3b)

According to the Gemara, a village that can be seen from or that is close to a walled city reads on the fifteenth of Adar, even though it was, itself, never surrounded by a wall. The *Rishonim* debate at length the relationship between "*samukh lo*" and "*nireh imo*." We will relate to one fundamental question that may impact upon the status of the outer neighborhoods of Jerusalem: Do satellite neighborhoods of a walled city observe Purim on the fifteenth of Adar simply because of their proximity to the walled city, because they appear to be part of the walled city,[4] because they are in the city boundary,[5] or because they actively share in the municipal responsibilities,[6] and are viewed as attached to the city?[7]

This question arose in the years between 1948 and 1967, when the Old City of Jerusalem was under Jordanian rule and there was no Jewish presence in that part of the city. R. Yitzchak Herzog, who served as Chief Rabbi of Israel from 1937 until his death, recorded the discussions held by the Rabbinical Council (Mo'etzet HaRabbanut) of the Israeli Rabbinate in 1949, immediately preceding the first Purim after the Old City of Jerusalem fell into Jordanian control.[8] R. Tzvi Pesach Frank addressed this issue as well in his *Har Tzvi*.[9] Their discussions focused upon a difficult passage in the Talmud Yerushalmi (Y. Megilla 1:1), as well as different archeological theories regarding the route of the original wall of Jerusalem. These sources imply that the laws of a walled city and its satellite neighborhoods may not apply to a city void of Jewish inhabitants. R. Herzog and R. Frank concluded that the neighborhoods of the "New City" should continue to read on the fifteenth of Adar. By the great kindness of God, the entire city of Jerusalem was miraculously returned to the Jewish people in 1967, and, God willing, this question will forever more remain a historical, rather than a practical one.

This question has also arisen since the reunification of Jerusalem in 1967 and the ensuing building of Jewish neighborhoods outside of Jerusalem's Old City across many hills and valleys. The *posekim* have had to determine whether the residents of these neighborhoods should observe Purim on the fourteenth or fifteenth. R. Shlomo Yosef Zevin (1888–1978) expresses his amazement that R. Tukatchinsky would, each year, call for residents of Jerusalem's "New City" (the neighborhoods beyond a *mil* from the Old City) to read on the fourteenth, even though common custom did not follow his view.[10] To this day, in R. Tukatchinsky's yeshiva, Yeshivat Etz Chayim, the Megilla is read on the fourteenth, although by someone who lives outside of Jerusalem.[11] Others maintain that all areas within a contiguous stretch of development from the Old City read on the fifteenth. Nowadays, all of Jerusalem's neighborhoods have been connected to the Old City through residential expansion, thus rendering this last question irrelevant. Indeed, two recent Chief Rabbis of Jerusalem – R. Shalom Messas (1908–2003)[12] and R. Yitzchak Kulitz (1922–2003) – ruled that the outer neighborhoods of Jerusalem should read the Megilla on the fifteenth. Some (including R. Shlomo Zalman Auerbach[13]) maintained that any neighborhood that pays municipal taxes to Jerusalem and is connected to the city with an *eiruv* should be considered "*samukh*" and thus read on the fifteenth. Common custom appears to follow this position.

ONE WHO TRAVELS TO AND FROM A WALLED CITY ON PURIM

With the return of the Jewish people to Israel in large numbers toward the end of the nineteenth century, the establishment of the State of Israel, and the reunification of Jerusalem, the once-theoretical questions regarding one who travels from a walled city to an unwalled city on Purim have taken on critical practical importance. In turn, the *posekim* have discussed this issue in great depth. We will attempt to briefly summarize the basic laws and guidelines relevant to this issue.

For the purpose of our discussion, a person categorized here as a "*ben ir*" (resident of an unwalled city) must read the Megilla and observe Purim on the fourteenth of Adar, while the term "*ben kerakh*" (resident of a walled city) refers to someone who must observe the holiday on the fifteenth of Adar. The Mishna establishes that a person's presence in a city even for a single day can, under certain circumstances, define a person as either a *ben kerakh* or *ben ir*:

> A resident of an [unwalled] city who has gone to a walled city or [a resident] of a walled city who has gone to an [unwalled] city: If he intends to return to his own place, he reads according to the rules of his own place, and otherwise he reads with the rest. (Megilla 19a)

The Gemara, commenting on this mishna, states:

> Rava said: This rule applies only if he intends to return on the night of the fourteenth, but if he does not intend to return on the night of the fourteenth, he reads with the rest.
>
> Rava said: From where do I derive this ruling? For it is written, "Therefore do the Jews of the unwalled cities that dwell in the unwalled cities" [Esther 9:19]. Since it is written, "The Jews of the unwalled cities," why then should it be further written, "that dwell in the unwalled cities"? *This teaches that one who is a resident of an unwalled city for one day is called a resident of an unwalled city*. We have proved this for the resident of an unwalled city. How do we know that it applies also to residents of a walled city? It is reasonable to suppose that since a resident of an unwalled city for one day is called a resident of an unwalled city, *a resident of a walled city for one day is called a resident of a walled city.*

Thus, a resident of Jerusalem who finds himself in an unwalled city on the night of the fourteenth – meaning, when the night ends at sunrise of the fourteenth – is obligated to observe the laws of Purim on the fourteenth.

Rava's comments address only the situation of a resident of a walled city who travels to an unwalled city, whose status is determined by his location on "the night of the fourteenth." Rava does not, however, address the opposite case of a resident of an unwalled city who finds himself in a walled city. Does the morning of the fourteenth determine his status as well, or is his status determined by his location on the morning of the fifteenth? Additionally, the Gemara does not discuss the fascinating question of whether one could theoretically be obligated to observe Purim on both days, or not at all, by traveling from one kind of city to the other.

Rashi argues that where one is located on the morning of the fifteenth is also a determining factor:

> They only taught that the resident of a walled city (*ben kerakh*) who went to an unwalled city and intends to return to his place [the walled city] reads on the fifteenth and not on the fourteenth, but the same applies regarding the resident of an unwalled city (*ben ir*) who went to a walled city. If he plans to return on the night of the fifteenth so that he will not be there [in the walled city] on the day of the fifteenth, he is not regarded as being a resident of a walled city for the day, and so he reads on the fourteenth in accordance with the obligation of his city.[14]

Rashi explains that while a person's location at sunrise on the morning of the fourteenth determines whether he reads in the unwalled city or not, one's location at sunrise on the morning of the fifteenth determines whether one must read on Shushan Purim. Rosh explains Rashi's approach:

> He did not wish to interpret Rava's words as referring also to a resident of an unwalled city who went to a walled city, because it does not stand to reason that if he is in a walled city on the fourteenth, he is governed by the obligation of [Megilla] reading of a walled city, and so he must remain there on the fifteenth and read with them.... Inasmuch as the time of reading of walled cities has not yet arrived, why should their obligation of [Megilla] reading apply to him?[15]

Accordingly, a resident of Jerusalem who finds himself in an unwalled city on the fourteenth but plans on being in Jerusalem on the fifteenth would read on the fifteenth in Jerusalem. A resident of an unwalled city who finds himself in Jerusalem on the fourteenth and plans on returning home before Shushan Purim should read the Megilla on the fourteenth in Jerusalem. If he is in Jerusalem on the morning of the fifteenth, he should read the Megilla on the fifteenth. Many *Rishonim* concur with Rashi's interpretation and halakhic conclusion.[16]

Rosh himself, however, along with *Tur*,[17] disagrees, maintaining that the morning of the fourteenth determines everyone's status, regardless of the situation. If one wakes up in an unwalled city on the morning of the fourteenth, then he must read the Megilla on that day. However, if one rises in Jerusalem on the morning of the fourteenth, then he must read the Megilla in Jerusalem on the fifteenth, even if he is a resident of an unwalled city. As Rosh writes:

> The wording of the gemara implies that Rava refers to the entire mishna, and this is indeed proven in the Yerushalmi. Rava's words can be applied to the entire mishna: Just as the resident of a walled city is regarded as a resident of an unwalled city if he is there on the night and part of the day of the fourteenth, which is the time when residents of the unwalled city read [the Megilla], and he becomes bound by their obligation, similarly, a resident of an unwalled city who went to a walled city and is there for part of the day of the fourteenth – since at the time when residents of his city are obligated to read [the Megilla] he is not there with them, he is no longer bound by the obligation to read [the Megilla] as it applies to the residents of his city.

Raavad agrees with Rosh, but adds that in order to become obligated to read on the fifteenth, one must remain in the walled city through the fifteenth. If the traveler returns to the unwalled city after the morning of the fourteenth, he will be exempt from reading the Megilla altogether![18] To summarize, while Rashi maintains that one's status is determined by his location at dawn on the fourteenth (for a *ben ir*) and the fifteenth (for a *ben kerakh*), Rosh maintains that one's location on the morning of the fourteenth determines if one should read on the fourteenth or fifteenth.

What conceptual issue underlies this debate between Rashi and Rosh? Seemingly, Rashi views these two days of Purim as two separate festivals. Therefore, one's status on the fourteenth or fifteenth of Adar depends upon whether he awoke inside or outside of Jerusalem. Rosh, however, likely believes that the fourteenth of Adar is considered Purim for the residents of walled cities as well, even if practically they observe the holiday on the next day. According to Rosh, a *ben kerakh* omits *Taḥanun* on the fourteenth of Adar not merely as a sign of identification with his brethren in unwalled cities, who observe Purim that day, but rather because even for the *ben kerakh*, that day is fundamentally Purim as well.

The *Shulḥan Arukh* follows Rashi's view that the status of a *ben kerakh* is determined by his location on the morning of the fifteenth,[19] and the *Mishna Berura*[20] and most other *Aḥaronim* concur.

A second question concerns the role played by one's intention with regard to this halakha. The *Rishonim* address the situation of a resident of a walled city who visits an unwalled city on the fourteenth, intending to return to his walled city before morning, but who was delayed and remained in the unwalled city. Must he celebrate Purim on the fourteenth, in accordance with his location on the morning of the fourteenth, or on the fifteenth, as he had intended to be in a walled city on the morning of the fifteenth?

Rashi and Baal HaMaor rule that one's identity is fully determined by his physical presence in a given place on Purim morning.[21] Other *Rishonim,* however, insist (based on the Gemara's formulation and Rif's interpretation) that one's status is determined based on where he had intended to be at the critical time (as discussed above).[22] Among those who recognize the importance of intention, we find a debate as to whether the determining factor is one's intention upon leaving home (Rosh, *Tur*), or his intention as Purim begins on the night of the fourteenth (Ramban, Ran). The *Shulḥan Arukh* rules:

> A resident of an unwalled city who travels to a walled city, or a resident of a walled city who travels to an unwalled city – if his intention was to return to his place by the time of the reading [of the Megilla], and he was delayed and did not return, then he reads in his place. [Similarly,] if he did not have in mind to return until after the time of the [Megilla] reading, he should read with the people of the place in which he is found.[23]

The *Mishna Berura* explains, as we noted above, that the *Shulḥan Arukh* accepts Rashi's view that the critical moment that determines one's obligation is the morning of the fourteenth for a *ben ir* and the morning of the fifteenth for a *ben kerakh*. Furthermore, the *Mishna Berura* adds, the *Shulḥan Arukh* follows the view of the *Rishonim* who maintain that one's intention upon leaving home regarding his location at the critical moment (the morning of the fourteenth or the fifteenth) determines his identity with respect to the obligation of Megilla.[24] Many *Aḥaronim*, including *Ḥazon Ish*[25] and R. Tzvi Pesach Frank,[26] concur.

SUMMARY OF THE LAWS OF A TRAVELER

It is evident that the halakhot of a traveler on Purim are extremely complex and confusing! Indeed, a cursory perusal of the responsa literature and contemporary halakhic compendia reveals numerous different approaches and conclusions that can leave the reader quite perplexed.

However, based upon what we have seen, we can succinctly summarize the basic guidelines as follows:[27]

> If a resident of Jerusalem (a walled city) traveled to an unwalled town with the intention of remaining there after dawn of the fourteenth, and he indeed remained in the unwalled city through dawn, he should observe Purim on the fourteenth of Adar. However, if his plans changed and he returned to Jerusalem before dawn, he should not observe Purim on the fourteenth.[28] If the traveler intends to return to Jerusalem before dawn, then he should not observe Purim on the fourteenth, even if, in the end, he remained in the unwalled city through the morning of the fourteenth. In such a case, however, some authorities advise reading the Megilla without a *berakha* on the fourteenth, in deference to the opinions (Rashi, Baal HaMaor) that base one's status solely on his physical location.[29]

In the opposite case, if a resident of an unwalled city travels to Jerusalem before the morning of the fourteenth with the intention of returning before dawn, he should observe Purim on the fourteenth regardless of whether or not he actually returned home before dawn. If his intention upon leaving home was to remain in Jerusalem until after dawn on the fourteenth and to return only after dawn on the fifteenth, than he should celebrate Purim on the fifteenth of Adar.

Is it possible for one to become obligated in *both* days of Purim? If one leaves an unwalled city after dawn on the fourteenth of Adar and plans to stay in Jerusalem until after dawn the following day, should he observe two days of Purim? Seemingly, according to Rosh, one can only incur one obligation, depending on his location on the morning of the fourteenth. According to Rashi, however, could such a person be obligated on both days?

The Talmud Yerushalmi teaches that one who "uproots his residency" (*akar dirato*) can be obligated to observe two days of Purim, or be exempt from Purim altogether, depending on whether he moves to or from a walled city (Megilla 2:3). On the basis of this passage, R. Shlomo Zalman Auerbach contends that a traveler can indeed be obligated to celebrate Purim twice.[30] However, some authorities recommend in such a case that one hear the *berakhot* on the Megilla from someone else on the second day, rather than reciting them himself.

In contrast, R. Tzvi Pesach Frank understands the Yerushalmi's comment as referring only to those who move residences permanently, and not to travelers; thus, it would not apply to our case. Moreover, R. Frank claims that the talmudic dictum, "a resident of a walled city for one day is called a resident of a walled city," is limited in scope and application, and it only applies to one who has yet to hear the Megilla is his own home town. However, one who visits a village on the fourteenth and returns to his home in a walled city for the fifteenth would indeed read again on the fifteenth, as that is where he really lives.[31]

If a Jerusalem resident travels to an unwalled city on the morning of the fourteenth, planning to remain there until at least the morning of the fifteenth, must he observe Purim at all? While some *Aḥaronim* write that he should still observe Purim on the fourteenth by default, as his intention was not to observe Purim in Jerusalem on the fifteenth,[32] it appears that according to many *Rishonim*, one would most likely be entirely exempt from observing Purim in such a case. Interestingly, R. Tzvi Pesach Frank writes that in this case, one should preferably gather ten people and read the Megilla on the fourteenth with a *berakha* in Jerusalem; if this is not possible, he should read it privately without a *berakha*.[33] Clearly, one should avoid this scenario so that he does not miss out on the wonderful holiday of Purim! It should be noted that in any situation where one's obligation is in doubt, he should not read the Megilla on behalf of others who are clearly obligated to observe Purim that day.

CHAPTER 40

Seudat Purim, Matanot LaEvyonim, and *Mishlo'aḥ Manot*

INTRODUCTION

Toward the end of the Megilla, we read that Mordekhai sent letters to the Jews of the provinces of Aḥashveirosh, announcing the establishment of the Purim festival. He wrote:

> That they should keep yearly the fourteenth day of the month Adar, and the fifteenth day of the same, the days wherein the Jews had rest from their enemies, and the month which was turned unto them from sorrow to gladness, and from mourning into a good day; that they should make them days of feasting and gladness, and of sending portions one to another, and gifts to the poor. (Est. 9:20–22)

Mordekhai enacted three components to the Purim celebration: "feasting and gladness" (*seudat Purim*), "sending portions one to another" (*mishlo'aḥ manot*), and "gifts to the poor" (*matanot la'evyonim*). In this chapter, we will discuss the details and parameters of each of these mitzvot, including the specific obligation of "*ḥayav inish livsumei*" – to become inebriated on Purim.

SEUDAT PURIM

The festive meal of Purim, the *seudat Purim,* is one of the central components of the Purim holiday, both experientially and halakhically. Indeed, the Megilla itself characterizes the days of Purim as "days of feasting and gladness." When should one conduct this festive meal? The Gemara records:

> Rava said: one who eats the festive Purim meal at night has not fulfilled his obligation. What is the reason? It says: "Days of feasting and gladness."

> R. Ashi was sitting in front of R. Kahana; it became dark, and the Rabbis did not come. He said to him: Why didn't the Rabbis come? Maybe they were busy with the festive Purim meal. He [Rav Kahana] said: Was it not possible for them to eat [their Purim meal] the previous night? He [R. Ashi] responded: Did you not hear that which Mar said in the name of Rava: one who eats the festive Purim meal at night has not fulfilled his obligation? (Megilla 7b)

Rava clearly rules that the festive meal must be eaten during the day of Purim, and not the previous night. Most *Rishonim*[1] rule in accordance with this gemara. The *Mordekhai,*[2] however, cites Raavya (R. Eliezer b. Yoel HaLevi) as arguing that just as the Megilla is read both at night and again during the day, one should similarly conduct a festive meal both at night and during the day. Apparently, he recognized an additional, albeit lower level of the mitzva that requires holding a meal at night as well. The *Shulḥan Arukh*[3] rules that the meal must be eaten during the day, although Rema also writes that one should "rejoice at night as well, and slightly increase in one's meal."[4]

In addition, Rema records that it is customary to begin the Purim meal in the afternoon, after praying the Minḥa service.[5] The *Mishna Berura* explains that this is because people are generally busy delivering *mishlo'aḥ manot* during the morning hours.[6] In many communities, especially where people must work on Purim, it is customary to begin the festive meal very late in the afternoon. Rema rules that the majority of the meal should be eaten during the day, and speaks very critically of those who begin late and eat most of their meal after dark.

Very often, the Purim meal is concluded only after nightfall, giving rise to the question of whether one should insert *Al HaNissim* in *Birkat HaMazon.* The *Orḥot Ḥayim,*[7] cited by the *Hagahot Maimoniyot,*[8] rules that *Al HaNissim* should be inserted even if the meal extended into the nighttime hours. *Tur,*[9] however, cites his father, Rosh,[10] as ruling that one should not insert *Al HaNissim* after dark. Maharil records that the custom in Ashkenaz followed the first opinion.[11] The *Shulḥan Arukh* cites both views, and Rema adds that it is customary to insert *Al HaNissim.*[12]

Peri Megadim lauds the practice of those who eat the *seudat Purim* in the morning.[13] Rema, citing the *Sefer HaMinhagim*, rules that this should certainly be done when Purim falls on Friday.[14]

What should one eat at the festive Purim meal? *Magen Avraham* writes, "We have not found [a source indicating] that one is obligated to eat bread on Purim."[15] Accordingly, the *Birkei Yosef*[16] and *Eliya Rabba*[17] rule that one need not eat bread at the *seudat Purim*. Others, however, maintain that one must eat bread at the Purim meal, just as one must eat bread at Yom Tov meals.[18] This is the view accepted by the *Arukh HaShulḥan*[19] and Netziv.[20]

This question may impact upon another issue – whether or not one who forgets to insert *Al HaNissim* must repeat *Birkat HaMazon*. The *Mishna Berura* cites a debate regarding this issue.[21] The *Magen Avraham*[22] and *Peri Megadim*[23] note that those who require one to eat bread at the Purim meal should also require one to repeat *Birkat HaMazon* if he forgot *Al HaNissim*, as the requirement of recitation of *Al HaNissim* was created as a result of the obligation to eat bread. Conversely, those who do not require eating bread should not demand that one repeat *Birkat HaMazon* in this case. The *Arukh HaShulḥan*, however, contends that even those who require the consumption of bread would not demand that one who omits *Al HaNissim* repeat *Birkat HaMazon*, as *Birkat HaMazon* should be treated no more stringently than the *Shemoneh Esreh*; one who forgets to add *Al HaNissim* in the *Shemoneh Esreh* does not repeat the prayer, despite the fact that the inclusion of *Al HaNissim* is clearly obligatory.[24] The *Mishna Berura* applies the principle of "*safek berakhot lehakel*" – one should not recite a *berakha* if there is some uncertainty as to whether it is warranted. Hence, in light of the different views surrounding this issue, one who forgets to add *Al HaNissim* in *Birkat HaMazon* should not repeat *Birkat HaMazon*.

Must one eat meat at the Purim meal? Rambam[25] and *Shulḥan Arukh*[26] strongly imply that one must eat meat at the Purim *seuda*; some *posekim* even express uncertainty as to whether one fulfills the obligation by eating poultry![27] *Magen Avraham*, however, questions whether one must actually eat meat.[28] The *Aḥaronim* relate this issue to the question of whether one must eat meat on Yom Tov to fulfill the commandment of *simḥat Yom Tov*.[29]

Another component of the festive Purim meal is drinking wine, a halakha to which we devote the next section.

ḤAYAV INISH LIVSUMEI: THE OBLIGATION TO DRINK WINE ON PURIM

The Gemara teaches:

> One is obligated to become intoxicated (*ḥayav inish livsumei*) on Purim until he cannot distinguish between "cursed is Haman" and "blessed is Mordekhai." Rabba and R. Zeira held the festive Purim meal together. They got drunk, and Rabba slaughtered R. Zeira. The next day, he prayed for him and he was resurrected. The next year, [Rabba] said to him: Let us hold the festive Purim meal together. [R. Zeira] said to him: Miracles do not occur every hour. (Megilla 7b)

This startling passage raises many questions. Maharsha (R. Shmuel Eidels, 1555–1631) writes in his commentary to this passage that Rabba certainly did not kill R. Zeira, but rather forced him to drink excessively, which made him ill. Maharsha suggests that the unusual term "*shaḥtei*" ("slaughtered") employed by the Gemara refers to what Rabba did to R. Zeira's throat – forcing him to drink.

From a practical halakhic perspective, of course, the more pressing question is how we must understand the Gemara's initial statement. Is there really an obligation to become inebriated on Purim, and if so, to what extent? The *Rishonim* take different approaches in interpreting this passage and determining the halakha. Baal HaMaor cites Rabbeinu Efraim as explaining that the Gemara brings the story of Rabba and R. Zeira to contradict and reject the initial statement requiring drinking on Purim. Accordingly, Baal HaMaor rules that there is no obligation to drink on Purim.[30] Ran concurs.[31]

Many other *Rishonim*, however, including Rif[32] and Rosh,[33] cite this passage verbatim, implying that while the story of Rabba and R. Zeira may serve as a warning against excessive intoxication, halakha fundamentally accepts the Gemara's initial statement. Interestingly, Rambam writes:

> How does one fulfill this obligation of the [Purim] meal? He should eat meat and arrange a meal according to his means, and *drink wine until he becomes inebriated and falls asleep as a result.*[34]

Rambam adds that one should drink until he falls asleep, while omitting the Gemara's description of drinking "until one cannot distinguish between 'cursed is Haman' and 'blessed is Mordekhai.'" Why does Rambam reformulate the Gemara's dictum, and does his new formulation alter the demands of this mitzva?

Rema seems to have understood that when one drinks until he falls asleep, he thereby fulfills the requirement to drink until he cannot distinguish between "cursed is Haman" and "blessed is Mordekhai."[35] The *Arukh HaShulḥan*, in contrast, explains that according to Rambam, the story of Rabba and R. Zeira serves to modify the initial statement and reject the extreme obligation first proposed by the Gemara. In other words, while one should become mildly intoxicated on Purim, excessive inebriation is not mandated – and therefore not permitted![36] The *Orḥot Ḥayim* similarly rejects the opinion that mandates complete inebriation, writing that one should merely "drink more than one is accustomed." He also rules that becoming completely inebriated constitutes a serious sin.[37]

Tur[38] and the *Shulḥan Arukh*,[39] following Rif and Rosh, cite the talmudic passage verbatim. The *Arukh HaShulḥan* actually expresses astonishment that they rule in accordance with Rif and Rosh, rather than the more moderate positions of other *Rishonim*.[40] Rema writes:

> And some say that one need not drink that much, and should rather drink more than he is accustomed to and then sleep, and by sleeping he cannot distinguish between the cursed Haman and blessed Mordekhai. Regardless of whether one drinks a lot or a little, he should focus his heart toward the heavens.

Many *Aḥaronim*, including the *Mishna Berura*[41] and *Arukh HaShulḥan*,[42] advocate following Rema's ruling.

When does one fulfill this mitzva? Rambam,[43] followed by *Tur* and *Shulḥan Arukh*,[44] imply that this mitzva is part of the obligation to participate in a festive Purim meal. R. Shimon Sofer, in his *Hitorerut Teshuva*,[45] infers from the fact that R. Zeira refused to attend Rabba's Purim meal the next year that the drinking must accompany the Purim meal. If so, given that the *Shulḥan Arukh* explicitly rules that one can fulfill the mitzva of *seudat Purim* only during the day,[46] the practice of drinking on Purim night is highly questionable.

Assuming that one wishes to reach some level of inebriation, is there a "preferred drink" that he should use for this purpose? The *Shulḥan Arukh* does not specify any particular beverage. However, some *Rishonim* explain that the halakha of drinking on Purim is intended to commemorate the feasts that took place during the Purim story, which included indulgence in wine. This would certainly indicate a preference for wine over other drinks. Rashi,[47] Rambam,[48] Roke'aḥ,[49] and Radbaz[50] also explicitly mention drinking wine, and some prove from these sources that one should preferably use wine in fulfilling this mitzva.[51]

R. Moshe Sternbach suggests that one should conduct the meal over wine to fulfill the obligation of "*mishteh*," which indicates specifically wine. Nevertheless, he may also drink other alcoholic beverages if he enjoys them.[52] *Biur Halakha* similarly cites the *Eliya Rabba*, who explains that since the miracle of Purim occurred as result of "*mishtaot*," feasts characterized by drinking – including the first feast, which led to Vashti's demise, and the feast at which Aḥashveirosh ordered Haman's execution – we commemorate those miraculous events through drinking wine.[53] Although women are included in all of the mitzvot of Purim, some sources suggest that it is inappropriate for women to become intoxicated.[54]

Several *Rishonim* expressed great concern regarding this mitzva. The *Orḥot Ḥayim*, for example, writes that full inebriation is certainly prohibited, "and there is no greater sin, as it leads to sexual impropriety, bloodshed, and other sins."[55] Some explain that the Gemara does not obligate drinking, but merely presents it as a *mitzva be'alma*, a mere good deed; one certainly fulfills the day's mitzvot even without drinking.[56] Furthermore, R. Avraham Danzig writes in his *Ḥayei Adam*:

> If one believes that drinking on Purim will interfere with his performance of any mitzva, such as reciting *Birkat HaMazon*, Minḥa, or Maariv, or if he will behave in a boorish manner, it is preferable that he not drink [or become inebriated] as long as his motives are proper.[57]

A famous talmudic statement allows one to alter the truth regarding "*puraya*," which is traditionally understood as referring to private sexual matters (Bava Metzia 23b). Maharsha, however, explains this term as referring to Purim:

> "*Befuraya*" – as a person is obligated to become intoxicated, the Rabbis would customarily lie, saying that they could not distinguish [between "cursed is Haman" and "blessed is Mordekhai"] even if they were not inebriated enough and could distinguish.[58]

Apparently, one should not feel pressured to become inebriated, and may even lie if necessary to avoid drinking. *Biur Halakha* concludes his discussion of this topic by citing the following comments of Me'iri:

> We are certainly not commanded to demean ourselves through joy, as we are not commanded to engage in a celebration of frivolity and nonsense, but rather through joy that brings about love of God and thanksgiving for the miracles that He wrought for us.[59]

It is worth noting that while one who is intoxicated may recite *Birkat HaMazon*,[60] the halakha differs when it comes to *tefilla*. The *Shulḥan Arukh* writes:

> One who drinks a *revi'it* of wine should not pray until he removes the wine [until its effects wear off]. And if he drank more but he is able to speak before the king, then if he prays [the *Amida*], his prayer fulfills his obligation. [However,] if he is unable to speak before the king and prays, his prayer is an abomination, and he must repeat his prayer when the wine is removed from him.[61]

One should therefore recite the Minḥa prayer before one's *seudat Purim*, and must be mindful to properly recite the Maariv prayer after the meal.

MATANOT LA'EVYONIM

As noted above, the Megilla relates that Mordekhai instructed the Jewish people to "make them [the days of Purim] days of feasting and gladness, and of sending portions one to another, and gifts to the poor" (Est. 9:22). R. Yair Chayim Bacharach (1639–1702, author of *Ḥavot Yair*) writes in his work *Mekor Ḥayim* that one should fulfill the mitzva of *mishlo'aḥ manot* before giving *matanot la'evyonim,* since the verse lists *mishlo'aḥ manot* before *matanot la'evyonim.*[62]

Others disagree, however.[63] In fact, the *Yesod VeShoresh HaAvoda*[64] and R. Yaakov Emden[65] write that one should actually give *matanot la'evyonim* before Shaḥarit on Purim morning! *Tur* and *Shulḥan Arukh*[66] record the laws of *matanot la'evyonim before* the laws of *mishlo'aḥ manot,* perhaps suggesting that *matanot la'evyonim* should be given first. Moreover, Rambam writes:

> It is better for a person to increase his gifts to the poor than to increase the size of his Purim meal or *mishlo'aḥ manot.* For there is no greater and more admirable joy than to gladden the hearts of the destitute, orphans, widows, and converts. One who gladdens the hearts of the misfortunate is likened unto the Divine Presence.[67]

The Gemara teaches that *matanot la'evyonim* entails giving two "gifts" to two separate people – as Rashi explains, a total of two gifts, one to each person (Megilla 7a).

What is the minimum that one must give for each gift? Ritva writes that one should give at least two *perutot* (coins), one for each gift.[68] Similarly, Rashi asserts that there is no minimum amount for *matanot la'evyonim,* as it is a form of charity, and one should give as much as one likes.[69] Others require that one give a more significant gift.[70] The *Shaarei Teshuva* cites the ruling of the *Zera Yaakov* that one should give a minimum of "three eggs," meaning the amount of a small meal.[71]

Rambam writes that one may give either money or food to fulfill this mitzva,[72] But *Or Same'aḥ* writes that one should not give clothing.[73] The *Turei Even* suggests that although one may indeed give food, the Gemara indicates that it is preferable to give money;[74] he notes that one reason that the Megilla is not read on Shabbat relates to the problem of giving money as *matanot la'evyonim* on Shabbat (Megilla 4a), which clearly presumes that money is the preferred means of fulfilling this mitzva.

Who is considered an "*evyon*" (poor person) for the purposes of this mitzva? Based upon the standard definition of a "poor person" who may take public charity funds,[75] one who is unable to support himself and his family or a person who faces exorbitant expenses for medical care or other needs may receive *matanot la'evyonim*.[76] Rambam[77] and *Shulḥan Arukh*[78] rule that we are not as discerning with people asking for charity on Purim as we are throughout the year, and all who "extend their hand" are given *matanot la'evyonim* on Purim. Ramban writes,[79] as do the *Tur*[80] and *Shulḥan Arukh*,[81] that one may give *matanot la'evyonim* to Jews and non-Jews alike in order to avoid "*eiva*" (enmity or animosity). The *Maḥzor Vitry*, however, records Rashi's harsh criticism of those who distribute *matanot la'evyonim* to their non-Jewish workers on Purim.[82] The *Shulḥan Arukh* rules that one who does not encounter a poor person on Purim may set aside the money and give it to them after Purim.[83]

It is customary to set aside money before Purim and give it to the appointed gabbaim, who serve as one's agents to distribute the *matanot la'evyonim* on Purim day. R. Yosef Engel claims that the identity of the giver must be known to the recipient, as the verse describes *matanot la'evyonim* as "gifts," which one generally gives expecting the recipient to know that he received it specifically from him.[84] Other *Aḥaronim*, however, reject this assertion, and even prefer to preserve the anonymity of the donor.

One should not give *matanot la'evyonim* from money already set aside as *maaser kesafim*.[85] Similarly, one should not give *matanot la'evyonim* to pay a debt, or to pay those whom he would ordinarily give a gift.[86] However, once one has fulfilled the minimum requirement of *matanot la'evyonim*, he may then add from his *maaser kesafim* to increase the sum or number of recipients.[87]

It is notable that giving charity often accompanies obligatory festivities. Rambam writes:

> When one eats and drinks [on Yom Tov], he is obligated to feed those less fortunate – the stranger, orphan, widow, and poor. One who locks his door and eats and drinks only with his family, neglecting the poor and those of bitter fortune, does not experience the joy of a mitzva but rather the enjoyment of one's belly![88]

Incorporating the less fortunate into our own celebrations is an integral part of religiously mandated "*simḥa*." Without this added dimension, one's happiness is merely physical, "the enjoyment of one's belly."

MISHLO'AḤ MANOT

A number of possible reasons have been suggested for the mitzva of *mishlo'aḥ manot* (sending portions one to another). Some relate the mitzva of *mishlo'aḥ manot* to the broader mitzva of the festive Purim meal, either in that it ensures that the less fortunate will have food for a festive meal or as it serves an extension of one's own personal obligation to hold a festive *seudat Purim*. The *Terumat HaDeshen*, for example, writes, "The reason for *mishlo'aḥ manot* is to ensure that each and every person has sufficient means to hold a proper Purim meal."[89] Similarly, Rambam writes,

> How should one fulfill the obligation of a festive meal? He should eat meat and assemble a proper meal according to his means, and drink wine until becoming inebriated.... And similarly, one is obligated to send two portions of meat or two cooked dishes of two types of food to his fellow.[90]

Rambam clearly implies that the mitzva of *mishlo'aḥ manot* stems from the obligation to partake of a festive meal.

Others, including *Manot HaLevi*, understand *mishlo'aḥ manot* as an independent mitzva instituted for the purpose of increasing friendship,[91] in the interest of rectifying the divisiveness that Haman observed among the Jewish people: "There is one nation scattered and dispersed among the [other] nations" (Est. 3:8).

This question may impact upon a number of practical halakhic issues. For example, what is the proper time for sending *mishlo'aḥ manot*? Rema rules that one must fulfill this mitzva during the day, and not on the night of Purim.[92] Instinctively, we might explain this ruling on the basis of the theory that associates *mishlo'aḥ manot* with the Purim meal, which would naturally require sending *mishlo'aḥ manot* specifically by day, when the Purim meal is eaten. In truth, however, it seems that the proper time for all the mitzvot of Purim is during the day (the nighttime Megilla reading being the exception), and we therefore cannot necessarily demonstrate the relationship between *mishlo'aḥ manot* and the *seudat Purim* from this halakha.

R. Aryeh Tzvi Frommer bemoans the practice of many to give *mishlo'aḥ manot* after sunset on Purim day, while still partaking of the Purim meal. He notes that *Terumat HaDeshen* might condone such a practice, as he associates *mishlo'aḥ manot* with the Purim meal; thus, as long as the meal is in progress, one may still fulfill the obligation of *mishlo'aḥ manot*. Nevertheless, R. Frommer writes, this position is not universally accepted, and one should not rely upon it.[93]

Can one fulfill this obligation by sending *mishlo'aḥ manot* before Purim on the assumption that it will be received on Purim (and it is indeed received on Purim)? Some suggest that according to *Terumat HaDeshen*, as long as the recipient benefits from the gift on Purim, the sender has fulfilled his obligation. According to *Manot HaLevi*, however, one must send the gift on Purim day itself, thereby demonstrating his affection for the recipient. This issue is debated by the *Aḥaronim*. Some maintain that the *mishlo'aḥ manot* must be received on Purim,[94] while others insist that it must actually be sent on Purim day.[95]

According to some authorities, one who lives in Jerusalem, where the mitzva of *mishlo'aḥ manot* is fulfilled on Shushan Purim (the fifteenth of Adar), should be careful to send *mishlo'aḥ manot* to a fellow Jerusalemite who also observes Shushan Purim. Conversely, one who lives outside Jerusalem should give *mishlo'aḥ manot* specifically to someone who observes Purim on the same day.

What must one send as *mishlo'aḥ manot*? The Gemara teaches:

> R. Yosef quotes a *baraita*: "Sending gifts from a man to his friend" – two presents to one man; "and gifts to the poor" – two presents, each to one or two people. (Megilla 7b)

Thus, this mitzva requires sending at least two gifts to at least one person.

What gifts qualify for this obligation? Rambam,[96] followed by the *Shulḥan Arukh*,[97] writes that one should send "two portions of meat or two cooked dishes of two types of food to his friend."

The *Mishna Berura* writes that one may even send a drink,[98] and the *Arukh HaShulḥan* adds that one may even send two drinks.[99] There is no source for the common misconception that one must send two foods requiring two different *berakhot*, although the two foods should be distinct and not two pieces of the same food.[100] Some write that the food must already be cooked and ready to eat,[101] while others maintain that one may even send uncooked foods.[102] The *Mishna Berura* cites both opinions.[103] Seemingly, those who relate the mitzva of *mishlo'aḥ manot* to the festive Purim meal might require that the food be ready to eat. Indeed, the work *Maase Rav* records the Vilna Gaon's ruling that one should send cooked items ready to be used for the Purim meal.[104]

R. Eliezer Yehuda Waldenberg suggests that this debate may also impact upon the size of the gift. According to *Terumat HaDeshen*, the giver should take into account the financial position of the recipient and whether he will potentially use the gift for his Purim meal. According to *Manot HaLevi*, however, the gift should reflect the position of the giver, in order to properly reflect his gesture of affection toward the recipient.[105]

The *Terumat HaDeshen* raises the interesting question of whether one may give clothing as *mishlo'aḥ manot*. He concludes, based upon his analysis cited above, that since *mishlo'aḥ manot* is intended to ensure proper provisions for the festive Purim meal, the contents of the *mishlo'aḥ manot* must be edible.[106]

Similarly, R. Menashe Klein questions whether one may send *ḥiddushei Torah* (written Torah insights) as *mishlo'aḥ manot*. He suggests that while this would certainly not suffice according to *Terumat HaDeshen*, it might qualify according to *Manot HaLevi*, who explains that *mishlo'aḥ manot* serves to increase friendship among people. Since some people enjoy *ḥiddushei Torah* more than material goods, it is possible that sending *ḥiddushei Torah* achieves the desired goal of *mishlo'aḥ manot* and thus fulfills the obligation.[107]

The *Aḥaronim* also question whether one fulfills the mitzva of *mishlo'aḥ manot* if the recipient declines ("*moḥel*") to accept the gift[108] and whether one may send a "gift with the condition that it be returned."[109] These questions may similarly depend upon whether the ultimate goal of the mitzva relates to the Purim meal or to increasing harmony among Jews.

The *Arukh HaShulḥan* comments that one does not fulfill the obligation if the recipient does not know that he received the *mishlo'aḥ manot*.[110]

R. Yaakov Ettlinger suggests that one should preferably send the *mishlo'aḥ manot* through a *shaliaḥ* – an agent – rather than personally, as the verse speaks of "sending" gifts, and not "giving."[111] The *Mishna Berura* cites this opinion.[112] This idea seemingly supports the notion that *mishlo'aḥ manot* serves to increase peace and harmony among the Jewish people, and should therefore include as many people as possible. If so, one need not send the gifts with an agent who is generally considered a valid "*shaliaḥ*" – meaning, an adult Jew – as the purpose of employing an agent here is not to discharge one's obligation, but rather to involve more people in the mitzva.

Women are equally obligated in *mishlo'aḥ manot* and *matanot la'evyonim*, as "they were also included in the miracle."[113] The *Magen Avraham* notes, however, that the women in his time were not strict about these obligations. To justify this practice, he suggests that while a widow should send her own *mishlo'aḥ manot* and *matanot la'evyonim*, a married woman fulfills her obligation through the *mishlo'aḥ manot* and *matanot la'evyonim* sent by her husband. The *Magen Avraham* concludes, however, that women should preferably act stringently in this regard and send their own *mishlo'aḥ manot* and *matanot la'evyonim*.[114]

The *Arukh HaShulḥan*, in contrast, writes that a husband and wife discharge their obligation by sending to one person, due to the principle of "*ishto kegufo*" (husband and wife are considered like one). Adult children, however – both boys and girls – are obligated to send *mishlo'aḥ manot* and give *matanot la'evyonim* independently, and do not fulfill the obligation through their parents.[115] Interestingly, *Peri Ḥadash* insists that women are *not* obligated in *matanot la'evyonim* and *mishlo'aḥ manot*, as the verse says "*ish lere'ehu*" ("a *man* to his neighbor").[116]

DAMAGES CAUSED ON PURIM; COSTUMES AND "SHPIELS"

Rema,[117] citing *Terumat HaDeshen*,[118] writes, "Some say that if one damages another as a result of the Purim festivities, he is exempt from paying." The *Mishna Berura*[119] cites *Baḥ*, who distinguishes in this regard between minor and major damages. He explains that people are not "forgiving" of major damages, even if they result from the Purim festivities, and therefore the guilty party must compensate the victim in the case of major damage. Furthermore, even if in some communities people may be forgiving of minor property damages, one must certainly avoid behavior that leads to embarrassing or humiliating others in any way.

Rema notes the custom to wear costumes on Purim, including men wearing women's clothing and vice versa, and justifies this behavior on the grounds that the intentions are for the day's festivities.[120] *Taz*, however, records that his father-in-law, *Baḥ*, sought to abolish this custom.[121] Certainly one who dresses up, and those who perform "Purim shpiels," should ensure that their actions are "*leshem Shamayim*" and in good taste. The *Aḥaronim* warn against excessive frivolity during the Purim celebrations.[122]

Pesaḥ

CHAPTER 41

Introduction to *Ḥametz* and the Laws of Pesaḥ

THE IMPORTANCE OF STUDYING THE LAWS OF PESAḤ PRIOR TO PESAḤ

The Talmud teaches that one should begin studying the laws of Pesaḥ thirty days prior to the holiday:

> We inquire about and investigate (*sho'alin vedoreshin*) the laws of Pesaḥ [beginning] thirty days prior. Rabban Shimon b. Gamliel says: Two weeks. What is the reasoning of the first view? Since Moshe rose on Pesaḥ and instructed concerning the Pesaḥ Sheni [which occurs thirty days later], as it says, "The Israelites shall perform the Paschal sacrifice in its set time," and then it says [introducing the concept of Pesaḥ Sheni], "There were people who were impure by reason of a corpse."[1]

Although this enactment may have originally related to the meticulous preparations necessary in order to bring the Paschal sacrifice before Pesaḥ (Avoda Zara 5b), the Rabbis retained this *takana* even after the destruction of the Temple.[2] The *Rishonim* cite a different passage, which records another ancient enactment: "Moshe instituted for Yisrael that they study the laws of Pesaḥ on Pesaḥ, those of *Atzeret* [Shavuot] on *Atzeret*, and those of *Ḥag* [Sukkot] on *Ḥag*" (Megilla 32a).

What is the difference, if any, between these two passages, and what is the reason for and the meaning of this second enactment? Most *Rishonim* explain that the passages refer to different laws. The second passage, which teaches that "Moshe instituted for Yisrael that they study the laws of Pesaḥ on Pesaḥ," instructs that one should study the laws of each specific festival *on* the festival itself.[3] What, therefore, is the intent of the first passage, "We inquire about and investigate (*sho'alin vedoreshin*) the laws of Pesaḥ [beginning] thirty days prior"?

Some explain that this passage instructs a teacher regarding the proper manner in which to prioritize questions.[4] The Tosefta records that when there are "Two [students] who ask, one on-topic and one off-topic, we deal [first] with the pertinent question" (Sanhedrin 7:5). Accordingly, Ran explains that during the thirty days prior to Pesaḥ, if a teacher must choose whether to address a question relating to the laws of Pesaḥ or another matter, he should relate to the question regarding Pesaḥ.[5]

Other *Rishonim* explain the gemara according to its simple understanding: One should review the laws of Pesaḥ for thirty days prior to Pesaḥ.[6] If so, does this passage refer exclusively to Pesaḥ, or to other festivals as well? *Beit Yosef* explains that because the laws of Pesaḥ are so numerous, including the proper grinding of wheat, the baking of *matzot, hagalat keilim,* and *biur ḥametz,* the Rabbis prescribed a full thirty days for one to properly study its laws. The halakhot of Sukkot, on the other hand, are less cumbersome and can be reviewed in a "day or two."[7] Alternatively, Rashi, in numerous places,[8] implies that this law applies to Sukkot as well.

R. Yoel Sirkis, in his *Bayit Ḥadash* commentary to the *Shulḥan Arukh,* disagrees with these approaches to understanding these gemarot. He insists that the two talmudic passages actually complement each other. The passage in Megilla does not mean to imply that one should study the laws of each holiday on the day itself, which is clearly, he reports, against common custom. Rather, the Gemara intends to teach that one should study the laws of each festival "near" it; in the case of Pesaḥ, according to the gemara in Pesaḥim, this means beginning thirty days prior.[9]

Incidentally, Rambam omits the passage that demands that one inquire and investigate the laws of Pesaḥ thirty days before Pesaḥ, but he does cite the obligation to study the laws of the festival on the day itself.[10] The *Aḥaronim* discuss this issue in depth. Some suggest that Rambam understood that the two passages cited above disagree, and he rules in accordance with the gemara in Megilla, which does not require one to study the laws of Pesaḥ thirty days prior to the festival.[11] Others explain that since *"sho'alin vedoreshin"* is merely preparatory, Rambam felt no need to codify it as obligatory. Alternatively, some propose that it is subsumed under the other laws that relate to the thirty days prior to Pesaḥ.[12]

According to Rambam and to those who believe that there are, indeed, two separate obligations, one might ask why one who properly prepares for the festival *before* the festival must study the laws of the festival on the festival itself. Some *Aḥaronim* explain that while the thirty days prior to the holiday are dedicated to preparing for it, learning about the festival on the festival itself fulfills a different and independent obligation – the obligation to relate to the day through *limud haTorah*. Indeed, the Gemara derives that one should divide one's time on Yom Tov between physical and spiritual enjoyment (Beitza 15b). As Rambam writes,

> Even though eating and drinking on Yom Tov is a positive commandment, one should not spend the entire day eating and drinking. Everyone must rise early to *batei knesset* and to *batei midrash*, where they learn and read Yom Tov portions in the Torah, and then return home to eat. They then return to *batei midrash* and learn until midday. After midday, they recite Minḥa and return home to eat and drink until nightfall.[13]

The proper celebration of a festival entails physical enjoyment, fulfilled through eating and drinking, and spiritual enjoyment, fulfilled through prayer and learning Torah. That learning, the Gemara suggests, should relate specifically to the day, thereby elevating one's spiritual connection to the festival.

THE PROHIBITIONS OF *ḤAMETZ*

Careful study of the laws of *ḥametz* reveals that they are both quantitatively and qualitatively more severe than the prohibitions against other forbidden foods. For example, in the *Mishneh Torah*, Rambam enumerates the various mitzvot and prohibitions relevant to Pesaḥ. Aside from the sixteen mitzvot associated with the *Korban Pesaḥ*,[14] he lists another six commandments that relate to *ḥametz*. He writes that it is biblically prohibited to eat *ḥametz* from midday of the fourteenth of Nissan (Deut. 16:3), as well as for all seven days of Pesaḥ (Ex. 13:3). He cites a separate prohibition of eating a mixture (*taarovet*) containing *ḥametz* for all seven days of Pesaḥ (Ex. 12:20).[15] He also cites the prohibition of "seeing" *ḥametz* in one's possession during the seven days of Pesaḥ (Ex. 13:7), and of having *ḥametz* "found" in one's possession during the seven days of Pesaḥ (Ex. 12:19). Rambam also lists a related positive commandment: the obligation to dispose of (*tashbitu*) leaven (*seior*) on the fourteenth of Nissan.

In addition, the Talmud teaches that it is prohibited to derive benefit from *ḥametz* (*issur hanaa*) (Pesaḥim 21b).[16] Finally, unlike other forbidden foods, the punishment incurred for eating *ḥametz* is *karet*. As Rambam rules,

> Anyone who intentionally eats a *kezayit* (olive-sized portion) of *ḥametz* on Pesaḥ from the beginning of the night of the fifteenth [of Nissan] until the conclusion of the day of the twenty-first [of Nissan] is liable for *karet*, as the Torah states, "Whoever eats leaven ... will have his soul cut off."[17]

Thus, a uniquely stringent picture of the prohibition of *ḥametz* emerges. Apparently, in contrast to other prohibited foods, the Torah demands that one should separate completely from and sever all ties to one's *ḥametz*. *Ḥametz* is portrayed as an "evil" entity, which one may not eat even in small quantities or in a mixture, nor derive benefit from, nor maintain any legal relationship with. One must search for it and destroy it.

What is so evil about *ḥametz*? This question has occupied Jewish thinkers for two thousand years. Interestingly, the prohibition of *ḥametz* is not limited to Pesaḥ. The Torah also forbids bringing *ḥametz* with one's *korbanot*:

> No meal offering that you offer to the Lord shall be with leaven (*ḥametz*), for you shall burn no leaven (*seior*) or honey in any fire offering to the Lord. (Lev. 2:11)

> And that which is left thereof shall Aharon and his sons eat; it shall be eaten without leaven in a holy place; in the court of the tent of meeting they shall eat it. It shall not be baked with leaven. I have given it as their portion of My offerings made by fire; it is most holy, as the sin-offering and as the guilt-offering. (Lev. 6:9–10)

The *Sefer HaḤinukh* seems to distinguish between these two prohibitions. Regarding *ḥametz* on Pesaḥ, the *Ḥinukh* insists that all of the mitzvot of Pesaḥ, including the obligation to eat *matza* and the prohibitions of *ḥametz*, serve to remind us of the hasty manner in which we left Egypt:

> In order that we remember forever the miracles that were done for us at the time of the Exodus, as well as what happened to us. Due to the rushed departure, we baked the dough into *matza* because we could not wait for it to rise.[18]

Regarding the prohibition of bringing *seior* and *ḥametz* as a *korban*, however, the *Ḥinukh* explains that the rejection of *ḥimutz* (leavening), which occurs due to a delay in the process of making the dough, emphasizes the centrality of "*zerizut*," alacrity and enthusiastic diligence in the service of God. The *mizbe'aḥ* (altar) cannot tolerate anything that symbolizes sluggishness and laziness.[19]

Others, however, connect the two prohibitions and suggest overarching reasons for the rejection of *ḥametz*. Some, for example, view *ḥametz* as a symbol of idolatry (*avoda zara*), one of the most severe sins of the Torah. Indeed, R. Menachem Kasher (1895–1983) observes that the details of the prohibition of *ḥametz* resemble the laws of *avoda zara* in at least six ways.[20] What is the meaning of this similarity? Rambam points to a historical connection between *ḥametz* and ancient pagan worship:

> Due to the fact that the idolaters would sacrifice only leavened bread and they would offer up all manner of sweet food and would smear their animal sacrifices with honey… therefore, God warned us not to offer to Him any of these things, leaven or honey.[21]

The Jewish people thus confirm their absolute rejection of pagan worship as they commemorate leaving Egypt and becoming a nation by not eating, owning, or benefiting from *ḥametz*, and even destroying it.

Alternatively, the Zohar hints to a spiritual connection: "Whoever eats *ḥametz* on Pesaḥ is as if he prayed to an idol."[22] Similarly, the Talmud compares *seior,* a leavening agent such as sourdough or yeast, to the *yetzer hara,* the evil inclination.

> R. Alexandri would end his daily prayers with the following supplication: Master of the Universe, You know full well that it is our desire to act according to Your will. But what prevents us from doing so? The yeast in the dough (*seior shebe'issa*). (Berakhot 17a)

Seior, which causes a mixture of flour and water to rise, is viewed as a metaphor for the evil inclination, which rises within us. Along these lines, the *Sefer HaḤinukh* offers a second reason why the Torah prohibits bringing *seior* as a *korban*:

> And I heard another reason behind the prohibition of *seior* and honey. Since *seior* causes [the dough] to rise…therefore, we should distance ourselves from it, alluding to [the verse], "Every haughty person is an abomination to the Lord."[23]

R. David b. Solomon Zimra discusses the many stringencies of *ḥametz*. After attempting to attribute these stringencies to the similarity between *ḥametz* and idolatry, he writes:

> Therefore, I rely upon that which the Rabbis taught that *ḥametz* symbolizes the evil inclination, the "*seior shebe'issa*." Therefore, a person should utterly banish it from his midst and search for it in all of the inner chambers of his consciousness, as even the smallest amount is not nullified. And this is true and correct.[24]

What is the relevance of the evil inclination, as represented by *ḥametz,* to Pesaḥ, the festival that commemorates our redemption from the bonds of Egyptian slavery? We might suggest that upon attaining freedom from the physical slavery of Egypt, we reject the "fleshpots of Egypt" (Ex. 16:3), the emphasis on physicality, and instead embrace, as servants of the Lord, a life of simplicity. Our lives are now "theocentric"; God is at the center, and not our own will and desires. We eat, therefore, not *ḥametz,* but *matza,* "*leḥem oni,*" the simple, poor-man's bread.

The Torah does not prohibit *ḥametz* during the entire year; only in the presence of God at the altar, or as we commemorate our freedom, do we shun all traces of *ḥametz*. Without the *yetzer hara,* man would not build, procreate, or develop. Indeed, on Shavuot, when we commemorate the spiritual event of the giving of the Torah, we are commanded to offer the *shetei haleḥem,* two loaves of leavened bread (Ex. 23:17). The Torah is intended to be fulfilled in this world, entailing a lifelong personal and national struggle. We are to incorporate our "self," including our desires and aspirations, into the fulfillment of the Torah. On Pesaḥ we commemorate freedom from the evil inclination and our ability to worship God; on Shavuot we commemorate the giving of the Torah and the challenge of its fulfillment.

CHAPTER 42

The Definition of *Ḥametz*

IN ORDER TO determine whether an item may be eaten or possessed on Pesaḥ, we must first determine its halakhic status. In this chapter, we will study the definition of *ḥametz* and discuss different types of *ḥametz,* including flour mixed with fruit juices, *ḥametz nukshe,* a mixture containing *ḥametz* which is no longer fit for canine consumption, and the custom of refraining from eating "*gebrukts*."

DEFINITION OF *ḤAMETZ*

The Torah prohibits two forms of leaven, *ḥametz* and *seior,* both of which are created by mixing flour and water. *Ḥimutz* (leavening) occurs when a mixture of flour and water is left alone and the fermentation process begins. While a mixture of flour and water alone will eventually ferment and become *ḥametz,* yeast is often added to a mixture in order to hasten and increase the fermentation. *Seior,* a yeast or sourdough mixture, is *ḥametz* that is left to become sour and inedible. It contains a concentrated mixture of yeast and bacteria that can be used to leaven bread. In short, while *ḥametz* is intended to be eaten, *seior* is used for the preparation of leavened products.

The Gemara teaches that just as one can only fulfill the mitzva of eating *matza* with *matza* made of one of the five grains (wheat, spelt, barley, oats, or rye), only products made from these grains can become *ḥametz.* When these five grains come into contact with water, they may potentially become *ḥametz* even without the aid of a leavening agent such as yeast. Other substances, even those that can be used to create dough and bread, such as rice, beans, lentils, and other legumes, cannot become *ḥametz.*

At what point does this mixture of grain and water become *ḥametz*? This question is dealt with in two passages in the third chapter of Pesaḥim that discuss the definition of "*ḥimutz*" (leavening). One passage presents the physical characteristics of *ḥametz* (Pesaḥim 48b). The Mishna describes the leavening process: First, the dough becomes pale, similar to the appearance of a man whose hair stands on end out of fright. Next, cracks begin to develop on the dough's surface, described by the Mishna as "*karnei ḥagavim*" (locusts' antennae). The cracks then begin to grow and merge into each other.

The Rabbis distinguish between two types of dough, *seior* (not to be confused with *seor,* sourdough) *sourdough* and *sidduk* (*ḥametz*). Although both must be burned, one who eats *seior* is "not culpable," while one who eats *ḥametz* is "liable to *karet.*" They disagree, however, as to when dough is considered to be *seior,* and when it is considered to be *ḥametz.*

> What is *seior*? [When there are lines on the surface] like locusts' antennae. *Sidduk* is when the cracks have intermingled with each other; this is the view of R. Yehuda. But the sages maintain: Regarding both, one who eats [the mixture] incurs *karet.* And what is *seior*? When its surface has turned white, like [the face of] a man whose hair is standing on end [from fright].

R. Yehuda maintains that at the first stage, when the dough becomes pale, the dough is permitted *mideoraita* and is considered to be *matza*. When cracks begin to develop on the dough's surface, it is called *seior* and must be destroyed, although one who eats it does not incur *karet*. Only when the dough develops cracks that have spread and intermingled is the mixture considered to be *ḥametz*. The sages, as well as R. Meir, disagree.[1] They identify the first stage, when the dough is pale, as *seior*, which they claim is biblically prohibited, although one does not incur *karet* for eating it. The second and third stages are considered to be full *ḥametz*, punishable by *karet*.

The *Rishonim* and the *Shulḥan Arukh* rule in accordance with the sages and R. Meir regarding the definition of *ḥimutz*.[2] Therefore, one may not eat dough that becomes white and pale. Furthermore, eating it after it has developed cracks like a "locust's antennae" is forbidden and punishable by *karet*.

Another passage presents a different definition of *ḥametz* (Pesaḥim 48b). The Mishna discusses dough that does not display the common external signs of leavening:

> [Regarding] "deaf" dough (*batzek haḥeresh*) – if there is [a dough] similar to it which has become leaven, it is forbidden.

Even though this dough does not display signs of leavening, if dough which was kneaded at the same time became *ḥametz*, then this dough is also considered to be *ḥametz*. The Gemara continues to discuss this "deaf" dough:

> What if there is no [dough] similar to it? R. Abbahu said in the name of R. Shimon b. Lakish: [The period for fermentation is] as long as it takes a man to walk from the Migdal Nunia [Fish Tower] to Tiberias, which is a *mil*. Then let him say a *mil*? He informs us [in this manner] that the standard of a *mil* is as that from Migdal Nunia to Tiberias.

If the mixture remains for a period of a "*mil*" – that is, the time it takes to walk the distance of a *mil* (approximately a kilometer) – then we consider the dough to be *ḥametz* even without external indications. This period is generally understood to be approximately eighteen minutes long.[3]

This passage implies that not only physical characteristics determine whether dough is considered to be *ḥametz*; time may also be a criterion. The *Rishonim* dispute how to understand this mishna, as they discuss the the relationship between the physical indications of leavening and the time period of eighteen minutes.

Some *Rishonim* insist that this passage refers to a specific case, in which we suspect that the dough may have indeed leavened despite lack of physical indications. For example, Rashi[4] and Me'iri[5] explain that this "deaf" dough has changed slightly in appearance, but has not developed the classic signs of leavening. Rashi explains, "It is different, like a deaf person who has ears, but one cannot discern whether or not he hears." He adds that some explain that the dough is "hard as a rock" (*batzek haḥeres*), although it has not yet developed the cracks characteristic of leavening. In other words, had its appearance been normal, we would not have been concerned at all that it had leavened. However, since this dough looks different, although the classic signs of *ḥametz* have not developed, the Gemara teaches that after the time of a "*mil*" has passed, the dough should be considered *ḥametz*. According to Rashi and Me'iri, time itself is not an indication of leavening; we take the time lapsed into account only when a doubt regarding the dough arises.

Similarly, Raavad claims that while dough that has leavened produces a very distinct sound when it is hit, *batzek haḥeresh* produces a lower sound. This sound may be indicative of leavening, but we do not consider this dough to be *ḥametz* until dough kneaded at the same time has leavened or until the time of a *mil* has elapsed. Raavad, like Rashi and Me'iri, does not believe that time alone determines *ḥimutz* unless the dough itself shows ambiguous signs of leavening.

Other *Rishonim* disagree, and maintain that time alone is a criterion in determining whether dough has leavened. Rambam, for example, writes: "*Batzek haḥeresh* refers to a case in which one hits [the dough] with one's hand and it does not produce an 'echo sound,' as if it were deaf and does not respond after being called."[6] He understands that the Mishna refers to dough that displays no physical signs of leavening, but would still be considered *ḥametz* if dough kneaded at the same time has already leavened or if the time it takes to walk a *mil* has passed:

> As long as one is actively kneading the dough, even for the entire day, the dough does not become *ḥametz*. If, however, he stopped working the dough and let it be, and it reached a stage at which it will produce a sound if one hit it, it has become *ḥametz* and should be burned immediately. If, however, it does not produce a sound, if it has been left for the time it takes to walk a *mil*, it has leavened and should be burned immediately.[7]

Thus, according to Rambam, not only physical characteristics determine whether dough has become *ḥametz*; if a *mil* has elapsed, then the dough is considered to be *ḥametz* even without displaying any signs of leavening. Ritva offers a different interpretation of "*batzek haḥeresh*," but he agrees that dough that has been left for the time it takes to walk a *mil* is considered *ḥametz*, regardless of other indications (Pesaḥim 46a).

Until now, we discussed the physical characteristics of *ḥametz* and whether leaving dough for a period of time necessarily leads to *ḥimutz*. The *Rishonim* disagree regarding another aspect of the leavening process as well. The Gemara teaches, "As long as they are engaged [in working] on the dough, it does not come to fermentation" (Pesaḥim 48b). This passage implies that as long as the dough is kneaded or worked, *ḥimutz* cannot occur.

Rambam, as cited above, rules that as long as one works the dough, even for an entire day, the dough does not become *ḥametz*; some *Rishonim* understand that according to Rambam, one may even choose to knead the dough for longer than the time it takes to walk a *mil*.[8] Ritva agrees that as long as the dough is worked, it does not become *ḥametz*, but he states that one should preferably not work the dough for longer than the amount of time it takes to walk a *mil*.[9]

Other *Rishonim* disagree. R. Yehoshua Boaz b. Shimon Baruch (*Shiltei Gibborim*; d. 1557), for example, in his comments published on Rif,[10] cites R. Yishaya Di Trani (Riaz; d. 1280). Riaz, citing the Talmud Yerushalmi, writes that dough certainly becomes *ḥametz* after four *mil* (approximately seventy-two minutes), even if one continues to knead it. *Shibbolei HaLeket* also cites this view.[11]

Other *Rishonim* raise additional concerns related to the *ḥimutz* of this dough. Rosh, for example, writes that after the dough has already been worked, even if it is left for a short time, it may become *ḥametz* immediately.[12] In addition, *Terumat HaDeshen* discusses whether interruptions in the kneading process combine to reach the *shiur* of a *mil*, at which point the dough would be prohibited. He concludes that if one thoroughly works the dough, the eighteen-minute count begins anew with each interruption. Merely poking holes in the *matzot*, however, does not stall the process of *ḥimutz*.[13]

How do we rule regarding these questions? The *Shulḥan Arukh* writes:

> One should not leave dough without it being worked, even for a moment. As long as one is working the dough, even for the entire day, it does not become *ḥametz*. If one left the dough without working it for a *mil*, then it becomes *ḥametz*. The period of a *mil* is eighteen minutes.[14]

Rema adds:

> One should be stringent regarding the making of *matzot*, as one should be concerned that even brief interruptions [in working the dough] will combine to the time of a *mil* or that it will be in a warm place that hastens the leavening process.

The *Shulḥan Arukh* continues:

> After one is finished working the dough and it has warmed up in one's hands, if one does not continue working the dough, it will become *ḥametz* immediately…
>
> If it ferments until there are [visible] cracks, even if the cracks have not intersected, but rather one goes in one direction and another in another direction, it is considered to be *ḥametz* and one who eats it incurs the punishment of *karet*. However, if there are no cracks, but the dough becomes whitish…one who eats it is exempt.

The *Shulḥan Arukh* rules in accordance with the sages regarding the physical characteristics of *ḥametz*[15] and in accordance with the position of Rambam, who rules that even without the physical signs of leavening, dough that was left for more than eighteen minutes is considered *ḥametz*. He similarly rules like Rambam in permitting one to work the dough for the entire day, although the concerns of *Terumat HaDeshen* and Rosh are also recorded.

ḤAMETZ NUKSHE

In addition to the physical characteristics that indicate that a mixture is *ḥametz* and the quantity of time at which point the dough is assumed to have become *ḥametz*, the Rabbis were also concerned with the quality of the mixture. Dough that did not completely leaven or which never became fit for consumption may not acquire the same status as fully leavened dough. The Gemara refers to such substances as "*ḥametz nukshe*." We find two examples of *ḥametz nukshe* in the Talmud, although the relationship between these two types is subject to question.

As discussed above, the Mishna teaches that certain types of mixtures that appear in the course of the *ḥimutz* process are prohibited. According to R. Meir, once the dough's surface has become a pale white, it is rendered "*seior*"; the sages, who accept this opinion, refer to it as "*ḥametz nukshe*." One who eats this dough violates a biblical prohibition and receives *malkot*, but he does not incur the punishment of *karet*. R. Yehuda, however, maintains that dough that becomes pale is prohibited only *miderabbanan*; dough that develops early signs of *ḥimutz*, such as cracks that appear like locusts' antennae, is "*seior*" and prohibited, although one does not receive *karet* for eating it.[16] According to either opinion, it seems that "*seior*" is equivalent to "*ḥametz nukshe*" and refers to a mixture in which the process of *ḥimutz* was not completed.

Elsewhere, however, the Gemara seems to provide a different definition of *ḥametz nukshe* (Pesaḥim 43a). After listing a number of forbidden *ḥametz* mixtures (*taarovet ḥametz*), the Mishna notes examples of inedible substances that are similarly forbidden:

> The following [things] must be removed on Pesaḥ: Babylonian kutach, Median beer, Idumean vinegar, Egyptian zithom, the dyer's broth, cook's dough, and the scribes' paste. R. Eliezer said: Women's ornaments, too. This is the general rule: Whatever is of the species of grain must be removed on

> Pesaḥ. These are subject to a warning [i.e., biblically prohibited], but they do not incur *karet*. (Pesaḥim 42a)

The Gemara identifies the last three examples in the Mishna – dyer's broth, cook's dough, and scribes' paste – as "*ḥametz nukshe*." What is the common denominator between the two types of *ḥametz nukshe* – *seior* (in which *ḥimutz* is incomplete) and inedible *ḥametz* mixtures?

Rashi implies that *seior* is prohibited, like the examples in the Mishna, because it is not fit for consumption.[17] According to Rashi, both types of *ḥametz nukshe* are similar in that they are not edible. Others suggest the opposite reasoning: both *seior* and the other substances have not completed the process of leavening, which is why they are unfit for human consumption.[18] Most *Rishonim*, however, apparently understood that there are two types of *ḥametz nukshe*: substances that have not completely leavened and those that are not fit for human consumption. Neither is considered to be *ḥametz gamur*.[19]

While some *Rishonim* rule that *ḥametz nukshe* is prohibited *mideoraita*, in accordance with R. Meir's opinion,[20] most *Rishonim* rule in accordance with the view of R. Yehuda, who views *ḥametz nukshe* as a rabbinic prohibition. The *Shulḥan Arukh* rules that *ḥametz nukshe* is prohibited to eat *miderabbanan*,[21] and *Magen Avraham*[22] and *Mishna Berura*[23] conclude that one should dispose of *ḥametz nukshe* before Pesaḥ.

INEDIBLE *ḤAMETZ* AND *ḤAMETZ* NOT FIT FOR DOGS (*NIFSAL MEAKHILAT KELEV*)

As we saw above, *ḥametz nukshe*, which never fully leavened or which was never fit for human consumption, is prohibited *miderabbanan*; one may not eat it or even keep it in one's possession for the duration of Pesaḥ. However, *ḥametz* that was edible before Pesaḥ must be burned, even if it spoiled and became inedible. The Gemara teaches:

> If a loaf went moldy, he must destroy it, because it is fit to crumble and leaven many other doughs with it.... Our Rabbis taught: If a loaf went moldy and it became unfit for human consumption, yet a dog can eat it, it can be defiled

> with the uncleanness of eatables, if the size of an egg, and it may be burned together with an unclean [loaf] on Pesaḥ. (Pesaḥim 45b)

As long as *ḥametz* is still fit for canine consumption, it must be destroyed, even if it is unfit for human consumption.

Elsewhere, the Gemara rules that if *ḥametz* is severely burnt before Pesaḥ, it is permitted on Pesaḥ: "Rava said: If he charred it [in the fire] before its time, benefit [thereof] is permitted even after its time" (Pesaḥim 21b). Tosafot,[24] along with most *Rishonim,* assume that this gemara refers to *ḥametz* that has been so severely burnt that it is no longer fit even for canine consumption, and therefore need not be destroyed.

The *Rishonim* disagree as to whether this burnt *ḥametz* may be eaten or only owned. Ritva notes that the Gemara only mentions *hanaa* (deriving benefit) and not eating because it is not normal for a person to eat burnt bread;[25] it is in fact permitted, however, to eat such *ḥametz.* Ran explains that "one may even eat this, as it lost its status of bread before the prohibition of *ḥametz* could take hold."[26] Rosh, however, disagrees:

> Some wish to say that not only *hanaa* is permitted, but eating as well, as it is akin to dirt. But this does not seem correct, even though this person's intention [to eat the burnt *ḥametz*] is nullified in contrast to the intention of most people; still, since he eats it, it is prohibited.[27]

Taz explains that Rosh prohibits eating this spoiled *ḥametz,* from which one is permitted to derive benefit, based on the principle of "*aḥshevei*"; by deliberately eating this *ḥametz,* one has elevated its status, and, *miderabbanan,* rendered it fit for consumption.[28] *Taz* and *Mishna Berura*[29] assume that the *Shulkhan Arukh* agrees with Rosh. We will discuss the practical ramifications of these principles as they apply to medicines and cosmetics in chapter 44.

CHAPTER 43

Ḥametz Mixtures

In the previous chapter, we discussed the definition of *ḥametz,* its physical characteristics, and the status of dough that has not fully leavened or that is inedible. In this chapter, we will discuss the status of a mixture containing *ḥametz,* whether one should be concerned with the kashrut of eggs and milk on Pesaḥ, and the custom of refraining from eating *gebrukts.* The unique stringencies regarding *ḥametz,* as expressed in the laws of mixtures, further emphasize the necessity of completely separating oneself from all leavened products on Pesaḥ.

TAAROVET ḤAMETZ: ISSUR MASHEHU

In general, when a forbidden substance is mixed together with a permitted substance in a manner in which the two dissimilar items completely combine (*laḥ belaḥ*), the mixture is prohibited unless the forbidden substance is nullified by a 1/60 ratio, known as *bittul beshishim* (Ḥullin 97b).

Regarding *ḥametz,* however, the Gemara cites Rav, who teaches that when *ḥametz* is combined with a permitted substance on Pesaḥ, the entire mixture is forbidden, regardless of the amount of *ḥametz*:

> Rav said: *Ḥametz,* in its time [during Pesaḥ], whether [mixed] with its own kind or with a different kind, is forbidden; when not in its time, [if mixed] with its own kind, it is forbidden; [if with] a different kind, it is permitted.... This refers to a minute quantity [of *ḥametz*]. (Pesaḥim 29b)

The *Rishonim* question why the laws of *ḥametz,* according to Rav, are so much stricter than those of ordinary mixtures, to the degree that a mixture of dissimilar substances, which is usually *batel beshishim,* is not *batel* at all in the case of *ḥametz.* Rashi suggests that the sages added this extra stringency to *ḥametz* and not to other prohibited substances that are punishable by *karet,* such as *ḥeilev* (prohibited fats) and *dam* (blood), because in those cases, "one is accustomed to separate oneself from them. *Ḥametz,* however, one is not accustomed to separate oneself from, as one eats it throughout the year."[1]

Rambam offers a different reason, arguing that *ḥametz* is not subject to nullification (*bittul*) because it is a "*davar sheyesh lo matirin,*" a prohibited item that will eventually become permitted. The Talmud teaches that a non-kosher item that will become permitted after time, such as "*ḥadash*" (the new wheat that is prohibited until after the first day of Pesaḥ), cannot be nullified in a mixture (Beitza 3b). Some explain that this is because one should not rely upon *bittul* if he can simply wait until the item will be permitted. Therefore, in our case, since one could simply wait until after Pesaḥ is over in order to eat the *ḥametz,* there is no justification for relying upon *bittul.*[2]

The *Aḥaronim* suggest a number of practical differences between Rashi, who attributes this stringency to the severity of the prohibition of *ḥametz,* and Rambam, who defines *ḥametz* as a *davar sheyesh lo matirin.* For example, *ḥametz* is biblically prohibited on Erev Pesaḥ from noon until nightfall, although the punishment of *karet* is not incurred. The *Shulḥan Arukh* rules that if *ḥametz* is mixed into a mixture on Erev Pesaḥ, even after the sixth hour, the *ḥametz* is still *batel beshishim.*[3] The *Mishna Berura* explains that since the prohibition on Erev Pesaḥ is less severe than the prohibition of *ḥametz* during Pesaḥ, it can be nullified before Pesaḥ.[4] This leniency should apparently only apply according to Rashi's rationale; if *ḥametz* cannot be nullified due to the temporary nature of the prohibition, as Rambam argues, then this should apply on Erev Pesaḥ as well.

Similarly, the *Arukh HaShulḥan* suggests that *ḥametz nukshe* should be *batel beshishim,* as one who eats it does not incur *karet.* Since the prohibition of *ḥametz nukshe* is less severe, as we discussed in the previous chapter, *Ḥazal* did not apply the prohibition of mixtures to it, as per Rashi's suggestion. The *Arukh HaShulḥan* offers other differences between the two opinions as well.[5]

Interestingly, *She'iltot*[6] and Rabbeinu Tam[7] disagree with the opinions cited above and assert that *ḥametz* is actually *batel beshishim* even during Pesaḥ. Tosafot report, however, that Rabbeinu Tam did not actually accept this opinion in practice. The *Shulḥan Arukh* rules that *ḥametz* is not *batel* if it is mixed with permitted substances during Pesaḥ.[8]

Is it also prohibited to derive benefit from a mixture that contains a minute amount of *ḥametz*? Some *Rishonim* rule that one may derive benefit from such a mixture; *Ḥazal* only prohibited eating it.[9] Most *Rishonim,* however, disagree, and forbid deriving benefit from this mixture as well. The *Shulḥan Arukh* rules accordingly.[10]

What types of mixture are subject to this stringency? The *Rishonim* disagree as to whether this stringency also applies to a mixture of dry substances (*yavesh beyavesh*). For example, if a piece of *ḥametz* became mixed in with pieces of *matza* and cannot be discerned, what is the status of the mixture? Generally, a substance of *issur* in a *yavesh beyavesh* mixture is *batel berov,* nullified when mixed with a majority of kosher food. Rif implies that the stringency regarding *ḥametz* applies to dry mixtures as well; even a *mashehu,* a minute amount, of *ḥametz* in a dry mixture is not *batel.*[11] Rosh, however, limits the stringency to wet mixtures.[12] The *Shulḥan Arukh* cites both opinions regarding this question,[13] and the *Mishna Berura* concludes that the consensus of the *Aḥaronim* is to accept the first, more stringent view.[14]

As a result of this special stringency related to *ḥametz* mixtures, *Beit Yosef* cites earlier authorities who caution against drinking water from wells during Pesaḥ, especially from wells shared with non-Jews, lest there be pieces of *ḥametz* in the well. He writes that one should carefully filter out grains of wheat with a cloth, as the *ḥametz* is not nullified by the majority of water.[15] The *Mishna Berura* writes that while one may be lenient regarding grains of wheat, if bread fell into a pit of water, the entire pit is prohibited.[16]

In a similar vein, in recent years, *posekim* have questioned whether the water that comes from the Kinneret should be prohibited, lest pieces of bread cast into the Kinneret during Pesaḥ prohibit the entire lake. R. Asher Weiss cites numerous opinions that maintain that one need not be concerned with *ḥametz* that falls into a river, as opposed to a contained body of water. After discussing the relevant views of the

Aḥaronim, he notes that according to Mekorot (Israel's National Water Company), all water that is brought from the Kinneret is first exposed to a pool of fish, which consume organic material, then to a chemical process that breaks down organic material, and finally to chlorination, which kills bacteria and purifies the water. He concludes:

> In my humble opinion, the real answer to this question lies in a powerful rationale, which states that a river cannot be prohibited by a *mashehu* [of *ḥametz*]. Because if so, the entire ocean could be prohibited by a crumb of bread that fell in, and all of the world's water would be prohibited! And this is simply unacceptable, and logic does not tolerate this.[17]

The popular work *Piskei Teshuvot* also discusses this issue and cites five reasons to be lenient.[18]

ḤOZER VENEOR AND *NOTEN TAAM LIFGAM*

As we learned above, *ḥametz,* even in the smallest amount, prohibits an entire mixture. Not only do the normal laws of *bittul* not apply to *ḥametz,* but leniencies applied to other mixtures are similarly not applied to *ḥametz* according to some *Rishonim*. For example, as we learned above, if *ḥametz* is mixed with other substances before Pesaḥ, it can be *batel beshishim*. Rambam writes that although the *ḥametz* was *batel* before Pesaḥ and one may therefore own it during Pesaḥ, the mixture should not be eaten during Pesaḥ.[19] Rambam and other *Rishonim* maintain that the *ḥametz* is "*ḥozer veneor*" (literally, "wakes up again") during Pesaḥ and should therefore not be consumed. Rosh, however, disagrees.[20]

The *Shulḥan Arukh* cites both opinions.[21] Rema rules, in accordance with *Terumat HaDeshen,*[22] that while one may be lenient regarding wet mixtures, one should accept the strict opinion regarding dry mixtures.[23] Apparently, while *issur* mixed into a wet mixture "disappears" entirely, in a dry mixture, it is still present, only indistinguishable.

Due to the severity of the prohibition of *ḥametz* and the stringencies associated with mixtures of *ḥametz,* some have the custom to buy only products produced before Pesaḥ, when *ḥametz* is *batel*. Similarly, *matzot* are made before Pesaḥ so that one can rely upon the nullifcation of *ḥametz* in one's *matzot* if necessary. Some are even accustomed to purchase "eighteen-minute *matzot*." During the production of these *matzot*, the machines are stopped and cleaned every eighteen minutes to ensure that no dough that was caught in the machines is mixed into the *matzot*, even though any *ḥametz* would still be *batel beshishim*.

The *Rishonim* further discuss the applicability of the principle of "*noten taam lifgam*" to *ḥametz* mixtures. The Gemara states that if an *issur* has a detrimental impact on permitted food, "*noten taam lifgam*," the mixture is permitted. The Gemara presents two applications of this principle. The first involves actually mixing a non-kosher element into kosher food, which causes a detrimental effect upon the mixture. The second, which is more common and relevant, involves cooking in non-kosher pots that have not been used for non-kosher food for at least twenty-four hours (*eino ben yomo*). The Torah relates that after the conquest of Midian, Elazar HaKohen commanded the people to "*kasher*" any cooking utensils taken from the spoils (Num. 31:21–23), and the Gemara explains that the Torah is concerned with "*giulei nokhrim*," the taste of non-kosher food emitted from the cooking utensils. This concern only applies, however, to taste emitted from utensils within a day after they were used (*ben yomo*). After that day (*eino ben yomo*), the taste emitted from these utensils is regarded as *noten taam lifgam*, imparting detrimental taste, and the food is permitted. Therefore, *mideoraita*, utensils that have not been in contact with the *taam* of *issur* for a full day may be used.

The Gemara rules, however, that it is rabbinically prohibited to use a non-kosher utensil even after a day has passed, lest one come to cook in a vessel that is *ben yomo*. Thus, a *keli she'eino ben yomo* is still prohibited *miderabbanan*. *Bediavad*, however, if food is accidentally cooked in an *eino ben yomo* non-kosher pot, the food is permitted (Avoda Zara 65–8).

The *Rishonim* debate whether this leniency applies to *ḥametz* as well. Tosafot,[24] Rosh,[25] and the *Mordekhai*[26] rule that *noten taam lifgam* applies to all prohibited substances, including an *issur mashehu*, such as *ḥametz*. *Yerei'im*[27] and Rashba,[28] however, disagree, insisting that a small amount of *ḥametz* always prohibits the mixture, even if it is *noten taam lifgam*.

The *Shulḥan Arukh* adopts the lenient view,[29] while Rema records that it is customary to be strict.[30] Thus, if one accidentally cooks food on Pesaḥ in an *eino ben yomo* pot that was used for *ḥametz* before Pesaḥ, the *Shulḥan Arukh* would permit the food and Rema would prohibit it. Interestingly, the *Arukh HaShulḥan* asserts that the halakha is really in accordance with the more lenient view; therefore, one who rules leniently for the poor has not "lost out."[31] He also cites the *Ḥakham Tzvi,* who permits the food if the pot has not been used for at least twelve months.[32]

OWNING A *ḤAMETZ* MIXTURE

May one keep a *ḥametz* mixture in his possession during Pesaḥ? The Mishna teaches:

> *Eilu overin bePesaḥ* ["With these, one transgresses on Pesaḥ"; alternatively, "These are removed on Pesaḥ"]: Babylonian kutach, Median beer, Edomite vinegar, Egyptian beer, dyer's broth, cook's dough, and scribe's glue. R. Eliezer says: Also women's toiletries. (Pesaḥim 42a)

The first four examples are all mixtures containing *ḥametz,* or *taarovot ḥametz.*

Rabbeinu Tam understands "*ve'eilu overin*" as "these are to be removed." These mixtures must be removed because they cannot be eaten, but one does not violate *bal yeira'e* and *bal yimatzei* for owning a *ḥametz* mixture.[33] Rashi,[34] as well as Rambam,[35] interprets "*ve'eilu overin*" as "with these one transgresses." Thus, one who keeps a *ḥametz* mixture during Pesaḥ violates *bal yeira'e* and *bal yimatzei.*

The *Shulḥan Arukh* rules that one violates *bal yeira'e* and *bal yimatzei* by keeping a mixture containing *ḥametz* over Pesaḥ.[36] The *Mishna Berura*[37] and *Arukh HaShulḥan*[38] assume that the halakha is in accordance with R. Moshe HaKohen, who rules that one violates the prohibitions of owning *ḥametz* even for keeping a mixture that contains less than a *kezayit* of *ḥametz.*

All agree that if the *ḥametz* is *batel beshishim* (nullified by sixty parts of a permissible substance), owning it is prohibited only *miderabbanan*, as eating such a mixture is only rabbinically prohibited. Practically speaking, one must rid himself of all *ḥametz* before Pesaḥ. However, whether one violates *bal yeira'e* and *bal yimatzei* by owning *ḥametz* mixtures on Pesaḥ may affect whether a mixture owned by a Jew during Pesaḥ is prohibited as *ḥametz she'avar alav haPesaḥ*. Furthermore, even those who are hesitant to "sell" their *ḥametz* through the traditional *mekhirat ḥametz* are often more willing to sell mixtures, as one may not violate an *issur deoraita* by owning them.

TAAROVET ḤAMETZ UNFIT FOR CONSUMPTION

May one possess a mixture of *ḥametz* that is not fit for human consumption? The Tosefta writes, "Similarly, an eye salve, a compress, and a plaster into which *ḥametz* was placed do not need to be destroyed."[39] These mixtures, apparently made from *ḥametz* and other ingredients, may be kept on Pesaḥ.

Some *Rishonim*[40] understand this Tosefta as referring to substances that become unfit for canine consumption and are therefore permitted on Pesaḥ. Rambam, however, disagrees:

> However, a substance which contains a mixture of *ḥametz* but is not fit to be eaten may be kept on Pesaḥ. A substance which is not eaten by people or one which is generally not eaten by people, with which *ḥametz* has become mixed – for example, Tiriac and the like – although one may keep it [during Pesaḥ], eating it is prohibited until after Pesaḥ. Even though it contains only the smallest amount of *ḥametz*, eating it is forbidden.[41]

Rambam explains that a mixture containing *ḥametz* that becomes unfit for human consumption may be kept during Pesaḥ, although it may not be eaten.

What is the difference between *ḥametz gamur* – regarding which one violates *bal yeira'e* and *bal yimatzei* unless it becomes unfit for canine consumption – and a *taarovet ḥametz*, which one may keep once it becomes unfit for human consumption? R. Chaim Soloveitchik, in his novellae (*ḥiddushim*) on Rambam,[42] distinguishes between *ḥametz* and *taarovet ḥametz*. *Ḥametz* is itself a prohibited substance and, even spoiled, may still cause *ḥimutz* in different dough. Thus, in order to own it on Pesaḥ, it must be spoiled to the point that it is no longer fit even for canine consumption. However, a mixture, which is only prohibited because of the "taste" of *ḥametz* (*taam ke'ikkar*), is no longer forbidden to own once the taste is no longer fit for human consumption.

The *Shulḥan Arukh* rules in accordance with Rambam.[43] Based upon this ruling, it would seem that even one who refrains from using certain medicines and cosmetics on Pesaḥ does not need to sell them to a non-Jew, as they are certainly not fit for human consumption.

MILK AND EGGS ON PESAḤ: *ZEH VAZEH GOREM*

Some meticulous individuals buy, before Pesaḥ, all milk and eggs that they intend on using during Pesaḥ. There are numerous reasons for this custom. Some are concerned that *ḥametz* derivatives that are added to milk (such as vitamin D) may prohibit the milk. Vitamin D that is added before Pesaḥ is *batel beshishim* (nullified), but if it is added during Pesaḥ, the milk may be prohibited. Others are concerned that grains present while the cow is milked may fall into the milk; if they mix into the milk before Pesaḥ, they are certainly *batel*, while if they fall into the milk during Pesaḥ, they may prohibit the entire mixture.

The more interesting concern, however, relates to a halakhic principle called *zeh vazeh gorem*. The Talmud records:

> Has it not been taught: If a field has been manured with the manure derived from an idolatrous source or a cow has been fattened on beans derived from an idolatrous source, one *Tanna* concludes that the field may be sown and the cow slaughtered, while another concludes that the field must lie fallow and the cow grow lean. (Avoda Zara 49a)

The sages debate whether one may benefit from a field, or a cow, nourished by both permitted and prohibited substances.

The *Rishonim* suggest different understandings of this debate. Rashi[44] and Ran,[45] for example, suggest that the lenient opinion views this case as a type of mixture; since more than one source contributed to the nourishment of this object, the prohibited source is *batel*. Others explain that the lenient option maintains that when one can attribute the nourishment of the soil or the cow to *either* prohibited or permitted sources, one may attribute the nourishment to the permitted source (*gorem*), and the object is permitted.[46] The *Shulḥan Arukh* rules in accordance with the lenient opinion: *zeh vazeh gorem mutar*.[47]

The *Aḥaronim*, however, dispute whether this applies on Pesaḥ. Since the laws of mixtures on Pesaḥ are so strict, should we be strict regarding this principle as well? For example, if one bakes or cooks over a fire fueled by regular coals along with charcoal produced from *ḥametz* burned after midday on Erev Pesaḥ, from which one may not derive benefit, would the food be prohibited? *Magen Avraham* insists that in this case of *zeh vazeh gorem,* in which both the regular coals and the burnt *ḥametz* contribute to the baking or cooking of the food, the food would be prohibited.[48] Others, however, disagree.[49] R. Aryeh Leib Heller (1745–1812), in his responsa, *Avnei Miluim,* concludes in accordance with *Magen Avraham* regarding *ḥametz*.[50]

R. Avraham Danzig, in his *Nishmat Adam,* writes that he has heard that some prohibit milk from cows fed *ḥametz* on Pesaḥ based upon *Magen Avraham*'s ruling. R. Danzig concludes, however, that milk from such a cow, even one owned by a Jew, is permitted.[51] *Shaarei Teshuva* also discusses this issue, and concludes that one may certainly drink milk from a cow owned by non-Jews that was fed *ḥametz*.[52] The *Kitzur Shulḥan Arukh,* however, cites two views, and concludes that one should preferably avoid such milk.[53] The *Mishna Berura* also cites both opinions.[54]

In a lengthy responsum, R. Moshe Feinstein rules that milk from a cow fed *ḥametz* on Pesaḥ is permitted. He notes that while it may be appropriate for a "*baal nefesh*" to act stringently regarding milk from a cow owned by Jews, there is no reason at all to be strict if the cow was owned by non-Jews.[55] Accordingly, in the Diaspora, where one may assume that the milk came from cows owned by non-Jews, it would be permitted purchase and drink milk during Pesaḥ.

In Israel, where most cows are owned by Jews, Tnuva (Israel's leading producer of dairy products) requires that the *refatot* (cow sheds) are cleaned of *ḥametz*, and that cows are not fed *ḥametz*, well before Pesaḥ. In addition, milk is filtered shortly after it is taken from the cows, and one therefore need not be concerned that even a bit of *ḥametz* is found in one's milk during Pesaḥ.[56] Despite the unlikelihood of there being any problem in either Israel or the Diaspora, some are still accustomed to buy all of their dairy products before Pesaḥ in order to adhere to the strictest opinions cited above.

This discussion is relevant to eggs laid on Pesaḥ as well. Some are accustomed to buy eggs before Pesaḥ, fearing that they were washed with chicken feed, although R. Feinstein rejects this stringency.[57] Others fear that the stamp on the eggs contains *ḥametz*. The London Beth Din Kashrut Division reports that the ink used on eggs is made from two components, a coloring agent and a solvent. While the coloring agent is purely synthetic and does not present a problem for Passover, the solvents most commonly employed are isopropanol, ethanol, or a combination of both, which may contain *ḥametz*. They explain, however, that "the solvent is of such nature, that within a fraction of a second after applying the stamp, it completely evaporates. A moist stamp would lead to unwanted smudges. It is therefore very safe to assume, that not a trace of solvent remains within a short time of application to the egg." They conclude, "It is not certain if ethanol is used in stamping eggs. Even if ethanol is used, it is not certain that it is wheat derived. Even if wheat-derived ethanol was used, none of it remains after the ink has dried and it no longer constitutes part of the ink."[58]

GEBRUKTS

Some are accustomed to refrain from eating *matza* soaked in water, "*gebrukts*," on Pesaḥ. Interestingly, the Talmud cites R. Yose as ruling that one may fulfill the mitzva of eating *matza* on the first night of Pesaḥ by eating *matza* soaked in water (Pesaḥim 41a), and the *Shulkhan Arukh* rules accordingly.[59] If one can fulfill the obligation through eating soaked *matza*, then surely soaked *matza* should not pose a problem of *ḥametz*!

The source for the practice of avoiding *gebrukts* appears to be R. Shmuel b. R. Yosef's *Olat Shabbat* commentary on the *Shulḥan*

Arukh, published in 1681, where he expresses concern that flour may possibly have been left on the *matzot* and may ferment and become *ḥametz* if it comes into contact with water. Therefore, he writes, one should not cook *matza* during the week of Pesaḥ.[60] R. Avraham Gombiner (1633–1683), *Magen Avraham,* argues on this point and describes the comments of the *Olat Shabbat* as "*temuhim*" (perplexing).[61]

Interestingly, during the same century in Turkey, R. Chaim Benveniste (1602–1673) records in his commentary to the *Shulḥan Arukh,* the *Knesset HaGedola,* that there was a communal enactment against using *matza* meal to replace flour, lest one become confused:

> I heard in my childhood that once the wife of a knowledgeable man was frying fish in oil in a frying pan. It was then customary to cover the fish with flour before frying them in order that they should not stick to the pan. Since on Pesaḥ one cannot do this, his wife took baked *matza* and ground it up finely until it became like flour and then covered the fish. At that moment, a neighbor entered and saw this woman frying fish with that flour, and she thought that it was actual flour. The next day, this neighbor fried fish with actual flour. As this was happening, her husband entered and saw his wife frying fish in actual flour and rebuked her. She responded by relating what he wife of the scholar [her neighbor] did the day before.... He went to ask the neighbor and she related that God forbid [she should fry fish in real flour, but rather] she used *matza* meal. When the scholars of the town heard this, they made an enactment that people should not do this, due to "*marit ayin*" (how it appears) and that is the custom there until this very day.[62]

Over a hundred years later, R. Dov Ber of Mezeritch (1704/1710?–1772), a disciple of Baal Shem Tov known as the Maggid of Mezeritch, adopted this custom. His student, Shneur Zalman of Liadi, the founder of Chabad Hasidism, defends the practice of the *Olat Shabbat* in his *Shulḥan Arukh HaRav,* asserting that "there is a great reason behind this stringency." He writes, however, that one may be lenient on the last day of Yom Tov (in the Diaspora) because of *simḥat Yom Tov.*[63] This stringency is also discussed in depth by the *Shaarei Teshuva.*[64] The *Aḥaronim* discuss whether one who is accustomed not to eat *gebrukts* may change his custom and whether he must first perform *hatarat nedarim.*[65]

CHAPTER 44

Medicines and Cosmetics

THE STATUS OF medicines and cosmetics on Pesaḥ is a source of great confusion and controversy. Many of the questions asked each year regarding *ḥametz* relate to the permissibility of medicines and cosmetics on Pesaḥ, as some medicines and many cosmetics contain actual *ḥametz* or *ḥametz* derivatives. In this chapter, we will discuss whether one may use these products on Pesaḥ.

MEDICINES ON PESAḤ

The *kashrut* of medicines is an issue relevant not only on Pesaḥ, but all year round. Many medicines contain non-kosher ingredients, such as magnesium stearate, calcium stearate, and stearic acid, which may be derived from either animal or vegetable sources. Many liquid medicines contain glycerin, which is often produced from non-kosher animals, and gelatin, which many contemporary authorities view as non-kosher. In addition, many medicines and vitamins contain wheat starch, wheat gluten, malt extract, or other powders that contain starches that are often derived from wheat.

There are actually two questions that we must consider in this context. First, assuming that the medicine is not kosher, is ingesting medicine in pill or capsule form considered "eating"? Second, are medicines that are bitter and inedible prohibited at all? At the outset, we should note that one who suffers from a life-threatening condition must take medicine, no matter what the ingredients are, in order to preserve his life. *Pikuaḥ nefesh* (saving life) sets aside all prohibitions aside from *avoda zara, gilui arayot,* and *shefikhut damim* (idolatry, prohibited sexual relations, and murder). Our discussion is therefore relevant only to one whose life is not in danger.

AKHILA SHELO KEDEREKH AKHILATAN

Medicines in pill form are generally swallowed whole, and not chewed or eaten in a normal manner. Is ingesting non-kosher food in such a manner prohibited? The Talmud teaches:

> R. Abbahu said in R. Yoḥanan's name: [With regard to] all the prohibited articles of the Torah, we do not give lashes on their account except [when they are eaten] in the normal manner of their consumption. (Pesaḥim 24b)

R. Abbahu rules that one only violates the prohibition of eating or benefiting from prohibited substances when used in the "normal way." Based upon this principle, Rambam rules that one who is sick, but does not suffer from a life-threatening illness, may ingest a prohibited substance in a manner that affords him no satisfaction (*shelo kederekh hanaatan*). The *Shulḥan Aruch* rules accordingly.[1]

Thus, we must establish whether swallowing a pill or capsule is considered to be *akhila kederekh hanaatan* or *shelo kederekh hanaatan*. R. Yechezkel Landau, however, in his Responsa *Noda BiYehuda*, disagrees. He cites a talmudic passage that teaches, "Rava said: If he swallows *matza* [without chewing], he discharges his duty" (Pesaḥim 115b). R. Landau claims that if one can fulfill the obligation to eat *matza* through swallowing without chewing, then swallowing must be considered *kederekh hanaatan*. Therefore, swallowing a pill or capsule containing a non-kosher substance would be no different than ingesting that non-kosher substance normally.[2]

R. Shlomo Zalman Auerbach disagrees, however. He suggests that while swallowing food, even without chewing, may be considered "*kederekh akhilatan*," swallowing a pill or capsule, which is not a food item, is not considered to be "*kederekh akhilatan*" and would therefore be permitted for a person who is sick.[3] Most *posekim* agree with the view of R. Auerbach, and therefore someone who is ill may ingest a pill or capsule containing non-kosher ingredients. This reasoning does not apply to someone suffering from a "*meiḥush be'alma*" (slight discomfort).

NIFSAL ME'AKHILAT KELEV: MEDICINES THAT ARE NOT FIT FOR CONSUMPTION

Medicines containing non-kosher ingredients that are not fit for human consumption should be permitted for an additional reason based upon the well-known talmudic principle:

> Because it has been taught: "You shall not eat of anything that dies of itself (*neveila*); you may give it unto the stranger that is within thy gates" [Deut. 14:21] – whatever is fit for use by a stranger is called *neveila,* and whatever is unfit for use by a stranger is not called *neveila*. (Avoda Zara 67–8)

This passage implies that food substances that are not fit for human consumption are not prohibited.

Regarding Pesaḥ, however, we learned above that as long as a loaf is fit for canine consumption, it must be destroyed (Pesaḥim 45b). Once, however, the *ḥametz* is rendered unfit for canine consumption, it is permitted on Pesaḥ (Pesaḥim 21b).[4] As we have seen above, some *Rishonim,* such as Ran, maintain that this burnt *ḥametz* may be owned, or even eaten,[5] although Rosh, as explained by *Taz,* prohibits eating this spoiled *ḥametz,* and thus elevating its status, and, *miderabbanan,* rendering it "fit for consumption."[6]

The *posekim* discuss whether the principle of *aḥshevei,* discussed earlier, applies to medicines. R. Aryeh Leib Gunzberg writes in his *Shaagat Aryeh*:

> It seems to me that foods and drinks that are not fit for consumption are not permitted even for medicinal purposes, as since one eats it, *aḥshevinhu* (one elevates its status), similar to what Rosh wrote... and even though it is not even fit for canine consumption, and it is like the dust of the earth, it is still prohibited.[7]

R. Gunzberg applies the principle of *aḥshevei* to medicines, and therefore prohibits ingesting medicines that are not fit for normal consumption. Almost all modern *posekim,* however, including *Ḥazon Ish,*[8] *Yad Avraham,*[9] R. Moshe Feinstein,[10] R. Ovadia Yosef,[11] and R. Eliezer

Waldenberg,[12] rule that *aḥshevei* does not apply to medicines. Some explain that *aḥshevei* does not apply when one's intent is to attain the medicinal value of the substance. Some (*Ḥazon Ish,* for example) add that *aḥshevei* does not apply to a mixture containing *ḥametz,* but only to a piece of *ḥametz* that has become spoiled.

While the *posekim* cited above assume that pills and capsules are considered unfit for human consumption, R. Shlomo Zalman Auerbach challenges that assumption in a responsum written to R. Chaim Pinchas Scheinberg.[13] He notes that Rambam includes ear wax, nasal mucus, and urine as edible foods![14] Nevertheless, in the original letter, he comments, "I also do not know why many are so strict regarding this issue."[15]

In summary, it seems that the majority of contemporary authorities permit swallowing tasteless pills, even those which may contain *ḥametz,* on Pesaḥ. While some insist that only a *ḥoleh,* someone who is sick, should take this medicine, and not someone who merely suffers from a "*meiḥush,*" such as a headache or another slight discomfort, others rule that one may take pills or capsules to relieve any discomfort.[16]

Many *posekim,* reportedly including R. Moshe Feinstein, distinguish between tasteless pills and capsules, and liquid or chewable medicines that contain *ḥametz.* They argue that the latter forms of medicine, which have a pleasant taste, are prohibited according to all authorities. Others suggest that although liquid medicines and chewable tablets may have taste, they are certainly not considered an edible food item, both because of their taste and because they may be harmful if consumed in large quantities.[17]

Some authorities further distinguish between pills that are medicines and those that are vitamins and food supplements. Taking vitamins and food supplements, they claim, may be considered *kederekh akhilatan,* and *aḥshevei* should therefore apply. R. Herschel Schachter disagrees, however. He sees no distinction between pills taken as medicines and those that are food supplements; since both are inedible, both should be permitted.[18]

Over the past few decades, the kosher consumer has become accustomed to the annual lists that record the medicines that contain *ḥametz* and those that do not. These lists are certainly valuable in determining which liquid or chewable medicines or vitamins are *ḥametz*-free and which are not. Some, however, are careful that all pills and capsules that they ingest are also free of *ḥametz*, despite their apparent permissibility. Indeed, R. Waldenberg writes,

> Although tablets and capsules that contain substances that are not fit for consumption ... one may certainly permit one to swallow them on Pesaḥ for medicinal purposes ... but the Jewish people are holy, and they seek out every way possible to avoid mixtures containing *ḥametz*.[19]

Concern has been raised, however, that some people are unnecessarily stringent, discontinuing usage of their regular medicines during Pesaḥ as a result. Indeed, anyone taking antibiotics, those suffering from high blood pressure, heart disease, diabetes, kidney disorders, seizure disorders, blood clotting disorders, a pregnant woman suffering from toxemia or who is in active labor, and even a person suffering from severe depression must continue taking his or her medicines on Pesaḥ. An elderly person with the flu or an infant with fever must also take medication, regardless of its contents.

Recently, some major Kashrut organizations, such as the Orthodox Union (OU)[20] and the Chicago Rabbinical Council (CRC),[21] have rejected the use of such lists and ruled that all pills that are swallowed may be taken on Pesaḥ. Although pious individuals may wish to be stringent in this matter, it seems that the proper communal ruling should be to permit all medicines that come in tablet or capsule form.

In a similar vein, R. Shmuel Eliezer Stern, a member of the Badatz Ḥug Ḥatam Sofer, writes,

> Fear and reticence have penetrated the hearts of pious Jews, and they carefully investigate the medicines that they intend on using during Pesaḥ, that their names appear on the "redeeming list," so that, God forbid, they don't encounter a stumbling block, as it has become clear to them that this is akin to eating *ḥametz* on Pesaḥ.... As a result of this corrupt outlook, many Jews are endangering their lives, as Jews who fear the word of God and take special precautions regarding *ḥametz* question why they should use [these medicines] ... and they assume that it certainly won't harm them if they stop

> taking their medicines for the week of Pesaḥ.... And the facts on the ground prove that many older, sick people who need consistent medication suffer setbacks in their physical health.... And I know many people who, weeks after Pesaḥ, have still not returned to their former health.... And therefore I feel obligated to publicize ... that those who take medicines for health problems such as high blood pressure, diabetes, illnesses related to the heart, kidney, or other internal organs, and those who suffer from psychological problems, may take their medicines without any fear, regardless of whether they appear on the list. Furthermore, they should not even switch to a similar medicine that appears on the list, as the change may cause complications and medical problems that one may not have anticipated.... Those who act strictly are acting oddly (*min hamatmihim*), and will one day be accountable for their actions.[22]

One may certainly keep such medicines in one's possession during Pesaḥ. As we learned previously, mixtures containing *ḥametz* that are not fit for human consumption may be owned during Pesaḥ.

COSMETICS ON PESAḤ

Cosmetics are another source of great confusion on Pesaḥ. Is it prohibited to use cosmetics that contain *ḥametz*? The cosmetics in question include creams, ointments, salves, powders, sticks, colognes, perfumes, deodorant in liquid/stick/spray/roll-on form, shaving lotions, eye shadow, eye liner, and blush. They also include mouthwash, lipstick, and toothpaste.

As we noted above regarding medicines, the question of the "*kashrut*" of these products applies year-round as well. We will therefore first discuss the broader question of whether one may use non-kosher cosmetics at all. We will then question whether cosmetics should be viewed as *ḥametz*, or whether they have been spoiled and are no longer fit even for canine consumption.

The cosmetic products mentioned above can be used in two ways: orally and topically. Prohibited substances that are still edible may not be eaten, nor may they be placed into one's mouth with the intention of spitting them out.[23] Is it permissible to apply non-kosher substances to one's skin? The Talmud teaches that at times, we view *sikha* (anointing) as akin to *shtiya* (drinking). This is true on Yom Kippur, for example:

> How do we know that anointing is the same as drinking on Yom Kippur? Although there is no proof of this, yet there is a suggestion thereof, for it is said, "And it came into his inward parts like water, and like oil into his bones."[24]

Elsewhere, the Gemara teaches that anointing with oil produced from *teruma* is akin to drinking oil from *teruma* (Nidda 32a). Thus, regarding certain halakhot, anointing may be viewed as a form of "consumption."

The *Rishonim* debate whether this principle of "*sikha kashtiya*" applies to other prohibitions as well. Since soaps were, and still are, commonly made from non-kosher animal fat and salt, this question is quite relevant. Rabbeinu Tam rules that anointing is only akin to drinking regarding the laws of Yom Kippur, *teruma*, and other *issurei hanaa* (substances from which one may not derive benefit). One may, however, apply other *maakhalot assurot*, forbidden foods, to one's skin.[25] Some *Rishonim* rule that it is prohibited to apply these creams and oils for pleasure; it is, however, permitted for medicinal purposes.[26]

Rema, in discussing the use of soap on Shabbat, implies that one may use animal fat as soap during the week.[27] Gra, however, accepts the more stringent view, which prohibits anointing with a forbidden substance.[28] The *Biur Halakha* observes that the common custom is to permit using soaps from non-kosher animals, but if kosher soap is readily available, it is proper to use the kosher soap.[29]

Nowadays, soaps and shampoos are not fit for consumption. The *Arukh HaShulḥan* writes that this debate does not apply to inedible soaps. Furthermore, he observes that the accepted practice throughout the world is to use soap made with non-kosher ingredients.[30] R. Ovadia Yosef accepts this distinction and rules that one may use any soap, even that made from non-kosher substances.[31]

Assuming that we are not concerned with *sikha kashtiya*, and that one may freely apply non-kosher topical substances, we must determine whether cosmetic products may be categorized as *ḥametz*, which may not be owned and from which no benefit may be derived. Many cosmetic products contain alcohol. While isopropyl alcohol comes from petroleum, ethyl alcohol is made from the fermentation of starch, sugar, and other carbohydrates. Ethyl alcohol can be produced from grains, which would render it *ḥametz*, or from corn or other sources. In addition, some products contain other wheat derivatives.

In order to distinguish between alcohol that is intended for human consumption, which is generally highly taxed and regulated, and inexpensive alcohol used in cosmetics and cleaning solutions, all alcohol that is not intended for human consumption is denatured – that is, it contains additives that make it unfit for consumption, and even poisonous. Denaturing does not alter the chemical composition of the alcohol and the process of denaturation can be reversed, although different additives are often used to make this difficult.

Seemingly, denatured alcohol should be considered unfit for canine consumption, and products containing this alcohol should therefore be permitted to own and use on Pesaḥ. The *posekim,* however, raise a few concerns regarding the permissibility of denatured alcohol. Some insist that denatured alcohol is still considered fit for human consumption. R. Moshe Feinstein, for example, writes that "there are those who drink this with slight additions and modifications."[32] Indeed, much of the alcohol used in cosmetics is not "completely denatured," but "specifically denatured alcohol," which is less dangerous. In recent years, prisons have reported that prisoners ingest large quantities of hand sanitizers in order to become intoxicated.[33] Others suggest that since the process of denaturation can be reversed and the *ḥametz* itself was not chemically transformed, the alcohol itself is still considered fit for canine consumption. R. Tzvi Pesach Frank cites the *Divrei Eliyahu* – who rules that since the alcohol can be restored, we do not consider denaturation to permanently render it unfit for consumption – and the *Atzei Levanon,* who rules leniently. R. Frank concludes that one should not use denatured ethanol as cooking fuel during Pesaḥ.[34]

R. Chaim Elazar Shapira, the Munkatcher Rav, rejects both reasons cited above and rules that denatured alcohol is fundamentally permitted. He acknowledges, however, that the common custom is not to use denatured alcohol. R. Ovadia Yosef[35] also permits all denatured alcohol on Pesaḥ.

It is worth noting that whatever starch or sugar is most readily available in a given country is used for the production of ethanol. In America, corn is the main source of ethanol. In Brazil, if often comes from sugar cane. In Europe, we generally assume that about half of the ethanol is produced from *ḥametz*. Thus, the acceptability of cosmetics containing ethanol may depend on their place of origin.

Although the argument to permit perfumes and aftershaves made with denatured alcohol seems compelling, especially since much, if not most, of the ethyl alcohol produced today does not come from *ḥametz*, many are still accustomed to sell these products before Pesaḥ. R. Shimon Eider rules that one should be concerned with denatured alcohol found in liquids, such as perfumes, colognes, aftershaves, mouthwash, and liquid, spray, and roll-on deodorant. However, creams and other substances that contain denatured alcohol, such as ointments, salves, powders, nail polish, nail polish remover, hand lotions, shoe polish, and paint, are permitted. Furthermore, powders and other cosmetics, such as powdered and stick deodorants, eye shadow, eye liner, mascara, blush, and rouge are unfit for consumption and permitted on Pesaḥ.[36]

R. Moshe Feinstein writes that all dish detergent is inedible, and one may therefore use dish detergent that contains non-kosher ingredients year round.[37] R. Eider writes, however, that on Pesaḥ, one should only use dish detergent that is approved for use during Pesaḥ.[38]

Toothpaste, lipstick, and mouthwash are worthy of separate discussion, as they may not be *nifsal me'akhilat kelev* and are specifically used near or in one's mouth. R. Tzvi Pesach Frank,[39] as well as R. Soloveitchik and R. Moshe Feinstein,[40] assume that toothpaste is not edible, and one therefore need not be concerned if it contains prohibited ingredients. As a result, the common custom is not to demand toothpaste under rabbinic supervision during the year, despite the fact that most toothpastes contain non-kosher ingredients. Nevertheless, R. Feinstein rules that although toothpaste is inedible and the principle of *aḥshevei* would not apply even if one accidentally swallowed some, on Pesaḥ, one should still use toothpaste without any concern of *ḥametz* whenever possible.[41]

Others insist that toothpaste, especially toothpaste that comes in pleasant flavors, is considered fit for consumption. Therefore, even during the year one should purchase toothpaste that does not contain non-kosher ingredients. Furthermore, some are simply more hesitant about putting non-kosher ingredients, even those rendered inedible, into one's mouth. It is customary to use a new tube of toothpaste, as well as a new toothbrush, on Pesaḥ for fear that traces of *ḥametz* remain on used tubes or brushes.

R. Eider includes mouthwash among those liquids that often contain denatured alcohol, which, as discussed above, he maintains one should not consume on Pesaḥ.[42] The *Sefer Piskei Teshuvot,* however, assumes that any *ḥametz* contained in mouthwash is inedible, and one may therefore use unsupervised mouthwash on Pesaḥ.[43] R. Hershel Schachter similarly insists that mouthwash, and toothpaste, are inedible and permitted.[44]

The *posekim* disagree regarding the status of lipstick. R. Eider assumes that lipstick is not considered to be edible, although he does recommend using a fresh stick for Pesaḥ and cautions against using flavored lipstick. Others insist that one should only use lipstick that is completely free of *ḥametz* on Pesaḥ.

In summary, all varieties of blush, body soap, creams, eye shadow, eyeliner, face powder, foot powder, ink, lotions, mascara, nail polish, ointments, paint, shampoo, and stick deodorant are permitted for use on Pesaḥ. Even if they do contain *ḥametz,* it is certainly *nifsal me'akhilat kelev*. Many are accustomed not to use liquid deodorants, hairsprays, perfumes, colognes, and shaving lotions that contain denatured alcohol [which appears in the ingredients as "alcohol," "SD" (special denatured), or "SDA" (special denatured alcohol)]. The use of lipsticks, mouthwashes, and toothpastes that are not under Pesaḥ supervision is also subject to debate, and some refrain from using them as well.

CHAPTER 45

Kitniyot

POSSIBLY THE MOST well known, and certainly the most discussed stringency of Pesaḥ is the prohibition of *kitniyot*, which Ashkenazi Jews refrain from eating during the entire week of Pesaḥ. What is the source of this stringency? The Talmud teaches that just as one can only fulfill the mitzva of eating *matza* with *matza* made from one of the five grains (wheat, spelt, barley, oats, or rye), only these grains can become *ḥametz* when mixed with water (Pesaḥim 35a). Although one of the *Tanna'im*, R. Yoḥanan b. Nuri, maintains that "rice is a species of corn and *karet* is incurred for [eating it in] its leavened state, and a man discharges his obligation with it on Pesaḥ," this opinion is not accepted as halakha.

In fact, the Gemara reports that R. Huna did not accept the position of R. Yoḥanan b. Nuri, and would use beets and rice as the two cooked foods served at the Seder to commemorate the two sacrifices eaten during the times of the Temple: the *korban Pesaḥ* and the *ḥagiga*.

> Rava used to insist on beet and rice, since it had [thus] issued from the mouth of R. Huna. R. Ashi said: From R. Huna you may infer that none pay heed to the following [ruling] of R. Yoḥanan b. Nuri. For it was taught: R. Yoḥanan b. Nuri said: Rice is a species of corn and *karet* is incurred for [eating it in] its leavened state, and a man discharges his duty with it on Pesaḥ. (Pesaḥim 114b)

Rambam writes,

> The prohibition of *ḥametz* on Pesaḥ only applies to the five types of grain: two types of wheat, namely, wheat and spelt, and three types of barley, namely, barley, oats, and rye. But *kitniyot*, such as rice, millet, beans, lentils, and the like, are not subject to [the prohibition of] *ḥametz*. Even if a person kneads rice flour or the like with boiling water and covers it with a cloth until

> it rises like dough that ferments, it is permitted to be eaten, for this is not fermentation, but rather decay.[1]

Despite these passages, some sources indicate concern that substances other than the five grains can become "*ḥametz nukshe*" (partially leavened). Ritva, for example, cites opinions that suggest that although rice and millet cannot become *ḥametz gamur*, they can become *ḥametz nukshe*.[2] Similarly, Maharam Ḥalava explains that although rice and millet cannot become *ḥametz*, some types of *kitniyot* can become partially leavened.[3] As we mentioned, almost all *Rishonim*, and well as the *Shulḥan Arukh*, reject this view, and rule that only the five grains listed in the Mishna can become *ḥametz*.

However, during the early thirteenth century, the custom to refrain from eating legumes (*kitniyot*) developed in France and Provence (Southern France). R. Peretz b. R. Eliyahu (d. c. 1300) writes in his comments on the *Semak* (*Sefer Mitzvot Katan*):

> Regarding *kitniyot*, such as beans, lentils ... and the like, our rabbis practiced a prohibition not to eat them on Pesaḥ .... They did not practice a prohibition because of the fermentation itself, for they would not have erred in a matter that even school children know....
>
> And therefore it seems right to maintain the practice and forbid all *kitniyot* on Pesaḥ – not because of the fermentation itself, for it would be a mistake to say that, but rather because of a decree. Since *kitniyot* are a cooked dish, and grain too is a cooked dish, were we to permit *kitniyot*, people might come to mix them up.... And it is also something that is piled up ("*midi demidgan*"), like the five species [of grain]. There are also places where it customary to make bread from them as from the five species, and those who are not well versed in the Torah are therefore liable to mix them up.[4]

Rabbeinu Peretz describes this custom as a "*gezeira*" (rabbinic enactment), and not a result of misunderstanding regarding whether these foods leaven. He claims that people may confuse legumes with grains since they are cooked in a similar fashion, they are both used to make bread, and they are even gathered in a similar way.

Tur brings another reason for the prohibition of *kitniyot*:

mixed with water. In a responsum written four years later,[33] he prohibits using rapeseeds, equating them with mustard seeds, which are prohibited. R. Shalom Mordechai Schwadron, in his responsa, permits using oil from rapeseeds as long as the production process is entirely dry.[34]

While Ashkenazi kashrut organizations in America do not permit *shemen kitniyot* and consider canola to be *kitniyot,* some Ashkenazim in Israel use canola oil produced under Sephardic supervision. Under supervision, the seeds are checked for wheat grains before processing and water does not come into contact with the seeds before processing. Those who permit peanut oil, and certainly those who permit all oils derived from *kitniyot,* would certainly permit canola oil.

OWNING *KITNIYOT* AND *KITNIYOT* MIXTURES DURING PESAḤ

As mentioned above, *Terumat HaDeshen* writes that one may keep *kitniyot* in his possession during Pesaḥ, as it is not considered to be *ḥametz.*[35] Furthermore, one can also derive benefit from *kitniyot,* such as by using *kitniyot* oil in order to fuel a fire. Although Maharil cites the "*ḥasidim harishonim*" who refrained from deriving benefit from *kitniyot* on Pesaḥ,[36] Rema rules that one may keep *kitniyot* during Pesaḥ.[37]

Terumat HaDeshen further permits mixtures containing *kitniyot,* unlike mixtures containing *ḥametz,* and Rema rules that if *kitniyot* "fell into a cooked food (*tavshil*)" the mixture is permitted. The *Aḥaronim* rule that *kitniyot* are *batel berov* – they are nullified in a mixture with a majority of permitted food – and *shishim* (sixty parts of non-*kitniyot*) is not required,[38] although Rema implies that *kitniyot* are only permitted *bediavad,* after falling into a mixture. Some Aḥaronim even imply that one may deliberately nullify *kitniyot* in a mixture before Pesaḥ.[39] This is not the custom of most *kashrut* organizations.

Some recent Israeli authorities have suggested that products containing a minority of *kitniyot* oil and produced by those who do not refrain from eating *kitniyot* (Sephardi Jews) are permitted on Pesaḥ.[40] Aside from the reasons mentioned above, they add that the principle of "*ein mevatlin issur lekhatḥila*" (one may not intentionally create a mixture in which prohibited food is nullified) should not be applicable, as the products are produced for the Sephardic consumers as well.[41] Larger, global considerations regarding the preservation of the custom of *kitniyot* may also be relevant.

In recent years, as Jews of Ashkenzic and Sephardic descent live together and marry one another, the question of whether an Ashkenazi Jew, who does not eat *kitniyot,* may eat at the home of a Sephardi Jew on Pesaḥ has become more pressing. R. Ovadia Yosef concludes that one may even eat on utensils used for *kitniyot* within the past twenty-four hours.[42] Depending on the situation, one may also rely upon those opinions which permit *shemen kitniyot* and even mixtures when necessary.

KITNIYOT FOR THE SICK AND CHILDREN

The *posekim* question whether to permit *kitniyot* in times of great duress. *Ḥayei Adam,* for example, permits eating *kitniyot* when there is nothing else to eat. In the *Nishmat Adam,* he relates that in 1771, there was a great famine, and a *beit din* was convened in order to permit cooking *kitniyot* on Pesaḥ.[43] Others, such as Maharam Padua[44] and *Divrei Malkiel,*[45] concur. Similarly, the *Arukh HaShulḥan* suggests that the original custom to refrain from eating *kitniyot* was conditional; in a year of famine, when the poor are hungry, the communal leaders gather and permit eating *kitniyot* for that year.[46] R. Eleazar Fleckles (1754–1826), however, rejects this notion, arguing that since this custom has been accepted by all of Ashkenazi Jewry, "even Shmuel HaRamati and Eliyahu and his court… cannot permit rice and other *kitniyot* on Pesaḥ."[47]

Ḥayei Adam adds that in times of great need, for a person who is sick or for a child, one may permit *kitniyot.*[48] In recent years, halakhic authorities have grappled with whether vegetarians, or vegans, who intake most of their protein from products generally considered to be *kitniyot,* may eat *kitniyot* on Pesaḥ. One who must eat *kitniyot* on Pesaḥ should preferably use a separate pot and separate utensils.[49] One may use a pot that was used to cook *kitniyot* if twenty-four hours have passed since its last use.[50]

CHAPTER 46

Bal Yeira'e UVal Yimatzei and *Tashbitu*

BAL YEIRA'E UVAL YIMATZEI: PROHIBITIONS RELATING TO THE OWNERSHIP OF *ḤAMETZ*

In addition to not eating or deriving benefit from *ḥametz,* the Torah commands, "For seven days, no leavened matter shall be *found* (*yimatzei*) in your houses". (Ex. 12:19). Furthermore, the Torah adds: "And no leavened matter shall be *seen* (*yeira'e*) by you, nor shall any leaven [itself] be seen by you in all your borders for seven days" (Ex. 13:7). These prohibitions, which forbid *ḥametz* being "seen" or "found," are known as "*bal yeira'e uval yimatzei.*"

What are the differences between these seemingly similar prohibitions? What is the relationship between them? Based upon a careful reading of the verses, we can identify three differences between these prohibitions.

(1) *Bal yeira'e* relates to *ḥametz* that is "seen," while *bal yimatzei* prohibits all *ḥametz* that is "found," even if not seen.
(2) *Bal yeira'e* relates to *ḥametz* "in all of your borders," while *bal yimatzei* only prohibits *ḥametz* found in one's "house."
(3) *Bal yeira'e* relates to *ḥametz* that is "yours," while *bal yimatzei* seems to prohibit all *ḥametz.*

The Gemara notes these differences and suggests that "*bal yeira'e uval yimatzei*" are two different prohibitions (Pesaḥim 5b). It appears, according to this initial understanding, that *bal yeira'e* focuses upon one's relationship with *ḥametz,* characterized by ownership ("*lekha*"), and therefore not limited to one's house, while *bal yimatzei* focuses upon the *ḥametz* itself and its presence in one's house.

The Gemara, however, noting that the word "*seior*" appears in both verses, conflates these two prohibitions by means of a *gezeira shava*. The *Rishonim* disagree regarding whether this means that these prohibitions are thus considered essentially identical or whether there are still halakhic differences between them.[1] Regardless of which prohibition one violates, however, owning *ḥametz* on Pesaḥ is forbidden – whether visible or not, and whether it is found inside or outside of one's domain.

As mentioned above, *bal yeira'e* implies that one may not "own" *ḥametz*, while *bal yimatzei* implies that *ḥametz* may not even be "found" in one's domain. While the gemara cited above discusses how these two verses combine to teach the location of *ḥametz* that is prohibited, it does not explicate the type of relationship to *ḥametz* that is forbidden.

PROHIBITED RELATIONSHIP TO *ḤAMETZ*

The Talmud teaches that a Jew who takes responsibility for the *ḥametz* of a non-Jew violates *bal yeira'e uval yimatzei* (Pesaḥim 5b). Apparently, the Torah does not only prohibit "owning" *ḥametz*. If so, what type of relationship to *ḥametz* did the Torah prohibit? We may suggest a few understandings of this prohibition:

(1) The Torah forbids "ownership" ("*lekha*") of *ḥametz*, but the prohibition of *bal yimatzei* expands the definition of "ownership" ("*yimatzei*") in regards to *ḥametz*.

(2) The Torah forbids maintaining a "relationship" with *ḥametz* – *ḥametz* that is "found" (*yimatzei*), and which one has a vested interest in preserving ("*lekha*").

(3) The Torah prohibits both "ownership" ("*lekha*") of *ḥametz*, as well as maintaining a "relationship" to *ḥametz* (*yimatzei*).

We will briefly examine this question in light of three issues discussed by the *Rishonim*: the type of responsibility that constitutes a violation of *bal yeira'e uval yimatzei*, whether one violates *bal yeira'e uval yimatzei* for *ḥametz* entrusted to a non-Jew, and whether one violates *bal yeira'e uval yimatzei* for *ḥametz* entrusted to a fellow Jew.

A NON-JEW'S *ḤAMETZ* ENTRUSTED TO A JEW

The *Rishonim* discuss whether and when accepting responsibility for a non-Jew's *ḥametz* constitutes a violation of *bal yeira'e*. Generally speaking, the Talmud speaks of three models of responsibility. The highest level of responsibility is one who accepts upon himself to pay even for damages incurred through events beyond his control, known as "*onasin*." This is the responsibilty of a *sho'el*, a borrower; no matter what the cause of damage, the borrower commits to replace the damaged object. The next level of responsibility is that of one who accepts upon himself to pay for a lost or stolen object. This is the responsibility of a *shomer sakhar*, one who is paid to watch an object. The lowest level is that of one who simply commits not to be negligent in watching the object, known as *peshia*. This is the level of responsibility of a *shomer ḥinam*, one who watches an object without being paid.

Tosafot rule that only one who accepts upon himself the responsibility of a borrower violates *bal yeira'e uval yimatzei*, as this type of responsibility is akin to a type of ownership.[2] Rosh, on the other hand, cites *Behag*, who insists that even one who accepts upon himself a minimal level of responsibility like a *shomer ḥinam* violates *bal yeira'e uval yimatzei*.[3] While Tosafot clearly maintain that one only violates *bal yeira'e uval yimatzei* for owning *ḥametz* on some level, *Behag* apparently believes that even a minimal legal relationship with *ḥametz* is forbidden, as one maintains a vested interest in its preservation.

Rosh also cites Ri, who maintains that only one who accepts upon himself responsibility for the object in case of it being stolen or lost, like a *shomer sakhar*, violates *bal yeira'e uval yimatzei*. It seems that Ri can be understood in either manner. "Responsibility" in the case of the *ḥametz* being stolen or lost can be understood as a serious interest in the *ḥametz* or as a form of quasi-ownership.[4]

Interestingly, the *Rishonim* also disagree as to whether or not this *ḥametz*, owned by the non-Jew but entrusted to the Jew, must be in the

Jew's possession in order to violate *bal yeira'e uval yimatzei*. The Gemara cites a Tosefta, which states:

> Our Rabbis taught: If a Gentile enters a Jew's courtyard with [leavened] dough in his hand, he [the Jew] is not obliged to remove it. If he deposits it with him, he is obliged to remove it; if he assigns a room to him [for the dough], he is not obliged to remove it. (Pesaḥim 6a)

The *Rishonim* debate why he is not obligated to remove the *ḥametz* if "he assigns a room to him" – that is, if the *ḥametz* is not kept in the Jew's possession. Rashi explains that if he assigns a room to him, then he has not accepted upon himself *aḥrayut* (responsibility).[5] Rif and Rambam do not even cite this case, implying, like Rashi, that this case does not present a new principle, but is rather a case in which the Jew did not accept responsibility.

Rabbeinu Tam,[6] Rosh,[7] and Ran,[8] however, disagree. They explain that although the Jew accepted upon himself *aḥrayut*, since the *ḥametz* is not in his possession, he does not need to remove it. These *Rishonim* apparently maintain that in order for *ḥametz* to be considered to be "found" in one's possession, he must not only be interested in the preservation of the *ḥametz*, but it must also be physically found in his possession. "*Matzui*" (found) implies that the Jew maintains a special interest in the *ḥametz* and it is physically located in his domain.

ḤAMETZ ENTRUSTED TO A NON-JEW OR A JEW

May we apply the same logic presented above to a case in which a Jew entrusted *ḥametz* to a non-Jew? In other words, just as a Jew entrusted to watch a non-Jew's *ḥametz* may violate *bal yeira'e uval yimatzei* due to his relationship with the non-Jew's *ḥametz*, do we say that if a Jew entrusts his *ḥametz* to a non-Jew under the same conditions he does not violate *bal yeira'e uval yimatzei*, as the non-Jew is now responsible for his *ḥametz*?

Rosh cites the *Geonim*, who accept this symmetry,[9] but he concludes in accordance with other *Rishonim*,[10] who maintain that the owner is always held accountable for his *ḥametz*, no matter whose possession it is in. Apparently, they disagree as to whether one who "owns" *ḥametz* is always accountable or if only one whose *ḥametz* is "found" violates *bal yeira'e uval yimatzei.*

Although some *Rishonim* assume that this debate would apply to *ḥametz* that is entrusted to a Jewish *shomer* as well,[11] Gra disagrees, arguing that one always violates *bal yeira'e uval yimatzei* for Jewish-owned *ḥametz* found in one's possession, regardless of whether one accepted upon oneself responsibility or not.[12]

In summary, the *Rishonim* disagree as to whether one must maintain some degree of "*baalut*" (ownership), and possibly even possession, or whether maintaining a personal and vested interest in the *ḥametz* suffices in order to violate *bal yeira'e uval yimatzei.*

The *Shulḥan Arukh* rules that one who owns *ḥametz,* regardless of where it is found, violates *bal yeira'e uval yimatzei.* Furthermore, one who is responsible for *ḥametz,* even if it is not found in his possession, also violates *bal yeira'e uval yimatzei.*[13] *Magen Avraham* writes that if a Jew accepts responsibility for a non-Jew's *ḥametz* that remains in the non-Jew's possession, he does not violate *bal yeira'e uval yimatzei.*[14] The *Shulḥan Arukh* also cites two opinions regarding the level of responsibility necessary – i.e., *shomer ḥinam* or *shomer sakhar.* These questions may be relevant in determining whether the *ḥametz* is considered *ḥametz she'avar alav haPesaḥ* and is forbidden after Pesaḥ.

OWNING STOCKS IN COMPANIES THAT OWN *ḤAMETZ*

This discussion may also be relevant to the question of whether one may own stocks in a company which owns *ḥametz* during Pesaḥ. R. Yitzchak HaLevi Ettinga discusses this question. He concludes: "It seems that [the shareholders] are guilty of no wrongdoing if they did not sell their shares."[15] Similarly, R. David Zvi Hoffmann (1843–1921) reports in his *Melamed LeHo'il* that this question was asked on an exam in the Hildesheimer Seminary, and that all of the students ruled leniently. He relates that R. Hildesheimer wrote on all the exams that they ruled correctly.[16]

R. Shaul Weingort, a student at the Seminary who was later responsible for bringing R. Yechiel Yaakov Weinberg, *Seridei Esh,* to Switzerland after WWII, wrote an article on this topic, which was later printed in *Yad Shaul,* a volume of Torah articles published in his memory after his death in a tragic train accident. He concludes that the shareholders are not considered to be owners of the corporate assets, and therefore do not violate *bal yeira'e uval yimatzei.*[17]

While some question whether a shareholder ownership is really considered ownership, at least regarding *ḥametz,* others equate this case to one who accepts responsibility for a non-Jew's *ḥametz* found in the possession of the non-Jew and rule accordingly. R. Yitzchak Yaakov Weiss[18] and R. Moshe Sternbuch[19] prohibit owning shares in a company that owns *ḥametz.* However, they both permit selling the shares as part of the customary *mekhirat ḥametz* before Pesaḥ. Indeed, many modern *mekhirat ḥametz* documents include the sale of stock shares.

MIXTURES

Does *bal yeira'e uval yimatzei* apply to *ḥametz* mixtures as well? The Mishna teaches, "*ve'eilu overin bePesaḥ,*" that one may not keep a *ḥametz* mixture in one's possession during Pesaḥ (Pesaḥim 42a). The *Rishonim* disagree, however, regarding how to understand the phrase "*ve'eilu overin*" and whether the Mishna refers to a biblical or rabbinic prohibition.

Rashi, for example, understands that "*ve'eilu overin*" means that those who keep these *ḥametz* mixtures during Pesaḥ ***violate*** *bal yeira'e uval yimatzei.*[20] Rabbeinu Tam, on the other hand, explains that "*ve'eilu overin*" means that "these should be ***removed*** from the table"; in other words, while one does not violate *bal yeira'e uval yimatzei,* one must remove *ḥametz* mixtures from one's possession.[21] Ran agrees that although one does not violate *bal yeira'e uval yimatzei* for keeping *ḥametz* mixtures during Pesaḥ, one must destroy – "*ve'eilu overin*" – these mixtures *miderabbanan.* Those who do not sell *ḥametz gamur* to a non-Jew before Pesaḥ are nevertheless often inclined to sell *ḥametz* mixtures due to this debate.

Finally, as we mentioned previously, *ḥametz* mixtures that are inedible may be kept during Pesaḥ.[22]

MITZVAT TASHBITU

In addition to the prohibition of *bal yeira'e uval yimatzei*, the Torah also commands that one should "destroy" *ḥametz*.

> Seven days shall you eat unleavened bread; on the first day, you shall put away ("*tashbitu*") leaven out of your houses; for whoever eats leavened bread from the first day until the seventh day, that soul shall be cut off from Israel. (Ex. 12:15)

The *Rishonim* debate how one fulfills the mitzva of *tashbitu*. Some *Rishonim* explain that *tashbitu* refers to the physical removal or destruction of *ḥametz*. Tosafot, for example, insist that *tashbitu* entails destroying *ḥametz*.[23] Similarly, Maharam Ḥalava and Rabbeinu David explain that *tashbitu* refers to physically emptying one's house of *ḥametz*, beginning with the "*bedikat ḥametz*."

Rashi disagrees, explaining that one fulfills the mitzva of *tashbitu* through *bittul*. He cites the Targum, which translates *tashbitu* as "*tevatlun*," "nullify," as support for his position. Rashi writes that "*bittul*" refers to "negation in the heart" ("*bittul balev*").[24] In other words, one fulfills *tashbitu* through merely negating the importance of *ḥametz* and one's relationship to it. Tosafot, incidentally, insist that "*bittul*" refers to the renunciation of ownership, known as "*hefker*."

Rashi's position is rather difficult to comprehend. How, why, and when would psychological negation suffice? Ramban, who also accepts the efficacy of *bittul*, writes:

> There are three methods of disposing of *ḥametz*, as the Torah says that one should not see *ḥametz* in our possession. Therefore, one should burn or totally destroy *ḥametz*, and that is the best method … and if one performs *bittul* through speech, one has also fulfilled the commandment.[25]

According to Ramban, while *bittul* may be a valid form of *tashbitu*, physical destruction through burning or another method is preferable. Rambam seems to disagree, however. He writes:

> There is a positive commandment to destroy (*lehashbit*) *ḥametz* before the time in which it becomes prohibited to eat, as it says, "on the first day ye shall put away (*tashbitu*) leaven out of your houses," and we have learned that the "first" refers to the fourteenth.... And what is the "*hashbata*" described by the Torah? One should nullify *ḥametz* in his heart, and resolve in one's heart, that he has no *ḥametz* in his possession at all and that all *ḥametz* in his possession is like dirt and is akin to something of no use.[26]

Rambam strongly implies two points. First, the manner of fulfilling *tashbitu* is through psychological/spiritual negation. Second, each person should actively fulfill this mitzva. If so, we might ask how *bittul* prevents the prohibitions of *bal yeira'e* and *bal yimatzei*. And what does this imply about the prohibitions of *ḥametz*?

Seemingly, Rambam understands that *ḥametz* transcends the recognized, formal prohibitions of forbidden foods. Ultimately, the Torah prohibited having any "relationship" with *ḥametz*. Therefore, not only is it prohibited to eat *ḥametz*, but *ḥametz* also may not be "seen" or "found" in one's possession. The most appropriate way to rid oneself of *ḥametz* is to separate from it psychologically and spiritually.

Ḥametz, according to this theory, represents a spiritual foe that must be battled both physically and spiritually. Indeed, as we discussed previously, the Gemara relates that "R. Alexandri would end his daily prayers with the following supplication: Master of the Universe, You know full well that it is our desire to act according to Your will; but what prevents us from doing so? The yeast in the dough." (Berakhot 17a)

Ḥametz represents something extremely negative, beginning with the "evil inclination," and, according to many, sharing characteristics of idolatrous practice, which we must rid ourselves of in every sense. This view of *ḥametz* apparently permeates Rambam's understanding of the prohibitions of *ḥametz* and his understanding of the mitzva of "*tashbitu*."

THE TIME AND NATURE OF THE MITZVA OF *TASHBITU*

The Gemara determines that the "first day" refers to the fourteenth of the month of Nissan, upon which the Pesaḥ offering is brought, and not the fifteenth, the first day of the festival (Pesaḥim 5a). While the Gemara offers different reasons as to why the "first day" must refer to the fourteenth of Nissan, partially depending upon the way in which the mitzva is to be fulfilled, all seem to agree to this interpretation.

This gemara, however, raises the following quandary: If *tashbitu* is fulfilled through *bedikat ḥametz* or *bittul,* then hasn't one already fulfilled the mitzva before its proper time? And if *tashbitu* is fulfilled through burning or destroying the *ḥametz,* then only one who is already in violation of the prohibition of owning *ḥametz* can fulfill *tashbitu*!

Seemingly, this question is related to a broader question concerning the nature of *tashbitu.* Does one fulfill *tashbitu* passively – that is, by not having any *ḥametz* in one's possession by noon of the fourteenth of Nissan – or actively, by destroying *ḥametz*? The *Minḥat Ḥinukh* raises this question, asking whether the mitzva of "*tashbitu*" refers to an obligation to actively destroy *ḥametz,* a "*maase,*" or to a responsibility to ensure that all *ḥametz* is disposed of before noon on the fourteenth, a "*totzaa.*"[27] In other words, does one fulfill "*tashbitu*" at noon on the fourteenth of Nissan if one has no *ḥametz* in one's possession or only through actively destroying the *ḥametz*?

As we noted above, Tosafot disagree with Rashi and assert that *tashbitu* is fulfilled through burning, not *bittul.*[28] As proof, they note that R. Akiva insists that "the first day" must refer to the fourteenth of Nissan; it cannot refer to the fifteenth, the first day of the festival, because it would then be prohibited to burn the *ḥametz* on Yom Tov (Pesaḥim 5a). Furthermore, if the nullification of *ḥametz* (*bittul*) cannot be performed after noon (*ḥatzot*), *tashbitu* must refer to the burning of *ḥametz.* Clearly, Tosafot assumes that the mitzva of *tashbitu* is fulfilled after *ḥatzot* on the fourteenth.

This position raises many difficulties, as one is not permitted to own *ḥametz* after *ḥatzot* on the fourteenth of Nissan. It seems that the Tosafot understand that the mitzva of *tashbitu* can be fulfilled only when a person inadvertently retains *ḥametz* in his possession after noon, and thereby violates the prohibitions of *bal yeira'e uval yimatzei*. One who follows the halakha precisely, according to Tosafot, may never fulfill "*tashbitu*," as it serves to "repair" the violation of owning *ḥametz*.

Interestingly, the *Mordekhai* cites the custom of those who would save *ḥametz* and burn it on the exact hour of noon in order to fulfill the mitzva in its fullest. Apparently, one may keep *ḥametz* for a short time after noon on Erev Pesaḥ, for enough time to fulfill the mitzva of *tashbitu*. Furthermore, these people clearly believed that *tashbitu* is incumbent upon every individual to fulfill.[29]

Rashi disagrees and claims that *tashbitu* is fulfilled before noon through *bittul*.[30] Maharam Ḥalava and Rabbeinu David, cited above, must also believe that *tashbitu* may be fulfilled before noon through the *bedikat ḥametz*. *Minḥat Ḥinukh* explains that Rashi must maintain that *tashbitu* does not refer to an active obligation to nullify *ḥametz*, but merely to a responsibility to ensure that one does not own any *ḥametz* by noon on the fourteenth.[31] Tosafot, on the other hand, who insist that the mitzva is fulfilled after *ḥatzot* on the fourteenth, must view the obligation as "active"; one must burn *ḥametz* in one's possession after the sixth hour.

R. Chaim Soloveitchik insists that Rambam also understands the mitzva of *tashbitu* in this manner.[32] He comments on Rambam's ruling that one who purchases *ḥametz* during the festival receives lashes for violating the prohibitions of owning *ḥametz* (*bal yeira'e* and *bal yimatzei*). He questions why one should receive lashes, as the general principle is that a negative commandment closely associated with a positive commandment ("*lav hanitak le'aseh*") intended to undo the damage done by violating the prohibition does not incur lashes upon its violation. How can one incur lashes for purchasing *ḥametz* during Pesaḥ if *bal yeira'e* is seemingly associated with *tashbitu*?

He concludes by referring to another fascinating debate. The Mishna cites different opinions as to whether one must destroy *ḥametz* through burning (R. Yehuda) or through any means of destruction (*ḥakhamim*) (Pesaḥim 21a). R. Chaim explains that while R. Yehuda clearly understands that *tashbitu* refers to an active commandment to burn *ḥametz,* the *ḥakhamim* must not view *tashbitu* as a mitzva with a specific action, but rather as a general obligation to ensure that one does not have any *ḥametz* in his possession after *ḥatzot.* Therefore, he explains, the *ḥakhamim* cannot view *tashbitu* as "linked to" or "associated with" a negative commandment, as its fulfillment is not mandated in an active manner.[33] Rambam ruled accordingly that one can, in fact, receive lashes for purchasing *ḥametz* on Pesaḥ.

In summary, while some *Rishonim* view *tashbitu* as a mitzva fulfilled passively through the pre-Pesaḥ preparations, others understand that one who has *ḥametz* in his possession after noon on the fourteenth of Nissan must actively destroy the *ḥametz.* The *Minḥat Ḥinukh* suggests that according to those who understand that *tashbitu* entails actively destroying *ḥametz* after noon on the fourteenth, the Rabbis enacted that one should fulfill this mitzva earlier, an hour before noon, from the fifth hour.

CHAPTER 47

Bedikat Ḥametz and *Biur Ḥametz*

BEDIKAT ḤAMETZ

The climax of the yearly pre-Pesaḥ cleaning is the *bedikat ḥametz.* Many gather their family; distribute feathers, wooden spoons, and candles; and search their homes for *ḥametz* that was either not found or intentionally hidden around one's house. The "ceremony" ends with the recitation of the *bittul ḥametz,* the nullification of *ḥametz,* and the *ḥametz* is set aside to be destroyed the next morning.

What is the source of and the reason for this search? When and how is it performed, and for what is one looking? The Mishna teaches that one should search one's house for *ḥametz* on the night of the fourteenth of Nissan (Pesaḥim 2a). Rashi explains that one must perform *bedikat ḥametz* in order to avoid violating the prohibitions of owning *ḥametz, bal yeira'e uval yimatzei.*[1] Many *Rishonim* find this interpretation difficult, especially in light of the gemara that states explicitly that the obligation of *bedikat ḥametz* must be *miderabbanan,* since one already fulfilled his biblical obligation through *bittul* (Pesaḥim 4a).[2] Thus, assuming that one has already nullified his *ḥametz,* what purpose does the *bedika* fulfill?

Ran explains that Rashi refers to the function of *bedikat ḥametz* on a biblical level. *Mideoraita,* he explains, one can avoid the prohibition of *bal yeira'e uval yimatzei* in one of two ways: *bittul* (nullification) or *bedika* (searching for *ḥametz*). Therefore, Rashi explains that through searching one's house for *ḥametz,* one avoids, *mideoraita,* the prohibition of owning *ḥametz* on Pesaḥ. *Miderabbanan,* however, the Rabbis insisted that one perform both a *bedika* and *bittul.*[3]

Others suggest that although *mideoraita* one may avoid the prohibition of *bal yeira'e uval yimatzei* through *bittul ḥametz, bedika* fulfills another mitzva – the obligation to physically remove *ḥametz* from one's home. This process, known as *biur ḥametz,* begins by searching one's home for *ḥametz*. Indeed, the blessing recited on *bedikat ḥametz* is not "*al bedikat ḥametz,*" but rather, "*al biur ḥametz.*" Rabbeinu David explains that although one could fulfill the mitzva of *tashbitu* through *bittul,* as we discussed previously, the Rabbis insisted that one should fulfill it through the physical removal of *ḥametz* as well.[4] Maharam Ḥalava also writes that one fulfills the biblical commandment of *tashbitu* through *bedikat ḥametz*. In fact, he even interprets the Targum's translation of *tashbitu*, "*tevatlun,*" as referring to "*bittul* from one's house," and not, as Rashi explains, to mental negation of the *ḥametz.*[5]

Tosafot offer a third explanation. They explain that although one can avoid the prohibition of owning *ḥametz* through *bittul,* the Rabbis insisted that one also search and remove *ḥametz* from his house in order that he should not come to eat *ḥametz* on Pesaḥ. Tosafot question why *ḥametz* should be different from other prohibited food, which one is not obligated to remove from one's home lest he come to eat it. They suggest that unlike other prohibited foods, one is accustomed to eating *ḥametz* during the year, and therefore the chances of inadvertently eating *ḥametz* on Pesaḥ are higher. Tosafot add that the Torah already demonstrates great stringency regarding *ḥametz*.[6]

R. David b. Solomon Zimra also questions why one must search for and remove *ḥametz* from one's home, and provides and interesting explanation:

> I rely [in my explanation] on what the Rabbis taught in their teachings that *ḥametz* on Pesaḥ is an allusion to the *yetzer hara*, and that is the leavening in the dough, and therefore a person must completely rid himself of it and search it out from all the recesses of his mind; even a minute amount is not insignificant.[7]

Radbaz concludes that the laws of *ḥametz* are similar to, and even more severe than, the laws of *avoda zara* (relating to objects of pagan worship). He therefore understands the laws of *ḥametz* in a broader context: *ḥametz* represents the *yetzer hara*, and therefore one must relentlessly work to remove it from one's midst.

THE EXTENT AND MANNER OF *BEDIKAT ḤAMETZ*

One of the most common questions regarding *bedikat ḥametz* relates to the extent to which one must search for every bit of *ḥametz*. The Gemara states that one must be concerned with dough in the cracks of a dough-trough, as the pieces may combine to the size of a *kezayit* (Pesaḥim 45b). This passage seems to imply that one must search for even the smallest pieces of *ḥametz*. However, the Gemara earlier questions why even one who already did *bedikat ḥametz* must recite the *bittul*, and explains that the *bittul* is not recited for the crumbs; one is not concerned about crumbs, since they are "*lo ḥashivi*," not important, and therefore one does not even need to nullify them (Pesaḥim 6b). This passage seems to imply that crumbs are insignificant and one need not nullify them. The question thus remains – must one search for even the smallest crumbs?

Some claim that while small pieces of dough in the dough-trough might stick together and combine to form a *kezayit* of dough, crumbs cannot, and therefore one need not search for crumbs.[8] *Magen Avraham*[9] and the Vilna Gaon[10] concur. Others, however, write that although one would not need to nullify these crumbs, one must search for and destroy them, lest someone come to eat them.[11] The *Shulḥan Arukh* writes: "The custom is to scrape the walls and chairs with which *ḥametz* had come in contact, and they [who follow this practice] have a basis on which to rely."[12] The *Mishna Berura*[13] cites the *Shulḥan Arukh HaRav,*[14] who writes that "the Jewish people are sacred and have the practice of conducting themselves stringently even with regard to crumbs." The *Shulḥan Arukh HaRav,* however, concludes that this does not apply to crumbs that have become dirty (i.e., on the floor), which no one will come to eat.

In most homes, it is common to begin cleaning well before Pesaḥ and then to perform a superficial search on the night of *bedikat ḥametz,* relying upon the earlier cleaning of the house. Is this practice proper? The *Mordekhai,*[15] based upon a Yerushalmi (Y. Pesaḥim 1:1), writes that even if one cleaned his home thoroughly before Pesaḥ, one should still perform a proper *bedikat ḥametz* in order not to differentiate between one *bedikat ḥametz* and another. The *Terumat HaDeshen* cites this *Mordekhai* and concludes that those who hide pieces of *ḥametz* before the search and end their *bedikat ḥametz* upon finding the pieces are acting incorrectly, as they did not perform a thorough search of the home.[16] Similarly, the *Shulḥan Arukh* rules that even if one cleaned his house thoroughly before Pesaḥ, he should still perform the *bedikat ḥametz.*[17]

Interestingly, *Shaarei Teshuva* cites Maharish, who describes how many people perform their *bedikat ḥametz*:

> Therefore, many people are lenient and check casually without searching properly in holes and cracks, since first they sweep, wash, and scour everything very well, and even if they wash and scour through a non-Jew, it stands to reason that they are trusted, for they are meticulous regarding cleanliness so as not to undermine themselves [their reputation].[18]

Although many are accustomed to rely upon this view, many *posekim* insist that one should carry out a proper and thorough search of one's home on the night of the fourteenth of Nissan.

THE TRAVELER AND ONE WHO SELLS HIS HOME BEFORE PESAḤ

Must someone who leaves his home before the evening of the fourteenth of Nissan, such as a student returning home for Pesaḥ or a family leaving their home for the festival, search their home for *ḥametz*? The Gemara discusses the case of one who rents his house to another Jew on the morning of the fourteenth of Nissan, Erev Pesaḥ:

> R. Naḥman b. Yitzchak was asked: If one rents a house to his neighbor from the fourteenth, upon whom [rests the duty] to make the search? [Does it rest] upon the landlord, because the leaven is his; or perhaps upon the tenant, because the forbidden matter exists in his domain?...We learned it: If one rents a house to his neighbor, if the fourteenth occurs before he delivers him the keys, the landlord must make the search; while if the fourteenth occurs after he delivers the keys, the tenant must make search. (Pesaḥim 4a)

According to this passage, the evening of the fourteenth of Nissan determines who is responsible to perform *bedikat ḥametz*. If the renter has already taken the key, then he must perform *bedikat ḥametz*, and if not, the responsibility rests upon the owner.

Although one might infer from this gemara that one who is not home at all on the night of the fourteenth is exempt from *bedikat ḥametz*, the Talmud states otherwise:

> One who embarks on a sea voyage or joins a departing caravan more than thirty days before Pesaḥ need not destroy the *ḥametz* [in his house], but one who leaves less than thirty days before Pesaḥ must remove the *ḥametz* [in his house]. (Pesaḥim 6a)

This passage states that one who leaves his home within thirty days of Pesaḥ must still search his home before he leaves. Seemingly, while this gemara teaches that one becomes obligated in *bedikat ḥametz* thirty days before Pesaḥ, the direct responsibility for each house is determined on the night of the fourteenth.

The *Shulḥan Arukh* rules that one who leaves his house within thirty days of Pesaḥ must still search his house for *ḥametz*.[19] The *Aḥaronim* debate whether one should recite the *berakha* upon this search; Rema rules that one should not recite the blessing.[20]

BEDIKAT ḤAMETZ FOR ONE WHO SOLD HIS ḤAMETZ

As discussed above, one who leaves his home within thirty days of Pesaḥ must perform *bedikat ḥametz* without a blessing the night before leaving. Some question whether selling one's home before Pesaḥ along with the *ḥametz* exempts him from the laborious task of *bedikat ḥametz*.

The *Tur* cites Raavya (*Avi Ezri*), who rules that if a Jew sells his house to a non-Jew within thirty days of Pesaḥ, he must perform *bedikat ḥametz* before he leaves, even though the non-Jew will bring *ḥametz* into the house. The *Tur* disagrees, explaining that since the non-Jew enters the home, the previous owner is not responsible to search, and he certainly renounces ownership of any *ḥametz* he leaves behind in the house.[21] The *Shulḥan Arukh* rules in accordance with *Avi Ezri*, while Rema rules like the *Tur*.[22] Therefore, those who follow the *Tur* and sell their house before the fourteenth of Nissan do not have to perform the *bedikat ḥametz*.

What about one who sells his house to a non-Jew on the morning of the fourteenth, on Erev Pesaḥ? The *Mishna Berura* writes:

> Regarding whether one must check the rooms that one intends to sell the next day to a non-Jew with the *ḥametz* contained in them, there are different opinions among the *Aḥaronim*. The opinion of *Mekor Ḥayim* and *Ḥayei Adam* is that one must check these rooms, since they are currently not sold and they are in the possession of a Jew. And even if they were sold, they are still not in his possession, and the keys are still in the control of the owner. *Binyan Olam*, however, disagrees; his view is that that one does not require *bedika* in this case, as the very fact that he is selling the next day to a non-Jew is a fulfillment of *tashbitu* and *biur*, and it is no worse than *ḥametz* which he found after searching the house, which he leaves for tomorrow and he need not destroy.... Similarly, in the response of Ḥatam Sofer,[23] he is lenient if one fulfills the mitzva of *bedika* in the other rooms...but one should be careful when he sells to explain that he is also selling all of the *ḥametz* in the rooms. Therefore, even though we should not criticize one who is lenient, one who sells his house on the thirteenth has done even better.[24]

The *Mishna Berura* records a debate regarding whether one must check rooms that he intends to sell the next day to a non-Jew. Although preferably one who wishes to be exempt from *bedikat ḥametz* should sell one's home or rooms before the fourteenth, those who sell their home (and its *ḥametz*) on the fourteenth of Nissan and do not perform *bedikat ḥametz* the evening before may rely upon the view of *Binyan Olam* and Ḥatam Sofer. Preferably, one should leave at least one room unsold or not rented in order to fulfill the mitzva of *bedikat ḥametz* on that room, and then sell or rent the rest of the home.

BITTUL ḤAMETZ

As we explained previously, the Gemara states that one fulfills his obligation, *mideoraita,* merely through reciting the *bittul ḥametz.* The Gemara adds, however, that even one who already searched his home should recite *bittul,* "lest he find a tasty loaf and [set] his mind upon it" (Pesaḥim 4a). The Gemara does not, however, specify which specific obligation one fulfills through reciting *bittul ḥametz.* Furthermore, the Gemara never explains what the precise legal meaning of the declaration of *bittul* is.

Tosafot explain that *bittul* is actually another word for *hefker,* the renunciation of one's ownership.[25] In other words, in order to avoid violating *bal yeira'e uval yimatzei,* one declares all *ḥametz* in his possession as ownerless. The *Rishonim,* including Tosafot, ask a number of questions on this interpretation. First, we do not find anywhere else that the term "*bittul*" refers to "*hefker.*" Second, the laws of *bittul* do not match the laws of *hefker.* For example, *hefker* is usually performed in front of three (Nedarim 45a), and *bittul* is performed alone. *Hefker* cannot be performed on Shabbat, as it is a type of business transaction, but when Erev Pesaḥ falls on Shabbat, *bittul* can be performed. Finally, *hefker* must be recited aloud, while *bittul* may be "said" in one's heart. While some explain each discrepancy and maintain that *bittul* can be understood as a classic form of *hefker,*[26] others note that in this case, merely withdrawing from and renouncing the *ḥametz* is sufficient, and therefore its laws are different from those of ordinary *hefker.*[27]

Rashi disagrees and explains that *bittul,* which is accomplished mentally (*"hashbata delev"*), is a fulfillment of the biblical commandment of *tashbitu.*[28] Indeed, Targum Onkelos translates *tashbitu* as *"tevatlun."* How is it possible that one fulfills *tashbitu* through merely mentally negating *ḥametz*? Ramban, as we noted previously, accepts the efficacy of *bittul,* but he writes:

> There are three methods of disposing of *ḥametz,* as the Torah says that one should not see *ḥametz* in our possession. Therefore, one should burn or totally destroy *ḥametz,* and that is the best method...and if one performs *bittul* through speech, one has also fulfilled the commandment.[29]

In other words, according to Ramban, while *bittul* may be a valid form of *tashbitu,* physical destruction through burning or another method is preferable. Furthermore, Ramban notes that in general, the prohibition of owning *ḥametz* on Pesaḥ is difficult to understand, since legally, once the *ḥametz* becomes *assur behanaa,* it is no longer considered to be in his possession. How can he then violate *bal yeira'e uval yimatzei*? He explains:

> *Bittul* works to remove it from the status of *ḥametz* and to consider it to be dirt, which is not edible. This mechanism is effective, based upon the words of R. Yishmael, who asserts that there are two things that, although they are not in the ownership of a person, the Torah treats them as if they are owned [Pesaḥim 6b]...which means to say that the Torah considered it to be his in order to violate these two prohibitions [*bal yeira'e uval yimatzei*] because his mind is upon it and he is interested in its preservation. Therefore, the person who aligns his thoughts with the Torah's intention and nullifies it in order that it should not be considered to have value but should rather be taken out of his possession completely, no longer violates these prohibitions.

By negating one's relationship to *ḥametz,* one avoids violating *bal yeira'e uval yimatzei* and fulfills the mitzva of *tashbitu.*

Although Ramban writes that one may fulfill *tashbitu* through *bittul, hefker,* or physical destruction, with physical destruction being the preferred method, Rambam seems to differ. He writes:

> There is a positive commandment to destroy (*lehashbit*) *ḥametz* before the time in which it becomes prohibited to eat, as it says, "on the first day you

> shall put away (*tashbitu*) leaven out of your houses," and we have learned that the "first" refers to the fourteenth.... And what is the "*hashbata*" described by the Torah? One should nullify *ḥametz* in his heart and resolve in one's heart that he has no *ḥametz* in his possession at all and that all *ḥametz* in his possession is like dirt and is akin to something of no use.[30]

Rambam strongly implies two points: First, the manner of fulfilling *tashbitu* is through psychological/spiritual negation. Second, he implies that each person should actively fulfill this mitzva. If so, we might ask how *bittul* prevents the prohibitions of *bal yeira'e* and *bal yimatzei*. And what does this imply about the prohibitions of *ḥametz*?

As we explained previously, Rambam apparently understands that *ḥametz*, which transcends the rules of other prohibited foods, represents a spiritual foe, and therefore must be battled through spiritual and mental negation. Practically, *bittul* is recited at night, after the *bedikat ḥametz*, and once again in the morning before the end of the fifth hour. At night, one only nullifies *ḥametz* that one has not found, while in the morning, one nullifies all *ḥametz*.

All adult men and women should recite the *bittul ḥametz*. The *Shulḥan Arukh* rules that one may appoint a *shaliaḥ*, an agent, to nullify one's *ḥametz*. Rema explains that the *shaliaḥ* would say: "Peloni's *ḥametz* should be *batel*."[31] The *Magen Avraham* notes that *Baḥ* disagrees and does not permit one to appoint a *shaliaḥ* for *bittul ḥametz*.[32]

Should married women recite the *bittul ḥametz*? The *Shulḥan Arukh* implies that a wife only nullifies *ḥametz* when her husband did not recite the *bittul*.[33] Seemingly, this is based upon the principle that "what a woman acquires automatically comes into the ownership of her husband" (Gittin 77b) – since a married woman's property is legally owned by her husband, he should be responsible to nullify the *ḥametz*. One might question, however, whether this principle is applicable nowadays, and therefore whether married women should recite their own *bittul ḥametz*.[34]

CHAPTER 48

Disposal and Sale of *Ḥametz*

BIUR ḤAMETZ

The Gemara records that while *mideoraita*, one may keep *ḥametz* until midday on the fourteenth of Nissan, the Rabbis enacted a "fence" to the Torah.[1] According to R. Meir, one may keep and eat *ḥametz* until the end of the fifth hour. R. Yehuda rules that one may eat *ḥametz* until the end of the fourth hour and must destroy it by the end of the fifth hour (Pesaḥim 11b). The halakha is in accordance with R. Yehuda.[2]

Regarding the proper manner in which to destroy *ḥametz*, the Mishna teaches:

> R. Yehuda said: There is no removal of leaven except by burning; but the sages maintain: He may also crumble and throw it to the wind or cast it into the sea. (Pesaḥim 21a)

According to R. Yehuda, *ḥametz* must be burned, while the sages maintain that one may even "crumble and throw it to the wind or cast it into the sea." The *Rishonim* discuss the conceptual underpinnings of this debate.

Tosafot[3] relate this argument to another mishna, which distinguishes between objects that are buried (or removed), known as "*nikbarin*" – such as a *shor haniskal, egla arufa,* and *basar beḥalav* – and those that must be burned, known as "*nisrafin*" – such as *teruma teme'a, orla,* and *kilei hakerem* (Temura 33b). The Gemara explains that one may not derive benefit from the ashes of items which are buried, while the ashes of objects that must be burned are permitted. Once one has fulfilled the mitzva of burning, *naasa mitzvatan* – their mitzva has been fulfilled, and their ashes may be used.

Based on this gemara, Tosafot explain that R. Yehuda and the sages disagree regarding whether we should categorize *ḥametz* as *nisrafin* or *nikbarin*. While R. Yehuda believes that *ḥametz* is categorized as "*nisrafin*," the sages view *ḥametz* as "*nikbarin*," and its ashes would still be prohibited. The *Tur* rules accordingly.[4] R. Chaim Soloveitchik develops this approach and defends the *Tur* in his *ḥiddushim* on Rambam.[5]

R. Akiva Eiger disagrees. He explains that there is no mitzva to dispose of objects that are *nikbarin*, but rather to remove them as a preventative measure – so that they will not be used. All agree, however, that one must destroy *ḥametz*. *Sefat Emet* agrees, arguing that both R. Yehuda and the sages agree that there is a mitzva to destroy the *ḥametz*; they only disagree about the proper means of doing so.[6]

The Mishna does not indicate whether the debate between R. Yehuda and the sages relates to *ḥametz* found during Pesaḥ or *ḥametz* left before Pesaḥ. The Gemara relates, "When is this? Before the time of removal; but at the time of removal, its 'putting away' is by any means" (Pesaḥim 12b). The *Rishonim* debate the meaning of the terms "before the time of removal" and "the time of removal."

Rashi explains that R. Yehuda and the sages disagree regarding the proper means of disposing of *ḥametz* before midday on the fourteenth of Nissan; afterward, all agree that one may dispose of *ḥametz* in any manner.[7] Rosh assumes that Rashi means that from the beginning of the sixth hour on Erev Pesaḥ, all agree that one may dispose of *ḥametz* in any manner.[8]

Rabbeinu Tam disagrees and explains that until and during the sixth hour, when "most people are involved [in disposing of] their *ḥametz*," all agree that one may dispose of one's *ḥametz* in any manner. After the sixth hour, however, R. Yehuda maintains that one must burn his *ḥametz*.[9] He cites the Yerushalmi in support of his view (Y. Pesaḥim 2:2). Baal HaMaor agrees fundamentally, but insists that R. Yehuda maintains that even from the fifth hour, an hour before midday, one must burn his *ḥametz*.[10] In summary, the *Rishonim* debate whether R. Yehuda requires one to burn his *ḥametz* before midday (Rashi), until the fifth hour (Rosh), from the fifth hour (Baal HaMaor), or after midday (Rabbeinu Tam). While some *Rishonim* rule in accordance with R. Yehuda,[11] others rule like the sages.[12] Interestingly, the Vilna Gaon insists that even the sages agree that the preferred method of disposing of *ḥametz* is through burning.[13]

The *Shulḥan Arukh* follows the view of the *Geonim* and Rambam, that *ḥametz* may be disposed of in any manner.[14] Rema records, however, that it is customary to burn *ḥametz,* like the opinion of R. Yehuda and those who maintain that R. Yehuda requires burning even before midday.[15]

The *Mishna Berura* mentions that one may throw his *ḥametz* to a place of *hefker* before the end of the fifth hour, and would then no longer need to burn the *ḥametz.*[16] R. Moshe Feinstein writes that one should not throw his *ḥametz* into his outdoor garbage can; since he owns the garbage can, the *ḥametz* is still in his possession. If one throws his *ḥametz* into a public garbage bin outside of one's property, then one does not have to destroy the *ḥametz.*[17]

Some burn the feather and the wooden spoon that are customarily used for *bedikat ḥametz,* and some also burn their lulavim and oils left over from Ḥanukka.

After burning one's *ḥametz,* one should recite the *bittul ḥametz.* Rema notes that one should recite the *bittul* only after one has already burned the *ḥametz,* so that one fulfills *biur ḥametz* while the *ḥametz* is still his.[18] Some also point out that one should not pour lighter fluid on the *ḥametz* itself, as that might render the *ḥametz* unfit for canine consumption (*nifsal me'akhilat kelev*), and there would therefore be no need to burn it.

ONE WHO FINDS *ḤAMETZ* DURING PESAḤ

Regarding one who finds *ḥametz* in his possession during Pesaḥ, the Talmud distinguishes between one who finds *ḥametz* on a day of Yom Tov and one who finds *ḥametz* on Ḥol HaMo'ed (or after midday of Erev Pesaḥ).

The Gemara teaches that one who finds *ḥametz* on Yom Tov should cover it with a vessel until the evening (Pesaḥim 6a). Rashi explains that the *ḥametz* is considered to be *muktze,* and therefore one would not be permitted to move it.[19] The *Rishonim* debate why one should not burn the *ḥametz* on Yom Tov, especially in light of the principle of *mitokh,* which permits one to perform on Yom Tov a *melekhet okhel nefesh,* a *melakha* necessary for the preparation of food, even for a non-food related purpose.[20]

Some *Rishonim* explain that the Gemara refers to a case in which one nullified his *ḥametz* properly. Therefore, one who finds *ḥametz* in his possession on Pesaḥ does not violate *bal yeira'e uval yimatzei,* and there is no pressing reason to destroy the *ḥametz.* The principle of *mitokh,* they explain, only applies if one has a "need," even a "slight need," for this *melakha,* such as carrying a child to shul on Yom Tov. However, since here there is no need to burn the *ḥametz,* it is *muktze* and one should dispose of it after Yom Tov. If, however, one did not nullify his *ḥametz* before Pesaḥ, the *ḥametz* is not considered to be *muktze,* and one may, and should, dispose of it on Yom Tov.[21]

Others insist that even if one did not nullify his *ḥametz* before Pesaḥ, he should still not move it on Yom Tov. Tosafot explain that since the *ḥametz* is considered to be *muktze* on Yom Tov, even in this case one should not burn it until the evening.[22] *Kesef Mishneh* suggests that the allowance of *mitokh* may not apply in this situation; burning *ḥametz* may not be a "need" that is "*shaveh lekhol nefesh*" (something that most people enjoy), which the Gemara (Ketubot 7a) requires in order to invoke *mitokh.*[23] Interestingly, Me'iri and the *Kol Bo* suggest that although one who did not nullify his *ḥametz* should not burn it on Yom Tov, he should set aside the prohibition of *muktze* and dispose of it in another manner.[24]

The *Shulḥan Arukh* rules that one who finds *ḥametz* in his house on Yom Tov should cover it with a vessel, and does not specify whether or not he nullified his *ḥametz* before Pesaḥ.[25] Gra explains that he rules in accordance with those who do not distinguish between one who has nullified his *ḥametz* and one who has not.[26]

One who finds *ḥametz* in his possession during Ḥol HaMo'ed should dispose of it immediately, either through burning or in another manner.

MEKHIRAT ḤAMETZ

Nowadays, almost every community offers a "*mekhirat ḥametz,*" the opportunity to sell one's *ḥametz* to a non-Jew before Pesaḥ, thereby avoiding the prohibition of *bal yeira'e uval yimatzei,* and then to buy back the *ḥametz* after the festival. This practice, although almost routine in many communities, has been the source of great halakhic controversy for hundreds of years.

R. Shlomo Yosef Zevin traces the development of this practice in his classic work on the festivals, *HaMo'adim BeHalakha.*[27] He identifies four historical/halakhic phases of *mekhirat ḥametz*: Selling *ḥametz* without the intention of repossessing it after Pesaḥ, selling the *ḥametz* with the intention of repossessing it after Pesaḥ, a private sale of *ḥametz* found in one's possession to a non-Jew, and the communal sale of *ḥametz* that remains in the possession of the Jew.

The Mishna, describing the earliest phase of this *mekhirat ḥametz,* teaches that before *ḥametz* becomes prohibited, one may eat it, feed it to one's animals, or sell it (Pesaḥim 21a). Similarly, the Gemara relates:

> It once happened that a certain man deposited a saddle-bag full of leaven with Yoḥanan of Hukok, and mice made holes in it and the leaven was bursting out. He then went before Rebbi. The first hour, he said to him, "Wait"; the second, he said to him, "Wait"; the third, he said to him, "Wait"; the fourth, he said to him, "Wait"; at the fifth, he said to him, "Go out and sell it in the market." (Pesaḥim 13a)

Apparently, one who was left with large amount of *ḥametz* before Pesaḥ and did not wish to destroy the *ḥametz,* as he would thus incur financial loss, would sell the *ḥametz* to a non-Jew.

The Mishna and Gemara refer to a case in which the owner did not repurchase the *ḥametz* after Pesaḥ, but the Tosefta records a situation in which one would sell his *ḥametz* and then repurchase and take possession of it again after Pesaḥ:

> A Jew and a non-Jew who were on a ship, and the Jew was in possession of *ḥametz* – he may sell the *ḥametz* to the non-Jew or give it to him as a gift and after Pesaḥ take [the *ḥametz*] back, as long has he gave it to him as a proper gift (*matana gemura*).[28]

Some *Rishonim* explain that the Tosefta refers to a case in which the Jew, because he is traveling on the eve of Pesaḥ, will not have any food for after the festival unless he performs this sale. Furthermore, *Beit Yosef*[29] cites *Behag*, who explains that the Tosefta refers to a case in which one does not intend to buy back the *ḥametz* afterward. While *Beit Yosef* himself disagrees, he notes that the Tosefta permits this practice only because the non-Jew actually took possession of the *ḥametz*.

R. Yisrael Isserlin (1390–1460) permits one to sell *ḥametz* to a non-Jew "outside of one's house" and then to repurchase it after Pesaḥ.[30] The *Aḥaronim* discuss whether the *Terumat HaDeshen* insisted that the non-Jew be outside of his house – that is, that he did not work for the Jew – or the *ḥametz*.

Over time, many people wished to sell their *ḥametz* to non-Jews without removing it from their property. For example, flour that may have become *ḥametz*, liquors, and other items are difficult to remove from one's property. R. Yoel Sirkis permits those with large quantities of commercial liquor produced from *ḥametz* to sell their stock to a non-Jew and give the non-Jew a key to the room in which it is stored.[31] Although this type of sale appears to be ideal, as it is personal and specific, it apparently became difficult to leave the sale of *ḥametz* up to each individual. Toward the beginning of the nineteenth century, a broader, more general sale of *ḥametz* developed, in which the members of a community would either sell their *ḥametz* to the *beit din* or appoint them as their agents to sell the *ḥametz* to a non-Jew.

Some question whether *mekhirat ḥametz* constitutes a *haarama*, a legal loophole, and, if so, whether one may rely upon it. R. Yosef Shaul Nathanson (1808–1875), for example, argues at length for the abolishment of this practice.[32] Ḥatam Sofer, however, defends the practice and rebukes anyone who casts doubt upon its legitimacy.[33] Although the sale of *ḥametz* has become standard in most communities, some rely upon *mekhirat ḥametz* only when necessary, such as a store-owner or one who owns large quantities of liquor. Some also insist that one should refrain from selling *ḥametz gamur* (real *ḥametz*),[34] but others disagree.[35] Some recommend that even those who dispose of all of their *ḥametz* before Pesaḥ, such as single men and women who live in dormitories, should still execute a *mekhirat ḥametz*, lest they forget to dispose of some *ḥametz* or keep certain items, unaware that they contain *ḥametz*.

The *Aḥaronim* also question the technicalities of the sale. For example, what is the most appropriate form of *kinyan*? The Mishna teaches that the acquisition of movable items must be done through physically transferring them (*meshikha* or *hagbaa*), and not merely through the transfer of money (*kinyan kesef*) (Kiddushin 26a). The Gemara discusses whether this is true regarding transactions between Jews and non-Jews as well (Bekhorot 13b). Tosafot write that since the final ruling is a matter of dispute, both in the Gemara and among the *Rishonim*, one should preferably perform both a physical transfer of the item as well as a monetary transfer when performing a transaction with a non-Jew for the sake of a mitzva.[36]

Since, in the case of *mekhirat ḥametz*, the *ḥametz* never leaves the possession of the Jew, another *kinyan* aside from *meshikha* or *hagbaha* must be employed. The Mishna teaches that one can transfer movable items as part of another transaction involving property, known as a *kinyan agav* (Kiddushin 26a). Based on this, the *Mishna Berura* recommends renting or selling part of one's property as part of the sale and including one's *ḥametz* in the transaction.[37] One therefore generally rents the room or cabinet in which the *ḥametz* is stored as part of the *mekhirat ḥametz*. In addition, the Gemara also discusses a transaction commonly used by local businessmen, a *kinyan situmta* (Bava Metzia 74a). Some explain that a *shetar* (contract document) is used for *mekhirat ḥametz*, even though a *shetar* cannot generally be used to transfer movable objects, as it may constitute a *kinyan situmta*. The *Mishna Berura* also recommends employing a *kinyan ḥalipin*, in which the non-Jew gives an item of his own in exchange for the *ḥametz*.[38]

Others note that while one generally pays the full price for what one purchases, the non-Jew does not pay the full price for all of the *ḥametz* that he buys. The *Mishna Berura* notes that although the sale reflects the full price of the *ḥametz*, the non-Jew simply gives a "down payment" at the time of the sale, and the balance is considered to be his debt.[39]

The *Aḥaronim* also discuss how to reacquire the *ḥametz* after Pesaḥ. While some suggest that the Jew takes back the *ḥametz* after Pesaḥ because the non-Jew has not yet paid the full balance of his debt, R. Shlomo Kluger,[40] as along with the *Mishna Berura*[41] and other *posekim*, insists that the *ḥametz* must be repurchased from the non-Jew.

In recent times, when travel has become increasingly common, especially travel to and from Israel for the festival, the *Aḥaronim* questioned what one should do if his *ḥametz* is located in a different time zone. For example, a person who lives in America and travels to Israel for Pesaḥ will begin celebrating Pesaḥ before the sale of *ḥametz* in America takes place. Conversely, one who travels from Israel to America will most likely reacquire his *ḥametz* while still observing Pesaḥ in America. Does the prohibition of *bal yeira'e uval yimatzei* follow the location of the *ḥametz* or the owner?

R. Yom Tov Lipman Halperin argues that the prohibition of *bal yeira'e uval yimatzei* follow the place of the *ḥametz* during Pesaḥ.[42] Many *Aḥaronim* disagree, however.[43] Although most *posekim* follow the place of the owner of the *ḥametz*, one should attempt to follow both opinions.[44]

May a Jew who owns a supermarket that continues to sell *ḥametz* during the festival sell his *ḥametz* to a non-Jew? R. Moshe Feinstein dealt with this question repeatedly, and he justified this practice with various conditions and stipulations.[45] R. Soloveitchik objected to such a sale, and the policy of the OU is not to sanction such a sale.[46]

Nowadays, it is customary for those who intend to sell their *ḥametz* to indicate on a *shetar harshaa*, a Statement of Authorization, which *ḥametz* they intend to sell and its location. By signing the document, one authorizes the rabbi to sell the *ḥametz* to a non-Jew.[47] While strictly speaking, one need not perform this *kinyan*, and one may authorize a sale verbally and even over the phone,[48] the rabbi generally performs a *kinyan sudar*, in which the seller lifts the rabbi's pen or kerchief, in order to demonstrate his seriousness regarding the sale. This practice is based upon Rambam, who records:

> It has become customary in the majority of places to perform a *kinyan* to confirm certain of the above matters and the like, even though it is not necessary. The witnesses say: "We performed a *kinyan* with so-and-so, confirming that he appointed so-and-so as an agent," "waived the debt that so-and-so owed him," or "nullified the protest he had issued concerning this bill of

> divorce," or the like. Such a *kinyan,* which is customarily performed with regard to these matters, is of no consequence except to demonstrate that the parties involved were not acting facetiously or in jest when making the statements, but had in fact made a resolution in their hearts before making the statements. Therefore, if a person says, "I am making my statements with a full heart, and I have resolved to do this," nothing else is necessary.[49]

Although this practice may be waived in case of need, one might question the propriety of performing *mekhirat ḥametz* "online," which has become very common in recent years. This interesting question awaits rabbinic consideration.

ḤAMETZ SHEAVAR ALAV HAPESAḤ

The Mishna teaches:

> One may derive benefit from *ḥametz* that belonged to a gentile during Pesaḥ; but *ḥametz* of a Jew [which remained in his possession over Pesaḥ] is forbidden, for the Torah says, "No leavening may be in your possession."[50]

The Gemara cites a debate between R. Yehuda and R. Shimon regarding the origin of this law. R. Yehuda maintains that *mideoraita,* one may not consume *ḥametz* owned by a Jew during Pesaḥ. R. Shimon disagrees; as Rava explains (Pesaḥim 29a), the Rabbis instituted a *kenas* (penalty) because this person violated the prohibition of *bal yeira'e uval yimatzei.* The halakha is in accordance with R. Shimon.

Ramban rules that we do not distinguish between one who inadvertently kept *ḥametz* over Pesaḥ and one who did so intentionally.[51] Similarly, Rambam writes:

> *Ḥametz* of a Jew that remained in his possession during Pesaḥ is forever forbidden from any benefit, and this matter is a fine instituted by the sages since the person transgressed the prohibition of "it shall not be seen nor found in your domain"; [therefore] they forbade it. Even if he left it over by mistake or against his will, [they instituted the fine] so that no person will leave over *ḥametz* in his domain during Pesaḥ in order to have it after Pesaḥ.[52]

The *Shulḥan Arukh* rules accordingly.[53] The *ḥametz* of a non-Jew is permitted after Pesaḥ, even for eating, but *ḥametz* of a Jew that remained in his possession over Pesaḥ, even if he left it over by mistake or against his will, is forbidden.

R. Feinstein writes that after Pesaḥ, one may purchase *ḥametz* from a supermarket owned by Jews at the point at which there is at least a 50% possibility that the food one buys was bought by the supermarket after Pesaḥ. Since *ḥametz she'avar alav haPesaḥ* is only *miderabbanan*, we invoke the principle of *safek derabbanan lekula*.[54]

Sefirat HaOmer — Shavuot

CHAPTER 49

Sefirat HaOmer: The Counting

THE TORAH COMMANDS in two places that one should count the days and weeks from the second day of Pesaḥ until the holiday of Shavuot:

> And you shall count for yourselves from the day after the Sabbath, from the day that you brought the sheaf of the wave offering; seven weeks shall there be complete. Count fifty days to the day after the seventh Sabbath; then you shall offer a new grain offering to the Lord. (Lev. 23:15–16)
>
> Seven weeks you shall number unto you; from the time the sickle is first put to the standing corn you should begin to number seven weeks. And you shall keep the Feast of Weeks unto the Lord your God after the measure of the freewill-offering of your hand, which you shall give, according as the Lord your God blessed you. (Deut. 16:9–10)

The *korban haOmer*, a sacrifice consisting of an "*omer*" of flour made from newly harvested barley, was brought on the second day of Pesaḥ. This *korban* signals the permissibility of the consumption of *ḥadash*, grains from the new harvest, which was forbidden until this offering. The *Sefirat HaOmer* begins on that day and continues until the holiday of Shavuot, when we offer the *shetei haleḥem*, two loaves made from newly harvested wheat. In this chapter, we will discuss the reasons for this mitzva, its source, and the manner in which it is performed.

REASONS FOR *SEFIRAT HAOMER*

The *Rishonim* offer different reasons for the mitzva of *Sefirat HaOmer*. They disagree as to whether to view this mitzva within its historical/agricultural context or within the framework of the period between the Exodus from Egypt and the impending giving of the Torah. R. David b. R. Yosef Abudraham offers the simplest explanation of this mitzva:

> The reason for which the Holy One, Blessed be He, commanded to count the *Omer* was because each Israelite was involved in his own harvest and each one was dispersed in his own threshing floor, and He commanded to count in order that they should not forget the time of their ascent for the festival (*aliya laregel*).[1]

The *Abudraham* explains that the farmer, who spends his time after Pesaḥ occupied with the wheat harvest, may lose track of time and forget to come to Jerusalem for the celebration of Shavuot. He is therefore commanded to count forty-nine days, after which he celebrates Shavuot in Jerusalem. Rabbeinu Yeruḥam explains the mitzva in this manner as well, suggesting that one counts at night because one is less burdened by the harvest at night.[2]

In the continuation of the passage cited above, the *Abudraham* offers another reason for the mitzva:

> Because the world is in distress between Pesaḥ and Shavuot over [the pending judgment of] the wheat and trees, as the Talmud describes in the beginning of Tractate Rosh HaShana.... Therefore, He commanded to count the days in order that we should remember the world's distress and return to Him with a full heart and plead before Him to have mercy on us and the creatures and the world, and that the wheat should be as it should be, as it is the source of our existence, and "if there is no flour, there is no Torah."

According this view, the counting of the *Omer* is not intended to remind the farmer of the upcoming festival, but rather to remind us of the precarious situation of the world during this time, so that we should pray for the sufficiency of the wheat harvest, upon which the world's sustenance depends.

In his *Guide for the Perplexed,* Rambam extends the importance of this mitzva beyond the practical significance for the ancient farmer:

> We count the days that pass since the preceding festival, as is done by one who waits for the coming of the human being he loves best and counts the

> days and hours. This is the reason for the counting of the *Omer* from the day when they left Egypt until the day of the giving of the Torah, which was the purpose and the end of their leaving.[3]

According to Rambam, we count the days from leaving Egypt until the receiving of the Torah because the entire purpose of the Exodus was to receive the Torah. The *Sefer HaḤinukh* agrees with this reason, adding that although it would seem to make more sense to count *down* the days until Shavuot, the Torah wants us to express our strong desire to reach the time of the giving of the Torah; one does not want to begin with the impression of so many days ahead of him.[4]

While Rambam and *Sefer Ḥinukh* explain that one counts in order to express his yearning for the Torah, Ran suggests that one counts in anticipation of receiving the Torah, just as the Jewish people counted from their freedom from Egypt until they received the Torah.[5] The reason suggested for the mitzva – focusing either on the the count between the *korban haOmer* until the *shetei haleḥem* or the time period between the Exodus from Egypt and the giving of the Torah – may impact upon whether the mitzva is considered binding *mideoraita* or *miderabbanan* after the destruction of the *Beit HaMikdash*, as we will see below.

THE SOURCE OF THE OBLIGATION OF *SEFIRAT HAOMER*

The Talmud states:

> Abaye said: It is the mitzva to count the days and also to count the weeks. The rabbis of the school of R. Ashi used to count the days as well as the weeks. Ameimar used to count the days but not the weeks, saying, "It is only in commemoration of Temple times (*zekher laMikdash*)." (Menaḥot 66a)

All agree that during the times in which the Temple stood, one was obligated to count both the days and the weeks. However, Ameimar maintained that after the destruction of the Temple, the counting of the *Omer* is only *zekher laMikdash*, as the *korban haOmer* and *shetei haleḥem* are no longer offered, and therefore one should perform the mitzva in an abridged form, by counting the weeks, and not the days. It remains unclear whether Abaye and R. Ashi, who maintained that one should count both the days *and* the weeks, nevertheless agreed that *Sefirat HaOmer* is only *zekher laMikdash* nowadays, or whether they disagreed with Ameimar's premise entirely, assuming that *Sefirat HaOmer* is still a biblical law even after the destruction of the Temple.

The *Rishonim* further debate whether *Sefirat HaOmer* is *mideoraita* or *miderabbanan* nowadays, and whether there is still a distinction between the counting of the days and the weeks. Rambam, for example, writes:

> There is a *mitzvat aseh* (positive obligation) to count seven complete weeks from the day of the bringing of the *Omer* [on the sixteenth of Nissan], as it says, "You shall count for yourselves, from the day following the Shabbat, seven weeks." There is a mitzva to count the days together with the weeks, as it says, "You shall count fifty days".... This mitzva applies to all males among Israel, in every place and at every time.[6]

Rambam clearly maintains that the obligation is *mideoraita* nowadays. Raavya[7] and *Shibbolei HaLeket*[8] concur. According to these *Rishonim*, Abaye and R. Ashi argue with Ameimar and maintain that *Sefirat HaOmer* remains a biblical obligation.

Others disagree. In discussing whether one may count the *Omer* during *bein hashemashot*, when one is in doubt whether it is day or night, Tosafot argue:

> It appears that when one is in doubt as to whether or not night has fallen one, he may recite the *berakha* [over *Sefirat HaOmer*] and need not wait until the time when night has definitely fallen, since this constitutes a situation of doubt concerning a rabbinic law [regarding which we rule leniently]. (Menaḥot 66a)

Tosafot apply the principle of *safek derabbanan lekula* to *Sefirat HaOmer*, clearly indicating its rabbinic origin in their opinion. Baal HaMaor agrees:

> Some have asked why we do not recite "*zeman*" [the *berakha* of *Sheheḥeyanu*] for *Sefirat HaOmer*.... Furthermore, why don't we count twice out of doubt,

> just as we observe two days of Yom Tov out of doubt? The governing principle is that we need not conduct ourselves stringently regarding *Sefirat HaOmer*, for it constitutes but a commemoration.[9]

Most *Rishonim* agree and clearly maintain that since we do not bring the *korban haOmer* nowadays, *Sefirat HaOmer* must only be a rabbinic obligation.[10]

Do these *Rishonim* distinguish between counting the days and the weeks, as Ameimar did, and count only the days? Baal HaMaor addresses this issue:

> It is only a commemoration, and this is the conclusion there in Menaḥot, that Ameimar counted days and not weeks, claiming that the mitzva is but a commemoration of the Temple. Although we count both days and weeks, this is a custom we have adopted.

Baal HaMaor fundamentally agrees that those who maintain that *Sefirat HaOmer* is only *miderabbanan* nowadays should distinguish between the counting of the days and the weeks, and he therefore concludes that the counting of weeks is only a "custom we have adopted." Most *Rishonim* disagree, however. Ran, for example, writes:

> Since Abaye and the school of R. Ashi counted both days and weeks, we follow their position, even though Ameimar argues with them.... Most commentators agree that nowadays, when we do not bring [the *Omer* offering] nor offer the sacrifice, *Sefirat HaOmer* is only a rabbinic obligation, in commemoration of the *Mikdash*.[11]

Apparently, even Abaye and the school of R. Ashi maintained that *Sefirat HaOmer* is a rabbinic obligation nowadays; they only argue with Ameimar regarding whether it should be observed differently from how it was in the *Mikdash*. In other words, they argue as to whether a mitzva that is instituted as a *zekher laMikdash* should be modeled exactly after the original mitzva.

If so, how are we to understand this debate between Ameimar and Abaye and the school of R. Ashi? R. Yitzchak Ze'ev Soloveitchik, known as the Brisker Rav, discusses this issue.[12] He distinguishes between two different types of enactments intended to serve as a *zekher laMikdash*. At times, the Rabbis instituted that one should continue fulfilling a mitzva just as it was fulfilled in the *Beit HaMikdash* in order to ensure that the particulars of that mitzva are not forgotten. However, the Rabbis also instituted certain practices that are intended to remind the Jewish people of the loss of the Temple and the lost opportunity to fulfill the mitzva. In other words, sometimes the enactment focuses upon the performance of the mitzva, while at other times, it focuses upon the mourning over the destruction of the Temple.

Abaye and the school of R. Ashi apparently maintained that the Rabbis instituted that one should continue to count the *Omer* just as it was done in the *Beit HaMikdash*. Ameimar, however, believed that the enactment was intended only to remind us of the loss of the Temple, and it is therefore sufficient to count the days.

While some *Rishonim* view *Sefirat HaOmer* as *mideoraita* and some understand it as being *miderabbanan*, others offer a third, middle position. Rabbeinu Yeruḥam, for example, maintains that during the time of the *Beit HaMikdash*, there are actually two separate mitzvot: the counting of the weeks and the counting of the days. The counting of the weeks is linked to the cutting of the *Omer*, as it says, "Count seven weeks from the beginning of the harvest of the standing grain" (Deut. 16:9). The counting of the days, however, is not dependent on the *Omer*. He therefore argues that nowadays, since we no longer offer the *korban haOmer* in the *Beit HaMikdash*, the counting of the days remains *mideoraita*, but the counting of the weeks is only *miderabbanan* – *zekher laMikdash*. Furthermore, he explains that since the counting of the weeks is only *miderabbanan*, it does not merit a separate *berakha*.[13]

Interestingly, *Sefat Emet* suggests a similar, yet opposite theory. He claims that the counting of the weeks mentioned in Deuteronomy relates to the holiday of Shavuot, while the counting of the days mentioned in Leviticus appears in the context of the *korban haOmer* and the *shetei haleḥem*. He proposes that neither of these two mitzvot – the mentioning of the days and the weeks – is applicable after the destruction for the Temple. Ameimar maintained that the counting that was relevant to the *Beit HaMikdash*, the counting of the days, should be observed *zekher laMikdash*. He concludes that after formulating this theory, he was shown opinion of Rabbeinu Yeruḥam, "whose words are not understood, and they are partially the opposite of what I wrote."[14]

Biur Halakha writes that although the position of the *Shulkhan Arukh* is that *Sefirat HaOmer* is a rabbinic mitzva, one should be careful to count the *Omer* after *tzeit hakokhavim,* in deference to those opinions that maintain that *Sefirat HaOmer* is a *mitzva mideoraita* even nowadays.[15]

Interestingly, the "*hineni mukhan umezuman*" paragraph customarily recited before counting the *Omer* reads, "I am hereby prepared and ready to fulfill the positive commandment of *Sefirat HaOmer,* as it is written in the Torah...." This declaration, which expresses one's intention to fulfill the commandment, implies that the obligation of *Sefirat HaOmer* is *mideoraita*. Not only is this point debatable, as demonstrated above, but it also seemingly contradicts the passage that is customarily said after counting the *Omer*: "O Compassionate One! May He return for us the Service of the Temple to its place speedily and in our time, Amen *selah*,"[16] which implies that *Sefirat HaOmer* is performed *zekher laMikdash*! While some *Aḥaronim* object to reciting either passage, others attempt to understand this common custom.

THE PROPER TIME FOR *SEFIRAT HAOMER*

The Mishna and the Gemara teach that the entire night is considered to be the proper time for the cutting and the counting of the *Omer* (Megilla 20b). Why is counting the *Omer* performed specifically at night?

Some suggest that the counting must be performed at night so that each day's counting is "complete," "*temimot*." The Gemara cites the following *baraita*:

> Perhaps the *Omer* should be cut and counted during the day? We are taught, "They should be seven complete weeks (*temimot*)" (Lev. 23:15). When can one attain seven complete weeks? When one starts to count at night. (Menaḥot 66a)

According to this source, one counts at night so that each day's count is "complete," including the entire day. Rabbeinu Tam maintains that even if the cutting of the *Omer* may be performed during the day, as we will discuss, the Torah specifically uses the term "*temimot*" to teach that the counting should be done at night.[17]

While Rabbeinu Tam clearly understands that the requirement of "*temimot*" applies to each night, one might suggest that it applies only the first evening, in order to create a complete count from beginning to end. R. Yehudai Gaon, for example, maintains that one who did not count the first night may not count on subsequent nights, as his counting can no longer be considered "*temimot*."[18] Similarly, some apply the notion of "*temimot*" to the conclusion of *Sefirat HaOmer* as well. The *Aḥaronim* write that one should not recite Kiddush and eat, or even recite Maariv, before *tzeit hakokhavim* of the evening of Shavuot so that the count will be complete.[19]

Some understand that "*temimot*" also requires that one count at the beginning of each night. Rambam mentions this requirement in his Commentary to the Mishna,[20] but not in his *Mishneh Torah*. *Tur* similarly writes, "The time for counting is the beginning of the night. If one forgot to count at the beginning of the night, one can count all night."[21]

The *Shulḥan Arukh* cites this as well, writing that one should count the *Omer* after *Tefillat Maariv*.[22] *Biur Halakha* cites R. Yaakov Emden, who insists, in his *Mor UKetzia*, that the *Shulḥan Arukh* referred to the practice years ago, when Maariv was recited before dark. Since *Sefirat HaOmer* must be performed at night, it obviously must follow Maariv. However, when Maariv is not recited before dark, one should certainly count the *Omer* before reciting Maariv. *Biur Halakha* disagrees, and it is common practice to count the *Omer* after Maariv, before *Aleinu*.[23]

The *Aḥaronim* debate why, in fact, we recite *Sefirat HaOmer* after Maariv. R. Moshe Feinstein notes that the principle of "*tadir veshe'eino tadir, tadir kodem*" (meaning that when we have two mitzva obligations, we perform the more frequent one first) dictates that Maariv should be recited first.[24] R. Shmuel Wosner, however, maintains that the principle of "*tadir veshe'eino tadir*" does not apply in this case. However, he agrees that even one who recites Maariv later in the evening should count the

Omer after Maariv; one should not become accustomed to separating *Sefirat HaOmer* from Maariv, lest he forget to count or lest he count twice. R. Shmuel Wosner suggests that one who prays alone, long after *tzeit hakokhavim,* may count the *Omer* early and recite Maariv later.[25] Some add that the mitzva of *Sefirat HaOmer* should preferably be fulfilled publicly, "*berov am,*" and this is another reason why it is recited in conjunction with Maariv.[26]

Alternatively, some suggest that we count the *Omer* at night because that is when the *ketzirat haOmer,* the cutting of the barley for the *Omer,* is performed.[27] Similarly, some *Rishonim* derive that one should stand for the *Sefirat HaOmer* by comparing the counting to the cutting of the *Omer,* as the verse describing the cutting of the *Omer* says it should be brought from the beginning of the harvest, when the grain is "*kama*" – standing.[28] The *Sefer HaYerei'im* cites this *derasha,* although he acknowledges that he is unsure of its origin.[29]

THE EARLIEST TIME FOR *SEFIRAT HAOMER*

When is the earliest time that one may count *Sefirat HaOmer*? Generally, we assume that while *tzeit hakokhavim* (the appearance of stars) marks the beginning of the evening, there is a *safek,* a halakhic doubt, whether to consider the period between *shekiat haḥama* (sunset) and *tzeit hakokhavim* as day or night. This question is of great relevance in places in which the congregation recites Maariv immediately after *shekia,* which is quite common outside of Israel.

The *Rishonim* address this question from two perspectives. First, as we discussed above, the *Rishonim* debate whether *Sefirat HaOmer* is a mitzva *mideoraita* or *miderabbanan* nowadays. Tosafot write that since *Sefirat HaOmer* is only a rabbinic mitzva, we employ the principle of *safek derabbanan lekula* and rule leniently, considering the period of *bein hashemashot* (*safek ḥasheikha*) to be nighttime. Thus, one may count the *Omer* with a *berakha* during *bein hashemashot.* Tosafot suggest that counting during *bein hashemashot* may even be preferable in order to fulfill the requirement of "*temimot,*" as we discussed above.[30]

Those *Rishonim* who maintain that *Sefirat HaOmer* is *mideoraita* would certainly disagree, but even Ran, who agrees that *Sefirat HaOmer* is *miderabbanan* nowadays, objects to deliberately entering into a situation of doubt, as Tosafot suggest. Furthermore, he questions whether one should count during *bein hashemashot* in order to fulfill the aspect of "*temimot*," which one would certainly not do during the time of the *Beit HaMikdash*, when the obligation is clearly *mideoraita*.[31]

The *Shulḥan Arukh* rules that those who are particular in their performance of mitzvot (*hamedakdekim*) wait until after *tzeit hakokhavim* to count, concluding, "It is proper to do so."[32] *Magen Avraham* writes that *bediavad*, one who counted during *bein hashemashot* has fulfilled his obligation,[33] but the *Mishna Berura* cites the *Eliya Rabba*, who recommends that one repeat the count without a *berakha* after *tzeit hakokhavim*.[34]

The *Arukh HaShulḥan* records that it is customary to wait until after *tzeit hakokhavim*, except on Fridays, when the entire congregation accepts Shabbat early.[35] R. Ovadia Yosef, however, rules that one may recite *Sefirat HaOmer* with the blessing immediately after *shekia*; he also describes this as the "*minhag Yerushalayim*," the custom in Jerusalem. He concludes, however, like the *Shulḥan Arukh*, that those who are meticulous should wait until *tzeit hakokhavim*, approximately fifteen minutes after *shekia*, and then count.[36]

SEFIRAT HAOMER FROM *PELAG HAMINḤA*

May one count *Sefirat HaOmer* even earlier, from *pelag haMinḥa* (the halfway point between *Minḥa ketana* and the end of the day – between ten and three quarter hours after day begins and one and one quarter hours before night)?

The *Shulḥan Arukh* cites the *Maḥzor Vitry*, who rules that one who prays with a community "while it is still day" should count the *Omer* without a blessing, and if he remembers later, he should count again with a *berakha*.[37] *Magen Avraham* explains that this works if one has in mind that if he remembers to count after dark, his intention

but one who omitted a different night may continue counting. Apparently, R. Soloveitchik suggests, R. Saadia Gaon maintains that by omitting the first number, the count never really begins. One who omits a different number, however, may continue to count, even though he made a mistake in the count. Similarly, *Biur Halakha*[68] cites R. Hai Gaon, who writes that if one forgot to count for an entire day, he should say on the next night, "Yesterday was the ____ day, and today is…" By mentioning the previous day, one restores the continuity lost by having omitted the previous day.

This interpretation may also enable us to answer *Minḥat Ḥinukh*'s question regarding one who became bar mitzva during the *Omer*. According to R. Soloveitchik, the *Sefer Ḥinukh* also maintains that the *Sefirat HaOmer* is made up of forty-nine separate mitzvot. However, the boy may only count with a blessing following his bar mitzva if he counted until now, creating the continuity necessary in order to continue counting.

THE LATEST TIME FOR *SEFIRAT HAOMER*

What if one forgot to count the *Omer* at night and during the day, but remembers during *bein hashemashot*? *Shaarei Teshuva*[69] cites the *Teshuvot Beit David*,[70] who rules that one who counts the previous day during *bein hashemashot* should count without a *berakha* on subsequent nights. He cites *Birkei Yosef*, who questions this ruling. Other *Aḥaronim* rule that he may count with a blessing the following night.[71] *Minḥat Yitzchak* qualifies that one should only rely upon this leniency during a time that all opinions define as *bein hashemashot*; one should not rely upon Rabbeinu Tam's time schedule for this issue.[72] R. Moshe Feinstein, for example, relies upon this leniency as long as one counts within nine minutes after *shekia*.[73]

What if one already recited the next day's Maariv before *shekia* and then remembered that he had not yet counted the previous day? Or what if one makes "early Shabbat," as many families do during the spring and summer, and remembered that he forgot to count the previous day's *Omer* only after he accepted Shabbat? Theoretically, one might distinguish between these two cases depending upon the dispute between *Taz* and Maharshal regarding whether accepting Shabbat transforms the time before sundown into the next day for matters not related to Shabbat, such as *aveilut, sukka,* and *nidda.*[74] *Shaarei Teshuva,*[75] however, along with R. Moshe Feinstein,[76] allows one to count in both cases and to continue to count with a blessing after *tzeit hakokhavim.*

WHO IS OBLIGATED TO COUNT *SEFIRAT HAOMER*?

Women

The Talmud rules in numerous places that women are exempt from "time-bound commandments" (*mitzvot aseh shehazeman geraman*) (Kiddushin 33b). Women are therefore exempt from certain mitzvot, such as *tefillin, tzitzit, sukka, arba minim,* shofar, and *Keriat Shema.* Seemingly, *Sefirat HaOmer,* which is performed between Pesaḥ and Shavuot and preferably at night, should be considered such a mitzva, and women should be exempt.

Indeed, Rambam[77] and the *Sefer HaḤinukh*[78] exempt women from the mitzva of *Sefirat HaOmer.* Ramban, however, enumerates mitzvot that are not time-bound and which women are therefore obligated to perform, including respecting and honoring parents, *bikkurim, ḥalla, kisui hadam, reishit hagez, matanot kehuna, perika ute'ina,* and *pidyon petter ḥamor* – as he summarizes, "most of the mitzvot." The mitzva of *Sefirat HaOmer* is included in this short list of examples of mitzvot that are not time-bound.[79] R. Malkiel Zvi b. R. Yona Tannenbaum (1847–1910)[80] and R. Soloveitchik[81] were so shocked by this opinion that they suggested that this must be a scribal error!

Indeed, is it possible to view *Sefirat HaOmer* as a commandment that is not time-bound and therefore one which women are obligated to perform? Perhaps we might argue that the mitzva of *Sefirat HaOmer* is not truly time-bound at all; the opinions that permit counting during the day view *Sefirat HaOmer* as a mitzva that is not bound by time, while those who maintain that the mitzva may only be performed at night, similar to the *ketzirat haOmer,* view *Sefirat HaOmer* as a *mitzvat aseh shehazeman gerama.*

Alternatively, we might suggest other reasons that *Sefirat HaOmer* is not a time-bound mitzva. R. Yechiel Yaakov Weinberg (1885–1966), for example, explains:

> In my humble opinion, the answer is simple. A *mitzvat aseh shehazeman gerama* is a mitzva that has a set time; the time is the frame within which the mitzva is fulfilled, such as *matza,* lulav, and *sukka* ... which is not the case regarding *Sefirat HaOmer*. [*Sefirat HaOmer*] is not a mitzva to count days, but rather to count the specific days between Pesaḥ and Shavuot, and it is not proper to say that the time has "caused" this mitzva.[82]

In other words, the time between Pesaḥ and Shavuot is not the time-frame within which one may fulfill this mitzva. Rather, these are the days that one must count in order to fulfill the mitzva. The time does not obligate or generate the mitzva, but rather *is* the mitzva itself!

R. Avraham Bornstein discusses this question in his *Avnei Nezer*. He suggests that just as women are obligated in all mitzvot related to the night of Pesaḥ, such as the prohibition to eat *ḥametz,* the mitzva to eat *matza,* and the mitzva of *sippur yetziat Mitzrayim,* women are naturally obligated to count the *Omer,* which begins "on the morrow after that day [of Pesaḥ]."[83] Although this interpretation is intriguing and raises the question as to the relationship between *Sefirat HaOmer* and Pesaḥ, it is doubtful that this is Ramban's intention. He labels *Sefirat HaOmer* as a mitzva that is not time-bound, not one which is time-bound but that women must still fulfill.[84]

Magen Avraham concludes that although women are exempt from *Sefirat HaOmer,* as it is a time-bound mitzva, "they have accepted it upon themselves as an obligation."[85] The *Minḥat Ḥinukh* disagrees,[86] and the *Mishna Berura* records that not only is this not the custom, but some even discourage women from reciting the blessing over *Sefirat HaOmer,* lest they forget to count on subsequent days.[87] It seems, however, that the custom nowadays is for women to count *Sefirat HaOmer* with a blessing.[88]

Beit Din

The Sifri notes one of the differences between the mitzva of *Sefirat HaOmer* as it appears in Leviticus and as it appears in Deuteronomy:

> "Seven weeks you shall number unto you" [Deut. 16:9–10] – in *beit din*. And how do we know that each and every individual must [also] count? It says, "And you shall count unto yourselves" [Lev. 23:15–16] – each and every person.[89]

This Sifri apparently maintains that the *Beit Din HaGadol* must count each day of the *Omer* leading up to Shavuot. We find a similar phenomenon, according to some opinions, regarding the years of the *Shemitta* cycles; Rambam rules that the *Beit Din HaGadol* must count each year of the *Shemitta* cycle, just as it must count the years of *Shemitta* leading up to the *Yovel*.[90] *Ḥizkuni* also clearly states that the Torah relates in the two different sources to two separate counts, one that is entrusted to the *Beit Din HaGadol* and the other, which is entrusted to the community (that is, the individuals).[91] R. Yerucham Fishel Perle, on the other hand, vehemently rejects this possibility.[92]

The possibility that the *Beit Din HaGadol* must also count the days of the *Omer* may be a minority opinion, but is intriguing, nonetheless. Why would the *Beit Din HaGadol* be commanded to count the days of the *Omer*? R. Soloveitchik explains that the *Beit Din HaGadol*, as the representative group of the Jewish people, is entrusted with the sanctification of the festivals. In fact, the Talmud distinguishes between Shabbat, whose sanctity is "fixed" by God and upon which we therefore recite the blessing, *Mekadesh HaShabbat* ("He who sanctifies the Shabbat"), and Yom Tov, which is sanctified by the Jewish people, who set the months and years and upon which we recite the *berakha*, *Mekadesh Yisrael VeHaZemanim* ("He who sanctifies Israel and the festivals") (Beitza 17a). R. Soloveitchik develops this idea further, claiming that Rambam maintains that the *Beit Din HaGadol* sanctifies the Jubilee year by counting each and every year of the *Shemitta* cycles.[93] Similarly, the *Beit Din HaGadol*, through their counting of the *Omer*, may also sanctify the Festival of Shavuot, especially since it is not identified by specific date, but rather by its relationship to Pesaḥ.[94] Indeed, the Torah says, "You should begin to number seven weeks, and you shall keep the Feast of Weeks" (Deut. 16:9–10); the counting of the weeks establishes the "Feast of Weeks" – Shavuot. While the individual counts each day between the *korban haOmer* and the *shetei haleḥem,* the *Beit Din HaGadol* counts each day leading up to Shavuot, sanctifying it thereby.

This intriguing idea may also explain the difference between the count of days that appears in Leviticus and the count of weeks that appears in Deuteronomy. The counting of the weeks relates to the Festival of Shavuot, while the counting of the days relates to the *korban haOmer* and the *shetei haleḥem*. We will return to this distinction shortly.

The distinctions between the personal and communal aspects of *Sefirat HaOmer* may also relate to the question, raised above, of whether *Sefirat HaOmer* should be considered to be a *mitzvat aseh shehazeman gerama*. R. Soloveitchik suggests that *Sefirat HaOmer* may not be considered a *mitzvat aseh shehazeman gerama* according to Ramban because women are certainly included in the communal sanctification of the holiday of Shavuot.

THE MANNER OF RECITING *SEFIRAT HAOMER* AND ONE WHO COUNTS INCORRECTLY

The *posekim* discuss the proper manner of reciting *Sefirat HaOmer* and whether counting incorrectly invalidates the *sefira*. As we mentioned above, the mitzva to count includes both the days and the weeks of the *Omer*. The *Mishna Berura* records that the *Aḥaronim* debate whether one who counted only the days has fulfilled his obligation. He concludes that one should count again without a *berakha,* but if one did not count again, he may continue counting the next evening with a *berakha.*[95]

Ḥayei Adam writes that one who counts the weeks but omits the days should similarly count again without the *berakha.*[96] The *Mishna Berura,* however, disagrees, ruling that one should count again with a blessing. One who realizes the next day that he counted only the weeks may continue to count with a blessing.[97] One who counts incorrectly should correct himself immediately, within the time known as "*tokh kedei dibbur*" – the amount of time it takes to say, "*Shalom aleikhem, Rebbe.*"

One must say "*hayom*," "today is," when counting the *Omer*. *Taz* rules that one who omits "*hayom*" has not fulfilled his obligation;[98] the *Shulḥan Arukh HaRav* rules that one must count again with a *berakha*,[99] and the *Mishna Berura* concurs.[100]

The *posekim* disagree as to whether one should say "*baOmer*" or "*laOmer*." Seemingly, "***la**Omer*" relates the counting to the offering of the *korban haOmer*, while "***ba**Omer*" refers to the time period leading up to Shavuot. As we discussed above, both ideas are firmly rooted in halakhic sources. Although Rema writes that one should say "*baOmer*,"[101] the *Mishna Berura* writes that most *Aḥaronim* rule that one should preferably say "*laOmer*," but adds that one fulfills his obligation with either version.[102]

One may count the *Omer* in any language, as long as he understands that language. Even one who counts in Hebrew but does not understand what he is saying may not have fulfilled his obligation, as "counting" implies that one understands what he is saying.[103] The *Mishna Berura* cites R. Yaakov Emden as disagreeing with this latter point.[104] One should preferably count again in a language that one understands.

Regarding many mitzvot performed through speech, such as Kiddush and *mikra Megilla*, we invoke the principle of "*shome'a keoneh*" – one who listens is akin to one who actally speaks. One can thus fulfill the mitzva through hearing the words of another person. Can one fulfill *Sefirat HaOmer* through the *sheliaḥ tzibbur*'s recitation? The *Mishna Berura* records that the *Aḥaronim* debate whether one can discharge his obligation of *Sefirat HaOmer* through hearing another person's count.[105] *Levush* notes that the verse commands, *Usefartem lakhem* – "and you should count for yourselves," implying that each and every person must count for his- or herself. Those *Aḥaronim* who disagree may maintain that this verse teaches that the mitzva of *Sefirat HaOmer* is incumbent upon each individual, as opposed to the *beit din*, but does not exclude the possibility of employing the principle of *shome'a keoneh*. Alternatively, they may maintain that one who hears someone else recite a text with the intention of discharging his obligation is literally akin to one who pronounces the words himself, therefore fulfilling the implication of the verse.[106] While it is customary for each individual to recite his or her own *Sefirat HaOmer,* one who can no longer recite the *berakha* should listen to the blessing of the *sheliaḥ tzibbur* and answer "Amen."

THE REQUIRED INTENTION FOR THE MITZVA OF *SEFIRAT HAOMER*

The *Shulḥan Arukh,*[107] based upon *Abudraham,*[108] rules that if one who has not yet counted is asked during *bein hashemashot* regarding the day of the *Omer,* he should respond, "Yesterday was..." Were he to respond properly, he would not be able to subsequently count with a *berakha.*

The *Aḥaronim* question this ruling. After all, the *Shulḥan Arukh* himself rules that, in general, "*mitzvot tzerikhot kavana,*" the performance of a mitzva requires certain intention.[109] In this case, the person who responds certainly does not have the intention to fulfill his obligation. Furthermore, it is likely that his intention was actually not to fulfill the mitzva, in which case we certainly should suspect that he did not fulfill his obligation.

Taz notes that if this person does not say "*hayom,*" there is certainly no reason for concern. He explains that the *Shulḥan Arukh* merely intended to suggest that one answer in a questionable manner; however, if one did, indeed, respond properly, he may still count afterward with the *berakha.*[110] The *Mishna Berura*[111] explains that according to *Magen Avraham,*[112] the *Shulḥan Arukh* was stringent because we invoke the principle of "*safek berakhot lehakel*" – in case of doubt, we are lenient regarding *berakhot* and do not recite them.

The *Mishna Berura*[113] also cites the *Eliya Rabba,* who distinguishes between *mitzvot deoraita,* which require special intention, and *mitzvot derabbanan,* such as *Sefirat HaOmer,* which do not require special intent. By responding properly to the questioner, one may thus have actually fulfilled his obligation to count. The *Mishna Berura* then cites the *Peri Ḥadash* and Gra, who both deny any distinction between *mitzvot deoraita* and *mitzvot derabbanan* in this regard and therefore explain that this passage in the *Shulḥan Arukh* must be according to the opinions who maintain that "*mitzvot ein tzerikhot kavana,*" that mitzvot do not require any special intention.

Practically, if one responded but did not say "*hayom*,"[114] if one responded during *bein hashemashot* and he ordinarily does not count the *Omer* until after *tzeit hakokhavim*,[115] if one did not mention the weeks,[116] or if one had explicit intention not to fulfill the obligation of *Sefirat HaOmer*,[117] he may, according to many, count later that evening with a blessing.

CHAPTER 50

Mourning Practices During the *Omer*

THE WEEKS BETWEEN Pesaḥ and Shavuot are characterized by excitement and anticipation as the Jewish people count from the Exodus from Egypt until the giving of the Torah, but they are also marked by the observance of *minhagei aveilut*, mourning practices. In this chapter, we will study the source, scope, and content of these practices. In addition, we will discuss Lag BaOmer, the thirty-third day of the Omer, which plays a central role in both halakha and *minhag* during this period.

MINHAGEI AVEILUT: THE SOURCE AND CONTENT

The Gemara relates:

> It was said that R. Akiva had twelve thousand pairs of disciples, from Gabbat to Antipatris; and all of them died at the same time because they did not treat each other with respect. The world remained desolate until R. Akiva came to our Masters in the South and taught the Torah to them. These were R. Meir, R. Yehuda, R. Yose, R. Shimon and R. Elazar b. Shammua, and it was they who revived the Torah at that time. A *Tanna* taught: All of them died between Pesaḥ and Shavuot. R. Ḥamma b. Abba or, some say, R. Ḥiyya b. Abin said: All of them died a cruel death. What was it? R. Naḥman replied: Diphtheria. (Yevamot 62b)

Ecclesiastes Rabba[1] and Genesis Rabba[2] record the same story, but only mention that they died "during the same period," and they attribute their death to "being stingy with their Torah" (*lefi she'einehem tzara*). R. Akiva urged his new students not to behave in such a manner, and in turn, "the world was filled with Torah."

Based on the Gemara, the *Geonim* cite an ancient custom of observing certain mourning customs between Pesaḥ and Shavuot (referred to as "*Atzeret*"):

> Know that this does not stem from a prohibition but from a mourning custom, for so said our sages: "R. Akiva had 12,000 pairs of disciples and they all died between Pesaḥ and *Atzeret* because they did not treat each other with respect"; and they further taught, "and they all died a cruel death from diphtheria." And from that time forward, the early sages had the custom not to marry during these days, but he who "jumps forward" and marries, we do not punish him by punishment or lashes, but if he comes to ask before the fact, we do not instruct him to marry. And as for betrothal, he who wants to betroth between Pesaḥ and *Atzeret* betroths, because the main joy is the [marriage] *ḥuppa* (canopy).[3]

In the Middle Ages, the *Rishonim* attributed other reasons to these mourning practices. Some ascribe the mourning practices to the precarious state of the Jewish people during this period, as they pray that God judges the world favorably.[4] Thus, these practices are intended to arouse *teshuva*, and not necessarily as an expression of mourning. Others attribute these *minhagei aveilut* to the destruction of the flourishing Jewish communities of France and Germany during the Crusades (eleventh and twelfth centuries). The *Sefer Assufot* (thirteenth-century Germany), for example, records that "people do not marry between Pesaḥ and *Atzeret*; this is because of the pain of the decrees, that the communities were killed in this entire kingdom." *Taz*[5] and the *Arukh HaShulḥan*[6] cite this reason as well.

Similarly, R. Yaakov Emden writes in his *Siddur Beit Yaakov*, "R. Akiva's students died and, due to our many sins, a number of communities were destroyed at the same time of year during the Crusades in Ashkenaz, and in 5408 in Poland." The latter refers to the Chmielnicki massacres, which took place in the spring of 1648.

Although some have objected to the observance of Yom HaSho'ah, the day of commemoration for the murder of six million Jews during the Holocaust, because it falls during the festive month of Nissan, these sources may indicate that remembering tragedies that befell the Jewish people specifically during the period of *Sefirat HaOmer* has its precedents.

Interestingly, neither Rambam, nor the *Maḥzor Vitry,* record mourning customs for this period.

MUSIC DURING *SEFIRAT HAOMER*

Which *minhagei aveilut* are observed during this time period? As noted above, the *Geonim* write that weddings are not held between Pesaḥ and Shavuot. *Tur* mentions this custom, adding that in some places, people also do not take haircuts.[7] The *Shulḥan Arukh* cites both of these customs.[8]

Interestingly, the *Geonim* seem to prohibit holding wedding ceremonies, but do not discuss attending weddings. It seems that the custom originally only proscribed getting married, and later, cutting one's hair. *Tur,* however, writes that it is customary "not to increase one's joy" (*leharbot besimḥa*) during this time. Does this imply that other practices should be prohibited as well? *Magen Avraham,*[9] cited by the *Mishna Berura,*[10] permits holding an engagement party (*seudat shidduḥin*), but adds that there should not be dancing (*rikkudim umeḥolot*). Thus, although a festive social gathering for a positive purpose is permitted, dancing is prohibited even in such a context.

Apparently, *Magen Avraham* understands the *Geonim*'s prohibition of weddings as relating to the festive environment caused by music. Does this custom cited by *Magen Avraham* to refrain from *rikkudim umeḥolot* include playing or listening to music as well? The *Arukh HaShulḥan,* who also permits social gatherings (*seudot reshut*) without dancing, adds that since dancing is prohibited, a fortiori, playing musical instruments is prohibited as well.[11]

R. Yitzchak Weiss also discusses this issue.[12] He first suggests that even if playing musical instruments does not technically fit into the activities prohibited during the *Omer*, if the community has already accepted upon themselves a certain stringency, the practice becomes prohibited, similar to a *neder* (vow). He then argues that playing music is indeed included in the prohibited activities of the *Omer*. He brings, for example, a responsum of R. Shalom Mordecai Schwadron,[13] who cites *Daat Kedoshim*'s warning that those who hold a wedding on Lag BaOmer should be careful to conclude the wedding music before sundown, as it is prohibited to continue playing during the *Omer* after nightfall. He also notes that *Magen Avraham* himself repeats that one should not engage in *rikkudim umeḥolot* regarding the laws of *Bein HaMetzarim* (the three weeks between *Shiva Asar B'Tammuz* and Tisha B'Av).[14] R. Weiss asserts that just as the *Aḥaronim* include a prohibition of playing instruments in the category of *rikkudim umeḥolot*,[15] the same applies during the *Omer*.

Numerous other *Aḥaronim*, including R. Moshe Feinstein,[16] R. Ovadia Yosef,[17] and R. Eliezer Waldenberg,[18] prohibit playing and listening to music, even from a radio, during the period of the *Omer*. Other recent authorities, however, have challenged the assumption that all music should be prohibited. First, we should note that the view of *Magen Avraham*, which is the first mention of a prohibition of *rikkudim umeḥolot* during the *Omer*, should most likely be viewed as a stringency added to a custom, even if it has become accepted practice. Second, *Magen Avraham* himself never mentioned a prohibition of listening to music, but only dancing, comparable to behavior at a wedding. Although refraining from *rikkudim umeḥolot* during the *Omer* may be the accepted custom, it is far from obvious that this custom includes playing or listening to music.

R. Shlomo Daichovsky argues that even during *Bein HaMetzarim*, the custom only prohibits music that leads to *rikkudim umeḥolot*, which would mean that playing classical music, for example, would be permitted. Furthermore, he argues that one should not compare the mourning practices observed during *Bein HaMetzarim* and those of the *Omer*. He therefore sees no reason to prohibit music that does not involve *rikkudim umeḥolot* during the period of the *Omer* (Teḥumin 21).

Similarly, R. Eliyahu Schlesinger, Rav of the Gilo neighborhood of Jerusalem and author of numerous works on halakha, vehemently disagrees with the stringent position. In a lengthy essay in which he defends his role in permitting the radio station Kol Simḥa to play calm and soothing music during the *Omer,* he argues that only music that leads to *rikkudim umeḥolot* is prohibited during the *Omer;* music that is spiritually uplifting and soothing to one's soul is certainly permitted. He insists that listening to music from a radio is part of the daily experience for many people, and can hardly be considered something that causes such great joy that it should be prohibited during the *Omer.* He marshals a host of contemporary *posekim,* not all whom wished to be identified, who agree with his view.

Seemingly, this approach would permit playing spiritually uplifting music or music appropriate for the time period (such as sad music on Yom HaZikaron). Furthermore, music played in the "background" and during exercising, and certainly music played while driving so that one should not fall asleep, should be permitted. Finally, one may learn to play music for professional reasons.[19]

There may be another reason to permit listening to music as well. Until this point, we have assumed, based on *Magen Avraham,* that while social gatherings are permitted during the *Omer,* music that may lead to *rikkudim umeḥolot,* and possibly even all music, would be prohibited. R. Soloveitchik, however, disagreed. He explained that the *aveilut* customs observed during the period of the *Omer,* as well as those observed during *Bein HaMetzarim,* must conform to some prior halakhic pattern.[20]

He notes that in the laws of *aveilut,* we generally speak of three periods of mourning: *shiva* (the seven-day period after the burial), *sheloshim* (the thirty days after burial), and the *yud-bet ḥodesh* (the twelve-month period after the death of a parent). R. Soloveitchik maintained that the mourning practices of *Sefirat HaOmer* conform to the halakhic category of "*yud-bet ḥodesh,*" the twelve-month period of mourning for one's parent. The laws that characterize the *yud-bet ḥodesh* include the prohibition of attending a "*beit hamishteh*"[21] and taking a haircut,[22] similar to the original two laws mentioned by the *Geonim* in the context of the *Omer.*

In comparing the laws of the *Omer* to that of the *yud-bet ḥodesh,* the *Geonim* fundamentally only prohibited social gatherings, known as *simḥat meriut*. Therefore, while a concert might be prohibited during the *Omer*, according to many, listening to music in private, or even attending a movie, is not. Conversely, social gatherings, even those without music, such as a baseball game, may also be prohibited, against the view of *Magen Avraham*.

Despite the custom to refrain from playing music and dancing during the *Omer*, *Magen Avraham* writes that *rikkudim umeḥolot* are permitted at a *seudat eirusin*, a meal held in honor of an *eirusin* (the halakhic betrothing, also known as *kiddushin*). Although parties held in honor of an engagement nowadays are not considered to be *seudot mitzva*, as they do not involve actual *eirusin*, many *posekim* permit playing music and dancing at other *seudot mitzva*, such as at a *sheva berakhot* for a wedding held on *Lag BaOmer*,[23] a *Brit Mila, Pidyon HaBen, bar/bat mitzva* (held on the actual day of the *bar/bat mitzva*), or even a *siyum masekhet*.[24] Others prohibit this even in these cases.[25]

HAIRCUTS AND SHAVING DURING *SEFIRAT HAOMER*

As mentioned above, it is customary to refrain from cutting one's hair during the *Omer*. Although this prohibition applies to both men and women, a married woman may cut hair that protrudes from her head covering, as well as trim her eyebrows, remove facial hair, and shave her legs.

May a man shave his face during the *Omer*? Many *Aḥaronim* equate shaving with cutting one's hair,[26] although they permit shaving – when necessary – for work.[27] This leniency may be more applicable outside of Israel. In Israel, where it is very common for people not to shave during the *Omer*, it may be less appropriate to rely upon this leniency.

Some permit shaving before Shabbat in its honor, based on the discussion regarding shaving before Shabbat during *Bein HaMetzarim*. The Talmud teaches that "during the week on which Tisha B'Av falls, it is prohibited to cut hair and to wash clothes, but it is permitted on Thursday for *kevod Shabbat*" (Taanit 26b). The *Rishonim* disagree as to whether the Gemara permits taking a haircut *and* laundering in honor of Shabbat or only laundering.[28] Rema rules that one may wear laundered clothing for Shabbat during the Nine Days (and implies that one may wash them as well).[29] *Magen Avraham*[30] explains that we do not permit haircuts before Shabbat, as people are not generally accustomed to taking a haircut every week, as they are to laundering (and bathing!). Ḥatam Sofer suggests that this rationale would imply that one who shaves daily would certainly be able to shave for Shabbat.[31]

Thus, according to some *Rishonim*, one may even take a haircut before Shabbat during the week of Tisha B'Av. Even according to those who only permit laundering, haircuts were only prohibited because one does not normally cut one's hair weekly. According to this argument, shaving before Shabbat may be permitted during *Bein HaMetzarim*, and accordingly, some authorities permit shaving before Shabbat during the period of the *Omer*.[32]

According to R. Soloveitchik, who equates the *aveilut* practices of the *Omer* to those of *yud-bet ḥodesh*, shaving would in fact be permitted daily throughout the *Omer*. This was his custom, and many of his students acted accordingly.

The *Mishna Berura* rules that when Rosh Ḥodesh Iyar falls on Shabbat, one may cut his hair (or shave) on Erev Shabbat.[33] He explains that the combination of Rosh Ḥodesh and Shabbat generates "*tosefet simḥa*" (extra joy) for which one may certainly cut one's hair in honor of the Shabbat.

The *posekim* disagree as to whether one may cut one's hair before Shabbat when Lag BaOmer falls out on Sunday. Should one take his first haircut only after Shabbat? This would seem to cause a lack of proper honor for Shabbat. Maharil writes that even in this case, one may not cut his hair on Friday.[34] Mahari Veil, however, disagrees and rules that one may cut his hair on Friday,[35] and Rema rules accordingly.[36]

PURCHASING NEW GARMENTS AND RECITING *SHEHEḤEYANU* DURING THE *OMER*

Maharil[37] cites the *Sefer Ḥasidim*,[38] who writes that during the period between *Shiva Asar B'Tammuz* and Tisha B'Av, one should avoid saying the *berakha* of *Sheheḥeyanu* on new fruit or new clothing. The *Shulḥan Arukh* rules accordingly.[39] Although some cite this custom regarding the period of the *Omer* as well,[40] *Maamar Mordekhai* criticizes those who refrain from saying *Sheheḥeyanu* during the *Omer*:

> Some have the practice of avoiding the recitation of *Sheheḥeyanu* during the period of *Sefira*, although I have not seen this in any work by a *Rishon* or *Aḥaron*. There is no doubt that this custom evolved [mistakenly] ... from [the halakhot] of *Bein HaMetzarim* [the Three Weeks].[41]

Maamar Mordekhai attributes this practice to those who mistakenly equate the period of the *Omer* with *Bein HaMetzarim*. The *Kaf HaḤayim*,[42] *Mishna Berura*,[43] and R. Ovadia Yosef[44] agree that one may recite *Sheheḥeyanu* during the *Omer*. Similarly, although some discourage moving into a new house during the *Omer*, most *posekim* are lenient.[45]

DURING WHICH DAYS ARE THE MOURNING CUSTOMS OBSERVED?

Different communities observe the *minhagei aveilut* during different parts of the *Omer* period. There are three basic approaches:

The Entire *Omer*

Shaarei Teshuva reports that Arizal would not take a haircut for the entire period of the *Omer*, until Erev Shavuot.[46] This, of course, is based upon the simple understanding of the Talmud's description of the death of the students of R. Akiva, "from Pesaḥ until *Atzeret*." Similarly, the *Mishna Berura* relates that some observe these *minhagei aveilut* for the entire period of the *Omer*, excluding Rosh Ḥodesh Iyar, Lag BaOmer, and from Rosh Ḥodesh Sivan until Shavuot.[47]

From Pesaḥ until Lag BaOmer

Many are accustomed to observe only the first part of this period. There are conflicting traditions regarding the days during which R. Akiva's students died. R. Yehoshua ibn Shuaib (1280–1340), a student of

Rashba, cites two possibilities in his *Derashot*.[48] According to one approach, based upon a midrash, the students of R. Akiva died until "*peros haAtzeret*," which is understood to refer to "half of a month," or at least fifteen days. Thus, *peros haAtzeret* falls on the thirty-fourth day of the *Omer*, fifteen days before the end of the count. Thus, assuming that the *minhagei aveilut* relate to the deaths of R. Akiva's students, one should observe the customs for the first thirty-four days of the *Omer*. R. Ibn Shuaib writes, however, that one may invoke the principle of "*miktzat hayom kekulo*" – part of a day counts as the entire day – which is applicable whenever the halakha demands that one count days (such as the seven clean days of a *zava gedola* and the seven days of mourning). Therefore, just as a mourner finishes the shiva on the morning of the seventh day, one may finish the mourning of the *Omer* period on the morning of the thirty-fourth day. The *Shulḥan Arukh* cites this opinion.[49]

Tur mentions the custom of those who cut their hair on the thirty-third day of the *Omer*, Lag BaOmer.[50] Apparently, they conclude that R. Akiva's students died until the thirty-third day of the *Omer*;[51] invoking the principle of "*miktzat hayom kekulo*," they cease to observe the mourning practices on the morning of Lag BaOmer itself. Gra explains that this is the basis for the opinion of Rema, who writes that Ashkenazim do not observe mourning customs on Lag BaOmer, but rather take haircuts and "rejoice a bit."[52]

Thirty-Three Days of Mourning

The *Derashot Ibn Shuaib* cites the opinion of the Tosafot – which appears in Maharil as well – that claims that the students of R. Akiva did not die on days in which "*teḥina*" (*taḥanun*) is not recited, i.e., on festive days.[53] There are sixteen such days during the *Omer* – seven days of Pesaḥ, three days of Rosh Ḥodesh [Iyar (2) and Sivan (1)], and seven Shabbatot. When subtracted from the forty-nine days of the *Omer*, we are left with thirty-three days upon which the students of R. Akiva died. Thus, the custom fundamentally is to observe mourning practices for thirty-three days. When are these thirty-three days observed?

Some observe these thirty-three days from the beginning of the *Omer*, i.e., the second day of Pesaḥ until Lag BaOmer. *Baḥ* explains that this is the reason behind the Rema's opinion, cited above.[54] Many communities, especially German communities, observed these thirty-three days during the "second half" of the *Omer*, as the Crusades occurred during the months of Iyar and Sivan. Some observe them from the second day of Rosh Ḥodesh Iyar until Erev Shavuot. Others begin from the first day of Rosh Ḥodesh (the thirtieth of Nissan) and observe until the third of Sivan, leaving out the three days before Shavuot, known as the "*sheloshet yemei hagbala*."

Based upon the calculation cited above, *Magen Avraham* cites a view that claims that one should observe *minhagei aveilut* on all days that R. Akiva's students died.[55] Therefore, aside from Pesaḥ, Shabbat, Rosh Ḥodesh, and Lag BaOmer, one should keep the mourning practices throughout the *Omer*. Rema, as he notes, clearly rejects this opinion, maintaining that the customs apply until Lag BaOmer. Rema states that one should not accept the leniencies of both opinions – for example, taking a haircut on Rosh Ḥodesh Iyar and after Lag BaOmer.[56]

Incidentally, in Israel, it is customary for many Ashkenazim to refrain from holding weddings until Rosh Ḥodesh Sivan, excluding, of course, Lag BaOmer.

May one who observes the second part of the *Omer*, from Rosh Ḥodesh Iyar until Shavuot (excluding Lag BaOmer), attend a wedding held after Lag BaOmer by one who observes the first part of the *Omer*? Conversely, may one who observes the first part of the *Omer* attend a wedding held before Rosh Ḥodesh Iyar? Although Ḥatam Sofer prohibits this,[57] as by participating one has not fully observed either part of the *Omer*, R. Moshe Feinstein[58] and R. Soloveitchik[59] permit it.

As we noted above, it is customary to suspend the mourning practices on the morning of Lag BaOmer by invoking the principle of *miktzat hayom kekulo*. Can that principle be employed at night as well? Indeed, it is quite common for weddings to be held on the eve of Lag BaOmer. *Beit Yosef*[60] cites Ramban, who applies the principle of *miktzat hayom kekulo* to the nighttime as well. Accordingly, one would be able to shave and get married on the evening of Lag BaOmer. In the *Shulḥan Arukh* however, he rejects this view.[61]

The *Eliya Rabba* writes that although one may act leniently regarding haircuts on the night of Lag BaOmer, he has not seen that people permit holding a wedding on the evening of Lag BaOmer. He concludes that on Erev Shabbat, in extenuating circumstances, one would be permitted to be married on the night of Lag BaOmer (i.e., Thursday night).[62] R. Moshe Feinstein argues the opposite approach: while one should be stringent and not apply the principle of *miktzat hayom kekulo* at night regarding shaving, one may apply it for a marriage, as marriage is a mitzva.[63] Some *Aḥaronim* endorse relying upon this view. Furthermore, the *Shulḥan Arukh HaRav* claims that those who do not recite *Taḥanun* at Minḥa before Lag BaOmer clearly believe that the entire day of Lag BaOmer is celebratory, and therefore one may get married at night without even invoking the principle of *miktzat hayom kekulo*![64]

One who is invited to a wedding on the evening of Lag BaOmer may certainly attend and may shave if his appearance would cause great discomfort.[65]

One who does not have a specific family custom may accept any of these *minhagim*. Some maintain that one may even change one's custom from year to year without *hatarat nedarim*.[66]

LAG BAOMER

As mentioned above, almost all communities suspend, or even cancel, the *minhagei aveilut* for Lag BaOmer. What is the uniqueness of Lag BaOmer? Lag BaOmer does not appear in rabbinic literature until the early fourteenth century. As we discussed, Me'iri relates that "according to the tradition of the *Geonim*… the plague ceased" on Lag BaOmer,[67] and the *Derashot R. Ibn huaib* cites a midrash that claims that the plague that killed the students of R. Akiva ended "*biferos haAtzeret*," which, according to some, refers to Lag BaOmer.

The *Peri Ḥadash* questions how Lag BaOmer, the day which apparently marks the deaths of the last of R. Akiva's students, can be considered a day of *simḥa*. He suggests that the *simḥa* relates to those students who did not die – the five students he began teaching afterward.[68] Indeed, Ḥida explains that on Lag BaOmer, R. Akiva began teaching these five students, the next generation of Torah scholars;[69] as the Midrash relates, when R. Akiva began teaching his five new students, "the world was filled with Torah."[70] Much of our Oral Tradition is based upon the teachings of these students, including R. Shimon b. Yoḥai.

Alternatively, R. Ḥayim Vital describes Lag BaOmer as the "*hillula*," the anniversary of the death, of R. Shimon b. Yoḥai, the *Tanna* to whom the Zohar is attributed.[71] *Benei Yissaschar* insists that R. Shimon b. Yoḥai was also born on Lag BaOmer.[72] Some suggest that R. Shimon b. Yoḥai "emerged from the cave" on Lag BaOmer.[73]

R. Ḥayim Vital relates that his teacher, Arizal, would visit the grave of R. Shimon b. Yoḥai at Meron, and even cut his son's hair there, on Lag BaOmer. The modern celebrations at Meron began in 1833 and to this day attract hundreds of thousands of visitors. Shai Agnon wrote this regarding these festivities:

> One who has not seen the festivities of Lag BaOmer at the grave of R. Shimon b. Yoḥai in Meron has never seen true joy. Jews, in droves, ascend with songs and instruments, and come to this place, from all of the cities of Israel and the lands of Edom and Yishmael, and stand there all night and day and learn ... and pray and recite psalms.[74]

Celebrations spread throughout Northern Africa and to hasidic communities in Russia and Poland and were often marked by the study of the Zohar.

Not everyone was pleased by the festivities at Meron. R. Moshe Sofer, for example, harshly criticizes the celebration. He suggests that although it may be permitted, and possibly obligatory, to establish a festive day in honor of one's being saved from a life-threatening situation, treating Lag BaOmer as a festival may violate the biblical prohibition of *bal tosef*! He further suggests that one should commemorate Lag BaOmer as the day that the manna began to fall, but not through festivities.[75]

Despite Ḥatam Sofer's objections, Lag BaOmer is observed around the world, often with bonfires accompanied by singing and dancing. The Jewish people celebrate the continuation of the Torah after the death of R. Akiva's students, and attempt to taste the depth and secrets of the Torah revealed by R. Shimon b. Yoḥai.

SEFIRAT HAOMER: A PERIOD OF HAPPINESS

Although we have discussed the custom of observing certain *minhagei aveilut* during this period and we noted that some commentators view this time as a period of judgment, Ramban asserts that the days between Pesaḥ and Shavuot are actually similar to Ḥol HaMo'ed:

> And you should count forty-nine days, and seven weeks, and sanctify the eighth day, like the eighth day of Sukkot, and these days which are counted in between are akin to Ḥol HaMo'ed, between the first and eighth of a festival…and that is why our Rabbis refer to Shavuot as "*Atzeret*" (a day of cessation), as it is similar to the eighth day of Sukkot, which is called "*Atzeret*."[76]

Ramban views Pesaḥ as the first festive day, Shavuot as the last day, and the entire interim period as a quasi-Ḥol-HaMo'ed. These days are thus fundamentally days of excitement, anticipation, and happiness leading up to the giving of the Torah on Shavuot.

The period of *Bein HaMetzarim* between *Shiva Asar B'Tammuz* and Tisha B'Av is categorically defined as a one of mourning. One who increases and intensifies his mourning for Yerushalayim and the *Beit HaMikdash* during this time is praiseworthy. The days of *Sefirat HaOmer*, however, are quite different. Indeed, R. Ovadia Yosef argues that "God forbid, one should not view the days of *Sefira* as days of tragedy," and refrain from reciting the *Sheheḥeyanu* blessing or from moving into a new house.[77] Therefore, one must strike a balance between the customary mourning practices – reminding us of the behavior that led to the death of R. Akiva's students, which was antithetical to the unity the Jewish people displayed before receiving the Torah[78] – and the festive nature of the period, as described by Ramban.

CHAPTER 51

Yom HaAtzma'ut and Yom Yerushalayim

INTRODUCTION

On the fifth of Iyar, 5708 (May 14, 1948) – three years after the conclusion of World War II and the destruction of European Jewry, fifty-one years after the First Zionist Congress, and close to two thousand years after the destruction of the second *Beit HaMikdash* – David Ben Gurion declared the independence of the State of Israel based upon the UN Partition Plan.[1] The next day, the armies of five Arab countries – Egypt, Syria, Jordan, Lebanon, and Iraq – attacked Israel, launching the War of Independence, which lasted close to a year.

Nineteen years later, shortly after Egyptian President Gamal Abdel Nasser expelled the United Nations Emergency Force (UNEF) from the Sinai Peninsula (May 1967), Egypt amassed 1,000 tanks and nearly 100,000 soldiers on the Israeli border. Jordan and Syria signed mutual defense treaties, and Iraqi tanks lined the Jordanian border. Fearing an imminent attack, Israel launched a preemptive strike on the Egyptian air force on June 5, 1967. Jordan responded by attacking Jerusalem, Netanya, and the outskirts of Tel Aviv. On June 9, Israel attacked the Syrian-controlled Golan Heights, from which Israeli settlements in the Galil had been shelled for the previous two decades.

By June 10, Israel had seized the Gaza Strip, the Sinai Peninsula, the Golan Heights, and the West Bank, including the Old City of Jerusalem, which had been under Jordanian control for nineteen years. Israel's territory grew by a factor of three.

The establishment of the State of Israel in 1948, representing the first Jewish autonomy in the Land of Israel in almost 2,000 years,[2] and the ensuing military victory signaled the return of *Am Yisrael* to Zion and the rescue of the Jewish people – those who lived in the Land of

Israel as well as those who now had a nation to which they could flee. The victory of the Six Day War not only saved the young country from almost certain defeat at the hands of its Arab neighbors, but returned Jerusalem and the Temple Mount to the Jewish people, as well as the heart of the biblical Land of Israel, including Judea and Samaria. For the religious Jew, such events demand a spiritual response. The Talmud teaches:

> The Holy One, Blessed be He, wished to appoint Ḥizkiyahu as the Messiah, and Sanḥeiriv as Gog and Magog, whereupon the Attribute of Justice said before the Holy One, Blessed be He: "Sovereign of the Universe! If You did not make David the Messiah, who uttered so many hymns and psalms before You, will You appoint Ḥizkiyahu as such, who did not hymn You in spite of all these miracles which You wrought for him?" (Sanhedrin 94a)

Ḥizkiyahu was due to be appointed the *Mashiaḥ*, but his lack of gratitude denied him, and the Jewish people, this opportunity.

Therefore, all who recognize God's hand in modern historical events feel obligated to respond – but how? What are the proper, permissible, or obligatory means of thanking *HaKadosh Barukh Hu*? In this chapter, we will discuss two issues raised regarding Yom HaAtzma'ut and Yom Yerushalayim – the establishment of a new holiday and the recitation of Hallel. At the outset, it is important to make clear that whether or not one embraces the recitation of Hallel or other practices on Yom HaAtzma'ut is not a litmus test of one's level of Zionism or commitment to the State of Israel. However, it behooves us all to acknowledge the historical and spiritual significance of these events and grapple with the proper means to respond.

THE ESTABLISHMENT OF NEW HOLIDAYS: *BAL TOSEF*

In 1949, a year after the establishment of the State of Israel, the Israeli government declared that the fifth of Iyar should be observed as a national holiday. In response, the Chief Rabbis of Israel, R. Yitzchak HaLevi Herzog and R. Ben-Zion Meir Hai Uziel, recommended to the Chief Rabbinate Council that the fifth of Iyar be observed as a "day [commemorating] the joy of the beginning of the redemption of the Jewish people." Since then, halakhic authorities discussed the legitimacy of the establishment of a holiday, Yom HaAtzma'ut, as a day of praise and thanksgiving.

This establishment of a new "festival" posed a great halakhic dilemma. Some suggested that instituting a festive day for the entire Jewish people to celebrate, even those who did not personally experience the miraculous events of 1948 or 1967, constitutes a violation of the biblical injunction of *bal tosef*, derived from the verse, "You shall not add [to the mitzvot]" (Deut. 4:2). In the Talmud, we find that this prohibition applies to adding parts to already existing mitzvot, such as adding an extra *parasha* to *tefillin*, wearing five *tzitzit* instead of four, or sitting in the *sukka* after the seventh day with the intention of fulfilling the mitzva, but Ramban implies that this injunction may also include adding a new holiday. He writes:

> And in my opinion, even creating a new mitzva by itself, such as the holiday which Yeravam made up [I Kings 12:33], violates this prohibition. And similarly, they said regarding the reading of the Megilla, "There were 180 prophets who prophesied for Israel, and they did not subtract or add to what is written in the Torah even one letter, except for the reading of the Megilla."[3]

Ramban alludes to the conclusion of the gemara, which describes how the sages found a biblical precedent for the establishment of the reading of the Megilla.

Others argued that this view of Ramban is not cited by other *Rishonim*. Indeed, we often see that the Rabbis instituted mitzvot. Rather, the distinction lies in whether these mitzvot are perceived as biblically obligatory, as Ramban himself mentions. Furthermore, Ramban may have only questioned the institution of the mitzva of *mikra Megilla*, and not the establishment of a festive day.[4] Finally, commemorating Yom HaAtzma'ut was not intended as an addition to the Torah, but rather an application of the well-established principles of *hakarat hatov* and giving *hodaa* to *HaKadosh Barukh Hu* for saving the Jewish people and giving them a country in Eretz Yisrael.

In grappling with this issue, numerous *posekim* looked for prior historical/halakhic precedents. Centuries earlier, the *Aḥaronim* debated whether a community may establish a personal "Purim," a day of thanksgiving commemorating a miraculous event that occurred, and whether the observance of such a day would be obligatory upon the residents of a given city even for generations afterward.

R. Moshe Alashkar (1466–1542) rules that a community certainly has this authority to establish a "Purim in order to publicize a miracle that happened on a specific day," and it is binding upon generations to come.[5] *Magen Avraham* cites this responsum.[6] R. Ḥezekiah da Silva, in his commentary to the *Shulḥan Arukh*, the *Peri Ḥadash*, confirms that numerous communities have instituted festive days in order to commemorate miraculous events. He cites R. Alashakr, but disagrees. He contends that nowadays, we rule that "*batla Megillat Taanit*" – the days enumerated by the chronicle *Megillat Taanit*, which commemorate joyful events that occurred to the Jewish people during the time of the Second Temple and were celebrated as festive days, are no longer in practice. Therefore, not only are these days not observed, but one may no longer institute holidays that commemorate festive events.[7]

R. Moshe Sofer, known as Ḥatam Sofer, rejects *Peri Ḥadash*'s argument. In a responsum written in 1805, he argues that although one may not establish a day that commemorates an event related to the *Beit HaMikdash*, one may certainly establish days that commemorate other miracles. Furthermore, the Talmud never meant to discourage or prohibit establishing festive days for cities or countries, but rather only a festival meant to be observed by the entire Jewish people.[8]

In fact, Ḥatam Sofer relates that the *Sefer Yosef Ometz* records a miracle that occurred in Frankfurt am Main on the twentieth day of Adar, and they established it as a festive day for generations to come.[9] He relates that his teacher, R. Natan Adler, as well as his community, which was located far away from the city, also observed this festive day. Interestingly, in a different responsum,[10] Ḥatam Sofer criticizes the celebration of the "*hilulla*" (Yahrzeit) of R. Shimon b. Yoḥai on Lag BaOmer in

Tzefat. He claims that this celebration may constitute the establishment of a holiday that is not in commemoration of a miraculous event, which even he maintains would be prohibited.

Indeed, throughout the Middle Ages and until modern times, communities have instituted their own festive days, often known as Purim Sheini or Purim Katan. R. Ovadia Hadaya (Jerusalem, 1890–1969) cites examples of numerous communities that observed their own local "Purims."[11]

R. Avraham Danzig, author of *Ḥayei Adam*, also rules in accordance with R. Alashkar, and relates that each year he celebrates the day his family was saved from a fire that destroyed his home and homes of others in 1804. He describes how they would light candles, as on Yom Tov, recite specific *Tehillim*, participate in a festive meal for those who learn Torah, and give money to charity. He called this day the "*Pulver Purim*," "Purim of the Gun Powder."[12]

R. Hadaya strongly argues in favor of establishing a festive day in commemoration of the establishment of the State of Israel.[13] Similarly, R. Meshulem Roth (1875–1963), a member of the Israeli Chief Rabbinic Council, authored a responsum on this subject. He argues that it is certainly permitted to establish a festive day that commemorates the salvation of the Jewish people, and that the quote from Ramban cited above referred to the establishment of a holiday without any purpose. He writes:

> Indeed, there is no doubt that that day [the fifth of Iyar] – which was established by the government and the members of the Parliament, the elected representatives of the people, as well as the majority of the great Rabbis to celebrate through the land, to commemorate our salvation and our freedom – it is a mitzva to make it [a day of] happiness and Yom Tov and to recite Hallel.[14]

HALLEL ON YOM HAATZMA'UT

The Talmud records the eighteen days upon which one recites the full Hallel (twenty-one days in the Diaspora, due to Yom Tov Sheni) (Arakhin 10a). Elsewhere, the Talmud seems to present contradictory evidence regarding the origins of Hallel (Berakhot 14a; Taanit 28b). The *Rishonim* therefore debate whether the recitation of this Hallel constitutes a biblical mitzva or a rabbinic one.

Rambam writes that the recitation of Hallel on the festivals and on Ḥanukka is only a mitzva *miderabbanan,*[15] but Ramban disagrees, arguing that Hallel on the festivals is either a *halakha leMoshe miSinai* or included in the fulfillment of the biblical obligation of *simḥa* (rejoicing) on the festival.[16] Raavad describes the obligation to recite Hallel as "*midivrei kabbala,*" from the prophets.[17]

In addition to these eighteen days, upon which the entire Hallel is recited, the Talmud mentions the custom of reciting Hallel on Rosh Ḥodesh and omitting two of its psalms (Taanit 29a). This "half-Hallel" is recited on Chol HaMo'ed Pesaḥ as well. The *Rishonim* debate whether one should recite a *berakha* upon reciting this Hallel or not, or whether to do so only when it is recited publicly. The custom of Ashkenazim is to say the blessing, while Sephardim omit the blessing.

While it seems intuitive that the Hallel recited on Ḥanukka is *miderabbanan,* Ḥatam Sofer writes:

> Commemorating the miracles that saved us from death which occurred on Purim, Ḥanukka, and the days enumerated in the *Megillat Taanit* is certainly *mideoraita*.... However, the quality and amount of commemoration is *miderabbanan.*[18]

In other words, Ḥatam Sofer maintains that through reciting Hallel on Ḥanukka or fulfilling the mitzvot on Purim, one fulfills a biblical commandment of commemorating deliverance from near death. While the Hallel recited on the festivals expresses one's *simḥat Yom Tov,* the Hallel of Ḥanukka relates directly to the miracle of Ḥanukka.

What is the source for this type of Hallel, and may it be recited on other occasions?

The Talmud teaches:

> And who recited this Hallel? The prophets among them ordained that Israel should recite it at every important epoch and at every misfortune – may it not come upon them! And when they are redeemed, they recite [in gratitude] for their redemption. (Pesaḥim 117a)

According to this passage, the prophets instituted that Hallel should be recited on every holiday and upon the redemption of the Jewish people from misfortune. Rashi explains that an example of such redemption from misfortune is Ḥanukka.[19]

To what extent does this source serve as a precedent for reciting Hallel upon being saved from danger? The *posekim* raise a number of issues. First, what kind of "redemption" obligates one to recite Hallel? R. Tzvi Hirsch Chajes (1805–1855), known as Maharatz Chajes, suggests that the Talmud refers only to the miracle of the flask of oil, and not to the military victory, because Hallel was only instituted because the miracle of the oil, which was a "*nes nigleh*," blatant and apparent to all.[20]

Some argue that the pronouncement of independence and the ensuing military victory do not constitute a "*nes nigleh*," and therefore do not qualify as deserving of Hallel according to this theory. Others argue that some sources indicate that Hallel may even be recited over a redemption that occurred through natural means.[21] Others simply maintain that the victory of the small Jewish army against the surrounding Arab states constitutes a "*nes nigleh*."

Second, when the Gemara states that upon being redeemed, "they" should say Hallel, of whom is the Gemara speaking? *Behag*, commenting on this gemara, writes:

> When our Rabbis remarked that there are eighteen occasions during the year on which the *individual* Jew recites Hallel, they did not mean to imply that it must be recited in private; rather... whenever we speak of the *entire house of Israel* as opposed to the individual Jew, they are not restricted to the eighteen occasions in the year, and they may recite Hallel whenever they are delivered from trouble.[22]

Similarly, Rabbeinu Tam writes:

> Hallel was introduced to be recited only on those occasions when *all of Israel has been saved* by a miracle; then, a new festival is introduced, and Hallel is recited together with its blessing – *but this is only if the miracle happens to all of Israel.*[23]

These *Rishonim* clearly limit the application of this gemara to cases in which *all* of Israel was saved, such as during the Ḥanukka miracle. This gives rise to the question of how we view the miraculous events of 1948 (or even 1967), and whether they can be said to have affected "all of Israel" in the same manner as the Ḥanukka miracle.

Me'iri, however, disagrees with this limitation:

> **Any person** who was delivered from trouble is allowed to establish a custom for himself to recite Hallel on that day every year, **but may not do so with a *berakha***. A similar ruling applies **to a community** [of the Jewish people]. This is, in fact, the institution of the prophets – to recite Hallel when delivered from trouble.

According to Me'iri, even an individual person or community that experiences salvation should recite Hallel, but without a *berakha*. Incidentally, Netziv limits the obligation to commemorate one's deliverance from danger to the time of the miracle, and not years later.[24]

In summary, we see that a number of *Rishonim* derive from the Talmud that if the entire nation is saved from danger, they may recite Hallel. They disagree as to whether this applies to individuals as well and whether this Hallel should be recited with a blessing.

May one invoke these sources in order to justify or mandate reciting Hallel on Yom HaAtzma'ut?[25] R. Ovadia Hadaya cites a responsum of R. Chaim Yosef David Azulai, Ḥida, who discusses a case in which a community wished to recite Hallel after escaping great misfortune.[26] Ḥida notes that the central halakhic codes of Rif, Rambam, and Rosh do not cite the passage from Pesaḥim. In addition, numerous *Rishonim* rule that a miracle that does not occur to an entire nation does not warrant Hallel, and even according to Me'iri, who would sanction it, this Hallel is recited without a blessing.

Based upon the above reasoning, R. Hadaya rules that Hallel should be recited without a blessing on Yom HaAtzma'ut. He adds that due to the precarious security situation, one should not recite Hallel with a blessing.[27] R. Ovadia Yosef also rules that Hallel may be recited without a blessing, as did R. Yitzchak Herzog (cited by R. Yosef).[28] R. Meshulem Roth, in the responsum cited above, argues that Yom HaAtzma'ut should be observed as a festive day, and that naturally one should recite the full Hallel, with a blessing, as well.[29]

The non-Zionist religious community, which in large part opposes the recitation of Hallel on Yom HaAtzma'ut (and Yom Yerushalayim), has not, for the most part, formulated its halakhic objections. R. Yitzchak Yaakov Weiss, former head of the Eida Ḥareidit, recorded his opposition to the establishment of Yom HaAtzma'ut and Yom Yerushalayim and to the recitation of Hallel.[30] In addition to his general belief that supporting the State of Israel constitutes heresy and his adherence to the doctrine developed by the former Satmar Rav, R. Yoel Teitelbaum, that the establishment of a Jewish State violates the "three oaths" that God made the Jewish people swear to uphold (including not returning to Israel by force, "*shelo yaalu baḥoma*") (Ketubot 111a), R. Weiss also raises halakhic objections. He, like R. Azulai, notes that the *Shulḥan Arukh* does not codify the passage from Pesaḥim, which teaches that the prophets established that one should recite Hallel when one is redeemed from danger. In addition, even according to that source, as we mentioned above, some limit it to a miracle experienced by the entire nation. Furthermore, he cites *Peri Ḥadash*, who opposed local annual festive commemorations.

Interestingly, R. Soloveitchik, whose recognition of the significance of the events of 1948 and 1967 is well documented,[31] objected to reciting Hallel, as he objected to any changes in the liturgy. He sanctioned, however, reciting half-Hallel, without a blessing and at the end of Shaḥarit, as this does not constitute a major change in the liturgy.[32]

Although we have seen different motivations for reciting Hallel without a blessing on Yom HaAtzma'ut, either due to doubt, because the *takana* of the prophets never included reciting a blessing over Hallel, or due to the undesirable security and spiritual situation of the State of Israel, we might suggest a different approach.

In addition to the eighteen days upon which one recites the full Hallel, one recites Hallel on the evening of Pesaḥ during the Seder. This Hallel has puzzled the commentators for centuries, as it appears to violate numerous classic halakhic norms: it is recited at night,[33] it is interrupted by the meal, and it is not preceded by a *berakha*. The *Rishonim* question the nature of this Hallel and why it does not conform to the classic models of Hallel.

R. Hai Gaon, as cited by the *Rishonim*, offers an intriguing explanation. He distinguishes between Hallel of the eighteen days, upon which one is obligated to read (*korei*) Hallel, and the Hallel of the Seder, which one is obligated to sing (*shira*) in response to the miraculous events of *yetziat Mitzrayim*.[34] This Hallel of "*shira*" is meant to be a spontaneous outburst of song expressing praise and gratitude to the Almighty for the redemption from Egypt. A *berakha* before such a Hallel is not only unnecessary, but also inappropriate, as it undermines and negates the very essence of this Hallel.

One might suggest the Hallel described by the Gemara in Pesaḥim, which one recites in response to a miracle, should also be "spontaneous," a "*shira*," and not preceded by a blessing. The closer one is to an event, the less formal and more "natural" the Hallel is. If so, then this model of Hallel, without a blessing, may actually be the more appropriate Hallel for Yom HaAtzma'ut. Those who pray in Religious Zionist communities in Israel on Yom HaAtzma'ut can testify to the genuine feeling of fervor and relevance with which Hallel is recited on that day.

While this discussion may be applied equally to Yom Yerushalayim, some believe that the victory of the Six Day War more closely resembles the redemption described by the Talmud. Therefore, the Chief Rabbinate, in a ruling signed by R. Unterman, R. Yitzchak Nissim, R. Zevin, and R. Yisraeli, ruled that Hallel should be recited with a blessing on Yom Yerushalayim.

YOM HAATZMA'UT AND THE MOURNING PRACTICES OF *SEFIRAT HAOMER*

Yom HaAtzma'ut falls out on the fifth of Iyar, during the customary period of mourning during which weddings, haircuts, and other public/festive events are forbidden. Do the Yom HaAtzma'ut celebrations suspend the *minhagei aveilut* of the *Omer*? R. Yitzchak Nissim (1896–1981), former Sephardic Chief Rabbi of Israel (1955–1972), ruled that one may hold weddings and take haircuts on Yom HaAtzma'ut.[35] His ruling is partially based on a ruling of R. Chayim Palagi (1788–1869), who records that in his city, certain individuals observed festive days commemorating a miraculous event that occurred to them during the *Omer*, upon which they would shave.[36] R. Hadaya rejects this argument and rules that one should continue his observance of the mourning practices of the *Omer*.[37] R. Soloveitchik also maintained that the mourning practices of the *Omer* should not be suspended in order to celebrate Yom HaAtzma'ut.[38] Many are accustomed to suspend the prohibition of live music, and even shaving, but refrain from taking a haircut, which would undermine the mourning for the duration of the *Sefira* period.

CONCLUSION

As demonstrated, one can certainly build a strong case in favor of establishing a day dedicated to praising God for the creation of the State of Israel, as well as the victory from near-certain national destruction of the Six Day War.

Over the past sixty-five years, rabbinic figures have grappled with the appropriate means of celebrating these days, including the recitation of the *berakha* of *Sheheḥeyanu*,[39] reading a portion from the prophets during the morning service, and reciting Hallel at night and/or during the day, and even at Minḥa time. Ultimately, *Klal Yisrael*, guided by their leaders, will determine the most fitting means of celebrating these days, and one should view, in retrospect, these attempts in their proper context – finding the proper means to offer thanksgiving to *HaKadosh Barukh Hu*.

CHAPTER 52

Shavuot

THE TORAH TEACHES that upon completing the counting of the *Omer,* the Festival of Shavuot is celebrated:

> Seven weeks you shall number unto you; from the time the sickle is first put to the standing corn you should begin to number seven weeks. And you shall keep the Feast of Weeks (*Ḥag HaShavuot*) unto the Lord your God after the measure of the freewill-offering of your hand, which you shall give according as the Lord your God blessed you. (Deut. 16:9–10)[1]

Shavuot not only commemorates the conclusion of the counting of the weeks of the *Omer,* but it also celebrates the wheat harvest (Ex. 23:16), and is therefore known as "*Ḥag HaKatzir,*" the Harvest Festival. The *shetei haleḥem,* two leavened loaves made from the new wheat harvest, are offered with the *Musaf* offering, and the festival is therefore also referred to as "*Yom HaBikkurim*" (Num. 28:26). The offering permits the use of new grains in the *Beit HaMikdash* and ushers in the season of the *Bikkurim,* the first fruits, which are brought to the *Beit HaMikdash* (Deut. 10:1–11).

In addition to the themes reflected by the biblical names given to this festival, the Rabbis refer to this festival as "*Atzeret*" (Rosh HaShana 1:2),[2] seemingly referring to the fact that it marks the conclusion of the Pesaḥ festival.[3] Indeed, as we have seen, Ramban asserts that Pesaḥ and Shavuot are comparable to the first and last days of Sukkot and Pesaḥ, and the days between Pesaḥ and Shavuot are actually similar to Ḥol HaMo'ed. It is logical then, that the description of Shavuot as "*Atzeret*" most likely refers to the religious/historical connection between Pesaḥ and Shavuot – the Jewish people left Egypt on Pesaḥ and received the Torah on Shavuot.

In addition to the agricultural and ritual reasons for the holiday cited above, we traditionally associate Shavuot with the giving of the

Torah. The Rabbis point to the uniqueness of Shavuot, as "it is the day upon which the Torah was given" (Pesaḥim 68b). In addition, the Torah reading of Shavuot (Ex. 19), as recorded by the Tosefta and cited in the Talmud (Megilla 31a), recounts the giving of the Torah. Furthermore, the Shavuot liturgy refers to the day as "*Zeman Matan Torateinu*" – the day upon which the Torah was given.

Numerous commentators have questioned why this aspect of Shavuot, *Matan Torah*, which is so central to our Shavuot celebration, is not mentioned in the Torah. In fact, the Talmud cites a debate between the *ḥakhamim* and R. Yose regarding whether the Torah was given on the sixth or seventh of Sivan (Shabbat 86b). According to R. Yose's opinion that *Matan Torah* took place on the seventh of Sivan, nowadays, when we always celebrate Shavuot on the sixth of Sivan (forty-nine days after the second day of Pesaḥ), we would actually be celebrating *Matan Torah* on the incorrect day!

These questions brought R. Yitzchak Abrabanel (1437–1508) to explain as follows in his commentary to the Torah:

> The Torah did not specify that the reason for the celebration for this festival is to remember the day of the giving of the Torah, as no festival was assigned to remember the giving of our Torah; because the Divine Torah and its prophecies, which are in our hands testify to themselves, and there is no need to dedicate a day to remember it. Rather, the reason for the Festival of Shavuot is because it is the beginning of the wheat harvest.[4]

R. Abrabanel does acknowledge that certain mitzvot and halakhot hint to the giving of the Torah on Shavuot. For example, the offering of the *shetei haleḥem* on Shavuot, which are made from leavened wheat, in contrast to Pesaḥ's *Omer* offering made from barley, indicates the Jewish people's spiritual poverty before receiving the Torah. He continues:

> [Although] there is no doubt that on this day the Torah was given, no festival was designated to remember it, just as you will find regarding *Yom Terua* [Rosh HaShana], upon which we say, "this is the day of the beginning of Your creation, a remembrance for the first day" [Rosh HaShana 27a], and despite this, God did not command that one should observe Rosh HaShana

as an anniversary of the creation of the world, rather as a "*Yom HaDin*" [day of judgment"].

The giving of the Torah is coincidental and secondary to the primary reason for the observance of Shavuot – the wheat harvest.

Others accept that the giving of the Torah plays a central role in the observance of Shavuot, but maintain that it was deliberately not mentioned by the Torah. R. Yitzchak b. Moshe Arama (c. 1420–1494) offers two reasons for this omission in his commentary to the Torah, the *Akeidat Yitzchak*. First, he suggests that like belief in the existence God, the giving of the Torah is so basic to Judaism that there is no reason to dedicate a day to its commemoration. Second, he proposes that the very nature of the Torah precludes designating a day of commemoration. He writes:

> The commemoration of the giving of the Torah cannot be limited to a particular time, like other matters connected with the festivals, but it is a precept that applies at all hours and times, as it is written, "This book of the Law shall not move from your mouth and you shall meditate in it day and night" [Josh. 1:8]. Every day, we are commanded that its contents should remain as fresh and as dear to us as on the day they were given, as it is written, "This day, the Lord your God has commanded you to do these statutes and judgments; you shall therefore keep them and do them."[5]

In other words, although the Torah may have been given on a specific historical date, we relate to Torah as if it is constantly given to us anew, and it is therefore not restricted or limited to a specific time. Indeed, the Midrash states:

> What is meant by "this day"? Had the Holy One, Blessed be He, not ordained these precepts for Israel till now? Surely this verse was stated in the fortieth year! Why does the Scripture therefore state, "this day"? This is what Moshe meant when he addressed Israel: Every day, let the Torah be as dear to you as if you had received it this day from Mt. Sinai.[6]

This beautiful midrash emphasizes the timeless nature of Torah, and how marking the anniversary of the giving of the Torah might ultimately reduce or minimize our relationship to the Torah.

Finally, R. David Zvi Hoffmann, in his commentary to Leviticus, explains why there are no mitzvot associated with Shavuot:

> No symbolic ritual was instituted for Shavuot to mark the Sinaitic Revelation, for the reason that it cannot be translated into the tangible language of symbol. The Children of Israel had been commanded to take heed "that you saw no likeness on the day that the Lord spoke unto you at Ḥorev from the midst of fire," so as not to become involved in any idolatrous, anthropomorphic conception of the Divinity. They were simply bidden to commemorate the historical experience. They would celebrate on the day of the giving of the Law the conclusion of the harvest as well, to give thanks to Him on bringing the first fruits to the Sanctuary and acknowledge that He is the Lord of all, to whom it was meet to pay homage and whose commandments they were to obey. By this they would reenact the promise they made on Sinai, "*naase venishma*" ("we shall do and hearken") [Ex. 24:7].

While it is impossible to commemorate the giving of the Torah with any symbols, we bring God our first fruits, give thanks to Him, and fulfill our promise to Him at Har Sinai – "*naase venishma*."

As R. Hoffmann observed, there are no halakhot or mitzvot specifically related to Shavuot. In fact, the *Shulḥan Arukh* dedicates only one chapter – at the end of the Laws of Pesaḥ – to the "Order of the Prayers on Shavuot."[7] The Jewish people, however, have enriched the Festival of Shavuot with many customs, which have themselves generated much Torah inquiry. In this chapter, we will investigate a number of these customs.

BRINGING IN SHAVUOT "EARLY"

The *Rishonim* record that the custom in Medieval Ashkenazic communities was to recite *Tefillat Maariv* after *pelag haMinḥa,* and not only after *tzeit hakokhavim,* in accordance with the position of R. Yehuda (Berakhot 26a). Based upon this custom and another passage in the Talmud that explicitly records the practice of reciting Kiddush on Shabbat before dark (Berakhot 26b), it was also customary to bring in Shabbat before dark in Ashkenazic communities until the modern era.

On Shavuot, however, it has become customary to begin the festival only after dark. What is the source of this practice? *Shela* writes in his *Shenei Luḥot HaBerit*:

> I received [a tradition] from my teacher, the Gaon R. Shlomo of Lublin, who received [this tradition] person to person from the Gaon R. Yaakov Pollack, [that one should] not make Kiddush and eat on the first night of Shavuot until after the stars have appeared. The reason is because it says regarding the counting [of the *Omer*], "Seven complete weeks there should be"; if one recites Kiddush while it is still day, one slightly detracts from the forty-nine days of *Sefirat HaOmer*, and Shavuot is supposed to be [observed] after the [full] count.[8]

This tradition dates back to R. Yaakov Pollack (1460–1561), the forefather of the Polish rabbinic tradition. Interestingly, R. Horowitz writes that even though one may not recite Kiddush before nightfall, one may still recite the evening prayers early, as even on Shabbat, one may recite the prayers of Motza'ei Shabbat.

R. Yosef Hahn (Frankfurt am Main, 1570–1637), a contemporary of R. Horowitz, records that he had not seen this practice in Germany. Furthermore, he argues that this practice is not only an unnecessary stringency, but it also takes away from the time one could learn at night, as the night is relatively short during the summer.[9] This seems to have been the practice in Germany thereafter as well, as R. Netanel Weil writes in his comments to Rosh, the *Korban Netanel*, that one may recite Kiddush and eat while it is still light on all festival days, including Shavuot.[10] *Magen Avraham*,[11] however, as well as *Peri Ḥadash*,[12] cite *Shela*, ruling that one should not recite Kiddush until after dark.

Although these early authorities only mention delaying Kiddush until evening, *Taz* records that the congregation delays beginning Maariv so that the count should be "complete."[13] R. Yaakov Emden, however, insists that, on the contrary, one should pray before dark in order to fulfill of the mitzva of adding from the weekday onto Shabbat and Yom Tov (*tosefet Shabbat*).[14]

R. Shimon Sofer, in his *Hitorerut Teshuva*, suggests a different reason to delay Maariv; we should wait until night to ensure that even those who will stay up the entire night will not forget to recite *Keriat*

Shema after dark, its proper time.[15] Similarly, R. Natan Gestetner suggests that Maariv is not recited until dark simply to ensure that people do not recite Kiddush before dark.[16] Numerous *Aḥaronim,* such as *Peri Megadim,*[17] the *Shulḥan Arukh HaRav,*[18] the *Kitzur Shulḥan Arukh,*[19] and the *Mishna Berura,*[20] rule that one should not recite Maariv until after dark.

R. Naftali Tzvi Yehuda Berlin, Netziv, offers another suggestion in his commentary to the Torah.[21] The Torah says that one observes Shavuot *"be'etzem hayom hazeh"* – "this very same day" – in order to teach that there is no mitzva of *tosefet Shabbat* on Shavuot. We learn that we should observe Shavuot after dark from this verse, and not in order to ensure than our "count" is complete.

DAIRY FOODS

One of the most well-known customs associated with Shavuot is the practice of eating dairy foods. R. Isaac Tyrnau (fourteenth to fifteenth century, Austria) records in his *Sefer HaMinhagim*[22] that this custom is alluded to by the verse, *"Minḥa **Ḥ**adasha **L**aShem **B**eShavuoteikhem"* (Num. 28:26), the first letters of which spell *"ḥalav"* – milk. This practice has generated much discussion in halakhic literature.

First, aside from the textual hint, what is the reason for this custom? Rema explains that in remembrance of the *shetei haleḥem,* the two loaves offered in the *Beit HaMikdash* on Shavuot, we wish to eat two loaves of bread at the meal. Since one is not permitted to use the same loaf of bread for both a dairy and meat meal,[23] we eat a dairy meal and then a meat meal, in order to ensure that two loaves are eaten.[24]

Magen Avraham offers another reason. He notes that the Zohar equates the seven weeks between Pesaḥ and Shavuot to the seven "clean days" (*shivat neki'im*) that a woman counts before purification. Just as the woman is "pure" after these seven days (after immersing in the *mikveh*), so too, the Jewish people are purified from the impurity of Egypt after *Sefirat HaOmer*. Milk is viewed, symbolcally, as antithetical to *tuma,* as a woman who produces milk and nurses generally does not menstruate. We therefore eat dairy foods on Shavuot.[25]

The *Mishna Berura*'s reason is possibly the most well known. He explains that after receiving the Torah, the Jewish people were no longer able to eat their meat; they had to properly slaughter and prepare new meat in kosher vessels. This process is time-consuming, and they therefore ate dairy products, whose halakhot are less intricate and which can be prepared in less time.[26] The *Mishna Berura*[27] also cites *Kol Bo*,[28] who explains that since the Torah is compared to milk and honey,[29] it is customary to eat dairy, and even honey, on Shavuot. The *Aḥaronim* offer additional reasons for this custom as well.

Second, this practice raises numerous halakhic concerns. For example, as we learned in chapter 3, one may be obligated to eat meat on Yom Tov as a fulfillment of the mitzva of *simḥat Yom Tov*. Even if one is not obligated to do so, many agree that it is certainly a mitzva to eat meat. The ancient practice of eating dairy on Shavuot seems to contradict this halakha! Indeed, even the *Sefer HaMinhagim* cited above writes that one should still eat meat on Shavuot, as "there is no happiness without meat" (Pesaḥim 109a).

R. Tzvi Hirsch Shapiro (1850–1930), the second Munkatcher Rebbe, discusses this issue at length in his *Darkhei Teshuva*.[30] He relates that some suggest eating a dairy meal at night and a meat meal during the day. This is the custom in many communities, and was the practice of R. Yaakov Yisrael Kanievsky (1899–1985), the Steipler Gaon.[31] R. Shapiro argues, however, that whether or not *simḥat Yom Tov* is biblically mandated at night is a debate among the *Aḥaronim*,[32] and it is therefore improper not to eat meat at night. In addition, Rema, cited above, implies that dairy food is meant to be eaten in addition to meat at the same meal in order to obligate two loaves. For this reason, the *Sefer Yosef Ometz* records that it is customary to eat dairy on the first day of Shavuot, but that one should eat meat afterward.[33]

The *Aḥaronim* note, however, that eating meat after dairy poses serious halakhic concerns, and therefore one should be careful not to violate the laws of *basar beḥalav* in fulfilling this custom. The Gemara (Ḥullin 105a) explicitly states that after eating cheese, one may eat meat. Rema, in his *Darkhei Moshe* commentary to *Tur*,[34] cites a responsum of Maharam of Rothenburg, who relates that he once found cheese between his teeth in between meals. He thereafter decreed upon himself to wait after eating cheese the same way he waits after meat, although he was lenient regarding chicken. The *Darkhei Moshe* continues to cite other sources that limit this stringency to cheese that has aged at least six months.[35] In his comments to the *Shulḥan Arukh*, R. Isserlis cites the custom of waiting after hard cheese, even before eating chicken. He notes, however, that others are lenient and says not to rebuke those who are lenient, as long as they do "*kinuaḥ*," "*hadaḥa*," and "*netilat yadayim*." He concludes, however, that "it is good to be stringent."[36]

How should one conduct himself if he wishes to eat both meat and milk at the same meal? Some write that one who does not eat hard cheese can simply clean and rinse one's mouth, and then eat meat at the same meal.[37] R. Ovadia Yosef writes that this is his practice.[38] Others insist that one should eat dairy and then recite the *Birkat HaMazon*,[39] in deference to the Zohar, which implies that one should not eat meat and cheese in the same meal.[40] Still others object to this practice, on the grounds that reciting *Birkat HaMazon* in between the meals constitutes a recitation of a "*berakha she'eina tzerikha*" (an unnecessary blessing),[41] but R. Moshe Feinstein endorses this practice.[42]

Darkhei Teshuva, cited above, offers a different suggestion:

> The preferred practice is the custom that I received from my teachers and my ancestors: to eat a dairy meal immediately after the morning prayers, during the Kiddush, without bread, but only as a "*seudat arai*." And then one should recite the blessing afterward, wait a bit more than an hour, and then eat the day meal with meat and wine. That is the preferred custom in my opinion, and with this, one fulfills one's obligation according to all.[43]

This custom also appears in the *Luaḥ Eretz Yisrae*l of R. Yechiel Michel Tukachinsky.

Interestingly, R. Yitzchak Ze'ev Soloveitchik, in his commentary to the Torah, suggests that the custom of eating milk and meat at the same meal affirms the commitment the Jewish people, who, unlike the angels, are able to fulfill the mitzvot with their bodies, with great zeal and alacrity.[44]

TIKKUN LEIL SHAVUOT

The earliest mention of the practice of staying up the entire night of Shavuot and learning Torah appears in the Zohar:

> Therefore, the pious in ancient times did not sleep that night but were studying the Torah, saying, "Let us come and receive this holy inheritance for us and our children in both worlds." That night, the Congregation of Yisrael is an adornment over them, and she comes to unite with the King. Both decorate the heads of those who merit this. R. Shimon said the following when the friends gathered with him that night: Let us come and prepare the jewels of the bride ... so that tomorrow she will be bejeweled ... and properly ready for the King.[45]

The Zohar connects the learning of Shavuot night to the "wedding" between the Jewish people and the Almighty.

Although this custom is not cited by R. Yosef Karo in the *Shulḥan Arukh,* there is written evidence of R. Karo holding a night of learning in Salonica, Greece, in 1533. *Shela* cites a letter from R. Shlomo Alkabetz, a friend of R. Yosef Karo's, and author of the *Lekha Dodi* prayer recited every Friday night, describing that evening and how it eventually led to R. Yosef Karo's move to Tzefat.[46]

By the seventeenth century, this practice was widespread, and *Magen Avraham* records the custom of staying awake all night on Shavuot:

> The Zohar says that the early pious ones would stay awake all night on Shavuot and learn Torah. Nowadays, our custom is for most learned people to do so. Perhaps the reason is based on the fact that the Israelites slept all night long and God had to wake them when He wanted to give them the Torah, as it says in the Midrash, and therefore we must repair this.[47]

There are different customs, however, regarding whether one should learn/recite the *Tikkun Leil Shavuot,* a collection of texts selected for study on Shavuot evening, or whether one should learn "whatever his heart pleases."

This practice of staying up all night has led to numerous and in-depth discussions regarding whether or not one who has not slept may recite the morning blessings. Concerning *netilat yadayim*, R. Yosef Karo writes that there is a doubt, and Rema rules that one should wash without a *berakha*.[48] The *Mishna Berura*, however, maintains that the *Aḥaronim* agree that if one uses the bathroom before Shaḥarit, one should then wash one's hands and recite the *berakha* of "*al netilat yadayim*."[49]

Since we follow the opinion that the *birkot hashaḥar*, the morning blessings, are recited regardless of whether or not one actually received the benefit described by the specific *berakha*, it would seem to follow that one should recite these *berakhot* even if one was awake all night, as they are a daily obligation. This, indeed, is the ruling of the *Arukh HaShulḥan*[50] and Arizal. The *Mishna Berura*, however, cites those who question whether one who did not sleep should recite "*Elokai neshama*" and "*hamaavir sheina*," and therefore suggests that one hear these *berakhot* from someone who has slept.[51]

The *Mishna Berura* cites a debate among the *Aḥaronim* regarding the *birkot haTorah*: *Ḥayei Adam*, *Peri Ḥadash*, and Gra rule that one should not say the *birkot haTorah* if one was awake all night, while *Magen Avraham* and *Eliya Rabba* rule that one should say the *berakhot*. Ideally, one should try to hear the *berakhot* from another person who has slept, but if this is not possible, one may have in mind that the second blessing preceding the morning *Keriat Shema* ("*Ahava Rabba*" in Ashkenazi congregations and "*Ahavat Olam*" in the Sephardic tradition) should exempt him from *birkot haTorah*. One should then study a verse or Mishna after one's *tefilla*.[52]

Interestingly, the *Mishna Berura*[53] cites the opinion of R. Akiva Eiger, who offers a brilliant solution to this quandary. He suggests that if one sleeps a *sheinat keva* (significant slumber) the day before, one may then recite *birkot haTorah* the next morning, even if one remained awake all night. He argues that, "*mimah nafshakh*," whichever opinion one follows, one would be so obligated – if the *berakha* is meant to be recited daily regardless of whether one slept, one should always recite it on Shavuot morning, and if is considered a *birkat hamitzva*, then it should be recited after any interruption, such as a long afternoon nap! Therefore, everyone would agree that in such a case one should recite *birkot haTorah* in such a case.

GREENERY

Another well-known custom of Shavuot is to adorn the *beit knesset* with greenery. Over the course of centuries, this custom developed in different directions, and numerous reasons were given for this practice. Some even expressed opposition to this practice.

It seems that this custom first developed in fifteenth-century Ashkenaz. R. Yaakov Moelin, known as Maharil, records that it was customary to cover the floor of the *beit knesset* with flowers, "*lesimḥat haregel*" (for the joy of the festival).[54] While Maharil speaks of adorning the *beit knesset,* the *Sefer Leket Yosher*[55] writes that his teacher, R. Yisrael Isserlin, author of the *Terumat HaDeshen,* put greenery on the floor of his home. It seems that the purpose of this early German custom was to beautify and refresh the *beit knesset,* or even one's house, in honor of the festival. Indeed, these sources emphasize that "*besamim,*" pleasant-smelling greenery, was placed on the floors.

Writing over a century later in Poland, Rema offers a different reason: "It is customary to place greenery in the *beit knesset* and the homes as a remembrance of the happiness of the giving of the Torah."[56] In what way does greenery remind us of the giving of the Torah? R. Mordekhai Yoffe explains in his *Levush Malkhut,* that the greenery reminds us of the plants that adorned Har Sinai, as the verse warns, "neither the flocks nor herds should feed before that mount" (Ex. 34:3) – implying that the mountain was filled with plant life.[57]

Magen Avraham offers a third reason.[58] He records that it is customary to place trees in the *beit knesset* on Shavuot to remind us that the fruits of the trees are judged on Shavuot (Rosh HaShana 1:2) and that we should pray for them.

Ḥayei Adam records that the Vilna Gaon abolished the custom of putting trees in the *beit knesset,* as it resembles the current custom of non-Jews.[59] Despite the Gaon's objections, however, it is common practice to adorn the *beit knesset* with greenery for Shavuot, and the *Aḥaronim* offer numerous defenses of this practice.

Fast Days

CHAPTER 53

The Four Fast Days

In his *Hilkhot Taaniyot*, Rambam discusses two types of *taaniyot* (fast days), each established to fulfill a different purpose. Some fast days are observed by an individual or a community and are declared in response to a personal or communal tragedy, including war, plague, famine, drought, and sickness:

> A positive scriptural commandment prescribes prayer and the sounding of an alarm with trumpets whenever trouble befalls the community. For when Scripture says, "Against the adversary that oppresses you, then you shall sound an alarm with the trumpets" [Num. 10:9], the meaning is: Cry out in prayer and sound an alarm against whatsoever is oppressing you, be it famine, pestilence, locusts, or the like.
>
> This procedure is one of the roads to repentance, for as the community cries out in prayer and sounds an alarm when overtaken by trouble, everyone is bound to realize that evil has come upon him as a consequence of his own evil deeds... and that his repentance will cause the trouble to be removed.[1]
>
> In addition, there is a rabbinic ordinance to fast whenever there is a difficulty that affects the community until there is a manifestation of divine mercy. On these fast days, we cry out in prayer, offer supplications, and sound the trumpets only. In the Temple, we sound both the trumpets and the shofar.[2]

According to Rambam, there is a biblical commandment to turn to God in prayer in a time of personal or communal need and a rabbinic ordinance to respond to crisis with fasting and repentance. Ramban agrees, as he writes:

> [This *derasha*]...may be instructing us that included in the service [of God] is that we should learn Torah, and pray to Him in times of crisis, and our eyes and hearts should be toward Him alone like the eyes of slaves to their masters, and this is similar to when the Torah writes, "And when you go to war in your land against the adversary that oppresses you, then you shall sound an alarm with the trumpets; and you shall be remembered before the Lord your God, and you shall be saved from your enemies." And it is a mitzva to respond to every crisis which the community will face by crying out to Him in prayer.[3]

In addition to this first type of fast, Rambam also discusses a second type of fast: the four fast days instituted to commemorate the different stages of the destruction of the Temple and the exile:

> There are days which are observed by all of Israel as fasts because tragic events happened on them, the object being to stir hearts and open the way to repentance and to remind us of our own evil deeds, and of our fathers' deeds, which were like ours, as a consequence of which these tragic afflictions came upon them and upon us. For as we remember these things, we ought to repent and do good, in accordance with the scriptural verse, "And they shall confess their iniquity and the iniquity of their forefathers" [Lev. 26:40], etc.[4]

Here, too, Rambam explains that the focus of the fast should be on repentance. However, while the first type of fast comes in response to an immediate crisis from which one seeks deliverance, the four fast days commemorate an ancient national tragedy, as well as the current national condition, with the intention of encouraging repentance for previous and current sins.

R. Soloveitchik notes that Rambam describes the two types of fasts differently: the first type of fast is "one of the roads to repentance," while the second type "stirs hearts and opens the way to repentance." He explains that only a clear and present crisis or tragedy directly triggers repentance as an attempt to save one from the current situation. A prior calamity, however, such as the destruction of the *Beit HaMikdash* and ensuing exile, merely inspires one to repent. Therefore, while a "communal fast" constitutes "one of the roads" of repentance itself, the four fasts serve to "stir hearts and open the way" to future repentance.[5] In the upcoming chapters, we will focus on the second category of fast days, the four fasts. We will discuss their origin and laws, and pay special attention to the numerous halakhot related to Tisha B'Av.

THE FOUR FASTS

In response to a query regarding the Jewish people's transition from exile to the period of the "Return to Zion" and the building of the Second Temple, the prophet Zechariah mentions four fasts that commemorate the events leading to and following the destruction of the First Temple: "The fast of the fourth month, and the fast of the fifth, and the fast of the seventh, and the fast of the tenth" (Zech. 8:19).

The Tosefta enumerates these events:

> The Rabbis expounded: It states, "Thus says the Lord of hosts: The fast of the fourth month, and the fast of the fifth, and the fast of the seventh, and the fast of the tenth shall be joy and gladness for the house of Judah, and cheerful seasons; therefore love truth and peace."
>
> "The fast of the fourth month" refers to the Seventeenth of Tammuz, when the [wall of the] city was breached.... The "fast of the fifth" is Tisha B'Av, the day upon which the *Beit HaMikdash* was burned.... The "fast of the seventh" is the day upon which Gedalia ben Aḥikam was murdered by Yishmael ben Netania. This is to teach you that, before God, the death of the righteous is equal to the destruction of the Temple.... The "fast of the tenth" is the Tenth of Tevet, when the king of Babylon laid siege to Jerusalem. (Sota 6:10)[6]

ASARA B'TEVET

According to this Tosefta, the fast of *Asara B'Tevet* (the tenth of Tevet) recalls the siege on the walls of Jerusalem by Nebuchadnezzar, the king of Babylon. Indeed, the Bible relates:

> And it came to pass in the ninth year of his reign, in the tenth month, in the tenth day of the month, Nebuchadnezzar king of Babylon came, he and all his army, against Jerusalem, and encamped against it; and they built forts against it round about. (II Kings 25:1)

Other biblical sources also refer to this event.[7]

Why does this event deserve to be commemorated by a communal fast day? The breaching of the walls of Jerusalem and the subsequent destruction of the First and Second Temples are certainly of great historical and spiritual importance. Similarly, the murder of Gedalia ben Aḥikam by a fellow Jew, which led to the cessation of any remnant of Jewish autonomy in Eretz Yisrael for almost two thousand years, also seems worthy of commemoration. However, the beginning of the siege on Jerusalem, which itself lasted almost three years, does not seem to demand an independent fast day!

Perhaps this fast day reminds us that the *beginning* of a process is indeed worthy of our attention; indeed, lack of proper response at an early juncture often affects the final result. The siege of Jerusalem was not only tragic because of its impact upon the city's inhabitants, but also because the Jewish people apparently did not respond to it in a manner that might have averted the final destruction.

We may suggest another dimension to this fast as well. The prophet Jeremiah portrays the Jewish people as unwilling to imagine the destruction of their city and Temple:

> Do not put your trust in illusions and say, "The Temple of the Lord, the Temple of the Lord, the Temple of the Lord are these [buildings]." Will you steal, and murder, and commit adultery, and swear falsely, and sacrifice to Baal, and follow other gods whom you have not experienced, and then come and stand before Me in this House which bears My name and say, "We are safe"? [Safe] to do all these abhorrent things! Do you consider this House, which bears My name, to be a den of thieves? (Jer. 7:1–15)

Since the Jews could not imagine their Temple being destroyed, they responded to the siege of Jerusalem with shock and astonishment. Indeed, the report of the siege, as related to Ezekiel, reflects the nation's disbelief:

> And the word of the Lord came unto me in the ninth year, in the tenth month, in the tenth day of the month, saying: "Son of man, write the name of the day, even of this selfsame day; this selfsame day the king of Babylon has invested Jerusalem." (Ezek. 24:1–2)

By emphasizing the day of the attack, God seems to speak to Ezekiel's sense of surprise that the siege of Jerusalem began: "The name of the day, even of this selfsame day; this selfsame day."

The fast of *Asara B'Tevet* reminds us of the false sense of security, both spiritual and physical, that took hold of the people prior to the destruction of the Temple. *Asara B'Teve*t challenges us to constantly examine ourselves and in whom we place our faith – and not to "put our trust in illusions."

Interestingly, the Tosefta also cites another view, which asserts that the "fast of the tenth" refers to the fifth of Tevet, the day upon which the bad tiding regarding the destruction of the Temple reached the Diaspora (nearly five months after it actually took place) (Sota 6:11; Rosh HaShana 18b). Ezekiel reports:

> And it came to pass in the twelfth year of our captivity, in the tenth month, on the fifth day of the month, that one who had escaped out of Jerusalem came unto me, saying, "The city is smitten." Now the hand of the Lord had been upon me in the evening, before he who escaped came; and He had opened my mouth against his coming to me in the morning; and my mouth was opened, and I was no more dumb. (Ezek. 33:21–2)

Thus, *Asara B'Tevet* may not commemorate a specific event, but rather the impact of the event upon our national morale. Even the shock and horror of *hearing* about the *ḥurban* are worth commemorating.

Aside from the siege upon the city, other sources, as well as the day's *Seliḥot,* attribute two other tragedies to the month of Tevet.[8] *Megillat Taanit* relates that on the eighth of Tevet in the third century BCE, seventy-two elders were forced to translate the Torah into Greek, as a result of which "darkness came to the world for three days." The Gemara records:

> Talmai [Ptolemy] gathered the seventy-two elders and brought them to seventy-two separate houses.... He commanded each one to "write the Torah of Moses your teacher." The Holy One, Blessed be He, gave each one counsel, and they all agreed to one [translation]. (Megilla 9a)

Record of this event also appears in the "Letter of Aristeas," a Hellenistic work of the second century BCE, which describes the Greek translation of the Hebrew Law by seventy-two interpreters who were sent to Egypt from Jerusalem at the request of the librarian of Alexandria. The translation became known as the Septuagint.

Some might find reason to celebrate this miraculous event, in which all seventy-two scholars produced identical translations of the Torah. Indeed, Philo of Alexandria (20 BCE–50 CE) records that Alexandrian Jewry celebrated this event each year.[9] The Rabbis, however, describe this day as tragic. Masekhet Soferim, which records this and a similar incident, says, "That day was as difficult for Israel as the day that the [Golden] Calf was made, as the Torah was unable to be interpreted properly" (Masekhet Soferim 1:7). The commentators discuss whether the Rabbis feared that this translation validated or endorsed the Greek language and culture, or whether it minimized the centrality of the Hebrew text of the Bible.

Other sources allude to another event that occurred on the ninth of Tevet, without specifying the specific incident. *Seder Rav Amram Gaon,* for example, simply writes, "On the ninth [of the month] – the Rabbis did not write what occurred."

Some explain that Ezra the Scribe died on the ninth of Tevet.[10] A commentary to the Vilna edition of *Megillat Taanit* states that "on the ninth of Tevet, 'that man' was born," a clear reference to Jesus of Nazareth. The early sources did not explicitly mention which "tragedy" occurred on the ninth of Tevet, fearing the repercussions if it became known that a fast was declared to commemorate his birth.[11]

In addition to the events enumerated above, in 1951, the Chief Rabbinate of Israel declared that *Asara b'Tevet* should be observed as "*Yom HaKaddish HaKelalli,*" the day upon which we should remember those who were murdered during the Holocaust and recite Kaddish for those whose date of death is unknown.

SHIVA ASAR B'TAMMUZ

The Talmud describes the events that occurred on the Seventeenth of Tammuz:

> Five things happened to our ancestors on the Seventeenth of Tammuz...: The Tablets [with the Ten Commandments] were broken, the daily [burnt]

> offering was stopped, the city was breached, Apostamos burned the Torah, and he placed an idol in the Temple. (Taanit 26b)

Although the Rabbis disagree regarding whether the Ten Commandments were given on the sixth or seventh day of Sivan, all agree that Moshe ascended Har Sinai on the seventh day and descended forty days later (Ex. 24:16-18) – on the seventeenth of Tammuz. Upon witnessing the nation's celebration of the Golden Calf, Moshe threw down the Tablets, smashing them to pieces.

The circumstances surrounding the cessation of the daily burnt offering, the *korban hatamid*, on the Seventeenth of Tammuz are unclear. Rambam writes that this refers to the time of the First Temple,[12] but both the Yerushalmi (Y. Taanit 4:5) and the Bavli (Bava Kama 82b) refer to an incident during the late Second Temple period.

Rashi explains that the government prohibited the offering of this sacrifice,[13] while R. Ovadia Bartenura suggests that they were unable to obtain sheep for the sacrifice during the siege on the city.[14] In his commentary to the Mishna, R. Yisrael Lipschitz (1782–1860) explains that R. Bartenura must be referring to the three-year siege of Jerusalem by Nebuchadnezzar at the time of the destruction of the First Temple.[15] R. Lipschitz offers another interpretation, pointing to a talmudic passage that records the story of the battle between the two Hasmonean heirs, Hyrcanus and Aristobulus:

> Our Rabbis taught: When the members of the Hasmonean house were contending with one another, Hyrcanus was within and Aristobulus without [the city wall]. [Those who were within] used to let down to the other party every day a basket of denarii, and [in return] cattle were sent up for the regular sacrifices. There was, however, an old man [among the besiegers] who had some knowledge in Grecian Wisdom and who said to them: "So long as the other party [are allowed to] continue to perform the service of the sacrifices, they will not be delivered into your hands." On the next day, when the basket of denarii was let down, a swine was sent up. When the swine reached the center of the wall, it stuck its claws into the wall, and Eretz Yisrael quaked over a distance of four hundred parasangs by four hundred parasangs. (Bava Kama 82b)

The Gemara clearly refers to an incident during the first century BCE, during the time of the Second Temple.

The identity of Apostamos, who "burned the Torah and placed an idol in the Temple" on the Seventeenth of Tammuz, as well as the details of this incident, have intrigued scholars for generations.

Some attempt to match this episode with other known incidents in which Torah scrolls were burned. Ancient sources mention at least three incidents during which a Torah was publicly destroyed. The Talmud relates that during the Hadrianic persecutions (130–138), R. Ḥanina b. Teradyon, one of the great Rabbis of his time, was wrapped in a Torah scroll and burned alive as punishment for teaching Torah (Avoda Zara 18b). Similarly, Flavius Josephus relates that a Roman soldier "seized the laws of Moses that lay in one of those villages and brought them out before the eyes of all present and tore them to pieces."[16] Others point to the burning of the Torah scroll by Antiochus Epiphanes, the Selucid king at the time of the Ḥanukka story.[17]

The *Tiferet Yisrael* suggests that the Talmud refers to the authoritative *sefer Torah* of Ezra. Alternatively, it may refer to a decree to destroy every *sefer Torah*. In any case, it clearly represents an attempt to eradicate the Torah from the Jewish people.

The circumstances of the placement of an idol in the Temple also generated scholarly debate. The text of the Talmud Bavli reads, "and *he* put up," implying that it was Apostamos who brought an idol to the Temple. This would seem to support the view that it was Antiochus Epiphanes, who erected a statue of the Olympian Zeus in the Temple, who also burned the *sefer Torah*. The Talmud Yerushalmi offers another suggestion based upon a variant text, "and there was put up," explaining that the Talmud refers to King Menashe, who also erected an idol in the Temple (II Kings 21:7).

The most well-known event that we mark on the Seventeenth of Tammuz is the breaching of the walls of Jerusalem. The Talmud notes that the prophet Jeremiah implies that the walls were breached on the ninth of Tammuz, not the seventeenth (Jer. 52:6). The Gemara explains that while the city was breached on the ninth of Tammuz before the destruction of the First Temple, the city was breached on the seventeenth during the siege on Jerusalem before the destruction of the Second Temple. Why does the fast commemorate the second breach of the city's walls and not the first? Ramban explains that the second destruction was more severe.[18] Others suggest that the destruction of the Second Temple ultimately affects us more directly, and its date is therefore commemorated.

Alternatively, the Talmud Yerushalmi suggests that the walls were breached during both sieges on the Seventeenth of Tammuz; the intensity of the siege during the first destruction led to scribal errors in the recorded history (Y. Taanit 4:5).

TZOM GEDALIA

The Bible relates that after Nebuchadnezzar destroyed Jerusalem and the Temple, he appointed Gedalia ben Aḥikam as the governor of Judea (II Kings 25 and Jer. 40–41). Aalis, the king of Ammon, sent Yishmael ben Netania, another Jewish refugee, to Mitzpa to assassinate Gedalia (and thereby destabilize the region for his benefit). Although Gedalia was forewarned of Yishmael's intentions, he did not believe the warnings and was subsequently killed by Yishmael.

> Now it came to pass in the seventh month that Yishmael the son of Netania, the son of Elishama, of the royal seed and one of the chief officers of the king, and ten men with him, came unto Gedalia the son of Aḥikam, to Mitzpa; and there they did eat bread together in Mitzpa. Then Yishmael the son of Netania arose, and the ten men that were with him, and they smote Gedalia the son of Aḥikam the son of Shafan with the sword and slew him, whom the king of Babylon had made governor over the land. Yishmael also slew all the Jews that were with him, even with Gedalia, at Mitzpa, and the Chaldeans that were found there, even the men of war. (Jer. 41:1–3)

The assassination of Gedalia ben Aḥikam in the month of Tishrei represents the completion of the *ḥurban,* the destruction of autonomous Jewish rule in Judea. The sages further note that the fact that we mourn over this individual alongside the fasts associated with the various stages of the destruction teaches that "the death of a righteous man is akin to the destruction of the house of God" (Taanit 28b).

Tzom Gedalia is observed on the third of Tishrei, immediately after Rosh HaShana. R. David Kimchi (Radak) insists that Gedalia ben Aḥikam was actually murdered on the first of Tishrei, on Rosh HaShana itself, but the Rabbis instituted that the fast day be observed on the third so as not to interfere with the celebration of the holiday.[19] In his opinion, the relationship between the fast and Rosh HaShana is purely coincidental. Maharsha (R. Shmuel Eliezer b. R. Yehuda HaLevi Edels; 1555–1632) arrives at a different conclusion:

> And furthermore, one should have in mind that as this [murder] occurred during the *Aseret Yemei Teshuva* [the Ten Days of Repentance between Rosh HaShana and Yom Kippur], Yishmael, who killed him, should have been aroused to repent. As he did not, he added a great sorrow to the Jewish people with the killing of Gedalia, who was a salvation for the nation of Israel.... Therefore, during this time in which we pray for life... on the third day of the days of repentance, upon which Gedalia was killed, we suffered a great blow, and therefore on this specific day, we should be extra concerned and request God's mercy.[20]

As we commemorate the actions of one who chose not to pursue the proper path, we affirm our commitment to leading a spiritual life.

THE STATUS OF THE FASTS NOWADAYS

In the chapter from Zechariah noted above, the prophet relates a fascinating incident. After the rebuilding of the Second Temple, the people asked Zechariah, "Should we weep in the fifth month, fasting as we have done over the years?" (Zech. 7:3). In other words, should they continue to observe the four fasts instituted after the destruction of the First Temple now that the Second Temple had been built? The prophet responded cryptically: "The fast of the fourth, fifth, seventh, and tenth months will become joyful and happy, pleasant feasts for the house of Judah, so love truth and peace" (8:19).

The Talmud attempts to clarify Zechariah's answer in the context of a discussion concerning the messengers that were sent out each month to notify those outside of Jerusalem regarding the day of the consecration of the new moon. The Gemara questions why the Mishna states that messengers were sent during the month of Av on account of the fast of Tisha B'Av, but not during the months of Tevet and Tammuz, which also contain fast days:

> Why were they not also sent for Tammuz and Tevet? Did not R. Ḥana b. Bizna say in the name of R. Shimon HaTzaddik: What is the meaning of the passage, "Thus said the Lord of Hosts: The fast of the fourth, and the fast of the fifth, and the fast of the seventh, and the fast of the tenth shall become in the house of Judah joy and gladness"? [Why are] they called fasts, and also days of joy and gladness? [This is what it means:] In the time of peace (*shalom*), they shall be for joy and gladness, but in the time when there is not peace (*ein shalom*), they are to be fasts…
>
> R. Papa said: [The verse in Zechariah] means: When there is peace (*shalom*), these days should be for joy and gladness; in the time of persecution (*gezeirat malkhut*), they shall be fast days; in times when there is neither persecution nor peace (*ein gezeirat malkhut ve'ein shalom*), people may fast or not, as they see fit. (Rosh HaShana 18a–b)

According to R. Papa, it was thus unnecessary to send out messengers to inform the people regarding Rosh Ḥodesh Tammuz and Tevet because the fasts in those months were not obligatory. Messengers were sent out on Rosh Ḥodesh Av, however, as Tisha B'Av is different; it remains obligatory because "multiple misfortunes befell us on that day" (Taanit 18b).

The Gemara leaves us with many questions. How should we define "*shalom*," the time period during which the fast is observed as a festival? How should we define a period of "*gezeirat malkhut*," during which one must observe the fasts? When a time period is defined as neither a period of "*shalom*" nor "*gezeirat malkhut*," may the people decide not to fast entirely? Who decides whether or not to observe the day? Is it possible for there to be "*shalom*" and "*gezeirat malkhut*"? Furthermore, how should we define our present situation, especially since the establishment of the autonomous State of Israel? Finally, why did the Rabbis legislate that, at least theoretically, the observance of the fast is dependent upon the will of the people?

Most *Rishonim* explain that "*shalom*," the state during which one must celebrate instead of fasting, refers to a time in which the *Beit*

HaMikdash stands.[21] However, the position of Rashi has generated much discussion. On the one hand, he explains that the mishna regarding the Rosh Ḥodesh messengers refers to the period after the destruction of the Temple, seemingly implying that after the destruction, the people may decide whether or not to fast, but only when the *Beit HaMikdash* stands are these fasts transformed into festivals.[22] On the other hand, when explaining the term "*shalom*," he writes, "'*Shalom*' is when the non-Jews do not have dominion over Israel."[23]

Some explain that "when the non-Jews do not have dominion over Israel" implies that there is a *Beit HaMikdash*.[24] Accordingly, Rashi fundamentally agrees with the other *Rishonim*. Others suggest, however, that according to Rashi, Jewish autonomy in the Land of Israel is sufficient to abolish the fasts entirely; the actual *Beit HaMikdash* would not be necessary to cause this change, according to that opinion.

R. Shimon b. Tzemaḥ Duran (1361–1444) writes that a time of "*gezeirat malkhut*" refers to a period of persecution, during which one must fast the entire day and observe all of the "afflictions," as we do on Tisha B'Av.[25] Interestingly, however, we do not have record of such practice during the many various persecutions of the Jewish people throughout the ages, including the Crusades, the Inquisition, the Expulsion from Spain, pogroms and blood libels, and the Holocaust.

The intermediate time period of "*ein gezeirat malkhut ve'ein shalom*" has also been the subject of much discussion. It seems that the mishna discussing the Rosh Ḥodesh messengers refers to the period after the destruction of the Temple, classifying it as a period of neither persecution nor peace during which observance of the fast days was dependent upon the will of the people.[26]

Ritva questions how the people could have abolished a fast instituted to commemorate the destruction of the Temple before the Temple was rebuilt. He therefore suggests an alternative understanding. While the fast itself must still be observed during a period of "*ein gezeirat malkhut ve'ein shalom*," the people may decide whether to observe the other stringencies of a fast day – such as beginning the fast the night before and abstaining from washing, anointing, wearing leather shoes, and sexual relations. Thus, the fasts themselves are certainly completely binding today, but communities never accepted these additional stringencies upon themselves.[27]

Most *Rishonim,* however, understand that during the period in which the community may "choose" to observe or not to observe these fasts, they may actually decide not to fast at all. Nowadays, we have accepted upon ourselves the fasts themselves, but not the additional stringencies.

During a time in which we have neither "*shalom*" nor "*gezeirat malkhut,*" who determines whether we should fast? Rosh writes that the "community" determines whether or not the fasts should be observed, and that "an individual should not separate from the community, as long as the community fasts."[28] Similarly, Ritva explains that the *beit din* decides whether the community should fast.[29]

What happens when "*gezeirot malkhut*" occur during a time of "*shalom*"? Rambam explains that the fasts were sometimes observed even during the period of the Second Temple.[30] *Tashbetz* insists that this Rambam must be based upon a scribal error,[31] but reliable manuscripts indicate otherwise. Rambam apparently maintains that "*shalom*" and "*gezeirat malkhut*" are not mutually exclusive, and may unfortunately exist side by side.

A careful examination of Rambam's view reveals that in his opinion, the fasts are all obligatory today, and not dependent upon custom or the will of the people.[32] In other words, the choice whether or not to fast was offered only during the time of the Second Temple; nowadays, all of the fasts are obligatory. Apparently, the fast days not only commemorate the destruction of the Temple, but also the precarious position of the Jewish people and their Temple – the potential to experience "*ḥurban*" at any moment. While the Temple stood, these fasts were observed during times of "*gezeirat malkhut,*" but not during periods of "*shalom.*" After the destruction of the Temple, however, all agree that the fasts must be observed.

The *Shulḥan Arukh,* however, concludes that nowadays the fasts are fundamentally "optional," but the Jewish people have accepted these fasts upon themselves as if they are obligatory. He stresses that "*ein lifrotz geder,*" one should not violate this well-established practice.[33]

The entire ruling of the prophet Zechariah seems strange. In the world of halakha, practices are usually deemed "permissible" or "prohibited." How are we to understand that the observance of these fasts was, at least for a time, dependent upon the will of the people?

As we noted above, it seems that the goal of these fasts is not simply to commemorate ancient tragedies. Rather, they are to be used as opportunities to stimulate and to honestly assess our behavior, both as individuals and as a nation. In the absence of a clear indication of *shalom* or *gezeirat malkhut,* we are called upon to determine on each and every fast day the extent to which we must repent. The fast days serve at an indicator, or litmus test, of the spiritual place of the Jewish people.

CHAPTER 54

Laws of the Minor Fast Days

IN THE PREVIOUS chapter, we discussed the origins of the four fast days. We distinguished between Tisha B'Av and the other three fasts, as "multiple misfortunes befell us on that day" (Taanit 18b). In this chapter, we will discuss the halakhot of these three minor fasts.

THE BEGINNING OF THE FAST: WAKING UP EARLY TO EAT OR DRINK

As we noted in the previous chapter, these three fast days, in contrast to Tisha B'Av, do not begin the night before and include only the prohibitions of eating and drinking. The fast begins at *alot hashaḥar* (dawn) and concludes at *tzeit hakokhavim* (when three medium stars can be discerned in the sky). One should consult a reliable *luaḥ* (time-chart) for these times.

Interestingly, Ramban maintains that all four fasts are fundamentally identical – they begin the night before, and one should observe the additional stringencies (regarding washing, anointing, marital relations, and wearing leather shoes). However, the fasts nowadays are only a "*reshut*," dependent upon the will of the people, and the people only accepted upon themselves to fast during the day. Nevertheless, the date of the fast begins the night before, and this has halakhic significance.[1] *Shela* suggests that those who are able should observe the entire fast; they should begin fasting the night before and observe the stringencies of a public fast day. (One should not abstain from wearing leather shoes, as this would be perceived as haughty.)[2]

Assuming that one does not begin fasting at sunset, until when may one eat the evening before the fast? The Talmud teaches:

> The sages taught: Until when may he eat and drink? Until daybreak. These are the words of R..... And the halakha is like R..... Abaye said: They only said this [about being able to eat in the morning before a fast] when he did not finish [his meal], but if he finished it, he may not eat.... Rava said: They only said this when he did not sleep, but if he slept, he may not eat. (Taanit 12a)

Abaye and Rava agree that once one has had "*heseḥ hadaat*" from eating, he may no longer eat, but they debate what constitutes this "*hesech hadaat*." According to Abaye, once one concludes the evening meal, one may no longer eat. According to Rava, only after one falls asleep is he prohibited from eating again. The halakha is in accordance with Rava,[3] and the *Rishonim* debate whether the sleep he refers to implies going to bed with the intent of waking up the next morning, or even falling asleep before dinner.

Some *Rishonim* explain this halakha based upon what we learned above. Fundamentally, the fast begins the night before. However, since the people accepted upon themselves to be able to eat the night before, the fast begins once one no longer intends to eat.

The Yerushalmi,[4] cited by Rosh,[5] adds that if one stipulated before going to sleep that he would wake up and eat, he may do so. The *Rishonim* debate whether one must make a stipulation in order to drink as well. Some *Rishonim* rule leniently, as one generally wakes up thirsty after sleeping and therefore has in mind to wake up and drink.[6] Rosh, however, rules that one must also stipulate his intention to drink water upon rising before daybreak.[7] The *Shulḥan Arukh* rules stringently,[8] but Rema rules that one need not stipulate intention to continue drinking.[9] The *Mishna Berura* writes that one should preferably stipulate intention to continue drinking even upon rising in the middle of the night, but *bediavad*, one who ordinarily drinks upon rising may still drink.[10]

"TASTING" AND BRUSHING TEETH ON A *TAANIT*

What constitutes forbidden "eating" or "drinking" on a *taanit*? The Talmud questions whether one who fasts must abstain only from "eating," or also from all "pleasure" to one's palate.

> Ashian, the *Tanna* of the school of R. Ammi, inquired of R. Ammi: May one who is observing a [voluntary] fast take a taste? Has he undertaken to abstain from eating and drinking, and this is really not such, or has he undertaken not to have any enjoyment, and this he obtains? He replied: He may taste, and there is no objection. It has been taught similarly: A mere taste does not require a blessing, and one who is keeping a [voluntary] fast may take a taste, and there is no objection. How much may he taste? R. Ammi and R. Assi used to taste as much as a *revi'it*. (Berakhot 14a)

The *Rishonim* debate whether this passage refers to a private fast that an individual accepts upon himself or even a public fast day.

Tosafot derive from the Gemara's language, "has he undertaken," that the passage refers to a private, voluntary fast.[11] The *Rishonim* discuss whether this "private fast" on which "tasting" is permitted includes fasts that are decreed upon the people in response to severe drought or only to a personal fast that an individual accepts upon himself.

On the other hand, Rosh and others explain that the Talmud permits tasting on all fast days, with the possible exception of Tisha B'Av and Yom Kippur.[12] On those days, tasting may violate the prohibition of "washing for pleasure," comparable to dipping one's finger in water on Yom Kippur,[13] or it may be forbidden simply because these days are more stringent, as reflected in the other "afflictions" observed on Yom Kippur and Tisha B'Av.[14] Some suggest that since the three minor fast days are dependent upon the community's will, they are considered to be a fast that people "accepted upon themselves," and we are therefore more lenient.[15]

The *Shulḥan Arukh* rules that one who is fasting may taste up to a *revi'it* on all fasts except for Tisha B'Av and Yom Kippur, as long as he expels the liquid from his mouth.[16] Interestingly, the *Shulḥan Arukh* later[17] cites the *Terumat HaDeshen,* who advises against rinsing out one's mouth on a fast day. The *Terumat HaDeshen* explains that since "tasting," in his opinion, is only permitted on a private fast day, one should refrain from rinsing out one's mouth on communal fasts.[18] The *Magen Avraham* points out the apparent contradiction: if the *Shulḥan Arukh* permits tasting on communal fasts, it would stand to reason that he would permit rinsing out one's mouth as well, unlike the position of the *Terumat HaDeshen.*[19]

To reconcile the two halakhot, the *Magen Avraham* suggests that the latter statement prohibiting washing out one's mouth refers to rinsing with more than a *revi'it.*[20] R. Mordechai Karmi, author of the *Maamar Mordekhai* commentary on the *Shulḥan Arukh,* was so troubled by this contradiction that he argues that R. Yosef Karo must be referring in his later statement to Tisha B'Av and Yom Kippur, while on an ordinary fast day, rinsing out one's mouth would be perfectly permitted![21] R. Ovadia Yosef describes any attempt to resolve this problem as "*sakanat derakhim*" – dangerous traveling.[22]

Rema adds that it is customary to be stringent and not permit tasting even on the minor fast days.[23] This ruling seems to be more in line with the *Terumat HaDeshen*'s position. However, in Rema's commentary to the *Tur,* the *Darkhei Moshe,* he notes that Maharil would wash out his mouth and then lean forward, so that water should not accidentally reach his throat. Apparently, Maharil maintained that even though one should not "taste" on the four fast days, one need not be concerned with washing out one's mouth.[24] The *Eliya Rabba* concurs.[25] The *Mishna Berura* writes that in cases of discomfort, one may wash his mouth out with water, as long as he is careful not to swallow any water; this is true even on Tisha B'Av![26] Similarly, *Minḥat Yitzchak* permits one to clean his month, even with toothpaste, when necessary.[27] Nowadays, it would seem that most people feel great discomfort when unable to brush their teeth in the morning, and would thus be permitted to brush their teeth or wash out their mouths on a fast day.

ONE WHO "FORGOT" THE FAST

What should one do if he only remembers that it is a fast day after reciting a *berakha* on a certain food? This question is related to the general question of what the proper procedure should be if one accidentally recited a blessing on a forbidden food, such as non-kosher items, dairy food after having eaten meat, or food that one has vowed not to eat. On the one hand, the food is prohibited, and one certainly does not want to eat it. On the other hand, one may not recite God's name in vain, even in a blessing, and one might therefore wish to eat the food so that the blessing should not be for naught. In order to resolve this problem, we must determine both the origin of the prohibition of reciting a *berakha levatala* (a blessing in vain), as well as the level of the prohibition of the food in question, and then assess which concern should prevail.

The *Rishonim* debate the origin of the prohibition of reciting a *berakha levatala*. The Gemara teaches (Berakhot 33a), "Whoever says an unnecessary blessing transgresses the command of 'You shall not take God's name in vain' [Ex. 20:6]." Elsewhere (Temura 4a), the Gemara further asserts that one who utters God's name in vain violates the command of "and you should fear the Lord your God" (Deut. 6:13). Most *Rishonim* maintain that the gemara should not be taken literally and that the prohibition is *miderabbanan*.[28] However, Rambam,[29] and consequently the *Shulḥan Arukh*,[30] imply that the prohibition may be *mideoraita*.

According to Rambam, in our case of mistakenly reciting a *berakha* over food on a fast day, one might be inclined to taste a small bit of the food in order not to recite a *berakha* in vain, as that prohibition is *mideoraita*, while the fast day is *miderabbanan*. According to Tosafot, however, perhaps one should not eat, especially on the four fasts whose origin may be "*midivrei kabbala*" (of prophetic origin). Therefore, one should rather simply say "*barukh shem kavod*" upon concluding the blessing.

R. Ovadia Yosef rules in accordance with Rambam, concluding that one should taste and swallow a bit of food in order to avoid the unnecessary blessing, and one may still be considered to be fasting in such a case.[31] The *Piskei Teshuvot* cites a number of *Aḥaronim* who conclude that one should not eat the food, but recommend tasting it without swallowing, thereby avoiding the question of a *berakha levatala* according to a number of opinions.[32] One who began the blessing but did not finish it should simply conclude "*lamdeini ḥukekha*," as this constitutes a verse from Tanakh (Ps. 119:12).

One who completely forgot about the fast and ate normally should still continue fasting the rest of the day. Furthermore, one need not make up the fast. Maharil, however, cited by the *Mishna Berura*,[33] instructs one who ate to make up the fast in order to attain atonement.

EXEMPTIONS FROM FASTING

On Yom Kippur, all adults are obligated to fast, unless fasting may endanger one's life (*pikuaḥ nefesh*). In such a situation, one should preferably eat or drink in small measurements (*shiurim*). On the minor fast days, however, certain people are exempt from fasting.

A sick person, even if his illness does not pose any danger to his life (*ḥoleh she'ein bo sakana*), as well as an elderly person who is weak and may become sick if he fasts, should not fast.[34] A sick person does not need to consider whether or not his condition will become dangerous; as long as he is sick, he is exempt from fasting.[35] Furthermore, one who is recovering from a sickness and fears that fasting may cause him to become sick again, or even one who fears that by fasting one will become sick, may eat and drink. For example, one who suffers from diabetes, severe migraine headaches, or kidney stones may eat or drink in order to prevent the onset of the condition. Those who must eat on a minor fast day should not indulge on meat and wine, however, but rather eat and drink only what is necessary for their health.

One who must continue to take medications on a fast day, such as antibiotics, or one who suffers from a chronic condition but is not presently sick and therefore must fast, should try to swallow his medicines without water. Some suggest that one who is unable to swallow medicines without water should mix a bit of water with a bitter substance and take the medicine with that water.[36] Swallowing a pill with a bit of mouthwash should also suffice. Rabbi Dr. Abraham S. Abraham, in his work on halakha and medicine, cites R. Shlomo Zalman Auerbach and R. Yehoshua Neuwirth as permitting one who is unable to swallow medicines with water to drink a bit of water with them.[37]

The *Aḥaronim* discuss whether one who must eat or drink on the minor fast days should eat or drink in small measurements (*shiurim*), as they should on Yom Kippur,[38] or whether this stringency is unnecessary on the minor fasts.[39] *Nishmat Avraham* writes in the name of R. Shlomo Zalman Auerbach that a healthy person who eats or drinks in order to avoid becoming sick should eat or drink in *shiurim*, as should a sick person who wishes to receive an *aliya* on the fast day.[40]

Although pregnant and nursing women are obligated to fast on Tisha B'Av, they are exempt from fasting on the three other minor fasts, and certainly on *Taanit Esther*.[41] Rema records that in Ashkenazic communities, pregnant women customarily fasted.[42] The *Arukh HaShulḥan* writes that pregnant women are permitted to fast, but if they are in great discomfort they may eat, even if the fast poses no danger to the mother or the fetus.[43] It is customary nowadays for pregnant and nursing women not to fast on these days.

While a "nursing mother" would seem to refer to one who is actually nursing, some *Aḥaronim*, such as R. Shalom Mordechai Schwadron,[44] as well as R. Ovadia Yosef,[45] exempt women from fasting during the entire twenty-four months after birth, the period identified by the Talmud as the time necessary for a woman to fully recover from birth (Nidda 9a).

While some authorities sought to exempt all women from fasting on the three minor fasts and *Taanit Esther* during all of their childbearing years,[46] this ruling seems difficult to rely upon under normal circumstances.

Must children abstain from eating on the minor fast days? The Talmud discusses the age at which a child should begin to fast on Yom Kippur, and for how long (Yoma 82). The *Mishna Berura* writes that while children are not obligated to fast on the minor fasts, even for a few hours, they should be taught to eat only simple foods necessary to maintain their health.[47] He repeats that children are exempt from fasting in his *Biur Halakha*.[48] R. Menachem Azaria da Fano (1548–1620), known as Rema MiFano, praises the custom to train children not to eat for a few hours on the minor fasts.[49]

BEHAVIOR ON A FAST DAY

As we have discussed, the fast days are intended to promote introspection and repentance. Indeed, R. Yisrael Meir Kagan, known as Ḥafetz Ḥayim after his work concerning the laws of *lashon hara*, warns that we should keep the essence of the day in its proper perspective:

> Therefore, a person must be attentive during these days, and examine one's ways and repent for them, because the essence [of the day] is *not* the fast, as it says regarding the people of Nineveh, "And God saw their actions, that they turned from their evil way" [Yona 3:10]. Our Rabbis taught: It does not say "their sackcloth" and "their fasts," but rather "their actions." The fast is merely a preparation for repentance, and therefore those people who fast but go about their ways and waste their time have grasped the minor part of the day and left the essence. However, repentance itself is not enough, as there is a commandment from the words of the prophets to fast.[50]

Indeed, as we learned above, in theory the fasts should be observed from the night before, with all of the stringencies associated with the fast of Tisha B'Av. Although it is customary not to observe those stringencies, their theoretical applicability should teach us something about how the day should be observed. Rambam notes this point in his halakhic description of proper behavior during the day:

> One who is fasting, whether in response to a calamity, or to a bad dream, or one who is fasting with the community for their crisis, should not engage in "*idunim*" (entertainment or delicacies). He should neither act in a

> light-hearted manner nor be happy and in good spirit. Rather, one should be in an apprehensive and mournful mood.[51]

While technically a fast merely requires that one abstain from eating and drinking, ideally one should limit one's physical pleasures and attempt to focus upon the essence of the day: repentance.

CHAPTER 55

Prayer on Fast Days

ANEINU

The Talmud teaches that on a public fast day, both the individual and the *sheliaḥ tzibbur* (prayer leader) should insert a special prayer, *Aneinu*, into the *Shemoneh Esreh*:

> R. Yehuda directed R. Yitzchak his son and expounded: An individual who accepts upon himself a fast should pray a "*tefillat taanit*" [*Aneinu*]. And where [in *Shemoneh Esreh*] should he say it? Between *Go'el* [the seventh blessing] and *Rofei* [the eighth blessing]. R. Yitzchak objected: Does an individual establish a blessing for himself? Rather, R. Yitzchak said: In *Shome'a Tefilla* [the fifteenth blessing]. And so did R. Sheshet say: In *Shome'a Tefilla*. And the halakha is: In *Shome'a Tefilla*, and the *sheliaḥ tzibbur* says it between *Go'el* and *Rofei*. (Taanit 13b)

Thus, while the *sheliaḥ tzibbur* inserts an additional *berakha* between the seventh and eighth blessings, an individual should insert *Aneinu* into the fifteenth blessing, *Shema Koleinu*.

The Yerushalmi records that *Aneinu* should be recited during all three prayers of the fast day: Maariv, Shaḥarit, and Minḥa:

> R. Yanai b. R. Yishmael [said] in the name of R. Shimon b. Lakish: Even an individual who decrees upon himself a fast must mention the nature of the

> occasion. And where should he mention it? R. Zeira [said] in the name of R. Ḥuna: He says it like the night of Shabbat and its day. (Y. Taanit 2:2)

The Bavli also implies that one should insert *Aneinu* at each prayer (Shabbat 24a), and most *Rishonim* rule accordingly.[1]

Baal HaMaor, however, disagrees, ruling that *Aneinu* should not be recited at night. He insists that "at a time during which one may eat, one should not [insert *Aneinu* into] the evening prayer." Indeed, Rashba, in his discussion of this opinion, asks, "How can one insert *Aneinu* in the evening prayer while one's belly is still full?!"

Ran explains that according to Rif, the fast fundamentally, although not practically, begins at night. Once one no longer intends to eat, the fast begins, and as we discussed above, if one awakens in the middle of the night without previously stipulating intent to eat, he is not be permitted to eat!

These *Rishonim* apparently disagree as to the nature of *Aneinu*. While Baal HaMaor views *Aneinu* as a *tefilla* recited as part of one's fast, Rif and Ran view *Aneinu* as, in the language of the Gemara, "*hazkarat me'ein hameora*," an expression of the nature of the day, which technically begins at night regardless of whether or not "one's belly is still full."

Rashi supports the position that *Aneinu* should be recited three times. However, he then cites the opinion of the *Geonim*, who record that they were not accustomed to saying *Aneinu* at night or in the morning, lest one not finish his fast and would therefore have retroactively lied in his prayers.[2] Rashba explains that the geonic position does not argue with the Yerushalmi's instruction to recite the prayer at every service, but rather reflects the weakness and inability to fast that has overcome some of the Jewish people.[3]

Ritva[4] and Tosafot[5] reject the concern of the *Geonim*. Even if one felt weak later in the day and ate, it would be considered an "*ones*," duress, and we would not consider his earlier prayer to be dishonest. These *Rishonim* report that the custom in France was for only the *sheliaḥ tzibbur* to insert *Aneinu* in the morning. They note that this practice does not seem to conform to either the Talmud or the *Geonim*! Ritva explains that "it is inconceivable that there is not at least one in the community who is fasting, so the *sheliaḥ tzibbur* may recite it," but an individual should not recite it until Minḥa.

The *Shulḥan Arukh* writes:

> Some say that an individual should not insert *Aneinu* except during Minḥa, lest he is afflicted by "*bulmus*" [a condition for which he must eat] and he turns out to have lied in his prayer. However, the *sheliaḥ tzibbur* should say it during Shaḥarit when he prays out loud, as some members of the community must be fasting. And on the four fast days, even an individual recites it in all of his prayers, as even if he would be afflicted by a "*bulmus*" and would eat, it is still appropriate to say "answer us (*Aneinu*) on our fast day," as the Rabbis established it as a day to fast.[6]

Rema adds:

> It is customary in our communities only to say *Aneinu* at Minḥa, except for the *sheliaḥ tzibbur*, who inserts it during the morning repetition.[7]

Ashkenazi Jews follow the practice cited by Rema and do not recite *Aneinu* until Minḥa. Most Sephardi communities do not recite *Aneinu* at night, in deference to the opinion of the Baal HaMaor, but do insert it in the morning.[8] Yemenite communities recite *Aneinu* even during Maariv.

MUST THE CONGREGANTS AND THE *SHELIAḤ TZIBBUR* BE FASTING IN ORDER TO RECITE *ANEINU*?

Rashba rules that the *sheliaḥ tzibbur* should not insert *Aneinu* in his repetition unless there are at least ten people in the congregation who are fasting.[9] Other *Rishonim* seem to disagree, however, implying that the *sheliaḥ tzibbur* may insert *Aneinu* even if only some of the congregation,[10] or even one member,[11] is fasting. Me'iri writes that as long as at least three people are fasting, it is considered to be a communal fast.[12]

The *Shulḥan Arukh* cites the view of Rashba requiring ten fasting members of the congregation.[13] The commentaries on the *Shulḥan Arukh*[14] cite Maharam b. Ḥaviv, author of the responsa *Kol Gadol*,[15] who insists that Rashba and *Shulḥan Arukh* refer only to a fast day that the community accepted upon themselves. On the four fast days, which are "*midivrei kabbala*," the *ḥazan* may certainly insert *Aneinu* in his repetition even if there are fewer than six or seven people fasting. The *Arukh HaShulḥan* also understood that as long as there are three people fasting, who will serve as the *sheliaḥ tzibbur* and participate in the Torah reading, *Aneinu* may be inserted.[16] The *Shaar HaTziyun*[17] notes that the *Peri Megadim*[18] and *Eliya Rabba*[19] disagree with this distinction and require that at least ten fasting people be present in order to insert *Aneinu* on the four fasts as well.

After citing Maharam b. Ḥaviv, the *Shaarei Teshuva* suggests that one should only insert *Aneinu* in the presence of at least six or seven fasting people, and then suggests that we may require a "noticeable majority," seven individuals, as we do for *Birkat HaMazon*.[20] In practice, while there should preferably be ten men fasting in order to insert *Aneinu* into the repetition, some maintain that seven fasting men are sufficient,[21] while others permit the insertion when there are only six.[22]

This question actually raises fundamental issues regarding who determines the nature of the day – the community or the calendar – as well as the extent to which the *ḥazan*'s repetition must reflect the congregation or the nature of the day.

Regarding the *sheliaḥ tzibbur* on a fast day, the *Tur* writes:

> R. Natan wrote that a *sheliaḥ tzibbur* who is not fasting should not pray [recite the repetition], since, as he is not fasting, he cannot say *Aneinu*. I do not know why, since he does not say "on this day of *my* fast," but rather, "on this fast day," and the fast is for others. Certainly, when possible, the *sheliaḥ tzibbur* should be one who is fasting. However, when not possible, it seems to me that he may say the repetition.[23]

Despite *Tur*'s objection, R. Yosef Karo, in his *Beit Yosef* and then in the *Shulḥan Arukh*,[24] rules in accordance with R. Natan and the *Geonim*.

While some *Aḥaronim* maintain that one who is not fasting cannot serve as the *sheliaḥ tzibbur* even in extenuating circumstances,[25] the *Arukh HaShulḥan* disagrees and rules that in such a situation one should act according to *Tur*; the *sheliaḥ tzibbur* should recite the repetition normally.[26] *Magen Avraham* writes that when necessary, even one who is not fasting may serve as the *sheliaḥ tzibbur* so that the community should not miss out on the *devarim shebikedusha*. However, he should say, "*beyom tzom hataanit hazeh*" ("on this fast day") instead of "*beyom tzom taaniteinu*" ("on *our* fast day"), and he should not recite a separate blessing but rather insert *Aneinu* into *Shema Koleinu*, the fifteenth blessing, as an individual does.[27] The *Mishna Berura*[28] and other *Aḥaronim*[29] concur.

ANEINU AND ONE WHO ACCIDENTALLY BROKE HIS FAST

It seems evident from the above discussion that one who is not fasting should not recite *Aneinu*.[30] What is considered "breaking one's fast" in this context? May one who accidentally broke his fast recite *Aneinu*? Generally, we define "*akhila*" (eating) as ingesting a "*kezayit*" of food (a quantity the size of an olive) within a specific quantity of time, known as *kedei akhilat peras* (the time it takes to eat half a loaf of bread). Similarly, we define "*shetiya*" as drinking a "*revi'it*" (a talmudic unit of liquid capacity, a quarter *log*) within a stipulated amount of time, either a *kedei akhilat peras* or the shorter time of *kedei shetiyat revi'it* (the time it takes to drink a *revi'it*).[31]

On Yom Kippur, however, "*akhila*" and "*shetiya*" are defined as eating a quantity equivalent to a "*kakotevet*" (a large date) or drinking a "*melo lugmav*" (cheekful). At that point, one is no longer considered "afflicting" oneself, as is required on Yom Kippur.

Which of these measurements apply to other fasts? The *Shulḥan Arukh* rules that one who consumed a *kezayit* of food has broken his fast and must fast again.[32] *Magen Avraham*, cited by the *Mishna Berura*,[33] explains that this refers to one who ate that amount within the typical halakhic time frame of *kedei akhilat peras*. Similarly, *Magen Avraham* asserts that one who drinks "*melo lugmav*," a cheekful, has broken the fast.

The *Aḥaronim* debate whether the *Shulḥan Arukh* refers only to a private fast that the individual accepted upon himself through a vow, or if his ruling includes the prescribed communal fasts as well.[34] Seemingly, once one has consumed a *kezayit* of food, a smaller quantity than a *kakotevet,* one should omit *Aneinu,* even though he must complete the fast.

KERIAT HATORAH (TORAH READING)

Masekhet Soferim records that we read "*Parashat VaYeḥal*" (Ex. 32:11–14, 34:1–10) on fast days other than Tisha B'Av (Masekhet Soferim 17:5). The Mishna records that it is also the custom to read the *haftara* of "*Dirshu Hashem BeHimatzo*" (Hos. 55).

Rambam rules that "*Parashat VaYeḥal*" is read at both Shaḥarit and Minḥa, but he makes no mention of a *haftara.*[35] *Abudraham* similarly makes no mention of a *haftara,* and *Beit Yosef* records that the custom in Sephardic lands is not to recite a *haftara* at Shaḥarit or Minḥa. He notes that Roke'aḥ[36] and *Kol Bo*[37] write that the *haftara* is recited at Minḥa, concluding that "each river should flow in its own direction."[38]

As expected, the *Shulḥan Arukh* makes no mention of reading a *haftara* on a *taanit tzibbur,* while Rema relates that the *haftara* of "*Dirshu*" is read at Minḥa.[39] R. Ovadia Hadaya rules in his *Yaskil Avdi* that a Sephardi praying Minḥa in an Ashkenazi *minyan* who is called up to read the *haftara* may recite the *haftara* with its blessings, as the matter is one of different customs and not of halakha.[40]

As we saw above regarding *Aneinu,* the special Torah reading and *haftara* should preferably be recited in the presence of ten men who are fasting; *bediavad,* even six or seven may suffice.

May an individual who is not fasting receive an *aliya*? Maharik rules that one who is not fasting should not be called up to the Torah.[41] The *Shulḥan Arukh* concurs,[42] as does *Taz,* who rules that if one who is not fasting was called to the Torah, he should not recite the blessings.[43] R. Akiva Eiger explains that the *keriat haTorah* of a *taanit* is part of the fast, and therefore one who is not fasting should not read or receive an *aliya.*[44] According to this opinion, a Kohen or Levite who is not fasting and is the only Kohen or Levite in the room should leave the room before the first *aliya* so that another person may be called up.

Others, however, disagree. R. Moshe Sofer, known as Ḥatam Sofer, relates how on Tisha B'Av of 1811, he was sick and unable to fast. He authored a *teshuva* regarding whether he could be called up for the Minḥa reading of *Parashat VaYeḥal.* He argues that Maharik's ruling is without precedent. Furthermore, in the case of Tisha B'Av, it is the day itself that obligates *keriat haTorah* – "*yoma ka garem*" – and not the fast. Thus, even someone who is not fasting may be called up to the Torah. He notes that *Baḥ* concurs.[45] Some *Aḥaronim* question whether Ḥatam Sofer's ruling and rationale would apply to the other three fasts as well. The *Arukh HaShulḥan* agrees that even one who is not fasting may be called up to the Torah.[46]

The *Mishna Berura,* who follows the ruling of the *Shulḥan Arukh,* concludes that if someone who is not fasting is called up to the Torah and would be severely embarrassed to reveal that he is not fasting, perhaps leading to the desecration of God's name, he may rely upon the lenient opinions and recite the *berakhot.*[47]

Magen Avraham notes that if the fast falls on a Monday or Thursday, even one who is not fasting may read from the Torah, despite the fact that *Parashat VaYeḥal,* and not the weekly *parasha,* is read.[48]

It is customary for the congregation to recite three of the verses from the reading out loud: "*Shuv meiḥaron apekha,*" "*Hashem, Hashem*" (the Thirteen Attributes of Mercy), and "*vesalaḥta.*" The *baal koreh* (Torah reader) should wait until after the congregation has finished their recitation before he reads these verses.

BIRKAT KOHANIM ON A PUBLIC FAST DAY

The Talmud teaches that just as a Priest may not perform his service in the *Beit HaMikdash* while intoxicated, he should similarly not "raise his hands" to bless the people after drinking alcohol (Taanit 26b). The Rabbis feared that the Priests, after eating their midday meal, may be intoxicated, and they therefore legislated that *Birkat Kohanim,* the priestly blessing, should not be recited at Minḥa.

The Mishna cites a debate whether *Birkat Kohanim* is recited at Minḥa of a fast day, when there is no such fear of intoxication. The Talmud rules in accordance with R. Yose, who insists that on a day in which Minḥa **and** *Ne'ila* are recited – on Yom Kippur, public fast days instituted during times of drought, and during the *maamadot* (the prayers of the communities whose representatives are serving in the Temple) – *Birkat Kohanim* is performed at *Ne'ila*, and **not** during Minḥa, lest one come to confuse Minḥa on these days with Minḥa on an ordinary weekday. The Gemara concludes: "And nowadays, why do the Kohanim 'raise their hands' at Minḥa on a fast day? Since it is close to sunset when they 'raise their hands,' it is similar to *Ne'ila*" (Taanit 26a). In other words, when Minḥa is recited on a fast day during the time of *Ne'ila*, close to nightfall, *Birkat Kohanim* may be said, as it would not be confused with an ordinary Minḥa. The *Shulḥan Arukh* rules:

> During a fast day when *Ne'ila* is not recited, since Minḥa is recited close to sunset, it is similar to the *Ne'ila* prayer and will not be confused with Minḥa of other days, and therefore they "raise their hands."[49]

This is relevant today specifically in Eretz Yisrael, where *Birkat Kohanim* is recited on a daily basis.

Ḥazon Ish suggests that once the Rabbis established that *Birkat Kohanim* may be recited at Minḥa of fast days, they did not distinguish between whether Minḥa is recited earlier or later in the day.[50] In fact, in the *Ḥazon Ish*'s *beit midrash*, *Birkat Kohanim* was recited during Minḥa of a fast day even when recited early.[51] Common custom, however, is in accordance with other *gedolei Yerushalayim*,[52] who ruled that *Birkat Kohanim* on a fast day should only be recited close to sunset.

CHAPTER 56

Bein HaMetzarim: The Three Weeks and the Nine Days

PROHIBITIONS DURING THE THREE WEEKS

Between the fast days of *Shiva Asar B'Tammuz* and Tisha B'Av, a three-week period of mourning, known as "*Bein HaMetzarim*" is observed. The Midrash understands the verse, "All [of Zion's] pursuers overtook her between the straits (*bein hametzarim*)" (Lam. 1:3) as referring to this three-week period of misfortune (Lamentations Rabba 1:29). In fact, the earliest reference to a three-week period of mourning over the loss of the *Beit HaMikdash* appears in Daniel, where the prophet relates:

> In those days I, Daniel, was mourning three whole weeks. I ate no pleasant bread, neither came flesh nor wine in my mouth, neither did I anoint myself at all, until three whole weeks were fulfilled. (Daniel 10:23)

Daniel recalls how he mourned for three weeks, abstaining from bread, wine, meat, and anointing.

Some of the earliest sources that record mourning customs of this time period attribute them to these verses. For example, *Shibbolei HaLeket* records in the name of R. Saadia Gaon that based upon these verses, some were accustomed to refrain from eating meat and drinking wine during the Three Weeks.[1] Similarly, the author of *Kol Bo* relates that he "saw precious women who refrain from eating meat and drinking wine... and they insist that they received this tradition from their mothers, generation after generation."[2] He attributes this to the cessation of the offering of the *korban tamid*, which occurred on *Shiva Asar B'Tammuz*.

According to custom, four basic prohibitions begin on *Shiva Asar B'Tammuz*. Ashkenazic practice prohibits holding weddings and taking haircuts during these three weeks, as this is a period of mourning for the *Beit HaMikdash* in preparation for Tisha B'Av. In addition, it is customary to refrain from reciting the *Sheheḥeyanu* blessing and to avoid unusually dangerous activities, as this is an inauspicious time period for the Jewish people.

What is the nature of the mourning during this time period? R. Soloveitchik insisted that these customs must conform to some previous halakhic pattern.[3] In the laws of *aveilut* for a parent, referred to by the Rabbis as "*aveilut ḥadasha*" ("new mourning"), we generally speak of three periods of mourning: first, *shiva* (the seven-day period after the burial), then *sheloshim* (the thirty days after burial), and then, the *yud-bet ḥodesh* (the twelve-month period after the death of a parent). R. Soloveitchik maintained that the mourning over the *Beit HaMikdash*, "*aveilut yeshana*" ("old mourning," commemorating a historic national disaster), follows the *opposite* pattern: the laws of Tisha B'Av closely resemble the laws of *shiva*, while the laws of *sheloshim* are similar to the laws of the Nine Days.

R. Soloveitchik suggested that the customary *aveilut* of the Three Weeks (as well as the *aveilut* of *Sefirat HaOmer*) conforms to the halakhic precedent of *yud-bet ḥodesh*. Indeed, the laws that characterize the *yud-bet Ḥodesh* include the prohibitions of attending a "*beit hamishteh*" (Mo'ed Katan 22b) and taking a haircut (Mo'ed Katan 22b).[4]

Other *Aḥaronim*, however, do not accept the premise that the *aveilut* practices of *Bein HaMetzarim* must be modeled after pre-existing categories; rather, a new custom developed over time. As we shall see, this difference of opinion may lead to sharp differences in halakhic application.

WEDDINGS

The Talmud teaches:

> We learned: During the week in which the Ninth of Av occurs, it is forbidden to cut the hair and to wash clothes.... And [in connection with this Mishna] it was taught: Before this time, the public must restrict their activities in commerce, building, and plantings, but it is permissible to betroth, although

> not to marry, nor may any betrothal feast be held. That was taught in respect to the period before that time. (Yevamot 43a)

According to this gemara, it is prohibited to cut hair and launder during the week in which Tisha B'Av falls, the "*shavua sheḥal bo*," and one may not marry during the "period before that time" – that is, during the entire Nine Days beginning with Rosh Ḥodesh Av. The *Shulḥan Arukh* cites this gemara, and Sephardic Jews are therefore accustomed not to hold weddings during the Nine Days.[5]

R. Isaac Tyrnau, in his *Sefer HaMinhagim*, records the custom to refrain from marrying during the entire Three Weeks. Rema cites this custom, and Ashkenazim follow this ruling.[6] This prohibition regarding weddings was interpreted in the broadest sense by some *Aḥaronim*. *Magen Avraham* writes, "It seems to me that it is prohibited to hold '*rikudim umeḥolot*' (dances) from *Shiva Asar B'Tammuz* until Tisha B'Av."[7]

The *Aḥaronim* differ as to the scope and nature of this extension. Based on his theory regarding the nature of the *aveilut* of the Three Weeks, R. Soloveitchik maintained that the custom prohibits whatever is prohibited during the period of *yud-bet ḥodesh*. During *yud-bet ḥodesh*, the mourner is prohibited from attending social gatherings whose enjoyment is a function of the participation of one's friends and acquaintances – *simḥat merei'ut* (Mo'ed Katan 22b).[8] Accordingly, playing instruments or listening to music privately would be permitted during the Three Weeks, while other public social gatherings – even those that do not involve music or dancing, such as a baseball game – might be prohibited.

Other *Aḥaronim* explain that it is specifically playing and listening to instruments and music that is prohibited, as it is inconsistent with the sense of sorrow we are supposed to experience during the Three Weeks, and this applies even to music outside of the context of "*rikudim umeḥolot*." *Biur Halakha* writes, however, that one who works as an entertainer for non-Jews at social gatherings or banquets may continue working until Rosh Ḥodesh Av.[9] Similarly, some *Aḥaronim* permit giving or taking instrument lessons until the week in which Tisha B'Av falls.[10]

Many other *Aḥaronim* equate the time-periods of the Three Weeks and *Sefirat HaOmer* (as R. Soloveitchik did) and therefore deal with them together. In recent years, there has been extensive discussion regarding listening to music from a radio or other electronic device in regard to both the Three Weeks and *Sefirat HaOmer*. R. Moshe Feinstein, who is generally inclined to prohibit all music after the destruction of the *Beit HaMikdash*,[11] as well as R. Ovadia Yosef,[12] prohibits listening to recorded music during the Three Weeks. R. Eliezer Waldenberg even prohibits recorded songs without musical accompaniment.[13]

R. Shlomo Daichovsky, former *dayan* (judge) on the Supreme Rabbinical Court of Israel, forcefully argues that there is no halakhic source to prohibit music, whether during the Three Weeks, the *Omer*, or even during the twelve-month mourning period after the loss of a parent.[14] He concludes that music that does not lead to "*rikudim umeḥolot*," as the *Magen Avraham* described, such as classical music, should certainly be permitted. He also reports that R. Moshe Feinstein permitted "background music" during the Three Weeks for the same reason.[15]

It thus seems that the type and function of the music is a determining factor. While the more festive and uplifting the music is, the more inclined we might be to prohibit it, music that is not necessarily celebratory or that serves as the background for exercising, driving, or in stores and offices, should be permitted.[16]

HAIRCUTS

The gemara cited above prohibits taking haircuts during the week in which Tisha B'Av falls. The *Shulḥan Arukh* rules accordingly,[17] and this is Sephardi practice. Ashkenazim, however, extend this prohibition to the entire three-week period as well.[18]

The two approaches cited above regarding the mourning customs of the Three Weeks play a central role here as well in the context of discussing the permissibility of shaving during this time. According to R. Soloveitchik, the mourning during the Three Weeks was modeled after the twelve-month mourning period for a parent. During the twelve months of mourning, it is only prohibited to take a haircut until "a friend admonishes him," until others note how disheveled he looks. Since we assume that an ordinarily clean-shaven person needs to shave again every day or two, we generally permit shaving during the *yud-bet ḥodesh*. R. Soloveitchik therefore similarly permitted shaving during *Bein HaMetzarim* until Rosh Ḥodesh Av.[19]

According to other *posekim*, however, even one who ordinarily shaves daily should refrain from shaving during the Three Weeks. R. Moshe Feinstein permits shaving in cases of potential monetary loss,[20] but cautions against shaving in order to avoid the ridicule of co-workers.[21]

May one shave or trim one's beard before Shabbat? Ḥatam Sofer suggests that one who ordinarily shaves daily should certainly be permitted to shave before Shabbat during the Three Weeks.[22] He notes that Rema writes that one may wear laundered clothes on Shabbat during the Nine Days,[23] implying that one may wash them as well. *Magen Avraham* cites *Darkhei Moshe* (Rema's commentary to the *Tur*), who records that the custom is to refrain from laundering even for Shabbat. To resolve the contradiction, *Magen Avraham* suggests that only if one does not have another shirt, one may wash one for Shabbat during the Nine Days. *Magen Avraham* distinguishes between laundering and haircuts, and concludes that we do not permit haircuts before Shabbat, as people are not generally accustomed to taking a haircut every week, as they are regarding laundering.[24] According to this logic, Ḥatam Sofer argues, one who is accustomed to cutting his hair weekly would be able to take a haircut before Shabbat during the Nine Days,[25] and one who usually shaves daily should be able to shave for Shabbat during the Three Weeks. Furthermore, *Biur Halakha*[26] cites R. Akiva Eiger, who notes that according to Tosafot, one may even take a haircut for Shabbat during the Nine Days. Based upon these sources, some *posekim* permit shaving before Shabbat during the Three Weeks.

A woman may trim hair that protrudes from her hair-covering during the Three Weeks and even during the week of Tisha B'Av.[27] Similarly, a woman may shave her legs even during the Nine Days.[28] The *Kitzur Shulḥan Arukh* writes that one may cut his nails until the week of Tisha B'Av.[29]

SHEHEḤEYANU

R. Yaakov b. Moshe Moelin, Maharil, cites the *Sefer Ḥasidim*,[30] who writes that, when possible, one should avoid reciting the blessing of *Sheheḥeyanu* during the Three Weeks on a new fruit or new clothing. However, when the cause of the obligation of *Sheheḥeyanu* cannot be postponed, such as the mitzva of *Pidyon HaBen*, one may recite the blessing.[31] The *Shulḥan Arukh* cites Maharil,[32] and Rema adds that if a specific new fruit will not be found after the Three Weeks, one may partake of it and recite the blessing.[33]

As a result of these rulings, many are accustomed not to purchase or wear new clothing on which one would ordinarily recite *Sheheḥeyanu* during the Three Weeks. Furthermore, one should refrain from purchasing furniture, appliances, or cars during this time, as one is required to recite *Sheheḥeyanu*. One who purchases a garment that must be altered may do so, and then wear the garment and recite the blessing after Tisha B'Av. Nowadays, it is customary to recite *Sheheḥeyanu* upon wearing the garment, and not upon buying it, and it would thus appear to be permitted to shop, without wearing or using what one buys, until Rosh Ḥodesh Av. New clothing that does not require one to recite *Sheheḥeyanu* – such as new shoes, undergarments, socks, and ordinary shirts – may be bought and worn until Rosh Ḥodesh Av.

Magen Avraham questions whether this stringency should apply on Shabbat,[34] and the *Mishna Berura* rules leniently, permitting one to wear new clothing or eat new fruits on Shabbat and to recite *Sheheḥeyanu*.[35]

Although it is customary to refrain from reciting *Sheheḥeyanu* during the Three Weeks, may the blessing, "*HaTov VeHaMetiv*" be recited? Seemingly, this may depend upon the nature of this blessing. The Gemara (Berakhot 59b), as well as the *Shulḥan Arukh*,[36] teaches that when more than one person benefits from an item – such as when one buys an item that may be used by the other members of one's household, or if one receives a gift (benefiting both the giver and receiver) (Y. Berakhot 9:3) – he should recite the blessing of *HaTov VeHaMetiv*. Is this blessing essentially the same as *Sheheḥeyanu*, just recited when more than one person benefits from the item, or is it a fundamentally a different blessing, focusing on the benefit others receive from the item? *Semak* argues that one recites *HaTov VeHaMetiv* in addition to *Sheheḥeyanu,*[37] indicating that in his view, the two blessings are fundamentally different. *Beit Yosef,* on the other hand, maintains that *HaTov VeHaMetiv* replaces the other blessing.[38] *Beit Yosef* may view these two blessings as fundamentally similar, or he may simply believe that in certain situations the Rabbis only mandated that one of the two blessings be recited, despite their differences.

R. Moshe Feinstein rules that while one should not purchase a car during the Three Weeks in order to avoid becoming obligated to recite *Sheheḥeyanu,* if one purchases the car in a manner that would require the blessing of *HaTov VeHaMetiv,* it would be permitted (until Rosh Ḥodesh Av).[39] Apparently, he maintains that *Sheheḥeyanu* and *HaTov VeHaMetiv* are fundamentally different blessings. *Shaarei Teshuva* seems to concur, as he rules that if one is given clothing during the Three Weeks, he may recite *HaTov VeHaMetiv.*[40] One who views these blessings as similar, with one simply being more expansive than the other, would also avoid reciting *HaTov VeHaMetiv* during the Three Weeks.

We may approach this question from a different perspective. Why do we refrain from reciting *Sheheḥeyanu* during the Three Weeks? *Magen Avraham* explains that the reason for this custom is not because of our mourning, as a mourner may recite *Sheheḥeyanu,* but rather because it is inappropriate to recite a blessing expressing gratitude to God for bringing us to this time during the unfavorable period of the Three Weeks.[41] Maharil, however, explains that one should refrain from reciting *Sheheḥeyanu* in order "*lema'et besimḥa,*" to minimize happiness.[42] We might suggest that according to *Magen Avraham,* it is specifically the formula of the blessing of *Sheheḥeyanu,* "Blessed are You… who has kept us alive, and sustained us, and enabled us to reach this moment," which causes the problem, while according to Maharil, both *Sheheḥeyanu* and *HaTov VeHaMetiv* would be problematic.

Interestingly, *Taz,*[43] *Biur HaGra,*[44] and the *Arukh HaShulḥan*[45] reject this custom entirely and permit the recitation of *Sheheḥeyanu* at least until Rosh Ḥodesh Av, at which point all purchases that generate happiness are prohibited.

WHEN DO THESE PROHIBITIONS BEGIN?

When do these prohibitions begin? For example, may one get married on the night of *Shiva Asar B'Tammuz*, as the fast does not actually begin until the next morning? As we explained in the previous chapter, the fast days really do begin the night before. According to most *Rishonim*, one should recite *Aneinu* at night; similarly, one who finishes eating and goes to sleep may not eat afterward, even if he wakes up before dawn.[46] It would follow that the prohibitions of the Three Weeks should begin at night. However, according to Baal HaMaor, who maintains that *Aneinu* should not be recited until morning, the "day" only begins the next morning, at which point one may not eat. According to this view, the prohibitions of the Three Weeks should begin only on the morning of the fast.

R. Moshe Feinstein contends that although the matter would seem to depend on this debate, since the entire prohibition is only based upon custom, even the *Rishonim* who maintain that the fast begins at night may still believe that the mourning practices should only begin when people begin to fast. Furthermore, as it is "only" a custom, we should follow the lenient opinion.[47]

R. Soloveitchik disagreed, ruling that one should treat the evening before the fast as the day itself. One should therefore not perform a wedding the night of *Shiva Asar B'Tammuz*.[48] He further notes that some suggest that although one may eat the on the evening before a fast, it is improper to eat meat.[49]

DANGEROUS SITUATIONS

Beit Yosef cites early *Rishonim* who warn against "walking alone between the fourth and ninth hours of the day, and hitting, even a teacher to his student, even with a belt," as these days are inauspicious for the Jewish people.[50] Rema cites this position as well.[51]

As we noted above, the Midrash connects the verse "All [of Zion's] pursuers overtook her 'between the straits' (*bein hametzarim*)" to this three-week period, the *Bein HaMetzarim*. For this reason, some

Aḥaronim recommend refraining from engaging in particularly risky activities during the entire Three Weeks.[52]

Furthermore, R. Alexander Susskind of Grodno writes in his *Yesod VeShoresh HaAvoda* that one should avoid pleasurable activities during the Three Weeks.[53] Some cite R. Chayim Palagi in his *Masa Ḥaim*, who records local legislation prohibiting taking walks in the orchards and along the river and sea during the Three Weeks. Based on this, some avoid taking vacations during the entire Three Weeks. While some are stringent upon themselves regarding risky or pleasurable activities, the halakha does not explicitly mention nor prohibit these types of activities during the Three Weeks.

THE NINE DAYS: MINIMIZING JOY DURING THE MONTH OF AV

The Mishna in Taanit presents the principle: "*Mishenikhnas Av memaatin besimḥa*" – with the arrival of the month of Av, we minimize joy. R. Papa elaborates:

> Therefore, a Jew who has any litigation with gentiles should avoid him during Av because his luck is bad. Rather, he should make himself available in Adar, when his luck is good. (Taanit 26b)

Furthermore, the Talmud in Yevamot cites a *baraita*:

> Before this time [before the week during which Tisha B'Av occurs], the public must minimize their activities in commerce, building, and plantings. But it is permissible to betroth, although not to marry, nor may any betrothal feast be held. (Yevamot 43a)

The *Aḥaronim* note that common practice is not to abstain from the behaviors listed in this latter passage.[54] The *Arukh HaShulḥan* notes that while the major codifiers of halakha – Rif, Rambam, and Rosh – all cite the mishna in Taanit prescribing that one should minimize joy during the month of Av, all omit the *baraita* from Yevamot, which enumerates the specific activities one should refrain from doing during the month of Av. He suggests that since the *baraita* only relates that "the public must minimize their activities in commerce, building, and planting," without employing the phrase "prohibited," which it used regarding taking haircuts and washing clothes, the Talmud did not intend to prohibit these activities, but rather merely to relate the self-imposed practice of the people. Accordingly, the *Arukh HaShulḥan* explains that we can understand the common practice not to completely refrain from these activities during the month of Av.[55]

The *Arukh HaShulḥan* further notes that the Mishna (Taanit 12b), and consequently Rambam,[56] prohibits engaging in these activities on communal fast days instituted in response to severe drought, and the laws on such days differ from those observed during the month of Av. During the month of Av, only commerce, building, and planting that are for *joyous* purposes are prohibited; these activities are all subsumed under the phrase "with the arrival of the month of Av, one minimizes joy."[57] In any case, *Tur*[58] writes that these activities should be avoided, and the *Shulḥan Arukh* rules that they are prohibited when done for joyous purposes.[59]

Practically speaking, one should refrain from unnecessary home and garden projects, as well as purchasing furniture, appliances, and other objects that are not necessary for one's business, but rather only for one's personal enjoyment. As we already discussed, it is customary to refrain from purchasing items upon which one recites the blessing of *Sheheḥeyanu* during the entire Three Weeks.

Building, planting, or purchasing for the sake of the public welfare,[60] in order to avoid financial loss,[61] or in order to prevent damage or physical harm are permitted.

LAUNDERING DURING THE NINE DAYS / *SHAVUA SHEḤAL BO*

The Mishna teaches that "During the week in which Tisha B'Av falls, haircutting and laundry are forbidden" (Taanit 26b). The Ashkenazic custom, as we have already noted, is to refrain from taking haircuts for the entire Three Weeks, beginning from *Shiva Asar B'Tammuz*.

As for laundering, the Talmud and the *Rishonim* discuss the definition and scope of this prohibition. First, the Talmud cites a debate regarding whether one may launder for future use:

> R. Naḥman said: This restriction only applies to the washing of clothes for immediate wear, but the washing of clothes for storing is permissible. R. Sheshet said: It is forbidden to wash clothes even for storing. R. Sheshet said: A proof for this is that the launderers in the house of Rav are then idle. (Taanit 29b)

Rashi explains that according to R. Sheshet, one should not launder at all, as "it appears as if one is distracted [from mourning] since he is involved in laundering."[62]

The *Rishonim* debate whether the prohibition of laundering includes wearing freshly laundered clothing as well. In the context of the laws of *aveilut,* Rashi writes that a mourner may wear clothing washed before the mourning period.[63] It is possible that during the week of Tisha B'Av, Rashi would thus permit wearing clothing laundered before the prohibition began. Some suggest that this is also Rambam's position.[64] Most *Rishonim* disagree, however, and prohibit wearing laundered clothing as well.[65]

The *Shulḥan Arukh* prohibits laundering clothing, as well as linens, handkerchiefs, tablecloths, and towels, for all purposes, as well as wearing clothing that was laundered before the week of Tisha B'Av.[66] Rema adds that one should not even give one's clothing to a non-Jewish launderer to have them cleaned during the Nine Days. Additionally, Rema records that Ashkenazim observe this prohibition for the entire Nine Days, and not just during the week of Tisha B'Av.[67]

The *Aḥaronim* record a number of leniencies regarding these laws. First, the *Mishna Berura* writes that one who has only one garment may launder his clothing from Rosh Ḥodesh Av until Shabbat (until the *shavua sheḥal bo*). Similarly, one whose clothing has all been soiled and has no other clothing to wear may wash his clothing; one need not buy extra clothing in order to have enough for the week. One who does not have clean clothing for Shabbat may launder his clothing.[68] The *posekim* disagree as to whether one who is traveling during the Nine

Days must bring along enough clothing in order to avoid the need to launder.[69]

Second, Rema cites *Beit Yosef,*[70] who permits washing cloth diapers for children, and he extends this leniency to all children's clothing.[71] The *Mishna Berura* writes that one should not wash a large quantity of clothing at once, and one should wash the clothing in private, and not in a public place (at the river or a laundromat).[72]

Third, although one may not wear freshly laundered clothing, it has become customary to wear one's freshly laundered clothing for a brief time before Rosh Ḥodesh, thereby permitting them during the Nine Days, just as a mourner may wear clothing which was previously worn for a short period by another person.[73] R. Yitzchak Yaakov Weiss cites those who permit throwing laundered clothing on the floor before wearing them during the Nine Days, as this is similar to wearing them before Rosh Ḥodesh.[74] Seemingly, if the garments were packed in a suitcase, they also lose the freshly laundered quality, and one should be permitted to wear them during the Nine Days.

Some *posekim* write that socks, underwear, and even shirts – which are classified as "*bigdei zei'a,*" clothes that are intended to absorb perspiration – may be worn during the Nine Days even without being worn previously. Some even permit wearing laundered clothing for the sake of an important meeting or for "*shiddukhim.*"[75] One may remove a small stain on one's clothing in order to avoid embarrassment.

A hospital may certainly launder sheets, towels, hospital garments, and the like, as the intention is to avoid the spread of disease and not for pleasure. Similarly, R. Eliezer Waldenberg writes that a hotel may change sheets for new guests, as this is similar to "washing in order to remove filth," which is also permitted during the Nine Days.[76] Furthermore, he adds that by washing sheets for new guests, the hotel fulfils the mitzva of *hakhnasat orḥim,* and washing for the sake of a mitzva is permitted.[77]

Rema writes that one does not change into Shabbat clothing for *Shabbat Ḥazon,* the Shabbat before Tisha B'Av,[78] But the *Arukh HaShulḥan* records that by his time, this ruling of Rema had not been observed for at least two or three generations.[79] The *Mishna Berura* similarly relates that in Vilna, the custom was in accordance with that of Gra, and even laundered clothing was worn on Shabbat.[80] The *Arukh HaShulḥan* suggests that generations ago, the difference between weekday and Shabbat clothing may not have been so noticeable, and they therefore would wear their weekday clothing on Shabbat. Nowadays, however, wearing weekday clothes on Shabbat would be akin to public mourning, and this practice is therefore not observed. He concludes by expressing his dissatisfaction with the current custom, and recommends adhering to the original ruling of Rema. The custom is in accordance with the *Mishna Berura*, however.

In addition to laundering clothing, the *Shulḥan Arukh* adds that one should not purchase, make, or wear new clothing during the *shavua sheḥal bo* (or the entire Nine Days for Ashkenazim).[81] Knitting and needlecraft is similarly prohibited,[82] but repairing a torn garment is permitted.[83]

BATHING

The Talmud does not mention that bathing, which is prohibited on Tisha B'Av, is also prohibited during the Nine Days, and especially during the week of Tisha B'Av. The Gemara briefly mentions a possible prohibition of bathing in the context of Erev Tisha B'Av, the day preceding the fast (Taanit 30a). Rambam, however, writes: "All of Israel has already become accustomed to refrain from eating meat on the week of Tisha B'Av, and they do not enter the bathhouse until after the fast."[84] The *Aḥaronim* note that Rambam refers only to the week of Tisha B'Av and that he restricts this custom to bathing in hot water (in a bathhouse).

R. Elazar of Worms (1160–1230) records in his Roke'aḥ that he asked R. Kalonymos of Rome whether one should abstain from bathing on Rosh Ḥodesh Av or the day before. Apparently, already in the eleventh century, German Jews abstained from bathing during the Nine Days. R. Kalonymos responded:

> One must refrain from washing from Rosh Ḥodesh Av, and it is forbidden on Rosh Ḥodesh itself, because it says, "[I will end all her rejoicing:] her

> festivals, new moons, and Sabbaths" [Hos. 2:13]. Before Rosh Ḥodesh, however, it is permissible.[85]

Apparently, this custom was prevalent in Ashkenazic communities, as it appears in the *Mordekhai*,[86] the *Or Zarua*,[87] and elsewhere. The *Terumat HaDeshen* assumes that some form of bathing is prohibited during the entire Nine Days, and questions whether "bathing in cold water, such as in the river" is permitted from Rosh Ḥodesh Av. He writes that although he recalls from his youth that people used to bathe in the river after Rosh Ḥodesh, he believed the custom was to refrain from bathing even in cold water, "and one who is stringent will be blessed."[88]

The *Shulḥan Arukh* cites both opinions, without relating to the temperature of the water.[89] R. Ovadia Yosef insists that the Sephardic *Rishonim*, including Rambam, Ramban, Raa,[90] and Ran,[91] all maintain that it is customary to refrain from bathing in hot water during the week of Tisha B'Av alone.[92] Rema, however, rules in accordance with the *Terumat HaDeshen* and maintains that it is customary to refrain from bathing even in cold water beginning from Rosh Ḥodesh.[93] The *Mishna Berura* comments that one may certainly wash his face, hands, and feet in cold water.[94]

One may certainly remove dirt from one's body, even with hot water.[95] Therefore, one who became soiled with paint, mud, or another substance may bathe in on order to clean himself.

The Talmud relates that R. Gamliel bathed on the first night after his wife's death, during the seven days of *aveilut*. In response to his students' queries, he asserted that since he was an "*istenis*," one who is particularly sensitive, he may wash even during the seven days of mourning (Berakhot 16b). The *Shulḥan Arukh* rules accordingly regarding bathing during *shiva*.[96]

It is undeniable that our level of personal hygiene in general, as well as the frequency of bathing and intolerance of bodily uncleanliness and odor, has evolved over the years. Furthermore, the climate of Eastern Europe during the Nine Days was significantly cooler than that of New York or Jerusalem.[97] It is thus plausible that the leniency of "*istinis*" should apply to many modern-day Jews during the Nine Days as well.

R. Moshe Feinstein permitted Yeshiva students to bathe on a hot summer day in order to remove their perspiration. In addition, one who cannot go to work with excessive body odor for reasons related to *parnassa* (one's livelihood) or one who feels he cannot go out in public because of *kevod haberiyot* (human dignity) may certainly shower.[98]

One who showers during the Nine Days should be careful to shower only for hygienic reasons, and not for personal pleasure. Therefore, it would be appropriate to bathe in cooler water and for a shorter period of time than usual.

Askenazic custom clearly prohibits swimming for pleasure during the Nine Days. As mentioned above, R. Ovadia Yosef maintains that it is only prohibited to bathe in hot water during the *shavua sheḥal bo*; he thus permits Sephardim to swim during the Nine Days, and even during the week of Tisha B'Av. Not all Sephardic authorities concur, however. R. Yosef Ḥayim b. Eliyahu al-Ḥakham, the *Ben Ish Ḥai*, records that it was customary in Baghdad to refrain from swimming, even in cold water, during the week of Tisha B'Av.[99] In his responsa, he describes how the children of Baghdad, where the average high temperature during August approaches 110 degrees, would swim in the Tigris River during the summer. He notes that those who began to learn how to swim before the Three Weeks and have yet to complete their sessions may continue swimming in the river even after Rosh Ḥodesh, as they are engaged in their "profession" and are not swimming for pleasure. He concludes that while it is still proper to be stringent in this matter, one should not criticize those who act leniently.[100] This may be the basis for those who permit "instructional swim" during the Nine Days.

May one bathe before *Shabbat Ḥazon*? Rema writes that one should not bathe even for Shabbat,[101] and the *Arukh HaShulḥan* severely censures those who are lenient.[102] Common custom, however, is to bathe regularly, with soap and shampoo, before *Shabbat Ḥazon*, as bathing for Shabbat constitutes a mitzva.[103]

Interestingly, as we have noted previously, R. Soloveitchik argued that the mourning practices of the Nine Days correspond to the laws of *sheloshim*, during which laundering and bathing are limited.

R. Soloveitchik suggested that nowadays, when we are not accustomed to prohibit bathing for the entire month after the burial of a close relative, it should follow that the custom to refrain from bathing during the Nine Days should no longer be applicable at all.

May one cut one's nails during the Nine Days? *Taz* prohibits cutting one's nails during the week of Tisha B'Av,[104] while the *Magen Avraham* permits it.[105] The *Mishna Berura* concludes that a woman may certainly cut her nails before immersing in the *mikveh,* and one may similarly cut one's nails before Shabbat.[106]

EATING MEAT AND DRINKING WINE

The Mishna teaches that at the *seuda mafseket,* the final meal eaten before the fast of Tisha B'Av, one should not eat meat nor drink wine (Taanit 26b). Aside from the *seuda mafseket,* the Talmud makes no mention of any prohibition of eating meat or drinking wine during the week preceding Tisha B'Av.

Early sources, however, record a custom to refrain from eating meat and drinking wine during this period. The *Shibbolei HaLeket,* for example, records in the name of R. Saadia Gaon that some were accustomed to refrain from eating meat and drinking wine.[107] Similarly, *Kol Bo* relates that he "saw precious women who refrain from eating meat and drinking wine... and they insist that they received this tradition from their mothers, generation after generation."[108] He attributes this to the cessation of the offering of the *korban tamid,* which occurred on *Shiva Asar B'Tammuz.* The *Mordekhai,*[109] Rambam,[110] Ramban,[111] and Rashba[112] also cite this custom.

R. Vidal of Tolouse (1300–1370), author of the *Maggid Mishneh* commentary on Rambam's *Mishneh Torah,* reports that this custom did not spread to his region, where people would eat meat until the day before Tisha B'Av.[113] The *Shulḥan Arukh* records these various customs:

> Some are accustomed not to eat meat or to drink wine during this week [of Tisha B'Av] ... and some add from Rosh Ḥodesh until the fast. And some add from *Shiva Asar B'Tammuz.*[114]

Ashkenazim follow the second view and refrain from eating meat and drinking wine from, and including, Rosh Ḥodesh Av.[115]

What is the reason for this custom? Some explain that since we minimize our joyous behavior during the month of Av, we should refrain from eating meat and drinking wine, which are foods traditionally associated with "*simḥa*" (happiness). Others attribute this custom to the abolishment of the daily *tamid* sacrifice, which occurred on *Shiva Asar B'Tammuz*. Alternatively, Gra relates this custom to the following fascinating talmudic passage:

> Our Rabbis taught: When the Temple was destroyed for the second time, large numbers in Israel became ascetics, committing themselves neither to eat meat nor to drink wine. R. Yehoshua entered a conversation with them and said to them: My sons, why do you not eat meat nor drink wine? They replied: Shall we eat flesh which used to be brought as an offering on the altar, now that this altar is in abeyance? Shall we drink wine which used to be poured as a libation on the altar, but now no longer? He said to them: If that is so, we should not eat bread either, because the meal offerings have ceased. They said: [That is so, and] we can manage with fruit. We should not eat fruit either, [he said,] because there is no longer an offering of first fruits. [They said:] Then we can manage with other fruits. [He said:] But we should not drink water, because there is no longer any ceremony of the pouring of water. To this they could find no answer.... It has been taught: R. Yishmael b. Elisha said: Since the day of the destruction of the Temple, we should by rights commit ourselves not to eat meat nor drink wine, only we do not lay a hardship on the community unless the majority can endure it. (Bava Batra 60b)

Gra explains that while R. Yishmael found it to be unrealistic to prohibit meat and wine forever, as a *beit din* does not create a legislation that the majority of the community is unable to follow, he fundamentally accepts the premise that we should not eat meat or drink wine after the destruction of the *Beit HaMikdash*. Therefore, for this minimal time before Tisha B'Av, it is appropriate to fulfill the sentiment expressed by R. Yishmael.[116]

Although abstention from meat during the Nine Days is only a custom, the *Mordekhai* writes[117] that one who eats meat during this period violates "One should not forgo the law of your mother" (Prov. 1:8).

The *Arukh HaShulḥan* adds that one who eats meat during these days violates a Torah prohibition, as this custom has attained the status of a communal vow.[118]

What type of meat is prohibited? *Kol Bo* writes that while it is customary not to eat meat during the Nine Days, one need not refrain from eating foods that were cooked with meat.[119] The *Shulḥan Arukh* cites this view.[120] The *Arukh HaShulḥan* concurs, explaining that the custom is not concerned with "*netinat taam*," the taste of meat, but rather with meat itself.[121] The *Mishna Berura* disagrees, however, and insists that the custom is to refrain from eating all meat mixtures.[122] All agree that pareve food cooked in a meat pot may be eaten.

One should refrain from drinking even diluted wine or grape juice during the Nine Days.[123] Rema writes that one may drink wine vinegar, as well as other alcoholic beverages, during the Nine Days.[124]

On what should one recite Havdala during the Nine Days? The *Shulḥan Arukh* rules that an adult may drink wine at Havdala,[125] and Gra explains that the nation did not accept upon itself not to drink wine at Havdala.[126] Rema disagrees, writing that the wine should preferably be given to a child.[127] The *Mishna Berura* explains that the wine must be given to a child old enough to understand Havdala – as the blessing over the wine is actually recited for him – but not yet old enough to understand the significance of mourning for Jerusalem.[128] While some drink wine, and some give the wine or grape juice to a child, the *Arukh HaShulḥan* recommends using beer ("*ḥamar medina*") for Havdala during the Nine Days.[129]

Incidentally, the *Magen Avraham* deduces, from Rema's ruling that the wine should be given to a child, that during the Nine Days, one may generally feed meat and wine to minors who do not yet understand the mourning over Jerusalem.[130] The *Mishna Berura,* however, disagrees.[131]

On Shabbat, one may eat meat and drink wine regularly, even if the fast begins immediately after Shabbat.[132] Before Shabbat, one may taste the food in preparation for Shabbat,[133] as it is a mitzva to taste the Shabbat food before Shabbat.[134] The *Shaarei Teshuva* cites the *Birkei Yosef* as permitting eating leftover Shabbat food for the *seudat melave malka*. He concludes, however, that we are not accustomed to eat meat after Shabbat during the Nine Days.[135] R. Moshe Feinstein similarly rules that even one who eats a full meat meal every Motza'ei Shabbat for *melave malka* should not eat meat during the Nine Days.[136]

One who is ill or weak and needs to eat meat to restore his or her strength, including a woman who has given birth or a pregnant or nursing mother, may eat meat during the Nine Days.[137]

May one eat meat on special occasions during the Nine Days? Rema writes:

> At a *seudat mitzva*, such as a *Brit Mila, Pidyon HaBen, siyum masekhet* (completion of a tractate), and the celebration of a betrothal, all who are part of the celebration may eat meat and drink wine, although one should limit and not add [the amount of people]. During the week of Tisha B'Av, only a small group should eat meat and drink wine.[138]

R. Yekutiel Yehuda Halberstam (1904–1995), the Klausenberger Rebbe, adds that a bar mitzva celebration held on the day of the boy's bar mitzva, or even delayed, is also considered a *seudat mitzva* if the boy speaks words of Torah, and the participants may eat meat.[139] Apparently, the custom was to exclude these events from the prohibition of partaking of meat and wine.

Many communities, as well as summer camps, are accustomed to holding "*siyumim*" during the Nine Days and serving meat. Indeed, the Talmud teaches: "Abaye said: May I be rewarded for that when I saw that a disciple had completed his tractate, I made it a festive day for the scholars" (Shabbat 118b). Some *Aḥaronim* severely censure those who deliberately hurry or slow down their learning in order to hold a *siyum* during the Nine Days. The *Arukh HaShulḥan*, for example, writes:

> How are we not ashamed and embarrassed! Indeed many of the non-Jews refrain from eating meat and milk and eggs for weeks, and the nation of Israel, regarding whom it says, "and you shall be sanctified," are unable to restrain themselves for eight days of the year in remembrance of our Temple.

He reports that he would deliberately postpone a *siyum* until after the Nine Days.[140] Some *Aḥaronim* permit rushing one's learning or leaving a section of the tractate until the Nine Days in order to hold a *siyum*, as long as eating meat is not one's primary intention.

Some further reproach participants in a *siyum* during the Nine Days who would not ordinarily participate in such an event during the rest of the year. R. Moshe Feinstein and R. Shlomo Zalman Auerbach, however, rule that in a summer camp or learning program, all the campers or participants, including the women, may participate in the *siyum*.[141]

What type of "completion" warrants a *seudat mitzva*? Rema explicitly mentions the completion of a tractate of Talmud,[142] but R. Reuven Margaliot (1889–1971) notes that Rema may have intended the completion of other books as well. He notes that some commentators take issue with Rema for permitting eating meat at the celebration of a betrothal, as the *Shulḥan Arukh* prohibits holding an engagement meal during this time.[143] To resolve this problem, some simply erase this phrase from the Rema,[144] but R. Margaliot suggests that a scribal error may have crept into this passage. He speculates that originally the text used the abbreviation "*vav, samekh, alef,*" which was later interpreted to refer to a *seudat eirusin* (engagement meal), but they originally indicated *vesefarim aḥerim*, "and other books." In other words, Rema may have intended that one may hold a *siyum* of a tractate or other books during the Nine Days.[145]

In any case, some *Aḥaronim* write that one may hold a *siyum* upon the completion of a book of Tanakh, a *seder* of Mishna (and possibly even a single tractate), or a section of the *Shulḥan Arukh*. Some add that such a *siyum* would only be considered a *seudat mitzva* if the topic was learned seriously, with proper attention and depth, and for a significant amount of time. R. Menashe Klein writes that one may hold a *siyum* upon the completion of a section of the *Shulḥan Arukh* or even a specific topic of study, such as *Hilkhot Shabbat*.[146] Similarly, the Rosh Yeshiva of Yeshivat Har Etzion, R. Yehuda Amital, permitted those who took their *smikha* exams during the Nine Days to celebrate with a meat meal.

THE TENTH OF AV

In the course of reconciling two seemingly conflicting verses regarding the day upon which the Temple was destroyed (II Kings 25:8–9, Jer. 52:12), the Talmud teaches:

> On the seventh day [of Av], the heathens entered the Temple and ate therein and desecrated it throughout the seventh and eighth, and toward dusk of the ninth, they set it to fire and it continued to burn the whole of that day.... And this is what R. Yoḥanan meant when he said: Had I been alive in that generation, I should have fixed [the mourning for] the tenth, because the greater part of the Temple was burned thereon. How will the Rabbis then [explain the contradiction]? The beginning of any misfortune is the greater moment. (Taanit 29a)

In fact, the Yerushalmi reports that R. Avin would fast on both the ninth and tenth of Av, and R. Levi would fast through the night of the tenth (Y. Taanit 4:6). Based upon this, *Abudraham* records that Rosh would not eat meat on the night of the tenth of Av,[147] and the *Hagahot Maimoniyot* writes that some wait until after midday on the tenth of Av.[148]

The *Shulḥan Arukh* writes that it is a "worthy custom not to eat meat or drink wine on the night and day of the tenth [of Av]."[149] Rema adds that some are stringent until midday, but not later.[150] Many *Aḥaronim* rule that one should not bathe or launder until this time as well, implying that the laws of the Nine Days extend until noon of the tenth of Av.[151] However, *Biur Halakha* cites the *Maamar Mordekhai*, who limits this stringency to meat and wine.[152]

When Tisha B'Av falls on Shabbat, in which case the fast is observed on Sunday, Rema writes that one may eat meat on the morning after the fast.[153] The *Mishna Berura* writes that one may cut one's hair even that evening.[154] Seemingly, one may launder as well.

When Tisha B'Av falls on Thursday, in which case the tenth of Av is on Friday, bathing, haircuts, and laundering are permitted in preparation for Shabbat (*kevod Shabbat*). Many *posekim* even permit these activities at night, immediately after the fast.[155] However, one should not consume meat or wine or engage in the above activities that are not necessary for Shabbat until after noon.

Even during a year in which Tisha B'Av does not fall on a Shabbat or Thursday, in extenuating circumstances, such as one who is leaving one's house early the next morning for an extended period of time, one may launder and wear clean clothes, relying upon the opinion of the *Maamar Mordekhai* cited above.[156]

CHAPTER 57

The Laws of Tisha B'Av

INTRODUCTION

The Mishna enumerates the tragedies that transpired on Tisha B'Av, a day of great misfortune:

> Five tragic events befell our forefathers...on the Ninth of Av.... On the Ninth of Av it was decreed that our forefathers should not enter the Land, the Temple was destroyed the first and the second time, Beitar was captured, and the city [Jerusalem] was plowed up. (Taanit 26a)

The laws of Tisha B'Av reflect two separate, and distinct, themes. On the one hand, Tisha B'Av is the prototypical, and most stringent, fast day. The Talmud emphasizes the severity of the fast of Tisha B'Av in comparison to the other communal fast days. Unlike the other three communal fasts instituted after the destruction of the *Beit HaMikdash*, which in times of "peace" need not be commemorated, Tisha B'Av is always observed, as "multiple misfortunes befell us on that day" (Rosh HaShana 18b). Therefore, the Gemara explains, messengers are sent out to notify those outside of Jerusalem regarding the precise day of Rosh Ḥodesh Av, and consequently of the proper day upon which to fast (Rosh HaShana 18a). Furthermore, unlike the other fast days, which are only observed "partially," the fast of Tisha B'Av begins the night before, and one must not only abstain from eating, but observe the other "afflictions" – the prohibition of washing, anointing, wearing shoes, and engaging in marital relations. In addition, the Torah portion of "*Parashat VaYeḥal*" (Ex. 32:11–14, 34:1–10), which is read on the other fast days at Minḥa, is read on Tisha B'Av as well.

On the other hand, Tisha B'Av is a day of mourning, a day of "*aveilut yeshana*" (Yevamot 43b). The *baraita* cited by the Talmud states, "All mitzvot that apply to a mourner during the seven days of mourning apply on Tisha B'Av" (Taanit 30a). We express this aspect of mourning throughout the day in our prayers and actions.

This phenomenon is found elsewhere in halakha. At times, we indeed find that multiple themes are commemorated on one day. For example, Yom Kippur is both a *mo'ed* (a festival), and a *taanit tzibbur* (a communal fast day).[1] Similarly, it seems that different themes make up the nature of Tisha B'Av. Tisha B'Av is both a fast day, similar to the other three fasts described by the prophet Zechariah, as well as a communal day of mourning for the tragedies that have befallen the Jewish people on this day and throughout our history. As we study the various laws of Tisha B'Av, we will encounter both aspects of this unique day.

EREV TISHA B'AV: *SEUDA MAFSEKET*

Before the fast begins, on Erev Tisha B'Av, one eats the *seuda mafseket*, the final meal before the fast begins. The Mishna describes the content of this meal. "On the eve of the Ninth of Av, one may not partake of a meal of two cooked foods, nor eat meat, nor drink wine" (Taanit 26b). Furthermore, the Gemara recounts the practice of R. Yehuda b. Illai:

> On the eve of the Ninth of Av, they brought to him dry bread with salt and he would take his seat between the [baking] oven and the [cooking] stove and eat, and he would drink with a pitcher full of water and he would appear as if a near relative were lying dead before him. (Taanit 30a)

Accordingly, Rambam writes, "He should eat [the *seuda mafseket*], and drink a pitcher of water, with worry, depression and weeping, as if a close relative is lying dead in from of him."[2]

What may one eat at this meal? As we saw, the Mishna prohibits eating meat and drinking wine, as these are important foods that arouse happiness. In addition, the Mishna states that one should not eat two cooked foods. While the *Aḥaronim* discuss how to define "two cooked foods," the *Shulḥan Arukh* simply writes that, when possible, one should eat dry bread with salt, along with water, for the *seuda mafseket*. In addition, he reports that "it is customary to eat lentils mixed with boiled eggs, which are a food of mourners."[3] Rema adds that some eat hard-boiled eggs, which are also a food of mourners, and that one should dip his bread into ashes.[4] The *Mishna Berura* suggests that one should declare, "This is the Tisha B'Av meal."[5]

Since this simple meal would probably not tide one over until the next day, the *seuda mafseket* is usually preceded by another meal. Rema writes:

> It is customary in these regions of Ashkenaz to eat a set meal before Minḥa, and then afterward to pray Minḥa and then eat the *seuda mafseket*. They are accustomed to increase this meal, in order that the fast should not be harmful, since we cease to eat during the day, like Yom Kippur.[6]

Interestingly, *Magen Avraham* suggests that the custom to eat a large meal before the *seuda mafseket* may be rooted in a different idea entirely. He writes that since Tisha B'Av was a day of celebration marked by a festive meal during the time of the Second Temple, the custom to partake of a set meal remains as a commemoration and hope for the future.[7]

The *Magen Avraham* also relates that some *Aḥaronim* (*Levush*, *Baḥ*, *Shela*) disapprove of the custom recorded by Rema and suggest eating this large meal, if necessary, before midday.[8] However, the *Eliya Rabba*,[9] cited by the *Mishna Berura*,[10] writes that as long as one's intentions are "for the sake of Heaven," he may partake of a larger meal after noon, as long as he leaves room for the *seuda mafseket*.

The *Shulḥan Arukh* rules that one may eat or drink after the *seuda mafseket* until the onset of the fast, unless one explicitly accepts upon himself not to eat anymore.[11] While Rema adds that a mental acceptance does not constitute acceptance of the fast,[12] the *Mishna Berura* writes that *Baḥ* and Gra disagree; he therefore recommends stating explicitly that one intends to eat or drink until sunset.[13]

The *Rishonim* mention a number of other customs associated with the *seuda mafseket*. The *Hagahot Maimoniyot*, for example, writes,

> Some of the great scholars of Ashkenaz ... and R. Sherira Gaon wrote as well, were accustomed not to recite the *zimun* with three during this meal; rather every individual should sit by himself, as it says, "Let him sit alone and keep silence" [Lam. 3:28]. So, too, the Ri and R. Meshulam would recite the Grace after Meals by themselves even when sitting amongst a group of three [which would ordinarily mandate reciting the *zimun*]. It is proper for three people not to sit together in order that they should not become obligated in the *zimun*.[14]

The *Shulḥan Arukh* rules accordingly, warning that three men should not sit together, in order not to become obligated to recite the *zimun*.[15] The *Mishna Berura* adds that even if they did sit together, they should still not say the *zimun*.[16]

Similarly, the *Terumat HaDeshen* writes that one should eat the *seuda mafseket* while sitting on the ground, although there is no need to remove one's shoes.[17] The *Shulḥan Arukh* records this custom as well.[18] Those who have difficulty sitting on the floor may sit on a chair, although they should preferably change their location.[19]

When Tisha B'Av falls on Sunday, the *seuda mafseket* is not held on Shabbat, and the restrictions mentioned above are not observed. One may eat meat and drink wine preceding the fast. However, one must stop eating before sunset.[20]

In addition to the laws of the *seuda mafseket*, Rema writes:

> It is customary not to learn [Torah] on the day before Tisha B'Av after midday, and therefore when Tisha B'Av falls out on Shabbat, we do not say Pirkei Avot. Similarly, one should not take walks on Erev Tisha B'Av.[21]

Magen Avraham upholds this custom[22] and suggests that one should only learn those passages that are permitted for study on Tisha B'Av.[23] Others challenge this custom, and even testify that they themselves learn after midday before Tisha B'Av.[24] When Tisha B'Av falls on Shabbat, when one may even eat meat and drink wine, one who learns Torah until nightfall is certainly in good company.[25]

Finally, just as one does not recite *Taḥanun* on Tisha B'Av,[26] as Tisha B'Av is called a "*mo'ed*" (Lam. 1:15), *Taḥanun* is not recited at Minḥa on Erev Tisha B'Av.[27]

THE FAST OF TISHA B'AV AND OTHER FASTS

As noted above, the fast of Tisha B'Av differs from the other three fast days. This is true quantitatively – regarding the length of the fast and the scope of its prohibitions – but also qualitatively.

We noted that on the minor fast days, in contrast to Yom Kippur, the ill are exempt from the fast. Not only does the halakha exempt a *ḥoleh she'ein bo sakana*, a sick person whose life is not in danger, there is also no need for him to eat in small quantities (*ḥatzi shiur*), as one must do on Yom Kippur. Moreover, we learned that a pregnant or nursing woman is also fundamentally exempt from fasting, although some are still accustomed to fast.

On Tisha B'Av, however, only the sick are exempt. Pregnant and nursing women are obligated to fast unless fasting poses a danger to the mother or fetus.[28] The *Arukh HaShulḥan* writes that pregnant (and nursing) women who are weak and whose fasting may lead to illness, even if not life threatening, are exempt from fasting on Tisha B'Av.[29] Therefore, a pregnant woman suffering from nausea, anemia (low hemoglobin), high or low blood pressure, or an infection need not fast. Furthermore, a pregnant woman who justifiably fears that fasting may cause a miscarriage, or even bleeding or early contractions, must certainly break her fast.

Fasting may be especially difficult for a nursing woman, as nursing causes a woman to lose fluids; by not drinking, she risks not producing enough milk for her child. R. Chaim Mordechai Margulies writes in his commentary to the *Shulḥan Arukh*, the *Shaarei Teshuva*, that if fasting will affect the quality of the mother's milk or diminish it, thereby posing a threat to the child, the mother may eat.[30] Similarly, *Ḥazon Ish* would instruct nursing mothers to break their fast if they feared that they would not be able to produce enough milk.[31]

THE PROHIBITIONS OF TISHA B'AV

Bathing and Anointing

The Talmud enumerates the other prohibitions of Tisha B'Av, aside from eating and drinking:

> Our Rabbis have taught: All the restrictions that apply to the mourner apply on Tisha B'Av: eating, drinking, bathing, anointing, the wearing of shoes, and marital relations, are forbidden thereon. (Taanit 30a)

Although this passage seems to equate the laws of Tisha B'Av with the laws of mourning, R. Soloveitchik noted that while a mourner may wash parts of his body in cold water,[32] on Tisha B'Av one may not even immerse one's finger into cold water.[33] The prohibition of "*reḥitza*" (bathing) is thus defined by the day's being a communal fast day, and not just a day of mourning.

Only washing for pleasure is prohibited; one may therefore wash his body if it is dirty,[34] after using the bathroom,[35] or for medicinal purposes.[36] In the morning or upon waking, one may wash *netilat yadayim* as usual, pouring the water until the joints at the end of one's fingers,[37] and one may wash in a similar fashion before prayer.[38] While preparing food, one may also wet one's hands.[39] One who experiences extreme discomfort from lack of washing (an "*istenis*") may wash his face.[40]

In our discussion of brushing teeth on a communal fast day, we concluded that on an ordinary fast day, one who experiences discomfort from not rinsing his mouth or brushing his teeth may do so. On Tisha B'Av, however, as well as on Yom Kippur, the *posekim* are more stringent. R. Moshe Feinstein even suggests that on Tisha B'Av, washing out one's mouth may be prohibited because of "*reḥitza*" (bathing).[41] *Minḥat Yitzchak* also prohibits rinsing one's mouth, but permits brushing teeth with "powder" in order to reduce discomfort. He further maintains that one may clean one's mouth in order to pray with "cleanliness."[42] The *Mishna Berura*, however, writes that even on Tisha B'Av, one who experiences "great discomfort" may wash out his mouth.[43]

One may dry his hands on a towel and then use the damp towel to clean his eyes and face, as the towel is not wet enough to impart enough water to wet something else (*tofe'aḥ al menat lehatpiaḥ*).[44] Rema writes that one may even soak cloths before Tisha B'Av, wring them out, and then use them to clean his face, hands, and feet.[45] This is permitted even if one's intention is for pleasure, as he already squeezed the water out of the cloths.

The Gemara also prohibits "anointing" for pleasure on Tisha B'Av, and one therefore may not rub oil, cream, soap, or perfume into his skin.[46] One may, however, rub oil on one's skin for medicinal purposes, use Vaseline for chapped lips, or bug repellents or anti-itch sprays. Moreover, one may use deodorant on Tisha B'Av, as one's intention is to prevent or remove odor.[47]

Wearing Leather Shoes

As we discussed in the context of the laws of Yom Kippur, there is a dispute as to whether the prohibition of "*ne'ilat hasandal*," wearing shoes, applies only to leather shoes or to other comfortable materials as well. Some *Rishonim* rule that one may not even wear comfortable wooden shoes on Tisha B'Av,[48] and some prohibit wooden shoes but permit shoes of other materials.[49] Most *Rishonim* rule that only leather shoes are prohibited.[50] While Rambam does not explicitly prohibit non-leather shoes on Yom Kippur, he explains the permissibility of wrapping a cloth around one's feet, as "the hardness of the ground reaches one's feet and he feels [as if] he is barefoot."[51] The *Shulḥan Arukh*, ruling leniently, writes:

> "The wearing of shoes" [which is prohibited] refers to [shoes of] leather. However, [shoes made of] a cloth, or wood, or cork, or rubber are permitted. Wooden shoes covered with leather are prohibited.[52]

Although some *Aḥaronim* suggest that one should be stringent and only wear shoes through which one can feel the ground,[53] which may be especially relevant nowadays, when many people wear comfortable shoes made from synthetic materials, the custom is to permit wearing any shoes not made from leather.

Marital Relations on *Tisha B'Av*

The Gemara prohibits marital relations on Tisha B'Av, just as they are prohibited for a mourner. R. Yosef Karo cites the *Hagahot Mordekhai*,[54] who rules that one should not even sleep in the same bed with one's wife on the night of Tisha B'Av.[55] The *Mishna Berura,* based upon the *Magen Avraham,* writes that one should avoid all physical contact with one's wife in the evening, as on Yom Kippur, although during the day it is permitted.[56] Some prohibit physical contact during the day as well.[57] *Taz* disagrees completely and permits physical contact even at night on Tisha B'Av and during the day on Yom Kippur.[58] Seemingly, all would agree that affectionate contact should be avoided during the entire day of Tisha B'Av.

Talmud Torah and *She'elat Shalom* (Greeting)

The Talmud teaches that in addition to fasting and refraining from certain physical pleasures, one should also refrain from studying Torah on Tisha B'Av: "It is also forbidden [thereon] to read the Torah, the Nevi'im and the Ketuvim, or to study the Mishna, Talmud, Midrash, halakhot, or *aggadot*" (Taanit 30a). The prohibition to study Torah apparently stems from a broader proscription from engaging in activities that bring about happiness. The Talmud raises two exceptions to the prohibition to learn Torah. First, the *Baraita* teaches:

> He may also read Lamentations, Job, and the sad parts of Jeremiah, and the school children are free [from school], for it is said: "The precepts of the Lord are right, rejoicing the heart" [Ps. 19:9].

Learning Torah is prohibited because it "rejoices the heart"; these portions, which sadden the heart, may therefore be studied.

Elsewhere, the Talmud derives that a mourner may not learn Torah or greet others from a verse in Ezekiel, in which God instructs the prophet to "remain quiet" ("*he'anek dom*") in anticipation of his wife's death (Mo'ed Katan 15a). This passage implies that the Talmud demands "silence" from the mourner and does not mention that a mourner may learn sad and depressing passages from the Torah. Perhaps we must distinguish between the prohibition of *talmud Torah* for a mourner, one experiencing *aveilut ḥadasha,* who is instructed to completely halt his normal activities and to silently contemplate his loss, and one observing *aveilut yeshana,* who must spend his day in grief and pain.

Some *Rishonim*, however, conflate the two categories. Tosafot, for example, report that in his youth, Rabbeinu Tam prohibited a mourner from learning any Torah. In his older years, however, he retracted and permitted a mourner to learn the passages which may be studied on Tisha B'Av.[59] The *Shulḥan Arukh* similarly rules that a mourner may study these passages.[60]

Which sections and topics may one learn on Tisha B'Av? The gemara cited above permits studying the books of Lamentations and Job, and well as the parts of Jeremiah that deal with the tragedy and punishment of the Jewish people. In addition, the *Shulḥan Arukh* permits learning the commentaries on Lamentations and Job, the Midrash of Lamentations, and the third chapter of the tractate Mo'ed Katan, which deals with the laws of mourning.[61] The *Aḥaronim* also permit learning the talmudic passages relating to the destruction of Jerusalem and the Temple in Gittin 55b–58a (known as the "*Kamtza and bar Kamtza*" section) and Sanhedrin 104,[62] as well as the Talmud Yerushalmi at the end of tractate Taanit.[63] Some also mention reading *Yossipon*, a popular chronicle of Jewish history compiled in the early tenth century that was at times falsely attributed to the Roman historian Josephus. One may also read historical accounts of the destruction of Jerusalem, as well as of other Jewish tragedies, including the Holocaust. Finally, the halakhot of Tisha B'Av and *aveilut* may also be studied.

Ramban,[64] and subsequently the *Shulḥan Arukh*,[65] permit the recitation of *korbanot* (*Parashat HaTamid*), as well as the "*Baraita* of R. Yishma'el," both of which precede *Pesukei DeZimra*. When these passages are said as prayers and not within the framework of *talmud Torah*, they do not arouse joy and are therefore permitted.

In addition to the five prohibitions of Tisha B'Av and the prohibition of *talmud Torah*, the Tosefta teaches that "there should be no greetings between friends on Tisha B'Av; and to those who do not know (*hedyotot*), one should [respond] quietly."[66] The *Rishonim*[67] and *Shulḥan Arukh*[68] rule accordingly. The *Mishna Berura* writes that one should even refrain from saying "good morning."[69] However, one may wish another person "*mazal tov*," and one may also shake another's hand.[70]

LAWS AND CUSTOMS OBSERVED UNTIL MIDDAY

All of the prohibitions that we have discussed thus far apply the entire day, until the conclusion of the fast. Other halakhot and customs are observed only until midday. The *Hagahot Maymoniyot* records the custom in France not to sit on benches until Minḥa, similar to a mourner who sits on the ground during the seven days of mourning.[71] The *Shulḥan Arukh* cites this custom as well, and writes that it is customary to sit on the ground until *Tefillat Minḥa*.[72] Rema adds that nowadays it is customary to sit on regular benches immediately after leaving the synagogue after Shaḥarit, although *kinot* are generally recited until a bit before midday.[73] *Magen Avraham* writes that one may sit on a pillow, as it is only a custom not to sit on benches.[74] In practice, many are accustomed to sitting on low benches or chairs, preferably lower than three *tefaḥim* (about twelve inches), until *ḥatzot* (midday).

The *Shulḥan Arukh* also records that some sleep on the ground with a rock under their heads on Tisha B'Av.[75] Rema comments that one should decrease his comfort in sleeping on Tisha B'Av night in some way. For example, one who is accustomed to sleeping with two pillows should sleep with one. There are even some who place a stone under their head at night, in remembrance of Yaakov, who "took from the stones of the place" (Gen. 28:11) and then prophetically foresaw the destruction of the Temple, according to the Midrash. Pregnant women, as well as those who would suffer extreme discomfort, need not do so.[76] In general, Rema advises that one should decrease one's comforts on Tisha B'Av.[77]

In addition to not sitting on benches, the Talmud teaches:

> Where it is the custom to do work on the Ninth of Av, we may do work, but where it is not the custom we may not; and everywhere the scholars refrain from work. It has been taught likewise: R. Shimon b. Gamliel says: [In this respect] let a man always consider himself a scholar that he may feel more strongly the fast.
>
> R. Akiva says: Anyone who does work on the Ninth of Av will never see in his work a sign of blessing. And the sages say: Anyone who does work on the Ninth of Av and does not mourn for Jerusalem, will not share in her joy,

> as it is said: "Rejoice with Jerusalem, and be glad with her, all you that love her; rejoice for joy with her, all you that mourn for her." (Taanit 30b)

This passage implies, the *Aḥaronim* explain, that one should avoid activities that divert one's mind from mourning.[78]

The *Shulḥan Arukh* cites these passages and adds that even in a place in which one does not work on Tisha B'Av, a non-Jew may work for him, even in his house. In addition, he writes that a "*davar haavud*," work which may incur a financial loss if not done, is permitted, although preferably after midday.[79] Rema reports that it is customary to refrain from any work that requires time to accomplish (*yesh ba shihui ketzat*) until after midday.[80]

The *Arukh HaShulḥan* emphasizes that whether or not one should work is dependent upon custom. In his time, because of the hardships of earning a living, it was customary to begin working after the morning prayers. However, he recommends that "God-fearing Jews" should open their shops only after midday.[81]

TALLIT AND *TEFILLIN* ON TISHA B'AV

One of the fascinating aspects of the Tisha B'Av prayers is the common custom not to wear *tefillin* at Shaḥarit. The Gemara teaches that a mourner does not wear *tefillin* on the first day of his mourning (Mo'ed Katan 15a).[82] When God commanded Ezekiel not to mourn for his wife, He told him, "Don your glory" (Ezek. 24:17). The Rabbis explain that God instructed Ezekiel to wear *tefillin*, which he ordinarily would not have done on the first day of mourning. This may be because the mourner's disheveled state is inappropriate for the *tefillin*,[83] or because wearing *tefillin*, "glory," inherently contradicts the intended appearance of a mourner.[84] Despite the apparent similarities between the practices of a mourner and the laws of Tisha B'Av, the Talmud makes no mention of not wearing *tefillin* on Tisha B'Av.

The *Rishonim* differ as to whether one should wear *tefillin* on Tisha B'Av. *Abudraham* cites Raavad, who rules that one should not wear *tefillin* on Tisha B'Av, but rather "it is better to place burnt ashes on one's head."[85] Similarly, Roke'aḥ[86] and R. Avraham HaRofeh[87] write that one should not wear *tefillin* on Tisha B'Av. Rosh cites his teacher, Maharam of Rothenburg:

> Rabbeinu Meir wrote: It seems that on Tisha B'Av one should not wear *tefillin,* similar to the first day of mourning, as there is no day more bitter than the day established for eternal mourning.[88]

This ruling is actually quite striking. According to these *Rishonim,* we set aside the biblical commandment of *tefillin* for the proper observance of Tisha B'Av! It seems that they maintain that wearing *tefillin* is simply inconsistent with one's mourning on Tisha B'Av or that *tefillin* may not be worn by one in such a state of bereavement. Thus, just as a mourner may not wear *tefillin,* we may not do so on Tisha B'Av.

Rambam records that "Some scholars are accustomed not to wear the *tefillin shel rosh* (the *tefillin* worn on the head) on Tisha B'Av."[89] Why did these scholars refrain specifically from the *tefillin shel rosh*? The Midrash notes the uniqueness of the *tefillin shel rosh,* the phylactery worn on the head.

> "All of the nations of the world will see that the name of God is on you" [Deut. 28:10] – R. Eliezer the Great says that this refers to *tefillin* on the head, since they are called glory (*pe'er*).[90]

This passage explicitly links the "*pe'er,*" which the Talmud teaches that a mourner is not to don, with the *tefillin shel rosh.* Thus, this source may support the custom cited by Rambam to refrain from wearing specifically the head phylactery on Tisha B'Av.

On the other hand, the *Geonim* record that it was customary in the "Two Yeshivas," Sura and Pumbedita, to wear *tefillin* on Tisha B'Av.[91] Rashba records that R. Hai Gaon concurred.[92] Ramban argues that the first day of mourning has a special and unique status, not to be compared with the mourning of Tisha B'Av.[93] Rashba, Ritva,[94] *Shibbolei HaLeket,*[95] *Or Zarua,*[96] *Manhig,*[97] and others agree.

The later *Rishonim* suggest an interesting compromise. The *Mordekhai* writes:

> On the Ninth of Av, one is permitted to wear *tefillin*, as it is a form of *aveilut yeshana*. However, R. Meir would not don *tefillin*, nor wrap himself with the *tallit* in the morning, because it says, "He has cast down from heaven unto the earth the beauty of Israel" [Lam. 2:1] – this is a reference to [one's] *tallit* and *tefillin*. However, in the afternoon, he dons his *tefillin* and wraps himself in *tzitzit*.[98]

R. Meir b. R. Yekutiel HaKohen of Rothenburg, a student of Maharam of Rothenburg and author of the *Hagahot Maimoniyot*, similarly reports that his teacher would wear *tefillin* in the afternoon. The *Shulḥan Arukh* records that this is the prevalent custom.[99] Ashkenazic communities follow this practice.[100]

What is the basis for such a custom? R. Chaim Yosef David Azulai, commonly known by the acronym of his name, Ḥida, explains that on the morning of Tisha B'Av, we observe the practices of the first day of mourning, while in the afternoon we act like on the rest of the days of the mourning period.[101] In other words, the intensity of the mourning diminishes as the day progresses.

Alternatively, we may suggest another distinction. We noted above that Tisha B'Av is made up of of two distinct themes: it is both a *taanit tzibbur* and a day of *aveilut*. While these two aspects of Tisha B'Av coexist, the theme of *aveilut* appears to dominate the morning experience; after midday, the intense *aveilut* wanes, and the *taanit tzibbur* emerges. For example, the *keriat haTorah* of Minḥa is identical to that of a communal fast day.

It is also customary to wear and recite the blessing upon the *tallit* at Minḥa. Some question whether one who removed his *tallit katan* ("*tzitzit*") the previous night should wear it until Minḥa without a blessing, or recite the blessing on them in the morning.[102] Some suggest sleeping in one's *tzitzit* in order to avoid this dilemma.

TISHA B'AV THAT FALLS ON MOTZA'EI SHABBAT

When Tisha B'Av is observed on Motza'ei Shabbat, when and how is Havdala performed? The *Rishonim* offer numerous possibilities. *Behag*, for example, as cited by Ramban,[103] suggests that one should say

Havdala on Shabbat itself, over a cup of wine, after *pelag haMinḥa*. He ultimately rejects this opinion, as by reciting Havdala he would also be accepting upon himself the next day's fast, and would then be prohibited from drinking the wine. Alternatively, the *Sefer HaManhig*[104] writes that one should recite Havdala on Motza'ei Shabbat, and then give the wine to a child to drink. Ramban[105] rejects this as well, arguing that this practice may lead to undesirable results.

Tosafot[106] cite R. Amram Gaon, who rules that one should recite Havdala on Sunday night, at the conclusion of the fast. Interestingly, Ramban[107] himself rules that since one was unable to recite Havdala on Motza'ei Shabbat, the obligation of Havdala has been lifted and there is no obligation whatsoever to recite Havdala after the fast.

The Shulḥan Arukh[108] rules that one one should recite Havdala over a cup of wine after the fast. The *Rishonim* disagree as to whether one should recite the blessing over the fire after Shabbat.[109] The Shulḥan Arukh[110] rules that one should recite the blessing over the fire after Shabbat; this blessing is usually recited before the reading of Lamentations.[111] The *Shulḥan Arukh* adds that one does not recite the blessing over the *besamim* at all. The *Aḥaronim* disagree as to whether this is due to a general custom of not bringing enjoyable fragrances into the house of a mourner, or more specifically because the blessing over the *besamim* was instituted on Motza'ei Shabbat in order to comfort one for the loss of one's "extra soul" (*neshama yeteira*), which may be inappropriate on Tisha B'Av.[112]

NOTES

INTRODUCTION

1 This topic is treated in greater depth in chapter 41.

2 My previous book, *Hilchot Tefilla: A Comprehensive Guide to the Laws of Daily Prayer* (OU Press/Yeshivat Har Etzion/KTAV Publishing House, 2010) follows a similar methodology.

3 *Sefer HaḤinukh*, Mitzva 16.

4 Avot 6:6.

CHAPTER 1

1 Rambam, *Hilkhot Shegagot* 1:1.

2 Rambam, *Hilkhot Yom Tov*, 1:2.

3 *Sefer HaḤinukh* 298.

4 See R. Michael Rosensweig, "*BeInyan Issur Melakha BeShabbat VeYom Tov*," Beit Yitzchak 5751.

5 See Beitza 14a regarding *toḥen*; 14b regarding *borer*; 23b regarding *tzad*; 29b regarding *meraked*; Shabbat 134a regarding *megaben*; see also Beitza 2b–3a regarding *kotzer* and *toḥen*.

6 *Hilkhot Yom Tov* 1:5–8.

7 Ibid., 3:12.

8 Rashi, Beitza 3a, s.v. *veyitlosh*; Eiruvin 39b, s.v. *pasak*.

9 Rosh, Beitza 3:1.

10 Ran, Beitza 12b.

11 Ex. 10:9; Lev. 16:39, 23:3, 28:31; Num. 29:7; Deut. 5:13.

12 Regarding Pesaḥ (Lev. 23:7), Shavuot (ibid., 23:21), Rosh HaShana (ibid., 23:25), and Sukkot (ibid., 23:35–36). See also Num. 16:8, 28:18, 25, 26, and 29:1, 12, 35; Ex. 12:16.

13 See Rashba, *Avodat HaKodesh, Beit Mo'ed,* 1:1.

14 See, for example, the opinion cited by Tosafot, Beitza 3a, s.v. *gezeira.*

15 *Oraḥ Ḥayim* 495:1–2.

16 The *Biur Halakha* notes, however, that Maharil disagrees with this leniency. In addition, the *Aḥaronim* disagree as to whether Rema permits one to intentionally wait until Yom Tov and then perform one of these labors with a *shinui;* the *Magen Avraham* (495:3) interprets Rema as permitting pushing off the *melakha,* while the *Mishna Berura* (495:10; *Shaar HaTziyun* 495:12) disagrees.

17 Rashi, Beitza 12a, s.v. *ela.*

18 Tosafot, Ketubot 7a, s.v. *mitokh;* see also 12a, s.v. *hakhi garas.*

19 Rid, Responsa 82.

20 See Ramban, Lev. 23:7.

21 *Shita Mekubetzet,* Ketubot 7a, s.v. *vezeh lashon shita yeshana.*

22 Tosafot, Shabbat 95a, s.v. *veharodeh.*

23 *Shaagat Aryeh* 102. Based on this assumption, he proves from the fact that it is permitted to cook on Rosh HaShana that there must be a mitzva of *simḥat Yom Tov* on that day.

24 *Sefer Yerei'im* 304.

25 *Hilkhot Yom Tov* 1:4.

26 *Maggid Mishneh,* ibid.

27 *Shulḥan Arukh* 518:1.

28 *Mishna Berura* 518:1.

29 Rabbeinu Ḥananel, Beitza 12a.

30 Tosafot, Beitza 12a s.v. *hakhi garsinan.*

31 Rosh, Beitza 1:18.

32 Interestingly, Maharshal (*Yam Shel Shlomo,* Beitza 1:34) sharply criticizes this practice. Although he allows small children to play ball, he maintains that for adults to play ball on Yom Tov in a public area is "child's play and frivolous behavior," or, in short, a "*minhag ra,*" and is not even considered to be a "*tiyul.*"

33 See Shabbat 130a, 131a–b, 133a; Eiruvin 102b–103b; Beitza 11b.

34 Ibid.

35 Rosh, Beitza 1:18.

36 *Beit Yosef* 518.

37 See *Semak* 282.

38 Rema 518:1. The *Aḥaronim* question this ruling. *Taz* (518:1) and *Magen Avraham* (518:2), for example, forcefully argue that one may not carry keys that are not

necessary for Yom Tov. The *Mishna Berura* (518:6) rules that one should preferably act in accordance with *Taz* and *Magen Avraham*. The *Arukh HaShulḥan* (518:5–6), however, defends Rema's position and rules that one may carry anything on Yom Tov that fulfills even the slightest purpose, such as keys to a safe that protects one's money or utensils that one fears will be stolen. He records that this is the common custom (*minhag haolam*).

39 Maharil 139.

40 See *Magen Avraham* 326:8 and *Mishna Berura* 326:21, for example.

41 *Minḥat Yitzchak* 6:32; *Shemirat Shabbat KeHilkhata* 14:11.

42 *Iggerot Moshe, Oraḥ Ḥayim* 4:74.

43 See *Biur Halakhah* 326:1; *Minḥat Yitzchak* 6:32; *Shemirat Shabbat KeHilkhata* 14:11.

44 Beitza 21b

45 Tosafot, Beitza 21b, s.v. *lo yiḥam.*

46 Rosh, Shabbat 3:7.

47 Ran, Beitza 11a, s.v. *veoseh.*

48 Rif, Beitza 11a.

49 *Hilkhot Yom Tov* 1:16.

50 See also Ramban, Shabbat 40a, s.v. *haditnan.*

51 *Shulḥan Arukh* 511:1–2.

52 Rema, ibid.

53 *Ḥazon Ovadia,* Yom Tov 1:12; see, however, *Mishna Berura* 511:12.

54 *Biur Halakha* 511, s.v. *yadav.*

55 Rema 511:2.

56 *Magen Avraham* 511:5.

57 *Shemirat Shabbat KeHilkhata,* chap. 14, n. 25. (R. Ephraim Greenblatt cites a similar rationale in the name of R. Chaim David HaLevi in his responsa, *Rivevot Efraim.*)

58 Ibid., chap. 19, n. 3.

59 Ibid., chap. 14, n. 21.

60 Ibid., 14:7.

61 See *Mishna Berura* 326:7.

62 *Shaar HaTziyun* 511:25. See also *Shemirat Shabbat KeHilkhata,* chap. 14, n. 25.

63 See *Shulḥan Arukh, Oraḥ Ḥayim* 326:10, and *Mishna Berura* 326:30.

64 For further discussion of this topic, see, for example, R. Moshe Feinstein, *Iggerot Moshe, Yoreh De'ah,* 2:49 and later in *Ḥoshen Mishpat* 2:76; R. Ovadia Yosef, *Yeḥave Daat* 5:39 and *Halikhot Olam* 1:265–266; R. Eliezer Waldenberg, *Tztiz Eliezer* 15:39; R. Moshe Stern, *Be'er Moshe* 6:160:9; and R. Efraim Greenblatt, *Rivevot Efraim* 8:586. In addition, the Rabbinic Council of America published a

response prohibiting smoking in 2006 (see http://www.rabbis.org/pdfs/Prohibition_Smoking.pdf, accessed February 1, 2012), with the approval of R. Dovid Cohen, R. Michael Rosensweig, R. Hershel Schachter, R. Gedalia Schwartz, and R. Mordechai Willig.

65 *Knesset Gedola, Oraḥ Ḥayim,* 608.

66 *Magen Avraham* 514:4.

67 Shabbat 39b

68 Beitza 2:10

69 *Ḥayei Adam* 95:13.

70 *Shaarei Teshuva* 511:5.

71 *Iggerot Moshe, Oraḥ Ḥayim* 5:34.

72 *The Laws of Yom Tov*, p. 108, n. 3.

73 *Orḥot Rabbeinu*, vol. 2, p. 105.

CHAPTER 2

1 For example, the Gemara prohibits cooking for non-Jews or for animals on Yom Tov; see Beitza 21a.

2 See also Beitza 21a.

3 Rif, Pesaḥim 15a; Rambam, *Hilkhot Yom Tov,* 1:15; Ramban, *Milḥamot Hashem,* Pesaḥim 14b–15a; Rosh, Pesaḥim 3:6.

4 Rabbeinu Efraim, cited by Ramban in *Milḥamot Hashem*; Baal HaMaor, Pesaḥim 14b–15a.

5 Rashi, Pesaḥim 46b, s.v. *mideoraita.*

6 Tosafot, Pesaḥim 47a, s.v. *ve'i.*

7 See Kiddushin 41a; see also *Haamek She'ala* 169.

8 Tosafot, Pesaḥim 46b, s.v. *Rabba.*

9 *Magen Avraham* 527.

10 See Rambam, *Hilkhot Yom Tov* 6:1; see also 1:9 and 1:15.

11 *Mishna Berura* 527:3; see also *Biur Halakha* 527.

12 Rashba, Beitza 17a, s.v. *memalei.*

13 Ran, Beitza 9b, s.v. *umiha.*

14 *Iggerot Moshe, Oraḥ Ḥayim* 2:103.

15 *Shemirat Shabbat KeHilkhata* 19:6, n. 14.

16 *Iggerot Moshe, Oraḥ Ḥayim* 5:35.

17 For example, see *Teshuvot VeHanhagot* 1:348.

18 *Tur* 503.

19 *Beit Yosef,* ibid.

20 *Hilkhot Yom Tov,* 1:10.

21 This is against the opinion of Roke'aḥ, 298.
22 Rashi, Beitza 17a, s.v. *memalei.*
23 *Shulḥan Arukh* 503:1.
24 *Mishna Berura* 503:5.
25 Ibid., 503:12.
26 See *Magen Avraham* 503:2 and *Mishna Berura* 503:7.
27 Baal HaMaor, Pesaḥim 14b.
28 *Mishnat Yaavetz* 36.
29 *Hilkhot Yom Tov* 6:2.
30 Raavad, ibid.
31 Ritva, Beitza 15b, s.v. *veoseh.*
32 Rosh, Beitza 2:1.
33 *Hagahot Maimoniyot, Hilkhot Yom Tov,* 6:2.
34 *Beit Yosef* 527.
35 *Tur* 527.
36 *Kol Bo* 59.
37 *Shulḥan Arukh* 527:14.
38 *Mordekhai* 671.
39 R. Yechezkel Landau suggests in his commentary on the Talmud (*Tzelaḥ,* Beitza 15b) that even R. Ashi accepts Rava's reason. Thus, even if the halakha is in accordance with R. Ashi, on Yom Tov Sheni, when R. Ashi's reason of ensuring proper respect for Yom Tov is no longer relevant, one may rely upon Rava and make an *Eiruv Tavshilin* in order to properly prepare for Shabbat.
40 *Sefer HaYashar, Ḥiddushim* 392; see also Tosafot, Beitza 17b, s.v. *amar* and *Siddur Rashi* 619.
41 Rif, Responsa 312; Rambam, *Hilkhot Yom Tov* 6:3; Ramban, *Milḥamot Hashem* 8a; Ran 10a, s.v. *amar Rava.*
42 Tosafot, Beitza 17b, s.v. *amar.*
43 *Shulḥan Arukh* 527:2.
44 *Shulḥan Arukh* 527:3.
45 Rema, ibid.
46 *Arukh HaShulḥan* 527:13.
47 Maharshal, Beitza 2:18.
48 Tosafot, Beitza 22a, s.v. *umadlikin.*
49 Rosh 2:16.
50 Ran 11a, s.v. *umidamrinan.*
51 *Mordekhai,* Beitza 672.
52 Rif, ibid.
53 *Hilkhot Yom Tov* 6:8.

54 *Shulḥan Arukh* 527:19.

55 *Magen Avraham* (528:2 and 667:2), citing Ran (9a, s.v. *tannu rabbanan*), implies that only actions necessary for the Shabbat meals are permitted. *Or Zarua* (*Hilkhot Yom Tov* 343:7) and R. Akiva Eiger (comments on *Magen Avraham*) insist that any action that may potentially provide benefit on Shabbat is permitted by the *Eiruv Tavshilin*. See also *Ḥazon Ovadia, Hilkhot Yom* Tov, p. 302.

56 *Shulḥan Arukh* 527:13.

57 *Tiferet Yisrael*, Beitza 2:1.

58 See, for example, Maharsham 2:36.

59 See *Minḥat Yitzchak* 7:36.

60 Rashi, Beitza 17a, s.v. *miyom*.

61 Ran 9b.

62 *Tur* 527.

63 *Baḥ* 527.

64 *Sefer HaIttur*, cited by *Tur* 527.

65 *Hilkhot Yom Tov* 6:14–15.

66 *Shulḥan Arukh* 527:22.

67 *Mishna Berura* 527:74.

68 Ibid., 527:75.

69 See, for example, Rambam, *Hilkhot Yom Tov* 6.

70 Rosh, Beitza 2:2. The *Korban Netanel* (7) explains, based on the Gemara, that one who forgets to prepare an *eiruv* a second time may no longer rely upon the rabbi's *eiruv*.

71 Rashi, Beitza 16b, s.v. *ledidaḥ*; Ran 9a, s.v. *hahu*.

72 *Beit Yosef* 527; see Rashba, Responsa 1:583.

73 *Arukh HaShulḥan* 527:16.

74 *Shulḥan Arukh* 527:7.

75 *Kaf HaḤayim* 527:48; see also *Mishna Berura* 527:22.

76 *Ḥayei Adam* 102:6.

77 *Arukh HaShulḥan* 527:18.

78 *Mishna Berura* 527:26.

79 *Shulḥan Arukh* 366:10; see *Mishna Berura* 527:34, who rules that if an adult from another family is not available, one's wife or children may make the acquisition.

80 See, for example, *Birkei Yosef* 527:10 and *Kaf HaḤayim* 527:35, 41.

81 *Eishel Avraham* 527:7.

82 *Maamar Mordekhai* 527:16.

83 *Mishneh Halakhot* 7:74.

84 *Ḥazon Ovadia, Hilkhot Yom Tov*, p. 278.

85 *Or LeTziyon*, vol. 3, 22:6.

86 See also *Minḥat Yitzchak* 7:36 and *Iggerot Moshe, Oraḥ Ḥayim* 5:20:26.
87 Rema 527:12.

CHAPTER 3

1 See Pesaḥim 108b and Tosafot, s.v. *yedei yayin*; see also *Yerei'im* 227 and Tosafot, Ḥagiga 8a, s.v. *vesamaḥta.*
2 Tosafot, Mo'ed Katan 14b, s.v. *aseh deyaḥid.*
3 *Hilkhot Yom Tov*, 6:17–18.
4 See R. Aryeh Pomeronchik, *Emek Berakha*, p. 108.
5 *Shaagat Aryeh* 65.
6 See also *Torat Refa'el* 92.
7 See *Yerei'im* 227, *Shaagat Aryeh* 65.
8 Tosafot, Pesaḥim 109a, s.v. *bameh*; *Yam Shel Shlomo*, Beitza 2:5; *Baḥ* 529; see also *Nimukei Oraḥ Ḥayim* 529.
9 *Hilkhot Yom Tov* 6:18.
10 *Yam Shel Shlomo*, Beitza 2:5.
11 *Baḥ* 529.
12 *Torah Temima*, Deut. 16:14.
13 *Beit Yosef* 529.
14 *Shulḥan Arukh* 529.
15 *Biur Halakha* 529, s.v. *keitzad*; *Yeḥave Daat* 6:33; *Iggerot Moshe, Oraḥ Ḥayim* 3:68, etc.
16 See, for example, *Leket Yosher* 157:3, *Ḥavot Ya'ir* 178; *Torah Temima*, Deuteronomy 16:14. See *Shevet HaLevi* 3:18, who records that it is not customary to insist upon eating beef on Yom Tov.
17 See *Darkhei Teshuva*, 89:19.
18 Shabbat 118; Rambam, *Hilkhot Yom Tov* 6:1; *Shulḥan Arukh* 529:1.
19 *Hilkhot Shabbat* 30:9.
20 *Tur* 529.
21 *Shulḥan Arukh* 529:1.
22 Ibid. See also *Hagahot Maimoniyot, Hilkhot Yom Tov* 6:20.
23 *Shiurim LeZekher Abba Mari*, vol. 2. See also *UVikashtem MiSham*, ft. 19 (pp. 210–11).
24 *Emek Berakha*, p. 108.
25 *Hilkhot Yom Tov* 6:19.
26 Ibid., 6:17
27 *Tur* 529.
28 *Shulḥan Arukh* 529:1.

29 See, for example, *Magen Avraham* 569, and *Mishna Berura* 529:1.

30 *Hilkhot Yom Tov* 6:20.

31 *Hilkhot Yom Tov* 6:18.

32 Rabbeinu Ḥananel, ibid.

33 Ritva, Rosh HaShana 16b and Sukka 27b; see also Rashba, Sukka 27b. See also *Penei Yehoshua* (Rosh HaShana 16b) who agrees that theoretically this mitzva might be fulfilled every day, and therefore, he claims, it is not a *mitzvat aseh shehazeman gerama* and women are obligated.

34 *Hilkhot Talmud Torah* 5:7.

35 Rashi, Ḥagiga 3a, s.v. *lehakbil.*

36 *Noda BiYehuda, Mahadura Tinyana, Oraḥ Ḥayim* 94.

37 Some insist that although one is not obligated to visit his teacher each festival, it is certainly praiseworthy to do so, and one is considered to have fulfilled a mitzva. See Sukka 10b; Rashi, s.v. *sheliḥei mitzva anan.*

38 *Sefer Ye'arot Devash*, p. 66.

39 *Shulḥan Arukh* 301:4; see also 554:12.

40 *Magen Avraham* 301:7.

41 *Kesef Mishneh, Hilkhot Talmud Torah* 5:7.

42 *Shevet Sofer* 17.

43 *Hilkhot Tumat Okhlin* 16:10.

44 *Sefer HaEshkol*, p. 3.

45 See, for example R. Natronai Gaon, cited in *Shaarei Teshuva* 175; Rosh, Yoma 8:24.

46 *Tur* 603.

47 *Tur* 606.

48 *Baḥ* 603. *Turei Even* explains that since the mizva to purify oneself before the *regel* is in order to enable one to offer sacrifices, therefore one is not obligated to purify oneself before Rosh HaShana and Yom Kippur.

49 *Beit Shmuel* 55:10.

CHAPTER 4

1 For more information, see Rambam, *Hilkhot Kiddush HaḤodesh* 5:3 and R. Avraham b. Ḥiyya's *Sefer HaIbbur*, citing R. Hai Gaon, who attributes the set calendar to Hillel in the year 358/9 CE; see also Sacha Stern, *Community and Calendar: A History of the Jewish Calendar, Second Century BCE-Tenth Century CE* (Oxford University Press, 2001).

2 See Rabbeinu Tam, *Sefer HaYashar, Ḥelek HaḤiddushim* 537, cited by Tosafot, Sukka 44b, s.v. *kan.*

3 See Ritva, Rosh HaShana 18a; Ran, Sukka 22a, s.v. *itmar*.

4 See *Hilkhot Berakhot* 11:16, *Hilkhot Yom Tov* 1:21 and 6:14, *Hilkhot Talmud Torah* 6:14, *Hilkhot Kiddush HaḤodesh* 5:6.

5 See Ritva, Rosh HaShana 18a.

6 Ritva, ibid.

7 *Teshuvot HaGeonim, musafiya* 1.

8 Rabbeinu Ḥananel, Beitza 5b.

9 Rif, Beitza 3a.

10 *Hilkhot Yom Tov* 1:21, *Hilkhot Kiddush HaḤodesh* 5:8.

11 Rosh, Beitza 1:4.

12 Baal HaMaor, Beitza 3a.

13 *Milḥamot Hashem*, Beitza 3a.

14 *Shulḥan Arukh* 601:2.

15 Pesaḥim 51a; Rambam, *Hilkhot Yom Tov* 1:22.

16 *Shulḥan Arukh, Yoreh De'ah* 399:2.

17 *Hilkhot Kiddush HaḤodesh* 5:4, 11–12.

18 *She'elat Yaavetz* 1:168; see *Piskei Teshuvot* 496:4, who cites those who questioned whether one should refrain from doing *melakha* on Yom Tov Sheni in Bnei Berak, and R. Yitzchak Ze'ev Soloveitchik, who was stringent regarding the New City of Jerusalem.

19 Rosh HaShana 18a, Sukka 43a.

20 *Sefer Eretz Yisrael* 7:4–5.

21 *Tzitz Eliezer* 3:23.

22 See *Sefer Yom Tov Sheni KeHilkhahto*, p. 172, citing R. Shlomo Zalman Auerbach and R. Yosef Shalom Elyashiv.

23 Rosh, Pesaḥim 4:4.

24 *Avkat Rokhel* 26.

25 *Shulḥan Arukh* 496:3.

26 See, for example *Mishna Berura* 496:13; *Iggerot Moshe, Oraḥ Ḥayim* 4:101; *Minḥat Yitzchak* 4:1–4, 9:54; *Minḥat Shlomo* 1:19; and others, as we shall see below.

27 *Magen Avraham* 497:7.

28 *Iggerot Moshe, Oraḥ Ḥayim* 3:74.

29 *Ḥayim Shaal* 1:55.

30 *Halakhot Ketanot* 4.

31 *Yeḥave Daat* 1:26; *Yabia Omer* 6:40.

32 *Magen Avraham* 468:12.

33 See *Piskei Teshuvot* 296:26, who presents these opinions.

34 *Iggerot Moshe, Oraḥ Ḥayim* 4:108.

35 *Arukh HaShulḥan*. Similarly, the Mishna (Bava Batra 7b) states: "How long must a man reside in a town to be counted as one of the townsmen? Twelve months."
36 Responsa *Geonei Mizraḥ UMaarav* 39.
37 See *Tzitz Eliezer* 9:30. See Also R. Yehuda Herzl Henkin, in his *Benei Banim* (3:3), who rules accordingly.
38 *Magen Avraham* 468:12; see also *Seridei Esh* 2:161, for example.
39 *Minḥat Shlomo* 1:19:7.
40 *Birkei Yosef* 496:4; see also *Shaarei Teshuva* 496:3.
41 *Ḥokhmat Shlomo, Oraḥ Ḥayim* 496.
42 *Iggerot Moshe, Oraḥ Ḥayim* 3:73.
43 *Shulḥan Arukh* 263:17.
44 *Shemirat Shabbat KeHilkhata* chap. 31, n. 80.
45 *Minḥat Shlomo* 1:19:3.
46 *Ḥakham Tzvi* 167.
47 *Shulḥan Arukh HaRav* 496:11.
48 Ibid.; see also *Mahadura Tinyana* 1:8.
49 *Reshimot Shiurim*, Sukka, p. 226.
50 *Yom Tov Sheni KeHilkhato*, p. 49, cites R. Bentzion Abba Shaul, who relates that the custom of Sephardim is in accordance with *Ḥakham Tzvi*. See also R. Natan Tzvi Friedman's *Netzer Matai* 10, and the view cited in *Minḥat Yitzchak* 8:59.
51 *Har Tzvi* 3:78.
52 *Ir HaKodesh VeHaMikdash* 19:11.
53 *Mo'adei HaRaaya*, pp. 143–4.
54 *Shulḥan Arukh HaRav Mahadura Tinyana* 1:8. See, however, 496:7–9.
55 See *Avnei Nezer, Oraḥ Ḥayim* 424; *Minḥat Elazar* 3:59.
56 *Shulḥan Arukh* 496:3.
57 *Mishna Berura* 496:5.
58 See, for example, *Har Tzvi* 2:78 and *Yeḥave Daat* 3:35; *Sefer Yom Tov Sheni KeHilkhato*, p. 83.
59 *Ḥayei Adam* 103:4.
60 Rashi, Pesaḥim 52a, s.v. *bayishuv*.
61 Tosafot, Pesaḥim 52a, s.v, *bayishuv*.
62 *Taz* 496:4.
63 *Magen Avraham* 496:2.
64 *Mishna Berura* 496:9.
65 *Iggerot Moshe, Oraḥ Ḥayim* 4:104.
66 See *Piskei Teshuvot* 496:10 and *Sefer Yom Tov Sheni KeHilkhato* 3:3.

CHAPTER 5

1 *Tur* 530.
2 Cited by Tosafot, Ḥagiga 18a, s.v. *ḥolo.*
3 *Mordekhai,* Mo'ed Katan 835.
4 Rabbeinu Tam; *Mordekhai*; Rosh, Mo'ed Katan 1:1; Me'iri, Mo'ed Katan 2a; *Tur* 530.
5 Ritva, Mo'ed Katan 13a.
6 Rashi, Mo'ed Katan 11b, s.v. *ela afilu*; Rashbam, Pesaḥim 118a, s.v. *kol hamevazeh*; *Sefer HaḤinukh,* mitzva 323; see also opinions cited by the *Yerei'im* 394; Me'iri, Mo'ed Katan 2a.
7 Mo'ed Katan 1a, s.v. *gemara*; see also *Maggid Mishneh, Hilkhot Yom Tov* 7:1.
8 Rashba, Avoda Zara 22a.
9 Ritva, Mo'ed Katan 2a.
10 *Hilkhot Yom Tov* 7:1.
11 *Keren Ora,* Mo'ed Katan 2a.
12 Similarly, the *Mishnat Yaavetz* (43), and *Sefer Mo'adim UZemanim* (4:296) explain that Rambam maintains that *mideoraita,* one is to treat Ḥol HaMo'ed as a *mikra kodesh,* as "it was a time when the *ḥagiga* sacrifices were brought in the Temple." The Rabbis, however, defined which *melakhot* were prohibited and which were permitted. Therefore, while one who treats Ḥol HaMo'ed as an ordinary weekday violates a biblical commandment, one who performs a specific *melakha* only violates a rabbinic prohibition, and therefore he receives "*makkot mardut.*"
13 The Yerushalmi, Mo'ed Katan 3:4, adds that one may write *tefillin* "in order to wear them."
14 *Mordekhai, Hilkhot Tefillin,* p. 13; Rosh, *Hilkhot Tefillin* 16; *Or Zarua* 1:589.
15 *Behag,* cited by Tosafot, Mo'ed Katan 19a, s.v. *Rabbi Yose*; Ri, cited by *Hagahot Maimoniyot, Hilkhot Tefillin* 4:1; Rashba, Responsa 1:690.
16 Ritva, Eiruvin 96a; *Semak* 153; *Tur* 31.
17 *Beit Yosef* 31.
18 *Shulḥan Arukh* 31:2.
19 Rema, ibid.
20 *Taz* 31:2; see also *Mishna Berura* 31:8 and *Arukh HaShulḥan* 31:4.
21 *Biur HaGra* 31:31; *Maase Rav* 174.
22 *Arukh HaShulḥan* 31:4.
23 *Shiurim LeZekher Abba Mari,* vol. 1, p. 109.
24 See *Kaf HaḤayim* 31:6.

CHAPTER 6

1 *Hilkhot Yom Tov* 7:1.
2 *Hilkhot Yom Tov* 6:17.
3 *Magen Avraham* 530:1.
4 Raavya, *Hilkhot Yom Tov* 750; *Orḥot Ḥayim, Hilkhot Ḥol HaMo'ed*; see also *Shulḥan Arukh* 188:7
5 See R. Dovid Zucker and R. Moshe Francis, *Hilkhot Ḥol HaMo'ed*, Biurim 1 and Teshuvot of R. Moshe Feinstein 1–2.
6 See Tosafot, Keritot 7a, s.v. *vekaru*; *Yerei'im* 317; *Magen Avraham* 530:1 and 664:3, who relates that Maharil would wear his Shabbat coat, and that many are accustomed to wear Shabbat clothing on Ḥol HaMo'ed.
7 *Shaar HaTziyun* 430:5.
8 *Tur* and *Beit Yosef* 531.
9 Ritva, Mo'ed Katan 14a.
10 Rema 531:8.
11 *Mishna Berura* 531:21 and *Biur Halakha*, s.v. *kola dam*.
12 *Shulḥan Arukh* 531:8.
13 Ibid., 546:5.
14 *Hagahot Maimoniyot, Hilkhot Yom Tov* 7:17; *Hagahot Asheri*, Beitza 3:1; Maharam of Rothenburg, *Hilkhot Semaḥot* 9.
15 *Tur* 531.
16 *Noda BiYehuda* 1:13; see also *Mahadura Tinyana* 99–101.
17 Ḥatam Sofer, *Oraḥ Ḥayim* 154.
18 See, for example, R. Ovadia Yosef, *Ḥazon Ovadia, Hilkhot Yom Tov*, p. 190; R. Shalom Messas, *Tevuot Shemesh, Oraḥ Ḥayim* 55–56; *Shemirat Shabbat KeHilkhata* 66:23.
19 *Iggerot Moshe, Oraḥ Ḥayim* 1:163.
20 *Nefesh HaRav*, pp. 189–90.
21 Rosh, Mo'ed Katan 3:21; *Nimukkei Yosef* 10b.
22 *Shulḥan Arukh* 534:1.
23 See *Ḥayei Adam* 110:2.
24 See *Shemirat Shabbat KeHilkhata* v. 2 chap. 66, n. 250. He cites R. Moshe Feinstein (*Hilkhot Ḥol HaMo'ed, Piskei Halakhot* 9), however, who disagrees.
25 R. Ovadia Yosef, *Yalkut Yosef, Hilkhot Yom Tov*, p. 198. See, however, R. Moshe Stern, *Be'er Moshe* 7:6, who writes that one should prepare enough undergarments for the entire festival, and in case of necessity, one should consult with a Rav.
26 Responsa *Sheraga HaMe'ir* 7:43.
27 *Iggerot Moshe, Oraḥ Ḥayim* 3:36:1.

28 *Shemirat Shabbat KeHilkhata* 66:72.

29 *Shemirat Shabbat KeHilkhata,* 66, n. 240. He cites R. Shlomo Zalman Auerbach, who suggests that one should preferably buy a new shirt rather than launder.

30 *Iggerot Moshe, Oraḥ Ḥayim* 3:36:4.

31 This is the view of R. Moshe Feinstein, as cited in *Hilkhot Ḥol HaMo'ed,* p. 34; R. Moshe Stern, *Be'er Moshe* 7:9, disagrees.

CHAPTER 7

1 *Kitzur Shulḥan Arukh* 128.

2 See Sanhedrin 104b.

3 *Pirkei DeRabbi Eliezer,* chap. 45.

4 See Rambam, *Hilkhot Teshuva* 3:4.

5 *Sefer HaManhig, Hilkhot Rosh HaShana* 24.

6 *Tur, Oraḥ Ḥayim* 581.

7 Rema, *Oraḥ Ḥayim* 581.

8 R. Yoel Sirkis, in *Baḥ* (*Oraḥ Ḥayim* 581), discusses which shofar blasts are sounded in Elul. Is it sufficient to sound only the "*tashrat*" series (*tekia, shevarim-terua, tekia*), or must one sound the two other types – "*tashat*" (*tekia, shevarim, tekia*) and "*tarat*" (*tekia, terua, tekia*) – so as not to create the misimpression that one need not blow all three sets on Rosh HaShana? In most congregations, it is customary to sound only the *tashrat* series after morning prayers.

9 *Tur, Oraḥ Ḥayim* 581.

10 *Shulḥan Arukh, Oraḥ Ḥayim* 581:1.

11 See *Mishna Berura* 581:6.

12 Rambam, *Hilkhot Tefilla* 1:1.

13 *Sefer HaMitzvot,* Positive Commandment 5.

14 Rashi, Berakhot 20b, s.v. *veḥayyavin.*

15 Rambam, *Hilkhot Taaniyot* 1:1–3.

16 *Redemption, Prayer, and Talmud Torah,* Tradition 17:2 (1978), pp. 67–68.

17 See *Eliyahu Zuta* 23.

18 *Seder Rav Amram* 2:59.

19 Rashba, Responsa 1:211.

20 *Tur, Oraḥ Ḥayim* 565.

21 *Shulḥan Arukh, Oraḥ Ḥayim* 565:5.

22 *Iggerot Moshe, Yoreh De'ah* 3:21.

23 *Kaf HaḤayim* 131:23.

24 Rema, *Oraḥ Ḥayim* 565:5.

25 *Taz,* ibid.; see also *Mateh Efraim* 581:21 and *Kitzur Shulḥan Arukh* 128:9.

26 *Mishna Berura* 565:13.

27 Ibid., 581:4. This is based on the Gemara (Sota 33a), which rules that although prayers, such as *Shemoneh Esreh*, may be recited in the vernacular, "One should never pray for his needs in Aramaic." See also *Shulḥan Arukh, Oraḥ Ḥayim* 101:4, who cites three possible interpretations of this gemara. Similarly, the *Mishna Berura* (101:19) rules that one should not recite Aramaic texts, such as "*Yekum Purkan*," when praying privately.

28 Maharal, *Netivot Olam, Netiv Avoda* 12.

29 Ḥatam Sofer, Responsa, *Oraḥ Ḥayim* 166.

30 *Shibbolei HaLeket*, 282.

31 *Shulḥan Arukh, Oraḥ Ḥayim* 581:1.

32 See Avoda Zara 3b.

33 *Shaarei Teshuva* 581:1.

34 *Magen Avraham* 565:5.

35 *Yeḥave Daat* 1:46.

36 *Iggerot Moshe, Oraḥ Ḥayim* 2:105.

37 See, for example, R. Shalom of Koldanov-Brahin, in his *Mishmeret Shalom* (41).

38 See, for example, R. Herschel Shachter's *MiPeninei HaRav*, pp. 120–121. It is worth noting, in this context, that R. Soloveitchik opposed saying *Seliḥot* in the morning (see B. David Schreiber, *Nora'ot HaRav*, VI (1997), pp. 240-245).

39 *Kitzur Shulḥan Arukh* 128.

40 See *Midrash Tehillim* 27:4.

41 *Likkutei Torah, Parashat Re'eh*, p. 32.

CHAPTER 8

1 *Hilkhot Megilla VeḤanukka* 3:6.

2 Tosafot, Mo'ed Katan 14, s.v. *aseh deyaḥid*.

3 *Hilkhot Yom Tov* 6:17–18.

4 Ibid.

5 *Shaagat Aryeh* 102.

6 *She'iltot, Parashat Ḥayei Sara* 15.

7 Ramban, *Mo'ed Katan* 24b.

8 *Shulḥan Arukh, Yoreh De'ah* 399:6. R. Soloveitchik addresses this issue as well in his *Shiurim LeZekher Abba Mari*.

9 Ibid., *Oraḥ Ḥayim* 597:1.

10 *Mishna Berura* 597:1.

11 Rema, *Oraḥ Ḥayim* 597:3.

12 *Terumat HaDeshen* 245.

13 *Mordekhai,* Rosh HaShana 708.
14 *Taz, Oraḥ Ḥayim* 597:1.
15 *Mishna Berura* 597:12.
16 Rosh, Rosh HaShana 4:14.
17 *Tur, Oraḥ Ḥayim* 582.
18 *Kitzur Shulḥan Arukh* 129:2.
19 *Yeḥave Daat* 2:69.
20 *Maase Rav* 207.
21 *Midrash Tehillim* 100, s.v. *ivdu.*
22 I heard this analysis in 1992 from R. Michael Rosensweig.

CHAPTER 9

1 *Sefer HaMitzvot,* Positive Commandment 137.
2 *Sefer HaḤinukh,* Mitzva 130.
3 Rambam, *Hilkhot Teshuva* 3:4.
4 *Sefer HaḤinukh,* Commandment 405.
5 Ramban, *Sefer HaMitzvot,* Positive Commandment 5.
6 Rambam, *Hilkhot Taaniyot* 1:1–3.
7 The Gemara also extends this principle to women, who are exempt from shofar because it is a *mitzvat aseh shehazeman gerama,* a time-bound positive commandment.
8 Me'iri 29.
9 R. Yonatan of Lunel, Rosh HaShana, 29a.
10 *Shulḥan Arukh* 589:2.
11 Rambam, *Hilkhot Shofar* 3:10.
12 Rambam, Responsa 142.
13 *Shulḥan Arukh, Oraḥ Ḥayim* 585:2.
14 Cited by Rosh 4:10.
15 *She'iltot* 171.
16 *Semag,* Positive Commandment 42.
17 This may be supported by Rabbeinu Tam's position regarding the *berakha* recited over eating in the *sukka,* as well as his position regarding women reciting a blessing over a *mitzvat aseh shehazeman gerama,* but this lies beyond the scope of our present discussion.
18 Rambam, *Hilkhot Shofar* 1:1, 3.
19 Ibid., 1:3.
20 *Hagahot Asheri* 4:14.
21 Rosh 3:11.

22 See Ran's discussion, 7b.
23 *Hilkhot Shofar* 2:4.
24 Maharam Alashkar, Responsa 10.
25 *Minḥat Ḥinukh*, Commandment 405.
26 R. Yonatan of Lunel 29b.
27 *Hilkhot Teshuva* 3:4.
28 Of course, R. Yonatan of Lunel's suggestion that the Torah commands us to transform Rosh HaShana into a "*yom terua*" fits in well with our previous discussion regarding the nature and experience of Rosh HaShana (see chapter 2).

CHAPTER 10

1 Incidentally, the word "*tzevi*," when used in early halakhic literature, refers to a "gazelle," the horns of which may be used for a shofar, and *not* to a deer, the antlers of which may not.
2 Incidentally, this passage clearly indicates that the shofar functions as a vessel for asking forgiveness.
3 Interestingly, Rashi implies that they disagree regarding the mode of prayer most appropriate for Rosh HaShana – hunched over, with one's face toward the ground, or looking up toward the heavens. Once again, the shofar's function as a vessel of prayer emerges. 4 *Hilkhot Shofar* 1:1.
5 See Tosafot, Rosh HaShana 26b, s.v. *shel ya'el*; Rashba; Ritva; Ran; Raavad, etc.
6 Ran 6a.
7 *Mordekhai* 714.
8 "*Shofar shel Rosh HaShana*," Sinai 69.
9 *Shulḥan Arukh, Oraḥ Ḥayim* 586:1.
10 See, for example, Ari Z. Zivotofsky, "Yemenite Shofar: Ideal for the Mitzva?" *The Journal of Halacha and Contemporary Society*, 53 (Pesach 5767/Spring 2007), pp. 106–124.
11 http://www.zootorah.com/essays/ExoticShofars.pdf (accessed September 16, 2012).
12 *Hilkhot Shofar* 3:1.
13 *Tur, Oraḥ Ḥayim* 590.
14 *Shulḥan Arukh, Oraḥ Ḥayim* 590:1.
15 Rif 10a.
16 See Ritva 34a.
17 *Hilkhot Shofar* 3:2.
18 See Ritva 34b.
19 *Shulḥan Arukh, Oraḥ Ḥayim* 588:3.

20 Ibid., 590:7–8.
21 Ad loc., s.v. *shalosh.*
22 Tosafot, ibid., s.v. *shiur;* Rosh 4:10.
23 *Hilkhot Shofar* 3:4; see also *Maggid Mishneh,* ad loc.
24 Raavad, ibid.
25 *Arukh HaShulḥan* 590.
26 *Shulḥan Arukh, Oraḥ Ḥayim* 590:3.
27 Some *Aḥaronim* (see *Sefat Emet,* Rosh HaShana 33b, *Siddur HaYaavetz, Dinei HaTekiot* 6; see also *Sefer Mo'adim UZemanim* 1:5) insist that one who lengthens that middle sound, i.e., the *terua* or *shevarim,* should lengthen the surrounding *tekiot* as well.
28 Ran 10b.
29 The *Mishna Berura* (*Shaar HaTziyun* 590:19) is inclined to believe that Rabbeinu Tam does not argue that the *shevarim-terua must* be blown in two breaths; he would agree that it may be blown in one breath.
30 See also Rosh 4:10.
31 *Shulḥan Arukh, Oraḥ Ḥayim* 590:4.
32 Rema, ibid.
33 *Shaar HaTziyun* 590:18.
34 *Arukh HaShulḥan* 590:13.
35 *Nefesh HaRav,* p. 206.
36 Rosh 4:10.
37 *Shulḥan Arukh, Oraḥ Ḥayim* 590:5.
38 Ibid., 586:6.
39 See *Piskei Teshuvot* 586:5.
40 *Shulḥan Arukh, Oraḥ Ḥayim* 588:2.
41 Ibid., 590:7–8.
42 Ibid.
43 Ibid., 590:9. *Taz* (588:2), citing *Levush,* argues that only the *toke'a* fails to fulfill his obligation if he inserts the wrong sound into a set. For the listener, he argues, this extra sound should not constitute an interruption, even according to Ramban, but rather a "pause." The *Aḥaronim* do not accept *Taz*'s distinction.
44 *Arukh HaShulḥan* 590:20.
45 *Mishna Berura* 590:34.

CHAPTER 11

1 Rosh HaShana 16b, s.v. *kedei.*
2 Ran 3a.

3 Rif 10b.
4 *Hilkhot Shofar* 3:10.
5 Rashba 16a.
6 Ritva 16a, 34a.
7 Ran 16a and 34a.
8 *Tur, Oraḥ Ḥayim* 585.
9 Tosafot, Pesaḥim 115a, s.v. *matkif.* Tosafot derive this from R. Ḥisda's position regarding the proper time to recite the blessing over the eating of *marror* at the Pesaḥ Seder.
10 Baal HaMaor, Rosh HaShana 10b.
11 Commentary on Lev. 23:24.
12 Commentary on Lev. 23:24 and in his *Derasha LeRosh HaShana.*
13 Recorded in *Harerei Kedem,* vol. I, chap. 29.
14 Rif 10b, Baal HaMaor 11a, Rambam *Hilkhot Shofar* 3:10, Rosh 4:10.
15 Cited by Ritva 34b; see also *Milḥamot HaShem* 11a.
16 *Shulḥan Arukh, Oraḥ Ḥayim* 592:1.
17 Ibid., 596:1; Ashkenazic practice is to lengthen the final *tekia,* known as the *tekia gedola.*
18 Tosafot, Rosh HaShana 32b, s.v. *shiur.*
19 As we discussed above, Rabbeinu Tam believes that a *tashrat* does not pose a problem of *hefsek,* interruption, because the halakha follows the *Rabbanan,* who allow one to hear even nine sounds over nine hours and still fulfill one's obligation. Thus, a *tashrat* works even if a *tarat* or *tashat* is really the proper method.
20 Rosh HaShana. *Ner Mitzva,* 17.
21 Tosafot, Rosh HaShana 33b, s.v. *shiur.*
22 *Mishna Berura* 596:2.
23 *Arukh HaShulḥan, Oraḥ Ḥayim* 596:1.
24 *Mishna Berura* 592:1.
25 *Otzar HaGeonim,* Rosh HaShana.
26 Rosh 4:13.
27 Rif 11a.
28 Rosh 4:12.
29 *Hilkhot Shofar* 3:11.
30 Cited by the *Hagahot Maimoniyot* 3:9.
31 Ran 11a.
32 *Shulḥan Arukh, Oraḥ Ḥayim* 592:3.
33 *Taz,* ibid., 2.
34 *Ḥazon Ish* 137:3–5.
35 *Kol Bo* 64.

36 *Penei Yehoshua*, Rosh HaShana 34b.
37 See R. Yitzchak Yaakov Weiss, *Minḥat Yitzchak* 3:44 and 4:47, and R. Eliezer Waldenberg, *Tzitz Eliezer* 11:45.
38 See *Mishna Berura* 55:8.
39 Cited by Ritva 34b.
40 Whether or not intention to fulfill the mitzva is required; see Rosh HaShana 26b.
41 *Baḥ, Oraḥ Ḥayim* 625.
42 *Milḥamot Hashem*, Berakhot 2b.
43 *Sefer HaIkkarim* 1:4.

CHAPTER 12

1 Rema 605.
2 Ibid.
3 See, for example, *Siddur Rashi* 211, Rosh, Yoma 8:25, *Tur* and *Shulḥan Arukh* 606. See also R. Yitzchak Tessler, "*Matai Lokin Malkot BeErev Yom HaKippurim*" Yeshurun, v. 11 (Elul 5762), who discusses when lashes were generally given.
4 *Hilkhot Teshuva* 2:10.
5 Rema 406:1.
6 *Mishna Berura* 406:11.
7 *Sefer Ḥafetz Ḥayim, Hilkhot Lashon Hara* 4:12.
8 See also *Mishna Berura* 606:3.
9 See *Sefer Mikhtavei HaḤafetz Ḥayim*, p. 11; *Tenuat HaMussar*, vol. 1, p. 636.
10 *Az Nidberu* 7:66.
11 See R. Moshe Harari's *Mikra'ei Kodesh, Hilkhot Yom HaKippurim*, p. 34, n.4.
12 *Ḥayei Adam* 144.
13 See Bava Kama 92a.
14 *Tur, Oraḥ ḥayim* 606.
15 *Pirkei DeRabbi Eliezer* 45.
16 See Rosh, Yoma 8:24; *Shibbolei HaLeket* 283; *Manhig* 52; Tosafot, Berakhot 22b.
17 See *Shibbolei HaLeket*, ibid., and R. Saadia Gaon, as cited by Rosh.
18 *Arukh HaShulḥan* 606:5.
19 *Shulḥan Arukh* 606:4.
20 Rema 606:4.
21 *Magen Avraham*, ibid., 8.
22 *Mishna Berura* 606:21.
23 See *Be'er Heitev*, ibid., 8.
24 Rashi, ibid., s.v. *shema*.
25 *Hilkhot Teshuva* 2:7.

26 Ran 6a, s.v. *tannu rabbanan.*
27 *Shulḥan Arukh* 607:1.
28 *Magen Avraham* 607:7 in the name of the *Shela.*
29 See *Maḥzor Masoret HaRav LeYom HaKippurim*, p. 42.
30 See Rosh, Yoma 8:25.
31 Yoma 81b, Rosh HaShana 9a, Pesaḥim 68b, Berakhot 8b.
32 Rashi, Yoma 81b, s.v. *kol.*
33 Rashi offers a similar interpretation in his commentary on Berakhot 8b, while he explains differently in Rosh HaShana 9a.
34 Rosh, Yoma 8:22.
35 *Shibbolei HaLeket* 307.
36 *Torah Temima*, Lev. 23, n. 97.
37 *Sedei ḥemed, Maarekhet Yom HaKippurim* 10:1.
38 See *ḥelkat Yaakov* 2:58; *Tzitz Eliezer* 7:32; *Mishneh Halakhot* 2:66.
39 Rabbeinu Yona, *Shaarei Teshuva* 4:8–10.
40 Ritva, Rosh HaShana 9a.
41 R. Akiva Eiger, Responsa 16.
42 See Reshash, Sukka 28b; *Minḥat ḥinukh* 313.
43 *Haamek She'ala* 167:12.
44 *Ketav Sofer* 112.
45 *Minḥat ḥinukh* 313:9.
46 *Ein Aya* 38.
47 *Ein Aya* 38.

CHAPTER 13

1 *Hilkhot Teshuva* 1:1.
2 *Minḥat ḥinukh* 364.
3 Pinchas H. Peli (1984), *On Repentance: The Thought and Oral Discourses of R. Joseph Dov Soloveitchik*, pp. 70–76.
4 Introduction to *Hilkhot Teshuva.*
5 *Hilkhot Teshuva* 2:6.
6 Ibid., 2:7.
7 Ramban, commentary on Deut. 30:11, s.v. *ki.*
8 *Shaarei Teshuva* 14.
9 Pinchas H. Peli (1984), *On Repentance: The Thought and Oral Discourses of R. Joseph Dov Soloveitchik*, p. 52.
10 The *Shulḥan Arukh* (607:2) rules that "one is not obligated to specify the sin; [however] if one wishes to specify, one may, and if he confesses silently, it is

proper to specify the sin." *Baḥ* (607) disagrees and rules that one must specify the sin. Incidentally, while *Tosafot Yeshanim* (Yoma 86b) writes that the *al ḥet sheḥatanu lefanekha* recited on Yom Kippur is considered to be a form of "*peirut haḥet*" (specification of the sin), Rema (607:2) disagrees, explaining that since the *al ḥet* appears in the *Maḥzor*, it is considered to be part of the *nusaḥ hatefilla*, and not a personal specification of one's sins. Therefore, many are accustomed to personalize the *al ḥet*, adding specific sins as one recites the set text.

11 *ḥibbur HaTeshuva* 1:10.

12 *Hilkhot Teshuva* 1:1.

13 Ibid., 2:7–8.

14 *Vikuaḥ Rabbeinu Yeḥiel MiParis*, found at http://www.hebrewbooks.org/31982 (accesed February 1, 2012).

15 Shlomo Ashkenazi, "*Minhagei Kol Nidrei.*" *Maḥanayim* 33, 1958.

16 Elizabeth Dilling, *The Jewish Religion: Its Influence Today* (1964). p. 48.

17 *Teshuvot HaGeonim, Shaarei Teshuva* 143.

18 Raavya, Yoma 528.

19 See Rosh, Yoma 8:28.

20 *Shibbolei HaLeket* 317.

21 *Hilkhot Nedarim* 13:23–25.

CHAPTER 14

1 Rashi, Yoma 74a, s.v. *shabbaton*; Rabbeinu Tam in Tosafot, Yoma 77*a*, s.v. *ditnan*; *Tosafot Yeshanim*, Yoma 73b; Rosh, Yoma 8:1; Ritva, Yoma 73b; *ḥinukh*, 313.

2 *Sefer Yerei'im* 420.

3 *Tosafot Yeshanim*, Yoma 73b.

4 *Haamek She'ala* 167.

5 Ran, Yoma 1a.

6 We find a similar idea regarding the prohibition of *melakha* (labor) on ḥol HaMo'ed, the intermediate days of a festival (see Tosafot, ḥagiga 18a, s.v. *ḥolo shel mo'ed* and Rambam, *Hilkhot Yom Tov* 7:1, as well as *Yerei'im* 274 and Ramban, Lev. 23:24.

7 *Hilkhot Shevitat Asor* 1:1, 4–5.

8 Ran, Yoma 1a, s.v. *yom*.

9 *Maggid Mishneh* 1:5.

10 *Sefer HaMitzvot*, Positive Commandment 164.

11 *Perush HaMishna*, Yoma 8:1.

12 *Pirkei DeRabbi Eliezer* 45.

CHAPTER 15

1 See *Shemirat Shabbat KeHilkhata* 39:18, for example.
2 Ḥatam Sofer, Responsa 6:16.
3 *Mishna Berura* 618:21.
4 *Arukh HaShulḥan, Oraḥ Ḥayim* 618:14.
5 R. Yitzchak Elchanan Spektor, as cited by R. Moshe Sternbach in *Teshuvot VeHanhagot* 2:289.
6 *Marḥeshet* 14.
7 See Ḥatam Sofer 6:23.
8 *Shulḥan Arukh, Oraḥ Ḥayim* 612:10.
9 Ran, Yoma 3b, s.v. *ḥutz.*
10 *Behag*; Ramban, *Torat HaAdam*; Rosh, Yoma 8:13.
11 *Shulḥan Arukh, Oraḥ Ḥayim* 218:7.
12 Ran, Yoma 3b, s.v. *venimtzenu.*
13 See *Nishmat Avraham, Oraḥ Ḥayim* 612:4.
14 *Iggerot Moshe, Oraḥ Ḥayim* 4:41.
15 *Mishna Berura* 618:21.
16 *Arukh HaShulḥan* 618:14.
17 *Haamek She'ala* 167:17.
18 See R. Yitzchak Zev Soloveitchik's (R. Chaim's son) *Ḥiddushei HaGriz, Hilkhot Shevitat HaAsor* 2:8, as well as R. Moshe Sternbach's *Moa'dim UZemanim* 1:60 and *Teshuvot VeHanhagot* 2:288.
19 *Hilkhot Shabbat* 2:14.
20 R. Shlomo Yosef Zevin, *Mo'adim BeHalakha.*
21 See R. Chaim Jachter, *Gray Matter*, p. 43.
22 See *Nishmat Avraham*, vol. 1, p. 310.
23 See also R. Moshe Sternbach, *Teshuvot VeHanhagot* 2:288.
24 *Arukh HaShulḥan, Oraḥ Ḥayim* 618:15.
25 *Shemirat Shabbat KeHilkhata* 39:6.
26 *Yeḥave Daat* 6:39.
27 *Shemirat Shabbat KeHilkhata* 39:8.
28 Ibid.
29 *Iggerot Moshe, Oraḥ Ḥayim* 3:91.
30 Rema, *Oraḥ Ḥayim* 613:9.
31 Tosafot, ibid., s.v. *af al pi.*
32 *Shenot Eliyahu,* Shabbat 9:4.
33 As cited in *Sefer Harerei Kedem*, p. 50.
34 *Hilkhot Shevitat Asor* 3:9.

35 Tosafot, Yoma 77b, s.v. *minayin*.
36 *Shulḥan Arukh, Oraḥ Ḥayim* 618:1.
37 *Biur Halakha* 554:15.
38 Yoma 77b.
39 *Hilkhot Tefilla* 7:8.
40 Ran, Yoma 2a, s.v. *vahevi*.
41 See Yoma 88.
42 Tosafot, Yoma 77b, s.v. *mishum*.
43 *Shulḥan Arukh, Oraḥ Ḥayim* 613:3.
44 Ibid., 613:4.
45 Ibid.
46 Ibid.
47 *Mishna Berura* 613:11, for example.
48 R. Shimon Eider's *Halachos of the Three Weeks*, p. 19.
49 *Minḥat Yitzchak* 4:109.
50 Baal HaMaor, Yoma 2a
51 Rif, Yoma 2a.
52 Rosh 8:7.
53 *Hilkhot Shevitat HaAsor* 3:7.
54 *Shulḥan Arukh, Oraḥ Ḥayim* 614:4.
55 *Moa'dim UZemanim* 6:28.
56 *Panim Me'irot* 2:28.
57 Ḥatam Sofer, *Hagahot* to *Shulḥan Arukh* 614.
58 *Mishna Berura* 614:5; see also *Arukh HaShulḥan* 614:5.
59 *Ḥazon Ovadia, Yamim Noraim*, p. 31.
60 *Shalmei Mo'ed*, p. 77.
61 *Sefer She'elot UTeshuvot Maharshag* 2:110.
62 *Mateh Efraim* 614; Maharam Schick 316.
63 *Kaf HaḤayim* 614:10.
64 *Sefat Emet* 78b.
65 Rema, *Oraḥ Ḥayim* 614:4.
66 *Mishna Berura* 614:12.
67 *Beit Yosef, Oraḥ Ḥayim* 614.
68 *Mordekhai, Mo'ed Katan* 934.
69 *Shulḥan Arukh, Oraḥ Ḥayim* 615.
70 *Taz*, ibid., 615:1.
71 *Mishna Berura* 615: 1.
72 See *Shulḥan Arukh, Yoreh De'ah* 195.

CHAPTER 16

1 Tosafot, Shabbat 114b; this opinion is attributed to R. Hai Gaon in *Teshuvot HaGeonim, Shaarei Teshuva* 67.

2 See Lev. 25:9–10.

3 See *Sefer HaIttur*, end of *Hilkhot Yom HaKippurim*, who suggests that we blow the shofar every year, as the exact calculation of the Yovel years is unknown.

4 Tosafot, Shabbat 114b.

5 Roke'aḥ 217.

6 *Kol Bo* 70; see *Teshuvot HaGeonim* cited above.

7 *Semag*, Negative Commandment 69.

8 See, for example, *Maḥzor Vitry* 356 and *Mordekhai*, Yoma 723.

9 *Shulḥan Arukh, Oraḥ Ḥayim* 623:6.

10 Ran, Shabbat 2a; *Mordekhai*, Yoma 727; *Semag*, Positive Commandment 67.

11 *Shulḥan Arukh, Oraḥ Ḥayim* 426:4.

12 See *Mishna Berura* 426:20, for example.

13 Rema, *Oraḥ Ḥayim* 426:4.

14 *Levush Malkhut, Oraḥ Ḥayim* 602.

15 *Eliyahu Zuta*, ibid.

16 *Eliya Rabba* 602:7.

17 *Maase Rav* 155.

18 *Mateh Efraim* 624:4.

19 *Mordekhai, Yoma* 727.

20 See Berakhot 52b–53a. Interestingly, the Tosefta (Berakhot 5:31) implies that preferably one should use a newly lit flame for Havdala of Motza'ei Shabbat. One might explain that a new flame better commemorates the first Motza'ei Shabbat, during which Adam HaRishon lit the first flame.

21 Rashi, ibid. See also Rambam, *Hilkhot Shabbat* 9:27.

22 *Maggid Mishneh, Hilkhot Shabbat* 29:27.

23 *Shulḥan Arukh, Oraḥ Ḥayim* 624:4–5.

24 *Sefer HaManhig*, p. 362.

25 Rema, *Oraḥ Ḥayim* 624:5; see also *Mishna Berura* ibid., 12.

26 Ostensibly, a "*ner neshama*" ("yahrtzeit candle") lit in memory of a deceased relative might pose a similar problem. It is customary, however, to recite Havdala over the *ner neshama*.

27 *Kol Bo* 70, *Sefer HaMeorot*, Berakhot 53a, *Sefer HaMikhtam*, Berakhot 53a.

28 *Shibbolei HaLeket* 322.

29 *Shulḥan Arukh, Oraḥ Ḥayim* 624:4.

30 Ibid., 624:5.

31 *Eliya Rabba* 624:6; *Ḥayei Adam* 145:40; *Arukh HaShulḥan* 624:6; *Kaf HaḤayim* 624:17.
32 *Mishna Berura* 624:7.
33 *Yeḥave Daat* 1:63.
34 *Iggerot Moshe* 4:122.
35 *Kol Bo* 41.
36 See *Abudraham, Seder Motza'ei Shabbat*; Rambam, *Hilkhot Shabbat* 29:29.
37 Maharil, Responsa 34; *Abudraham, Seder Tefillat Ne'ila.*
38 *Shulḥan Arukh, Oraḥ Ḥayim* 624:2.
39 *Baḥ,* ibid.; *Magen Avraham,* ibid., 1; *Taz,* ibid., 2.
40 *Mishna Berura* 642:5.
41 *Arukh HaShulḥan, Oraḥ Ḥayim* 642:1.
42 Raavya, Berakhot 8:141. Me'iri, Berakhot 53b, and *Nimukei Yosef,* Pesaḥim 54a, citing Raa, concur. See also Ritva, *Hilkhot Berakhot,* 8:23.
43 *Mishna Berura* 642:7.
44 See Rambam, *Hilkhot Shabbat* 12:1.
45 R. Tzvi Pesach Frank, *Har Tzvi* 2:114; R. Ovadia Yosef, *Yeḥave Daat* 2:39, et al.
46 R. Chaim Ozer Grodzinski; R. Eliezer Waldenberg, *Tzitz Eliezer* 1:20:13; R. Chaim Soloveitchik, et al. For a full treatment of this topic, see R. Howard Jachter's and R. Michael Broyde's "Electrically Produced Fire or Light in Positive Commandments," *Journal of Halacha & Contemporary Society,* XXI.
47 *Teshuvot VeHanhagot* 2:302.
48 *Tzitz Eliezer* 1:20:13:5.
49 Rema, *Oraḥ Ḥayim* 624:5.
50 *Shaarei Teshuva* 243.
51 *Maḥzor Vitry* 73; *Orḥot Ḥaim, Hilkhot Havdalat Shabbat* 33, et al.
52 Rema, *Oraḥ Ḥayim* 624:5.
53 Ibid.

CHAPTER 17

1 See Nehemiah 9:19.
2 Ramban, Lev. 23:43.
3 Rashbam, Lev. 23:43.
4 Commentaries to Lev. 23:43.
5 *Tur* and *Shulḥan Arukh* 625.
6 See also *Peri Megadim, Mishbetzot Zahav* 625:1.
7 *Baḥ* 625.
8 *Tur* 8.

9 Ibid., 25.
10 *Mishna Berura* 625:1.
11 *Bikkurei Yaakov* 3.
12 *Mishna Berura* 625:1.
13 Ḥatam Sofer, *Yoreh De'ah* 271.
14 *She'iltot* 169.
15 *Haamek She'ala*, ibid.
16 *Kitzur Shulḥan Arukh* 134:1; *Kaf Haḥayim* 625:11.
17 *Or Zarua, Hilkhot Tefillin* 583.
18 Tosafot, Sukka 46a, s.v. *nikhnas.*
19 Rambam, *Hilkhot Berakhot* 11:9; Ritva, Sukka 46a, et al.
20 See, for example, *Or Zarua* 2:316, citing *Behag.*
21 Rosh, Responsa 25:3.
22 *Mordekhai*, Sukka 769.
23 *Shulḥan Arukh* 641.
24 Rema 624:5.
25 *Shaarei Teshuva* 625.
26 *Magen Avraham* 625:1.

CHAPTER 18

1 *Ḥayei Adam* 146:3.
2 Sukka 2a; *Shulḥan Arukh* 633:8.
3 *Shulḥan Arukh* 630:9.
4 See Ritva, Sukka 16a.
5 *Hilkhot Sukka* 4:11.
6 Rosh, Sukka 1:6.
7 Ran, Sukka 2a s.v. *vegarsinan.*
8 *Shulkhan Arukh* 630:6.
9 *Mishna Berura* 630:30.
10 *Penei Yehoshua* 6b; *Arukh LaNer* 6b; see also R. Tzvi Pesach Frank's *Mikra'ei Kodesh*, Sukkot 1:7.
11 *Tur* 630.
12 *Shulḥan Arukh* 630:9.
13 R. Akiva Eiger, Responsa 12.
14 Ran, Sukka 9a.
15 Rabbeinu Ḥananel, Raavad, *Sefer HaIttur.*
16 *Hillkhot Sukka* 4:1.
17 *Shulḥan Arukh* 634:2.

18 *Mishna Berura* 634:1.

19 *Shulḥan Arukh* 630:2.

20 *Ḥazon Ish* (*Yoreh De'ah* 172:2) writes that this *tzurat hapetaḥ* should be composed of two vertical beams: one next to the *tefaḥ* of wall and one across from it.

21 *Mishna Berura* 630:9.

22 *Ḥazon Ish*, ibid.

23 See *Shaar HaTziyun* 3.

24 *Mishna Berura* 630:11.

25 *Peri Megadim, Mishbetzot Zahav* 630:3 and *Eishel Avraham* 630:7.

26 *Shulḥan Arukh* 630:3

27 *Mishna Berura* 630:16.

28 *Shemirat Shabbat KeHilkhata* p. 24 ft. 115; see also R. Tzvi Pesach Frank's *Mikra'ei Kodesh* 1:11.

29 Rif, 2b; Ran, ad loc., s.v. *she'amar*.

30 Eiruvin 15b; *Shulḥan Arukh* 362:4.

31 *Shulḥan Arukh* 362:10.

32 Rashi, Sukka 7b s.v. *mah*; see *Maggid Mishneh, Hilkhot Sukka* 4:12.

33 *Hilkhot Sukka* 4:12.

34 *Toldot Adam VeḤava* 5:1.

35 Ritva, 7b s.v. *amar*.

36 Rosh, Sukka 1:8.

37 *Hilkhot Sukka* 4:12; see *Ḥiddushei HaRav Chaim HaLevi Soloveitchik, Hilkhot Shabbat* 16:16.

38 *Shulḥan Arukh* 630:5.

39 *Taz* 630:6.

40 *Magen Avraham* 630:6.

41 *Mishna Berura* 630:22.

42 *Ḥazon Ish* 75:13.

43 *Mishna Berura* 630:23.

44 *Shulḥan Arukh* 630:5.

45 Rema 630:5.

46 *Mishna Berura* 630:28.

CHAPTER 19

1 *Shulḥan Arukh* 630:1. Interestingly, the *Or Zarua* (*Hilkhot Sukka* 289:2; see also *Hagahot Asheri* 1:24) cites a Yerushalmi that warns that one may not construct a *sukka* from materials that are *mekabel tuma* (objects that potentially may become *tamei*, ritually impure) – that is, materials that may not be used for *sekhakh*. This

position is troubling not only because the Gemara consistently implies that one may use objects that are *mekabel tuma* for walls, but also because our text of the Yerushalmi (1:6) implies precisely the opposite! Although *Baḥ* suggests that one should refrain from constructing the walls from materials that one may not use for *sekhakh*, the *Aḥaronim* reject this stringency.

2 *Shaar HaTziyun* 630:45.

3 *Shulḥan Arukh* 630:10.

4 *ḥazon Ish, Hilkhot Eiruvin* 13:6.

5 *Kiryat Sefer, Hilkhot Sukka,* chap. 4.

6 *Be'er Heitev* 630:10.

7 *ḥazon Ish, Oraḥ ḥayim* 52:14.

8 *Magen Avraham* 630:15.

9 *Emek Berakha,* Sukka 19.

10 *Mikra'ei Kodesh,* Sukka 1:2.

11 *Iggerot Moshe, Oraḥ ḥayim* 5:40:2.

12 *ḥazon Ish, Hilkhot Eiruvin* 13:6.

13 *Iggerot Moshe, Oraḥ ḥayim* 5:40:2.

14 *Yeḥave Daat* 3:46.

15 *Tur* 630.

16 *Shulḥan Arukh* 6:30.

17 *Mo'adim UZemanim* 1:84.

18 *Iggerot Moshe, Oraḥ ḥayim* 5:40:2.

19 *Sukka KeHilkhata,* chap. 4, n. 2; *ḥeiko Mamtakim* 630:42.

20 It is worth noting that the *Arukh HaShulḥan* (530:32) writes that *bediavad,* if one tied the canvas walls, the *sukka* is valid.

21 *Shulḥan Arukh* 630:10.

22 *Magen Avraham* 630; see also *Mishna Berura* 630:7.

23 Tosafot, Sukka *16b,* s.v. *befaḥot.*

24 Rashi, Sukka 21b, s.v. *she'ein.*

25 *Hasagot HaRaavad,* Sukka 10a.

26 Rashi, Sukka *21b,* s.v. *shemaamida.*

27 Raavad, Sukka 10a; Ritva 21b s.v. *veḥad;* Ran, 21b s.v. *matnitin.* Some question why it is forbidden to place *sekhakh* upon the legs of a bed while it is permitted to construct a *sukka* on the top of a tree, which is also invalid for *sekhakh.* Raavad (in *Hasagot HaRaavad,* Sukka 10a) suggests that since it is uncommon to use trees – which are attached to the ground and cannot be used as *sekhakh* – when building a *sukka,* the Rabbis saw no reason to prohibit "*maamid*" (supporting) on a tree. Alternatively, Ramban (*Milḥamot Hashem,* Sukka 10a) notes that the Rabbis prohibited supporting *sekhakh* on a material that is invalid for *sekhakh;* one who

builds a *sukka in* a treetop, however, does not place the *sekhakh* on the tree, but rather rests the *sukka on* the tree.

28 See Commentary on the Mishna, and note his omission of this halakha in the *Mishneh Torah*.

29 Baal HaMaor, Sukka 10a.

30 Raavya 631.

31 Maharil, Responsa 83.

32 Rosh, Sukka 1:1.

33 *Milḥamot Hashem*, Sukka 10a.

34 *Shulḥan Arukh* 630:3.

35 Ibid., 629:7.

36 See Sukka 14a.

37 *Taz* 629:10.

38 *Magen Avraham* 629:9.

39 *Arukh HaShulḥan* 629:19.

40 *Mishna Berura* 630:59; see also *Shaar HaTziyun* 60.

41 *Shulḥan Arukh* 629:8.

42 See *Mishna Berura* 629:26 and *Shaar HaTziyun* 51.

43 *ḥazon Ish* 143:2.

44 Rashi, 17a s.v. *pesula*.

45 Rashi, ibid., s.v. *paḥot*.

46 Ritva, Sukka 4a.

47 Ran, Sukka 2a; *Maggid Mishneh* 4:14.

48 *Hilkhot Sukka* 4:14.

49 See R. H. Reichman, *Reshimot Shiurim*, Sukka (4a).

50 *Shulḥan Arukh* 632:1, 633:6–7.

CHAPTER 20

1 Rashi, Sukka 2a, s.v. *delo shalta*.

2 Rosh, Sukka 1:13.

3 Rambam, *Hilkhot Sukka* 6:15.

4 R. Zvi Reichman, *Reshimot Shiurim* (Sukka), p. 5.

5 *Or Zarua*, *Hilkhot Sukka* 289:2; see also *Hagahot Asheri* 1:24. Our text of the Yerushalmi (1:6) actually indicates the opposite conclusion.

6 *Shulḥan Arukh* 629:1.

7 Rashi, ibid., s.v. *bivlai*.

8 *Hilkhot Sukka* 5:37.

9 *Arukh HaShulḥan* 629:5.

10 *Shevet HaLevi* 3:95.
11 *Tzitz Eliezer* 13:66.
12 *Sukka KeHilkhata*, p. 59 and *Sefer HaSukka HaShalem*, p. 270, citing Keilim 16:5.
13 Rashi, Sukka 11a, s.v. *pesula*
14 Ritva, Sukka 11a.
15 *Shulḥan Arukh* 629:18.
16 Rashi, Sukka 14a, s.v. *Rabbi Meir*.
17 Ritva, Sukka 14a, s.v. *amar*.
18 Ran, Sukka 7b.
19 See Bava Metzia 117a.
20 Rashba, Responsa 1:213.
21 *Magen Avraham* 632:1.
22 *Ḥayei Adam* 146:31.
23 Rosh, Sukka 1:37.
24 *Shulḥan Arukh* 629:6.
25 Rema, ibid.
26 See *Biur Halakha* 629:6.
27 *Mishna Berura* 629:18.
28 *Iggerot Moshe, Oraḥ Ḥayim* 1:177.
29 See Rambam, *Hilkhot Sukka* 5:6. This is the conclusion of R. Ovadia Yosef, *Yeḥave Daat* 1:64; see also *Piskei Teshuvot* 629:6. R. Yehuda Paris, "*Keshirat Sekhakh LaNetzaḥ al yedei Ḥutei Barzel*," *Teḥumin* 15, argues for the permissibility of tying down *sekhakh* with copper wire.
30 Responsa *Az Nidberu* 2:66.
31 *Tzitz Eliezer* 10:29.
32 R. Binyamin Zilber, Responsa *Az Nidberu* 2:66; R. Ovadia Yosef, *Ḥazon Ovadia*, p. 28; R. Shmuel Wosner, *Shevet HaLevi* 6:74; R. Shlomo Zalman Auerbach, *Halikhot Shlomo*, p. 128.
33 Rif, Sukka 8b.
34 *Hilkhot Sukka* 5:14.
35 Rosh, Sukka 1:32.
36 Ran, Sukka 8b.
37 Baal HaMaor, Sukka 7a.
38 *Hasagot Raavad*, Sukka 7a.
39 Ritva, Sukka 19a.
40 *Shulḥan Arukh* 632.
41 *Mishna Berura* 632:3.
42 *Hilkhot Sukka* 5:20.
43 Rosh, Sukka 1:33.

44 *Shulḥan Arukh* 631.

45 Ritva, Sukka *18a*, s.v. *amar Abaye*; Ran, Sukka 9a.

46 Rosh, Sukka *1:36*; Rabbeinu Yeruḥam, *Toldot Adam VeḤava* 8:1.

47 Rema 632:2.

48 Interestingly, R. Shlomo b. Yehoshua Adeni (early seventeenth century), in his commentary on the Mishna, *Melekhet Shlomo* (Sukka 2:1), suggests that although one may not sleep under a gap of less than three *tefaḥim*, one may eat there. The *Biur Halakhah* (632:2), however, rules that one should not distinguish between sleeping and eating.

49 Tosafot, ibid., s.v. *ilu*; Rosh, Sukka 1:33; *Shulḥan Arukh* 632:4.

50 *Bikkurei Yaakov* 632:9; *Mishna Berura* 632:19.

51 *Tur* 626–627.

52 *Eishel Avraham* 631:2.

53 *Bikkurei Yaakov* 631:5.

54 *Hagahot Maimoniyot, Hilkhot Sukka* 5:9.

55 *Mordekhai*, Sukka 1:732.

56 Rosh, Sukka 8:2.

57 *Eishel Avraham* 631:2.

58 *Bikkurei Yaakov* 631:4; see also *Hagahot Maimoniyot, Hilkhot Sukka* 5:9; *Ḥayei Adam* 146:18.

59 *Baḥ* 635.

60 *Shulḥan Arukh HaRav* 631:5.

61 *Ḥayei Adam* 146:18.

62 *Arukh HaShulḥan* 632:6.

63 *Mishna Berura* 632:6.

64 Rosh, Sukka 1:12.

65 *Baḥ* 631, 635.

66 Rashi, Sukka 22b, s.v. *kazuza*.

67 Tosafot, Sukka 22b, s.v. *kazuza*.

68 *Shulḥan Arukh* 631:1.

69 Ibid., 631:2.

70 Rema, ibid.

71 Rashi, ibid., s.v. *bésheḥavatan*.

72 Raavya 613.

73 Tosafot, Sukka 10a; Rosh 1:14.

74 *Shulḥan Arukh* 626:1.

75 *Biur Halakha*, ibid., s.v. *veyesh*.

76 *Tur* 626.

77 *Shulḥan Arukh* 626:3.

78 Rif, Sukka 10a; Rosh, Sukka 2:1; Rambam, Commentary on the Mishna, Sukka 2:1, *Hilkhot Sukka* 5:23; *Baḥ* 626.
79 Baal HaMaor, Sukka 10a.
80 *Milḥamot Hashem*, Sukka 10a.
81 Rashba, Responsa 1:55.
82 Rif, Rambam, *Semag*, Rosh, and *Shulḥan Arukh* 629:19, 627:4.
83 Me'iri, Sukka 10a.
84 Rosh, Sukka 1:18, for example.
85 See *Mishna Berura* 627:11 and *Shaar HaTziyun* 14–16.
86 Rema 627:4.
87 *Mishna Berura* 627:15.
88 *Hilkhot Sukka* 5:17.
89 *Mordekhai* 736.
90 See Tosafot, Sukka 10a.
91 Tosafot, ibid.
92 Rosh, Sukka 1:14.
93 *Tur* 629.
94 *Tur* 626.
95 *Beit Yosef* 629.
96 *Baḥ* 629.
97 *Shulḥan Arukh* 629:19.
98 *Magen Avraham* 629:25.
99 *Mishna Berura* 629:55.
100 *Shulḥan Arukh* 638:2.

CHAPTER 21

1 Rif 4b; Rambam, *Hilkhot Sukka* 5:9. Radbaz suggests that the Yerushalmi was explaining *Beit Shammai*'s position, in which case the passage is certainly rejected.
2 *Shibbolei HaLeket, Seder Ḥag HaSukkot* 337.
3 Ran, Sukka 1a.
4 *Beit Yosef* 446. It is worth noting, however, that most *Rishonim*, aside from R. Yehudai Gaon, do not say this explicitly, but rather merely cite the passage from the Yerushalmi.
5 *Shulḥan Arukh* 636:1.
6 *Magen Avraham* 636:1.
7 *Taz* 636:3.
8 *Mishna Berura* 636:4 and *Shaar HaTziyun* 4, citing the *Ḥayei Adam* and *Bikkurei Yaakov*; *Arukh HaShulḥan* 636:2.

9 R. Shlomo HaKohen of Vilna (1828–1905) discusses this topic at great length in his responsa *Binyan Shlomo* (43) and brings proofs to support the opinion that views this *ḥiddush* as a *mitzva min hamuvḥar* and not strictly required. In addition, he offers a unique and compelling explanation of the Yerushalmi. While most understand that the Yerushalmi maintains that even *Beit Hillel* prefers that a *sukka* be built with intent, the *Binyan Shlomo* argues that one should add to the *sukka* for an entirely different reason – in order to personally participate in the building of the *sukka*, in fulfillment of the principle of "*mitzva bo yoter mibisheluḥo.*" (As we discussed previously, some sources imply that building a *sukka* itself constitutes a mitzva.)

10 *Tur* 636.

11 *Shulḥan Arukh* 636:1.

12 *Sefer HaIttur, Hilkhot Sukka*; Rosh, Sukka 1:13; Ritva, Sukka 2:1; Me'iri, Sukka 9a.

13 See, for example, Rosh, Sukka *1:13* and *Korban Netanel,* ad loc. 20.

14 *Shulḥan Arukh* 636:1.

15 *Mishna Berura* 636:5; see also *Shaar HaTziyun* 4.

16 Rashi, Sukka 8b, s.v. *amar.*

17 Cited by Rosh, Sukka 1:12.

18 Ran, Sukka 4a. The *Aḥaronim* (*Baḥ, Taz,* and *Magen Avraham*) disagree regarding whether Rashi would agree with Ran.

19 *Shulḥan Arukh* 635

20 *Arukh HaShulḥan* 635:2.

21 *Binyan Shlomo* 43.

22 *Hilkhot Sukka* 5:9.

23 *Hagahot Maimoniyot, Hilkhot Sukka* 5:30.

24 Rema 635.

25 *Baḥ* 635.

26 *Magen Avraham* 635:4.

27 *Arukh HaShulḥan* 635:5.

28 *Taz* 635:4.

29 *Beit Yosef* 626.

30 *Orḥot Ḥayim, Hilkhot Sukka* 26.

31 *Beit Yosef* 626.

32 Rema 626:2–3.

33 See *Mishna Berura* 626:18.

34 Rashi, ibid., s.v. *al.*

35 *Arukh LaNer,* Sukka 9a. s.v. *shem.*

36 Rashba, Beitza 30b.

37 *Taz* 338.

38 *Tur* 639.
39 See Yoma 69.
40 *Oneg Yom Tov* 49.
41 *Biur HaGra* 639:22.
42 *Mishna Berura* 638:4.
43 *Hilkhot Sukka* 6:15.
44 Tosafot, Sukka 9a, s.v. *minayin.*
45 Rosh, Sukka 1:13.
46 *Shulḥan Arukh* 338:1.
47 Rema, ibid.
48 Tosafot, ibid., s.v. *sukka.*
49 *Shulḥan Arukh* 338:3.
50 Rema, ibid.

CHAPTER 22

1 *Sefer HaMitzvot,* Positive Commandment 168.
2 Ran, Sukka 12b, s.v. *matnitin.*
3 *Tur* 639.
4 Ritva, Sukka 27a.
5 *Shulḥan Arukh* 639:3.
6 *Mishna Berura* 639:22.
7 *Shulḥan Arukh* 639:2.
8 Tosafot, Sukka 27a, s.v. *teshvu.*
9 See *Shaarei Teshuva* 639:5.
10 *Mishna Berura* 639:21.
11 Rabbeinu Peretz, comment on *Semak* 93.
12 Rosh, Sukka 3:20.
13 Rema 639:2.
14 *Magen Avraham* 639:11.
15 *Taz* 472:2.
16 *Biur Halakha* 639, s.v. *lo yokhal.*
17 *Peri Megadim, Mishbetzot Zahav* 643 and *Eishel Avraham* 539:16; see also *Bikkurei Yaakov* 539.
18 Tosafot, Sukka 27a, s.v. *teshvu.*
19 Rosh, Sukka 3:15.
20 *Or Zarua* 301.
21 Maharil, *Hilkhot Sukkot* 18.
22 *Leket Yosher, Oraḥ Ḥayim,* p. 144.

23 *Magen Avraham* 539:12; Gra 539; *Shulḥan Arukh HaRav* 539:20; *Mishna Berura* 539:27.
24 See *Shulḥan Arukh* 471.
25 Rashba, Responsa 4:78.
26 "*Mitzvot tzerikhot kavana*"; see *Shulḥan Arukh* 60:4.
27 *Baḥ* 625; *Magen Avraham* 625; *Mishna Berura* 625.
28 *Minḥat Ḥinukh* 325.
29 *Atvan Deoraita*, chap. 11.
30 Responsa *Avnei Nezer, Oraḥ Ḥayim* 481.
31 R. Akiva Eiger, Sukka 25a.
32 *Yesod VeShoresh HaAvoda, Shaar HaIttun*, chap. 12.
33 *Hilkhot Sukka* 6:6.
34 Rif, Sukka 22a. See also R. Hai Gaon, as cited by Rosh, and *Orḥot Ḥayim, Hilkhot Sukka* 39.
35 *Hilkhot Sukka* 6:12.
36 See Rosh 4:3; *Torah Temima*, Leviticus 23:42, proposes that according to Rambam, one who eats in the *sukka* while standing has not fulfilled the mitzva.
37 Berakhot 1:13; see Rosh, Sukka 4:3; Tosafot, Berakhot 11b, s.v. *shekevar*.
38 *Shulḥan Arukh* 629:8.
39 *Taz* 639:20.
40 *Mishna Berura* 639:48.
41 *Ḥayei Adam* 147:15.
42 *Maamar Mordekhai* 639:8.
43 *Mishna Berura* 639:46.
44 See *Sefer HaSukka HaShalem*, p. 654.
45 See *Piskei Teshuvot* p. 639, n. 91.
46 Ritva, Sukka 45b.
47 Rosh, Sukka 4:3.
48 Me'iri, *Berakhot* 40b.
49 *Shulḥan Arukh* 643:3.
50 Maharil, *Minhagim, Hilkhot Ḥag HaPesaḥ*; see also *Sefer HaIttur, Hilkhot Matza UMarror*.
51 *Magen Avraham* 639.
52 *Sefer HaMikhtam* 27a; *Orḥot Ḥayim* 26.
53 Ibn Ezra, Ex. 12:15.
54 *Ḥizkuni*, Ex. 12:19.
55 Rosh, Responsa 23:3.
56 See Eiruvin 96b; *tefillin*, which are described as an "*ot*," are not worn on a day described as an "*ot*."

57 *Maase Rav* 185.
58 Ḥatam Sofer, Responsa, *Yoreh De'ah* 2:191.
59 *Arukh HaShulḥan* 475:18.
60 Baal HaMaor, Pesaḥim 26b–27a.
61 *Avnei Nezer, Oraḥ Ḥayim* 376.
62 Ḥatam Sofer, *Oraḥ Ḥayim* 639.
63 *Haamek Davar*, Lev. 23:6.
64 See Sukka 11b.

CHAPTER 23

1 See Ritva, Sukka 25a, s.v. *okhlin*. See also Ran, 11a s.v. *okhlin* and Raa 25a s.v. *okhlin*.
2 See, for example, Rashi 26a s.v. *tartei*; Tosafot 26a s.v. *tartei*; Rambam, *Hilkhot Sukka* 6:6; Ritva 26a s.v. *okhlin*.
3 *Shulḥan Arukh* 639:2.
4 Some *Rishonim* cite R. Avigdor Kohen Tzedek (*Shibbolei HaLeket* 444), who insists that on Shabbat and Yom Tov, *all* food is considered to be *akhilat keva*, as we see regarding the laws of *terumot* and *maasrot* (see Beitza 34b). Many *Rishonim* disagree (see, for example, *Maharaḥ Or Zarua*, Responsa 71). Similarly, some *Aḥaronim* (*Tzelaḥ*, Berakhot 49b; see also *Hagahot R. Akiva Eiger* 639:2 and the *Bikkurei Yaakov* 20) insist that we consider *all* bread eaten on Yom Tov to be an *akhilat keva*, regardless of its size, which must be eaten in the *sukka*. Most *Aḥaronim* (*Eliya Rabba* 11; *Magen Avraham* 639:10; *Mishna Berura* 639:23; see also *Seridei Esh* 2:41 and *Tzitz Eliezer* 16:20) do not distinguish between Shabbat and Ḥol HaMo'ed regarding *akhilat arai* and *akhilat keva*.
5 Rosh, Sukka 2:13.
6 Interestingly, some (see Me'iri, Sukka 26b, s.v. *umah*) suggest that one should still distinguish between fruits eaten as a snack and those eaten for a meal, and some *Aḥaronim* relate to this stringency (see *Ḥayei Adam* 147:3, who recommends being stringent when sitting down to eat fruit with other people).
7 *Shulḥan Arukh* 639:2.
8 Rema, ibid.; see also *Mishna Berura* 639:13.
9 Tosafot, Sukka 27a, s.v. *beminei*; Ritva, Sukka 27b, s.v. *veha*; *Tosafot Rabbeinu Peretz* cited by Rosh, Sukka 2:14.
10 Rosh; Tosafot, Pesaḥim 107b, s.v. *minei targima*; *Tur* 639.
11 *Shulḥan Arukh* 639:2.
12 See *Ḥayei Adam* 3 and *Bikkurei Yaakov* 15, for example.
13 *Mishna Berura* 639:15; *Biur Halakha*, s.v. *kava*; see also R. Ovadia Yosef, Responsa *Yeḥave Daat* 1:65.

14 *Mishna Berura* 639:16. Some *Aḥaronim*, due to this doubt, suggest that one should recite the blessing of *leishev basukka before* the blessing recited on the food. They fear that since the food itself may not warrant the blessing, but rather the sitting in the *sukka*, the blessing of *leishev basukka* may constitute an interruption between the blessing and eating the food. The common custom, however, is to recite the blessing upon eating more than a *kebeitza* of grain-based food (cooked or baked) *after* the blessing recited over the food.

15 *Baḥ* 639.

16 *Eliya Rabba* 639:13.

17 *Ḥayei Adam* 147:3.

18 See also Rashi, Sukka 20b s.v. *lo*, Rambam *Hilkhot Sukka* 6:5, and *Shulḥan Arukh* 639:1.

19 Ritva, Sukka 2a.

20 *Baḥ* 639.

21 *Mordekhai* 741; Rosh, Sukka 2:13; *Tur* 639.

22 *Shulḥan Arukh* 639:2.

23 Rema, ibid.

24 See *Biur Halakha*, ibid., s.v. *veyayin*. Interestingly, *Shaar HaTziyun* (29) suggests that even water drunk as part of a meal must be had in the *sukka*, regarding which he concludes, "*vetzarikh iyun*."

25 *Shulḥan Arukh, Oraḥ Ḥayim* 639:2. The *Mishna Berura* (11) cites the *Peri Megadim*, who defines a *sheinat arai* as the time it takes to walk 100 *amot*, or slightly under a minute.

26 See *Bikkurei Yaakov* 34, for example.

27 *Tosefet Maase Rav*, p. 13.

28 See *Mordekhai* 741; Me'iri, Sukka 26a.

29 Rema 639:2.

30 *Darkhei Moshe* 639.

31 See Raavya 646.

32 Rema, Responsa 29.

33 *Yerei'im* 421.

34 Rema 640:4.

35 *Mishna Berura* 640:18.

36 *Magen Avraham* 640:8.

37 *Taz* 640:9; see also *Darkhei Moshe*.

38 See *Mishna Berura* 640:18; see also *Leket Yosher*, who describes that this was the practice of his teacher, *Terumat HaDeshen*.

39 *Darkhei Moshe* 639.

CHAPTER 24

1 Rashi, Sukka 26a, s.v. *holkhei*; see also Tosafot, Sukka 26a, s.v. *holkhei*.
2 Rashba, Responsa 7:296.
3 See Ramban, Lev. 23:42.
4 Ritva, Sukka 28b.
5 See, for example, Me'iri, Sukka 26b, who cites *Ḥakhmei Lunel*; see also Tosafot, Berakhot 49b, s.v. *iy*.
6 Rashba, Responsa 4:78; Ritva, Sukka 26a, s.v. *ha de'amrinan*; see also Ran, Sukka 12b, s.v. *matni*.
7 See *Magen Avraham* 640:15; *Eliya Rabba* 640:23.
8 *Peri Megadim, Eishel Avraham* 640:15.
9 *Iggerot Moshe, Oraḥ Ḥayim* 3:93. In a later responsum (*Even HaEzer* 4:32), written in 1980 to R. Elyakim Ellinson, R. Feinstein defends his position, but suggests that one who visits the Land of Israel during Sukkot, a trip that generally entails great effort and expense, and who wishes to see as much of Israel as possible, may rely upon the exemption of *holkhei derakhim*, as his trip is not for "enjoyment," but rather a necessity.
10 *Ḥazon Ovadia*, Sukkot, pp. 166–8.
11 See, for example, R. Binyamin Zilber in his responsa *Az Nidbaru* 11:34.
12 See, for example, Baal HaMaor, Sukka 7a.
13 Rambam, *Hilkhot Shabbat* 30:13; Rif 7b; Rosh 1:35.
14 *Or Zarua, Hilkhot Sukka* 299.
15 Rema 640:3.
16 *Magen Avraham* 640:4.
17 Tosafot, Sukka 26a, s.v. *veḥayavin*.
18 Me'iri, Sukka 26a, s.v. *holkhei*.
19 Rema 640:8.
20 *Magen Avraham* 640:15.
21 See *Levush* 640:8; *Mishna Berura* 640:41–42; see also *Biur Halakha*, ibid.; *Arukh HaShulḥan* 640:17.
22 *Orḥot Ḥayim, Hilkhot Sukka* 33; see also *Sefer HaMikhtam*, Sukka 26a.
23 Rema 640:8.
24 *Levush* 640:8; see also *Ḥayei Adam* 147:22; *Mishna Berura* 640:40.
25 See http://www.vbm-torah.org/sukkot/suk-ral.htm (accessed October 10, 2012).
26 *Hilkhot Tzitzit* 3:11.
27 See, for example, Tosafot, Sukkot 26a, s.v. *holkhei*.
28 *Levush* 640:3; see also *Mishna Berura* 640:9 and *Arukh HaShulḥan* 640:3.
29 *Taz* 640:8; see also Maharik 178 and *Teshuvot HaGeonim, musafiya* 51.

30 *Levush* 640:3; see also *Shulḥan Arukh HaRav* 640:7 and *Mishna Berura* 640:7.

31 *Shulḥan Arukh* 640:3–4.

32 *Shevut Yaakov* 3:51.

33 *Shulḥan Arukh* 640:3.

34 Cited by Ritva 28b; see also Ramban, Lev. 23:42.

35 *Taz* 640:8.

36 *Baḥ* 625.

37 Rema 640:4.

38 *Terumat HaDeshen*, Responsa 93.

39 *Shulḥan Arukh* 640:4.

40 Rema, ibid.

41 *Tur* 640.

42 *Biur Halakha* 640.

43 Ran, Sukka *12a*, s.v. *ḥatan*.

44 Rema 640:4.

45 *Taz* 640:6.

46 Rashi Sukka 25b, s.v. *tzaara*.

47 Rema 639:2.

48 *Yerei'im* 421.

49 Rema 660:4.

50 *Ḥakham Tzvi* 94; see also *Shaarei Teshuva* 640:5; *Mishna Berura* 640:20; *Shaar HaTziyun* 25.

51 Gra, *Biur HaGra* 640:4, offers numerous examples in which discomfort may indeed invalidate the *sukka*; see *Shulḥan Arukh* 634:1, 633:9, 628:1.

52 *Mishna Berura* 640:18.

53 *Peri Megadim, Eishel Avraham* 640:6.

54 *Mishna Berura* 640:20; *Arukh HaShulḥan* 640:9.

55 Rema 640:4.

56 *Mishna Berura* 640:25 and 639:39.

57 Rema 639:7.

58 Rosh, Berakhot 7:23; Rashba, Responsa 4:75.

59 *Tur* 640.

60 Ran, Sukka 13a, s.v. *matnitin*.

61 Ritva, Sukka 29a, s.v. *tannu rabbanan*.

62 Radbaz, Responsa 6:320.

63 *Shulḥan Arukh* 639:6.

64 Hosea 4:6.

65 See Sukka 2b.

66 See Tosafot, Berakhot 49b, s.v. *iy*; Rosh, Berakhot 7:23; *Hagahot Asheri*, Sukka 2:20. See also Me'iri, Sukka 26a who reports that often, if it would rain on the first night of Sukkot, his teachers would "put their hats on their heads and eat in the *sukka*."

67 Rashba, Responsa 4:78; Ritva, Sukka 26a, s.v. *ha de'amrinan*.

68 Rema 639:5.

69 See, for example, *Hagahot R. Akiva Eiger* 639:7, which cites *Tzelaḥ*; see also *Mishna Berura* 639:35, who also discusses whether one should wait until midnight, in case it may stop raining.

70 *Taz* 639:17.

71 *Biur HaGra* 639:7.

72 *Sefer Maase Rav* 217.

73 See *Terumat HaDeshen* 95, who concludes that one who wishes to be stringent may eat a *kezayit* of bread in the *sukka before* concluding the meal; see Radbaz, Responsa 6:320.

74 *Mishna Berura* 639:36.

75 *Levush* 639:6.

76 *Arukh HaShulḥan* 639:24.

77 See Rema 639:7, who writes that even a bit of rain may justify returning to the house if one is sleeping in the *sukka*.

78 See Rosh HaShana 16b.

79 Tosafot, Sukka 25a, s.v. *sheluḥei*.

80 Raavad and Rif, Sukka 11b; see also Ran, Sukka 11a, s.v. *ve'ika*.

81 *Derisha, Yoreh De'ah* 341.

82 *Taz, Oraḥ Ḥayim* 108:1.

83 See *Shaar HaTziyun* 475:39.

84 Rema 38:8.

85 *Shulḥan Arukh* 640:7; see *Mishna Berura* 640:35.

86 See *Sefer Sukka KeHilkhata*, p. 130, n. 25.

CHAPTER 25

1 Rashi, Sukka 41a, s.v. *bamikdash*.

2 *Parashat Emor, parasha* 12.

3 *Kovetz Ḥiddushei Torah*, p. 114; see also R. Tzvi Reichman, *Reshimot Shiurim*, p. 115.

4 Rashi, Sukka 29b.

5 Tosafot, Sukka 29b, s.v. *ba'inan*.

6 Rosh, Sukka 3:1.

7 *Hilkhot Lulav* 8:9.

8 *Milḥamot Hashem,* Sukka 15a.

9 R. Soloveitchik attributes this explanation to his father, R. Moshe Soloveitchik. See also *Kovetz Ḥiddushei Torah* and *Reshimot Shiurim,* cited above.

10 The Gemara (Sukka 29b–30a) disqualifies a stolen lulav for an additional reason – *mitzva habaa be'aveira.*

11 *Shulḥan Arukh* 658:9.

12 Rema 649:5.

13 *Terumat HaDeshen* 100.

14 Rashi, Sukka 29b; Tosafot, Sukka 29b, s.v. *ba'inan*; Rosh, Sukka 3:1.

15 *Hilkhot Lulav* 8:9; see also *Raavad* 8:9, as well as in his *Hilkhot Lulav,* who claims that a *lulav hayavesh* (dried out lulav) is invalid for the entire week for a different reason. He cites the Yerushalmi (Sukka 3:1), which states, "Rav Avin in the name of R. Yuda b. Pazi said, *Yavesh* is disqualified on account of 'The dead shall not praise the Lord' (Ps. 115:17)."

16 *Shulḥan Arukh* 649:5.

17 Rema, ibid.

18 Rema 649:5. The *Mishna Berura* (649:36; see also *Magen Avraham* 648:9) notes that the *Aḥaronim* disagree as to whether an etrog whose *pitom* has fallen off is considered to be "*ḥaser*", and therefore valid for the rest of the week, or whether it is not considered to be "*hadar,*" in which case it would be disqualified all week according to some *Rishonim,* as we saw above. He concludes that one should preferably use a different etrog with an intact *pitom.*

19 See Rashi, Sukka 36b, s.v. *umesaninan*; Tosafot, Sukka 29b, s.v. *ba'inan* and 34b, s.v. *shetehe*; Rosh, Sukka 3:3.

20 Ritva, Sukka 29b, s.v. *bishlama.*

21 *Hilkhot Lulav* 8:9.

22 Ritva, Sukka 29a, s.v. *vekhol she'amarnu.*

23 *Shulḥan Arukh* 659:5; see *Mishna Berura* 649:50; R. Soloveitchik discusses this issue in his *Kovetz Ḥiddushei Torah,* p. 148.

24 Ritva, Sukka 11b.

25 Maharil, *Seder Tefillot Ḥag HaSukkot*; see *Kappot Temarim,* Sukka 36b, who relates that "*ḥasidim ve'anshei maase*" only use a leaf from the lulav.

26 *Yerei'im* 124; also cited in *Mordekhai,* Sukka 748.

27 *Shulḥan Arukh* 651:1.

28 *Tur* 651.

29 Rema 651:1; see also *Darkhei Moshe* 651; *Magen Avraham* 651:3.

30 *Eishel Avraham* 647.

31 *Mishna Berura* 651:8.

32 *Arukh HaShulḥan* 651:7.
33 Ḥatam Sofer, Sukka 36a; *Bikkurei Yaakov* 651:8.
34 See, for example, *Peri Megadim, Eishel Avraham* 651:3; *Bikkurei Yaakov* 651:5.
35 *Shaarei Teshuva* 651:3.
36 Rema 651:1.
37 *Magen Avraham* 651:5.
38 *Taz* 651:1; *Shulḥan Arukh HaRav* 651:11.
39 *Eliya Rabba* 651:6, *Kitzur Shulḥan Arukh* 136:8.
40 *Sefer Ḥayim UVerakha, Hilkhot Etrog VeLulav* 288.
41 *Kaf HaḤayim* 651:16.
42 Rambam, *Sefer HaMitzvot*, Positive Commandments 12–13; *Semag*, Positive Commandments 21–22; *Ḥinukh* 421–422.
43 Rif, Sukka 17a.
44 Ritva, Sukka 34b, s.v. *gemara*.
45 Rosh, Sukka 3:14.
46 *Hilkhot Lulav* 7:6.
47 Ran, Sukka 17a, s.v. *ve'af al gav*; see also Ritva 34b, s.v. *gemara*.
48 Tosafot, ad loc., s.v. *shetehei*.
49 See Tosafot, Menaḥot 27a, s.v. *ulekaḥtem*; *Or Zarua* 308; see also *Mordekhai*, Sukka 747 and *Hagahot Asheri*, Sukka 3:14.
50 Interestingly, the responsa *Oneg Yom Tov* (1) insists that all agree with the position of Ramban; Rosh, Ritva, and Rambam demand the presence of all four *minim* only for the sake of the *berakha*, lest one not actually take all four *minim*, in which case the blessing will be in vain.

Sefer HaMikhtam (Sukka 34b) offers an entirely different explanation of the entire passage. He explains that one who does not have all four *minim* must take whatever he has at the same time. However, if he has all four *minim* in his possession, he can take them consecutively, one after the other. Apparently, although taking one of the *minim* has no value, one may either take some of them together or all of them, even consecutively. He also cites Raavad, who writes that although one who does not have all four *minim* should not recite the blessing, he should still take them in order to "remember" the mitzva of *arba minim*.

51 *Shulḥan Arukh* 651:12.
52 Rema, ibid.
53 *Magen Avraham* 521:25; see also Ritva 35b.
54 One may ask a similar question regarding *Sefirat HaOmer*: is the mitzva fulfilled only after one has counted each of the forty-nine nights, or does each night constitute a new mitzva?
55 *Hilkhot Berakhot* 11:5–7.

56 *Or Zarua* 1:25.
57 See Rambam, *Hilkhot Berakhot* 1:3.
58 Rif, Pesaḥim 3b–4a; Rambam, *Hilkhot Berakhot* 11:7; Tosafot, Pesaḥim 7a, s.v. *al*; Rosh, Pesaḥim 1:10; et al.
59 Tosafot, Sukka 29a, s.v. *over*.
60 *Hilkhot Lulav* 7:6.
61 Ibid. See also Rosh, Sukka 3:33 and Ran, Sukka 20b, s.v. *mideparkhinan*.
62 *Biur HaGra* 651.
63 *Baḥ* 521.
64 *Shulḥan Arukh* 521:5.
65 *Biur HaGra* 521:5; *Sefer Arbaat HaMinim HaShalem*, p. 352, relates that this was the practice of *Ḥazon Ish*.
66 Rabbeinu Tam, *Sefer HaYashar*, Ḥiddushim 406; Rashba, Responsa 7:297; Ritva, Sukka 42a.
67 See Menaḥot 93b and Zevaḥim 52a.
68 Tosafot, Sukka 39a, s.v. *over*.
69 This phrase may be a scribal error, as other *Rishonim*, including *Tosafot HaRosh* (Sukka 39a, s.v. *mevarekh*), use the similar phrase, "*sheyarei hamitzva*."
70 *Hilkhot Lulav* 7:9.
71 Rosh, Sukka 3:26.
72 Me'iri, Sukka 37b.
73 Rashi, Sukka 39b, s.v. *kedei*.
74 See, for example, Tosafot, Pesaḥim 7b, s.v. *be'idana*.
75 I Chr. 16:33–34.
76 Tosafot, Sukka 37b, s.v. *behodo*.
77 Rosh, Sukka 3:26.
78 Similarly, Ramban (*Sefer HaMitzvot, shoresh* 9), who suggests that the Hallel recited on the festivals is of biblical origin, cites a talmudic passage as proof: "Is it possible that the Jewish people slaughtered their Passover sacrifices and took their lulav bundles without singing a hymn to God?" (Pesaḥim 117a).
79 *Hilkhot Lulav* 7:10.
80 *Shulḥan Arukh* 652:1.
81 *Magen Avraham* 652:3.
82 See, for example, *Mishna Berura* 621:34.
83 *Piskei Teshuvot* 652:3, n. 12.
84 Tosafot, Sukka 39a, s.v. *over*.
85 *Ḥayei Adam* 148:11; *Mishna Berura* 651:26.
86 *Bikkurei Yaakov* 651:20. See *Shaar HaTziyun* 651:32, who disagrees.
87 *Arukh HaShulḥan* 651:14.

CHAPTER 26

1 Rambam, *Hilkhot Lulav* 7:23–24.

2 Rashi, Sukka 43b, s.v. *vehevium*; Tosafot, Sukka 45a, s.v. *zokfin*.

3 Rashi, Sukka 43b, s.v. *vehevium*; see also *Or Zarua* 315.

4 Rambam, *Hilkhot Lulav* 7:23; Ran, Sukka 22a, s.v. *uvegemara*; see also *Or Zarua* 315.

5 Rashi, Sukka 43b, s.v. *sheluḥei*; see also Tosafot, s.v. *sheluḥei*.

6 See Keilim 1:9.

7 *Or Zarua* 2:315; see also *Shita Mekubetzet*, Menaḥot 27b; Responsa *Ri MiGash* 43, and possibly Rambam, *Hilkhot Lulav* 7:22–3; see also *Tosafot Yom Tov* 4:5.

8 *Yalkut Shimoni*, Ps. 703.

9 Ritva, Sukka 43b, s.v. *ufarkinan*; see also Ran, Sukka 21b, s.v. *garsinan*.

10 *Siddur R. Saadia Gaon*, p. 238.

11 *Otzar HaGeonim*, Sukka 43b.

12 *Shibbolei HaLeket, Seder Ḥag HaSukkot* 469.

13 *Shaarei Teshuva* 751:20.

14 *Tur* 759–760; see *Iggerot Moshe, Oraḥ Ḥayim* 3:99.

15 *Sefer Ḥasidim* 730 relates that R. Saadia Gaon would travel to Eretz Yisrael each year in order to encircle the Mount of Olives (or, possibly, *on* the Mount of Olives) seven times on Hoshana Rabba, the seventh day of Sukkot.

16 *Shulḥan Arukh* 760.

17 Rema, ibid.

18 *Mishna Berura* 760:9.

19 See *Abudraham, Seder Tefillat Sukkot*, for example.

20 *Kol Bo* 72.

21 Commentary on the Mishna, Sukka 4:5 and *Hilkhot Lulav* 7:20–21.

22 Rashi, Sukka 42b, s.v. *vehevium* and 44b, s.v. *ḥavit*.

23 See *Midrash Tanḥuma* (Buber), *Parashat Emor* 28.

24 See also *Teshuvot HaGeonim, Shaarei Teshuva* 340, where R. Tzemaḥ Gaon suggests that hitting the *aravot* to the ground atones for sins committed through one's speech.

25 *Mo'adei HaRaaya*, p. 128.

26 Leviticus Rabba 30:12.

27 See Sukka 43b.

28 *Teshuvot HaGeonim, Shaarei Teshuva* 340.

29 *Mo'adim UZemanim*, vol. 1, p. 179.

30 See Rashi, Sukka 44a, s.v. *minhag*.

31 *Tur* 664.

32 Rambam, *Hilkhot Lulav* 7:22; Rosh, Sukka 4:1, et al.
33 *Shulḥan Arukh* 664:2.
34 Rambam, *Hilkhot Berakhot* 11:16.
35 See Taanit 28b.
36 Rabbeinu Tam, cited by Tosafot, Sukka 44b, s.v. *kan*.
37 Raavya 699; Rosh 4:1.
38 Rabbeinu Ḥananel 44b; Rambam, *Hilkhot Lulav* 7:20.
39 *Shulḥan Arukh* 664:6.
40 *Mishna Berura* 664:21.
41 *Tur* 764.
42 Rema 764:4.
43 *Mishna Berura* 764:16.
44 Ibid., 764:17.
45 Rashi, Sukka 44b, s.v. *aleh*.
46 Ran, Sukka 22a, s.v. *vekhama*.
47 *Shulḥan Arukh* 664:4.
48 Ibid., 764:3.
49 Rema 764:7.
50 *Mishna Berura* 764:26–27.
51 Ibid., 760:8.
52 *Shulḥan Arukh* 764:4.
53 Rema, ibid.
54 *Arukh HaShulḥan* 764:2, 7.
55 Leviticus Rabba 37; *Midrash Tehillim* 17:5.
56 Hos. 58:2.
57 Zohar, vol. 3, p. 31b.
58 *Shibbolei HaLeket* 371; *Sefer HaManhig, Hilkhot Etrog* 38.
59 *Tur* 664.
60 See *Magen Abraham* 664.
61 See *Arukh HaShulḥan* 664:11.
62 *Arukh HaShulḥan*, ibid., for example.
63 Rema 667:1.

CHAPTER 27

1 See also Zech. 14:9 and 16–17, who describes how the nations of the world will one day celebrate the Festival of Sukkot and worship God in Jerusalem.
2 Rashi, Num. 29:36.
3 *Ḥizkuni*, Lev. 23:36.

4 The ballot was used in order to determine which of the twenty-four "*mishmarot hakehuna*" received the *korbanot* on Shemini Atzeret, as it is on other festivals. During the first seven days of the festival, however, no ballot was necessary, as the "*parei haḥag*" were sufficient to provide for all of the Priests.

5 The *Sheheḥeyanu* blessing is recited, even though it was already recited on the first day of the festival. This stands in contrast to Pesaḥ, when *Sheheḥeyanu* is only recited once, on the first day.

6 The *Rishonim* disagree as to the implication of "*regel bifnei atzmo*." In one place, Rashi (Sukka 48a, s.v. *regel*) explains that Shemini Atzeret is separate in that one does not sit in a *sukka*. Elsewhere (Rosh HaShana 4b, s.v. *pazar*), however, Rashi writes that "*ein shem Ḥag haSukkot alav*" – the eighth day does not bear the *name* of the Festival of Sukkot. Tosafot (Rosh HaShana 4b, s.v. *pazar*) explain that in *Birkat HaMazon* and *Tefilla*, one mentions "*Shemini Atzeret*," and not "*Ḥag HaSukkot*." Early Sephardic *Rishonim*, such as Rabbeinu Ḥananel (Sukka 48a) and Rif (Sukka 23a) explain that Shemini Atzeret is a "*regel bifnei atzmo*" in that if one buries a close relative, over whom he must mourn, before the festival, the first day of Sukkot cancels the *shiva* (seven days of mourning), and Shemini Atzeret cancels another seven days of the period of mourning. Therefore, upon concluding the entire festival, one has already counted twenty-one days (seven days before the beginning of the festival, seven days of Ḥol HaMo'ed, and Shemini Atzeret) of the thirty-day period of mourning (*sheloshim*). Rabbeinu Tam (Tosafot, Sukka 48a, s.v. *regel*) disagrees, and offers another explanation: "*Regel bifnei atzmo*" refers to the obligation to sleep in Jerusalem (*lina*) during the time of the *Beit HaMikdash* on the night of Shemini Atzeret. Ramban (Sukka 48a) rejects all these explanations and explains that Shemini Atzeret is a "*regel bifnei atzmo*" in that one who is exempt from bringing the *olat re'iya* and the *shalmei ḥagiga* on the first day of Sukkot – for example, one who converted during Ḥol HaMo'ed or a minor who became an adult during Ḥol HaMo'ed – is obligated to bring these *korbanot* on Shemini Atzeret. Furthermore, according to the opinion that maintains that one violates "*bal te'aḥer*" (the prohibition of not fulfilling one's vows) after three "*regalim*" have passed, one would be in violation after two *regalim* and the seven days of Sukkot pass.

7 See Num. 29:36. On Shemini Atzeret the descending pattern of bull offerings, from thirteen to seven, stops, and only one bull is offered.

8 The "*shir*" (psalm) recited in the *Beit HaMikdash* by the Levites on Shemini Atzeret (Ps. 12) also differed from the pattern of songs recited by the Levites throughout the festival (See Sukka 55a.).

9 The *Rishonim* differ as to whether "*berakha*" refers to the unique formula inserted in one's prayers (Rabbeinu Tam, Tosafot, Sukka 48a, s.v. *regel*) or to the blessing

recited for the "life of the King" at the end of the festival (Rashi, Yoma 3a, s.v. *berakha le'atzmo*; see also Tosefta, Sukka 4:10 and Rashi, Sukka 48a, s.v. *berakha*).

10 Rif, Sukka 23a; Rashi, Rambam, *Seder Tefillot*; Sukka 47b, s.v. *birkat*; Rosh, Sukka 4:5, et al.

11 *Shulḥan Arukh* 668:1. Gra notes that the Talmud does refer to Shemini Atzeret as a "*ḥag*" (*Biur HaGra* 668:2); Ran cites the Yerushalmi, which implies that in the language of the Torah, Shemini Atzeret is not referred to as a "*ḥag*" (Ran, Nedarim 49a).

12 Rema 668:1.

13 Maharshal, Responsa 64.

14 *Taz* 668:1.

15 *Arukh HaShulḥan* 668:1.

16 *Birkei Yosef* 668.

17 *Shaarei Teshuva* 668:2.

18 *Ḥayei Adam* 28:15.

19 *Arukh HaShulḥan* 668:1.

20 *Iggerot Moshe, Oraḥ Ḥayim* 3:97.

21 *Birkei Yosef* 668; see also R. Ovadia Yosef, *Yabia Omer* 4:51.

22 See *Kaf HaḤayim* 668:3, for example.

23 R. Betzalel Zolty (*Mishnat Yaavetz, Oraḥ Ḥayim* 71) discusses this question at length, and suggests other issues that may be subject to this debate.

24 See Eiruvin 96a.

25 Maharshal, Responsa 68.

26 *Taz* 678.

27 Sukka 46b–47a. See R. Yehuda b. Kalonymus's *Yiḥusei Tanna'im VeAmora'im* (ed. Y. L. Maimon), pp. 329–330 for a different understanding of the Gemara's conclusion.

28 Cited in *Kesef Mishneh, Hilkhot Mila* 3:6. Interestingly, the *Kesef Mishneh* cites R. Meir HaLevi Abulafia, Rama, who dismisses this responsum, and notes that despite the fact that every Yom Tov Sheni is a *safeika deyoma*, Kiddush and other blessings are still recited. He suggests that when the *berakha* would interfere with or undermine another biblical law, then a blessing is not recited. Reciting the blessing over the *sukka on* Shemini Atzeret would undermine the sanctity of Shemini Atzeret by implying that it is actually a weekday, and it is therefore forbidden.

29 Rif, Sukka 22b–23a.

30 *Ḥinukh* 323.

31 See Tosafot, Sukka 47a, s.v. *metav*.

32 See Shabbat 23a.

33 Ran, Sukka 22b.

34 *Mordekhai*, Sukka 772; see also *Hagahot Asheri*, Sukka 4:5.

35 *Beit Yosef* 668.

36 *Darkhei Moshe* 668.

37 *Maase Rav* 216.

38 *Mishna Berura* 668:6.

39 *Shulḥan Arukh* 668:1.

40 *Maḥzor Vitry* 384; see also Maharil, *Hilkhot Lulav* 6.

41 See, for example, *Minḥat Elazar* 4:31; *Arukh HaShulḥan* 668:3–5.

42 *Korban Netanel*, Sukka 4:7.

43 Tosafot, Sukka 47a, s.v. *metav*.

44 See *Tur* 688.

45 Prof. Chaim Soloveitchik ("*Olam KeMinhago Noheg: Review Essay.*" AJS Review 23:2 [1998]: 223–234) offers a different explanation. He writes:

> In Poland, however, the frequently bitter autumn cold made *sukka*-sitting a genuine burden. Jews had sacrificed much for their religion, and no one dreamed that severe chills suspended the demands of religion, and Jews dutifully sat in *sukkot* throughout the Sukkot holiday. Shemini Atzeret, however, was a different matter. *Sukka*-eating on that day was clearly a second-class commandment. Evidence – it did not even merit a blessing, unlike all other second-day mitzvot. And by the 1640s, the laxity of *sukka*-sitting on Shemini Atzeret was widespread in Poland, as the remarks of the super-commentators on the *Tur* and *Shulḥan Arukh* clearly indicate.

46 *Minḥat Shlomo* 1:19:1; see also *Minḥat Yitzchak* 9:54.

47 *Yeḥave Daat* 2:76.

48 See Responsa *BeTzel HaḤokhma* 5:146.

49 See Avraham Yaari, "*Toldot Ḥag Simḥat Torah*," Mosad Ha-Rav Kook, Jerusalem: 1964.

50 Benjamin of Tudela, *The Itinerary of Benjamin of Tudela: Travels in the Middle Ages*, trans. Marcus Nathan Adler (1907), p. 70.

51 *Hilkhot Tefilla* 13:5.

52 B.M. Levin, *Otzar Ḥilluf Minhagim Bein Eretz Yisrael UVein Bavel* (1942), p. 98.

53 *Shaarei Teshuva* 314.

54 Ibid.; see also Beitza 36b.

55 *Sefer HaEshkol* 21; *Sefer HaManhig, Hilkhot Sukka* 54; *Abudraham, Seder Tefillot Sukkot*; *Orḥot Ḥayim, Hilkhot Keriat Sefer Torah* 58.

56 *Maḥzor Vitry* 385.

57 See Deut. 16:15.

58 *Abrabanel, Parashat Vayak'hel.*

59 *Toldot Ḥag Simḥat Torah*, p. 355.

CHAPTER 28

1 See Bava Batra 3b.

2 *Hilkhot Megilla VeḤanukka* 3:1–3.

3 *Oraḥ Ḥayim* 670

4 See, for example, http://www.torahweb.org/torah/2006/moadim/rros_chanukah.html (accessed October 10, 2012).

5 *Hilkhot Ḥanukka* 3:6.

6 *Yoreh De'ah* 233 and *Oraḥ Ḥayim* 191 and 208.

7 *Maase Nissim* 1.

8 See Rambam, *Sefer HaMitzvot, shoresh* 1 and *Hilkhot Ḥanukka* 3:5–6. Ramban disagrees in his comments on the *Sefer HaMitzvot,* arguing that Hallel must be of biblical origin. He suggests that it may either be a *halakha leMoshe miSinai* or an expression of the biblical obligation to rejoice on the festivals (*simḥat Yom Tov*). Raavad, in his comments on Rambam, suggests that Hallel may be "*midivrei kabbala,*" from the prophets, which is implied by the gemara in Arakhin cited above. See also *Shaagat Aryeh* 69, who rules that Hallel is only *miderabbanan,* and therefore, if one is in doubt whether he recited Hallel, he need not repeat it (as we maintain that *safek derabbanan lekula*).

9 Rema, *Oraḥ Ḥayim* 695:4.

10 *Hilkhot Ḥanukka* 3:14.

11 For a more thorough discussion of this topic, see R. Refael Shapiro (1837–1921), *Torat Refa'el, Hilkhot Pesaḥ* 75; R. Shlomo HaKohen, Responsa *Binyan Shlomo, Oraḥ Ḥayim* 61; and R. Ovadia Yosef, Responsa *Yabia Omer, Oraḥ Ḥayim* 6:45 and *Yeḥave Daat* 1:78.

12 See Tosafot, Berakhot 45a, s.v. *al.*

13 *Hilkhot Berakhot* 3:13.

14 Ibid., 30.

15 *Levush Tekhelet* 208:12.

16 See *Harerei Kedem,* vol.1, pp. 302–302; see also *Haggada Shel Pesaḥ MiBeit Levi,* p. 233.

17 See Berakhot 49a and *Shulḥan Arukh, Oraḥ Ḥayim* 188:6–7.

18 See his posthumously published *Iggerot HaGrid, Hilkhot Berakhot* 3:13; see also *Harerei Kedem,* cited above.

19 *Levush* 670:2.

20 *Taz* 670:3.

21 Rema 670:1.

22 *Hilkhot Ḥanukka* 3:3.

23 See Ran Shabbat 10a.

24 See R. Yaakov Moshe Toledano, *Sarid UFalit*, p. 8 and *Ner Maarav*, p. 199.
25 *Tur* 670.
26 See *Ḥakham Tzvi* 87.
27 The *Sefer Ḥasidim* (121) even suggests that men should also refrain from work.
28 *Mishna Berura* 670:4.
29 *Levush* 640.

CHAPTER 29

1 Rashi, Megilla 4a, s.v *she'af hen*.
2 Tosafot, Megilla 4a, s.v. *she'af hen*.
3 Tosafot, Pesaḥim 108b, s.v. *hayu*.
4 Tosafot, Megilla 4a, s.v. *she'af hen*.
5 Ḥatam Sofer, Responsa, *Oraḥ Ḥayim* 185.
6 Tosafot, Pesaḥim 108b.
7 *Sefer HaYashar*, Responsa 70.
8 *Oraḥ Ḥayim* 291:6.
9 See *Mishna Berura* 26.
10 As we shall see in the next chapter, this question is only relevant according to the Ashkenazic practice, according to which each person kindles his or her own lights. According to Sephardic custom, only one person, usually the head of the household, lights in any case.
11 Maharshal, Responsa 85.
12 *Eliya Rabba* 671.
13 *Mishna Berura* 671:9.
14 *Iggerot Moshe, Oraḥ Ḥayim* 109; see Rema 677:3.
15 Ḥatam Sofer, Shabbat 21b.
16 *Mishmeret Shalom* 48:2.
17 *Nefesh HaRav*, p. 226.
18 *Mikra'ei Kodesh, Hilkhot Ḥanukka*, addendum 7, p. 154.

CHAPTER 30

1 *Hilkhot Megilla VeḤanukka* 4:1.
2 Ran, Shabbat 10a.
3 Tosafot, ibid.
4 Cited in Ran, Shabbat 21b.
5 *Hilkhot Ḥanukka* 4:3.

6 Ibid., 4:2.

7 Ran, Shabbat 21b.

8 Ritva, ibid.

9 Maharil, Responsa 145.

10 *Shulḥan Arukh, Oraḥ Ḥayim* 671:2.

11 Rema, ibid.

12 See, for example, *Taz* 671:1.

13 R. Ovadia Yosef, *Yeḥave Daat* 6:43; R. Shlomo Zalman Auerbach, *Shalmei Mo'ed*, p. 204. R. Auerbach even believes that students whose parents light in a different time zone should still refrain from lighting on their own; R. Yosef disagrees (see *Ḥazon Ovadia*, Ḥanukka, p.150).

14 R. Ovadia Hadaya, *Yaskil Avdi* 7, p. 386; *Ḥazon Ish* and R. Elyashiv, cited in *Yemei Hallel VeHodaya*, p. 277; R. Shalom Mashash and R. Avrum Shapiro, cited in *Peninei Halakha, Zemanim*, p. 281.

15 *Peri Megadim, Mishbetzot Zahav* 671:1 and R. Akiva Eiger, *Mahadura Tinyana* 13.

16 *Ḥiddushei HaGriz, Hilkhot Ḥanukka* 4:1.

17 See *Sefat Emet* 21b.

18 The *Mishna Berura* (672:6) cites a debate between *Beit Yosef* (citing *Orḥot Ḥayim*) and *Peri Megadim* as to whether one who lights one candle with a *berakha* and later receives additional candles should light the new candles with a *berakha*. *Beit Yosef* implies that if one did not have the additional candles in mind when he recited the *berakha*, he should recite the *berakha* again upon kindling the new lights, implying that the *mehadrin min hamehadrin* fulfillment is an independent mitzva. *Peri Megadim*, however, disagrees. *Magen Avraham* (651:23) discusses this issue and rules in accordance with *Beit Yosef*. This debate reflects the basic question of whether the additional lights constitute an integral part of the basic mitzva or are merely a *hiddur*, a means of enhancing the mitzva, but not part of the mitzva itself.

19 The *Rishonim* and *Aḥaronim* question whether one should preferably rekindle the light or if this is entirely unnecessary (all agree it is permissible). The *Or Zarua* (322) concludes that it is certainly meritorious to rekindle the lights. The *Leket Yosher* (*Oraḥ Ḥayim*, p. 151) records that it is customary to rekindle the lights, since in any event one may not derive benefit from the leftover oil, but he implies that there is no intrinsic value in relighting the candles. Rema (673:3) writes that one who wishes to act stringently and rekindle the light should not recite a new *berakha*.

20 Rashba, Responsa 1:539.

21 *Shulḥan Arukh* 673:3.

22 *Taz* 673:8.

CHAPTER 31

1 See Tosafot, Berakhot 2b, s.v. *dilma*; Shabbat 35a, s.v. *terei*; Pesaḥim 94a, s.v. *R. Yehuda.*

2 See *Beit Yosef, Yoreh De'ah* 69.

3 *Shulḥan Arukh* 459:2.

4 Rema 261:1.

5 See Maharam Alashkar, Responsa 96, citing R. Sherira Gaon and R. Hai Gaon.

6 *Biur HaGra, Oraḥ Ḥayim* 261:2.

7 *Hilkhot Ḥanukka* 4:5. See *Arukh HaShulḥan* 472:4 and *Biur Halakha,* s.v. *lo* and *velo*

8 Responsa 1:127.

9 Rashba, Shabbat 21b; Ran, Shabbat 9a.

10 Tosafot, Menaḥot 20b, s.v. *nifsal.*

11 Rosh, Shabbat 2:3.

12 *Shulḥan Arukh* 672:1.

13 *Biur HaGra,* ibid., s.v. *sof.*

14 *Mishna Berura* 672:1.

15 See R. Yechiel Michel Tukachinsky, *Ir HaKodesh VeHaMikdash* 3, 25:9.

16 R. Aryeh Tzvi Frumer (1884–1943), a pre-war Polish authority who was killed in Majdanek, recommends providing enough oil in at least one candle to last until one half-hour after Rabbeinu Tam's *tzeit hakokhavim,* or approximately 102 minutes after sunset; see *Eretz Tzvi,* 121.

17 R. Eliyahu Schlesinger, *Mitzvat Ner Ish UVeito,* pp. 334–343, defends this practice, despite its lack of support in the *Rishonim.*

18 See *Yalkut Yosef, Mo'adim,* p. 208.

19 See *Sefer Orḥot Rabbeinu,* 35; see also R. Moshe Sternbach, *Teshuvot VeHanhagot* 2:134.

20 *Iggerot Moshe, Oraḥ Ḥayim* vol. 4, 101:6.

21 R. Shimon Eider, *Halachos of Ḥanukka.*

22 *Peri Megadim* 672:1.

23 *Magen Avraham* 672:5.

24 *Shevut Yaakov* 2:40.

25 *Ḥayei Adam* 124:20.

26 *Arukh HaShulḥan* 672:4.

27 *Hilkhot Ḥanukka* 4:5.

28 Rashba, Shabbat 21b and Ran, Shabbat 9a.

29 Cited in the *Beit Yosef* 672.

30 See *Kaf HaḤayim* 672:3.

31 See, for example, *Mishna Berura* 672:3.
32 See Tosafot, Shabbat 21b, s.v. *de'i;* Rosh, Shabbat 2:3; Rambam, *Hilkhot Ḥanukka* 4:5.
33 Ibid., 2:3.
34 Tosafot, Shabbat 21b, s.v. *de'i.*
35 See *R"i Porat* cited by Tosafot.
36 Rashba, Shabbat 21b, s.v. *veha.*
37 See Megilla 20b.
38 *Shulḥan Arukh* 672:2.
39 *Shulḥan Arukh* 672:6.
40 Rosh, Shabbat 2:7.
41 *Shulḥan Arukh* 672:2.
42 *Magen Avraham* 672:4.
43 See Tosafot, Rashba, Rosh, Ran, and others.
44 Rema 672:2.
45 Rashba, Shabbat 21b.
46 Maharshal, Responsa 85.
47 *Hilkhot Ḥanukka* 4:2.
48 *Tur* 672.
49 *Mishna Berura* 672:6.
50 *Magen Avraham* 672:6.
51 *Arukh HaShulḥan* 672:7.
52 See *Shaar HaTziyun* 17.
53 *Iggerot Moshe, Oraḥ Ḥayim* 4, 105:7.
54 *Shalmei Mo'ed*, p. 218.
55 *Yalkut Yosef, Mo'adim*, p. 218, and *Ḥazon Ovadia*, Ḥanukka, p. 64.
56 One might question whether *pirsumei nissa* to non-Jews also justifies lighting with a *berakha*. In explaining the phrase "until there is no wayfarer in the street," the Gemara identifies these "wayfarers" as "the Tarmodians." Rashi explains that the Tarmodians were people assigned the job of collecting firewood to sell; they would stay in the market until all the merchants had returned home. It is unclear whether we are concerned with publicizing the miracle to the non-Jewish Tarmodians or to the Jews who would return to the market to purchase wood from them. Rif (9a) explains that Tarmodians were not a nationality, but rather people who sold a type of wood called "*tarmuda*," implying that they may have been Jewish merchants.

R. Moshe Feinstein (*Iggerot Moshe, Oraḥ Ḥayim* 4, 105:7) writes that publicizing the miracle to non-Jews does not fulfill *pirsumei nissa*. In contrast, R. Shimon Sofer writes in his Responsa *Hitorerut Teshuva* (3, 457:1) that even one who lives among non-Jews should light outside in order to publicize the miracle, as we are certainly interested in publicizing God's greatness to non-Jews (see Ezek. 38:23).

57 See, for example, *Mo'adim UZemanim* 2:141 and *Mikra'ei Kodesh* 4:1.

58 Ritva, Shabbat 21b.

59 According to *Sefer Uvdot VeHanhagot LeBeit Brisk*, vol. 2, p. 99, R. Yitzchak Ze'ev Soloveitchik agreed that *ad shetikhle* is defined as an objective *shiur* of a half-hour, but he nevertheless arranged for his candles to burn until the later hours as a *hiddur*.

60 Ramban, Pesaḥim 7a.

61 See *Ḥovat HaDar* chap. 1 fn. 50, who raises this question. See *Shevet HaLevi* 4:64 and *Rivevot Efraim* 4:163:12 (who cites R. Moshe Feinstein).

62 *Shevet HaLevi* 4:64.

63 R. Ovadia Yosef, *Yeḥave Daat* 3:51; R. Binyamin Zilber, *Az Nidberu* 3, 30:3; R. Yitzchak Ze'ev Soloveitchik, *Uvdot VeHanhagot LeBeit Brisk*.

64 *Shevet HaLevi* 4:66.

65 See *Halikhot Bat Yisrael* 21:9.

66 See *Halachos of Ḥanukka*, p. 34.

67 Maharshal, Responsa 85.

68 *MiPeninei HaRav*, p. 147.

69 Me'iri, Shabbat 21b.

70 *Halikhot Shlomo*.

71 Maharshal, Responsa 85 (*Kitzur Dinei Ḥanukka*).

72 See *Shaar HaTziyun* 14.

73 See R. Joseph Yospa Hahn, *Yosef Ometz*, a collection of laws and customs of the Frankfurt community, chap. 1166; and *Yalkut Yosef, Mo'adim*, p. 211. See also *Halikhot Shlomo, Mo'adei HaShana* page 299, where R. Shlomo Z. Auerbach permits eating a snack before lighting.

CHAPTER 32

1 Rashi, Shabbat 21b, s.v. *mibeḥutz*.

2 Tosafot, ibid., s.v. *mitzva*.

3 *Hilkhot Ḥanukka* 4:1.

4 Rif, Shabbat 9b.

5 *Hilkhot Ḥanukka* 3:3.

6 Rosh, Shabbat 2:4.

7 *Shulḥan Arukh* 671:5.

8 Cited in *Az Nidberu* 5:39.

9 *Teshuvot VeHanhagot* 2, 342:2.

10 See *Yemei Hallel VeHodaa* 8:5:2 and *Mikra'ei Kodesh*, Ḥanukka, pp. 25–6.

11 *Mikra'ei Kodesh* 17.

12 *Beit Yosef* 671. Interestingly, R. Yaakov Yishayahu Blau, in his compendium on the laws of Ḥanukka, *Ḥovat HaDar* (chap.1, n. 16) questions whether a resident of a loft whose doorway opens to a courtyard or a stairwell that cannot be seen from the *reshut harabbim*, should also light in his window.

13 Rashi, Shabbat 21b, s.v. *hasakana*; See Tosafot, Shabbat 45a, s.v. *mekamei*.

14 Ritva, Shabbat 21b.

15 *Or Zarua* 323.

16 *Shibbolei HaLeket* 185.

17 See *Levush* 671:8, *Ḥayei Adam* 154:12, and *Arukh HaShulḥan* 671:24.

18 *Iggerot Moshe, Oraḥ Ḥayim* 4:125.

19 See R. Yaakov Emden, *She'elat Yaavetz* 1:149.

20 *Minḥat Yitzchak* 6:61.

21 *Devar Yehoshua*, 40.

22 See R. Ovadia Hadaya, *Yaskil Avdi* 8, 10:2; R. Ovadia Yosef, cited in *Yalkut Yosef*, pp. 231–2.

23 *Har Tzvi, Oraḥ Ḥayim* 2:114.

24 *Az Nidberu* 6, 12:2.

25 *Maadanei Shlomo*, p. 109.

26 Rema 672:2.

27 *Shaar HaTziyun* 671:42.

28 *Ḥazon Ish, Oraḥ Ḥayim* 65:52, 90:2.

29 See, for example, Ritva, Shabbat 21b.

30 *Shulḥan Arukh* 671:7.

31 Ibid.

32 *Mishna Berura* 671:34.

33 See *Yemei Hallel VeHodaa*, p. 62.

34 *Magen Avraham* 671:8; *Arukh HaShulḥan* 24; *Iggerot Moshe, Yoreh De'ah* 4:125.

35 Rosh, Shabbat 2:5.

36 Ritva, Shabbat 21b; see also *Mordekhai*, Shabbat 266.

37 *Shulḥan Arukh* 671:6.

38 *Mordekhai* 268.

39 *Shulḥan Arukh* 671:6.

40 *Mishna Berura* 671:26.

41 *Peri Ḥadash* 671:6.

42 Ran, Shabbat 10a.

43 *Shulḥan Arukh* 677:1.

44 *Magen Avraham* 677:1.

45 *Kaf HaḤayim,* 677.
46 Maharil, Responsa 145.
47 *Darkhei Moshe* 677.
48 *Mishna Berura* 677:7.
49 *Magen Avraham* 677:3.
50 *Ner Ish UVeito,* p. 368.
51 *Terumat HaDeshen* 101.
52 Maharil, Responsa 145.
53 *Beit Yosef* 677.
54 *Eliya Rabba* 677:4.
55 Rema 677:3.
56 *Levush* 677:1.
57 *Taz* 677:1.
58 *Magen Avraham* 677:1.
59 *Mishna Berura* 677:15.
60 *Taz* 677:2.
61 *Tur* 677.
62 Rashba, Responsa 1:542.
63 *Shulḥan Arukh* 677:1.
64 Rema 677:1.
65 Of course, one who travels alone may rely upon his family's lighting at home, if necessary.
66 *Ḥovat HaDar,* chap. 1, n. 65.
67 *Yemei Hallel VeHodaa,* p. 274, in the name of R. Shlomo Zalman Auerbach.
68 *Iggerot Moshe, Yoreh De'ah* 3, 14:5 and *Oraḥ Ḥayim* 4, 70:3.
69 *Minḥat Yitzchak* 7:48.
70 *Az Nidberu* 5, 38:2.
71 *Shevet HaLevi* 3:83.
72 *Iggerot Moshe, Oraḥ Ḥayim* 4, 70:3.
73 See *Teshuvot VeHanhagot* 2 342:11.
74 Cited by R. Shimon Eider, *Halachos of Ḥanukka,* p. 37.
75 *Mikra'ei Kodesh,* Ḥanukka, p. 100, n. 101.
76 R. Yosef Zvi Rimon analyzes this question at length in his "*Ner Ḥanukka LaḤayal VeLaMetayel*" (*BeOrekha Nireh Or,* 2004).
77 Tosafot, Sukka 46b, s.v. *haro'eh.*
78 Rashi, Shabbat 23a, s.v. *haro'eh.*
79 *Hilkhot Ḥanukka* 4:1.
80 Ran, Shabbat 10a, s.v. *amar.*
81 *Taz* 677:2.

82 *Iggerot Moshe, Yoreh De'ah* 3, 14:5.
83 *Halikhot Shlomo*, p. 257.
84 Maharsham, Responsa 4:146.
85 *Arukh HaShulḥan* 677:5.
86 See http://www.vbm-torah.org/Chanukkah/05chanal.htm (accessed February 1, 2012).
87 *Tzitz Eliezer* 15:29.
88 *Az Nidberu* 6:75.
89 *Tzitz Eliezer* 15:29.
90 *Mikra'ei Kodesh*, Ḥanukka p. 18, n. 3.
91 *Ḥazon Ovadia*, p. 156.
92 *Sefer HaIttur*, Ḥanukka 114.
93 See Megilla 29a.
94 Rivash 111.
95 *Mikhtam*, Pesaḥim 101b; *Abudraham, Seder Maariv shel Shabbat.*
96 *Shibbolei HaLeket* 185.
97 *Shulḥan Arukh* 671:1.
98 Rema 671:1.
99 R. Moshe Feinstein, *Iggerot Moshe, Oraḥ Ḥayim* 1:190.
100 R. Ovadia Yosef, *Yeḥave Daat* 2:77.
101 *Minḥat Yitzchak* 6 65:3.
102 *Tzitz Eliezer* 15:30; 22:37:1.
103 *Az Nidberu* 5:37.
104 *Yabia Omer* 7, 57:6; *Ḥazon Ovadia*, p. 47.
105 *Az Nidberu* 6, p. 137; *Ḥazon Ovadia*, p. 47.

CHAPTER 33

1 *Shulḥan Arukh* 676:1.
2 *Arukh HaShulḥan* 676:1.
3 *Mishna Berura* 676:1.
4 Rashi, ibid., s.v. *haro'e*; *Or Zarua* 325; Rambam, *Hilkhot Ḥanukka* 3:4.
5 See Ritva, Shabbat 23a.
6 Rosh 2:8; *Hagahot Maimoniyot* 3:1 in the name of R. Simḥa and Raavya.
7 *Mordekhai* 267.
8 Maharshal, Responsa 85.
9 *Baḥ* 676.
10 Rashba, Shabbat 23a, s.v. *haro'e*; Ran, Shabbat 10a, s.v. *amar*; *Tur* 676.
11 Tosafot, Sukka 46a, s.v. *haro'e.*

12 *Shulḥan Arukh* 676:3.
13 *Taz* 676:4.
14 *Magen Avraham* 676:1.
15 See Ritva 23.
16 This view is supported by a passage from Masekhet Soferim 20:4.
17 Rema 676:2.
18 *Nefesh HaRav*, p. 225.
19 Me'iri, Shabbat 23a.
20 *Shaar HaTziyun* 676:3.
21 *Biur Halakha* 692.
22 *Peri Ḥadash* 676:1.
23 *Iggerot Moshe, Oraḥ Ḥayim* 1:190; 5:43:2.
24 *Yabia Omer* 6: 42:2.
25 Masekhet Soferim 20:4.
26 Rosh, Shabbat 2:8.
27 *Tur* 676.
28 *Nefesh HaRav*, p. 224.
29 Rema 676:4.
30 *Shulḥan Arukh* 676:4.
31 See *Magen Avraham* 676:3 and *Taz* 676:5.
32 See *Peri Megadim* 676, *Mishbetzot Zahav* 5, and *Eishel Avraham* 3.
33 *Mishna Berura* 676:8.
34 *Leket Yosher* 1, p. 152.
35 Rema 671:4.
36 *Rav Pe'alim* 4:30.
37 *Peri Ḥadash* 671:4.
38 *Magen Avraham* 671:3.
39 *Mishna Berura* 671:15.
40 *Mordekhai*, Shabbat 268.
41 Maharil 40.
42 Maharik, *shoresh* 183.
43 *Terumat HaDeshen* 106.
44 *Levush* 676:5.
45 *Maase Rav* 232.
46 *Biur HaGra, Oraḥ Ḥayim* 676:5.
47 *Shulḥan Arukh* 676:5.
48 See R. Shlomo Zalman Auerbach, as cited in *Shalmei Mo'ed*, p. 225.

CHAPTER 34

1 See, for example, Tosafot, Shabbat 23a, s.v. *mereish*; *Mordekhai* 278.

2 Me'iri, Shabbat 21a, s.v. *mimah*; *Kol Bo* 44.

3 See Rif, Rambam, Rosh, and *Tur*.

4 Rema 673:1. In the *Darkhei Moshe*, 671, he describes using wax candles as a "*mitzva min hamuvḥar*". See also *Eliya Rabba* 673:2 and *Mateh Moshe* 990.

5 *Ner Mitzva*, s.v. *vekatav haRosh*.

6 *Yemei Hallel VeHodaa*, p. 106, n. 21.

7 *Mayim Ḥayim*, *Oraḥ Ḥayim* 79.

8 *Ner Mitzva*, p. 8.

9 *Hilkhot Shabbat* 12:1.

10 *Har Tzvi*, *Oraḥ Ḥayim* 2:114:2.

11 *Kaf HaḤayim* 673:19.

12 *Be'er Moshe* 6:58; *Yabia Omer*, *Oraḥ Ḥayim* 3:35. For more on this topic, see Rabbis Howard Jachter and Michael Broyde's articles in the *Journal of Halacha and Contemporary Society* (vols. 21 and 25) and R. Feitel Levin's "*Ḥanukiya Ḥashmalit*" in *Teḥumin* 9. See also R. Shlomo Zalman Auerbach's essay, *Meorei Esh* (*perek* 5, *anaf* 2), where he deals with this topic extensively.

13 Rashi, ibid., 21a, s.v. *ve'assur*.

14 Ran, Shabbat 9a.

15 Rashba, Shabbat 21b.

16 Baal HaMaor, Shabbat 9a.

17 Ibid.

18 *Tur* 673.

19 *Shibbolei HaLeket* 185.

20 Rosh, Shabbat 2:6.

21 *Shulḥan Arukh* 673:1.

22 *Magen Avraham* 673:2.

23 *Taz* 673:3.

24 Ritva, Shabbat 21b, s.v. *amar Rava*.

25 Me'iri, Shabbat 21b, s.v. *ner Ḥanukka*; see below.

26 *Arukh HaShulḥan* 673:7, *Mishna Berura* 673:11.

27 *Shulḥan Arukh* 672:2.

28 Rif, Shabbat 9a.

29 *Mishna Berura* 672:8.

30 Maharshal, Responsa 83.

31 Tosafot, Shabbat 23a, s.v. *shema*.

32 *Tur* 674.

33 *Shulḥan Arukh* 674:1.
34 Rema, ibid. The *Shaarei Teshuva* (674:1) cites authorities who refute this point.
35 *Mishna Berura* 674:1.
36 Rashi, ibid, s.v. *ner* and *ve'ika*; Ran 9b, s.v. *tannu rabbanan*; Baal HaMaor, Rif 9a; Me'iri 21b; *Kol Bo* 44; see also *Eliya Rabba* 671:10.
37 *Mordekhai* 269; Ritva, Shabbat 21b; Rambam, *Hilkhot Ḥanukka* 4:8; see also *Levush* 681:5.
38 *Shulḥan Arukh* 671:5.
39 Ibid., 673:1.
40 *Darkhei Moshe* 673, who cites Maharil; *Beit Yosef* 673, who cites Rabbeinu Yeruḥam.
41 *Shulḥan Arukh* 673:1.
42 Rema, ibid.
43 *Arukh HaShulḥan* 673:9.
44 See, for example, *Mateh Moshe* 984.

CHAPTER 35

1 See, for example, Ritva to Taanit 29a.
2 Both Rambam (Taaniyot 5:6) and *Shulḥan Arukh* (551:1) cite the passage regarding the reducing of joy during the month of Av.
3 See Rashi ad loc.
4 *Hilkhot Tefilla* 13:22.
5 *Oraḥ Ḥayim* 685.
6 *Shulḥan Arukh, Oraḥ Ḥayim* 282:4.
7 *Mishna Berura* 685:2.
8 *Sefer HaḤinukh*, 105.
9 See also Masekhet Soferim 21:3.
10 Rema 694:1.
11 *Hilkhot Shekalim* 1:1, 8.
12 Incidentally, historical and archeological evidence testifies to the observance of this commandment in Israel and abroad during the Second Temple period.
13 *Hilkhot Shekalim* 1:7.
14 R. Ovadia Bartenura, Shekalim 1:3.
15 *Tosafot Yom Tov*, Shekalim 1:4.
16 *Magen Avraham* 694:3.
17 *Torah Temima*, Ex. 30 n. 24.
18 *Kaf HaḤayim* 694:27.
19 *Mishna Berura* 694:5.
20 *Kaf HaḤayim* 794:20.

21 Rema 694:1.
22 *Tzitz Eliezer* 13:72.
23 *Kaf HaḤayim* 694:23.
24 *Maase Rav* 233.
25 See *Kaf HaḤayim* 694:23, *Tzitz Eliezer* 13:72, and *Minḥat Elazar* 1:30.
26 Rema 694:1.
27 *Magen Avraham* 694:2.
28 See R. Ovadia Yosef, *Yeḥave Daat* 1:86.
29 *Shulḥan Arukh, Yoreh De'ah* 249.
30 *Magen Avraham* 694:1.
31 *Sefer HaMitzvot,* Positive Commandment 189; see also *Hilkhot Melakhim* 5:5.
32 Cited in *Harerei Kedem* 1:185.
33 *Sefer HaḤinukh,* 603.
34 Ibid.
35 Ḥatam Sofer, *Even HaEzer* 1:119.
36 See *Sefer Ḥareidim,* Positive Commandment 84:21.
37 Rambam, *Sefer HaMitzvot,* Positive Commandment 189.
38 *Shela, Parashat Ki Tetzei.* See also *Magen Avraham* 60.
39 *Hilkhot Melakhim* 5:5.
40 *Sefer HaḤinukh,* 603.
41 See Tosafot, Megilla 17b, s.v. *kol* and Berakhot 13a, s.v *belashon.*
42 *Terumat HaDeshen* 108.
43 *Magen Avraham* 685.
44 *Mishna Berura* 685:16.
45 *Harerei Kedem* 1:185.
46 Berakhot 3a, s.v. *ve'idi.*
47 *Shulḥan Arukh* 685:7.
48 Rema, ibid.
49 *Taz* 685:3.
50 *Minḥat Elazar* 2:1.
51 *Peri Ḥadash* 67:1.
52 *Meishiv Davar, Oraḥ Ḥayim* 47.
53 See R. Ovadia Yosef's discussion in *Yeḥave Daat* 3:53.
54 *Mishna Berura* 685:18.
55 Two scholarly studies have recently been published regarding this question. Both R. Mordechai Breuer ("*Mikraot Sheyesh Lahem Hekhre'a,*" Megadim 10) and Y. Pankover (*Minhag UMesora: Zekher Amalek BeḤamesh O Shesh Nekudot,*" in Bar Ilan University's *Iyunei Mikra UFarshanut* 4) conclude that the proper reading is "*zeikher*" and that early texts support this conclusion.

56 See R. Tzvi Pesach Frank, *Mikra'ei Kodesh*, Purim 7; *Minḥat Yitzḥak* 3:9 and 4:47:3; *Yabia Omer* 6:11; *Halikhot Shlomo* 18:1.
57 *Marḥeshet* 22:3; *Avnei Nezer, Oraḥ Ḥayim* 509.
58 *Sefer HaḤinukh*, 603.
59 *Minḥat Ḥinukh*, ibid.
60 *Minḥat Yitzchak* 9:68.
61 *Torat Ḥesed, Oraḥ Ḥayim* 37.
62 *Mo'adei Yeshurun, Hilkhot Purim* 1:3, n. 9.

CHAPTER 36

1 *She'iltot, Parashat Vayak'hel* 67.
2 *Shulḥan Arukh* 686.
3 *Shibbolei HaLeket* 194.
4 Rosh, Megilla 1:1.
5 Cited by Ran, Taanit 7a.
6 *Hilkhot Taaniyot* 5:5.
7 *Shulḥan Arukh* 686:2.
8 *Harerei Kedem*, p.188.
9 *Hilkhot Taaniyot* 1:14.
10 *Piskei Teshuvot* 686:2.
11 *Hilkhot Taaniyot* 5:9.
12 See Rambam, *Hilkhot Megilla* 2:18.
13 *Hilkhot Megilla* 5:5.
14 *Shulḥan Arukh* 686:2.
15 *Kol Bo* 45. See *Shibbolei HaLeket*, Purim, 194, who severely criticizes this practice.
16 *Shiurei HaRav*, pp. 175–80.
17 *Shibbolei HaLeket* 194.

CHAPTER 37

1 See Megilla 2a.
2 See *Behag*, cited by *Beit Yosef*, 690; R. Amram and R. Gershom, as cited by *Hagahot Maymoniyot, Hilkhot Megilla* 1:10.
3 *Shulḥan Arukh* 690:17
4 *Beit Yosef* 690.
5 Rashi, Megilla 5a, s.v. *R. Assi*.
6 Rosh, Megilla 1:6.

7 Baal HaMaor, Megilla 3a.
8 Rif, Megilla 3a.
9 *Hilkhot Megilla* 2:8.
10 *Orḥot Ḥayim, Hilkhot Megilla* 24.
11 *Arukh HaShulḥan* 690:25.
12 Cited by Rosh, Megilla 1:6.
13 Tosafot, Megilla 4a, s.v. *ḥayav*.
14 *Hilkhot Megilla* 1:3.
15 Cited by the *Mordekhai*, Megilla 781.
16 Tosafot, Megilla 4a, s.v. *ḥayav*.
17 *Noda BiYehuda, Mahadura Kama, Oraḥ Ḥayim* 41.
18 This is the explanation of *Turei Even* (R. Aryeh Leib b. Asher Gunzburg) for *Behag*'s opinion that women cannot exempt men from their obligation. *Turei Even* contends that while a man's obligation in Megilla originates from *divrei kabbala*, a woman's obligation is based on the principle of *af hein hayu beoto ha'nes* and is rabbinic in origin. Since she has a lower level of obligation, a woman cannot discharge the higher obligation of a man. See *Turei Even*, Megilla 4a, s.v. *nashim*. This is discussed in the next chapter.
19 *Mikra'ei Kodesh*, Purim, 29.
20 *Marḥeshet* 1:22:9. *Marḥeshet* explains that according to *Behag*, a woman cannot discharge a man's obligation of Megilla because women are exempt from the Hallel component of Megilla. Accordingly, at least theoretically, a woman should be able to read the Megilla for a man on Purim night, when their obligations are identical. In the next chapter, we note that the suggestions of R. Frank and *Marḥeshet* were made in the context of theoretical talmudic discourse regarding one interpretation of *Behag*, and therefore have little practical relevance.
21 Ran, Megilla 1a, s.v. *ela*.
22 *Shulḥan Arukh* 692:1.
23 Rema, 692:1.
24 *Magen Avraham* 692:1. *Biur Halakha* discusses whether the holiday of Purim itself mandates reciting *Sheheḥeyanu*, as do the other festivals.
25 Rif, Megilla 3a.
26 See *Orḥot Ḥayim*, Megilla 23; Me'iri, Megilla 2b.
27 *Terumat HaDeshen* 109.
28 *Shulḥan Arukh* 692:4.
29 *Peri Ḥadash* 687.
30 *Yabia Omer, Oraḥ Ḥayim* 1:43.
31 *Shulḥan Arukh* 692:4.
32 *Magen Avraham* 692:7.

33 *Mishna Berura* 692:16.
34 Tosafot, Megilla 4a, s.v. *pasak*; Maharil 56.
35 Rif, Megilla 3a; Rosh, Megilla 1:7; Rambam, *Hilkhot Megilla* 2:12.
36 *Shulḥan Arukh* 690:17.
37 *Mishna Berura* 690:55–56.
38 *Shaar HaTziyun* 690:50.
39 Ran, Megilla 12a.
40 *Abudraham, Hilkhot Birkat HaMitzvot.*
41 *Arukh HaShulḥan* 690:5.
42 *Shulḥan Arukh* 690:17.
43 Maharil 56.
44 *Magen Avraham* 690:19.
45 See *Shulḥan Arukh* 284:6.
46 *Magen Avraham* 284:20.
47 *Tur, Oraḥ Ḥayim* 692 and *Beit Yosef* and *Baḥ*, ad loc.
48 *Beit Yosef, Oraḥ Ḥayim* 692.
49 *Orḥot Ḥayim, Hilkhot Megilla* 7.
50 Rema 692:1.
51 *Eliya Rabba* 692:8. The *Biur HaGra* 692:1 also implies that the *berakha* may be recited without a quorum.
52 *Arukh HaShulḥan* 692:5.
53 Ibid.
54 *Shulḥan Arukh* 692:1.
55 *Beit Yosef, Oraḥ Ḥayim* 689.
56 *Shulḥan Arukh* 690:6.
57 *Tur, Oraḥ Ḥayim* 690.
58 Ran, Megilla 5b; see *Shulḥan Arukh* 690:14.
59 Rashba, Responsa 467.
60 Ran, Megilla 5b.
61 *Shiltei Gibborim*, Megilla 5a.
62 See *Biur Halakha* 690 s.v. *aval.*
63 See *Shulḥan Arukh* 690:15.
64 Rema 690:14.
65 *Sefer HaManhig, Hilkhot Megilla.*
66 *Sefer Maharil, Minhagim.*
67 See http://www.biu.ac.il/JH/Parasha/tetzaveh/pare.pdf (accessed February 1, 2012).
68 Rema 690:17.

CHAPTER 38

1 Rambam, *Hilkhot Megilla* 1:1; Rashi, Arakhin 3a, s.v. *laatuyei*; R. Yishaya Di Trani (Riaz) in *Shiltei HaGibborim*, to Rif, Megilla 4a; Ritva, Megilla 4a; *Or Zarua* 2:368; Me'iri, Megilla 5a.

2 Tosefta Megilla 2:4.

3 Tosafot, Megilla 4a, s.v. *nashim*; Rosh, Megilla 1:4.

4 See *Semag, Divrei Soferim, asei* 4; Ritva, Megilla 4a, s.v. *she'af hen*.

5 See Megilla 23b.

6 Tosafot, Sukka 38a, s.v. *be'emet ameru*.

7 *Kol Bo*, 45.

8 *Shulḥan Arukh, Even HaEzer* 21:1

9 *Shulḥan Arukh, Oraḥ Ḥayim* 75:2–3.

10 Rosh, Megilla 1:17.

11 *Mordekhai*, Megilla 779.

12 *Marḥeshet* 1:22:9.

13 See Megilla 14a.

14 See Megilla 4a.

15 *Turei Even*, Megilla 4a, s.v. *nashim*.

16 R. Tzvi Pesach Frank, *Mikra'ei Kodesh*, Purim 29.

17 *Shulḥan Arukh* 689:2.

18 See *Ben Ish Ḥai, Shana Rishona, Parashat Tetzave* 2; and *Kaf HaḤayim, Oraḥ Ḥayim* 689:14.

19 *Yeḥave Daat* 3:51 and 4:34; see also R. Yitzchak Yosef's *Yalkut Yosef*, vol. 5, pp. 287–289.

20 Rema 689:2.

21 None of the *Rishonim* who cite *Behag* or the *posekim* who accept his ruling suggest a distinction between the nighttime and daytime Megilla readings. Indeed, the theories cited above from the *Marḥeshet* and *Turei Even* appear to have been offered as theoretical interpretations of *Behag*, and not as practical suggestions or rulings. Therefore, there seems to be little basis to support the *practice* proposed by R. Avraham Weiss ("Women and the Reading of the Megillah," *Torah UMadda Journal*, 8 (1998–1999), pp. 295–397) and R. Daniel Landes ("The Reading of the Megilla on Purim Night," at http://www.pardes.org.il/online_learning/halacha/Megillah_reading.php, accessed February 1, 2012) allowing a woman to publicly read the Megilla for men on Purim night. (See R. Aaron Cohen's response, "Women Reading Megilla for Men: A Rejoinder," in the *Torah UMadda Journal*, 9 (2000), pp. 248–63, as well as R. Aryeh Frimer's critique of their approach,

http://www.daat.ac.il/daat/english/tfila/frimer2.htm (accessed February 2, 2012).

22 Tosefta Megilla 2:4.

23 Tosafot, Sukka 48a.

24 *Korban Netanel,* Megilla 1:30.

25 *Tosafot HaRosh,* Sukka 38a.

26 *Mishna Berura* 689:2 and *Shaar HaTziyun* 15.

27 R. Yehuda Henkin, *Equality Lost: Essays in Torah Commentary, Halacha and Jewish Thought* (Urim Publications, Jerusalem 5759/1999).

28 *Magen Avraham* 689:6.

29 As we will see, however, Rema (690:18) raises the possibility that a group of ten women suffice to meet this preferred standard.

30 *Mishna Berura* 689:1.

31 *Benei Banim* 2:10.

32 *Yabia Omer, Oraḥ Ḥayim* 8:56:4. See R. Aryeh Frimer's comprehensive discussion of the various views on this subject, in his article, "Women's Megilla Readings," http://www.daat.ac.il/daat/english/tfila/frimer2.htm (accessed February 2, 2012).

33 *Mordekhai,* Megilla 779.

34 Raavya, Megilla 569.

35 Rema 689:2.

36 *Peri Ḥadash* 689:2.

37 *Maase Rav, Hilkhot Purim* 246.

38 R. Aryeh Frimer, in "Women's Megilla Readings," http://www.daat.ac.il/daat/english/tfila/frimer2.htm (accessed February 2, 2012), cites a host of modern authorities who rule in accordance with Rema, including R. Shlomo Zalman Auerbach (cited in *VeAleihu Lo Yibol* I, *Oraḥ Ḥayim* 433), R. Yehoshua Neuwirth (*Madrikh Hilkhati LeAḥayot BeVatei Ḥolim,* chap. 10, Purim, no. 3), R. Yechiel Michel Tukatchinsky (*Luaḥ Eretz Yisrael,* Purim), R. Chaim David Halevi (*Mekor Ḥayim LeBenot Yisrael,* sec. 34, no. 8), and R. Moshe Harari (*Mikra'ei Kodesh,* Purim 9:9). He then cites others who rule in accordance with *Peri Ḥadash* and the Vilna Gaon, such as R. Ovadia Yosef (*Yabia Omer, Oraḥ Ḥayim* 1:44 and 8:22:27), R. Moshe Sternbuch (*Mo'adim UZemanim* 2:171 and *Teshuvot VeHanhagot* 3:228).

39 See, for example, *Magen Avraham* 585:3 and *Ḥayei Adam* 141:7.

40 *Shulḥan Arukh* 690:18.

41 Rema 690:18.

42 See *Piskei Teshuvot* 690:11 and R. Aryeh Frimer's comprehensive treatment of this question at http://www.daat.ac.il/daat/english/tfila/frimer2.htm (accessed February 1, 2012).

43 *Mishna Berura* 590:61.
44 *Peri Ḥadash* 590:18.
45 See *Ḥazon Ish* 155:2; *Ir HaKodesh VeHaMikdash* 26:2; *Mikra'ei Kodesh*, Purim 50; *Yabia Omer* 6:46.

CHAPTER 39

1 Ramban, Megilla 2a.
2 In doing so, they based themselves upon a biblical precedent. See Megilla 7a and Y. Megilla 1:5.
3 Ran, Megilla 1a.
4 *Ḥiddushei HaRan*, Megilla 3a s.v. *vekhol*.
5 Ran, Megilla 2a s.v. *amar*.
6 Ritva, Megilla 2b s.v. *ela*.
7 Me'iri, Megilla 2b s.v. *af al pi*.
8 *Heikhal Yitzchak* 63–5.
9 *Har Tzvi, Oraḥ Ḥayim* 2:131.
10 *Mo'adim BaHalakha*, p. 237, n. 25.
11 *Mikra'ei Kodesh*, Purim, p. 100.
12 *Shemesh UMagen* 1:51–52, 2:16–7.
13 *Halikhot Shlomo* 20:8-9.
14 Rashi, Megilla 19a, s.v. *shanu*.
15 Rosh, Megilla 2:3.
16 Rif 6a, as understood by Ran; Ramban in *Milḥamot Hashem*, Ran 6a; Riaz as cited by *Shiltei Gibborim*, 6a; Rambam, *Hilkhot Megilla* 1:10, as understood by *Maggid Mishneh* and *Kesef Mishneh*.
17 *Tur* 688.
18 Rif, Megilla 6a.
19 *Shulḥan Arukh* 688:5.
20 *Mishna Berura* 688:12.
21 Baal HaMaor, Megilla 6a.
22 Rif 6a; Ramban, *Milḥamot Hashem*, 6a; Rosh 2:3; 6a; *Tur* 688.
23 *Shulḥan Arukh* 688:5.
24 *Mishna Berura* 688:12.
25 *Ḥazon Ish, Oraḥ Ḥayim* 152:6. *Ḥazon Ish* adds one important condition to this halakha – one's intention is significant only if he is already in the new location at nightfall (*tzeit hakokhavim*) of the fourteenth or fifteenth. If, however, a resident of a walled city is in his walled city for the beginning of the evening, and then at some point in the evening travels to an unwalled city and stays there into

the morning, he still reads the Megilla on the fifteenth, as he began the day in his walled city. Most authorities, however, disagree, and rule in accordance with the *Mishna Berura,* who implies that the location where one intends to be on the morning of the fourteenth or fifteenth determines his status, regardless of where he began the night.

26 *Har Tzvi, Oraḥ Ḥayim* 119.

27 We assume here that the halakha is in accordance with Rashi – the critical moment of obligation is on both the morning of the fourteenth and that of the fifteenth. Some *Aḥaronim* suggest being stringent and reading, without a blessing, in deference to the opinion of Rosh.

28 This follows the position of *Taz* and the *Mishna Berura*; according to *Ḥazon Ish,* even if his plans change, he observes Purim on the fourteenth.

29 *Ir HaKodesh VeHaMikdash*; *Har Tzvi* 2:128.

30 *Minḥat Shlomo* 1:23:4.

31 *Har Tzvi, Oraḥ Ḥayim* 2:118–9.

32 *Mishna Berura* 688:12; *Kaf HaḤayim* 688:29.

33 *Har Tzvi, Oraḥ Ḥayim* 2:128:11, 20–21.

CHAPTER 40

1 See, for example, Rambam (*Hilkhot Megilla* 2:14), Rashba (Megilla 4a), and Ritva (Megilla 4a).

2 *Mordekhai,* Megilla 787.

3 *Shulḥan Arukh* 695:1.

4 Rema 695:1.

5 Ibid.

6 *Mishna Berura* 695:8.

7 *Orḥot Ḥayim, Hilkhot Purim* 35.

8 *Hagahot Maimoniyot, Hilkhot Megilla* 2:14.

9 *Tur, Oraḥ Ḥayim* 695.

10 Rosh, Responsa 22:6.

11 Maharil, *Hilkhot Purim* 15

12 *Shulḥan Arukh* and Rema 695:2.

13 *Eishel Avraham* 5.

14 Rema 695:2.

15 *Magen Avraham* 695:9.

16 *Birkei Yosef* 695.

17 *Eliya Rabba* 695:7.

18 See *Shulḥan Arukh, Oraḥ Ḥayim* 529:1.

19 *Arukh HaShulḥan* 695:7.
20 *Haamek She'ala* 67:1, attributing this view to R. Aḥai Gaon.
21 *Mishna Berura* 695:15.
22 *Magen Avraham* 695:9.
23 *Peri Megadim* 695:9.
24 *Arukh HaShulḥan* 695:12.
25 *Hilkhot Megilla* 2:15.
26 *Shulḥan Arukh* 696:6.
27 See *Yeḥave Daat* 6:33.
28 *Magen Avraham* 696:15.
29 See above, chap. 3.
30 Baal HaMaor, Megilla 3b.
31 Ran, ibid.
32 Rif, Megilla 3b.
33 Rosh 1:8.
34 *Hilkhot Megilla* 2:15.
35 Rema 695:2.
36 *Arukh HaShulḥan* 695:3.
37 *Orḥot Ḥayim, Hilkhot Purim.*
38 *Tur* 695.
39 *Shulḥan Arukh* 695:2.
40 Rema 695:5.
41 *Mishna Berura* 695:5.
42 *Arukh HaShulḥan* 695:5.
43 *Hilkhot Megilla* 2:15.
44 *Tur* and *Shulḥan Arukh* 605.
45 *Hitorerut Teshuva* 1:6.
46 *Shulḥan Arukh* 695:1.
47 Rashi, Megilla 7b, s.v. *livsumei.*
48 *Hilkhot Megilla* 2:15.
49 Roke'aḥ 237.
50 Radbaz 1:462.
51 See, for example, R. Menashe Klein, *Mishneh Halakhot* 5:83.
52 *Mo'adim UZemanim* 2:190.
53 *Biur Halakha* 695:2.
54 See Ketubot 65a, Pesaḥim 109a, and *Mo'adim UZemanim*, ibid.
55 *Orḥot Ḥayim, Hilkhot Purim.*
56 Raavya 2:564.
57 *Ḥayei Adam* 155:30.

58 Maharsha, ibid.
59 *Biur Halakha* 695 s.v *ad.*
60 *Shulḥan Arukh* 185:4.
61 *Shulḥan Arukh* 99:1.
62 *Mekor Ḥayim, Oraḥ Ḥayim* 695.
63 See, for example, R. Betzalel Stern (1911–1989), *BeTzel Ha-Ḥokhma* 6:81.
64 *Yesod VeShoresh HaAvoda* 12:6.
65 *Siddur R. Yaakov Emden.*
66 *Tur* and *Shulḥan Arukh* 694–5.
67 *Hilkhot Megilla* 2:17.
68 Ritva, Megilla 7a.
69 Rashi, Responsa 293; *Shibbolei HaLeket* 202.
70 See Maharsha, *Ḥiddushei Aggadot*, Megilla 7a.
71 *Shaarei Teshuva* 695:1.
72 *Hilkhot Megilla* 2:16.
73 *Or Same'aḥ*, ibid.
74 *Turei Even*, Megilla 7a.
75 *Shulḥan Arukh, Yoreh De'ah* 253:2.
76 See *Piskei Teshuvot* 694:2.
77 *Hilkhot Megilla* 2:16.
78 *Shulḥan Arukh* 694:3.
79 Cited by *Nimukei Yosef*, Bava Metzia 48b.
80 *Tur* 694.
81 *Shulḥan Arukh* 694:3.
82 *Maḥzor Vitry* 245.
83 *Shulḥan Arukh* 694:4.
84 *Gilyon HaShas*, Shabbat 10b.
85 See Rema, *Yoreh De'ah* 249:1.
86 *Arukh HaShulḥan* 694:4.
87 R. Ovadia Yosef, *Yeḥave Daat* 1:87.
88 *Hilkhot Yom Tov* 6:18.
89 *Terumat HaDeshen* 111.
90 *Hilkhot Megilla* 2:15.
91 See, for example, Ḥatam Sofer, *Oraḥ Ḥayim* 1:196, citing R. Shlomo Alkavetz's *Manot HaLevi.*
92 Rema 695.
93 *Eretz Tzvi* 121.
94 *Be'er Heitev* 695:7; *Ḥelkat Yaakov* 1:102.
95 *Arukh HaShulḥan* 695:17.

96 *Hilkhot Megilla* 2:15.
97 *Shulḥan Arukh* 695:4.
98 *Mishna Berura* 695:20.
99 *Arukh HaShulḥan* 695:14.
100 Ibid.
101 *Magen Avraham* 695:11; *Ḥayei Adam* 135:31; *Arukh HaShulḥan* 695:15.
102 *Peri Ḥadash* 695; *Yeḥave Daat* 6:45.
103 *Mishna Berura* 695:20.
104 *Maase Rav* 249; see also *Peri Ḥadash* 695.
105 *Tzitz Eliezer* 8:14.
106 *Terumat HaDeshen* 111.
107 *Mishneh Halakhot* 4:91.
108 See Rema 695; Ḥatam Sofer, *Oraḥ Ḥayim* 1:196.
109 *Peri Megadim* 694:11.
110 *Arukh HaShulḥan* 695:16.
111 *Binyan Tziyon* 44.
112 *Mishna Berura* 695:18.
113 *Shulḥan Arukh* 695:4 and *Mishna Berura* 695:25.
114 *Magen Avraham* 695:14.
115 *Arukh HaShulḥan* 694:2.
116 *Peri Ḥadash* 695; see also the comments of the Vilna Gaon 695:4.
117 Rema 695:2.
118 *Terumat HaDeshen* 110.
119 *Mishna Berura* 695:13.
120 Rema 696:4.
121 *Taz, Yoreh De'ah* 182.
122 See *Mishna Berura* 696:31 and *Arukh HaShulḥan* 695:10.

CHAPTER 41

1 Pesaḥim 6a–b, citing Num. 9:2, 6.
2 Tosafot, ibid., s.v. *vehatnan*.
3 *Beit Yosef* (429) writes that on the day itself, one should study the reasons why we observe the particular *ḥag*. In addition, he suggests that one should learn the laws relating to Yom Tov.
4 See Rashba, Megilla 4a; Ritva, Megilla 4b; Ran, Pesaḥim 2b; Me'iri, Pesaḥim 6a.
5 See Rambam, *Hilkhot Talmud Torah* 2:8.
6 See R. Aḥai Gaon, *She'iltot, Tzav* 78; Rashi, Rosh HaShana 7a, s.v. *atei* and Bava Kama 113a, s.v. *berigla*; Tosafot, Megilla 4a., s.v. *mai irya*; Roke'aḥ 244.

7 *Beit Yosef* 429.
8 Berakhot 30a; Sukka 9a; Bava Kama 113a; Sanhedrin 7a.
9 *Baḥ* 429.
10 *Hilkhot Tefilla* 13:8.
11 *Ora VeSimḥa, Hilkhot Ḥametz UMatza* 2:19.
12 See Pesaḥim 4a; Rambam, *Hilkhot Ḥametz UMatza* 2:19.
13 *Hilkhot Yom Tov* 6:19.
14 Introduction to *Hilkhot Korban Pesaḥ.*
15 Ramban, in his comments on Rambam's *Sefer HaMitzvot* (Negative Commandment 198), disagrees, arguing that there is no separate prohibition of a *taarovet ḥametz.*
16 The *Amora'im* argue regarding the source of this prohibition:

Ḥizkiya states: What is the source from which we learn that it is forbidden to derive benefit from *ḥametz*? The Torah states [Ex. 13:3]: "And *ḥametz* should not be eaten"; that is, it is not permitted [to be used to derive benefit that leads to] eating. The reason is because the Torah says, "And *ḥametz* should not be eaten," and not, "And he should not eat *ḥametz*." Had it said that, I might have thought that it is [only] prohibited to eat, but one may derive benefit from it. R. Abbahu states: Wherever the Torah states, "He should not eat" or "Do not eat," a prohibition against eating and deriving benefit is implied, unless the Torah instructs otherwise.

Regarding other prohibited foods, Rambam (*Hilkhot Maakhalot Assurot* 8:15) cites the view of R. Abbahu, who teaches that whenever the Torah states, "Do not eat," it includes the prohibition of deriving benefit from prohibited foods unless instructed otherwise. It is therefore curious that regarding *ḥametz* (*Hilkhot Ḥametz UMatza* 1:2), Rambam seems to cite the position of Ḥizkiya. The *Aḥaronim* discuss this issue in great depth, noting that Rambam felt it necessary to enlist a separate, independent source to prohibit benefiting from *ḥametz.*

A similar situation is found when Rambam records the prohibition of eating less than a *kezayit* of *ḥametz,* known as "*ḥatzi shiur*:" "Eating even the slightest amount of *ḥametz* itself on Pesaḥ is forbidden by the Torah, as it states [Ex. 13:3], 'Do not eat [leaven].' Nevertheless, [a person who eats *ḥametz*] is not liable for *karet,* nor must he bring a sacrifice for anything less than the specified measure, which is the size of an olive" (*Hilkhot Ḥametz UMatza* 1:1). Here, too, the *Aḥaronim* note that Rambam cites an independent source for this prohibition, despite the fact that R. Yoḥanan (Yoma 73b) already prohibits eating an amount less than a *kezayit* of all prohibited foods.

17 *Hilkhot Ḥametz UMatza* 1:1, citing Ex. 12:15.
18 *Ḥinukh* 11.

19 *Ḥinukh* 117.

20 *Torah Sheleima,* vol.19, appendix 20; see also *Haggada Sheleima,* appendix 7. He notes that both *ḥametz* and *avoda zara* share the unique prohibition against possession, they must both be destroyed, and one may not derive benefit from them. In addition, both *ḥametz* and *avoda zara* cannot be nullified in a *taarovet* (a mixture of permissible and prohibited foods), and both *ḥametz* and *avoda zara* (in certain circumstances) may be "nullified" through an oral declaration (*bittul*). Finally, just as we check our houses for *ḥametz* (*bedikat ḥametz*) before Pesaḥ, the Jewish people were commanded to search the Land of Israel for remnants of idolatry (Rambam, *Hilkhot Avodat Kokhavim* 7:1).

21 *Guide for the Perplexed* 3:46; see also *Hilkhot Avoda Zara* 1:1.

22 Zohar 2:182.

23 Mitzva 117, citing Prov. 16:5.

24 Radbaz, Responsa 3:546.

CHAPTER 42

1 R. Meir's view is presented in Pesaḥim 43a and 48b.

2 *Shulḥan Arukh* 451:2.

3 *Terumat HaDeshen* 167; *Shulḥan Arukh* 459:2.

4 Rashi, Pesaḥim 48b, s.v. *batzek.*

5 Me'iri, Pesaḥim 48b, s.v. *batzek.*

6 Commentary on the Mishna, Pesaḥim 3:2.

7 *Hilkhot Ḥametz UMatza* 5:13.

8 See Ran, Pesaḥim 15a; see also Rashba, Responsa 1:124 who concurs.

9 Ritva, Pesaḥim 48b.

10 *Shiltei Gibborim,* Pesaḥim 15b.

11 *Shibbolei HaLeket, Hilkhot Pesaḥ* 211.

12 Rosh, Responsa 14:4.

13 *Terumat HaDeshen* 123.

14 *Shulḥan Arukh* 459:2.

15 That is, it is forbidden and punishable by *karet* to eat the mixture once it has developed cracks like a "locust's antennae," and dough that becomes white and pale is considered to be "*seior.*"

16 The Gemara (Ḥullin 23b) offers two explanations of why one is exempt from *malkot* for eating such dough: either there is a *safek* (doubt) regarding whether it is truly *ḥametz* or not, and therefore one cannot be liable for eating it, or it is considered to be its own stage of leavening (*birya*) – it is not matza, but not yet

ḥametz. The *Aḥaronim* discuss whether R. Yehuda believes that this dough is prohibited *mideoraita* or *miderabbanan*.

17 Pesaḥim 43a, s.v. *seior*.

18 See *Minḥhat Barukh* 44.

19 Although *ḥametz nukshe* is not *ḥametz gamur*, the *Rishonim* disagree regarding the relationship between *ḥametz nukshe* and *ḥametz gamur*. This question is even more significant, of course, for R. Meir, who prohibits *ḥametz nukshe mideoraita*. For example, Rashi (s.v. *ve'eilu*) explains that all forms of *ḥametz* mentioned by the Mishna are subject to *bal yeira'e*, but Tosafot (s.v. *ve'eilu*) disagree. According to Rashi, although the punishment may be different, we relate to *ḥametz nukshe* no differently than to *ḥametz gamur*, and *bal yeira'e* thus applies. Tosafot, however, view *ḥametz nukshe* as a separate and qualitatively more lenient category, regarding which not all of the laws of *ḥametz* apply. R. Yehuda, as noted above, maintains that *ḥametz nukshe* is only rabbinically prohibited, and the *Rishonim* debate whether one must rid himself of *ḥametz nukshe* before Pesaḥ according to his opinion (Ran, Pesaḥim 13a, s.v. *lefikhakh*) or not (*Tur* 442).

20 Baal HaMaor and Raavad, Pesaḥim 13a in Rif.

21 *Shulḥan Arukh* 459:2, 447:12.

22 *Magen Avraham* 442:1. *Magen Avraham* insists that if the *ḥametz* is not fit at all for human consumption, it is not even considered *ḥametz nukshe*. Indeed, other prohibited foods that are not edible are generally not prohibited (Avoda Zara 67b–68a). Thus, *ḥametz nukshe* refers only to mixtures that are barely edible. The *Minḥat Barukh* (44) disagrees, arguing that if *ḥametz* that is barely edible is permitted *mideoraita* and prohibited *miderabbanan*, then the laws of *ḥametz* are actually more lenient than the laws of other prohibited foods, which are prohibited *mideoraita* even if they are barely edible!

23 *Mishna Berura* 442:2.

24 Tosafot, ibid., s.v. *ḥarakho*.

25 Ritva, ibid.

26 Ran, Pesaḥim 5b.

27 Rosh, Pesaḥim 2:1.

28 *Taz* 442:8.

29 *Mishna Berura* 442:43.

CHAPTER 43

1 Rashi, Pesaḥim 29b, s.v. *shelo*. Rashi also maintains that Rav rules in accordance with R. Yehuda, who prohibits all mixtures of similar substances (*min bemino*); he

simply extended this stringency to all mixtures of *ḥametz* due to the prohibition's more severe nature.

2 *Hilkhot Maakhalot Assurot* 16:9. The *Rishonim* challenge this assertion for numerous reasons. The *Mordekhai* (Pesaḥim 553), for example, suggests that since *ḥametz* will become prohibited again the next year, it cannot be considered to be a *davar sheyesh lo matirin*. Ran (Nedarim 52a) offers an entirely different understanding of *davar sheyesh lo matirin.*

3 *Shulḥan Arukh* 447:2.

4 *Mishna Berura* 447:15.

5 *Arukh HaShulḥan* 447:3.

6 *She'iltot, Parashat Tzav* 3:80.

7 Tosafot, Pesaḥim 30a, s.v. *amar rav.*

8 *Shulḥan Arukh* 447:1.

9 Ran, Avoda Zara 37a, s.v. *vegarsinan,* cites Raavad and Ramban, who rule that one may derive benefit from this mixture.

10 *Shulḥan Arukh* 447:1.

11 Rif, Avoda Zara 30a.

12 Rosh, Avoda Zara 5:30.

13 *Shulḥan Arukh* 447:9.

14 *Mishna Berura* 447:95.

15 *Beit Yosef* 467.

16 *Mishna Berura* 467:62, 67.

17 *Haggada Shel Pesaḥ Minḥat Asher.*

18 *Piskei Teshuvot* 467:14.

19 *Hilkhot Ḥametz UMatza* 4:12.

20 Rosh, Pesaḥim 2:65.

21 *Shulḥan Arukh* 447:4.

22 *Terumat HaDeshen* 114.

23 Rema 447:4.

24 Tosafot, 66a s.v. *mikhlal.*

25 Rosh, Avoda Zara 5:6.

26 *Mordekhai,* Avoda Zara 567.

27 *Yerei'im* 52.

28 Rashba, Responsa 1:499.

29 *Shulḥan Arukh* 447:10.

30 Rema, ibid.

31 *Arukh HaShulḥan* 447:21.

32 *Ḥakham Tzvi* 75.

33 Tosafot, Pesaḥim 42a s.v. *ve'eilu overin.*

34 Rashi, ibid., s.v. *ve'eilu.*

35 *Hilkhot Ḥametz UMatza* 4:8. The commentators on Rambam disagree as to when one violates *bal yeira'e* and *bal yimaztei. Maggid Mishneh* questions whether one only violates the prohibition of owning *ḥametz* if he keeps a mixture containing a significant amount of *ḥametz* – that is, a *kezayit bikhedei akhilat peras* [the size of an olive or more with the combined volume of three (Rashi) or four (Rambam) eggs] – or even a mixture containing less (R. Moshe HaKohen, cited by *Maggid Mishneh* and *Kesef Mishneh* 4:8). Among the *Rishonim*, Maharam Ḥalava (Pesaḥim 43a) rules that one only violates the biblical prohibition of owning *ḥametz* for a mixture containing a *kezayit bikhedei akhilat peras,* while Rabbeinu David (ibid., 42a) believes that any mixture containing a *kezayit* of *ḥametz* is prohibited to own *mideoraita.*

36 *Shulḥan Arukh* 442:1.

37 *Mishna Berura* 442:1.

38 *Arukh HaShulḥan* 442:12.

39 Tosefta, Pesaḥim 3:2.

40 Raavad, *Hilkhot Ḥametz UMatza* 4:10–11; Raavan, cited by Rosh, Pesaḥim 3:10.

41 *Hilkhot Ḥametz UMatza* 4:8, 12.

42 *Hilkhot Maakhalot Assurot* 15:1.

43 *Shulḥan Arukh* 442:4.

44 Rashi, Avoda Zara 49a, s.v. *ve'amar.*

45 Ran, Avoda Zara 21b.

46 Tosafot, Rabbeinu David, Pesaḥim 26b.

47 *Shulḥan Arukh, Yoreh De'ah* 142:11.

48 *Magen Avraham, Oraḥ Ḥayim* 445:5; see also *Taz, Yoreh De'ah* 142:4.

49 See *Shulḥan Arukh, Yoreh De'ah* 142:4, 7; Shakh, ad loc. 10, and in his *Nekudot HaKesef.*

50 *Avnei Miluim* 6–7; regarding *avoda zara,* he rules in accordance with Shakh. See *Shulḥan Arukh HaRav* 445:10 (and *Kunteras Aḥaron* 445:6), who discusses this issue as well.

51 *Nishmat Adam, Hilkhot Pesaḥ,* 9.

52 *Shaarei Teshuva* 448:15.

53 *Kitzur Shulḥan Arukh* 117:13.

54 *Mishna Berura* 448:33.

55 *Iggerot Moshe, Oraḥ Ḥayim* 1:147. R. Feinstein wrote this responsum in Russia in 1935, shortly before immigrating to the United States, and at the end of this responsum, he alludes to the persecution he experienced at the hands of the Soviets.

56 See http://kashrut-tnuva.co.il/milk_page.php?actions=show&id=208 (accessed February 1, 2012).

57 *Iggerot Moshe, Oraḥ Ḥayim* 3:61.

58 See http://www.kosher.org.uk/faq.htm (accessed February 1, 2012).

59 *Shulḥan Arukh* 461:4.

60 *Olat Shabbat* 453:73. R. Shmuel b. R. Yosef's two-volume commentary on the *Shulḥan Arukh*, the *Olat Tamid* and the *Olat Shabbat*, is often quoted by other commentaries on the *Shulḥan Arukh*, such as *Magen Avraham*. Originally published in 1681, it was never printed a second time.

61 *Magen Avraham* 458:1.

62 *Knesset HaGedola* 461; *Beit Yosef*, s.v. *anu*.

63 *Shulḥan Arukh HaRav* 460:6.

64 *Shaarei Teshuva* 460:10.

65 *Ḥayei Adam* 127:7; *Iggerot Moshe, Oraḥ Ḥayim* 3:64.

CHAPTER 44

1 *Shulḥan Arukh, Yoreh De'ah* 155:3.

2 *Noda BiYehuda Mahadura Kama, Yoreh De'ah* 35.

3 *Minḥat Shlomo* 1:17. R. Auerbach concludes by questioning whether the definition of "sick" here is equivalent to the category of "*ḥoleh she'ein bo sakana*" found in the laws of Shabbat, which is generally defined as one who is sick with an illness that is not life-threatening, or whether even one who is only slightly ill may take such medicine.

4 See also Tosafot, Pesaḥim 21b, s.v. *ḥarakho*.

5 Ritva, Pesaḥim 21b; Ran on Rif, Pesaḥim 5b.

6 *Taz* 442:8.

7 *Shaagat Aryeh* 75.

8 *Ḥazon Ish, Oraḥ Ḥayim* 116:8.

9 *Yad Avraham, Yoreh De'ah* 84:17.

10 *Iggerot Moshe, Oraḥ Ḥayim* 2:92.

11 *Yeḥave Daat* 2:60.

12 *Tzitz Eliezer* 10:25.

13 *Minḥat Shlomo* 1:17.

14 *Hilkhot Tumat Okhelin* 10:2.

15 *Moriah* 75.

16 For example, see R. Ovadia Yosef, *Yeḥave Daat* 2:60 and *Yalkut Yosef, Hilkhot Mo'adim*, p. 362; *Shemirat Shabbat KeHilkhata* 40:74–75.

17 See http://www.crcweb.org/Sappirim/Sappirim%2014%20%28Oct%202008%29.pdf (accessed February 1, 2012).
18 Orthodox Union Daf HaKashrus 12:2, available at http://www.ou.org/pdf/daf/5764/Daf%2012-2.pdf (accessed February 1, 2012).
19 *Tzitz Eliezer* 10:25:20.
20 See http://oukosher.org/index.php/passover/article/5708/ (accessed February 1, 2012).
21 See http://www.kashrut.com/Passover/CRC_Policy_on_Medicines.pdf (accessed February 1, 2012).
22 *Madrikh Kashrut, Ḥug Ḥatam Sofer*, 1993.
23 Rema, *Yoreh De'ah* 108:5.
24 Shabbat 86a, citing Ps. 109:19.
25 Tosafot, Nidda 32a, s.v. *vekashemen*; Tosafot, Yoma 77b, s.v. *ditenan.*
26 See, for example, *Sefer HaTeruma* 238.
27 Rema 326:10.
28 *Biur HaGra*, s.v. *o bishe'ar ḥeilev.*
29 *Biur Halakha* 326:10, s.v. *bishe'ar ḥeilev.*
30 *Arukh HaShulḥan, Yoreh De'ah* 117:29.
31 *Yeḥave Daat* 4:43.
32 *Iggerot Moshe, Oraḥ Ḥayim* 3:62.
33 See, for example, http://www.freerepublic.com/focus/chat/2348007/posts (accessed February 1, 2012). Similarly, the *Economist* (November 29, 2008 p. 13) reports that "moonshine and 'dual purpose' liquids, such as perfume and windscreen wash, make up a significant proportion of alcohol consumption" in Russia.
34 *Mikra'ei Kodesh*, Pesaḥ 54.
35 *Yalkut Yosef*, Mo'adim p. 360.
36 *Halachos of Pesach* pp. 25–26.
37 *Iggerot Moshe, Yoreh De'ah* 2:30.
38 *Halachos of Pesach*, pp. 25–26.
39 *Har Tzvi, Yoreh De'ah* 95.
40 *Halachos of Pesach*, p. 27, n. 108.
41 Ibid.
42 Ibid., p. 26.
43 *Piskei Teshuvot* 442:10.
44 Orthodox Union Daf HaKashrus 12:2.

CHAPTER 45

1 *Hilkhot Ḥametz UMatza* 5:1. Dr. B. P. Munk (*Teḥumin* 1, pp. 97–99) describes the chemical difference between a process of *ḥimutz* (leavening) and *sirḥon*

(spoiling). The wheat flour contains an enzyme called beta-amylase, which breaks down the starch into glucose (sugar), which is then converted into alcohol. When the alcohol evaporates (producing a pleasant smell), the dough rises. Rice, however, lacks beta-amylase. Although other enzymes contained in rice generate a slow process of fermentation, another enzyme causes the dough to decay before the process is completed. This is why the sages explain that rice does not ferment, but rather decays.

2 Ritva, Pesaḥim 35b.

3 Maharam Ḥalava, Pesaḥim 35b.

4 *Hagahot Rabbeinu Peretz* 222.

5 *Oraḥ Ḥayim* 453.

6 *Hagahot Rabbeinu Peretz* 222.

7 *Or Zarua* 2:256.

8 Rabbeinu Yeruḥam, *nativ* 5, 3:41:1.

9 *Sefer Maharil, Minhagim, Hilkhot Maakhalot Assurot BePesaḥ*, s.v. [16] *kitnit*.

10 *Tur*; *Hagahot Maimoniyot*, chap. 5; and *Mordekhai*, chap. *kol shaa*

11 Rema 453:1.

12 *Mor UKetzia* 453.

13 *Terumat HaDeshen* 453.

14 *Hilkhot Kilayim* 1:8.

15 Maharil, *Minhagim, Maakhalot Assurot BePesaḥ* 19.

16 *Darkhei Moshe* and Rema 464.

17 *Hilkhot Kilayim* 2.

18 *Taz* 453:1.

19 *Mikra'ei Kodesh* 2:60.

20 *Iggerot Moshe, Oraḥ Ḥayim* 3:63.

21 *Nishmat Adam*, Pesaḥ, 20.

22 *Nishmat Adam* 33; *Avnei Nezer, Oraḥ Ḥayim* 373.

23 *Terumat HaDeshen* 113

24 Rema 453:1

25 *Be'er Yitzchak* 11.

26 *Marḥeshet, Oraḥ Ḥayim* 3. See also Maharsham 1:183.

27 *Oraḥ Mishpat*, pp. 108–14.

28 *Mikra'ei Kodesh* 2:60.

29 *Minḥat Yitzchak* 3:138.

30 *Iggerot Moshe, Oraḥ Ḥayim* 3:63.

31 R. Tzvi Pesach Frank, *Mikra'ei Kodesh* 2:60; *Ḥelkat Yaakov* 97, *Seridei Esh* 1:50.

32 *Avnei Nezer* 533.

33 Ibid., 373.

34 Maharsham 1:183.

35 *Terumat HaDeshen* 113.

36 Maharil, Responsa 25.

37 Rema 453:1.

38 *Ḥayei Adam* 127; *Mishna Berura* 453:9.

39 See *Peri Ḥadash* OC and *Be'er Yitzchak* 11.

40 See the responsa of *Eretz Ḥemda, Shut BeMareh HaBazak* (4:51) and R. Yehuda Price, "*Kitniyot BePesaḥ,*" *Teḥumin* 13. This position is attributed to R. Dov Lior (*Derekh Chevron* OC 499), R. Nachum Rabinovitz, and R. Yaakov Ariel as well.

41 Seemingly, this might depend on the question of whether one may eat food containing a minority of non-kosher ingredients (less that 1/60) produced by non-Jews. See *Noda BiYehuda, Yoreh De'ah* 56 and Rashba, Responsa 2:214.

42 *Yeḥave Daat* 5:32.

43 *Ḥayei Adam* 127:1.

44 Maharam Padua 48.

45 *Divrei Malkiel* 1:28.

46 *Arukh HaShulḥan* 453:5.

47 *Teshuva MeAhava* 259.

48 *Ḥayei Adam* 7.

49 Maharam Schick, *Oraḥ Ḥayim* 241.

50 *Kaf HaḤayim* 453:27.

CHAPTER 46

1 Some *Rishonim* insist that there may still be differences. For example, Raa (cited by Ritva, Pesaḥim 5b) and Rabbeinu David (Pesaḥim 5b, s.v. *ne'emar*) explain that both *bal yeira'e* and *bal yimatzei* apply in one's house and outside of one's domain. However, *bal yeira'e* only applies to *ḥametz* which is visible, while *bal yimatzei* applies to both visible and hidden *ḥametz*. Ritva (Pesaḥim 5b) cites a more extreme position, which posits that while the *gezeira shava* equates these two prohibitions regarding ownership – i.e., the *ḥametz* must either be owned or under one's *aḥrayut* (responsibility) – they are still different regarding location. For hidden *ḥametz* in one's home, one only violates *bal yimatzei*, and for visible *ḥametz* outside of one's domain, one only violates *bal yeira'e*. Accordingly, one does not violate either prohibition for hidden *ḥametz* outside of one's domain! The *Kesef Mishneh* (*Hilkhot Ḥametz UMatza* 1:3) understands that the Gemara only intended to equate these two prohibitions in one direction – whenever one violates *bal yeira'e*, one also violates *bal yimatzei*. However, if the *ḥametz* is hidden, one only violates *bal yimatzei*. Others disagree. Rambam (*Hilkhot Ḥametz*

UMatza 4:1–2), for example, implies that the prohibitions are identical, despite that fact that he lists them separately in his *Sefer HaMitzvot* (Mitzvot 200, 201).

2 Tosafot, Shavuot 44b, s.v. *shomer*.

3 Rosh, Pesaḥim 1:4.

4 Rambam (*Hilkhot Ḥametz UMatza* 4:4) agrees, but adds that even if the non-Jew forces the Jew to pay in case it is stolen or lost, he violates *bal yeira'e uval yimatzei*. Rambam clearly cannot maintain that this relationship is defined as a type of ownership. Rather, he violates *bal yeira'e uval yimatzei* because of his personal interest in the *ḥametz*.

5 Rashi, ibid., s.v. *yiḥed*.

6 Tosafot, ibid., s.v. *yiḥed*.

7 Rosh, Pesaḥim 1:6.

8 Ran, Pesaḥim 2b.

9 Rosh, Pesaḥim 1:4.

10 See Rambam 4:1, for example.

11 See Rosh, Pesaḥim 1:4.

12 *Biur HaGra* 443:2.

13 *Shulḥan Arukh* 440.

14 *Magen Avraham* 440:1.

15 Mahari HaLevi 2:124.

16 *Melamed LeHo'il, Oraḥ Ḥayim* 91.

17 *Sefer HaZikaron, Yad Shaul*.

18 *Minḥat Yitzchak* 3:1.

19 *Mo'adim UZemanim* 3:269, n. 1.

20 Rashi, ibid., s.v. *ve'eilu*.

21 Tosafot, ibid., s.v. *ve'eilu*.

22 Rambam, *Hilkhot Ḥametz UMatza* 4:88; *Shulḥan Arukh* 442:1.

23 Tosafot, Pesaḥim 4b, s.v. *mideoraita*.

24 Rashi, ibid.

25 Ramban, Pesaḥim 4b.

26 *Hilkhot Ḥametz UMatza* 2:1–2.

27 *Minḥat Ḥinukh*, Mitzva 9.

28 Tosafot, Pesaḥim 4b, s.v. *mideoraita*.

29 See also Tosafot, Pesaḥim 29b s.v. *R. Ashi*. Interestingly, Baal HaMaor (Pesaḥim 7a) asserts that according to R. Shimon (Pesaḥim 28a), who permits eating *ḥametz* until nightfall, not only may one eat *ḥametz* after the sixth hour, but by eating *ḥametz*, one actually fulfills the mitzva of *tashbitu*!

30 Rashi, Pesaḥim 4b.

31 Incidentally, Ramban, in describing the mitzva of *tashbitu*, writes that "God intended that one's *ḥametz* should be destroyed or nullified by noon…" Clearly, he also focuses upon the "result," that one should not have any *ḥametz* in one's possession by noon, and not upon the act of destruction itself.

32 *Hilkhot Ḥametz UMatza* 1:3.

33 The *Minḥat Ḥinukh* rejects this understanding of the debate between R. Yehuda and the *ḥakhamim*.

CHAPTER 47

1 Rashi, Pesaḥim 2a, s.v. *bodkin*.

2 Furthermore, the Gemara implies that had one not done *bittul ḥametz*, one might indeed violate *bal yeira'e* and *bal yimatzei*! Tosafot (Pesaḥim 21a, s.v. *ve'i*) assert that one does not violate *bal yeira'e uval yimatzei* for *ḥametz she'eino yadua*, *ḥametz* whose existence is unknown. Other *Rishonim* assume that one does violate *bal yeira'e uval yimatzei* for *ḥametz she'eino yadua*, but they disagree as to whether and how *bedikat ḥametz* helps. Ran (Pesaḥim 1a, s.v. *ela*), for example, explains that the Torah recognizes probability ("*samkha Torah al haḥazakot*"), and therefore only after one has searched his house thoroughly can he safely assume that he does not own any more *ḥametz*. Seemingly, if one missed some *ḥametz* during the search, he would be considered a *shogeg*, one who inadvertently violates a commandment. Rabbeinu David (Pesaḥim 2a, s.v. *ela*) explains that "the Torah was not given to angels," and therefore one is certainly not responsible for *ḥametz* found after a thorough search. *Tur* (*Oraḥ Ḥayim* 433) disagrees and insists that if one finds *ḥametz* in one's home after searching, he retroactively violates *bal yeira'e uval yimatzei*. The *Shulḥan Arukh HaRav* (433:12 and *Kuntras Aḥaron* 433:5) disagrees and argues that after performing *bedikat ḥametz*, one no longer violates *bal yeira'e uval yimatzei* and is considered to be an *ones*.

3 Ran, Pesaḥim 1a, s.v. *bodkin*.

4 Rabbeinu David, Pesaḥim 2a, s.v. *bodkin*.

5 Maharam Ḥalava, ibid., s.v. *bodkin*.

6 Tosafot, ibid., s.v. *or*. The *Aḥaronim* debate whether this comment is meant to explain why *ḥametz* should be different from other prohibited foods, or whether Tosafot is offering another explanation for *bedikat ḥametz* – the Rabbis followed the Torah's lead in demanding that one remove *ḥametz* from one's house.

7 Radbaz, Responsa 3:546.

8 See Maharam Ḥalava 6b, for example.

9 *Magen Avraham* 460:1.

10 *Biur HaGra* 460:11.

11 *Shulḥan Arukh HaRav* 442:28, *Ḥayei Adam* 119:6.
12 *Shulḥan Arukh* 442:6–7.
13 *Shaar HaTziyun* 442:52 and *Mishna Berura* 442:33.
14 *Shulḥan Arukh HaRav* 442:30.
15 *Mordekhai*, Pesaḥim 535.
16 *Terumat HaDeshen* 133.
17 *Shulḥan Arukh* 433:11.
18 *Shaarei Teshuva* 433.
19 *Shulḥan Arukh* 436:1.
20 Rema, ibid.
21 *Tur* 436. *Avi Ezri* apparently views *bedikat ḥametz* as a "*ḥovat gavra*" – a personal obligation to search one's house, even if he will not own it on Erev Pesaḥ. *Tur*, however, understands the obligation to be a "*ḥovat bayit*" – an obligation incumbent upon the house, to be fulfilled by its owner on Erev Pesaḥ.
22 *Shulḥan Arukh* and Rema 436.
23 Ḥatam Sofer 131.
24 *Mishna Berura* 436:32.
25 Tosafot, ibid., s.v. *mideoraita*.
26 Raavya 417, for example.
27 Ran 1a, s.v. *umihu*; Maharam Ḥalava 6b, s.v. *amar*.
28 Rashi, Pesaḥim 4b, s.v. *bevittul*.
29 Ramban, Pesaḥim 4b.
30 *Hilkhot Ḥametz UMatza* 2:1–2.
31 *Shulḥan Arukh* and Rema 334:4.
32 *Baḥ* 334:9.
33 *Shulḥan Arukh* 434:4.
34 See R. Chaim Jachter, *Gray Matter*, vol. 3, p. 139.

CHAPTER 48

1 As mentioned previously, many *Rishonim* explain that one fulfills the mitzva of *tashbitu* by destroying one's *ḥametz*. Although some *Rishonim* believe that one can fulfill *tashbitu* through *bittul*, or even by declaring one's *ḥametz hefker*, all agree that one who does not perform *bittul* until midday of the fourteenth of Nisan must certainly destroy his *ḥametz*.
2 *Shulḥan Arukh* 443.
3 Tosafot, Pesaḥim 21b, s.v. *behadei*.
4 *Tur* 455.
5 *Hilkhot Ḥametz UMatza* 1:3.

6 *Sefat Emet*, Pesaḥim 21a.
7 Rashi, Ibid.
8 Rosh, Pesaḥim 2:3.
9 Tosafot, Pesaḥim 12b, s.v. *eimatai.*
10 Baal HaMaor, Pesaḥim 5a in Rif.
11 Tosafot, Pesaḥim 27b, s.v. *ein*; Rashi, *Siddur Rashi* 356; Rosh, Pesaḥim 2:3; *Semag* 39; *Semak* 98, et al.
12 Rosh, Pesaḥim 2:3; Ritva, Pesaḥim 27b; Ran, Pesaḥim 5a; Baal HaMaor, ibid.; Rif, Pesaḥim 5a; and Rambam 3:11.
13 *Biur HaGra* 445:1.
14 *Shulḥan Arukh* 445:1.
15 See *Mishna Berura* 445:6.
16 *Mishna Berura* 445:18.
17 *Iggerot Moshe, Oraḥ Ḥayim* 3:57.
18 Rema 434.
19 Rashi, Pesaḥim 6a, s.v. *kofeh.*
20 See Beitza 12a.
21 Ran, Pesaḥim 2b; s.v. *homotzei*; Rashba, Responsa 1:61; *Or Zarua*, 2:256.
22 Tosafot, Ketubot 7a, s.v. *mitokh.*
23 *Hilkhot Ḥametz UMatza* 3:8.
24 *Kol Bo* 48.
25 *Shulḥan Arukh* 446:1.
26 *Biur HaGra* 446:1.
27 *HaMo'adim BeHalakha*, Pesaḥ, chap. 4.
28 Tosefta, Pesaḥim 2:12.
29 *Beit Yosef* 448.
30 *Terumat HaDeshen* 1:120.
31 *Baḥ* 448.
32 *Sho'el UMeishiv*, Tinyana 2:7.
33 Ḥatam Sofer, *Oraḥ Ḥayim* 113.
34 See, for example, *Nefesh HaRav*, p. 177, citing R. Soloveitchik.
35 R. Moshe Feinstein, cited in *Halakhos of Pesaḥ*, p. 123, n. 44.
36 Tosafot, Avoda Zara 71a, s.v. *Rav Ashi.*
37 *Mishna Berura* 448:19.
38 *Mishna Berura* 448:19.
39 *Biur Halakha* 448:3, s.v. *bedavar.*
40 *HaElef Lekha Shlomo, Oraḥ Ḥayim* 221.
41 *Biur Halakha* 448:3, s.v. *mekhira.*
42 *Teshuvot Oneg Yom Tov* 36.

43 See *Piskei Teshuvot* 443:1.

44 See *Iggerot Moshe, Oraḥ Ḥayim* 4:94–95.

45 *Iggerot Moshe, Oraḥ Ḥayim* 1:149, 2:91 and 4:95.

46 http://www.oukosher.org/index.php/common/article/1377993 (accessed February 2, 2012).

47 R. Yehuda Herzl Henkin, in Responsa *Benei Banim* (1:13), criticizes the practice of some to attach pages of signatures to the *shetar harshaa*. He insists that the Statement of Authorization appear on each page.

48 See *Shulḥan Arukh, Ḥoshen Mishpat* 182:1; see also *Piskei Teshuvot* 448 n. 72.

49 *Hilkhot Mekhira* 5:12–13.

50 Pesaḥim 28a, citing Ex. 13:7.

51 Ramban, Pesaḥim 31b.

52 *Hilkhot Ḥametz UMatza* 1:4.

53 *Shulḥan Arukh* 448:3.

54 *Iggerot Moshe, Oraḥ Ḥayim* 4:96.

CHAPTER 49

1 *Sefer Abudraham, Tefillot Pesaḥ.*

2 *Toldot Adam VaḤava* 5:4.

3 *Guide for the Perplexed* 3:43.

4 *Sefer HaḤinukh*, mitzva 306.

5 Ran, Pesaḥim 28a.

6 *Hilkhot Temidin UMusafin* 7:22–4.

7 Cited in the *Or Zarua* 329.

8 *Shibbolei HaLeket* 234.

9 Baal HaMaor, Pesaḥim 28a.

10 See, for example, Rosh, Pesaḥim 10:40, and Ran, Pesaḥim 28a.

11 Ran, Pesaḥim 28a.

12 *Ḥiddushei HaGriz*, Menaḥot 66a.

13 *Toldot Adam VeḤava* 5:4. R. Yerucham Fishel Perle (*Sefer HaMitzvot LeRasag*, Mitzva 51) discusses these two points, challenging and strongly disagreeing with Rabbeinu Yeruḥam's assumption that a mitzva instituted as a *zekher laMikdash* does not warrant a blessing before its performance. Regarding the possible difference between the counting of the days and the weeks, he demonstrates that while many *Rishonim* actually view the counting of the weeks as the central mitzva and the counting of the days as secondary, others view the counting of the days as the primary mitzva and the counting of the weeks as secondary. R. Soloveitchik (*Nefesh HaRav*, p. 191) discusses this issue as well.

14 Rambam (*Sefer HaMitzvot* 161) explicitly rejects the possibility that the counting of the days and the weeks constitute two separate mitzvot. He writes:

Do not be misled to consider [the counting of days and weeks as] two commandments because of the statement of our sages, "It is a mitzva to count the days and it is a mitzva to count the weeks." [They use the expression, "It is a mitzva"] because for any mitzva that has many parts, it is a "mitzva" [we are commanded] to do each part. If the sages would have said, however, "Counting the days is a mitzva, and counting the weeks is a mitzva," they would be considered two separate commandments. This is clear to anyone who thinks carefully about the wording; because when it is said that there is an "obligation" to do a certain act, that expression does not necessarily indicate that it is a separate commandment. The clear proof of this [that counting the days and weeks are not separate commandments] is that we count the weeks every single night by saying, "It is this number of weeks and this number of days." If [counting] the weeks would be a separate commandment, [the sages] would have established them to be counted only on those nights which [complete] the weeks. They also would have established two blessings: "[Blessed are You God, King of the universe,] who has sanctified us with His commandments and commanded us to count the days of the *Omer*," and, "...to count the weeks of the *Omer*." This is not the case; rather the mitzva is to count the days and weeks of the *Omer* as was commanded.

According to Rambam, the counting of the weeks and of the days together make up one single mitzva.

15 *Biur Halakha* 489:1.

16 See Tosafot, Megilla 20b.

17 Tosafot, Megilla 20b, s.v. *kol.*

18 Cited in *Behag* 71.

19 *Magen Avraham,* 494; *Taz* 494. The *Siddur Yaavetz* actually insists that one daven early in order to fulfill the mitzva of *tosefet Yom Tov,* adding on to Yom Tov.

20 Commentary on the Mishna, Menaḥot 10:3.

21 *Tur* 489.

22 *Shulḥan Arukh* 489:1.

23 *Biur Halakha* 489:1.

24 *Iggerot Moshe, Oraḥ Ḥayim* 4:99.

25 *Shevet HaLevi* 6:53.

26 *Shela,* Pesaḥim 3a, cited by *Be'er Heitev* 489:20.

27 Rabbeinu Yeruḥam, *Toldot Adam VeḤava* 5:4; *Tosafot HaRosh,* Megilla 20b s.v. *kol.*

28 Deut. 16:9; Rosh, Pesaḥim 10:41.

29 *Sefer Yerei'im* 261.

30 Tosafot, Menaḥot 66a, s.v. *zekher*.
31 Ran, Pesaḥim 28a.
32 *Shulḥan Arukh* 489:2.
33 *Magen Avraham* 489:6.
34 *Mishna Berura* 489:15.
35 *Arukh HaShulḥan* 489:7.
36 *Yeḥave Daat* 1:23.
37 *Shulḥan Arukh* 489:3.
38 *Magen Avraham* 489:7. *Taz* (489:6) disagrees, and objects to performing a mitzva in this manner. Rather, he explains, he only counts the first time so as not to give the impression that he does not wish to count with this community, but he has in mind not to discharge his obligation.
39 See *Mishna Berura* 489:16, who explains that this case refers to a community that prays after *shekia*. In his *Biur Halakha*, however, he cites *Aḥaronim*, such as *Levush*, who understand that the *Shulḥan Arukh* refers to a community of "*amei haaretz*," who may forget to count the *Omer* after dark; they therefore count, with a blessing, after *pelag haMinḥa*. *Olat Tamid* writes that one who counts after *pelag haMinḥa* should count again after dark, but without a blessing.
40 *Shulḥan Arukh* 489:4.
41 *Behag* 12 (see also as cited by Ran, Megilla 7a, s.v. *mikan*); Me'iri, Megilla 20b.
42 Rambam, *Hilkhot Temidin UMusafin* 7:23.
43 Rabbeinu Tam, Tosafot, Megilla 20b (see *Tosafot HaRosh*, ibid. who cites Rabbeinu Tam as ruling that one who forgets to count at night may count with a *berakha* during the day); *Semag*, Positive Commandment 199.
44 Raavya 2:526; *Mordekhai*, Megilla 803; Rabbeinu Yeruḥam, *netiv* 5, part 4; Rosh, cited by *Tur* 489.
45 See, for example, Ran, Megilla 7a, s.v. *mikan*.
46 *Mordekhai*, Megilla 803, citing R. Yaakov b.Yakar; see Berakhot 26a.
47 *Shulḥan Arukh* 489:7.
48 *Mishna Berura* 489:34.
49 Mitzva 306.
50 *Behag*, chap. 12.
51 *Beit Yosef* 480.
52 *Sefer HaMakhria* 29.
53 *Shulḥan Arukh* 489:8.
54 See *Terumat HaDeshen* 37.
55 *Mishna Berura* 489:38.
56 *Avnei Nezer, Oraḥ Ḥayim* 2:539.
57 *Shaarei Teshuva* 489:20.

58 *Ketav Sofer* 99.
59 *Minḥat Elazar* 3:60.
60 *Arukh HaShulḥan* 489:15.
61 *Tzitz Eliezer* 14:55.
62 The *Aḥaronim* also question whether a slave or a non-Jew who counted *Sefirat HaOmer* and was subsequently freed or converted may continue to count with a blessing, but there may be other considerations in these cases.
63 *Shulḥan Arukh* 489:8.
64 *Mishna Berura* 489:45.
65 Tosafot, Megilla 20b, s.v. *kol halayla*.
66 Reshash (Megilla 20b) notes that other *Rishonim* cite *Behag* as ruling that one who forgets to count at night should count the next day with a blessing. See *Behag*, chap. 12.
67 *Tur* 489.
68 *Biur Halakha* 489:8.
69 *Shaarei Teshuva* 489:20.
70 *Teshuvot Beit David, Oraḥ Ḥayim* 102.
71 *Beit Shlomo* 1:102.
72 *Minḥat Yitzchak* 9:57.
73 See *Iggerot Moshe, Oraḥ Ḥayim* 4:62.
74 See *Taz* 668.
75 *Shaarei Teshuva* 489:20.
76 *Iggerot Moshe, Oraḥ Ḥayim* 4:99:3.
77 *Hilkhot Temidin UMusafin* 7:20.
78 *Sefer HaḤinukh* 306.
79 Ramban, Kiddushin 33b.
80 *Divrei Malkiel* 3:5.
81 *Nefesh HaRav*, p. 191.
82 *Seridei Esh* 2:90.
83 *Avnei Nezer, Oraḥ Ḥayim* 384.
84 R. Yerucham Fishel Perle, in his momentous commentary on R. Saadia Gaon's list of the 613 mitzvot (end of the introduction), offers another explanation. He suggests that a mitzva is considered to be a *mitzvat aseh shehazeman gerama* only if time determines whether or not the mitzva can be performed. However, if a mitzva can theoretically be performed any time, but other factors determine that it can only be performed on certain days, it is not considered to be a time-bound mitzva. *Sefirat HaOmer* is dependent not upon specific days, but rather upon the bringing of the *korban haOmer* on Pesaḥ and the *shetei haleḥem* on Shavuot, and it is therefore not considered a time-bound mitzva. Furthermore, he suggests that

15 *Hilkhot Megilla VeḤanukka* 3:6.
16 *Sefer HaMitzvot, shoresh* 1.
17 Raavad, *Hilkhot Megilla VeḤanukka,* 3:6.
18 Ḥatam Sofer, *Oraḥ Ḥayim,* 208; see also *Yoreh De'ah* 233 and *Oraḥ Ḥayim* 191.
19 Rashi, ibid., s.v. *ve'al.*
20 Maharatz Chayot, Shabbat 21b.
21 Rambam, *Hilkhot Megilla VeḤanukka* 3:2; Megilla 14a.
22 *Hilkhot Lulav,* p. 35.
23 Cited in Tosafot, Sukka 44b.
24 Commentary on the *She'iltot,* 26.
25 See R. Shmuel Katz, "*HaRabbanut HaRashit VeYom HaAtzma'ut,*" in *HaRabbanut HaRashit LeYisrael: Shivim Shana LeYisuda, Samḥuta, Peuloteha, Toldoteha,* part 2 (Jerusalem: Heikhal Shlomo, 2002). R. Katz discusses the various opinions of the Chief Rabbis and the Rabbinical Council.
26 *Ḥayim She'al* 2:11.
27 *Yaskil Avdi, Oraḥ Ḥayim,* 10:7. He adds that one should recite Hallel at the conclusion of *Tefillat Shaḥarit.*
28 *Yabia Omer, Oraḥ Ḥayim,* 6:41.
29 R. Roth adds, however, that since this practice would be considered to be innovative, one should recite the blessing only after receiving the approval of "the majority of the great Rabbis."
30 *Minḥat Yitzchak* 10:10.
31 See *Kol Dodi Dofek,* for example.
32 *Nefesh HaRav,* p. 96.
33 The Mishna (Megilla 20b) teaches that Hallel is recited only by day.
34 R. Yitzchak Ze'ev Soloveitchik, in his *Ḥiddushei HaGriz,* Ḥanukka 3:4, elaborates upon this distinction.
35 *Sinai* (April-May, 1958).
36 *Mo'ed LeKhol Ḥai* 6.
37 *Yaskil Avdi* 6:10.
38 *Nefesh HaRav,* p. 97.
39 *Kol Mevasser* 1:21.

CHAPTER 52

1 See also Ex. 34:22.
2 See also *Onkelos,* Num. 28:26.
3 See *Pesikta DeRav Kahana, pesikta* 28.
4 Abrabanel, Lev. 23.

5 *Akeidat Yitzchak*, Lev. 23.
6 Tanḥuma, *Parashat Ki Tavo*.
7 *Shulḥan Arukh* 494.
8 *Shenei Luḥot HaBerit*, Masekhet Shavuot.
9 *Yosef Ometz* 850.
10 *Korban Netanel*, Pesaḥim 10:2.
11 *Magen Avraham* 494.
12 *Peri Ḥadash* 494.
13 *Taz* 494.
14 *Siddur Yaavetz*.
15 *Hitorerut Teshuva* 56.
16 Responsa *Lehorot Natan* 7:31.
17 *Mishbetzot Zahav* 494, s.v. *me'aḥarin*.
18 *Shulḥan Arukh HaRav* 494:2.
19 *Kitzur Shulḥan Arukh* 120:11.
20 *Mishna Berura* 494:1.
21 *Haamek Davar*, Lev. 23:21.
22 *Hagahot UMinhagim*, *Ḥag HaShavuot*.
23 See *Shulḥan Arukh*, *Yoreh De'ah* 89:4.
24 Rema 494:3.
25 *Magen Avraham* 494:6.
26 *Mishna Berura* 494:12.
27 Ibid., 494:13.
28 *Kol Bo* 52.
29 See Song. 4:11.
30 *Darkhei Teshuva*, *Yoreh De'ah* 89:19.
31 *Orḥot Rabbeinu*, vol. 2, p. 98.
32 As discussed by the *Shaarei Teshuva* 529:4.
33 *Sefer Yosef Ometz* 854.
34 *Darkhei Moshe*, *Yoreh De'ah* 89.
35 Ibid., 89:2.
36 Rema, *Yoreh Dea'h* 89:2.
37 See *Magen Avraham* 494:6; *Mishna Berura* 494:12.
38 *Ḥazon Ovadia*, Yom Tov, p. 318.
39 See *Be'er Heitev* 494:8, citing the *Knesset Gedola* and *Shela*.
40 Zohar, *Parashat Mishpatim*.
41 See *Oraḥ Mishor* as cited by the *Darkhei Teshuva*.
42 *Iggerot Moshe*, *Oraḥ Ḥayim* 1:160.
43 *Darkhei Teshuva*, *Yoreh De'ah* 89:19.

44 *Ḥiddushei HaGriz al HaTorah, Parashat Yitro.*
45 Zohar, *Parashat Emor* 88a.
46 *Shela,* Masekhet Shavuot.
47 *Magen Avraham* 494.
48 *Shulḥan Arukh* and Rema 4:13.
49 *Mishna Berura* 4:30 and in *Biur Halakha,* s.v. *veyitlem.*
50 *Arukh HaShulḥan* 46:13.
51 *Mishna Berura* 46:24.
52 Ibid., 47:28.
53 Ibid.
54 Maharil, *Minhagim, Hilkhot Shavuot,* 2; see also *Sefer HaMinhagim* of R. Isaac Tyrnau, *Hagahot UMinhagim, Ḥag HaShavuot.*
55 *Leket Yosher,* vol. 1, p. 150.
56 Rema 494:3.
57 *Levush Malkhut* 494.
58 *Magen Avraham* 494:5.
59 *Biur HaGra* 131:13; see also *Maase Rav* 196:2.

CHAPTER 53

1 *Hilkhot Taaniyot,* 1:1–2.
2 Ibid., 1:4.
3 Ramban, comments to *Sefer HaMitzvot,* Positive Commandment 5.
4 *Hilkhot Taaniyot,* 5:1
5 *Harerei Kedem,* vol. 2, p. 280.
6 See also Rosh HaShana 18b.
7 See Ezek. 24:1–2; Jer. 52:4–6.
8 See *Behag* 18; *Seder Rav Amram Gaon, Seder Taanit; Maḥzor Vitry* 271; *Siddur Rashi* 541; *Kol Bo* 63; *Tur* 580.
9 *De Vita Mosis* 2:7:41, cited by L. Feldman, *Jew and Gentile in the Ancient World,* p. 52.
10 See *Kol Bo* 63.
11 This commentary is cited in a footnote to the Maḥon Yerushalayim edition of the *Tur* (580). See also Prof. Shnayer Leiman, "Scroll of Fasts: The Ninth of Tebeth," *Jewish Quarterly Review,* 74:2 (October, 1983), pp. 174–95, who investigated this question extensively.
12 *Hilkhot Taaniyot,* 5:2.
13 Rashi, Taanit 26b.
14 R. Ovadia Bartenura, Taanit 4:6.

15 *Tiferet Yisrael* 4:6.
16 *Antiquities of the Jews* 20:5:4. This soldier was later beheaded by the Roman procurator Cumanus, "out of fear lest the multitude should go into a sedition."
17 See Maccabees 1:1:56.
18 *Torat HaAdam, Shaar HaEvel, Inyan Aveilut Yeshana.*
19 Radak, Jer. 41:1.
20 Maharsha, Rosh HaShana 18b.
21 Rabbeinu Ḥananel 18b; Ramban, *Torat HaAdam, Shaar Aveilut Yeshana,* 243; *Tur* 550.
22 Taanit 18b, s.v. *de'amar.*
23 Ibid., s.v. *sheyesh shalom.*
24 For example, see R. E. Lichtenstein's notes to Ritva, Rosh HaShana 18b, n. 366.
25 *Tashbetz* 2:271.
26 See *Turei HaEven,* ibid.
27 Ritva, Megilla 5a, Rosh HaShana 18b.
28 Rosh, Rosh HaShana 1:6.
29 Ritva, Rosh HaShana 18b.
30 Rambam, Commentary on the Mishna, Rosh HaShana 1:3.
31 *Tashbetz* 2:271.
32 See *Hilkhot Taaniyot* 5:5 and *Maggid Mishneh*; see Frankel edition of Rambam.
33 *Shulḥan Arukh* 550.

CHAPTER 54

1 Ramban, *Torat HaAdam, Inyan Aveilut Yeshana*
2 See *Shaar HaTziyun* 550:9.
3 *Shulḥan Arukh* 564. *Beit Yosef* cites a debate regarding whether one who falls asleep at his meal, and did not intend to sleep for the night, may continue to eat. The *Mishna Berura* writes that although the *Shulḥan Arukh* implies that he rules stringently, many *Aḥaronim* rule that one who literally fell asleep at one's meal may finish his meal upon awaking.
4 Y. Taanit 1:4.
5 Rosh, Taanit 1:14; see also Tosafot, Taanit 12b.; *Mordekhai* 626.
6 *Mordekhai* 626; *Or Zarua* 2:406; *Kol Bo* 71.
7 Rosh, Responsa 27:7.
8 *Shulḥan Arukh* 564.
9 Rema, ibid.
10 *Mishna Berura* 564:6.
11 Tosafot, Taanit 14a, s.v. *o dilma.*

12 Rosh, Taanit 1:15, in the name of R. Yehuda of Barcelona.

13 Ritva, Taanit 12a.

14 *Korban Netanel,* Taanit 12a.

15 See Rivash 287; *Biur HaGra* 567.

16 *Shulḥan Arukh* 567:1.

17 Ibid., 567:3.

18 *Terumat HaDeshen* 158.

19 *Magen Avraham* 567:6.

20 Ibid.

21 *Maamar Mordekhai* 567.

22 *Yalkut Yosef, Mo'adim,* p. 534.

23 Rema 567:1.

24 *Darkhei Moshe* 567:2.

25 *Eliya Rabba* 567:5.

26 *Mishna Berura* 11.

27 *Minḥat Yitzchak* 4:109.

28 Tosafot, Rosh HaShana 33a; Rabbeinu Tam cited by Rosh, Kiddushin 1:49; *Sefer HaḤinukh,* mitzva 430.

29 *Hilkhot Berakhot,* 1:15.

30 *Shulḥan Arukh* 215:4.

31 *Yabia Omer, Yoreh De'ah* 2:5:6–8.

32 *Piskei Teshuvot* 568. The *Shaarei Teshuva* (568:1) discusses this issue as well.

33 *Mishna Berura* 568:8.

34 *Mishna Berura* 554:11; *Ḥayei Adam* 135:2.

35 *Shulḥan Arukh* 554:4.

36 *Piskei Teshuvot* 554:8.

37 *Nishmat Avraham* 5:554:1.

38 *Biur Halakha* 554:6, citing the *Pitḥei Olam*; *Marḥeshet* 1:14.

39 *Avnei Nezer* 54; *Arukh HaShulḥan* 554:7; *Shevet HaLevi* 4:56; *Tzitz Eliezer* 10:25:16.

40 *Nishmat Avraham* 4:554:1.

41 *Shulḥan Arukh* 554:5, 550:1.

42 Rema, ibid.

43 *Arukh HaShulḥan* 550:1.

44 *Daat Torah* 550.

45 *Yeḥave Daat* 1:35.

46 See *Piskei Teshuvot* 550:1.

47 *Mishna Berura* 550:5.

48 *Biur Halakha* 550:1.

49 Rema MiFano 111.
50 *Mishna Berura* 549:1
51 *Hilkhot Taaniyot* 1:14.

CHAPTER 55

1 *Teshuvot HaGeonim, Shaarei Teshuva* 77; Rif, Taanit 4a; Ran and Ramban on Rif; Ritva, Shabbat 24a; Rashba, Responsa 1:142, 387.
2 Rashi, Shabbat 24a, s.v. *arvit*.
3 Rashba, Responsa 1:142.
4 Ritva, Shabbat 24, s.v *ve'im*.
5 Tosafot, Taanit 11b. s.v. *lan*.
6 *Shulḥan Arukh* 565:3.
7 Rema, ibid.
8 *Yalkut Yosef*, Mo'adim p. 536.
9 Rashba, Responsa 1:81.
10 Rosh, Shabbat 2:15.
11 Tosafot, Shabbat 24a.
12 Me'iri, Megilla 2a.
13 *Shulḥan Arukh* 566:3.
14 *Shaarei Teshuva* 566:4, *Mishna Berura* 566:15.
15 Responsa *Kol Gadol* 14.
16 *Arukh HaShulḥan* 566:7.
17 *Shaar HaTziyun* 566:15.
18 *Mishbetzot Zahav* 7.
19 *Eliya Rabba* 566:4.
20 *Shaarei Teshuva* 566:4.
21 *Ishei Yisrael* 44:5.
22 *Yeḥave Daat* 1:79; *Piskei Teshuvot* 676. R. Ovadia Yosef points out that even *Shaarei Teshuva* himself rules elsewhere (*Shaarei Efraim* 8:108) that one may insert *Aneinu* even if there are only six who are fasting.
23 *Tur* 566. R. Natan's opinion can be found in the *Seder R. Amram HaShalem* (*Seder Taanit*), as well as in the geonic collection of responsa, *Shaarei Teshuvot* (50), in the name of R. Hai Gaon, as well as in other geonic sources.
24 *Shulḥan Arukh* 566:5.
25 See *Taz* 566:7.
26 *Arukh HaShulḥan* 566:10.
27 *Magen Avraham* 566:7.
28 *Mishna Berura* 566:18.

29 See *Ishei Yisrael* 44:8.
30 See *Biur Halakha* 565:1.
31 See *Shulḥan Arukh* 612:10; *Mishna Berura* 612:31 and 210:1.
32 *Shulḥan Arukh* 567:1.
33 *Mishna Berura* 567:5.
34 See *Piskei Teshuvot* 568:1 and *Yalkut Yosef, Mo'adim* p. 536.
35 *Hilkhot Tefilla* 13:18.
36 Roke'aḥ 211.
37 *Kol Bo* 62.
38 *Beit Yosef* 565.
39 *Shulḥan Arukh* and Rema 565.
40 *Yaskil Avdi* 6:9; see also *Yalkut Yosef*, Mo'adim, p. 546.
41 Maharik, *shoresh* 9.
42 *Shulḥan Arukh* 566:6.
43 *Taz* 566:7.
44 R. Akiva Eiger, Responsa 24. Interestingly, he questions whether the *keriat haTorah* of Minḥa on Yom Kippur stems from the *kedushat hayom*, the sanctity of the day, in which case one who was not fasting would be able to receive an *aliya*, or from its status as a fast day, in which case he would not. (Whether or not the reading at Minḥa of Yom Kippur is chanted to the Yom Tov or daily tune may depend upon this question as well.)
45 *Baḥ*, end of 566.
46 *Arukh HaShulḥan* 566:11.
47 *Mishna Berura* 566:21.
48 *Magen Avraham*, 566:8
49 *Shulḥan Arukh* 129:1.
50 *Ḥazon Ish, Oraḥ Ḥayim* 20.
51 See *Mo'adim UZemanim* 7:248.
52 See R. Tukatchinsky in his *Luaḥ Eretz Yisrael*; R. Shlomo Zalman Auerbach as cited in *Halikhot Shlomo*, chap. 10, n. 21.

CHAPTER 56

1 *Shibbolei HaLeket* 263.
2 *Kol Bo* 62.
3 See, for example, *Shiurei HaRav, Inyanei Tisha B'Av*, p. 20–21 and *Nefesh HaRav*, p. 191.
4 *Shulḥan Arukh* and Rema, *Yoreh De'ah* 390:4.
5 *Shulḥan Arukh* 561:2.

Notes

6 Rema, ibid.
7 *Magen Avraham* 561:10.
8 Rambam, *Hilkhot Avel* 6:6.
9 *Biur Halakha* 551.
10 *Tzitz Eliezer* 16:19.
11 *Iggerot Moshe, Oraḥ Ḥayim* 1:166 and *Yoreh De'ah* 2:137.
12 *Yeḥave Daat* 6:34.
13 *Tzitz Eliezer* 15:33.
14 *Teḥumim* 21.
15 See also Maharam Schick, *Yoreh De'ah* 368 and *Ḥelkat Yaakov* 1:62.
16 The permissibility of listening to music at all since the destruction of the *Beit HaMikdash* is beyond the scope of this chapter. Seemingly, however, there is extra reason to be stringent during the period of mourning of the Three Weeks.
17 *Shulḥan Arukh* 551:3.
18 Rema, ibid.; *Sefer HaMinhagim, Ḥodesh Tammuz..*
19 Incidentally, R. Soloveitchik also permitted shaving during *Sefirat HaOmer*.
20 *Iggerot Moshe, Oraḥ Ḥayim* 4:102.
21 *Iggerot Moshe, Ḥoshen Mishpat* 1:93.
22 Ḥatam Sofer, *Yoreh De'ah* 348.
23 Rema, *Oraḥ Ḥayim* 551:3.
24 *Magen Avraham, Oraḥ Ḥayim* 551:14.
25 This is, in fact, the opinion of Tosafot, Taanit 29.
26 *Biur Halakha* 551.
27 *Mishna Berura* 551:79.
28 R. S. Eider, *Halachos of the Three Weeks*, quoting R. Moshe Feinstein.
29 *Kitzur Shulḥan Arukh* 122:5.
30 *Sefer Ḥasidim* 840.
31 Maharil, *Hilkhot Shiva Asar B'Tammuz VeTisha B'Av.*
32 *Shulḥan Arukh* 551:17.
33 Rema, ibid.
34 *Magen Avraham* 551:42.
35 *Mishna Berura* 551:98; see *Shaar HaTziyun* 99.
36 *Shulḥan Arukh* 223:5.
37 Cited by *Tur* 223.
38 *Beit Yosef* 223.
39 *Iggerot Moshe, Oraḥ Ḥayim* 3:80.
40 *Shaarei Teshuva* 551:18.
41 *Magen Avraham* 551:42.
42 Maharil, *Hilkhot Shiva Asar B'Tammuz VeTisha B'Av.*

43 *Taz* 551:7.
44 *Biur HaGra* 551:17.
45 *Arukh HaShulḥan* 551:38.
46 Ramban, *Milḥamot Hashem,* Taanit 3a.
47 *Iggerot Moshe, Oraḥ Ḥayim* 1:168.
48 *Nefesh HaRav,* p. 196.
49 *Torat HaShelamim, Hilkhot Nidda* 185:10.
50 *Beit Yosef* 551.
51 Rema 551:18.
52 See *Piskei Teshuvot* 551:46, n. 240.
53 *Yesod VeShoresh HaAvoda* 3:9.
54 *Beit Yosef* 551; *Taz* 551:1.
55 *Arukh HaShulḥan* 551:1–3.
56 *Hilkhot Taaniyot* 3:8.
57 Indeed, *Tur* (551), who does cite the *baraita* in Yevamot, brings two interpretations as to whether *all* trade, building, and planting are prohibited, or only those activities that are for joyous purposes. *Beit Yosef* rules that they are prohibited only when they are performed for joyous purposes, in accordance with the Yerushalmi (Taanit 4:6).
58 *Tur* 551.
59 *Shulḥan Arukh* 551:1.
60 *Mishna Berura* 551:12.
61 The *Mishna Berura* (551:11) explains that we are lenient regarding business transactions because even according to the more stringent opinion, one may work "*kedei parnassato,*" for one's livelihood. We generally assume that all work is for one's livelihood, although the *Mishna Berura* implies that it may be inappropriate to engage in business matters that can be delayed until after the Nine Days.
62 Rashi, s.v. *afilu.*
63 Cited by Tosafot, Mo'ed Katan 24b, s.v. *birkat aveilim.*
64 See *Leḥem Mishneh, Hilkhot Taaniyot* 5:6.
65 Ramban, *Torat HaAdam, Inyan Aveilut Yeshana,* s.v. *matnitin;* Ran, Taanit 9b, s.v. *ukavus;* Rashba, Responsa 1:187.
66 *Shulḥan Arukh* 551:3.
67 Rema 551:4.
68 *Mishna Berura* 551:29, 32.
69 *Piskei Teshuvot* 551:21.
70 *Beit Yosef* 551.
71 Rema 551:14.
72 *Mishna Berura* 551:83.

73 Tosafot, Mo'ed Katan 24b; *Orḥot Ḥayim*, p. 584; Rema, *Yoreh De'ah* 389:1.
74 *Minḥat Yitzchak* 10:44.
75 See *Piskei Teshuvot* 551:17.
76 *Tzitz Eliezer* 13:61.
77 Rema 551:3.
78 Rema 551:1.
79 *Arukh HaShulḥan* 551:11.
80 *Mishna Berura* 551:6.
81 *Shulḥan Arukh* 551:6–7.
82 R. Shimon Eider, *Halachos of the Three Weeks*, p. 11.
83 *Iggerot Moshe, Oraḥ Ḥayim* 3:79.
84 *Hilkhot Taaniyot* 5:6.
85 Roke'aḥ 312.
86 *Mordekhai*, Taanit 638.
87 *Or Zarua* 2:414.
88 *Terumat HaDeshen* 150.
89 *Shulḥan Arukh* 551:16.
90 Raa, *Pekudat HaLevi'im*, Taanit 29a.
91 Ran, Taanit 9b, s.v. *mutar*.
92 *Yabia Omer, Oraḥ Ḥayim* 5:41; *Yeḥave Daat* 1:38.
93 Rema 551:16.
94 *Mishna Berura* 551:94.
95 *Arukh HaShulḥan* 551:37.
96 *Shulḥan Arukh, Yoreh De'ah* 381:3.
97 The average high temperature during August in Krakow, Poland, home of Rema, is 64 degrees Fahrenheit; in Lithuania, it is around 70 degrees. In New York City and Jerusalem, the average August high temperature is around 85 degrees!
98 *Iggerot Moshe, Even HaEzer* 3:84.
99 *Ben Ish Ḥai*, Deut. 16.
100 *Rav Po'alim, Oraḥ Ḥayim* 4:29.
101 Rema 551:6.
102 *Arukh HaShulḥan* 551:36.
103 Shabbat 25a; *Shulḥan Arukh* 260:1.
104 *Taz* 551:13.
105 *Magen Avraham* 551:11.
106 *Mishna Berura* 551:20.
107 *Shibbolei HaLeket* 263.
108 *Kol Bo* 62.
109 *Mordekhai*, Taanit 639.

110 *Hilkhot Taaniyot* 5:6.
111 Ramban, *Torat HaAdam, Inyan Aveilut Yeshana,* s.v. *matnitin.*
112 Rashba, Responsa 1:306.
113 *Maggid Mishneh, Hilkhot Taaniyot* 5:6.
114 *Shulḥan Arukh* 551:9.
115 *Mishna Berura* 551:58.
116 Gra, *Oraḥ Ḥayim* 551:11.
117 *Mordekhai,* Taanit 639.
118 *Arukh HaShulḥan* 551:23.
119 *Kol Bo* 62.
120 *Shulḥan Arukh* 551:10.
121 *Arukh HaShulḥan* 551:24.
122 *Mishna Berura* 551:63.
123 *Shaarei Teshuva* 19.
124 Rema 551:9, 11.
125 *Shulḥan Arukh* 551:10.
126 Gra, ibid.
127 Rema, ibid.
128 *Mishna Berura* 551:68, 70.
129 *Arukh HaShulḥan* 551:26.
130 *Magen Avraham* 551:31.
131 *Mishna Berura* 551:70.
132 *Shulḥan Arukh* 552:10.
133 *Mekor Ḥayim* 551:9.
134 *Magen Avraham* 250:1.
135 *Shaarei Teshuva* 11.
136 *Iggerot Moshe, Oraḥ Ḥayim* 4:21:4.
137 *Arukh HaShulkhan* 551:26.
138 Rema 551:1.
139 *Divrei Yatziv, Oraḥ Ḥayim* 2:238.
140 *Arukh HaShulḥan* 551:28. See also *Eliya Rabba* 551:26; *Mishna Berura* 551:73; *Kaf HaḤayim* 551:161; *Piskei Teshuvot* 551:38.
141 Cited in *Nitei Gavriel* 18:7.
142 Rema 555:1.
143 *Shulḥan Arukh* 551:2.
144 See *Magen Avraham* 34.
145 *Nefesh Ḥaya* 555:1.
146 *Mishneh Halakhot* 6:166.
147 *Seder Tefillat HaTaaniyot.*

148 *Hagahot Maimoniyot, Taaniyot* 5:10.
149 *Shulḥan Arukh* 558:1.
150 Rema, ibid.
151 Maharshal, Responsa 92; *Magen Avraham* 558:1; *Eliya Rabba* 558:2; *Mishna Berura* 558:3.
152 *Biur Halakha*, s.v. *ad.*
153 Rema, 558:1.
154 *Mishna Berura* 558:4.
155 See *Piskei Teshuvot* 558:3, n. 17.
156 *Nitei Gavriel* 41:16.

CHAPTER 57

1 The *Aḥaronim* discuss whether the afternoon Torah reading of Yom Kippur reflects the *taanit tzibbur* aspect of the day – in which case only one who is fasting should receive an *aliya* – or the *mo'ed* aspect of the day, in which case anyone may ascend to the Torah.
2 *Hilkhot Taaniyot* 5:9.
3 *Shulḥan Arukh* 552:5–6.
4 *Shulḥan Arukh* 552:5–6.
5 *Mishna Berura* 552:16. This is based on the practice of Rav as recorded in Y. Taanit 4:6.
6 Rema 552:9.
7 *Magen Avraham* 552:11.
8 *Magen Avraham* 552:10.
9 *Eliya Rabba* 552:12.
10 *Mishna Berura* 552:22.
11 *Shulḥan Arukh* 553:1.
12 Rema, ibid.
13 *Mishna Berura* 553:2.
14 *Hagahot Maimoniyot, Hilkhot Taaniyot* 5:7:30.
15 *Shulḥan Arukh* 552:8.
16 *Mishna Berura* 552:19.
17 *Terumat HaDeshen* 1:151.
18 *Shulḥan Arukh* 552:7.
19 *Kaf HaḤayim* 552:38.
20 *Shulḥan Arukh* and Rema, *Oraḥ Ḥayim* 552:10.
21 Rema 553:2.
22 *Magen Avraham* 553:7.

23 As per *Shulḥan Arukh* 554:1.
24 *Mishna Berura* 554:8; *Biur Halakha* in the name of Maharshal and Gra; *Arukh HaShulḥan* 553:4.
25 *Taz* 553:2; *Mishna Berura* 553:10.
26 *Shulḥan Arukh* 559:1.
27 *Shulḥan Arukh* 552:12.
28 *Shulḥan Arukh* 554:5.
29 *Arukh HaShulḥan* 554:7.
30 *Shaarei Teshuva* 554:6.
31 See *Piskei Teshuvot* 554:6.
32 *Shulḥan Arukh, Yoreh De'ah* 381:1.
33 *Shulḥan Arukh* 554:7.
34 Ibid., 554:9.
35 *Kitzur Shulḥan Arukh* 124:7.
36 *Shulḥan Arukh* 554:14.
37 Ibid., 554:10.
38 *Mishna Berura* 554:21.
39 Ibid., 554:19.
40 Ibid., 554:22.
41 See R. Shimon Eider, *The Halachos of the Three Weeks*, p. 19.
42 *Minḥat Yitzchak* 4:109.
43 *Mishna Berura* 567:11.
44 *Shulḥan Arukh* 554:11. If one must actually clean one's eyes in the morning, it is permitted to do so normally, as it is no different from washing any other part of the body that has become soiled.
45 Rema 554:14.
46 See *Shulḥan Arukh* 554:15.
47 *Biur Halakha* 554 s.v. *sikha.*
48 See, for example, Baal HaMaor, Yoma 2a s.v. *vesandal.*
49 Rashi/Tosafot.
50 Rif, Yoma 2a; Ran, ibid.; Rosh, Yoma 8:7; *Tur* 614.
51 *Hilkhot Shevitat Asor* 3:7.
52 *Shulḥan Arukh* 554:16.
53 See, for example, *Mishna Berura* 614:5 and *Arukh HaShulḥan* 614:2–5.
54 *Hagahot Mordekhai,* Mo'ed Katan.
55 *Beit Yosef* 554 and *Shulḥan Arukh* 554:18.
56 *Mishna Berura* 554:27.
57 *Kitzur Shulḥan Arukh* 124:12.
58 *Taz* 615:16.

59 Tosafot, Mo'ed Katan 21a, s.v. *ve'assur*.
60 *Shulḥan Arukh, Yoreh De'ah* 484:4.
61 *Shulḥan Arukh, Oraḥ Ḥaim* 554:2.
62 See, for example, *Mishna Berura* 554:3.
63 *Kitzur Shulḥan Arukh* 124:5.
64 *Torat HaAdam, Inyan Aveilut Yeshana.*
65 *Shulḥan Arukh* 554:4.
66 Tosefta, Taanit 3:12.
67 Rosh, Taanit 4:37; Ramban, *Torat HaAdam*; Rambam, *Hilkhot Taaniyot* 5:11.
68 *Shulḥan Arukh* 554:20.
69 *Mishna Berura* 554:41.
70 *Har Tzvi, Yoreh De'ah* 290.
71 *Hagahot Maimoniyot, Hilkhot Taaniyot* 5:11.
72 *Shulḥan Arukh* 559:3.
73 Rema, ibid.
74 *Magen Avraham* 559:2.
75 *Shulḥan Arukh* 550:2.
76 *Mishna Berura* 550:7
77 Rema 550:2.
78 See *Mishna Berura* 454:43, for example.
79 *Shulḥan Arukh* 554:22–24.
80 Rema 554:22.
81 *Arukh HaShulḥan* 554:21.
82 See also 21a.
83 Rashi, Berakhot 11a, s.v. *alma*.
84 Rashi, Sukka 25b, s.v *mi-deamar*.
85 *Abudraham, Seder Tefillat HaTaaniyot.*
86 Roke'aḥ 310.
87 Cited by the *Shibbolei HaLeket* 270.
88 Rosh, Taanit 4:7.
89 *Hilkhot Taaniyot* 5:11. Regarding the position of Rambam himself, Rabbeinu Yeruḥam (cited by *Beit Yosef* 555) argues that according to Rambam, one should *not* wear *tefillin* on Tisha B'Av. *Maggid Mishneh* (*Hilkhot Taaniyot* 5:11) and Me'iri (Taanit 30a) however, maintain that Rambam implies that wearing *tefillin* on Tisha B'Av is superfluous, but it is permitted.
90 *Pesikta Zutrata*, Ex. 13:9.
91 *Shaarei Teshuva* 155, 266.
92 Rashba, Responsa 5:214.
93 Taanit 30a and in his *Torat HaAdam, Inyan Aveilut Yeshana.*

94 Ritva, Taanit 30a.

95 *Shibbolei HaLeket* 270.

96 *Or Zarua* 2:439.

97 *Sefer HaManhig, Hilkhot Tisha B'Av.*

98 *Mordekhai, Taanit* 637.

99 *Shulḥan Arukh* 555:1.

100 In deference to the talmudic statement that one who reads *Keriat Shema* without *tefillin* is akin to one who testifies falsely (Berakhot 14b), the *Be'er Heitev* notes that some people would pray at home on Tisha B'Av, while wearing their *tallit* and *tefillin*, and then come to synagogue to recite *kinot*. Many report that the custom of the Kabbalists of Jerusalem – as established by R. Sar Shalom Sharabi (1720–1777), the Rashash, Rosh Yeshiva of the kabbalist Beit El Yeshiva – is to wear *tallit* and *tefillin* for Shaḥarit, even publicly; see *Yeḥave Daat* 2:64.

101 *Birkei Yosef* 555:1.

102 *Mishna Berura* 555:2.

103 Ramban, *Torat HaAdam, Inyan Aveilut Yeshana.*

104 *Sefer HaManhig, Tisha B'Av* 21.

105 *Torat HaAdam*, ibid.

106 Tosafot, Pesaḥim 107a, s.v. *ameimar*. See also *Maḥzor Vitry* 267 and *Behag*, as cited the Ramban.

107 See also Rashba, Responsa 1:117 and Ritva, Taanit 30b.

108 *Shulḥan Arukh* 556:1. See also *Magen Avraham* 556:2, *Eliya Rabba* 556:4, and *Ḥayei Adam* 126:6. Radbaz (Responsa 2:642) disagrees.

109 Me'iri (Taanit 30b) writes that one should not recite the blessing over fire after the fast, as the fire of the *Beit HaMikdash* was extinguished on this day. Others, however, including Raavya (3:890) and the *Hagahot Maimoniyot* (end of *Hilkhot Taaniyot, Minhagei Tisha B'Av*) rule that one should recite the blessing over fire, *borei meorei ha'esh*, after Shabbat.

110 *Shulḥan Arukh* 556:1.

111 *Taz* 556:1, who cites *Abudraham.*

112 *Beit Yosef* 556. See also Shakh (*Yoreh De'ah* 265:12). The *Shaar HaTziyun* (556:1) writes that according to the first reason, one should not smell pleasant fragrances at all on Tisha B'Av

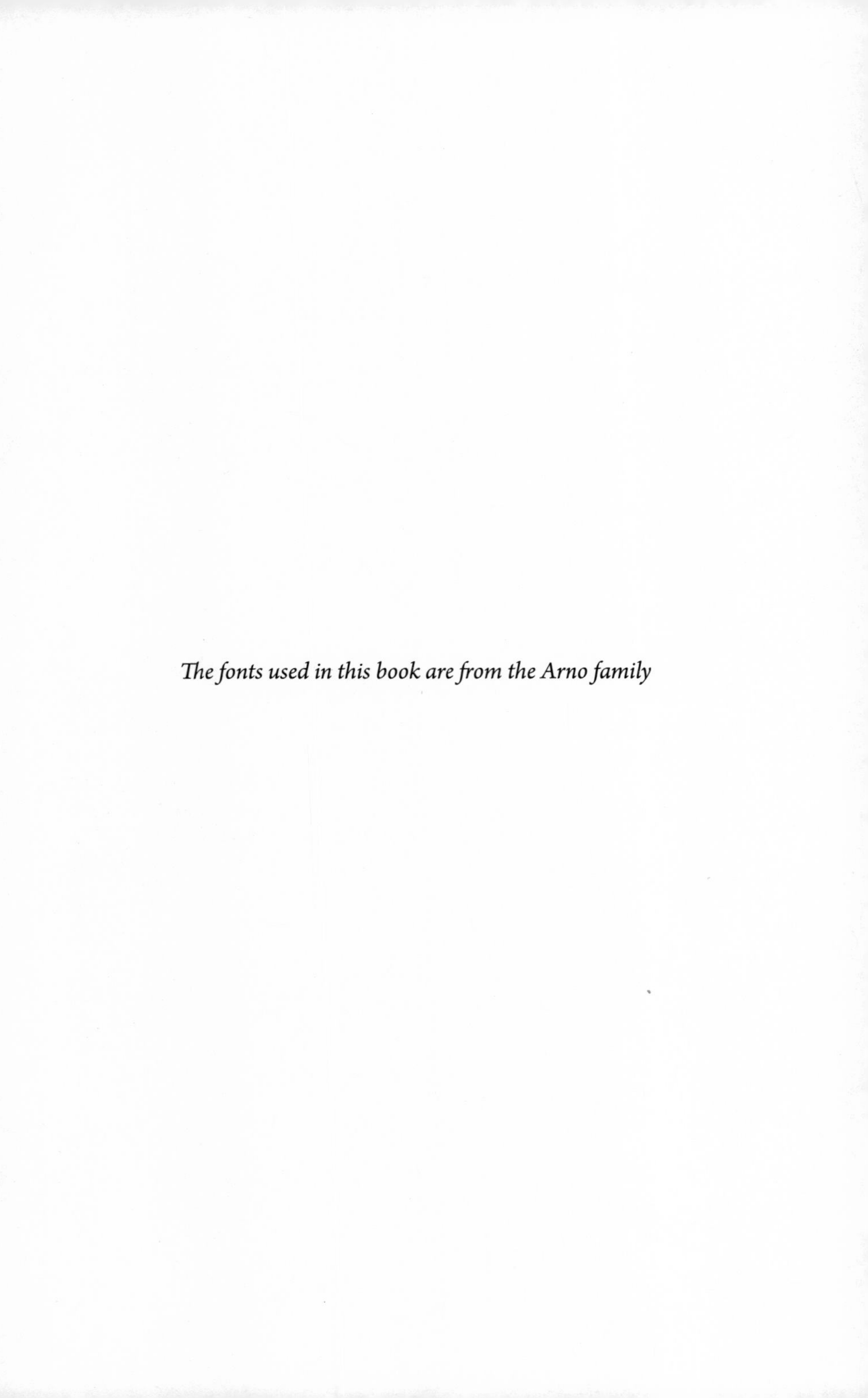

The fonts used in this book are from the Arno family

Maggid Books
The best of contemporary Jewish thought from
Koren Publishers Jerusalem Ltd